HOLLYWOOD
MUSIC INDUSTRY
DIRECTORY

3RD EDITION 2006

FROM THE PUBLISHERS OF

THE REPORTER

EDITORIAL OFFICES

5055 Wilshire Blvd., Los Angeles, CA 90036
Phone 323.525.2369 or 800.815.0503
Fax 323.525.2393
www.hcdonline.com

Jeff Black ....VP, Information Services

EDITORIAL

Matt Hayes ....Sr. Research Editor, Directories
L. M. Siegel ....Research Editor, Directories
Ben Taylor ....Research Associate
David Siegel ....Research Associate
Carla Green ....Production Manager
Samira Mahjoub ....Software Engineer

SALES AND MARKETING

Valencia McKinley ....Senior Director, Sales
Betsy Ahlstrand.......................Manager, Marketing
Jia-Juh Yuh ....Coordinator, Sales

THE REPORTER

Robert J. Dowling ....Editor-in-Chief and Publisher
Tony Uphoff ....VP, General Manager
Matthew King ....VP, Strategic Planning

vnu business publications
usa

Michael Marchesano......................................President & CEO
Robert Dowling ....Group President, Film & Performing Arts
Mark Holdreith...................................Group President, Retail
John Kilcullen ....Group President, Music & Literary
Richard O'Connor............Group President, Travel, Performance,
Food Service & Real Estate/Design
Michael Parker..........Group President, Marketing/Media & Arts
Joanne Wheatley............................VP, Information Marketing
Karen Palmieri ....VP, Manufacturing & Distribution

vnu business media

Michael Marchesano......................................President & CEO
Derek Irwin ....Chief Financial Officer
Greg Farrar ....President – VNU Expositions
Toni Nevitt ......President – eMedia and Information Marketing
Michael Alicea ....Senior VP/Human Resources
Joellen Sommer............................VP/Business Management
Deborah Patton ....VP/Communications
Howard Appelbaum ....VP/Licensing & Events
Jonathan Gordon ....Director, Business Planning
& Development

THIRD EDITION 2006

CONTENTS

ASSOCIATIONS & GUILDS

Academy of Country Music (ACM)
www.acmcountry.com
Supports, promotes and enhances the advancement of country music worldwide.
4100 W. Alameda Ave., Ste. 208
Burbank, CA 91505
Phone   818-842-8400
Fax   818-842-8535
Email   info@acmcountry.com

Academy of Motion Picture Arts and Sciences (AMPAS)
www.oscars.org
Honorary organization of motion picture professionals founded to advance the arts and sciences of motion pictures.
8949 Wilshire Blvd.
Beverly Hills, CA 90211-1972
Phone   310-247-3000
Fax   310-859-9351
              310-859-9619
Sid Ganis, President

Academy of Television Arts & Sciences (ATAS)
www.emmys.tv
Nonprofit corporation for the advancement of telecommunications arts and sciences.
5220 Lankershim Blvd.
North Hollywood, CA 91601
Phone   818-754-2800
Fax   818-761-2827

Alliance of Canadian Cinema, Television & Radio Artists (ACTRA)
www.actra.ca
Labor union founded to negotiate, safeguard, and promote the professional rights of Canadian performers working in film, television, video, and all recorded media.
625 Church St., 3rd Fl.
Toronto, ON M4Y 2G1 Canada
Phone   800-387-3516
              416-489-1311
Fax   416-489-8076
Email   national@actra.ca
              info@actratoronto.com

American Composers Forum
www.composersforum.org
Serves composers and performers of serious non-commercial or art music.
332 Minnesota St., Ste. E-145
St. Paul, MN 55101
Phone   651-228-1407
Fax   651-291-7978
Email   mail@composersforum.org
G.A. Dibrell, VP/Managing Director

American Disc Jockey Association (ADJA)
www.adja.org
Promotes ethical behavior, industry standards and continuing education for members.
20118 N. 67th St., Stes. 300-605
Glendale, AZ 85308
Phone   888-723-5776
Email   office@adja.org

American Federation of Musicians (AFM)
www.afm.org
Labor union representing professional musicians. Additional offices in Washington, DC and Ontario.

National Headquarters
1501 Broadway, Ste. 600
New York, NY 10036
Phone   212-869-1330
Fax   212-764-6134

Los Angeles
3550 Wilshire Blvd., Ste. 1900
Los Angeles, CA 90010
Phone   213-251-4510
Fax   213-251-4520

American Federation of Television & Radio Artists (AFTRA)
www.aftra.org
Labor organization representing broadcast performers.

Los Angeles
5757 Wilshire Blvd., Ste. 900
Los Angeles, CA 90036
Phone   323-634-8100
Fax   323-634-8126

New York
260 Madison Ave., 7th Fl.
New York, NY 10016
Phone   212-532-0800
Fax   212-532-2242
Christopher de Haven, Administrative Assistant

American Guild of Musical Artists (AGMA)
www.musicalartists.org
Union representing classical artists, opera singers, ballet dancers, stage managers, and stage directors.
1430 Broadway, 14th Fl.
New York, NY 10018
Phone   212-265-3687
Fax   212-262-9088
Email   agma@musicalartists.org

American Guild of Variety Artists (AGVA)
Labor union representing performers in Broadway, off-Broadway, and cabaret productions, as well as theme park and nightclub performers.

Los Angeles
4741 Laurel Canyon Blvd., Ste. 208
Valley Village, CA 91607
Phone   818-508-9984
Fax   818-508-3029
Email   agvawest@earthlink.net

New York
363 Seventh Ave., 17th Fl.
New York, NY 10001
Phone   212-675-1003
Fax   212-633-0097

American Music Conference
www.amc-music.org
Promotes the benefits of music education, supports efforts to preserve music in the schools and helps raise the national standard of these education programs.
5790 Armada Dr.
Carlsbad, CA 92008
Phone   760-431-9124
              800-767-6266
Fax   760-438-7327
Email   sharonm@namm.com
              info@amc-music.org

American Society of Young Musicians (ASYM)
www.asymusicians.org
National nonprofit organization committed to the enrichment of young musicians; Sponsor of the annual ASYM Spring Benefit Concert and Awards.
6100 Wilshire Blvd., Ste. 230
Los Angeles, CA 90048
Phone   310-358-8301
Fax   310-358-8304
Email   info@asymusicians.org

American Women in Radio & Television (AWRT)
www.awrt.org
National organization supporting the advancement of women in the communications industry.
8405 Greensboro Dr., Ste. 800
McLean, CA 22102
Phone   703-506-3290
Fax   703-506-3266
Email   info@awrt.org

ASCAP (Los Angeles)
www.ascap.com
Performing rights organization representing composers, lyricists, songwriters, and music publishers
7920 Sunset Blvd., 3rd Fl.
Los Angeles, CA 90046
Phone   323-883-1000
Fax   323-883-1049
Email   info@ascap.com
Marilyn Bergman, President/ Chairman of the Board
John LoFrumento, CEO
Todd Brabec, Executive VP, Membership Group
Nancy Knutsen, Sr. VP, Film & TV Music
Jeanie Weems, VP, Creative/ Film & TV Special Projects
Michael Kerker, Assistant VP, Musical Theater
Kevin Coogan, Sr. Director, Film & TV Music
Shawn LeMone, Sr. Director, Research & Technology/ Film & TV/LA Membership
Diana Szyszkiewicz, Sr. Director, Distribution & Membership Projects/LA Membership
Pamela Allen, Director, Film & TV Music
Mike Todd, Director, Film & TV Music
Charlyn Bernal, Film & TV Music Representative
Darren Cusanovich, Executive Assistant
Jennifer Flett, Executive Assistant

ASCAP (Nashville)
www.ascap.com/nashville
2 Music Square West
Nashville, TN 37203
Phone   615-742-5000
Fax   615-742-5020
Connie Bradley, Sr. VP

ASCAP (New York)
www.ascap.com
1 Lincoln Plaza
New York, NY 10023
Phone   212-621-6000
Fax   212-721-0955
Marilyn Bergman, President/ Chairman of the Board
John LoFrumento, CEO
Michael Kerker, Assistant VP, Musical Theater
Sue Devine, Sr. Director, Film/TV Music
Jumee Park, Executive Assistant

Association of Independent Music Publishers (AIMP)

www.aimp.org
Educates and informs local music publishers about current industry trends and practices through meetings, forums and workshops.

Los Angeles
PO Box 69473
Los Angeles, CA 90069
Phone   818-771-7301
Email   lainfo@aimp.org
         nyinfo@aimp.org

New York
c/o Burton Goldstein & Company, LLC
156 W. 56th St., Ste. 1803
New York, NY 10019
Phone   212-582-7622
Fax   212-582-8273

Association of Independent Video and Filmmakers (AIVF)

www.aivf.org
Nonprofit membership organization serving local, national and international filmmakers, including documentarians and experimental artists.
304 Hudston St., 6th Fl.
New York, NY 10013
Phone   212-807-1400
Fax   212-463-8519
Email   info@aivf.org
Bo Mehrad, Information Services Director

Association of Talent Agents (ATA)

www.agentassociation.com
Nonprofit trade association for talent agencies representing clients in the motion picture and television industries, as well as literary, theatre, radio, and commercial clients.
9255 Sunset Blvd., Ste. 930
Los Angeles, CA 90069
Phone   310-274-0628
Fax   310-274-5063
Shellie Jetton, Administrative Director

Audio Engineering Society (AES)

www.aes.org
A professional society devoted to audio technology.
60 E. 42nd St., Ste. 2520
New York, NY 10165
Phone   212-661-8528
Fax   212-682-0477
Email   hq@aes.org

Axis of Justice

www.axisofjustice.org
Nonprofit organization whose purpose is to bring together musicians, fans of music, and grassroots political organizations to fight for social justice together.
PO Box 29426
Los Angeles, CA 90029
Email   politics@axisofjustice.org
         volunteer@
         axisofjustice.org
Jake Sexton, Political Director

The Blues Foundation

www.blues.org
Nonprofit corporation with over a hundred affiliated Blues organizations and membership spanning twenty-four countries. The Foundation serves as the umbrella organization for Blues music.
49 Union Ave.
Memphis, TN 38103
Phone   901-527-2583
Fax   901-529-4030
Email   jay@blues.org
Jay Sieleman, Executive Director

Blues Music Association

www.bluesmusicassociation.com
Trade organization explores and expands work opportunities for professional Blues musicians.
PO Box 3122
Memphis, TN 38173
Phone   901-572-3843
Email   info@
         bluesmusicassociation.com

BMI (Los Angeles)

www.bmi.com
8730 Sunset Blvd., 3rd Fl.
Los Angeles, CA 90069
Phone   310-659-9109
Fax   310-657-6947
Doreen Ringer Ross, VP, Film & TV Relations
Linda Livingston, Sr. Director, Film & TV Relations
Ray Yee, Sr. Director, Film & TV Relations
Ivanne Deneroff, Associate Director, Film & TV Relations
Liane Mori, Associate Director, Media Relations

BMI (New York)

www.bmi.com
320 W. 57th St.
New York, NY 10019
Phone   212-586-2000
Fax   212-246-2163
Frances W. Preston, President Emerita
Del R. Bryant, President/CEO
Alison Smith, Sr. VP, Performing Rights
Phillip R. Graham, Sr. VP, Writer/Publisher Relations

California Arts Council (CAC)

www.cac.ca.gov
State organization encouraging artistic awareness, expression, and participation reflecting California's diverse cultures.
1300 I St., Ste. 930
Sacramento, CA 95814
Phone   916-322-6555
         800-201-6201
Fax   916-322-6575
Mary Beth Barber, Communications Director

Clear, Inc.

www.clearinc.org
Organization of clearance and research professionals working in the film, television, and multimedia industries.
PO Box 628
Burbank, CA 91503-0628
Fax   413-647-3380
Email   info@clearinc.org

Country Music Association (CMA)

www.cmaworld.com
Organization dedicated to bringing poetry and emotion of country music to the world.
One Music Circle South
Nashville, TN 37203
Phone   615-244-2840
Fax   615-726-0314

Entertainment Industries Council Inc.

www.eiconline.org
Nonprofit organization founded in 1983 by leaders in the entertainment industry to provide information, awareness and understanding of major health and social issues among the entertainment industries and to audiences at large.
10635 Santa Monica Blvd., Ste. 100
Los Angeles, CA 90025
Phone   310-446-7818
Fax   310-446-7819
Email   eicwest@eiconline.org

Film Music Network

www.filmmusicworld.com
Organization for film and television music professionals, including supervisors, composers, editors and contractors.
13101 Washington Blvd., Ste. 466
Los Angeles, CA 90066
Phone   310-909-8418
         800-774-3700
Fax   310-496-0917
Email   info@filmmusicworld.com

Gospel Music Association (GMA)

www.gospelmusic.org
Organization founded for the purpose of supporting, encouraging and promoting the development of all forms of Gospel music.
1205 Division St.
Nashville, TN 37203
Phone   615-242-0303
Fax   615-254-9755

Hollywood Radio & Television Society (HRTS)

www.hrts.org
Recognized as the entertainment industry's premiere networking and information forum. Through the signature Newsmaker Luncheon Series and other HRTS events, provides industry executives the opportunity to stay abreast of current trends while also staying connected to other key entertainment industry leaders.
13701 Riverside Dr., Ste. 205
Sherman Oaks, CA 91423
Phone   818-789-1182
Fax   818-789-1210
Email   info@hrts.org
Andy Friendly, President, Board of Directors
Dave Ferrara, Executive Director

International Alliance of Theatrical Stage Employees (IATSE)

www.iatse-intl.org
Union representing technicians, artisans and craftpersons in the entertainment industry including live theatre, film and television production and trade shows.

Los Angeles
10045 Riverside Dr.
Toluca Lake, CA 91602
Phone   818-980-3499
Fax   818-980-3496

New York
1430 Broadway, 20th Fl.
New York, NY 10018
Phone   212-730-1770
Fax   212-730-7809

International Bluegrass Music Association (IBMA)

www.ibma.org
Organization dedicated to promoting high standards of professionalism, a greater appreciation of Bluegrass music and the success of the worldwide Bluegrass community.
2 Music Circle South, Ste. 100
Nashville, TN 37203
Phone   615-256-3222
         888-438-4262
Fax   615-256-0450
Email   info@ibma.org

International Music Products Association (NAMM)

www.namm.com

Unifies, leads, and strengthens the global music products industry to increase active participation in music making.

5790 Armada Dr.
Carlsbad, CA 92008
Phone   760-438-8001
Fax   760-438-7327
Email   info@namm.com

International Press Academy

www.pressacademy.com

Association of professional entertainment journalists.

9601 Wilshire Blvd., Ste. 755
Beverly Hills, CA 90210
Phone   310-271-7041
Fax   818-787-3627
Email   info@pressacademy.com

Latin Academy of Recording Arts & Sciences (LARAS)

www.latingrammy.com

Membership-based association composed of musicians, producers, engineers and other technical recording professionals who are dedicated to improving the quality of life and the cultural condition for Latin music and its makers.

311 Lincoln Blvd., Ste. 301
Miami Beach, FL 33139
Phone   305-672-4060
Fax   305-672-2076
Email   florida@grammy.com

The Norman Lear Center

www.learcenter.org

A multidisciplinary research and public policy center exploring implications of the convergence of entertainment, commerce, and society.

USC Annenberg School of Communication
Los Angeles, CA 90089
Phone   213-821-1343
Fax   213-821-1580
Email   enter@usc.edu

Lifebeat - The Music Industry Fights AIDS

www.lifebeat.org

National nonprofit organization dedicated to reaching America's youth with the message of HIV/AIDS prevention. Lifebeat mobilizes the talents and resources of the music industry to raise awareness and to provide support to the AIDS community.

630 Ninth Ave., Ste. 1010
New York, NY 10036-3708
Phone   212-459-2590
Fax   212-459-2892
Email   info@lifebeat.org

Los Angeles Music Network (LAMN)

www.lamn.com

Promotes career advancement, continued education and communication among music industry professionals. Sponsors industry gatherings, workshops, private dinners and seminars with top executives. Provides professional development opportunities and career services, such as job listings and a mentor network, to our members.

PO Box 2446
Toluca Lake, CA 91610-2446
Phone   818-769-6095
Email   info@lamn.com

Music for America

www.musicforamerica.org

Dedicated to providing the cultural capital and political savvy for our generation to reinvent progressive politics.

660 York St., Ste. 101
San Francisco, CA 94110

Music Managers Forum (MMF)

www.mmfus.org

Organization dedicated to furthering the interests of managers and their artists in all fields of the music industry including live performance, recording and publishing.

PO Box 444, Village Station
New York, NY 10014
Phone   212-213-8787
Fax   212-213-9797
Email   info@mmfus.org

Music Video Production Association (MVPA)

www.mvpa.com

Nonprofit trade organization made up of music video production and post production companies, as well as editors, directors, producers, cinematographers, choreographers, script supervisors, computer animators and make-up artists involved in the production of music videos.

201 N. Occidental Blvd.,
Bldg. 7, Unit B
Los Angeles, CA 90026
Phone   213-387-1590
Fax   213-385-9507
Email   info@mvpa.com

*Andrea Clark, Executive Director
Amy E, Administrative Director*

Musicares

www.musicares.com

Ensures that music people have a compassionate place to turn to in times of need. Provides critical assistance, treating each case with integrity and confidentiality. Programs provide much-needed services and resources to individuals in the music community who are confronted by a wide range of financial, medical and personal emergencies.

3402 Pico Blvd.
Santa Monica, CA 90405
Phone   310-392-3777
Fax   310-392-2187
Email   musicares@grammy.com

Musicians Assistance Program (MAP)

www.map2000.org

Nonprofit national organization which helps musicians and industry pros recover from drug and alcohol abuse.

817 Vine St., Ste. 219
Hollywood, CA 90038
Phone   888-MAP-MAP1
          323-993-3197
Fax   323-993-3198
Email   mapoffice@aol.com

Musicians Contact Service

www.musicianscontact.com

Job finding service for professional musicians.

PO Box 788
Woodland Hills, CA 91365
Phone   818-888-7879
Email   info@musicianscontact.com

Nashville Association of Talent Directors (NATD)

www.n-a-t-d.com

Professional entertainment organization comprised of industry professionals involved in all aspects of the music and entertainment industries.

PO Box 23903
Nashville, TN 37202-3903
Phone   615-662-2200 (x*410)
          615-297-0100
Email   info@n-a-t-d.com

Nashville Songwriters Association International (NSAI)

www.nashvillesongwriters.com

Consists of songwriters from all genres of music who are committed to protecting the rights and future of the profession of songwriting and to educate, elevate and celebrate the songwriter.

1710 Roy Acuff Place
Nashville, TN 37203
Phone   615-256-3354
          800-321-6008
Fax   615-256-0034
Email   nsai@
          nashvillesongwriters.com

Alicia Jones, Membership Director

National Academy of Popular Music/Songwriters Hall of Fame

www.shof.org

Founded in 1969, the Songwriters Hall of Fame is dedicated to recognizing and honoring the accomplishments and lives of those men and women who create the popular songs that serve as the soundtrack of our lives.

330 W. 58th St., Ste. 411
New York, NY 10019-1820
Phone   212-957-9230
Fax   212-957-9227
Email   songwritershalloffame@
          compuserve.com

National Academy of Recording Arts & Sciences (NARAS)

www.grammy.com

Organization dedicated to improving the quality of life and cultural condition for musicians, producers, and other recording professionals. Provides outreach, professional development, cultural enrichment, education and human services programs. Sponsors The Grammy Awards.

The Recording Academy
3402 Pico Blvd.
Santa Monica, CA 90405
Phone   310-392-3777
Fax   310-392-2306
Email   losangeles@grammy.com

National Association for Campus Activities (NACA)

www.naca.org

Links the higher education and entertainment communities in a business and learning partnership.

13 Harbison Way
Columbia, SC 29212
Phone   803-732-6222
Fax   803-749-1047
Email   memberservices@naca.org

National Association of Broadcasters (NAB)

www.nab.org

Full-service trade association representing the interests of free, over-the-air radio and television broadcasters.

1771 North St. NW
Washington, DC 20036
Phone   202-429-5300
Fax   202-429-4199
Email   nab@nab.org

National Association of Composers

www.music-usa.org

Produces member concerts, newsletter and the Young Composers competition.

PO Box 49256
Barrington Station
Los Angeles, CA 90049
Phone   310-838-4465
Email   nacusa@music-usa.org

National Association of Record Industry Professionals (NARIP)

www.narip.com

Promotes continued education, career advancement and collegiality among record executives.

PO Box 2446
Toluca Lake, CA 91610
Phone   818-769-7007
Email   info@narip.com
Tess Taylor, President

National Association of Recording Merchandisers (NARM)

www.narm.com

Non-Profit trade association representing retailers, wholesalers, record labels and distributors of pre-recorded music in the U.S.

9 Eves Dr., Ste. 120
Marlton, NJ 08053
Phone   856-596-2221
Fax   856-596-3268
Email   dichter@narm.com
Jim Donio, President

National Association of Talent Representatives (NATR)

www.agentassociation.com
New York, NY
Phone   212-262-5696
Phil Adelman, President

National Conference of Personal Managers (NCOPM)

www.ncopm.com

Association for the advancement of personal managers and their clients.

Los Angeles
PO Box 609
Palm Desert, CA 92261-0609
Phone   310-492-5983

New York
330 W. 38th St., Ste. 904
New York, NY 10018
Phone   212-245-2063
Fax   212-245-2367
Daniel Abrahamsen, Executive Director, Eastern Division
Candee Barshop, Executive Director, Western Division

National Music Council

www.musiccouncil.org

Founded in 1940 and chartered by the 84th Congress in 1956, the National Music Council represents the United States to the International Music Council/UNESCO. The Council acts as a clearing house for the joint opinion and decision of its members and is dedicated to strengthening the importance of music in our life and culture.

425 Park St.
Upper Mountclair, NJ 07043
Phone   973-655-7974
Fax   973-655-5432
Email   sandersd@
              mail.montclair.edu

National Music Publishing Association (NMPA)

www.nmpa.org

The NMPA's mandate is to protect and advance the interests of music publishers and their songwriter partners in matters relating to the domestic and global protection of music copyrights. The NMPA is the leading trade association in the United States for music publishers, and advocates for their interests, as well as for their songwriter partners, by protecting, upholding, and advancing their valuable copyrights.

101 Constitution Avenue NW, Ste. 705 East
Washington, DC 20001
Phone   202-742-4375
Fax   202-742-4377
Email   pr@nmpa.org

Nosotros/Ricardo Montalban Foundation

www.nosotros.org

Organization established to improve the image of Latinos/Hispanics as they are portrayed in the entertainment industry, both in front of and behind the camera, as well as to expand employment opportunities within the entertainment industry. Producers of The Golden Eagle Awards.

650 N. Bronson Ave., Ste. 102
Hollywood, CA 90004
Phone   323-466-8566
              (President's Office)
              323-465-4167
              (Nosotros/Theatre Office)
Fax   323-466-8540

Rap Coalition

www.rapcoalition.org
www.rapcointelpro.com

Nonprofit advocacy group supporting artists.

99 S. 2nd St., Ste. 274
Memphis, TN 38103
Phone   917-501-6100
Email   rapcoalition@aol.com

Recording Industry Association of America (RIAA)

www.riaa.com

Strives to protect artistic freedom, combat record piracy and expand market opportunities. Also awards the gold, platinum and multi-platinum sales certificates.

1330 Connecticut Ave. NW, Ste. 300
Washington, DC 20036
Phone   202-775-0101
Fax   202-775-7253

Recording Musicians Association (RMA)

www.rmala.org

Nonprofit organization of studio musicians and composers.

817 Vine St., Ste. 209
Hollywood, CA 90038-3716
Phone   323-462-4762
Fax   323-462-2406
Email   info@rmaweb.org
Ximena Marin, Executive Administrator

The Red Hot Organization

www.redhot.org

The leading AIDS fighting organization in the music industry.

Email   redhotorganization@
              yahoo.com

Rock the Vote

www.rockthevote.org

Dedicated to protecting freedom of expression and mobilizing young people to get out and vote.

Los Angeles
10635 Santa Monica Blvd., Ste. 150
Los Angeles, CA 90025
Phone   310-234-0665
Fax   310-234-0666
Email   info@rockthevote.org

Washington, DC
1313 L St., NW, 1st Fl.
Washington, DC 20005
Phone   202-962-9710
Fax   202-962-9715

SESAC (Los Angeles)

www.sesac.com

Nonprofit performing rights organization of songwriters, composers and music publishers.

501 Santa Monica Blvd., Ste. 450
Santa Monica, CA 90401
Phone   310-393-9671
              877-831-0533
Fax   310-393-6497
Email   progers@sesac.com
Pat Rogers, Sr. VP, Corporate Relations/Artist Development
James Leach, Director, Writer/Publisher Relations
JJ Cheng, Director, SESAC Latina
Hugo Gonzalez, Associate Director, SESAC Latina
Alissa Nurko, Coordinator, Writer/Publisher Relations
Alex Perez, Coordinator, SESAC Latina

SESAC (Nashville)

www.sesac.com
55 Music Square East
Nashville, TN 37203
Phone   615-320-0055
Fax   615-329-9627
Tim Fink, Associate VP, Writer/Publisher Relations
John Mullins, Associate Director, Writer/Publisher Relations
Shannan Neese, Associate Director, Writer/Publisher Relations
Mandy Reilly, Assistant

SESAC (New York)

www.sesac.com
152 W. 57th St., 57th Fl.
New York, NY 10019
Phone   212-586-3450
Fax   212-489-5699
Email   llorence@sesac.com
Trevor Gale, VP, Writer/ Publisher Relations
Linda Lorence, VP, Writer/ Publisher Relations

SOCAN (The Society of Composers, Authors and Music Publishers of Canada)
www.socan.ca
41 Valleybrook Dr.
Toronto, ON M3B 2S6, Canada
Phone 416-445-8700
 800-557-6226
Fax 416-445-7108
Email socan@socan.ca
Andre LeBel, CEO
Joel Grad, Executive VP/CFO
*France LeFleur, VP, Licensing/
 GM, Quebec & Atlantic Division*
*Kent Sturgeon, VP, Member
 Management/GM, West Coast
 Division*
*Doreen Cable, VP, External
 Relations*
*Tom Flannery, VP, Business
 Development*
Jeff King. VP, Member Operations
*C. Paul Spurgeon, VP, Legal
 Services/General Counsel*
Randy Wark, VP, Human Resources
*Marian Wilson, VP, Information
 Technology*

Society of Composers & Lyricists
www.filmscore.org
www.thescl.com
*Nonprofit volunteer organization
advancing the professional
interests of lyricists and
composers of film and television
music.*
400 S. Beverly Dr., Ste. 214
Beverly Hills, CA 90212
Phone 310-281-2812
Fax 310-284-4861

Society of Professional Audio Recording Services
www.spars.com
*Organization dedicated to
sharing hands-on business
information about recording
facility ownership, management
and operations.*
PO Box 770845
Memphis, TN 38177-0845
Phone 800-771-7727
 901-747-3111

Society of Stage Directors & Choreographers (SSDC)
www.ssdc.org
*Union representing directors and
choreographers of Broadway
national tours, regional theatre,
dinner theatre and summer stock,
as well as choreographers for
motion pictures, television and
music videos.*
1501 Broadway, Ste. 1701
New York, NY 10036-5653
Phone 212-391-1070
 800-541-5204
Fax 212-302-6195

Sweet Relief Musicians Fund
www.sweetrelief.org
*Relief organization offering
grants to musicians suffering from
serious illness, disability or other
conditions.*
4150 Riverside Dr., Ste. 212
Burbank, CA 91505
Phone 818-563-5140
Fax 818-563-5144
Email info@sweetrelief.org

Talent Managers Association (TMA)
www.talentmanagers.org
*Nonprofit organization
promoting and encouraging
the highest standards of
professionalism in the practice
of talent management.*
4804 Laurel Canyon Blvd.,
Ste. 611
Valley Village, CA 91607
Phone 310-205-8495
Fax 818-765-2903
Steven Nash, President
Betty McCormick Aggas, VP

U.S. Copyright Office
www.copyright.gov
*Promotes progress of the arts
and protection for the works of
authors; Web site serves the
copyright community of creators
and users, as well as the general
public.*
Library of Congress
101 Independence Avenue S.E.
Washington, D.C. 20559
Phone 202-707-3000
 202-707-9100 (Hotline)

Women in Music - National Network
www.womeninmusic.com
*Nonprofit membership
organization designed to
promote the recognition of
women in music through
services, education and
networking resources.*
31121 Mission Blvd., Ste. 300
Hayward, CA 94544
Phone 510-232-3897
Fax 510-215-2846
Email admin@womeninmusic.com

Women's Image Network (WIN)
www.winfemme.com
www.thewinawards.com
*Nonprofit corporation
encouraging positive portrayals
of women in theater, television
and film.*
2118 Wilshire Blvd., Ste. 144
Santa Monica, CA 90403
Phone 310-229-5365
Email info@winfemme.com
Phyllis Stuart, Founder
Joy Tuttle, Event Producer
Xochitl Gonzales
Grace Sutherin

HOLLYWOOD MUSIC INDUSTRY DIRECTORY

To submit your company for a free listing in the
HOLLYWOOD MUSIC INDUSTRY DIRECTORY, complete and return
this application form along <u>with a brief bio and/or company profile.</u>
All listings are at the discretion of the editor.

Phone 323-525-2348 • Fax 323-525-2393 • www.hcdonline.com

COMPANY _____ C/O _____

STREET _____ CITY _____ STATE _____ ZIP _____

PHONE _____ FAX _____

PUBLISHED EMAIL _____ WEBSITE _____

UNPUBLISHED EMAIL _____ UNPUBLISHED FAX _____

YOU ARE...
(check one)

☐ RECORD COMPANY/LABEL ☐ MUSIC PUBLISHER ☐ MUSIC SUPERVISOR

☐ MUSIC PRODUCER ☐ MUSIC LICENSING/CLEARANCE ☐ RECORDING STUDIO

Artist Roster (Partial list or attach full roster) _____

_____

Distributor _____

Labels _____

Genres

☐ ALL GENRES ☐ ADULT CONTEMPORARY ☐ ALTERNATIVE ☐ AMERICANA ☐ BLUEGRASS

☐ BLUES ☐ CHILDRENS ☐ CHRISTIAN ☐ CLASSICAL ☐ COUNTRY

☐ ELECTRONICA ☐ FOLK ☐ GOSPEL ☐ HARDCORE ☐ JAZZ

☐ LATIN ☐ METAL ☐ NEW AGE ☐ POP ☐ PUNK

☐ R&B ☐ RAP/HIP-HOP ☐ REGGAE ☐ REGGAETON ☐ ROCK

☐ ROOTS ☐ URBAN ☐ WORLD

Recent Soundtracks or Soundtrack Contributions _____

_____

Submission Policy _____

Comments _____

S
T Include Principals, Dept. Heads, complete A&R Staff, and key Maketing, Publicity, Public Relations and Licensing personnel.
A NAME _____ TITLE _____
F NAME _____ TITLE _____
F NAME _____ TITLE _____
     NAME _____ TITLE _____
     NAME _____ TITLE _____

(Please list additional names on separate sheet of paper)

SUBMITTED BY _____ DATE _____

HOLLYWOOD MUSIC INDUSTRY DIRECTORY

To submit your company for a free listing in the
HOLLYWOOD MUSIC INDUSTRY DIRECTORY, complete and return
this application form along <u>with a brief bio and/or company profile.</u>
All listings are at the discretion of the editor.

Phone 323-525-2348 • Fax 323-525-2393 • www.hcdonline.com

COMPANY _____ C/O _____

STREET _____ CITY _____ STATE _____ ZIP _____

PHONE _____ FAX _____

PUBLISHED EMAIL _____ WEBSITE _____

UNPUBLISHED EMAIL _____ UNPUBLISHED FAX _____

YOU ARE...
(check one)

❑ AGENCY   ❑ MANAGEMENT COMPANY

TYPES OF CLIENTS REPRESENTED
(check all that apply)

❑ MUSICAL ARTISTS

❑ ALL GENRES	❑ ADULT CONTEMPORARY	❑ ALTERNATIVE	❑ AMERICANA	❑ BLUEGRASS
❑ BLUES	❑ CHILDRENS	❑ CHRISTIAN	❑ CLASSICAL	❑ COUNTRY
❑ ELECTRONICA	❑ FOLK	❑ GOSPEL	❑ HARDCORE	❑ JAZZ
❑ LATIN	❑ METAL	❑ NEW AGE	❑ POP	❑ PUNK
❑ R&B	❑ RAP/HIP-HOP	❑ REGGAE	❑ REGGAETON	❑ ROCK
❑ ROOTS	❑ URBAN	❑ WORLD		

❑ MUSIC PRODUCERS   ❑ MUSIC SUPERVISORS   ❑ FILM/TV COMPOSERS   ❑ LYRICISTS

❑ SONGWRITERS   ❑ STUDIO MUSICIANS   ❑ STUDIO VOCALISTS   ❑ STUDIO ENGINEERS/TECHNICIANS

❑ OTHER _____

Client List (Use separate sheet for additional clients) _____

_____

Submission Policy _____

S NAME _____ TITLE _____

T NAME _____ TITLE _____

A NAME _____ TITLE _____

F NAME _____ TITLE _____

F NAME _____ TITLE _____

(Please list additional names on separate sheet of paper)

ADDITIONAL COMMENTS _____

_____

SUBMITTED BY _____ DATE _____

SECTION **A**

DISTRIBUTORS & LABELS

— **Distributors**

— Labels

Asterisks (*) next to companies denote new listings.

101 DISTRIBUTION
2375 E. Camelback Road, 5th Fl.
Phoenix, AZ 85016
PHONE 602-357-3288
FAX 602-357-3288
EMAIL . . . . .weworktogether@101distribution.com
SECOND EMAIL . . . . .intelligence@101distribution.com
WEB SITE www.101distribution.com
GENRES   All Genres
COMMENTS   Distributor

Damon Evans . . . . .Executive Director

ACTIVATE ENTERTAINMENT
11328 Magnolia Blvd., Ste. 3
North Hollywood, CA 91601-3705
PHONE 818-505-0669
EMAIL . . . . .jay@2activate.com
WEB SITE www.2activate.com
GENRES   Alternative - Pop - Punk - Rap/Hip-Hop -
                          Rock - Urban
SUBMISSION POLICY   CD with photo, bio and accomplish-
                          ments

Jay Warsinke . . . . .President
Perry Sagliocci . . . . .Film & TV

AEC ONE STOP GROUP
4250 Coral Ridge Dr.
Coral Springs, FL 33065
PHONE 800-329-7664
WEB SITE . . . . .www.aent.com
GENRES   All Genres

Eric Dreyfuss . . . . .Domestic Accounts
Heather Peach . . . . .Chain Accounts
Nelson Perez . . . . .Independent Distribution

ALLEGRO CORPORATION
14134 NE Airport Way
Portland, OR 97230-3443
PHONE 503-257-8480/800-288-2007
FAX 503-257-9061/503-256-4615
EMAIL .mailcs@allegro-music.com
WEB SITE .www.allegro-music.com
GENRES   Classical - Jazz - Pop - World

Joe Micallef . . . . .Chairman/CEO (x2063)
Vince Micallef . . . . .President/COO (x2061)
Rico Micallef . . . . .Executive VP (x2058)
Damon Sgobbo . . . . .VP, North American Sales (x2139)
Chris Scofield . . . . .Label Manager (x2009)
Forrest Faubion . . . . .Product Manager, Non-Classical (x2035)
Bill Tennant . . . . .Product Manager, Classical (x2108)
John Shaw . . . . .Director, Warehouse Operations (x2003)
Amelia Dupree . . . . .Customer Service Manager (x2055)
Pete Foley . . . . .MIS Manager (x2026)
Ted Lambeth . . . . .Inventory Manager (x2057)

ALTERNATIVE DISTRIBUTION ALLIANCE (ADA)
72 Spring St., 12th Fl.
New York, NY 10012
PHONE 212-343-2485/818-977-0552
FAX 212-343-7977
EMAIL . . . . .distribution@ada-music.com
WEB SITE . . . . .www.ada-music.com
GENRES   Alternative
COMMENTS   West Coast office: 3300 Pacific Ave.,
                          Burbank, CA 91505

Andy Allen . . . . .President
David Lee Galanida . . . . .Western Sales Manager (818-953-2112)
Hyla Urbany . . . . .Eastern/Central Sales Manager (212-991-5111)

APPLE ITUNES
1 Infinite Loop
Cupertino, CA 95014
PHONE 408-996-1010
WEBSITE . . . . .www.apple.com
GENRES   All Genres
COMMENTS   Digital distribution

Steven Jobs . . . . .Chairman/CEO

AROUND THE WORLD MUSIC
17208 Braxton St.
Granada Hills, CA 91344-1515
PHONE 818-360-8088
FAX 818-366-8353
EMAIL . . . . .weissworld@socal.rr.com
GENRES   Adult Contemporary - Alternative -
                          Classical - Electronica - Folk - Jazz -
                          Latin - New Age - Pop - Roots - World
COMMENTS   Distributor in Southeast Asia only:
                          Singapore, Malaysia, Thailand, Hong
                          Kong, Taiwan, Philippines, Indonesia

Bob Weiss . . . . .President
Pielak Chang . . . . .Managing Director

ARROW DISTRIBUTING COMPANY
11012 Aurora Hudson
Streetsboro, OH 44241
PHONE 800-321-3660/330-528-0405
FAX 330-528-0423
EMAIL . . . . .mminfo@arrdis.com
SECOND EMAIL . . . . .mee@arrdis.com
WEB SITE . . . . .www.arrdis.com
GENRES   Alternative - Hardcore - Metal - Pop -
                          Punk - R&B - Rap/Hip-Hop - Rock -
                          Urban
COMMENTS   Distributor and wholesaler

Wes Lowe . . . . .VP, Sales & Marketing
Matt Earley . . . . .Sales, Independent Distribution

ARTIST1STOP
3734 Osage St.
Denver, CO 80211
PHONE 877-247-5046/303-433-9779
FAX 303-433-8808
EMAIL . . . . .info@artist1stop.com
WEB SITE www.artist1stop.com
GENRES   All Genres

Abel Arroyo . . . . .Manager

ARTISTDIRECT.COM
10900 Wilshire Blvd, Ste. 1400
Los Angeles, CA 90024
PHONE 310-443-5360
FAX 310-443-5361
WEB SITE . . . . .www.artistdirect.com
GENRES   Alternative
COMMENTS   Online distributor

Jon Diamond . . . . .CEO
Nick Turner . . . . .President
Bill Weiman . . . . .Sales

AUSTIN RECORD DISTRIBUTORS
PO Box 312
Austin, TX 78767
PHONE 512-451-9770
FAX 512-451-9770
EMAIL . . . . .ausrec@realtime.net
WEB SITE www.mosaicsandmore.net/ard3table4.html
GENRES   Blues - Country - Folk - Jazz - R&B -
                          Rock - Roots
COMMENTS   Local Artists

Susan Jarrett . . . . .Owner

DISTRIBUTORS

BALBOA RECORDS CO.
10900 Washington Blvd.
Culver City, CA 90232
PHONE 310-204-3792
FAX 310-204-0886
EMAIL . . . . .contacto@balboarecords.com
WEB SITE . . . . .www.balboarecords.com
GENRES   Latin - World

Fernando Sanchez . . . . .Controller

*BAYSIDE ENTERTAINMENT DISTRIBUTION
885 Riverside Pkwy.
West Sacramento, CA 95605
PHONE 916-371-2800/800-525-5709
FAX 916-371-1995
WEB SITE . . . . .www.baysidedist.com
GENRES   All Genres

Rory Musil . . . . .Product Manger (x218)
Mike Regan .National Sales (x206)
Ray Copeland . . . . .Audio Buyer (x246)
Brian Kimball . . . . .Account Rep (951-312-3411)
Jim McCall . . . . .Account Rep (770-831-6226)
Carl Michelakos . . . . .Account Rep (770-736-1224)
Jimmy White . . . . .Account Rep (310-378-7625)

BIG DADDY MUSIC DISTRIBUTION
162 N. Eighth St.
Kenilworth, NJ 07033
PHONE 908-653-9110
FAX 908-653-9114
EMAIL . . . . .info@bigdaddymusic.com
WEB SITE .www.bigdaddymusic.com
GENRES   All Genres
COMMENTS   Distributor

Burt Goldstein . . . . .President (bigburt@bigdaddymusic.com)
Doug Bail . . . . .VP (doug@bigdaddymusic.com)
Mike Dunkerley . . . . . . .Product Manager (mike@bigdaddymusic.com)
Larry Germack . . . . .National Sales (larry@bigdaddymusic.com)
Gary Gutmann . . . . .Indie Sales (gary@bigdaddymusic.com)
Rob Meagher . . . . .Warehouse Manager
Steve Palmer . . . . .Chicago/Midwest Sales (sbprep@aol.com)
Ed Richter . . . . .Seattle/Portland Sales (edmrich@aol.com)
Brad Tyrrell . . . . .West Coast Sales
George Castanza . . . . .Label Acquisition

BURNSIDE DISTRIBUTION CORP.
3158 E. Burnside St.
Portland, OR 97214
PHONE 503-231-8943/503-231-0876
FAX 503-238-2020/503-231-0420
EMAIL . . . . .sales@bdcdistribution.com
WEB SITE . . . . .www.bdcdistribution.com
GENRES   All Genres
COMMENTS   Warehouse: 3647 SE 21st Ave.,
                         Portland, OR 97202

Terry Currier . . . . .President
Bill McNally . . . . .VP
Frank Brandon .Operations Manager
Jill McNamera . . . . .Markeitng Director
Keith Westmoreland . . . . .Marketing Director
Bob Beland . . . . .Sales, Los Angeles (310-390-9709)
Diane Bizier . . . . .Sales, Southwest
Matt Brown . . . . .In-House Sales
Derek Brown .Warehouse Manager
Bill Brownlee . . . .Sales, Central & North Central States (913-341-8739)
Ric Curtice . . . . . . .Sales, Northern CA & Northern NV (925-461-5056)
Barry Fisch . . . . .Sales, NY & CT (516-827-5431)
Dan Hogan . . . . .Sales, Southern CA & Southern NV
Alexis Kelley . . . . .Sales, Southeast (770-441-7844)
Steve Palmer . .Sales, Chicago, St. Louis & Kansas City (773-334-7078)
Clay Pasternack . . . . .Sales, Midwest (440-333-2208)
Bill Pierce . . . . .Sales, Minnesota (952-831-5663)
George Romansic . . . . .Sales, Washington (206-282-4820)
Brenna Sheridan . . . . .Data & Inquiry Manager
Jim Williams . . . . .Sales, Hawaii (808-595-5218)

CAROLINE DISTRIBUTION
104 W. 29th St.
New York, NY 10001
PHONE 212-886-7500
FAX 212-643-5563
EMAIL . . . . .distribution@caroline.com
SECOND EMAIL .sales@caroline.com
WEB SITE . . . . .www.carolinedist.com
GENRES   Alternative - Electronica - Metal - Punk -
                         Urban

Rick Williams . . . . .General Manager
Michael Bull .VP, Label Relations
Mercedes Ramos . . . . .Finance Director
Marc Weitz . . . . .Director, Strategic Sales & Marketing
Kenny Butler . . . . .Distribution Center Manager
Natalie Chavez . . . . .West Coast Sales Manager
Arthur Nalis . . . . .East Coast Sales Manager
Niall Rafferty . . . . .Finance Analyst
Isa Shulman . . . . .West Coast Marketing Manager
Chad Tait . . . . .Digital Sales & Marketing Manager
Ken Kamber . . . . .IT Manager

CARROT TOP DISTRIBUTION, LTD.
935 W. Chestnut St., Ste. LL15
Chicago, IL 60622
PHONE 312-432-1194
FAX 312-432-1351
EMAIL . . . . .ctd@carrottoprecords.com
WEB SITE . . . . .www.ctdltd.com
GENRES   Country - Pop - Reggae - Rock
SUBMISSION POLICY   See Web site
COMMENTS   Also Indie Rock; 15,000 title catalog

Patrick Monaghan . . . . .President

CEGI DISTRIBUTORS
PO Box 9965
Canoga Park, CA 91309
PHONE 818-725-2611
FAX 818-998-3763
EMAIL . . . . .clout@cloutent.com
SECOND EMAIL .cegi@cloutent.com
WEB SITE . . . . .www.cloutent.com
GENRES   Alternative - Gospel - Jazz - New Age -
                         Pop - R&B - Rap/Hip-Hop - Reggae -
                         Urban

Desi Hill . . . . .CEO
Mike James . . . . .VP, Promotions
Terry Williams . . . . .VP, Product Management
Paula Williams . . . . .VP, Urban Marketing
Terri Yates . . . . .VP, Business Affairs

CENTRAL SOUTH DISTRIBUTION, INC.
3730 Vulcan Dr.
Nashville, TN 37211
PHONE 615-833-5960
FAX 615-331-2501
WEB SITE . . . . .www.centralsouthdistribution.com
GENRES   Christian - Gospel

Chuck Adams . . . . .President
Randy Davidson . . . . .CEO
J.P. Bennett . . . . .VP, Distribution
Greg Davidson . . . . .VP, Finance
Charles Adams Jr. . . . . .National Director, Field Sales
Kim Eason . . . . .Marketing Director
Terry Woods . . . . .Director, Distribution
Judy Copeland . . . . .Sales Manager
Jamie Warden . . . . .National Accounts Manager

CHOKE DISTRIBUTION
PO Box 4694
Chicago, IL 60680
PHONE 773-539-5411
EMAIL . . . . .info@choked.com
WEB SITE . . . . .www.choked.com
GENRES   Hardcore - Punk - Rock

Chuck . . . . .No Title
Todd . . . . .No Title

CISCO MUSIC
9347 Eton Ave.
Chatsworth, CA 91311
PHONE 818-678-1688/212-213-8197
FAX 818-678-1686/212-213-8559
WEB SITE . . . . .www.ciscomusic.com
GENRES   Classical - Electronica - Folk - Jazz -
                              New Age - Pop - Rap/Hip-Hop - Rock -
                              Urban
COMMENTS   East Coast office: 114 E. 32nd St., Ste.
                              1201, New York, NY 10016

Glenn Berry . . . . .Manager (NY)
Shelley Danta . . . . .Production Services
Abey Fonn . . . . .Controller
Robert Pincus . . . . .Domestic & Audiophile Sales
Richard Sanchez . . . . .Buyer
Robert Sliger .International Sales
James Vincent . . . . .Buyer
Chris Williams . . . . .Inventory Control

CITY HALL RECORDS
101 Glacier Pt., Ste. C
San Rafael, CA 94901
PHONE 415-457-9080
FAX 415-457-0780
EMAIL .info@cityhallrecords.com
WEB SITE . . . . .www.cityhallrecords.com
GENRES   All Genres
COMMENTS   Distributor of independent music

Robin Cohn . . . . .Founder
Grace Cohn . . . . .Human Resources
Walter Zelnick . . . . .Ambassador

CRYSTAL CLEAR DISTRIBUTION
10486 Brockwood Rd.
Dallas, TX 75238
PHONE 214-349-5057
FAX 214-349-3819
EMAIL . . . . .info@crystalcleardistribution.com
WEB SITE . . . . .www.crystalcleardistribution.com
GENRES   Alternative - Country - Metal - Punk -
                              Rock - Roots
SUBMISSION POLICY   Does not accept unsolicited submissions
COMMENTS   Subsidiary: C.E.D. Entertainment
                              Distribution

Marcia Banasik . . . . .Sales & Marketing Representative
Chelsea Callahan . . . . .Sales & Marketing Representative

DARLA
2107 Camino Cantera
Vista, CA 92084
PHONE 760-631-1731
FAX 760-454-1625
EMAIL . . . . .orders@darla.com
WEB SITE . . . . .www.darla.com
COMMENTS   Online retailer

James Agren . . . . .President
Chandra Tobey . . . . .VP

EMI MUSIC MARKETING
1750 N. Vine St.
Hollywood, CA 90028
PHONE 323-462-6252
GENRES   All Genres
COMMENTS   Second office: 5750 Wilshire Blvd., Los
                              Angeles, CA 90036, phone: 323-692-
                              1100

Ronn Werre . . . . .President, Sales & Distribution
Phil Quartararo . . . . .Executive VP, EMI Music North America
Herb Agner . . . . .VP, Catalog Marketing
Andrew Boughton . . . . .VP, Finance & Business Development
Tom Cartwright . . . . .VP, Product Development
Kenny Di Dia . . . . .VP, Marketing
Bill Gagnon . . . . .VP, Catalog Sales & Marketing
Bob O'Neill . . . . .VP, Legal & Business Affairs
Giulio Proietto . . . . .VP, Finance & Business Development (Wilshire)
Rachna Bhasin . . . . .Sr. Director, International & Digital Sales
Stacey Freeman . . . . .Sr. Director, Product Development
Tonya Puerto . . . . .Sr. Director, Licensing (Wilshire)
Stephanie Sprester Ribeiro . . . . .Sr. Director, Sales & Marketing,
                                                             Special Markets
Lisa Wohl . . . . .Sr. Director, Creative & Soundtracks (Wilshire)
Maureen Bacon . . . . .Director, International Licensing (Wilshire)
Jennifer Ballantyne . . . . .Director, Media & Marketing
Jesse Flores . . . . .Director, Urban Marketing
Melanie Halbach . . . . .Director, National Independent Retail Sales
Linda Kalkin . . . . .Director, Label Marketing
Michael Ruthig . . . . .Director, Product Development
Mark Spenner . . . . .Director, Development, Digital Sales
Aaron Striegel . . . . .Director, Catalog Sales
Jody Glisman-Best . . . . .Associate Director, Radio
Rayshon Harris . . . . .Manager, Product Development
John Owen . . . . .Product Manager
Janine Popoli . . . . .Manager, National Marketing & Merchandising

FAT BEATS DISTRIBUTION
110 Bridge St., 3rd Fl.
Brooklyn, NY 11201
PHONE 718-875-8191
FAX 718-875-9297
EMAIL . . . . .info@fatbeats.com
WEB SITE . . . . .www.fatbeats.com
GENRES   Electronica
COMMENTS   Distributor, label, retailer

Joseph Abajian . . . . .Owner

FONTANA DISTRIBUTION
10 Universal City Plaza, Ste. 400
Universal City, CA 91608
PHONE 877-878-3668
EMAIL . . . . .info@fontanadist.com
WEB SITE . . . . .www.fontanadistribution.com
COMMENTS   Distributor of established independent
                              music labels

Steve Pritchitt .General Manager
Ken Gullic . . . . .VP, Sales
Bryan Mead . . . . .VP, Marketing
David Zierler . . . . .Director, Business Development

FORTE DISTRIBUTION LLC
PO Box 35
Paramus, NJ 07653-0035
PHONE 732-745-0530
FAX 732-745-0532
EMAIL .info@fortedistributionllc.com
GENRES   Classical - Jazz - World
COMMENTS   Distributor

Jack DeSalvo . . . . .President
Barry Bender . . . . .National Sales Director, West Coast (319-338-1758)
David Osenberg . . . . .Director, Marketing

DISTRIBUTORS

GALAXY MUSIC DISTRIBUTORS
2400 Josephine St.
Pittsburgh, PA 15203
PHONE 412-481-8600/800-542-5422
FAX 412-481-1969/800-542-8863
EMAIL . . . . .info@galaxymusic.com
SECOND EMAIL . . . . .international@galaxymusic.com
WEB SITE . . . . .www.galaxymusic.com

Eugene Jakiela . . . . .CEO
George Balicky . . . . .VP, National Sales & Business Development
Mark Graham . . . . .VP, Information Technology
Tim Jakiela . . . . .VP, Credit
Wayne Jakiela . . . . .VP, Sales
Kevin Jakiela . . . . .VP, Operations
John Artale .Purchasing Manager
Kevin Malloy . . . . .Sales Manager

GLOBAL VILLAGE RECORDS & FILMS
c/o Creative Network-Nicoletti Music
PO Box 2818
Newport Beach, CA 92659
PHONE 714-328-9693
EMAIL . . . . .nicolettico@cox.net
LABELS   California International - Global Village
                       - Streetwise
GENRES   All Genres

Joseph Nicoletti . . . . .President/CEO

GOLDENROD MUSIC, INC.
1310 Turner St.
Lansing, MI 48906
PHONE 517-484-1712
FAX 517-484-1771
EMAIL . . . . .music@goldenrod.com
WEB SITE . . . . .www.goldenrod.com
GENRES   Electronica - Folk - New Age - World
SUBMISSION POLICY   Mail press kits to Attn: Submissions
COMMENTS   Women's music

Terry Grant . . . . .President
Susan Frazier . . . . .Sales Manager
Alana Marcum .Sales, Midwest/West
Melinda Pierce . . . . .Sales, East/South (860-871-8332)

GROOVE DISTRIBUTION
1164 N. Milwaukee Ave.
Chicago, IL 60622
PHONE 773-435-0250
FAX 773-435-0252
EMAIL . . . . .dirkv@groovedis.com
WEB SITE . . . . .www.groovedis.com
GENRES   Electronica - Jazz

Dirk van den Heuvel . . . . .President/General Manager (x123)

HANDLEMAN COMPANY
500 Kirts Blvd.
Troy, MI 48084
PHONE 248-362-4400
FAX 248-362-3615
EMAIL . . . . .corporate.info@handleman.com
WEB SITE . . . . .www.handleman.com

Stephen Strome . . . . .Chairman/CEO
Thomas C. Braum Jr. . . . . .CFO
Bob Sausa . . . . .CIO
Lynn Dutney . . . . .VP, Finance
Mark Heidel . . . . .VP, Field Sales
Wade Rohrer . . . . .VP/Account Executive
Angelique Strong Marks . . . . .VP, Corporate Legal Counsel
Mike Barker . . . . .Assistant VP, International Operations
Frank Ralko . . . . .Assistant VP, US Operations
Bill Tucker . . . . .GM, Distribution (Toronto)
Dirk Lopour . . . . .Field Sales Director
Jonathan Stickel . . . . .Director, Finance
Karen Thornton . . . . .Director, Budgeting & Forecasting
Tony Vecchiato . . . . .Director, Business Continuity
Maggie Gruber . . . . . . .Manager, Center for Performance Management
Chris Kwant . . . . .National Team Assortment Manager

IMAGE ENTERTAINMENT, INC.
20525 Nordhoff St., Ste. 200
Chatsworth, CA 91311
PHONE 818-407-9100
FAX 818-407-9331
EMAIL . . . . .license@image-entertainment.com
WEB SITE . . . . .www.image-entertainment.com
GENRES   All Genres

Martin Greenwald . . . . .CEO
David Borshell . . . . .COO
Jeff Farmer . . . . .CFO
Barry Gordon . . . . .Sr. VP, Acquisitions

INDEPENDENT ONLINE DISTRIBUTION ALLIANCE (IODA)
665 Third St., Ste. 305
San Francisco, CA 941037
PHONE 415-777-4632
FAX 415-777-4633
EMAIL . . . . .info@iodalliance.com
WEB SITE . . . . .www.iodalliance.com
GENRES   All Genres
COMMENTS   Digital distributor

Kevin Arnold . . . . .CEO
Stephen Bronstein . . . . .COO
Eril Gilbert . . . . .VP, Content Acquisition
Tim Mitchell . . . . .VP, Business & Product Development
Jonathan Earp . . . . .VP, Business Affairs

INNOVATIVE DISTRIBUTION NETWORK (IDN)

10 East 40th St., Ste. 3110
New York, NY 10016
PHONE 212-683-0467
FAX 212-683-1350
WEB SITE . . . . .www.idndist.com
SECOND WEB SITE . . . . .www.aent.com
ARTIST ROSTER   Orgy - Brotha Lynch Hung - Joe
     Bonamassa - Sue Foley - Proof - Walter
     Trout - Slum Village
LABELS   D1 Music - Rounder - Jet Star -
     Casablanca - Domo - 215 Records -
     Justin Time - Louisiana Red Hot - LKS
     Entertainment - Ruf - Siccmade - Iron Fist
     - Newhouse
GENRES   All Genres
COMMENTS   Division of Alliance Entertainment

Lou DeBiase . . . . .VP, Sales & Marketing/General Manager
     (loudeb@aent.com)
Jim Freeman . . . . .VP, Advertising/Marketing & Business Affairs
     (jimfre@aent.com)
Nelson Perez . . . . .Director, Operations (nelper@aent.com)
Rosalie Labate . . . . .Customer Service (800-329-7664 x4518,
     roslab@aent.com)
Josh Lichter . . . . .Assistant, Sales & Marketing (joslic@aent.com)

KANDAMERICA INC.

134 Laporte St.
Arcadia, CA 91006
PHONE 626-445-7700
FAX 626-445-0066
EMAIL . . . . .keizo@kandamerica.com
WEB SITE . . . . .www.kandamerica.com

Keizo Fujimoto . . . . .President
B. Landmark . . . . .VP

LUMBERJACK MORDAM MUSIC GROUP

PO Box 434
Toledo, OH 43697-0434
PHONE 419-726-3930/877-LUMBERJACK
FAX 419-726-3935/916-641-8989
EMAIL .info@lumberjack-online.com
SECOND EMAIL . . . . .info@mordamrecords.com
WEB SITE . . . . .www.lumberjack-online.com
SECOND WEB SITE . . . . .www.mordamrecords.com
GENRES   Hardcore - Punk
COMMENTS   West Coast office: 731 N. Market Blvd.,
     Unit R, Sacramento, CA 95834

Dirk Hemsath . . . . . .President (dirk.hemsath@lumberjackmordam.com)
Mark Hemsath . . . . .CFO
Chris Hnat . .Marketing/Advertising (chris.hnat@lumberjackmordam.com)
Lindsay Falcone . . . . .Exclusive Label Manager
     (lindsay.falcone@lumberjackmordam.com)
Dawn Marshman . . . . .Exclusive Label Relations
     (dawn.marshman@lumberjackmordam.com)
Emily Hemsath . . . . .Director, Sales & Marketing
     (emily.hemsath@lumberjackmordam.com)
Andy Leitner . . . . .Director, Operations & Systems
Sarah Echler . . . . .Web Site Orders/Mail/Phone Orders
     (sarah.echler@lumberjackmordam.com)
Eric Fernald .Developing Label Manager
     (eric.fernald@lumberjackmordam.com)
Lori Stout . . . . .Store Sales (lori.stout@lumberjackmordam.com)

MUSIC DESIGN

4650 N. Port Washington Rd.
Milwaukee, WI 53212
PHONE 414-961-8380
FAX 414-961-8381
WEB SITE .www.musicdesign.com
GENRES   Children's - Classical - Jazz - New Age -
     World
SUBMISSION POLICY   Send one copy of CD, video or DVD
     along with label, marketing, pricing
     and/or distribution info via mail; Attn:
     New Title Department

Dan Godden . . . . .GM

MUSIC FORCE MEDIA GROUP

4658 Wortser Ave.
Sherman Oaks, CA 91423
PHONE 818-789-4483
FAX 818-789-4489
EMAIL . . . . .sindrome@pacbell.net
WEB SITE . . . . .www.bigdeal.com
SECOND WEB SITE . . . . .www.sin-drome.com
GENRES   All Genres

Henry Marx . . . . .President
Norman Russell . . . . .Production Director

MUSICRAMA

43-01 22nd St., 6th Fl.
Long Island City, NY 11101
PHONE 718-389-7818
FAX 718-383-5152
EMAIL . . . . .info@musicrama.com
WEB SITE . . . . .www.musicrama.com
GENRES   All Genres

Mark Jarzabek . . . . .President
Duncan Hutchison .President, MDM
Charles Jarzabek . . . . .VP
Karen Karaca . . . . .Director, National Accounts
Aron Hunt .West Coast Sales Representative

NAIL DISTRIBUTION

14134 NE Airport Way
Portland, OR 97230
PHONE 503-257-8480
FAX 503-257-9061
EMAIL .info@naildistribution.com
WEB SITE . . . . .www.naildistribution.com
SECOND WEB SITE . . . . .www.allegro-music.com
LABELS   Heinz - PUSA Inc. - Amulet - crank! - K
     Records - Decretly Canadian - Yoho -
     Wildhive - Cornerstone RAS - +80 more
GENRES   Alternative - Folk - Hardcore - Jazz -
     Punk - Rap/Hip-Hop - Rock - World
SUBMISSION POLICY   Accepts unsolicited label packs with 10
     or more releases

Chris Scofield .Label Manager (x2009)
Ted Lambeth .Inventory Manager (x2057)
Jason Smithling . . . . .Inside Sales Representative (x2053)
Amy Welch . . . . .Inside Sales Representative (x2056)
Diane Podolak . . . . .Media Coordinator (x2054)

NAPSTER/NAPSTER LIVE
9044 Melrose Ave.
Los Angeles, CA 90069
PHONE 310-281-5761
FAX 310-281-5788
EMAIL . . . . .michelles@napster.com
SECOND EMAIL . . . . .gregg.ogorzelec@napster.com
WEB SITE . . . . .www.napster.com
GENRES　　　　　　　　　All Genres
COMMENTS　　　　　　　Online distribution

Chris Gorog . . . . .Chairman/CEO
Michelle Santosuosso . . . . .VP, Music Programming
Micah McKinney . . . . .Sr. Director, A&R
Gregg Ogorzelec . . . . .Director/Music Programmer

NAVARRE CORPORATION
7400 49th Ave. North
New Hope, MN 55428
PHONE 763-535-8333
FAX 763-533-2156
EMAIL . . . . .info@navarre.com
SECOND EMAIL . . . . .jaugustin@navarre.com
WEB SITE . . . . .www.navarre.com
GENRES　　　　　　　　　All Genres
COMMENTS　　　　　　　Distributes music, software, video
　　　　　　　　　　　　games, DVDs

Eric H. Paulson . . . . .Chairman/President/CEO
Michael Bell . . . . .CEO, Encore
Brian Burke . . . . .President, Navarre Distribution Services
Cary Deacon . . . . .President/COO, Navarre Corp.
Bob Freese . . . . .Sr. VP/GM, Navarre Entertainment Media
John Turner . . . . .Sr. VP, Global Logistics
Jim Colson . . . . .VP, Business Affairs
Joyce Fleck . . . . .VP, Marketing & Sales
Margot McManus . . . . .VP, Human Resources
Haug Scharnowski . . . . .VP, Corporate Relations
Rick Vick .VP, Merchandising
Lina Shurslep . . . . .Chief Information Officer
Cindy Chinn . . . . .Director, Product Development
Mike Cornette . . . . .Director, Content
Vito Lazauskas . . . . .Eastern Director, Sales
Ed Maxin . . . . .Western Director, Sales
Chris Smith . . . . .Director, Marketing
Ken Persing . . . . .Manager, E-Commerce
Al Engleman . . . . .National Sales Manager, Video & Video Games
Brad Kearin . . . . .Sales Manager, Software & Major Music
Chris Stone . . . . .National Sales Manager, New Business
Jada Augustin . . . . .Account Executive, E-Commerce

THE ORCHARD
100 Park Ave., 17th Fl.
New York, NY 10017
PHONE 212-201-9280
FAX 212-201-9203
EMAIL . . . . .info@theorchard.com
SECOND EMAIL . . . . .firstname@theorchard.com
WEB SITE . . . . .www.theorchard.com
GENRES　　　　　　　　　Alternative - Blues - Christian - Classical
　　　　　　　　　　　　- Country - Electronica - Folk - Gospel -
　　　　　　　　　　　　Jazz - Latin - New Age - Pop - R&B -
　　　　　　　　　　　　Rap/Hip-Hop - Reggae - Rock - Roots -
　　　　　　　　　　　　Urban - World
SUBMISSION POLICY　　　Open acceptance policy
COMMENTS　　　　　　　Specializes in digital distribution for inde-
　　　　　　　　　　　　pendent record labels

Richard Gottehrer . . . . .Founder/Chairman
Greg Scholl . . . . .President/CEO
Scott Cohen . . . . .Founder/VP, International
Jason Ojalvo . . . . .VP, Marketing & Merchandising
Steve Haase . . . . .VP, Business Development
Brad Navin . . . . .VP, Content Acquisition

OUTSIDE MUSIC INC.
25 Defries St.
Toronto, ON M5A 3R4 Canada
PHONE 416-461-0655
FAX .416-364-3616/416-461-0973
WEB SITE .www.outside-music.com
LABELS　　　　　　　　　Saddle Creek - Sub Pop - Ninja Tune -
　　　　　　　　　　　　Varese Sarabande - Barsuk - Yep Roc
GENRES　　　　　　　　　All Genres

Peter Hardman . . . . .VP, Sales & Marketing
Lloyd Nishimura . . . . .A&R
Mark Di Pietro . . . . .Director, Outside Music Label
Stephanie Hardman . . . . .Director, Media Relations
Maureen Spillane . . . . .Marketing
Kat Stewart . . . . .Publicity
Darryl Weeks . . . . .Publicity

PROVIDENT MUSIC GROUP
741 Cool Springs Blvd.
Franklin, TN 37067
PHONE 615-261-6500
FAX 615-261-5916
EMAIL . . . . .pr@pmgsonybmg.com
WEB SITE .www.providentmusic.com
LABELS　　　　　　　　　Essential Records - Reunion Records
　　　　　　　　　　　　(Beach Street Records) - Brentwood
　　　　　　　　　　　　Records - Brentwood Kids - Benson
　　　　　　　　　　　　Records
GENRES　　　　　　　　　Christian
COMMENTS　　　　　　　Distributes to Christian retail

Terry A. Hemmings . . . . .President/CEO
Robert Beeson . . . . .Sr. VP, A&R, Provident Label Group
Dean Diehl . . . . .Sr. VP, Marketing, Provident Label Group
Skip Bishop . . . . .VP, Mainstream Promotion & Marketing
Andrew Patton . . . . .VP, National Promotions, Provident Label Group
Jacquelyn Marushka Smith . .VP, Public Relations, Provident Music Group
　　　　　　　　　　　　　　　　　(615-261-6475)
Nina Williams . . . . .VP, Label Operations, Provident Label Group

RED INK
79 Fifth Ave., 15th Fl.
New York, NY 10003-3034
PHONE 212-404-0786
FAX 212-404-0685
EMAIL . . . . .howard_gabriel@redmusic.com
WEB SITE . . . . .www.redmusic.com
DISTRIBUTOR　　　　　　All Genres
COMMENTS　　　　　　　Independent
　　　　　　　　　　　　Marketing/Distribution/Artist/Label
　　　　　　　　　　　　Development

Howard Gabriel . . . . .Sr. VP/General Manager
Danny Buch . . . . .VP, Promotions & Marketing

RED MUSIC DISTRIBUTION
79 Fifth Ave., 15th Fl.
New York, NY 10003
PHONE 212-404-0600
FAX 212-404-0619
EMAIL . . . . .redmusic@redmusic.com
WEB SITE . . . . .www.redmusic.com
GENRES   All Genres

Robert Morelli .Executive VP/General Manager
Alan Becker . . . . .Sr. VP, Product Development
Howard Gabriel . . . . .Sr. VP/GM, RED Ink
Danny Buch . . . . .VP, Promotion & Artist Development
Dean Fine .VP, Inventory Management
Lynn Hazan-DeVaul . . . . .VP, Finance
Laura Marques . . . . .VP, Marketing
Marla Shatz . . . . .VP, International Sales & Marketing
Lou Tatulli .VP, Sales & Marketing
Tony Timpano . . . . .VP, Business & Legal Affairs
Frank Falkow . . . . .Sr. Director, National Field Sales
Russell Fink . . . . .Sr. Director, New Media
Wardell Mahone . . . . .Sr. Director, Urban Marketing
Paul Reitz . . . . .Director, Catalog Sales & Marketing

REDEYE DISTRIBUTION
449-A Trollingwood Rd.
Haw River, NC 27258
PHONE 336-578-7300/877-733-3931
FAX 336-578-7388
EMAIL . . . . .info@redeyeusa.com
SECOND EMAIL . . . . .firstname@redeyeusa.com
WEB SITE . . . . .www.redeyeusa.com
SUBMISSION POLICY   No unsolicited material

Stephen Judge . . . . .Director, A&R and Distribution (x211)
Lori Miller . . . . .Marketing Director (x216)
Greg Broom . . . . .Director, Purchasing (x214)
Steve Dixon . . . . .Sales Director (708-763-0894)
Chris Brandstetter . . . . .Indie Store Sales Representative (530-661-1150)
Fergus Denham . .International Sales Representative (44-208-852-8391)
Ryan Dimock . . . . .Alternative Media (x204)
Kate Dockins . . . . .National Accounts, Northeast (518-456-7722)
Perry Harrell . . . . . . .Indie Store & New Business Representative (x295)
Greg Horne . . . . .National Accounts, Midwest (630-820-9492)
Steven King . . . . .National Accounts, West Coast (916-442-5530)
Nathan McKinney . . . . .Indie Store Sales Representative (x210)
William Paris . . . . . . .Indie Store Sales Representative (201-683-3650)
Angie Carlson . . . . .Publicity (x209)
Dave Jackson . . . . .Manufacturing Coordinator (x221)
Alyson Miller . . . . .Controller/HR (x212)

REVOLVER USA DISTRIBUTION
2745 16th St.
San Francisco, CA 94103
FAX 415-241-2421
EMAIL . . . . .revolver@midheaven.com
SECOND EMAIL . . . . .revolverusa@yahoo.com
WEB SITE . . . . .www.midheaven.com
GENRES   All Genres

ROAD TO RUIN DISTRIBUTION
2208 Meyer Pl.
Costa Mesa, CA 92627
PHONE 949-274-1857
FAX 949-548-0683
EMAIL . . . . .roadtoruindistro@comcast.net
WEB SITE . . . . .www.roadtoruindistro.com
GENRES   Punk

Pat Grindstaff . . . . .Label Manager
Josh Barnes . . . . .Store Sales (619-294-3627)

ROCK BOTTOM DISTRIBUTION
3400 Corporate Way, Ste. G
Duluth, GA 30096
PHONE 770-814-8868
FAX 770-497-9206
GENRES   All Genres

Frank Rochman . . . . .President

RUNT DISTRIBUTION
PO Box 2947
San Francisco, CA 94126
PHONE 510-540-4104
FAX 510-540-4105
EMAIL . . . . .labels@runtdistribution.com
SECOND EMAIL . . . . .info@runtdistribution.com
WEB SITE . . . . .www.runtdistribution.com
LABELS   4 Men With Beards - Water Records -
                          Plain Recordings - Isota - DBK Works -
                          Antenna Farm
GENRES   Alternative - Bluegrass - Blues - Country
                          - Folk - Jazz - Punk - R&B - Rap/Hip-
                          Hop - Reggae - Rock - Roots - World
COMMENTS   Vinyl

Filippo Salvadori . . . . .CFO
Pat Thomas . . . . .A&R/Promotion

RYKO DISTRIBUTION
30 Irving Pl., 3rd Fl.
New York, NY 10003
PHONE 212-287-6100/800-808-RYKO
EMAIL . . . . .distribution@rykogroup.com
WEB SITE . . . . .www.rykodistribution.com
SECOND WEB SITE . . . . .www.rykodisc.com
GENRES   All Genres

Jim Cuomo . . . . .President

SELECT-O-HITS
1981 Fletcher Creek Dr.
Memphis, TN 38133
PHONE 901-388-1190
EMAIL . . . . .info@selectohits.com
WEB SITE . . . . .www.selectohits.com
GENRES   All Genres

Kathy Gordon . . . . .Advertising
Gary Barnard . . . . .Distribution

SMASH!
1636 W. 139th St.
Gardena, CA 90249-3003
PHONE 310-352-3055
FAX 310-352-4209
EMAIL . . . . .frontdesk@smashdist.com
WEB SITE . . . . .www.smashdist.com
GENRES   Punk

Reed Chaffey . . . . .US Buyer

SONY BMG SALES ENTERPRISE
550 Madison Ave.
New York, NY 10022
PHONE 212-833-8000
WEB SITE . . . . .www.sonybmg.com
GENRES   All Genres

Bill Frohlich . . . . .Co-President
Jordan Katz . . . . .Co-President

SOUTHERN RECORDS, INC.

PO Box 577375
Chicago, IL 60657
PHONE 773-235-5030
FAX 773-235-5025
EMAIL . . . . .info@southern.com
WEB SITE . . . . .www.southern.com
ARTIST ROSTER   90 Day Men - Vi - Karate - Tight
                       Phantomz - William Elliott Whitmore -
                       Dianogah - Darediablo - Todd - Rex -
                       Geoff Farina - Crucifix - Chumbawamba
                       - Frightwig - Him - Lustre King - Prong -
                       Slow Loris - Smoothies - Cat on Form -
                       Beekeeper - Atombombpocketknife -
                       Action Time - Antisect - Lungleg - Bob
                       Tilton - Billie Mahonie Stratford
                       Mercenaries - Sweep the Leg Johnny -
                       Ten Grand - Lapse
GENRES   Bluegrass - Punk - Rock - Roots
SUBMISSION POLICY   Need both master and synch contracts
                       and one-month lead time; For demos
                       email info@southerrecords.com
COMMENTS   Also Indie Rock and Americana music;
                       Distributor

Danielle Soto . . . . .President (djs@southern.com)
Scot Diamond . . . . .Wholesale Manager, Sales & Marketing
                       (scotd@southern.com)
Brendan Joyce . . . . .Wholesale Sales (brendanj@southern.com)
Chris Jern . . . .Retail Manager, Sales & Marketing (chris@southern.com)
James Lechocki . . . . .Retail Sales (jamesl@southern.com)
James McArdle . . . . .Accounts (jmcardle@southern.com)
James Zepsy . . . . .Warehouse Manager (zespy@southern.com)
Brent Fuscaldo . . . . .Label Assistant (brent@southern.com)

SUMTHING ELSE MUSIC WORKS

9 E. 45th St., 3rd Fl.
New York, NY 10017-2425
PHONE 212-818-0047
FAX 212-818-0048
WEB SITE . . . . .www.sumthing.com

Nile Rodgers .Owner (212-420-8700)
Barry Roberts . . . . . . .General Manager/A&R (broberts@sumthing.com)
Sooze Plunkett Green . . . . .Assistant to Nile Rodgers

SUPER D

17822 Gillette Ave., Ste. A
Irvine, CA 92614
PHONE .949-225-1170/866-666-1170
FAX 949-724-5162
WEB SITE . . . . .www.sdcd.com
COMMENTS   Northern California office: 725 Main St.,
                       Ste. 107, Woodland, CA 95695, phone:
                       530-668-3470, fax: 530-668-3476

Bruce Ogilvie . . . . .Co-Owner
Jeff Walker . . . . .Co-Owner

SYNERGY DISTRIBUTION

3650 Osage St.
Denver, CO 80211
PHONE 303-433-7557/877-247-5044
FAX 303-433-8228
EMAIL . . . . .info@synergydistribution.com
WEB SITE . . . . .www.synergydistribution.com
GENRES   All Genres
COMMENTS   East Coast office: 1747 First Ave., 3rd
                       Fl., New York, NY 10128, phone: 212-
                       369-2554, fax: 212-369-2559

Paul Schulman   General Manager (pschulman@synergydistribution.com)
Abel Arroyo . . .Artist One-Stop Manager (x1404, abel@artist1stop.com)
Danny Birch . . . . .Inventory & Product Set-up Specialist
                       (x1403, dbirch@synergydistribution.com)
Matt Blanks . . . . .Graphic Design/Webmaster
                       (x1406, mblanks@synergydistribution.com)

UNIVERSAL MUSIC & VIDEO DISTRIBUTION

10 Universal City Plaza, Ste. 400
Universal City, CA 91608
PHONE 818-777-4400
WEB SITE . . . . .www.umusic.com
SECOND WEB SITE . . . . .www.umvd.com
GENRES   All Genres

Jim Urie . . . . .President, UMVD (818-777-8806)
Mike Davis . . . . .Executive VP, UMVD (818-777-4120)
Tom O'Malley   Executive VP/CFO, Visual Entertainment (818-777-8729)
Bob Schnieders . . . . .Executive VP, Customer Operations, UMVD
                       (818-225-7686)
Mavis Takemoto . . .Executive VP, Administration, UMVD (818-777-4528)
Cliff O'Sullivan . . . . .Sr. VP, Marketing, UMVD (818-777-5727)
Susan Roberts . . . . .Sr. VP, New Media, UMVD (818-777-6025)
Rick Buehler . . . . .VP, Sales, Visual Entertainment (818-777-1097)
Mike Gillespie . . . . .VP, National Sales, UMVD (818-777-5786)
Rich Grobecker . . . . .VP, Field Sales, UMVD (MA) (603-893-0412)
Ken Gullic . . . . .VP, Sales, Fontana (818-777-5554)
LJ Hayden . . . .VP, Retail Partnership Marketing, UMVD (818-777-9803)
Jason Kleve . . . . .VP, Sales Analysis, UMVD (818-777-5600)
Rhoda Lawrence . .VP, Urban Sales & Marketing, UMVD (818-777-7262)
Yolanda Macias . . . . .VP, Business Development & Acquisitions,
                       Visual Entertainment (818-777-8115)
Bryan Mead . .VP, Marketing & Label Relations, Fontana (818-777-6802)
Joy Slusarek . . . . .VP, National Sales, UMVD (818-777-9823)
Soumya Sriraman . . . .VP, Marketing & Operations, Visual Entertainment
                       (818-777-0534)
Kim Sullivan . . .VP, Sales (Rental), Visual Entertainment (818-777-9381)
Chris Vanole . . . . .VP, Finance, UMVD (818-777-9373)
Steve Pritchitt . . . . .General Manager, Fontana (818-777-6938)
Abe Claiborne . . . . . . .Manager, College & Lifestyle Marketing, UMVD
                       (818-777-2597)
Mike Marshino   Manager, Artist Development, Associated Labels, UMVD
                       (818-777-0023)
Nydia Laner . . . . .Sr. Director, Latin Sales, Rack & Retail, UMVD
                       (818-777-9986)
Chris Ayears . . . . .Director, Urban Marketing & Sales, Fontana
                       (818-777-0568)
Dave Blomsterberg . . .National Sales Director, Fontana (818-777-0575)
Nancy Dean . . . .Director, Sales Administration, UMVD (818-777-4009)
Mary Escobedo . . . . .Director, Latin Sales, Visual Entertainment
                       (818-777-6430)
Rob Hershenson . . .Director, Merchandising & Creative Services, UMVD
                       (818-777-0569)
Michael Jakary . .Director, Artist Development, Universal/Motown, UMVD
                       (818-777-6191)
Joe Kara . .Director, Artist Development, Island Def Jam (818-777-0567)
Chris Morrison . . .Director, Country Marketing, UMVD (818-777-8805)
LaShawn Norton . . . .Director, Artist Development, Geffen/Verve, UMVD
                       (818-777-4122)
Tom Overby . . . . . . .Director, Rock Marketing, Fontana (818-777-6166)
Vince Szydlowski . .Director, Catalog, Classics, Jazz & Associated Labels,
                       UMVD (818-777-8607)
Josh Tario . . . . . . .Director, Artist Development, Interscope/A&M, UMVD
                       (818-777-0277)
Scott Van Horn . . .Director, Catalog, Classics, Jazz & Associated Labels,
                       UMVD (NY) (212-445-3203)
David Zierler . . . . . .Director, Business Development & Finance, Fontana
                       (818-777-3438)

DISTRIBUTORS

WEA CORP.
3400 W. Olive Ave.
Burbank, CA 91505
PHONE 818-238-6500/212-275-4500
FAX 818-562-9165
WEB SITE . . . . .www.wea.com
SECOND WEB SITE . . . . .www.wmg.com
GENRES   All Genres
COMMENTS   East Coast office: 75 Rockefeller Plaza,
                              New York, NY 10019

Edgar Bronfman Jr. . . . . .Chairman/CEO, Warner Music Group
Lyor Cohen   Chairman/CEO, US Recorded Music, Warner Music Group
John Esposito . . . . .President (212-275-1462)
Kelly Diamond . . . . .Sr. VP, Sales & Marketing Services
Rick Froio . . . . .Sr. VP, Sales (212-275-2510)
Steve Corbin . . . . .VP, Catalog Sales
John Dalton . . . . .VP, Lifestyle Sales
Robert Turner . . . . .Director, Country & Christian Music (Nashville)
Billy Fields .Director, Sales (212-275-2785)
Brian Hay . . . . .Regional Sales Director, Minneapolis
Jack Klotz . . . . .Regional Sales Director, Atlanta
Rick Orr . . . . .Regional Sales Director, Los Angeles

WORKSHEET

DATE	PROJECT	CONTACT	NOTES

Available online at www.hcdonline.com

SECTION **A**

DISTRIBUTORS & LABELS

- Distributors
- **Labels**

Asterisks (*) next to companies denote new listings.

456 ENTERTAINMENT, LLC
The Soho Bldg., 110 Greene St., 3rd Fl.
New York, NY 10012
PHONE 212-925-5500
FAX 212-925-5690
EMAIL . . . . .info@456entertainment.com
WEB SITE www.456entertainment.com
DISTRIBUTOR   Fontana Distribution
ARTIST ROSTER   Vast - The UN - Seymour Glass - Last of
                           the Famous - Chico & Coolwadda -
                           Sean Baker - Mis-Teeq
GENRES   Alternative - Rap/Hip-Hop - Rock
SUBMISSION POLICY   Mail CD, bio, photo, and any relevant
                           sales and touring info to Attn: A&R
                           Department

Carson Daly . . . . .CEO
Jonathan Rifkind . . . . .CEO
John B. Davis . . . . .President
Michael Cirelli Esq. . . . . .Business Affairs
Samantha Pogue . . . . .Director, Marketing

5 POINTS RECORDS
12 W. 37th St., 6th Fl.
New York, NY 10018
PHONE 212-629-7595
FAX 212-629-0017
WEB SITE www.5pointsrecords.com
GENRES   Alternative - Electronica - Pop - Rock

David Nichtern . . . . .President (x31, dn@5pointsrecords.com)
Nadine Steaman . . . .Director, Sales (x32, nadine@5pointsrecords.com)
Troy Martin . . . . .Creative Director/Production Director
                           (x30, troy@5pointsrecords.com)
Chris Child . . . .Composer/Producer/Engineer (x23, chris@nudgie.com)
Van Wilson . . . . . . .Executive Assistant (x15, van@5pointsrecords.com)

604 RECORDS
101-1001 W. Broadway, Unit 362
Vancouver, BC V6H 4E4 Canada
PHONE 604-879-7320
EMAIL . . . . .info@604records.com
WEB SITE www.604records.com
ARTIST ROSTER   The Suits - Tommy Lee - The Years -
                           Theory of a Deadman - Thornley - Tin
                           Foil Phoenix - The Organ - Marianas
                           Trench - The Solution
GENRES   Rock

Chad Kroeger . . . . .Co-Owner/A&R
Jonathan Simkin . . . . .Co-Owner/A&R
Julie Baldwin . . . . . . .Director, Marketing, Promotions & Artist Relations
Delia Reaveley . . . . .Sr. Executive Assistant
Amber Lockhart .Executive Assistant
Kesi Parker . . . . .A&R Administration

A&M RECORDS
2220 Colorado Ave., 5th Fl.
Santa Monica, CA 90404-3506
PHONE 310-865-1000
FAX 310-865-6270
EMAIL . . . . .firstname.lastname@umusic.com
DISTRIBUTOR   Universal Music & Video Distribution
ARTIST ROSTER   Sheryl Crow - Sting - Black Eyed Peas
GENRES   Pop - Rap/Hip-Hop - Rock - Urban
COMMENTS   See also Interscope Geffen A&M

Ron Fair . . . . .President
Michelle Thomas . . . . .GM
Tony Ferguson . . . . .A&R
Erica Grayson . . . . .Urban A&R
Deb Fenstermacher . . . . .Marketing
Tiffany Johnson . . . . .Assistant, Marketing
Deonna Simone Perry . . . . .Assistant, A&R

ABSOLUTELY KOSHER RECORDS
1412 10th St.
Berkeley, CA 94710-1512
PHONE 510-525-7791
FAX 510-525-7791
EMAIL . . . . .macher@absolutelykosher.com
WEB SITE . . . . .www.absolutelykosher.com
DISTRIBUTORS   Fontana Distribution - Revolver USA
                           Distribution
ARTIST ROSTER   Bottom of the Hudson - Franklin Bruno -
                           The Court and Spark - Rob Crow - The
                           Dead Science - Eltro - The Extra Glenns
                           - Frog Eyes - Get Him Eat Him - Jack
                           Hayter - The Jim Yoshii Pile-Up -
                           Jukeboxer - The Mountain Goats - Okay
                           - Optiganally Yours - P.E.E. - Pinback -
                           The Places - Summer at Shatter Creek -
                           The Swords Project - Shooby Taylor -
                           Telegraph Melts - Thingy - Two Guys -
                           Virginia Dare - The Wrens - Xiu Xiu
SUBMISSION POLICY   Physical demos only, no MP3s or links

Cory Brown . . . . .Owner
Joe Finlaw . . . . .Director, Operations

ACE FU RECORDS
322 W. 14th St., Ste. 1A
New York, NY 10014
PHONE 212-352-8052
FAX 212-352-8052
EMAIL . . . . .office@acefu.com
WEB SITE . . . . .www.acefu.com
ARTIST ROSTER   Acid Mothers Temple & the Cosmic
                           Inferno - Oneida - An Albatross - The
                           Dears - Officer May - The Vexers -
                           Pinback - Secret Machines - Ex Models -
                           Olive Grain - Ted Leo & the Pharmacists
                           - Tarot Bolero - Diving Bell - California
                           Stadium - Chisel

Eric Speck . . . . .President (sketch@acefu.com)
Kate Blumm . . . . .General Manager (kate@acefu.com)
Davie Kaufmann . . . . .Operations (davie@acefu.com)
JT Hamilton . . . . .Sales Manager (jtham@acefu.com)
Tai Morita . . . . .Office Manager (tai@acefu.com)

ACONY RECORDS
PO Box 40100
Nashville, TN 37204
PHONE 615-269-9072
FAX 615-269-9066
WEB SITE . . . . .www.aconyrecords.com
DISTRIBUTOR   Ryko Distribution
ARTIST ROSTER   Gillian Welch
GENRES   Folk - Roots
RECENT SOUNDTRACKS   Steal Me - Trust the Man - Into the West
SUBMISSION POLICY   Open

Lori Condon . . . . .General Manager
Norm Parenteau . . . . .A&R
Karen Macmillan . . . . .Sales & Marketing

LABELS

ACOUSTIC DISC RECORDS
PO Box 4143
San Rafael, CA 94913
PHONE .415-454-1187/800-221-3472
FAX 415-459-2815
EMAIL . . . . .publicity@acousticdisc.com
SECOND EMAIL . . . . .sales@acousticdisc.com
WEB SITE . . . . .www.acousticdisc.com
DISTRIBUTOR   KOCH Entertainment Distribution
ARTIST ROSTER   David Grisman Quintet - Old School
                             Freight Train
GENRES   Bluegrass - Blues - Classical - Folk - Jazz
RECENT SOUNDTRACKS   Grateful Dawg
SUBMISSION POLICY   Call prior to sending; Acoustic music
                             only

David Grisman . . . . .President/Director, A&R
Harriet Rose . . . . .Distribution Manager/Sales
Rob Bleetstein . . . . .Director, Promotions & Publicity
Craig R. Miller . . . . .Director, Business Affairs

AEZRA RECORDS
14040 N. Cave Creek Rd., Ste. 110
Phoenix, AZ 85022
PHONE 602-482-6518
FAX 602-765-6824
EMAIL . . . . .info@aezra.com
WEB SITE . . . . .www.aezra.com
ARTIST ROSTER   Crea - Chomsky - Magna-Fi - Sera -
                             Toadies - Robin Trower - John Price -
                             Cavier - Billy Miles - Ross Golan -
                             Molehead

Julie Preger . . . . .CEO
Michael Preger . . . . .COO/General Manager
Eric Cheroske . . . . .President
Paige Cheroske . . . . .CFO
Allen Jacobi . . . . .VP, Business Affairs
Paul Yeskel . . . . .VP, Promotions & Marketing
Juanita Stephens . . . . .VP, Artist Development & Publicity
Judy Libow . . . . .Director, Promotion
Rob Sides . . . . .Director, Sales
Trevor Lane . . . . .Net Music Promotions, LLC
Sam Kaiser . . . . .MVP Entertainment
Lydia Chavez . . . . .Head, Production
Paul Barger . . . . .Artist Relations
Bret Vesely . . . . .Artist Relations
Jeff Criden . . . . .Northeast Regional Promotion
Dee Ann Metzger . . . . .West Regional Promotion
John Nagara . . . . .Southeast Regional Promotion
Steve Walker . . . . .Northwest Regional Promotion
Mason Munoz . . . . .Marketing

AFTERMATH ENTERTAINMENT
2220 Colorado Blvd.
Santa Monica, CA 90404
PHONE 310-865-7642/310-865-7641
FAX 310-865-7068
WEB SITE .www.aftermathmusic.com
DISTRIBUTOR   Universal Music & Video Distribution
GENRES   Rap/Hip-Hop - Urban

Dr. Dre . . . . .President (310-865-7648)
Kirdis Postelle . . . . .General Manager
Angelo Sanders . . . . .Director, A&R
Wendell Cage . . . . .Project Coordinator
Larry Chatman . . . . .Production Coordinator

THE AIRPLAY LABEL
PO Box 851
Asbury Park, NJ 07712
PHONE 732-681-0623
FAX 732-681-0623
EMAIL .airplaypete@hotmail.com
LABELS   Airplay - Pop2K
GENRES   Alternative - Blues - Jazz - Latin - Pop -
                             R&B - Rap/Hip-Hop - Rock - Roots -
                             World
SUBMISSION POLICY   Accepts unsolicited material

P.P. Mantas . . . . .President
Jefferson Powers . . . . .CEO/VP

ALIEN8 RECORDINGS
PO Box 666, Station R
Montréal, PQ H2S 3L1
PHONE 514-284-3605
EMAIL . . . . .alien8@alien8recordings.com
WEB SITE www.alien8recordings.com
DISTRIBUTOR   Southern Records, Inc.
ARTIST ROSTER   Aube - Daniel Menche - David Kristian -
                             Francisco López - Keiji Haino - Knurl -
                             Les Georges Leningrad - Lesbians on
                             Ecstasy - Loren MazzaCane Connors -
                             M.S.B.R. - Masonna - Merzbow -
                             Molasses - Monstre - set fire to flames -
                             Shalabi Effect - Soft Canyon - Tanakh -
                             The Unicorns - Tomas Jirku

Sean O'Hara . . . . .Co-Owner
Gary Worsley . . . . .Co-Owner

ALIVE RECORDS
PO Box 7112
Burbank, CA 91510
PHONE 818-729-9096
FAX 818-729-9235
EMAIL . . . . .promo@bomprecords.com
WEB SITE . . . . .www.alive-totalenergy.com
ARTIST ROSTER   The Bloody Hollies - The Black Keys -
                             Two Gallants - Turpentine Brothers -
                             Detonations - Rosetta West - Boyskout -
                             Red Tyger Church - The Master Plan -
                             The Michelle Gun Elephant - Big
                             Midnight
LABELS   Alive - Total Energy
GENRES   Pop - Punk - Rock
SUBMISSION POLICY   Send demos to PO Box

Patrick Boissel . . . . .No Title

ALLIED ARTISTS
273 W. Allen Ave.
San Dimas, CA 91773-1439
PHONE 626-330-0600
FAX 626-961-0411
EMAIL . . . . .info@alliedartists.net
WEB SITE . . . . .www.alliedartists.net
ARTIST ROSTER   Coolio - Luis Cardenas- Renegade -
                             David Hasselhoff - David Burrill -
                             Resonance - Cablejuice
GENRES   Pop - Rap/Hip-Hop - Rock
SUBMISSION POLICY   Accepts unsolicited material

Robert Fitzpatrick . . . . .President
Greg Hammond . . . . .President, Allied Artist International
Ashley Posner . . . . .General Counsel
Danny Ramos . . . . .VP, A&R (x3)
Jerry Sifuentes . . . . .Public Information Officer
Jim Weda . . . . .Alternative Media Coordinator

ALLIGATOR RECORDS
PO Box 60234
Chicago, IL 60660
PHONE 773-973-7736
FAX 773-973-2088
EMAIL . . . . .bob@allig.com
WEB SITE . . . . .www.alligator.com
DISTRIBUTOR   Ryko Distribution
ARTIST ROSTER   Mavis Staples - Holmes Brothers - Shemekia Copeland - Koko Taylor - Hound Dog Taylor - Albert Collins
GENRES   Blues
RECENT SOUNDTRACKS   Angel Eyes - Primal Fear - Heaven's Prisoners

Bruce Iglauer . . . . .President/Director, A&R (boss@allig.com)
Bob DePugh . . . . .Director, Licensing
Bill Giardini . . . . .Director, International Sales
Matt LaFollette . . . . .Director, Artist Relations/Artist Management
Chris Levick .Assistant to President

ALTERNATIVE TENTACLES RECORDS
PO Box 419092
San Francisco, CA 94141-9092
PHONE 510-596-8981
FAX 510-596-8982
EMAIL . . . . .info@alternativetentacles.com
WEB SITE . . . . .www.alternativetentacles.com
DISTRIBUTOR   Lumberjack Mordam Music Group
ARTIST ROSTER   Jello Biafra - The Melvins - Skarp - Ludicra - Akimbo - Pansy Division - Fleshies - The Phantom Limbs - Wesley Willis - Comets on Fire - Lard - eX-Girl - Greg Palast - The Evaporators - Jim Hightower - Noam Chomsky - Leftover Crack - Buzz Oven - Slim Cessna
GENRES   Alternative - Country - Hardcore - Metal - Pop - Punk - Rock
SUBMISSION POLICY   Submit demos to Jello Biafra

Dave Adelson . . . . . .General Manager (dave@alternativetentacles.com)
Jello Biafra . . . . .A&R (jello@alternativetentacles.com)
Maiko Hara . . .Radio/Retail Marketing (retail@alternativetentacles.com)
Matt Harvey . . . . .Publicity (press@alternativetentacles.com)
Jesse Townley . . . . . . .Mail Order (mailorder@alternativetentacles.com)

AMERICAN BLOOD RECORDINGS
1123 Broadway, Ste. 317
New York, NY 10010
PHONE 212-367-0826
FAX 212-807-9288
EMAIL . . . . .scott@americanbloodrecordings.com
WEB SITE . . . . .www.americanbloodrecordings.com
GENRES   Alternative - Hardcore - Pop - Punk - Rap/Hip-Hop - Rock - Urban
SUBMISSION POLICY   Accepts demos, will contact if interested

Scott Egbert . . . . .GM/A&R

AMERICAN GRAMAPHONE
9130 Mormon Bridge Rd.
Omaha, NE 68152
PHONE 402-457-4341
FAX 402-457-4332
EMAIL . . . . .mailbox@amgram.com
WEB SITE . . . . .www.mannheimsteamroller.com
DISTRIBUTOR   Select-O-Hits
ARTIST ROSTER   Mannheim Steamroller
SUBMISSION POLICY   Does not accept submissions

Chip Davis . . . . .President
Brian Ackley . . . . .COO
Dwight Montjar . . . . .Director, Sales
Dan Wieberg . . . . .Director, Promotions
Mary Allen . . . . .Assistant

AMHERST RECORDS, INC.
1762 Main St.
Buffalo, NY 14208
PHONE 716-883-9520
FAX 716-884-1432
EMAIL . . . . .info@amherstrecords.com
WEB SITE . . . . .www.amherstrecords.com
ARTIST ROSTER   Doc Severinsen - Stylistics - Spyro Gyra - Van McCoy - Della Reese - Glenn Medeiros
GENRES   Jazz - R&B
RECENT SOUNDTRACKS   Charlie's Angels 2: Full Throttle

Leonard Silver . . . . .President/CEO
Larry Silver . . . . .Executive VP
Dave Colson . . . . .VP
Rose Rupert . . . . .A&R/National Promotions

LABELS

LABELS

ANGEL/EMI CLASSICS/VIRGIN CLASSICS
150 Fifth Ave., 6th Fl.
New York, NY 10011
PHONE 212-786-8600
WEB SITE .www.angelrecords.com
DISTRIBUTOR   EMI Music Marketing
ARTIST ROSTER   Sarah Brightman - Bernadette Peters -
                     Anoushka Shankar - Ravi Shankar - Jay
                     Ungar & Molly Mason - Eroica Trio - Sir
                     Simon Rattle - Mstislav Rostropovich -
                     Nigel Kennedy - Itzhak Perlman - Sasha
                     Sitkovetsky - Deborah Voight - Angela
                     Gheorghiu - David Daniels - Ian
                     Bostridge - Leif Ove Andsnes -
                     Emmanuel Pahud - Sarah Chang - Han
                     Na Chang - Thomas Ades - Maksim -
                     Maxim Vengerov
GENRES   Adult Contemporary - Classical - Jazz -
                     World
SUBMISSION POLICY   No unsolicited material accepted
COMMENTS   Broadway

Bruce Lundvall . . . . .CEO, EMI Jazz & Classics
Tom Evered . . . . .Sr. VP/General Manager Jazz & Classics
Mark Forlow . . . . .VP, Classics
Saul Shapiro . . . . .VP, Sales, EMI Jazz & Classics
Gordon Jee . . . . .Director, Creative, EMI Jazz & Classics
Tara Chiari . . . . .Product Manager, Angel
Chris Cofoni . . . . .Coordinator, A&R Administration, EMI Jazz & Classics
Sharon Russell . . .Manager, International Marketing, EMI Jazz & Classics

ANTHEM RECORDS
189 Carlton St.
Toronto, ON M5A 2K7 Canada
PHONE 416-923-5855
FAX 416-923-1041
EMAIL . . . . .sro-anthem@sro-anthem.com
WEB SITE . . . . .www.anthementertainmentgroup.com
ARTIST ROSTER   Rush - The Tea Party
GENRES   Rock
SUBMISSION POLICY   Mail all submissions to the attention of
                     the A&R department; No emails

Ray Danniels . . . . .President

ANTICON RECORDS
5290 College Ave., Ste. C
Oakland, CA 94618
PHONE 510-655-3819
EMAIL . . . . .mrhiphop@anticon.com
WEB SITE . . . . .www.anticon.com
DISTRIBUTOR   Revolver USA Distribution
GENRES   Rap/Hip-Hop

Baillie Parker . . . . .Label Manager/Co-Owner (mrhiphop@anticon.com)
Shaun . . . . .Street Promotions (shaun@anticon.com)

APPLESEED RECORDINGS
PO Box 2593
West Chester, PA 19380
PHONE 610-701-5755
FAX 610-701-9599
EMAIL . . . . .info@appleseedrec.com
SECOND EMAIL . . . . .jim@appleseedrec.com
WEB SITE . . . . .www.appleseedrec.com
DISTRIBUTOR   KOCH Entertainment Distribution
ARTIST ROSTER   Al Stewart - Pete Seeger - Tom Paxton -
                     Eric Andersen - Roger McGuinn - Holly
                     Near - Donovan
GENRES   Folk - Latin - World
RECENT SOUNDTRACKS   Cold Mountain - Chrystal

Jim Musselman . . . . .President
Alan Edwards . . . . .Public Relations (215-628-4562)

ARBORS RECORDS
2189 Cleveland St., Ste. 225
Clearwater, FL 33765
PHONE 727-466-0571/800-299-1930
FAX 727-466-0432
EMAIL . . . . .info@arborsrecords.com
WEB SITE .www.arborsrecords.com
DISTRIBUTOR   Allegro Corporation
GENRES   Jazz

Mat Domber . . . . .President
Rachel Domber . . . . .VP
David Florczyk . . . . .Customer Sales & Distribution
Claudia Florczyk .Executive Assistant

ARDENT
2000 Madison Ave.
Memphis, TN 38104-2794
PHONE 901-725-0855
FAX 901-725-7011
EMAIL . . . . .info@ardentrecords.com
WEB SITE .www.ardentrecords.com
SECOND WEB SITE . . . . .www.ardentstudios.com
ARTIST ROSTER   Todd Agnew - Brother's Keeper -
                     Jonah33 - Skillet - Joy Whitlock
GENRES   Christian - Rock

John Fry . . . . .President
Aislynn Rappé . . . . .Coordinator, Creative & Marketing

ARENA ROCK RECORDING CO. (ARRCO)
17 SE Third Ave., #405
Portland, OR 97214
PHONE 503-233-3775
EMAIL . . . . .greg@arenarockrecordingco.com
SECOND EMAIL . . . . .takinaride@aol.com
WEB SITE .www.arenarockrecording.com
DISTRIBUTOR   Redeye Distribution
ARTIST ROSTER   The Autumn Defense - Calla - The
                     Carlsonics - Creeper Lagoon - The
                     Gloria Record - Grand Mal - Minus the
                     Bear - Mono - On!Air!Library! - Ovian -
                     Pilot to Gunner - Solex - Superdrag -
                     Swords - Worm is Green
GENRES   Alternative - Pop - Rock

Greg Glover . . . . .Partner
Dan Ralph . . . . .Partner

ARHOOLIE PRODUCTIONS, INC.
10341 San Pablo Ave.
El Cerrito, CA 94530
PHONE 510-525-7471
FAX 510-525-1204
EMAIL . . . . .info@arhoolie.com
WEB SITE . . . . .www.arhoolie.com
DISTRIBUTOR   KOCH Entertainment Distribution
ARTIST ROSTER   Flaco Jiminez - Freddy Fender -
                          Beausoleil - The Campbell Brothers -
                          Sonny Boy Williamson - Lightnin'
                          Hopkins - Big Mama Thornton - Johnny
                          Otis - Charlie Musselwhite - Clifton
                          Chenier - Carter Family - Del McCoury -
                          Sacred Steel - Lydia Mendoza
LABELS   Arhoolie - Folklyric
GENRES   Bluegrass - Blues - Christian - Country -
                          Folk - Jazz - Latin - Roots - World
SUBMISSION POLICY   Contact by telephone before submitting
COMMENTS   Publishing; Affiliated with Tradition Music
                          Co.

Chris Strachwitz . . . . .President
Tom Diamant . . . . .Label Manager/Publicity
Annie Johnston . . . . .Office Manager

ARK 21 RECORDS
14724 Ventura Blvd., PH
Sherman Oaks, CA 91403
PHONE 818-461-1701
FAX 818-461-1704
WEB SITE www.ark21.com
DISTRIBUTOR   Universal Music & Video Distribution
LABELS   Mondo Melodia - Pagan Records
GENRES   Alternative

Miles Copeland III . . . . .Chairman
Barbara Bolan . . . . .General Manager
Stevo Glendinning   . . . .Sr. VP/A&R (323-512-4083, sglen@ark21.com)
John Bevilacqua . . . . .Director, Production & Marketing

ARTEMIS RECORDS
130 Fifth Ave., 7th Fl.
New York, NY 10011
PHONE 212-433-1800
FAX 212-414-1703
WEB SITE . . . . .www.artemisrecords.com
ARTIST ROSTER   Steve Earle - Sugarcult - Better Than Ezra
                          - Jaguar Wright - The Pretenders - Ruff
                          Ryders - Alan Parsons - Jill Sobule
LABELS   Popularity
GENRES   Alternative - Country - Folk - Pop -
                          Reggae - Rock

Daniel Glass . . . . .President/CEO (212-433-1837,
                                               dglass@artemisrecords.com)
Greg Barbero . . . . .President, Artemis Classics
Chris Scully . . . . .CFO
Jeanne Drewson . . . . .VP/General Counsel (212-433-1813)
Brady Brock . . . . .VP, Publicity (212-433-1810)
Lisette Rioux . . . . .VP, Marketing & Artist Development
Thom Storr . . . . .VP, Marketing Services & International
John McDonald . . . . .Head, Sales (212-433-1849)
Alison Hearne . . . . .National Director, Rock Promotion
David Coke . . . . .Director, Finance & Administration
Lauren Scicolone . . . . . . .Director, West Coast Promotion & Marketing
Manny Simon . . . . .Director, Promotion/International Marketing

ARTS & CRAFTS
3110 American Dr.
Mississauga, ON 14V 1T2 Canada
PHONE 905-364-3261
FAX 905-364-3244
EMAIL . . . . .raiseyourhands@arts-crafts.ca
SECOND EMAIL .jeffrey@arts-crafts.ca
WEB SITE . . . . .www.arts-crafts.ca
ARTIST ROSTER   The American Analog Set - New Buffalo
                          - The Most Serene Republic - Apostle of
                          Hustle - Stars - Feist - Broken Social
                          Scene - Jason Collett - Valley of the
                          Giants
GENRES   All Genres

Jeffrey Remedios . . . . .Co-Owner

ASIAN MAN RECORDS
PO Box 35585
Monte Sereno, CA 95030
PHONE 408-395-0662
FAX 408-395-5952
WEB SITE . . . . .www.asianmanrecords.com
DISTRIBUTOR   Lumberjack Mordam Music Group

Mike Park . . . . .Owner
Skylar Suorez . . . . .Promotions (skylar@asianmanrecords.com)

ASPHODEL LTD.
763 Brannan St.
San Francisco, CA 94103
PHONE 415-863-3068
FAX 415-863-4973
EMAIL . . . . .info@asphodel.com
WEB SITE . . . . .www.asphodel.com
DISTRIBUTOR   Revolver USA Distribution
GENRES   Electronica - R&B - Rap/Hip-Hop
COMMENTS   Experimental

Mitzi Johnson . . . . .President/CEO
Naut Humon . . . . .A&R
Teresa Rice . . . . .Controller
Chris Dixon . . . . .Distribution

ASTRALWERKS RECORDS
104 West 29th St., 4th Fl.
New York, NY 10001
PHONE 212-886-7500
FAX 212-643-5573
EMAIL . . . . .astralwerks@astralwerks.com
SECOND EMAIL . . . . .feedback@astralwerks.net
WEB SITE . . . . .www.astralwerks.com
DISTRIBUTORS   Caroline Distribution - EMI Music
                          Marketing
ARTIST ROSTER   A Band of Bees - Air - Athlete - Audio
                          Bullys - Basement Jaxx - Ben Watt - The
                          Beta Band - Beth Orton - Brian Eno -
                          Cassius - Caesars - The Chemical
                          Brothers - The Concretes - Fatboy Slim -
                          Gabin - The Golden Republic - Ed
                          Harcourt - Gemma Hayes - Kings of
                          Convenience - K-Os - Kraftwerk - Miss
                          Kittin - Phoenix - Placebo - Radio 4 -
                          Royksopp - Sleepy Jackson - Turin Brakes
                          - VHS or Beta - West Indian Girl
LABELS   Astralwerks - Caroline - Honest Jon's
GENRES   Alternative - Electronica - Rock - World
SUBMISSION POLICY   Open

Errol Kolosine . . . . .General Manager (212-886-7521,
                                               errol@astralwerks.com)
Glenn Mendlinger . . . . .Label Manager (212-886-7507,
                                               glenn@astralwerks.com)
Joshua Graver . . . . . . .National Director, Advertising & Merchandising
                          (212-886-7591, emily.silman@astralwerks.com)
                                                              (Continued)

LABELS

ASTRALWERKS RECORDS (Continued)

Dave Lombardi . . . . National Director, Promotion (212-886-7506, dave.lombardi@astralwerks.com)
Lisa Smith-Craig . . . . Production Director (212-886-7510, lisac@astralwerks.com)
Alison Tarnofsky . . . . Publicity Director (212-886-7573, alison@astralwerks.com)
Nick Clift . . . . Senior Project Manager (212-886-7520, nick@astralwerks.com)
Brian Beck . . Project Manager (212-886-7619, beckb@astralwerks.com)
Katie Deatrick . . . . Publicity Manager (212-886-7575, katie@astralwerks.com)
Scott Kanov   Project Manager (212-886-7511, scottk@astralwerks.com)
Morgan Kazan . . . . Retail Marketing Coordinator (212-886-7597, morgan.kazan@astralwerks.com)
Lawrence Lui . . . . Project Manager (212-886-7510, lawrence@astralwerks.com)
Jared Patterson . . . . New Media Marketing (212-886-7522, jared.patterson@astralwerks.com)
Paul Rocha . . West Coast Marketing Coordinator (323-468-8627 x207, paul.rocha@astralwerks.com)
Emily Silman . . . . Radio Marketing Manager (212-886-7591, emily.silman@astralwerks.com)
Anna Swank . . . . New Media Webmaster (212-886-7595, anna@astralwerks.com)
Dayna Talley . . . West Coast Radio Promotion Manager (323-468-8627, dayna@astralwerks.com)
Ashley Warren . . . . Project Manager (212-886-7515, ashley@astralwerks.com)
Krista Crews . . . . Licensing/A&R/Asst. to GM (212-886-7502, krista.crews@astralwerks.com)
Catherine Licata . . . . Production Assistant (212-886-7598, catherine.licata@astralwerks.com)

ASTROLUX

3055 Overland Ave., Ste. 200
Los Angeles, CA 90034-3431
PHONE 310-838-1995
FAX 310-838-9280
DISTRIBUTOR   Universal Music & Video Distribution
GENRES   Alternative - Folk - Pop - Rock

Brad Benedict . . . . .Co-President
Gary Stamler . . . . .Co-President

ATLAN-DEC/GROOVELINE RECORDS

2529 Green Forest Court, PO Box 1676
Snellville, GA 30078
PHONE 877-751-5169/770-985-1686
FAX 877-751-5169
EMAIL . . . . .atlandec@prodigy.net
WEB SITE . . . . .www.atlan-dec.com
DISTRIBUTORS   Crystal Clear Distribution - Independent
                     Online Distribution Alliance (IODA)
ARTIST ROSTER   Shawree - Furious D - Mark Cocker - Jus
                     Skillz - BlackJack - LowLife - Randi
GENRES   Country - Jazz - R&B - Rap/Hip-Hop -
                     Urban
SUBMISSION POLICY   Accepts unsolicited material

Wileta Hatcher . . . . .A&R Representative
James Hatcher . . . . .A&R Representative

ATLANTIC RECORDS GROUP

1290 Avenue of the Americas
New York, NY 10104
PHONE 212-707-2000/818-238-6800
FAX 212-405-5475
EMAIL . . . . .firstname.lastname@atlanticrecords.com
WEB SITE . . . . .www.atlanticrecords.com
DISTRIBUTOR   WEA Corp.
LABELS   Asylum - Atlantic - Bad Boy - Elektra -
                     LAVA - Nonesuch - Vice - VP
GENRES   All Genres
COMMENTS   West Coast office: 3400 W. Olive,
                     Burbank, CA 91505

Ahmet Ertegun . . . . Founding Chairman (212-707-2350)
Craig Kallman . . . . .Chairman/CEO (212-707-2300)
Julie Greenwald .President (212-707-2222)
Andrea Ganis . . . . . .Executive VP, National Promotion (212-707-2230)
Ronnie Johnson . . . . .Executive VP (212-707-2276)
Tom Aaron . . . . .Sr. VP, International (212-707-2755)
Mike Caren . . . . .Sr. VP, A&R (818-238-6811)
Doug Cohn . . . . .Sr. VP, Video Promotion (212-707-2110)
Mike Easterlin . . . . . .Sr. VP, Promotion, Lava Records (212-707-2207)
Michael Kushner . . . . . .Sr. VP, Business & Legal Affairs (212-707-2624)
Morace Landy . . . . .Sr. VP, Urban Promotion (212-707-2551)
John McMann . . . . .Sr. VP, Promotion (212-707-2085)
Michael Pollack . . . . .Sr. VP/General Counsel (212-707-3028)
Ron Poore . . . . .Sr. VP, Rock Promotion (212-707-2519)
Sheila Richman . . . . .Sr. VP, Media Relations (212-707-3063)
Samantha Schwam . . . . Sr. VP/CFO (212-707-2666)
Nikke Slight . . . . .Sr. VP, New Media (212-707-2213)
Livia Tortella . . . . .Sr. VP, Marketing (212-707-2986)
Adam Abramson . . . . .VP, Sales (212-707-2333)
Liz Barrett . . . . .VP, Creative Services (212-707-2465)
David Burrier . . . . .VP, Marketing (212-707-2265)
Josh Dern . . . . .VP, New Media Operations (212-707-2394)
Greg Dorfman . . . . . . .VP, Rock Formats, Lava Records (212-707-2116)
Erik Ford . . . . .VP, Promotion (212-707-2442)
Mark Fritzges . . . . .VP, Promotion (412-331-6172)
Mary Gormley . . . . .VP, A&R (212-707-2720)
Camille Hackney . . . . .VP, Strategic Marketing (212-707-3111)
Marni Halpern . . . . . .VP, Pop Promotion, Lava Records (212-707-2077)
Kyambo Joshua . . . . .VP, A&R (212-707-2052)
Bob Kaus . . . . .VP, Media Relations & Communications (212-707-2026)
Joy Larocca . . . . .VP, Finance (212-707-2695)
Jon Lewis . . . . .VP, Promotion (212-707-3123)
James Lopez . . . . .VP, Urban Marketing (212-707-2280)
Jack McMorrow .VP, Sales (212-707-2509)
Lea Pisacane .VP, Promotion (212-707-2215)
Gee Roberson . . . . .VP, A&R (212-707-2352)
Craig Rosen . . . . .VP, A&R Administration (212-707-2139)
John Rubeli . . . . .VP, A&R (818-238-6813)
Margo Scott . . . . .VP, Business & Legal Affairs (212-707-2520)
Janet Stampler . . . . .VP, New Media (212-707-2306)
Tom Storms . . . . .VP, A&R (818-238-6815)
Ari Taitz   VP/Assistant Counsel, Business & Legal Affairs (212-707-2284)
Deborah Urbont . . . . .VP, Adult Format (212-707-2224)
Diane Van Horn . . . . .VP, Video Promotion (212-707-3144)
Dane Venable . . . . .VP, Marketing (212-707-3059)
Chris Webby . . . . .VP, Artist Development (212-707-3106)
Danny Wimmer . . . . .VP, A&R (212-707-2252)
Rana Alem . . . . .Sr. Director, National Promotion (212-707-3112)
Joi Brown . . . . .Sr. Director, Urban Marketing (212-707-2275)
Tommy Delaney . . . . .Sr. Director, Rock Promotion, Lava Records (212-707-2824)
Johnny DeMairo . . . . .Sr. Director, A&R/Promotion (212-707-2261)
Cara Donatto . . . .Sr. Director, Media & Artist Relations (212-707-3060)
Leslie Dweck . . . . . . .Sr. Director, A&R Administration (212-707-3336)
Glenn Fukushima   Sr. Director, Media & Artist Relations (818-238-6833)
Rob Gold . . . . .Sr. Director, Creative Services (212-707-2367)

(Continued)

ATLANTIC RECORDS GROUP (Continued)

Janice Israel . . . . .Sr. Director, Finance (212-707-2820)
Josh Lerman . . . . .Sr. Director, International (212-707-2857)
Leigh Lust . . . . .Sr. Director, A&R (212-707-3076)
Sydney Margetson Sr. Director, Media & Artist Relations (212-707-2262)
Gihan Salem   . . . .Sr. Director, Media & Artist Relations (818-238-2232)
Nick Stern   . . . . .Sr. Director, National Media Relations (212-707-2051)
Anne Declemente . . . . .Associate Director, A&R Administration
(212-707-2133)
Odell Nails Associate Director, Business & Legal Affairs (212-707-2620)
Corey Williams   Associate Director, A&R Administration (212-707-2626)
Scott Bergman .Director, Sales (212-707-2041)
Phil Botti . . . . .Director, Video Production (212-707-2225)
Greg Burke . . . . .Director, Art (212-707-3037)
Brian Corona . . . . .Director, AAA Promotion (818-238-6838)
Tim Dalbec . . . . .Director, Promotion (818-238-6842)
Christina Dittmar . . . . .Director, Creative Services (212-707-2476)
Chris Goyette . . . . .Director, Promotion Operations (212-707-2058)
Al Harmon . . . .Director, Business Affairs Administration (212-707-2560)
Lindsay Harris . . . . .Director, Strategic Marketing (818-238-6827)
Anthony Ko . . . . .Director, Production (212-707-2260)
Lynn Kowaleski . . . . .Director, Creative Services (212-707-2479)
Michele Mahoney . . . . .Director, Finance/Marketing Administration
(212-707-2304)
Samantha Rhulen . . . .Director, Business & Legal Affairs (212-707-2122)
Steve Robertson . . . . .Director, A&R (407-788-8501)
Tara Tzoucalis . . . . .Director, International (212-707-2712)
Brett Dumler   Midwest Regional Manager, Lava Records (630-678-5217)
Tommy Muzzillo South Regional Manager, Lava Records (863-709-8722)
Ken Pittman . . . . .West Coast Regional Manager, Lava Records
(818-238-6904)
Beth Simione . . . . .New England Regional Manager, Lava Records
(781-229-2150)
Chris Stang Northeast Regional Manager, Lava Records (212-401-0645)
Ray Vaughn . . .South Regional Manager, Lava Records (214-821-7298)
Jamie Willis . . . . .Northwest Regional Manager, Lava Records
Kevin Young   Midwest Regional Manager, Lava Records (216-221-5389)
Paul Davidson . . . . .Promotion Assistant, Lava Records (212-707-2106)
Erica Zafiriou . . . . . .Promotion Assistant, Lava Records (212-707-2155)
Jill Kaplan . . . . .Commissioner, Video (212-707-2238)

ATO RECORDS

157 Chambers St., 12th Fl.
New York, NY 10007-3533
PHONE 212-233-6646
FAX 212-233-6648
EMAIL . . . . .info@atorecords.com
WEB SITE . . . . .www.atorecords.com
DISTRIBUTOR   Sony BMG Sales Enterprise
ARTIST ROSTER   David Gray - Patty Griffin - Gov't Mule -
                       North Mississippi Allstars - Ben Kweller -
                       My Morning Jacket - Amandla! - Vusi
                       Mahlasela - Jem - Mike Doughty -
                       Gomez
GENRES   Alternative - Rock
RECENT SOUNDTRACKS   The O.C. - Win a Date with Tad
                       Hamilton - Wonderfalls - Crossing
                       Jordan - Six Feet Under - Life As We
                       Know It
SUBMISSION POLICY   Open policy; Send to Attn: Sam Shah
COMMENTS   Joint venture with RCA Records

Dave Matthews . . . . .Founder
Coran Capshaw . . . . .Founder
Michael McDonald . . . . .President (michael@atorecords.com)
Chris Tetzeli .VP (tetz@musictoday.com)
John Biondolillo . . . . .Label Manager

AVENUE RECORDS

1801 Avenue of the Stars, Ste. 421
Los Angeles, CA 90067
PHONE 310-312-0300/646-424-1600
FAX 310-479-1356/646-424-1680
DISTRIBUTOR   WEA Corp.
GENRES   Jazz - R&B - Rock
SUBMISSION POLICY   No unsolicited material
COMMENTS   East Coast office: 276 Fifth Ave., Ste.
                        507, New York, NY 10001

Jerry Goldstein . . . . .CEO (310-824-6393)
Glenn Stone . . . . .Executive VP (646-424-1600)
Richard March . . . . .Production Manager/A&R (LA) (310-823-6393)
Peter Durando . . . .Director, Administration & Licensing (646-424-1600)

AWARE RECORDS

2336 W. Belmont Ave.
Chicago, IL 60618-6423
PHONE 773-248-4210
FAX 773-248-4211
WEB SITE . . . . .www.awarerecords.com
ARTIST ROSTER   Mat Kearney - John Mayer - Five for
                       Fighting - Bleu - Wheat - Kyle Riabko
GENRES   Adult Contemporary - Alternative - Pop -
                       Rock
RECENT SOUNDTRACKS   Win a Date with Tad Hamilton
SUBMISSION POLICY   No unsolicited materials
COMMENTS   In cooperation with Columbia Records

Gregg Latterman . . . . .President
Steve Smith . . . . .VP, A&R (steve@awarerecords.com)
Mark Cunningham . . . . .VP, Marketing (mark@awarerecords.com)
Scott Burton . . . . .VP, Promotions (scott@awarerecords.com)
Jenn Uhen . . . . .Rep. Coordinator (jenn@awarerecords.com)
Jason Ienner . . . . .Marketing (jienner@awarerecords.com)
Tyler Hagenbuch . . . . .Assistant (tyler@awarerecords.com)
Caroline Linder . . . . .Assistant (caroline@awarerecords.com)
Brenden Mulligan . . . . .Assistant (brenden@awarerecords.com)

AXBAR RECORDS

5230 San Pedro Ave.
San Antonio, TX 78212
PHONE 210-829-1909
EMAIL . . . . .axbar@stic.net
WEB SITE . . . . .www.axbarmusic.com
LABELS   Axbar - Charro - Trophy - Prince - JATO
GENRES   Bluegrass - Country - Gospel

Joe Scates . . . . .Owner/General Manager

BACK PORCH/NARADA
4650 N. Port Washington Rd.
Milwaukee, WI 53212
PHONE 414-961-8350
FAX 414-961-8351
EMAIL .info@backporchrecords.com
SECOND EMAIL . . . . .friends@narada.com
WEB SITE .www.backporchrecords.com
SECOND WEB SITE . . . . .www.narada.com
DISTRIBUTOR   Music Design
ARTIST ROSTER   John Hammond - Neville Brothers - Paul
                          Thorn - Over the Rhine - Subdudes - Lily
                          Holbrook
GENRES   Blues - Country
SUBMISSION POLICY   No unsolicited submissions accepted

David Neidhart .Sr. VP, Sales & Marketing
Rich Denhart . . . . .Sr. Director, A&R (x308, denhartr@narada.com)
Michael Bailey . . . . .A&R Representative (x310, baileym@narada.com)
Dan Harjung . . . . . .A&R Representative (x311, harjungd@narada.com)

BAD BOY ENTERTAINMENT
1710 Broadway
New York, NY 10019
PHONE 212-381-1540
FAX 212-381-1599
EMAIL . . . . .firstinitiallastname@badboyworldwide.com
WEB SITE . . . . .www.badboyonline.com
DISTRIBUTOR   Warner Music Group (WMG)
ARTIST ROSTER   Mase - Mario Winans - Notorious B.I.G.
                          - P. Diddy - B5 - Boyz N da Hood - Carl
                          Thomas - Babs - Chopper aka Young
                          City - Black Rob - Ness - 8 Ball and
                          MJG - Cheri Dennis - Shannon Jones -
                          Jordan McCoy - Aasim
GENRES   Pop - Rap/Hip-Hop - Urban

Sean Combs . . . . .CEO
Derek Ferguson . . . . .CFO
Harve Pierre . . . . .Executive VP
Vashta Dunlap . . . . .VP, Human Resources & Operations
Candi Shand . . . . .VP, Marketing Administration
Anne-Marie Stripling . . . . .VP, Video Promotion
Shawn Prez . . . . .Promotions Director
Jason Wiley . . . . .Director, Marketing
Natasha Aarons . . . . .Executive Assistant to Mr. Pierre
Carla Guerrero . . . . .Executive Assistant to Mr. Pierre

BADMAN RECORDING CO.
1388 Haight, Ste. 211
San Francisco, CA 94117
PHONE 415-255-1609
EMAIL .info@badmanrecordingco.com
WEB SITE . . . . .www.badmanrecordingco.com
SUBMISSION POLICY   No unsolicited demos

Dylan Magierek . . . . . .Licensing/A&R (dylan@badmanrecordingco.com)
Adam Farrell . . . . .Street Team
Sue Kim . . . . .Retail Marketing
Dana Laraovitz . . . . .Publicity

BAR/NONE RECORDS
PO Box 1704
Hoboken, NJ 07030
PHONE 201-770-9090
FAX 201-770-9920
EMAIL . . . . .info@bar-none.com
WEB SITE . . . . .www.bar-none.com
DISTRIBUTOR   KOCH Entertainment Distribution
GENRES   Alternative

Glenn Morrow .Owner/President
Michael Hill . . . . .A&R
Mark Lipsitz .Marketing Director
Rob Cukierman . . . . .Press/Radio

BARSUK RECORDS
PO Box 22546
Seattle, WA 98122
PHONE 206-322-7785
FAX 206-762-0152
WEB SITE . . . . .www.barsuk.com

Josh Rosenfeld . . . . .President
Van Irker . . . . .International
Wes Howerton . . . . .Radio & Tour Marketing
Ever Kipp . . . . .Publicist

BEACH STREET RECORDS
5200 Old Harding Rd.
Franklin, TN 37064
PHONE 615-799-2229
FAX 615-799-9312
WEB SITE . . . . .www.beachstreetrecords.com
ARTIST ROSTER   Casting Crowns - Josh Bates
GENRES   Christian

Mark Miller . . . . .President
Frank Miller . . . . .VP
Jenna Roher . . . . .A&R Administration
Dianna Luster . . . . .Accounts
Ron Harris . . . . .No Title

BEEZWAX RECORDS
PO Box 4816
Elkhart, IN 46514
PHONE 574-266-4343
FAX 253-399-9305
EMAIL .buzz@beezwaxrecords.com
WEB SITE .www.beezwaxrecords.com
ARTIST ROSTER   Uncle Art - Bill Boris - Catman & the All
                          Niters - Lori Bell - Grant Levin -
                          Franklin/Clover/Seales - Joe Robinson -
                          Bob Guthrie Quartet - James Rogers
                          Band
GENRES   Blues - Jazz
SUBMISSION POLICY   Accepts submissions by mail
COMMENTS   Brass

David A. Seyboldt . . . . .President
Bill Boris . . . . .A&R
Rafe Bradford . . . . .A&R

THE BEGGARS GROUP
17-19 Alma Rd.
London SW18 1AA United Kingdom
PHONE 44-208-871-9912
FAX 44-208-871-1766
EMAIL . . . . .beggars@beggars.com
WEB SITE . . . . .www.beggars.com
LABELS   Beggars Banquet - XL Recordings - 4AD
                                - Too Pure - Matador - Mantra - Wiiija
GENRES   Alternative - Pop - Rock
COMMENTS   Distributed by Vital

Martin Mills . . . . .Chairman, Beggars Group
Roger Trust . . . .Label Head, Beggars Banquet (rogertrust@beggars.com)
Simon Wheeler . . . . .Head of New Media, Beggars Group
Janice Chaplin . . . . .Assistant

THE BEGGARS GROUP CANADA
333 King St. East
Toronto, ON M5A 3X5 Canada
PHONE 416-362-1377
FAX 416-362-1410
EMAIL . . . . .canada@beggars.com
WEB SITE . . . . .www.beggarsgroup.ca
GENRES   Alternative - Pop - Rock

Robert Ansell . . . . .No Title

THE BEGGARS GROUP (US)
625 Broadway, 12th Fl.
New York, NY 10012
PHONE 212-995-5882
FAX 212-995-5883
EMAIL . . . . .banquet@beggars.com
WEB SITE . . . . .www.beggars.com
DISTRIBUTOR   Alternative Distribution Alliance (ADA)
LABELS   4AD - Mantra - Mo' Wax - Too Pure -
                                Wiiija - XL - Matador
GENRES   Alternative - Rock

Lesley Bleakley . . . . .CEO
Lisa Gottheil . . . . .VP, Publicity, Beggars US
Matt Harmon .VP, Marketing, Beggars US
Dick Huey . . . . .Consulting VP, New Media, Beggars US
Jennifer Lanchart . . . . .Film & TV, Beggars US
Rusty Clarke . . . . .National Sales Director, Beggars US
Jeremy Goldstein . . . . .National Director, Radio, Beggars US
Dan Gallo . . . . .Production, Beggars US
Rob Guthrie .Royalty Analyst, Beggars US
Sujan Hong . . . . .Online Marketing, Beggars US
Lucy Hurst . . . . .Publicity, Beggars US
Alex Moreno . . . .Marketing Coordinator, Video Promotions, Beggars US
Fred Navarrete . . . . .Radio Promotions, Beggars US
Miwa Okumura . . . . .Product Manager, Beggars US
Christy Simpson .Marketing, Beggars US
Euvin Weeber . . . . .Product Manager, Beggars US
Adam Carroll . . . . .Finance Manager, Beggars US
Peter Jacobson . . . . .Retail/Sales Coordinator
Sara Hruska . . .Receptionist, Office Manager, Street Teams, Beggars US

BETTER LOOKING RECORDS
11041 Santa Monica Blvd., Ste. 302
Los Angeles, CA 90025
FAX 208-728-4271
EMAIL . . . . .info@betterlookingrecords.com
WEB SITE . . . . .www.betterlookingrecords.com
DISTRIBUTOR   Alternative Distribution Alliance (ADA)
ARTIST ROSTER   Goldrush - Tristeza - The Album Leaf -
                                The Jealous Sound

David Brown . . . . .Publicity/Advertising/Air Drums
                                (holidaymatinee@mac.com)
Paul "opie" Fischer . . . . .Marketing/Sales/Air DJ-ing
                                (paul@betterlookingrecords.com)

*BIFOCAL MEDIA
PO Box 50106
Raleigh, NC 27650-0106
PHONE 919-696-3892
EMAIL . . . . .charles@bifocalmedia.com
WEB SITE . . . . .www.bifocalmedia.com
ARTIST ROSTER   Braid - The Cherry Valence- Continent -
                                Crash Smash Explode - Des Ark - The
                                Firebird Band - Goner - Kerbloki - The
                                Kickass - The Ladderback - Legend of
                                the Overfiend - The Party of Helicopters
                                - The Secret Life of Machines - Serotonin
                                - Utah!
GENRES   Electronica - Hardcore - Punk - Rap/Hip-
                                Hop

Charles Cardello . . . . .Owner
Brad Scott . . . . .Owner

BIG3 ENTERTAINMENT
6090 Central Ave.
St. Petersberg, FL 33707
PHONE 727-343-1840
FAX 727-384-5195
EMAIL . . . . .info@big3entertainment.com
WEB SITE www.big3entertainment.com
ARTIST ROSTER   Lil Eddie - Cheap Trick - DJ X - Rick
                                Derringer - Joey
LABELS   Big3 Records
GENRES   Country - Electronica - Jazz - Latin -
                                Rock
COMMENTS   WE Productions, Jam Management,
                                Mojo Rizin Publishing

William Edwards . . . . .Owner/Chairman
Maryann Pascal . . . . .President
Thomas Gribbin . . . . .Executive VP
Duvid Leach . . . . .General Manager
Jim "Pinky" Beeman . . . . .VP/Chief Engineer

BIRDMAN
PO Box 50777
Los Angeles, CA 90050
PHONE 323-259-1529
FAX 323-340-8986
EMAIL . . . . .drbutcher@sbcglobal.net
SECOND EMAIL . . . . .info@birdmanrecords.com
WEB SITE . . . . .www.intheredrecords.com
SECOND WEB SITE . . . . .www.birdmanrecords.com
DISTRIBUTOR   Revolver USA Distribution
ARTIST ROSTER   In the Red: The Dirtbombs - Blacktop -
                                The Fuse! - The Cuts - The Ponys;
                                Birdman: The Warlocks - Boredoms -
                                The Twilight Singers
LABELS   In the Red - Birdman - Sepia Tone - M80
GENRES   Pop - Rock

Larry Hardy . . . . .General Manager

LABELS

BLACKHEART RECORDS GROUP
636 Broadway, Ste. 1210
New York, NY 10012
PHONE 212-353-9600
FAX 212-353-8300
EMAIL . . . . .bhrecords@aol.com
WEB SITE . . . . .www.blackheart.com
SECOND WEB SITE . . . . .www.joanjett.com
ARTIST ROSTER   Joan Jett & the Blackhearts - The
                       Eyeliners - The Vacancies
GENRES   All Genres - Alternative - Punk - Rock

Kenny Laguna . . . . .President
Lauren Varga . . . . .General Manager
Karol Kamin . . . . .Head, Licensing
Julie Rader . . . . .Head, Media & Promotions
Elliot Saltzman . . . . .Tour Manager

BLIND PIG RECORDS
PO Box 2344
San Francisco, CA 94126
PHONE 415-550-6484/773-772-0043
FAX 415-550-6485/773-772-2115
EMAIL . . . . .pigpen@blindpigrecords.com
SECOND EMAIL . . . . .info@wholehoginc.com
WEB SITE . . . . .www.blindpigrecords.com
DISTRIBUTOR   Ryko Distribution
ARTIST ROSTER   Elvin Bishop - Harper - Tommy Castro -
                       Renee Austin - Bill Perry - Rod Piazza -
                       Popa Chubby - Albert Cummings - Nick
                       Curran - Rev. Billy C. Wirtz
RECENT RELEASES   Big Bill Morganfield - Renee Austin
GENRES   Blues - Roots
SUBMISSION POLICY   No unsolicited demos
COMMENTS   Publisher; Chicago office: PO Box
                       18461, Chicago, IL 60618-0461

Edward Chmelewski . . . . .Co-Owner/President (SF)
Jerry DelGiudice . . . . . .Co-Owner (Chicago) (jerry@wholehoginc.com)
Jim Netter . . . . . . .General Manager (Chicago) (jim@wholehoginc.com)
Luke Welsh . . . . .Director, Marketing, Retail Relations & Radio Promotion
                       (Chicago) (luke@wholehoginc.com)
Debra Regur . . . . .Publicist (SF) (pigpress@blindpigrecords.com)
Terry DelGiudice . . . . .Office Manager/Bookeeper (Chicago)
Sean Tripi . . . . .Office Manager (SF)

BLOODSHOT
3039 W. Irving Park Rd.
Chicago, IL 60618-3538
PHONE 773-604-5300
FAX 773-604-5019
EMAIL . . . . .bshq@bloodshotrecords.com
WEB SITE . . . . .www.bloodshotrecords.com
ARTIST ROSTER   The Waco Brothers
GENRES   Alternative - Blues - Country - Jazz -
                       Rock

Rob Miller . . . . .Owner (rob@bloodshotrecords.com)
Nan Warshaw . . . . .Owner (nan@bloodshotrecords.com)

BLUE JACKEL ENTERTAINMENT
PO Box 87
Huntington, NY 11743
PHONE 516-624-6095
FAX 516-624-6096
EMAIL . . . . .bluejackel@earthlink.net
DISTRIBUTOR   WEA Corp.
ARTIST ROSTER   Tony Martinez - William Cepeda - Maria
                       Ochoa - Monica Salmaso
GENRES   Electronica - Folk - Jazz - Latin - Roots -
                       World
RECENT SOUNDTRACKS   Catalano Veloso - Tieta
SUBMISSION POLICY   Send to Jack O'Neil
COMMENTS   Producer; Blue Jackel Publishing, Jackel
                       Publishing

Jack O'Neil . . . . .Owner
Nina Gomes O'Neil .Label Manager

BLUE WAVE RECORDS
3221 Perryville Rd.
Baldwinsville, NY 13027
PHONE 315-638-4286
FAX 315-635-4757
EMAIL . . . . .bluewave@localnet.com
WEB SITE . . . . .www.bluewaverecords.com
DISTRIBUTORS   Burnside Distribution Corp. - Select-O-
                      Hits
ARTIST ROSTER   Downchild Blues Band - Kim Simmonds
                      - Jony James Blues Band - Kim Lembo -
                      The Kingsnakes - Jimmy Cavallo
GENRES   Blues
SUBMISSION POLICY   Accepts unsolicited material
COMMENTS   Publishing; Licensing

Greg Spencer . . . . .President

BMG LABEL GROUP, US
550 Madison Ave.
New York, NY 10022
PHONE 212-833-8000
WEB SITE . . . . .www.sonybmg.com
LABELS   Arista - J Records - Jive Records - LaFace
                      - So So Def - RCA - RLG - Verity -
                      Zomba

Clive Davis . . . . .Chairman/CEO, BMG, Label Group, US
Charles Goldstuck . . . . .President/COO, BMG, Label Group, US
Joe Galante . . . . .Chairman, RLG/Nashville
Richard Sanders . . . . . . .Executive VP/General Manager, RCA Records
Max Siegel . . . . .President, Verity/VP, Zomba Label Group
Barry Weiss . . . . .President/CEO, Zomba Label Group

BOMP! RECORDS
PO Box 7112
Burbank, CA 91510
PHONE 818-729-9096
FAX 818-729-9235
EMAIL . . . . .promo@bomprecords.com
WEB SITE . . . . .www.bomp.com
ARTIST ROSTER   BBQ - The Black Lips - The Brian
                      Jonestown Masacre - The Coffin Lids -
                      Dead Meadow - Hard-Ons - Hell on
                      Heels - John Sparrow - The Lovetones -
                      The S'Cool Girls - The Telescopes - The
                      Warlocks
GENRES   Pop - Rock

Patrick Boissel . . . . .No Title
Suzy Shaw . . . . .No Title
Bangle Juice . . . . .Promotions

BOREALIS RECORDS
225 Sterling Rd., Unit 19
Toronto, ON M6R 2B2 Canada
PHONE 416-530-4288/877-530-4288
FAX 416-530-0461
EMAIL . . . . .info@borealisrecords.com
WEB SITE . . . . .www.borealisrecords.com
DISTRIBUTORS   Burnside Distribution Corp. - KOCH
                     Entertainment Distribution
ARTIST ROSTER   The Bills - Ron Hynes - Le Vent du Nord
                     - Nancy White
GENRES   Bluegrass - Blues - Folk - Roots
SUBMISSION POLICY   Include CD, bio and touring plans
COMMENTS   Celtic, Americana, Singer/Songwriter;
                     Also distributed by Proper Distribution

Bill Garrett . . . . .Partner
Grit Laskin . . . . .Partner
Linda Turu . . . . .Manager

BOTTLED MAJIC MUSIC
121 W. 27th St., Ste. 1004
New York, NY 10001
PHONE 212-645-3627
FAX 212-367-8315
EMAIL . . . . .info@bottledmajic.com
WEB SITE . . . . .www.bottledmajic.com
ARTIST ROSTER   Okra-Tone: Demolition String Band -
                     Hazeldine - Earl King - Lynn Miles - John
                     Mohead - Gil Parris - John Sinclair -
                     Chris Smither - Lorette Velvette - Wolfe;
                     Rooster Blues: Roosevelt "Booba" Barnes
                     & The Playboys - D.C. Bellamy - Lady
                     Bianca - Eddie Campbell - Eddy "The
                     Chief" Clearwater - Willie Cobbs - Larry
                     Davis - Willie King - Big Daddy Kinsey
LABELS   Okra-Tone Music - Rooster Blues Music
GENRES   Blues - Country - Folk - Roots

Robert Johnson . . . . .President (rjohnson@bottledmajic.com)
Anita Anderson . . . . . . .Tour Promotion (aanderson@bottledmajic.com)
Jeff Loh . . . . .Retail Promotion (jloh@bottledmajic.com)

BRASSHEART MUSIC/DREAM A WORLD ENTERTAINMENT
256 S. Robertson Blvd., Ste. 2288
Beverly Hills, CA 90211-2898
PHONE 323-932-0534
FAX 323-937-6884
EMAIL . . . . .brassheartmusic@aol.com
WEB SITE .www.brassheartmusic.com
SECOND WEB SITE . . . . .www.dreamaworld.com
DISTRIBUTOR   Music Design
LABELS   Dream A World: Kids Creative Classics
GENRES   All Genres - Children's
SUBMISSION POLICY   No unsolicited submissions
COMMENTS   Additional distribution by EMI/Music
                     Design - DeVorss & Co.; Publisher;
                     Licensing

Bunny Hull . . . . .President (brassheartmusic@aol.com,
                                              bunny@dreamaworld.com)

BRIDGE NINE RECORDS
35 Congress St.
Salem, MA 01970
PHONE 978-745-7199
FAX 978-745-4265
EMAIL . . . . .chris@bridge9.com
WEB SITE www.bridge9.com
DISTRIBUTOR   Caroline Distribution
ARTIST ROSTER   Outbreak - Death Before Dishonor -
                     Blue Monday - Champion - Have Heart
GENRES   Hardcore
SUBMISSION POLICY   Be familiar with label before submitting
                     demo

Chris Wrenn . . . . .Owner
Max Powers . . . . .Marketing
Jeff Jawk . . . . .Manufacturing & Design
Mike Melillo . . . . .Webmaster/Manufacturing

BROKEN BOW RECORDS
c/o Cummins Station
209 10th Ave. South, Ste. 230
Nashville, TN 37203
PHONE 615-244-8600
FAX 615-244-3700
EMAIL . . . . .info@brokenbowrecords.com
WEB SITE .www.brokenbowrecords.com
DISTRIBUTOR   RED Music Distribution
ARTIST ROSTER   Chad Austin - Robert Lee - Craig
                     Morgan - Lila McCann - Joe Diffie -
                     Sherrie Austin - Elbert West - Jason
                     Aldean - Megan Mullins - Fidel
                     Hernandez
GENRES   Country
SUBMISSION POLICY   Address submissions Attn: Larry Shell

Benny Brown . . . . .President/CEO
Brad Howell . . . . .General Manager
Paul Brown . . . . .Sr. VP, Operations
Jim Yerger . . . . .Sr. VP, Marketing (530-276-9837)
Jon Loba . . . . .VP, National Promotion
Larry Shell . . . . .VP, A&R
Rick Shedd . . . . .Director, Sales, Retail Marketing & Manufacturing
Lee Adams . . . . .National Co-Director, Promotion
Shelley Hargis . . . . .National Co-Director, Promotion
Layna Bunt . . . . .Director, Regional Promotion (West Coast)
JoJamie Hahr . . . . .Director, Regional Promotion (Southeast)
Summer Harman . . . . .Director, Publicity
Tina Crawford . . . . .A&R/Promotion Coordinator
Tonya Johnson . . . . .Receptionist/Administrative Assistant
Jenifer Snyder .Publicity Assistant

BROKEN ELBOW RECORDS
12534 Valley View St., Ste. 160
Garden Grove, CA 92845
PHONE 714-449-2406
EMAIL . . . . .info@brokenelbow.com
WEB SITE . . . . .www.brokenelbow.com
ARTIST ROSTER   Jeff Platts - Tex Strange & the One-Night
                     Stand Band
GENRES   Christian - Country - Roots
SUBMISSION POLICY   Does not accept unsolicited material

Jeff Platts . . . . .Owner

LABELS

BROOKLYN BOY ENTERTAINMENT, LLC
Box 3029
Venice, CA 90294-3029
PHONE 310-827-1819
FAX 310-564-0444
EMAIL . . . . .info@brooklynboy.com
WEB SITE . . . . .brooklynboy.com
ARTIST ROSTER   Kashif
GENRES   Jazz - R&B - Urban
SUBMISSION POLICY   Solicited only

Kashif . . . . .Owner

*BRUNSWICK RECORDS
524 Broadway
New York, NY 10012
PHONE 212-352-1500
FAX 305-661-4625
WEB SITE . . . . .www.brunswickrecords.com
DISTRIBUTOR   KOCH Entertainment Distribution
GENRES   R&B

Paul Tarnopol . . . . .President

BUENA VISTA MUSIC GROUP
500 S. Buena Vista St.
Burbank, CA 91521
PHONE 818-560-5670
FAX 818-560-3230
EMAIL .firstname.lastname@disney.com
LABELS   Hollywood Records - Lyric Street Records - Walt Disney Records

Bob Cavallo . . . .Chairman, Buena Vista Music Group (818-560-1800)
Mitchell Leib . . . . .President, Music & Soundtracks, Walt Disney Pictures/Television & Buena Vista Music Group (818-560-5124)
David Agnew   Executive VP/General Manager, Buena Vista Music Group (818-560-6406)
Ken Bunt . . . . . . .Sr. VP, Marketing, Hollywood Records (818-560-6161)
Justin Fontaine . .Sr. VP, Promotion, Hollywood Records (818-560-5521)
Carolyn Javier . . . . . . .Sr. VP, Business Affairs, Buena Vista Music Group
Abbey Konowitch . . . . . . .Sr. VP/General Manager, Hollywood Records (818-560-7575)
Jon Lind . . . . .Sr. VP, A&R, Hollywood Records (818-560-2595)
Geoffrey Weiss . . . . . .Sr. VP, A&R, Hollywood Records (818-560-2017)
Curt Eddy . . . . .VP, Sales, Hollywood Records (818-560-7415)
Lillian Matulic . . . . . .VP, Publicity, Hollywood Records (818-560-6197)
Cary Prince . . . . .VP, International, Buena Vista Music Group (818-973-7552)
Rob Souriall . . . . .VP, Strategic Marketing, Hollywood Records (818-560-7380)

BURNSIDE RECORDS
1522 N. Ainsworth St.
Portland, OR 97217
PHONE 503-231-0876
FAX 503-231-0420
EMAIL .music@burnsiderecords.com
WEB SITE .www.burnsiderecords.com
LABELS   Burnside - Sideburn
GENRES   Blues - Roots

Susan Stewart . . . . .No Title

CALLIOPE ENTERTAINMENT LLC
43 Chestnut Woods Rd.
Redding, CT 06896
PHONE 203-938-5544
FAX 203-938-5533
EMAIL . . . . .info@soniadada.com
WEB SITE . . . . .www.soniadada.com
DISTRIBUTOR   Sony BMG Sales Enterprise
ARTIST ROSTER   Sonia Dada - John Lee Hooker
GENRES   Blues - Rock

Brayton Fogerty . . . . .No Title
Michele Tayler . . . . .No Title

CALVIN RECORDS
701 W. Hwy. 7
Excelsior, MN 55331
PHONE 952-541-0099
FAX 952-541-9111
EMAIL . . . . .info@calvinrecords.com
WEB SITE www.liquid8records.com
ARTIST ROSTER   Fear Factory - Tim Bowman
LABELS   Calvin - Tribute Sounds - Liquid 8
GENRES   All Genres

Michael Catain . . . . .CEO
Mark Heyert . . . . .VP, Sales
Eric Foss . . . . .Director, Licensing
Bobby Z . . . . .A&R

CANDLEBONE
12811 Bonaparte Ave.
Los Angeles, CA 90066
PHONE 310-822-8062
EMAIL . . . . .info@candlebone.com
WEB SITE . . . . .www.candlebone.com
GENRES   Alternative
COMMENTS   Distributed by B.D.C. (US) & Shellshock (Europe)

Moris Tepper . . . . .No Title

CANTALOUPE MUSIC
80 Hanson Pl., Ste. 702
Brooklyn, NY 11217
PHONE 718-852-7755
FAX 718-852-7732
EMAIL . . . . .info@cantaloupemusic.com
WEB SITE . . . . .www.cantaloupemusic.com
ARTIST ROSTER   Alarm Will Sound - Bang on a Can - Arnold Dreyblatt - Ethel - Michael Gordon - Gutbucket - Icebreaker - Phil Kline - David Lang - Lisa Moore - So Percussion - Toby Twining - Julia Wolfe - Evan Ziporyn
GENRES   Classical - Electronica - Jazz - New Age - Punk - Rock - World
SUBMISSION POLICY   Submit by US mail or email address above

Ken Thomson . . . . .Label Manager (kt@cantaloupemusic.com)
Ian Quay . . . . .Licensing & Retail Manager (ian@cantaloupemusic.com)

CAPITOL RECORDS
1750 N. Vine St
Los Angeles, CA 90028
PHONE 323-462-6252/212-786-8000
FAX 323-469-4542/212-253-3099
EMAIL . . . . .firstname.lastname@capitolrecords.com
WEB SITE . . . . .www.capitolrecords.com
DISTRIBUTOR   EMI Music Marketing
GENRES   Alternative - Classical - Jazz - Pop - Rock
COMMENTS   East Coast office: 150 Fifth Ave., New
                     York, NY 10011

Andrew Slater . . . . .President/CEO (323-462-6252)
Bruce Lundvall . . . . .President, Jazz/Classical (212-786-8600)
Mark DiDia . . . . .Executive VP (323-462-6252)
Jon Polk . . . . .Executive VP (323-462-6252)
John Boulos . . . . .Sr. VP, Promotion
Ambrosia Healy . . . . .Sr. VP, Publicity (323-871-5373)
Ron Laffitte . . . . .Sr. VP, A&R (323-871-5765)
John Ray . . . . . . .Sr. VP Legal/Business Affairs (323-871-5088)
Ike Youssef . . . . .Sr. VP/CFO (323-871-5345)
Joy Feuer . . . . .VP, Field Sales (323-871-5788)
Ken Lucek . . . . .VP, Promotion
Julian Raymond . . . . .VP, A&R (323-871-5260)
Maggie Sikkens . . . . .VP, A&R Administration (323-871-5277)
Louie Bandak . . . . .Sr. Director, A&R (323-871-5101)
Bobbie Gale . . . . .Sr. Director, Publicity (323-871-5118)
Judi Kerr . . . . .Sr. Director, Publicity (323-871-5375)
Laurel Stearns . . . . .Sr. Director, A&R (323-871-5792)
Nancy Burgess . . .Director, Marketing & Merchandising (323-871-5786)
Jamie Feldman . . . . .Director, A&R (323-871-5087)
Jonna Terrasi . . . . .Director, A&R Administration (323-871-5297)
Brian Wittmer .Director, A&R Research
David Walsh . . . . .A&R Administration (323-871-5799)
Hazel Eckles . . . . .Assistant to Andrew Slater
Anita Contreras . . . . .Assistant to Julian Raymond
Siobhan Davis . . . . .Assistant to Ron Laffitte

CAPITOL RECORDS NASHVILLE
3322 West End Ave., 11th Fl.
Nashville, TN 37203
PHONE 615-269-2000
EMAIL . . . . .firstname.lastname@emimusic.com
WEB SITE . . . . .www.capitol-nashville.com
SECOND WEB SITE . . . . .www.emimusic.com
DISTRIBUTOR   EMI Music Marketing
ARTIST ROSTER   Keith Urban - Trace Adkins - Dierks
                    Bentley - Chris Cagle - Jennifer Hanson
                    - The Jenkins Jamie O'Neal - Chris
                    LeDoux - Amber Dotson - Ryan Shupe &
                    the Rubber Band - Eric Chuch - Luke
                    Bryan - Kenny Rogers - Emily West
GENRES   Country

Mike Dungan . . . . .President/CEO (615-269-2020)
Tom Becci . . . . .COO (615-269-2096)
Fletcher Foster . . . . .Sr. VP, Marketing (615-269-2068)
Jimmy Harnen . . . . .VP, Promotions (615-269-2030)
Bill Kennedy . . . . .VP, Sales (615-269-2083)
Larry Willoughby . . . . .VP, A&R (615-269-2037)
Joanna Carter . . . . . . .Sr. Director, Artist Development (615-269-2060)
Autumn House . . . . .Director, A&R (615-269-2072)
Judy McDonough . . .Director, Media & Public Relations (615-269-2032)
Betsy Morley . . . . .Director, A&R Administration (615-269-2038)
Dixie Weathersby . . .Director, Media & Public Relations (615-269-2087)
Dottie Chamberlin . . . . . . .Assistant to Mike Dungan (615-269-2090)

CARGO MUSIC, INC.
4901-906 Morena Blvd.
San Diego, CA 92117
PHONE 858-483-9292
EMAIL . . . . .info@cargomusic.com
WEB SITE . . . . .www.cargomusic.com
GENRES   Alternative - Country - Hardcore - Metal
                    - Pop - Rock
SUBMISSION POLICY   Accepts unsolicited submissions
COMMENTS   Also a distributor

Sharon Goodis . . . . .Label Manager

CASABLANCA RECORDS
745 Fifth Ave., Ste. 800
New York, NY 10151
PHONE 212-471-4000
FAX 212-471-4090
WEB SITE .www.casablanca-music.com
ARTIST ROSTER   Corey Gunz - Lindsay Lohan
GENRES   Pop - R&B - Rap/Hip-Hop - Urban
RECENT SOUNDTRACKS   Shall We Dance - Bride and Prejudice -
                    Bree Larson

Thomas Mattola . . . . .President
Edward Woods . . . . .Executive VP, Urban Music

CASH MONEY RECORDS
PO Box 6257
Metairie, LA 70009
PHONE 504-835-2676
FAX 504-835-3676
WEB SITE .www.cashmoney-records.com
DISTRIBUTOR   Universal Music & Video Distribution
LABELS   Roun' Table Entertainment

Ronald Williams . . . . .President/CEO
Bryan Williams . . . . .COO
Merlin Bobb . . . . .CEO, Roun' Table Entertainment
Michelle Diaz . . . . .CFO
Vernon Brown . . . . .Business Manager
Kim Williams . . . . .Publicist

CASTLE RECORDS
30 Music Square West, Ste. 102
Nashville, TN 37203
PHONE 615-401-7111
EMAIL . . . . .castlerecords@castlerecords.com
WEB SITE . . . . .www.castlerecords.com
GENRES   Country - Gospel - Pop - R&B -
                    Rap/Hip-Hop
SUBMISSION POLICY   See Web site for submission procedure

Ed Russell . . . . .CEO/President
Peggy Tresco . . . . .Director, Publishing
Ben Wright . . . . .Director, A&R
Joe Khoury . . . . .A&R
Ron Treat . . . . .Engineering
Debbie Wallin . . . . .Publishing Marketing Assistant

LABELS

CENTURY MEDIA

2323 W. El Segundo Blvd.
Hawthorne, CA 90250-3315
PHONE 323-418-1400
FAX 323-418-0118
EMAIL . . . . .mail@centurymedia.com
SECOND EMAIL . . . . .firstname@centurymedia.com
WEB SITE . . . . .www.centurymedia.com

DISTRIBUTOR	Caroline Distribution
ARTIST ROSTER	God Forbid - Napalm Death - Nevermore - The Haunted - Arch Enemy - Diecast - Lacuna Coil - Shadows Fall
LABELS	Liquor & Poker - Abacus - Nuclear Blast - Olympic
GENRES	Hardcore - Metal - Rock
RECENT SOUNDTRACKS	Resident Evil - Hellboy
SUBMISSION POLICY	Accepts unsolicited demos

Marco Barbieri . . . . .President (x113)
Phil Hinkle . . . . .A&R (x109)
Branden Linnell . . . . .Publishing (x121)

CHAIN DRIVE RECORDS

1411 N. Sierra Bonita Ave., #3
Hollywood, CA 90046
PHONE 323-525-2348

ARTIST ROSTER	manSaveman - The Larrys
GENRES	Blues - Punk - Rock - Roots
SUBMISSION POLICY	No unsolicited submissions

Jeff Squigley . . . . .Owner/A&R

CHIAROSCURO RECORDS

830 Broadway
New York, NY 10003
PHONE 845-279-4828
FAX 845-279-5025
WEB SITE . . . . .www.chiaroscurojazz.com
SECOND WEB SITE . . . . .www.downtown-sound.com

LABELS	Downtown Sound
GENRES	Jazz
SUBMISSION POLICY	No unsolicited submissions at this time

Hank O'Neill . . . . .President
Andrew Sordoni . . . . .CEO
Jon Bates . . . . .VP, Operations

CLAIRECORDS

1812 J St., #1
Sacramento, CA 95814
PHONE 916-551-1597
FAX 240-352-4784
EMAIL . . . . .susan@clairecords.com
SECOND EMAIL . . . . .heather@clairecords.com
WEB SITE . . . . .www.clairecords.com

DISTRIBUTORS	Carrot Top Distribution, Ltd. - Choke Distribution - Revolver USA Distribution
ARTIST ROSTER	Air Formation - Airiel - Catapult - Con Dolore - Eau Claire - Ecstasy of Saint Theresa - Electro Group - The Flatmates - The Frenchmen - Hartfield - Highspire - Isobella - Malory - Mean Red Spiders - Monster Movie - Paik - Park Avenue Music - Pia Fraus - Sciflyer - Secret Shine - Silver Screen - St. Avalanche - Stella Luna - thebrotherkite

Heather Sostrom . . . . .No Title (heather@clairecords.com)
Dan Sostom . . . . .No Title (dan@clairecords.com)

CLEOPATRA RECORDS

11041 Santa Monica Blvd., #703
Los Angeles, CA 90025
PHONE 310-477-4000
FAX 310-312-5653
EMAIL . . . . .cleoinfo@cleorecs.com
WEB SITE . . . . .www.cleorecs.com

DISTRIBUTOR	Navarre Corporation
LABELS	Cleopatra - Deadline - X-Ray - Stardust - Hypnotic - Purple Pyramid - Goldenlane - Magick
GENRES	Blues - Country - Electronica - Jazz - Metal - Rap/Hip-Hop - Rock
SUBMISSION POLICY	Contact before submitting material
COMMENTS	Additional genres: Gothic, Industrial and Reggaeton

Brian Perera . . . . .CEO
Tim Yasui . . . . .VP/General Manager (tim@cleorecs.com)
Jeff Gray . . . . . . .Licensing & Creative Services (cleoinfo@cleorecs.com)
Jason Myers .A&R, Hard Rock & Metal
Ali O. . . . . .Publicity (ali@cleorecs.com)
Ken Tighe . . . . .Marketing

CMH RECORDS

2898 Rowena Ave., Ste. 201
Los Angeles, CA 90039
PHONE 323-663-8073
FAX 323-669-1470/323-669-1471
EMAIL . . . . .info@crosscheckrecords.com
WEB SITE . . . . .www.cmhrecords.com
SECOND WEB SITE . . . . .www.crosscheckrecords.com

DISTRIBUTORS	Cargo Music, Inc. - Choke Distribution - Handleman Company - Lumberjack Mordam Music Group - Navarre Corporation - Select-O-Hits - Super D
ARTIST ROSTER	CMH: Pine Mountain Railroad - Wanda Jackson - Cache Valley Drifters - Carolina Road - Larry Cordle; Crosscheck: Street Dogs - Vice Dollsogs; Urabon: Dr. Octagon (Kool Keith)
LABELS	Crosscheck - Vitamin - Urabon - Rockwell - Dwell - Scufflin' - IED
GENRES	Bluegrass - Country - Gospel - Punk - Rap/Hip-Hop - Rock - Roots
SUBMISSION POLICY	Mail submissions to: CMH Records, PO Box 39439, Los Angeles, CA 90039

David Haerle . . . . .President
Joel Spielman . . . . .President, Crosscheck Records
April McClellan . . . . .A&R/Promo

COLUMBIA RECORDS (LOS ANGELES)

c/o Sony BMG Music Entertainment
2100 Colorado Ave.
Santa Monica, CA 90404
PHONE 310-449-2100
FAX 310-552-1350
EMAIL . . . . .firstname.lastname@sonybmg.com
WEB SITE . . . . .www.columbiarecords.com

LABELS	Aquemini - Columbia International - DMZ - DV8 - Facility - Game - Lapis Music - Loud - Ravenous - Rise - Roc-A-Bloc - Sucka Free - Urban Wolves
GENRES	Classical - Jazz - Pop - R&B - Rap/Hip-Hop - Rock

Tim Devine . . . . .Sr. VP, A&R/General Manager, West Coast
Barbara Jones .Sr. VP, Product Marketing
David Andreone . . . . .VP, A&R
Angelica Cob Baehler . . . . .VP, Media
Bob Semanovich .VP, Product Marketing
Robert Shahnazarian Jr. . . . . .VP, Core Production Services
Tom Muzquiz . . . . .Director, Media
Hilari Farrell . . . . .A&R Project Manager
April Baldwin . . . . .A&R Administration
Nancy Matalon . . . . .A&R Administration

*COLUMBIA RECORDS (NASHVILLE)

1400 18th Avenue South
Nashville, TN 37212
PHONE 615-858-1300
WEB SITE . . . . .www.columbiarecords.com

ARTIST ROSTER	Van Zant - Brice Long - Ashley Monroe - Montgomery Gentry - Buddy Jewell - Mary Chapin Carpenter - Trent Willmon - Jessi Alexander - Shelly Fairchild - Rodney Crowell
GENRES	Country

Larry Pareigis .Sr. VP, Radio Promotion
Tom Moran .National Director, Promotion

COLUMBIA RECORDS (NEW YORK)

550 Madison Ave.
New York, NY 10022-3211
PHONE 212-833-8000
FAX 212-833-5401
EMAIL . . . . .firstname.lastname@sonybmg.com
WEB SITE . . . . .www.columbiarecords.com

LABELS	Aquemini - Columbia International - DMZ - DV8 - Facility - Game - Lapis Music - Loud - Ravenous - Rise - Roc-A-Bloc - Sucka Free - Urban Wolves
GENRES	All Genres

Steve Barnett . . . .Chairman, Columbia Records Group (212-833-5335)
Steve Greenberg . . . . .President, Columbia Records
Stu Bergen . . . .Executive VP, Alternative Music/Sr. VP, Columbia Records Group (212-833-8030)
Jim Burruss . . . . .Sr. VP, Promotion/Operations (212-833-4541)
Ron Cerrito . . . . . . .Sr. VP, Alternative/Rock Promotion (212-833-7563)
Mitchell Cohen . . . . .Sr. VP, A&R (212-833-4015)
Pete Cosenza . . . . .Sr. VP, Promotion/Adult Format (212-833-8986)
Fran DeFeo . . . . .Sr. VP, National Media (212-833-5784)
John Doelp . . . . .Sr. VP, A&R Operations (212-833-4623)
Marcia Edelstein . . . . .Sr. VP, Creative Marketing (212-833-8618)
Gary Fisher . .Sr. VP, Video Promotion/TV Programming (212-833-5971)
Denise Gatto . . . . .Sr. VP, Release Planning (212-833-4137)
Jeff Jones . . . . .Sr. VP, Jazz/Legacy Recordings (212-833-8430)
Barbara Jones . . . . .Sr. VP, Marketing (310-449-2160)
Steve Lillywhite . . . . .Sr. VP, A&R (212-833-8671)
Yvette Noel-Schure . . . . . . .Sr. VP, Media, Sony Urban (212-833-4483)
Liz Pokora . . . . .Sr. VP, Pop Promotions (212-833-5119)
Denis Venturino . . . . .Sr. VP, Finance & Operations (212-833-5107)
Steve Yegelwel . . . . .Sr. VP, A&R (212-833-7244)
Lee Anne Callahan . . . . .VP, Video Promotion (212-833-5507)
Nick Cucci . . . . .VP, Product Marketing (212-833-5545)
Lee Dannay .VP, A&R (212-833-4684)

(Continued)

COLUMBIA RECORDS (NEW YORK) (Continued)

John DiMaio . . . . .VP, Alternative Rock Promotion (212-833-4464)
Liana Farnham . . . . .VP, Tour Marketing (212-833-8578)
Mark Feldman . . . . .VP, Jazz Marketing (212-833-5013)
Joe Guzik . . . . .VP, Rock Promotion (212-833-5897)
Rocco Lanzilotta . . . . .VP, Creative Marketing (212-833-5133)
Greg Linn . . . . .VP, Product Marketing (212-833-4746)
Elaine Locatelli . . . .VP, Adult Contemporary Promotion (212-833-4680)
Claire Mercuri . . . . .VP, Media (212-833-5121)
Kevin Patrick .VP, A&R (212-833-7311)
Matt Pinfield . . . . . . .VP, A&R/Artist Development (212-833-8683)
John Vernile . . . . . . .VP, Adult Promotion & Marketing, Columbia Jazz/Legacy Recordings (212-833-4765)
Lisa Wolfe . . . . .VP, Promotion & Marketing (212-833-5807)
Dave Watson National Director, Promotion (Cleveland) (440-729-4188)
Nick Casinelli . . . . .Sr. Director, A&R (212-833-4404)
Tony Ferguson . . . . . . .Sr. Director, Media, Sony Urban (212-833-4595)
Garrett Schaeffer . . . . . .Sr. Director, Product Marketing (212-833-7020)
Julie Stillman . . . . .Sr. Director, Top 40 Promotion (212-833-8522)
Benny Tarantini . . . . .Sr. Director, Publicity (212-833-5858)
Trina Tombrink . . .Sr. Director, Adult Formats Promotion (212-833-8505)
Tim Holmes . . . . .Director, Editorial Services (212-833-7476)
Carolyn Scarbrough . . . . . . .Director, Media Relations (212-833-4146)
Nina Webb . . . . .Director, Product Marketing (212-833-8325)
Edwin Banacia Associate Director, Media, Sony Urban (212-833-5072)
Tony Cammarota . . . . .Associate Director, Promotion (212-833-5611)
Jane Mathangani . . . . .Associate Director, Promotion (212-833-5871)
Becca Callaway . . . . .A&R Manager (212-833-7029)
Maria Egan . . . . .A&R Manager (212-833-5746)
Maureen Kenny . . . . .A&R Manager (212-833-7557)
Benjamin Simone . . . . .A&R Manager (212-833-7526)
Tracey Chilandese . . . . .Manager, Top 40 Promotion (212-833-5036)
Bettie Levy . . . . .Manager, Video Promotion (212-833-4267)
Brady Bedard . . . . .Radio Promotion (Atlanta) (770-392-1844)
Geoffrey DeWilde . . . . .Radio Promotion (Denver) (720-946-0989)
Andy Flick . . . . .Radio Promotion (Dallas) (214-378-0536)
Jonathan Jacobs . . . . .Radio Promotion (Minneapolis) (952-921-5165)
Pam Kaye . . . . .Radio Promotion (NY) (516-827-3738)
Jeremy Rubin . . . . .Radio Promotion (SF) (415-884-5045)
Lynne Salivaris . . . . .Radio Promotion (DC) (301-572-2444, x111)
Mike Scheid . . . . .Radio Promotion (Chicago) (847-640-4335)
David Shaw . . . . .Radio Promotion (Boston) (401-233-1544)
Hilary Stafford . . . . .Radio Promotion (LA) (310-449-2479)
Rich Tardanico . . . . .Radio Promotion (Miami) (954-431-0076)

COMMOTION RECORDS

126 Fifth Ave., 7th Fl.
New York, NY 10011
PHONE 212-243-2100
FAX 212-243-2329
EMAIL . . . . .info@arecordcommotion.com

DISTRIBUTOR	Ryko Distribution
RECENT SOUNDTRACKS	Hotel Rwanda - Murderball - Mysterious Skin - Happy Endings - Code 46 - My Architect - A Slipping-Down Life - The Cooler
COMMENTS	Music Supervisor

Tracy McKnight . . . . .Partner
Walter Yetnikoff . . . . .Partner
Aram Goldberg . . . . .No Title

LABELS

COMPADRE RECORDS
708 Main St., Ste. 720
Houston, TX 77002
PHONE 713-228-3847
FAX 713-228-3843
EMAIL . . . . .info@compadrerecords.com
WEB SITE . . . . .www.compadrerecords.com
DISTRIBUTOR   RED Music Distribution
ARTIST ROSTER   Billy Joe Shaver - James McMurtry - Suzy
                      Bogguss - Flaco Jimenez - Kate
                      Campbell - Kevn Kinney - Julie Lee -
                      Lonesome River Band - Townes Van
                      Zandt - Hayes Carll - Mike McClure
GENRES   Bluegrass - Country - Folk - Rock

Brad Turcotte . . . . .President
Logan Rogers . . . . .VP/Director, A&R (615-423-2038)
Jenni Finlay . . . . .Manager, Publicity
Marc Harkness . . . . .Creative Design Manager
Blythe Leger . . . . .Secondary Marketing Coordinator

COMPASS RECORDS
916 19th Ave. South
Nashville, TN 37212
PHONE 615-320-7672
FAX 615-320-7378
EMAIL . . . . .info@compassrecords.com
WEB SITE . . . . .www.compassrecords.com
DISTRIBUTOR   Ryko Distribution
ARTIST ROSTER   Allison Brown Quartet - Pierce Pettis -
                      The Waifs - Drew Emmitt - Lunasa -
                      Thea Gilmore - Paul Brady - Victor
                      Wooten - Kate Rusby - Colin Hay -
                      Glenn Tilbrook
GENRES   Bluegrass - Folk - Jazz - Pop - Roots -
                      World

Alison Brown . . . . .President/Owner (alison@compassrecords.com)
Garry West . . . . .VP, A&R/Owner (garry@compassrecords.com)
David Haley . . . . .Licensing & Clearance

COMPENDIA MUSIC GROUP
210 N. 25th Ave., Ste. 1200
Nashville, TN 37203
PHONE 615-277-1800
FAX 615-277-1801
EMAIL . . . . .rpepin@compendiamusic.com
WEB SITE . . . . .www.compendiamedia.com
DISTRIBUTOR   KOCH Entertainment Distribution
LABELS   Compendia - Light Records - Intersound
                      Records - Life2 Records
GENRES   Adult Contemporary - Christian -
                      Country - Gospel - Jazz - Pop - R&B -
                      Rock

Michael Olsen . . . . .President, Compendia Music Group
Mick Lloyd . . . . .VP/General Manager, Compendia Records/
                                              Intersound Records
Phillip White . . . . .VP/General Manager, Light Records, Life2
Ric Pepin . . . . .VP, Marketing & Promotion, Compendia Records/
                                              Intersound Records
Terry Donovan . . . . .VP, Sales, Compendia Music Group
Michelle S. Duffie . . . . .Director, Marketing, Light Records
Kendall Duffie . . . . .Director, A&R & Promotion, Light Records
Tammy Hillebrand . . . . .Director, International Licensing,
                                              Compendia Music Group
Crystal McLin . . . . .Director, Publicity, Light Records
Glenn Meadows . . . . .Director, Media, Compendia Music Group
Holly Nelson . . . . .Director, Creative Services, Compendia Music Group
Tracy Wallner . . . . .Art Director, Compendia Music Group
Paul Colson . . . . .Coordinator, Marketing & Promotions,
                                              Compendia Records/Intersound
Amy Larson . . . . .Royalties Manager, Compendia Music Group
Jada Gunn . . . . .Artist Relations, Light Records
Jake Shores . . . . .Graphic Designer
Brittainy Spaht . . . . .Office Manger, Compendia Music Group
Lori Gerlach . . . . .Administrative Assistant

CONCORD RECORDS
100 N. Crescent Dr., Ste. 275
Beverly Hills, CA 90210
PHONE 310-385-4455
FAX 310-385-4466
EMAIL . . . . .info@concordrecords.com
WEB SITE . . . . .www.concordrecords.com
DISTRIBUTOR   Universal Music & Video Distribution
ARTIST ROSTER   Howard Alden - Karrin Allyson - Patti
                      Austin - Jimmy Bruno - Gary Burton -
                      Kenny Burrell - Peter Cincotti - Chick
                      Corea - Joey DeFrancesco - Pete
                      Escovedo - Michael Feinstein - Nneena
                      Freelon - Robben Ford - Scott Hamilton -
                      Marian McPartland - Monica Mancini -
                      Barry Manilow - Tania Maria - Ozomatli
                      - Eddie Palmieri - John Patitucci - Dave
                      Samuels & The Caribbean Jazz Project -
                      Poncho Sanchez Latin Jazz Band - Diane
                      Schuur - George Shearing - Keely Smith
                      - Curtis Stigers - Dave Weckl
LABELS   Concord Jazz - Concord Picante -
                      Fantasy - Stretch Records - Feinery -
                      Peak - Playboy Jazz - The Jazz Alliance
GENRES   Adult Contemporary - Blues - Jazz - Latin
                      - R&B - Rock - World
SUBMISSION POLICY   No unsolicited submissions

Glen Barros . . . . .President
John Burk . . . . .Executive VP
Lawrence Blake . . . . .Sr. VP, Business Affairs/GM
Joel Amsterdam . . . . .VP, Publicity
Abbey Anna . . . . .VP, Product Development
Joyce Castagnola . . . . .VP, Sales
Margi Cheske . . . . .VP, Marketing
David Morrell . . . . .VP, Promotion
Nick Phillips . . . . .VP, Artist & Catalog Development
Andrew Flad . . . . .Director, International Sales & Marketing
Mary Hogan . . . . .Director, A&R Administration
Jo Foster . . . . .Director, Publicity
Deb Rosner . . . . .Director, Licensing & Special Markets

CONCRETE RECORDINGS, INC.
8306 Wilshire Blvd., Ste. 487
Beverly Hills, CA 90211
PHONE 310-358-2773
FAX 323-852-4926
EMAIL . . . . .jay@concreterecordingsinc.com
WEB SITE . . . . .www.concreterecordingsinc.com
SECOND WEB SITE . . . . . .www.myspace.com/concreterecordingsinc
ARTIST ROSTER   Young Spook - Knee-Hi - Rudy - St.
                      James - Hypnotik - Ice Blag - The
                      Renegades - Rachel Murray - Indojah
GENRES   Alternative - Classical - Gospel - Jazz -
                      Latin - Pop - R&B - Rap/Hip-Hop -
                      Urban
SUBMISSION POLICY   No unsolicited material accepted

Jay Atkins . . . . .CEO
Kayanta Culbert . . . . .Director, A&R, Urban
Darnell Davis . . . . .A&R
Marco Durham . . . . .A&R/Street Team
DJ D. Evans . . . . .A&R
Brent Hoover . . . . .A&R/Promotions
Conrad Williams . . . . .A&R
Ronald Milligan .Assistant to CEO

CONNOISSEUR RECORDS
8730 Sunset Blvd., Ste. 175
Los Angeles, CA 90069
PHONE 310-360-7700/203-227-1978
FAX 310-854-5936/203-227-2373
WEB SITE . . . . .www.conncos.com
ARTIST ROSTER   Beyond Bob
GENRES   Alternative - Rock
COMMENTS   East Coast office: 136 Main St., Ste.
                         202, Westport, CT 06880

Dan Hubbert . . . . .President
Michael O. Driscoll . . . . .Westport
Lenore Hermann . . . . .Westport
Charles G. Lelievre . . . . .Westport
Cana Sharai . . . . .LA
Jeffrey D. Warshaw . . . . .Westport

*CONTANGO RECORDS
244 Fifth Ave., #2215
New York, NY 10001
PHONE 212-561-0598
FAX 212-591-6723
EMAIL . . . . .michael@contangorecords.com
SECOND EMAIL . . . . .warren@contangorecords.com
ARTIST ROSTER   Whitestarr - Lost Boyz - Mr. Cheeks
GENRES   Rap/Hip-Hop - Rock
SUBMISSION POLICY   Only send full press kit with photos and
                         music to above address
COMMENTS   Looking for bands with past success and
                         track record

Warren Gumpel . . . . .Partner
Michael "Shoop" Harrison . . . . .Partner

COOL MUSIC GROUP
PO Box 10162
North Hollywood, CA 91606
PHONE 310-364-1704
WEB SITE . . . . .www.coolmusicgroup.com
SECOND WEB SITE . . . . .www.coolmediagroup.com
ARTIST ROSTER   Invisible Poet Kings - Trevor McShane -
                         Michael Jarrett - Shoofly - Michael
                         Richard - Barry Keenan
GENRES   Alternative - Blues - Country -
                         Electronica - Jazz - Latin - Metal - Pop -
                         R&B - Rap/Hip-Hop - Rock
SUBMISSION POLICY   Accepts submissions sent only to our PO
                         Box; Present your best three songs with
                         lyrics in CD format; Cassettes not
                         accepted
COMMENTS   Additional genre: Rock En Espanol;
                         Company is also an E Label (Digital
                         downloads primarily) as well as a Music
                         Publishing Company

Jeff Hirshtick . . . . .No Title
Neville Johnson . . . . .No Title
Barry Keenan . . . . .No Title
Greg Philippi . . . . .No Title

CRASH MUSIC, INC.
4025 E. Chandler Blvd., Ste. 70B-3
Phoenix, AZ 85048
PHONE 480-496-9634
FAX 480-496-9638
EMAIL . . . . .info@crashmusicinc.com
WEB SITE . . . . .www.crashmusicinc.com
DISTRIBUTORS   Caroline Distribution - RED Music
                         Distribution
ARTIST ROSTER   Flotsam & Jetsam - Texas Is on Fire -
                         Enforsaken - Abeyance - Divine Empire -
                         Metalium - Holy Moses
GENRES   Metal - Rock

Mark Nawara .President/Director, Crash USA
                         (mark@crashmusicinc.com)
Ralph Graupner . . . . .Director, Crash Europe (49-69-9855-8368,
                         ralph@crashmusicinc.com)
Jackie Bubrowski . .Direct Sales/Accounting (jackie@crashmusicinc.com)
Andrew Norris . . . . .Promotion (andrew@crashmusicinc.com)

CRAVEDOG RECORDS
1522 N. Ainsworth
Portland, OR 97217
PHONE 503-233-7284/866-469-9820
FAX 503-234-5305
EMAIL . . . . .info@cravedog.com
WEB SITE . . . . .www.cravedog.com
DISTRIBUTOR   Burnside Distribution Corp.
ARTIST ROSTER   Bingo - Fernando - Little Sue - Luther
                         Russell - Warren Pash
GENRES   Country - Pop - Rock
COMMENTS   CD Manufacturing

Todd Crosby . . . . .Founder
Tony Trause . . . . .General Manager
Matt Gannon . . . . .Graphic Designer
Michael Fitzgerald . . . . .Customer Service
Russell Short . . . . .Customer Service

CRC JIANIAN RECORDS
1680 Vine St., Ste. 1200
Hollywood, CA 90028
PHONE 323-960-0830
FAX 323-960-0840
EMAIL . . . . .info@chinarecords.net
WEB SITE . . . . .www.chinarecords.net
GENRES   World
SUBMISSION POLICY   Email for permission
COMMENTS   Representing the largest catalog of
                         Chinese music from China Record
                         Corporation

Frank Mayor . . . . .CEO
Peter Jansson . . . . .COO
Jackie Subeck . . . . .VP, Music
Nana Lee . . . . .VP, International

CRESCENT MOON RECORDS
420 Jefferson Ave.
Miami, FL 33139
PHONE 305-695-7000
FAX 305-695-7113
WEB SITE . . . . .www.crescentmoonrecords.com
SECOND WEB SITE . . . . .www.estefanenterprises.com
GENRES   Latin - Pop - R&B

Emilio Estefan Jr. . . . . .Chairman
Iosvanny Castillo . . . . .Director, A&R (305-695-7000)
Janet De Armas . .Assistant to Owner (jdearmas@estefanenterprises.com)

CURB RECORDS INC.
47 Music Square East
Nashville, TN 37203
PHONE 615-321-5080/818-843-2872
FAX 615-327-1964/818-843-4659
EMAIL .firstinitiallastname@curb.com
WEB SITE . . . . .www.curb.com
DISTRIBUTOR   WEA Corp.
LABELS   Curb Records - Curb/Asylum Records
GENRES   Christian - Country - Latin - Pop
SUBMISSION POLICY   No unsolicited material
COMMENTS   West Coast office: 3907 W. Alameda
                    Ave., Burbank, CA 91505

Mike Curb . . . . .Chairman
Carole Curb . . .President, Curb Entertainment International Corporation
                    (818-843-2872 x149)
Dennis P. Hannon Executive VP/General Manager (615-321-5080 x319)
Harley Hatcher . . .Sr. VP, Publicity/Special Projects (818-843-2872 x153)
Tracy Moore . . . . .Sr. VP, Business Affairs (818-843-2872 x129)
John Butler . . . . .VP, Christian Promotion (615-321-5080 x349)
Liz Cavanaugh . . . . .VP, Publicity/Media Relations (615-321-5080 x316)
Benson Curb . . . . .VP, Sales (615-321-5080 x322)
Carson James . . . . .VP, Country Promotions, Curb Records
                    (615-321-5080 x376)
Doug Johnson . . . . .VP, A&R (615-321-5080 x211)
Jeff Tuerff . . . . .VP, Marketing (615-321-5080 x340)

CUTTING RECORDS
16 Penn Plaza, Ste. 1518
New York, NY 10001-1820
PHONE 212-868-3154
FAX 212-868-1061
EMAIL . . . . .info@cuttingnyc.com
WEB SITE . . . . .www.cuttingnyc.com
ARTIST ROSTER   Fulanijo - Son Callejeros - E-Real -
                    Guanabanas - KHZ
LABELS   Propane - Cutting Latino
GENRES   Electronica - Latin - Rap/Hip-Hop
RECENT SOUNDTRACKS Shaft - Playstation
SUBMISSION POLICY   Accepts unsolicited material

Amado Marin . . . . .President (amado@cuttingnyc.com)
Louie Garcia . . . . .General Manager (louie@cuttingnyc.com)
Aldo Marin . . . . .VP, A&R (aldo@cuttingnyc.com)
Ernie Nieves . . . . .Publicity/Licensing (ernien@cuttingnyc.com)
Joey Ruiz . . . . .Promotion (jruiz@cuttingnyc.com)

CYCLOTRON RECORDS
6351 Wilshire Blvd.
Los Angeles, CA 90036
PHONE 323-852-1215/323-717-2395
EMAIL . . . . .info@cyclotronrecords.com
WEB SITE . . . . .www.cyclotronrecords.com
GENRES   Alternative - Pop - Rock
SUBMISSION POLICY   Accepts unsolicited material

Chris Simental . . . . .Owner/Producer

DAEMON RECORDS
PO Box 1207
Decatur, GA 30031
PHONE 404-297-0109
FAX 404-297-0709
EMAIL . . . . .hello@daemonrecords.com
WEB SITE . . . . .www.daemonrecords.com
DISTRIBUTOR   KOCH Entertainment Distribution
ARTIST ROSTER   Magnapop - Girlyman - Utah Phillips -
                    Bambix - Athens Boys Choir - Cordero -
                    Paul Melancon - John Trudell - Gerard
                    McHugh - Moto Litas - Amy Ray -
                    Nineteen Forty-Five - Mrs. Fun - Rose
                    Polenzani - Danielle Howle & the
                    Tantrums - ph Balance - Terri Binion -
                    Ellen James Society - James Hall -
                    Rock*A*Teens - New Mongrels - Jesus
                    Christ Superstar - Lift - Honor - The
                    Oblivious - Snow Machine - Michelle
                    Malone - The Great Unknowns
GENRES   Folk - Pop - Rock
SUBMISSION POLICY   See Web site for info

Amy Ray . . . . .President
Andrea White . . . . .Label Manager (andrea@daemonrecords.com)
Stacey Singer . . . . .Publicist/Retail (stacey@daemonrecords.com)

DANCING CAT RECORDS
PO Box 639
Santa Cruz, CA 95061
PHONE 831-429-5085
FAX 831-423-7057
EMAIL . . . . .ml@dancingcat.com
SECOND EMAIL . . . . .firstnamelastinitial@dancingcat.com
WEB SITE . . . . .www.dancingcat.com
SECOND WEB SITE . . . . .www.georgewinston.com
DISTRIBUTOR   Sony BMG Sales Enterprise
ARTIST ROSTER   George Winston
GENRES   World
SUBMISSION POLICY   Submissions not accepted
COMMENTS   Hawaiian Slack Key Guitar; Publishing

Cathy Econom . . . . .President/Artist Manager (x204)
Belinda Au . . . . .VP, Legal/Business Affairs (x205)
Gail Korich . . . . .Director, Contract Administration (x218)
Jennifer Ramsay . . . . .Director, Marketing (x215)
C. Taylor-Shultes . . . . .Director, Benefit Concerts (x207)

DAYLIGHT RECORDS
550 Madison Ave., 20th Fl.
New York, NY 10022-3211
PHONE 212-833-8000
FAX 212-833-7339
WEB SITE . . . . .www.daylightrecords.com
ARTIST ROSTER   Good Charlotte - Anastacia - Phantom
                    Planet - Delta Goodrem - Cyndi Lauper
                    - Cheyenne Kimball - The Jonas Brothers
GENRES   Pop - Rock

David Massey . . . . .President (212-833-7188,
                    david_massey@sonymusic.com)

LABELS

DEAD TEENAGER RECORDS
2323 N. 51st St.
Seattle, WA 98103
PHONE 206-282-4210
FAX 206-286-0111
EMAIL . . . . .deadteenagerrecords@gmail.com
WEB SITE .www.deadteenager.com
DISTRIBUTOR   NAIL Distribution
ARTIST ROSTER   Speedealer - Camarosmith -
                          Flamethrower - Angry Amputees - TAD -
                          Filthy Jim - Bible of the Devil - Manfall -
                          Aiden - Players Club - Voodoo Organist
                          - ZEKE
GENRES   All Genres

Ben Rew . . . . .President/A&R

DECCA U.S.
c/o Universal Music Group
825 Eighth Ave., 19th Fl.
New York, NY 10019
PHONE 212-333-8000
FAX 212-603-3919
WEB SITE . . . . .www.decca.com
LABELS   Decca - Decca Black - Philips
GENRES   Classical
RECENT SOUNDTRACKS   The Motorcycle Diaries - Vanity Fair -
                          Finding Neverland

Chris Roberts . . . . .Chairman
Marc Johnston . . . . .Sr. VP, UCG
Randy Dry . . . . .VP, Marketing
Brian Drutman . . . . .Sr. Director, Decca Broadway

DEEP ELM RECORDS
PO Box 36939
Charlotte, NC 28236-6939
PHONE 803-631-6319
EMAIL . . . . .info@deepelm.com
WEB SITE . . . . .www.deepelm.com
DISTRIBUTOR   Lumberjack Mordam Music Group
ARTIST ROSTER   Latterman - Desert City Soundtrack -
                          Lock and Key - Burns Out Bright - Clair
                          de Lune - Eleven Minutes Away -
                          Secondhand Stories - Settlefish -
                          Surrounded - Sounds Like Violence - Fire
                          Divine
GENRES   Alternative - Hardcore - Punk - Rock
SUBMISSION POLICY   Listens to all submissions; Will contact
                          the artist if interested; No calls

John Szuch . . . . .Owner, A&R

DEF JAM RECORDS
SEE The Island Def Jam Music Group

DEFINITIVE JUX
147 W. 24th St., #5
New York, NY 10011
PHONE 212-243-5351
FAX 212-367-8280
EMAIL . . . . .info@definitivejux.net
WEB SITE .www.definitivejux.net
DISTRIBUTOR   Caroline Distribution
ARTIST ROSTER   El-P - Aesop Rock - RJD2 - Mr. Lif - Murs
                          - C Rayz Walz - The Perceptionists - Rob
                          Sonic - Hangar 18 - S.A. Smash - Cage
GENRES   Rap/Hip-Hop

Jaime Meline . . . . .Co-Founder
Amaechi Uzoigwe .Co-Founder
Jesse Ferguson .Label Manager
Jay Drake . . . . .Promotion & Marketing

DELICIOUS VINYL
6607 Sunset Blvd.
Los Angeles, CA 90028
PHONE 323-465-2700
FAX 323-465-8926
EMAIL . . . . .dvinyl@earthlink.net
WEB SITE .www.deliciousvinyl.com
DISTRIBUTOR   WEA Corp.
ARTIST ROSTER   Mr. Vegas - Fatlip - The Ben Astrop
                          Project - Bucwheed - Cecile - Chop
                          Black - The Pharcyde - The Brand New
                          Heavies - Tone-Loc - Young MC
GENRES   Folk - R&B - Rap/Hip-Hop - Reggae -
                          Rock - Urban

Michael Ross . . . . .President
Carmen Ridley Claus . . . . .General Manager
David Leiman . . . . .Sr. VP, Licensing for Film, TV, Advertising
Ty Flournoy .Product Manager

DEVIL IN THE WOODS
PO Box 579168
Modesto, CA 95357
PHONE 209-521-3489
FAX 209-521-3489
EMAIL . . . . .mc@devilinthewoods.com
WEB SITE .www.devilinthewoods.com
ARTIST ROSTER   Fiver - Frank Jordan - Meow Meow -
                          Minmae - The Workhouse

Mike Cloward . . . . .Owner/Operator (mc1@devilinthewoods.com)
Chris Watson . . . . .Label Manager/A&R

DFA RECORDS
225 W. 13th St.
New York, NY 10011
PHONE 212-989-1038 x222
FAX 212-741-4197
EMAIL . . . . .dfaweb@dfarecords.com
WEB SITE .www.dfarecords.com
ARTIST ROSTER   Black Dice - LCD Soundsystem - The
                          Juan McLean - The Rapture - Delia
                          Gonzalez & Gavin Russom - Pixeltan -
                          Black Leotard Front - Hot Chip
SUBMISSION POLICY   Submit by mail

Jonathan Galkin . . . . .No Title
James Murphy . . . . .No Title
Justin Miller . . . . .No Title
Tim Goldsworthy . . . . .No Title

DIESEL ONLY RECORDS, LLC
PO Box 720508
Jackson Heights, NY 11372
PHONE 718-565-2497
EMAIL . . . . .info@dieselonly.com
WEB SITE .www.dieselonly.com
GENRES   Country - Roots

Jeremy Tepper . . . . .No Title

LABELS

DIM MAK RECORDS
PO Box 348
Hollywood, CA 90078
PHONE 323-957-3096
FAX 323-957-2858
EMAIL .dimmak@dimmak.com
SECOND EMAIL . . . . .ana@dimmak.com
WEB SITE . . . . .www.dimmak.com
DISTRIBUTOR   Touch and Go/Quarterstick
ARTIST ROSTER   Neon Blonde - From Monument to
                      Masses - Bloc Party - The Rakes - Grafitti
                      - The Blood Brothers - Lion Fever - Neon
                      Blonde - DDM
GENRES   Pop - Punk - Rap/Hip-Hop - Rock
SUBMISSION POLICY   Accepts unsolicited material

Steve Aoki . . . . .Owner
Ana Calderon . . . . .Label Manager

DIRRTY RECORDS
468 N. Camden Dr., #200
Beverly Hills, CA 90210
PHONE 310-860-5609
FAX 310-860-5600
EMAIL . . . . .info@dirrtyrecords.com
WEB SITE .www.dirrtyrecords.com
DISTRIBUTOR   Burnside Distribution Corp.
GENRES   Rock
RECENT SOUNDTRACKS   Wildboys (MTV)
SUBMISSION POLICY   Accepts unsolicited material
COMMENTS   UK office: 145-157 St. John St.,
                      London, England EC1V 4PY

Cynthia Lawes . . . . .President

DISCHORD RECORDS
3819 Beecher St. NW
Washington, DC 20007
PHONE 703-351-7491
FAX 703-351-7582
EMAIL . . . . .dischord@dischord.com
WEB SITE . . . . .www.dischord.com
COMMENTS   Documenting DC Punk Rock

Alec Bourgeois . . . . .Advertising/Radio Stations

WALT DISNEY RECORDS
500 S. Buena Vista St.
Burbank, CA 91521-6235
PHONE 818-560-1000
EMAIL . . . . .firstname.lastname@disney.com
WEB SITE .www.disneyrecords.com
DISTRIBUTOR   Universal Music & Video Distribution
GENRES   Children's - Pop
RECENT SOUNDTRACKS   50th Anniversary: A Musical History of
                      Disneyland Box Set - Disneymania 3 -
                      Cheetah Girls - The Incredibles
COMMENTS   Soundtracks - Tween/Teen Pop

Robert Marick . . . . .General Manager/Sr. VP, Walt Disney Records
Jay Landers . . . . .Sr. VP, A&R
Maria Kleinman . . . . .VP, Media Relations
Ted Kryczko . . . . .VP, Product Development
Susan Van Hosen . . . . .VP, Sales
Damon Whiteside . . . . .VP, Marketing
Kelly Hugunin . . . . .Director, Marketing
Dani Markman . . . . .Director, A&R

DIVERSITY RECORDS, LTD.
109 C St. SE
Quincy, WA 98848
PHONE 509-787-5202
EMAIL . . . . .info@diversityrecords.net
WEB SITE .www.diversityrecords.net
GENRES   Bluegrass - Folk - Rock
COMMENTS   Specializes in live recordings

Paul Weitzel . . . . .Owner

DIVINE RECORDINGS
9292 Civic Center Dr.
Beverly Hills, CA 90210
PHONE 310-205-3120
FAX 310-859-2897
EMAIL . . . . .info@divinerecordings.com
WEB SITE .www.divinerecordings.com
GENRES   Rock

Ozzy Osbourne . . . . .CEO
Sharon Osbourne . . . . .President
Michael Guarracino . . . . .General Manager
John Fenton . . . . .Director, Operations

DOMINO RECORD CO. LTD.
45 Main St., Ste. 604
Brooklyn, NY 11201
PHONE 718-797-4229
WEB SITE .www.dominorecordco.com
DISTRIBUTOR   Caroline Distribution
LABELS   Franz Ferdinand - Clinic
GENRES   Rock
COMMENTS   UK office: PO Box 47029, London
                      SW18 1WD

Kris Chen . . . . .Label Manager

DOMO RECORDS, INC.
11340 W. Olympic Blvd., Ste. 270
Los Angeles, CA 90064-1697
PHONE 310-966-4414
FAX 310-966-4420
EMAIL . . . . .domo@domo.com
WEB SITE . . . . .www.domo.com
SECOND WEB SITE . . . . .www.kanpairecords.com
DISTRIBUTOR   Innovative Distribution Network (IDN)
ARTIST ROSTER   Kitaro - Nawang Khechog - Randy
                      Armstrong - Uma - Dave Eggar -
                      Benedetti & Svoboda - Chuck Barris -
                      Agatsuma - The Yoshida Brothers - Luis
                      Villegas - Steve Reid - Luis Perez - Steven
                      DeRuby - Peas - Appogee - Fumio -
                      Hoppy Kamiyama - Akasau - Little Plastic
                      Pilots - Indicia - Prototokyo - Test Shot
                      Starfish - Steve Jablonsky - Twelve Girls
                      Band
LABELS   Cocoro Sounds - Domo Anime - Kanpai
                      Records
GENRES   Classical - Electronica - Folk - Jazz -
                      New Age - Pop - Rock - World
SUBMISSION POLICY   Send to Dino Malito's attention

Eiichi Naito . . . . .President (eiichi@domo.com)
Dino Malito . . . . .General Manager/VP, A&R (dino@domo.com)
Howard Sapper . . . . .VP, Business & Legal Affairs

DOUBLE-TIME JAZZ/DOUBLE-TIME RECORDS

PO Box 1244, 1211 Aebersold Dr.
New Albany, IN 47151-1244
PHONE 800-293-8528
FAX 812-923-1971
EMAIL .dtjazz@doubletimejazz.com
SECOND EMAIL . . . . .info@doubletimejazz.com
WEB SITE . . . . .www.doubletimejazz.com
SECOND WEB SITE . . . . .www.doubletimerecords.com
DISTRIBUTOR   City Hall Records
GENRES   Jazz

Jamey D. Aebersold . . . . .No Title
Julia Aebersold . . . . .No Title

DRAG CITY

PO Box 476867
Chicago, IL 60647
PHONE 312-455-1015
FAX 312-455-1057
EMAIL . . . . .info@dragcity.com
SECOND EMAIL . . . . .press@dragcity.com
WEB SITE . . . . .www.dragcity.com
ARTIST ROSTER   AZITA - Bonnie "Prince" Billy - Faun
       Fables - The Fucking Champs - Ghost -
       David Grubbs - Joanna Newsom - Neil
       Michael Hagerty & the Howling Hex -
       Neil Hamburger - High Llamas - King
       Kong - Papa M - Red Krayola - Alasdair
       Roberts - (Smog) - US Maple - Weird
       War - White Magic - Pearls & Brass - Six
       Organs of Admittance - PG Six - RTX -
       Gary Higgins - Silver Jews - Edith Frost
GENRES   Pop - Rock

Zach Cowie . . . . .Publicity (zach@dragcity.com)
Leslie Vlazny . . . . .Tour Press, Direct Sales (leslie@dragcity.com)
Rian Murphy . . . . .Sales (sales@dragcity.com)
Scott McGaughey . . . . .Production (scott@dragcity.com)
Brett Sova . . . . .Shipping, Mail Order (brett@dragcity.com)

DREYFUS RECORDS

19 W. 44th St., Ste. 1108
New York, NY 10036
PHONE 212-398-5859
FAX 212-944-1631
WEB SITE . . . . .www.dreyfusrecords.com
ARTIST ROSTER   Jean Michel Jarre - Michel Petrucciani -
       Jean-Michel Pilc - Roy Haynes - Bireli
       Lagrene - Ahmad Jamal - Klement
       Julienne
GENRES   Jazz

Francis Dreyfus . . . . .Owner

DRIVE-THRU RECORDS

PO Box 55234
Sherman Oaks, CA 91413
PHONE 818-883-9985
FAX 818-883-9978
EMAIL .richard@drivethrurecords.com
SECOND EMAIL . . . . .peter@drivethrurecords.com
WEB SITE . . . . .www.drivethrurecords.com
DISTRIBUTOR   Sanctuary Records Group North America
ARTIST ROSTER   Finch - Jenoah - The Starting Line -
       Senses Fail - RX Bandits - Something
       Corporate - New Found Glory - The
       Early November - Allister - Steel Train -
       Home Grown - I Can Make A Mess Like
       Nobody's Business - An Angle - Socratic
       - Halifax - Hellogoodbye - Morning Call
       - I Am the Avalanche - David Melillo -
       House of Fools - Adelphi
LABELS   Drive-Thru - Rushmore
GENRES   Alternative - Folk - Pop - Punk - Rock
SUBMISSION POLICY   Unsolicited submissions accepted via US
       mail; Do not call or email; Will call if
       interested

Richard Reines . . . . .Owner
Stefanie Reines . . . . .Owner
Kristine Ripley . . . . .General Manager
Peter Verdell . . . . .Assistant, A&R

DRT ENTERTAINMENT

45 W. 21st St., 4th Fl.
New York, NY 10010
PHONE 646-437-5000
EMAIL . . . . .info@drt-entertainment.com
WEB SITE . . . . .www.drtentertainment.com
DISTRIBUTOR   Navarre Corporation
GENRES   Rock

Ron Urban . . . . .Co-Principal
Ted Green . . . . .Co-Principal
Derek Schulman . . . . .Co-Principal

DUALTONE

DUALTONE MUSIC GROUP INC.

1614 17th Ave. South
Nashville, TN 37212
PHONE 615-320-0620
FAX 615-320-0692
EMAIL . . . . .info@dualtone.com
WEB SITE . . . . .www.dualtone.com
ARTIST ROSTER   Chely Wright - The Greencards - Robin
       Ella - Bobby Bare - The Peasalls Sisters -
       Carey Ott - David Ball - Jim Lauderdale
       - BR5-49 - Charlie Robison - Deryl Dodd
       - Jeff Black - Roger Creager - Hayseed
       Dixie - The Silos - Mark Olson - Victoria
       Williams - Chris Knight - Cowboy Jack
       Clement - Nitty Gritty Dirt Band -
       Norman Blake
GENRES   Bluegrass - Country - Folk - Gospel -
       Roots
RECENT SOUNDTRACKS   Deadwood - Daltry Calhoun
SUBMISSION POLICY   No unsolicited material

Dan Herrington . . . . .Co-President
Scott Robinson . . . . .Co-President
Lanie Miller . . . . .Head, Publicity
Paul Roper . . . . .Director, Sales & Marketing
Anita Gorevski . . . . .Manager, Business Finance/Affairs
Joey Luscinski . . . . .Manager, Production & Operations
Lori Kampa . . . . .Promotion

LABELS

DUST-TO-DIGITAL
PO Box 54743
Atlanta, GA 30308
FAX 435-603-2438
EMAIL . . . . .info@dust-digital.com
WEB SITE . . . . .www.dust-digital.com
GENRES   Blues - Rock - Roots

Lance Ledbetter . . . . .President

EAGLE ROCK ENTERTAINMENT, INC.
22 W. 38th St., 7th Fl.
New York, NY 10018
PHONE 212-354-1040
FAX 212-354-1041
WEB SITE . . . . .www.eaglerockent.com
SECOND WEB SITE . . . . .www.eagle-rock.com
DISTRIBUTOR   RED Music Distribution
ARTIST ROSTER   Sebastian Bach. - Jack Casady - Deep
                          Purple - The Duke - Candy Dulfer - Hot
                          Tuna - James Last - The Levellers -
                          Shane McGowan - Yngwie Malmsteen -
                          ohGr - Overkill - Phoebe Snow -
                          Testament - George Thorogood - Twisted
                          Sister - Beautiful Creatures - Nashville
                          Pussy - Slave to the System
LABELS   Spitfire Records - Eagle Records - Eagle
                          Vision - Eagle Eye Media - Eagle Media
                          Productions
GENRES   Blues - Metal - Rock
SUBMISSION POLICY   No unsolicited material accepted
COMMENTS   UK office: 22 Armoury Way, London
                          SW18 1EZ United Kingdom; phone: 44-
                          20-8870-5670, fax: 44-20-8874-2333

Mike Carden . . . . .President, Operations, North America
Robert Gill . . . . .VP, Operations, North America
Stacy Poole . . . . .VP, Finance
Amanda Saldarelli . . . . .Director, Production
Cathy Nevins . . . . .VP, Communications &Publicity
Pete Tsakiris . . . . .Art Director
David MacMillan . . . . .Director, Canadian Operations
Tom Smith . . . . .Sr. Director, Promotions & Marketing
Fred Kelly . . . . .Co-National Sales Director
Alonzo Marrow . . . . .Co-National Sales Director

EASY STAR RECORDS
PO Box 602, Midtown Station
New York, NY 10018
PHONE 212-736-2160
FAX 347-823-4437
EMAIL . . . . .easystar@easystar.com
WEB SITE . . . . .www.easystar.com
ARTIST ROSTER   Easy Star All-Stars - John Brown's Body -
                          Sugar Minott - Sister Carol - Frankie
                          Paul - Luciano - Half Pint - The African
                          Brothers - Ranking Joe - Tristan Palma -
                          The Meditations - Junior Demus - Sluggy
                          Ranks - Gary "Nesta" Pine - Ossie
                          Dellimore - Rob Symeonn
GENRES   Reggae

Remy Gerstein . . . . .Principal
Michael Goldwasser . . . . .Principal
Lern Oppenheimer . . . . .Principal
Eric Smith . . . . .Principal

ECKO RECORDS
485 N. Hollywood St.
Memphis, TN 38112
PHONE 901-320-9250
FAX 901-320-9251
EMAIL . . . . .ecko@eckorecords.com
WEB SITE . . . . .www.eckorecords.com
DISTRIBUTOR   Select-O-Hits
ARTIST ROSTER   Denise LaSalle - Lee Shot Williams -
                          Sheba Potts-Wright - Bill Coday - Rick
                          Lawson - Carl Sims - O.B. Buchanan -
                          Donnie Ray - Dr. Feelgood Potts -
                          Lorraine Turner
GENRES   Blues - R&B

John Ward . . . . .President

ECM RECORDS
825 Eighth Ave., 19th Fl.
New York, NY 10019
PHONE 212-333-1016
FAX 212-445-3509
EMAIL . . . . .ecmny@umusic.com
WEB SITE . . . . .www.ecmrecords.com/usa
DISTRIBUTOR   Universal Classics Group
ARTIST ROSTER   Keith Jarrett - Jan Garbarek - The
                          Hilliard Ensemble - András Schiff -
                          Charles Lloyd - John Abercrombie -
                          Meredith Monk - Kim Kashkashian - Tord
                          Gustavsen Trio - Tomasz Stanko
LABELS   ECM - ECM New Series - Watt - Xtrawatt
GENRES   Classical - Jazz - World
SUBMISSION POLICY   Does not accept unsolicited demo pack-
                          ages

S. Humphries-Berne . . . . .Label Director (212-333-8449)
Tina Pelikan . . . . .Publicity Director (212-333-1405)
Daniel Giffen . . . . .ECM Coordinator (212-333-1016)

EDMONDS RECORDS GROUP
1635 N. Cahuenga Blvd., 6th Fl.
Los Angeles, CA 90028-6201
PHONE 323-860-1520
FAX 323-860-1537
GENRES   Pop - Urban

Tracey Edmonds . . . . .Co-President (tracey@edmondsent.com)

EENIE MEENIE RECORDS
8316 Melrose Ave.
Los Angeles, CA 90069
PHONE 323-653-8890
FAX 323-653-6885
EMAIL . . . . .info@eeniemeenie.com
WEB SITE . . . . .www.eeniemeenie.com
ARTIST ROSTER   Seksu Roba - DJ Me DJ You - Irving -
                          From Bubblegum to Sky - The Faraway
                          Places - The High Water Marks - Blue-
                          Eyed Son - Pine*Am - Ulysses - Oranger

Reiko Kondo . . . . .No Title (reiko@eeniemeenie.com)
April Shunn . . . . .No Title (april@eeniemeenie.com)
Noelle Bell . . . . .No Title (noelle@eeniemeenie.com)
Chris Rodriguez . . . . .No Title (chris@eeniemeenie.com)
Simone Snaith . . . . .No Title (simone@eeniemeenie.com)

ELECTRO-FI
40 Beaverdale Rd.
Toronto, ON M8Y 3Y4 Canada
PHONE 416-251-3036
FAX 416-259-5445
EMAIL . . . . .info@electrofi.com
WEB SITE . . . . .www.electrofi.com
ARTIST ROSTER   Mark Hummel - Curley Bridges - Snooky
                                       Pryor - Mel Brown - Fruteland Jackson -
                                       Paul Oscher - Sam Myers - Kenny Blues
                                       Boss Wayne
GENRES   Blues - Roots
COMMENTS   US mailing address: PO Box 191,
                                         LaSalle Station, Niagara Falls, NY
                                       14304

Andrew Galloway . . . . .President
Gary Collver . . . . .Operations Manager

ELEVATOR MUSIC
PO Box 628
Bronxville, NY 10708
PHONE 914-779-2392
FAX 914-509-5870
WEB SITE . . . . .www.elevatormusic.com
ARTIST ROSTER   Les Baton Rouge - Tedio Boys - Pist -
                                       Parkinsons - Thumper - Independents
GENRES   Punk - Rock
SUBMISSION POLICY   No unsolicited submissions

Fernando Pinto . . . . . . .Label Manager (fernando@elevatormusic.com)
Bob D'Aprile . . . . .Publicity (bob@elevatormusic.com)

ELEVEN THIRTY RECORDS
449-A Trollingwood Rd.
Haw River, NC 27258
PHONE 336-578-7300
FAX 336-578-7388
WEB SITE .www.eleventhirtyrecords.com
DISTRIBUTOR   Redeye Distribution

Stephen Judge . . . . .A&R Director
Glenn Dicker . . . . .Label Manager/Publicity Director
Steve Gardner . . . . .Radio Director
Tor Hansen . . . . .Sales & Marketing Director/A&R

EMI GOSPEL
101 Winners Circle
Brentwood, TN 37024-5009
PHONE 615-371-6800
FAX 615-371-6985
DISTRIBUTOR   EMI Music Marketing
ARTIST ROSTER   Vanessa Bell Armstrong - LaShun Pace -
                                       Darwin Hobbs - Myron Butler & Levi -
                                       Darrell McFadden & The Disciples -
                                       Darrel Petties & Strength In Praise -
                                       Antonio Neal - Micah Stampley - Vicki
                                       Yohe - Canton Jones - Mr. Del - V3 - Tri-
                                       City Singers - Smokie Norful - Kierra
                                       Sheard - New Birth Choir - Aaron
                                       Neville - Mighty Clouds of Joy - Darlene
                                       McCoy - T.D. Jakes
LABELS   EMI Gospel - Dexterity Sounds - Pure
                                       Springs - Tell It - Holy Hip Hop
GENRES   Gospel
SUBMISSION POLICY   By email only, no packages

Ken Pennell . . . . .President (kpennell@emicmg.com)
Larry Blackwell . . . . . . .VP/General Manager (lblackwell@emicmg.com)
Brandon Egerton . . . . .A&R Manager (begerton@emicmg.com)
Karen Scott . . . . .Director, Marketing
Eboni Funderbunk . . . . .Manager, National Radio Promotions

EMI GROUP PLC
27 Wrights Lane
London W8 5SW United Kingdom
PHONE 44-0-20-7795-7000
FAX 44-0-20-7795-7001
WEB SITE . . . . .www.emigroup.com
SECOND WEB SITE . . . . .www.emimusicpub.com
COMMENTS   EMI Music (New York Office):
                                       150 Fifth Ave.
                                       New York, NY 10011
                                       phone: 212-786-8600
                                       fax: 212-786-8849

                                       EMI Music Publishing:
                                       1290 Avenue of the Americas
                                       New York, NY 10104
                                       phone: 212-492-1200
                                       fax: 212-492-1865

Eric Nicoli . . . . .Chairman, EMI Group plc
Martin Stewart . . . . .CFO, EMI Group plc
Alain Levy . . . . .Chairman/CEO, EMI Music
David Munns . . . . . . .Vice Chairman & Chairman/CEO, North America,
                                                  EMI Music
Stuart Ells . . . . .COO/Regional Director, EMI Music
Tim Maunder . . . . .CFO, EMI Music
Martin Bandier . . . . .Chairman/CEO, EMI Music Publishing
Roger Faxon . . . . .President/COO, EMI Music Publishing

EMI JAZZ & CLASSICS
150 Fifth Ave., 6th Fl.
New York, NY 10011
PHONE 212-786-8600
WEB SITE . . . . .www.bluenote.com
DISTRIBUTOR   EMI Music Marketing
ARTIST ROSTER   Patricia Barber - Bob Belden - Terence
                                       Blanchard - Ron Carter - Bill Charlap -
                                       Bob Dorough - Dr. John - Kurt Elling -
                                       Rachelle Ferrell - Al Green - Stefon
                                       Harris - Lena Horne - Paul Jackson Jr. -
                                       Norah Jones - Joe Lovano - Madredeus
                                       - Wynton Marsalis - Pat Martino - Bobby
                                       McFerrin - Jackie McLean - Medeski,
                                       Martin & Wood - Marisa Monte - Jason
                                       Moran - Van Morrison - Greg Osby -
                                       Dianne Reeves - Renee Rosnes -
                                       Gonzalo Rubalcaba - Jacky Terrasson -
                                       Erik Truffaz - Chucho Valdes -
                                       Cassandra Wilson
LABELS   Blue Note Records
GENRES   Jazz - World
SUBMISSION POLICY   No unsolicited material accepted

Bruce Lundvall . . . . .CEO, EMI Jazz & Classics
Tom Evered . . . . .Sr. VP/General Manager, EMI Jazz & Classics
Zach Hochkeppel . . . . .VP, Marketing, EMI Jazz & Classics
J.R. Rich . . . . .VP, Publicity, Blue Note
Saul Shapiro . . . . .VP, Sales, EMI Jazz & Classics
Gordon Jee . . . . .Director, Creative, EMI Jazz & Classics
Eli Wolf . . . . .Director, A&R, EMI Jazz & Classics
Michael Cuscuna . . . . .A&R Consultant, Blue Note
Shanieka Brooks . . . . .Product Manager, Blue Note
Perry Greenfield . . . . .Product Manager, Blue Note
Sharon Russell . . .Manager, International Marketing, EMI Jazz & Classics

EMI MUSIC NORTH AMERICA
150 Fifth Ave.
New York, NY 10011
PHONE 212-786-8000
WEB SITE . . . . .www.emigroup.com
GENRES   All Genres

Alain Levy . . . . .Chairman/CEO, EMI Music
David Munns . . . . .Chairman/CEO, EMI Music North America
Ronn Werre . . . . .President, EMI Music Marketing
Ivan Gavin . . . . .COO, EMI Music North America
Colin Finkelstein . . . . .CFO, EMI Music North America
Adam Klein . . . . .Executive VP, Strategy & Development
Phil Quartararo . . . . .Executive VP, EMI Music North America
Victoria Bassetti . . . . . . .Sr. VP, Worldwide Industry & Government Affairs
Ted Cohen . . . . .Sr. VP, Digital Development & Distribution
Susan Feingold . . . . .Sr. VP, Legal & Business Affairs
Alasdair McMullan . . . . .Sr. VP, Legal Affairs
Jeanne Meyer . . . . .Sr. VP, Corporate Communications
Thomas Ryan . . . . .Sr. VP, Mobile & Digital Business Development

EMI TELEVISA MUSIC
404 Washington Ave., Ste. 700
Miami Beach, FL 33139-6606
PHONE 305-674-7529
FAX 305-674-7546
EMAIL . . . . .emilatin@emimusic.com
WEB SITE . . . . .www.emimusic.com
DISTRIBUTOR   EMI Music Marketing
GENRES   Latin

Marco Bissi . . . . .President/CEO, EMI Music Latin America
Rodolfo Lopez-Negrete . . . . .President, EMI Televisa Music
Ed McCardell . . . . .VP, Business Affairs
Fernando Sanchez . . . . . . .VP, Regional Mexican Music Division
Enna Alcaine . . . . .Executive Assistant/Office Manager

EPIC RECORDS GROUP
550 Madison Ave.
New York, NY 10022-3211
PHONE 212-833-8000/310-449-2100
EMAIL . . . . .firstname.lastname@sonybmg.com
WEB SITE . . . . .www.epicrecords.com
GENRES   All Genres - Alternative - Electronica -
                         Pop - Rap/Hip-Hop - Rock
COMMENTS   West Coast office: 2100 Colorado Ave.,
                         2nd Fl., Santa Monica, CA 90404-3504

Charlie Walk . . . . .President, Epic Records Group (212-833-5900)
Andrea Finkelstein . . . . .Sr. VP, A&R Administration (212-833-4103)
Ben Goldman . . . . .Sr. VP, A&R, East Coast (212-833-4687)
Harvey Leeds . . . . .Sr. VP, Artist Development (212-833-8661)
Lois Najarian . . . . .Sr. VP, Publicity (212-833-7983)
Lee Stimmel . . . . .Sr. VP, Marketing (212-833-8743)
Kaz Utsunomiya . . . . .Sr. VP, Epic A&R, West Coast (310-449-2944)
Lisa Markowitz . . . . .VP, Press, East Coast (212-833-5483)
Ron Mirro . . . . . . .VP, Finance/Administration (212-833-4147)
Julie Smith . . . . .VP, Strategic Marketing (212-833-4849)
Kenny Salcido . . . . .Director, A&R, West Coast (310-449-2575)
Peter Cohen . . . . .Manager, A&R, West Coast (310-449-2872)
Amy Levin . . . . .Manager, Epic Records Group (212-833-5626)
Dan Davis . . . . .A&R, East Coast
Mike Flynn . . . . .A&R, West Coast (310-449-2100)
Andrew Gould .A&R (212-833-8703)

EPIC RECORDS NASHVILLE
1400 18th Ave. South
Nashville, TN 37212
PHONE 615-858-1300
WEB SITE . . . . .www.sonynashville.com
ARTIST ROSTER   Gretchen Wilson - Patty Loveless - Jon
                         Randall - Miranda Lambert - Jace Everett
                         - Susan Haynes
GENRES   Country

Bill Macky . . . . .VP, National Promotion
Buffy Cooper . . . . .Director, National Promotion
Rick Hughes .Southeast Promotion
Bo Martinovich . . . . .Midwest Promotion
Larry Santiago . . . . .West Coast Promotion
Chad Schultz . . . . .Southwest Promotion
Elizabeth Sledge . . . . .Northeast Promotion
Jason Rockhill . . . . .Promotion Coordinator

EPITAPH
2798 Sunset Blvd.
Los Angeles, CA 90026
PHONE 213-413-7353
FAX 213-413-9678
EMAIL . . . . .hector@epitaph.com
SECOND EMAIL . . . . .chris@hell-cat.com
WEB SITE . . . . .www.epitaph.com
SECOND WEB SITE . . . . .www.hell-cat.com
DISTRIBUTOR   Alternative Distribution Alliance (ADA)
ARTIST ROSTER   I Am Ghost - Neko Case - Matchbook
                         Romance - DangerDoom - Bettye LaVette
                         - HorrorPops - The Frames - Jolie
                         Holland - Pennywise - Nekromantix -
                         Bad Religion - Tom Waits - Dropkick
                         Murphys - The Coup - Nick Cave & the
                         Bad Seeds - Sage Francis - From First to
                         Last - Suicide Girls - Blackalicious -
                         Orange - Bad Religion - Some Girls -
                         The Slackers - Tim Fite - Refused - Day
                         of Contempt - The Lost Patrol Band -
                         Randy
LABELS   Epitaph - Anti - Hellcat - Burning Heart
GENRES   Punk - Rap/Hip-Hop - Rock
RECENT SOUNDTRACKS   Motion City Soundtrack

Brett Gurewitz . . . . .Owner, Epitaph & Hellcat Records
Tim Armstrong .Owner, Hellcat Records
Andy Kaulkin . . . . .President, Anti
Dave Hansen . . . . .General Manager
Jeff Abarta . . . . .Artist Relations
Kerri Borsuk . . . . .Advertising/Lifestyle Marketing
Matt McGreevey . . . . .Internet Marketing
Jen Santoro . . . . .Retail Marketing
Jon Strickland . . . . .Sales
Hector Martinez . . . . .Director, Tour Publicity
Hilary Okun . . . . .Director, Publicity

EQUAL VISION RECORDS
PO Box 38202
Albany, NY 12203-8202
PHONE 518-458-8250
FAX 518-458-1312
EMAIL . . . . .info@equalvision.com
WEB SITE . . . . .www.equalvision.com
DISTRIBUTOR — RED Music Distribution
ARTIST ROSTER — Alexisonfire - Armor For Sleep - Bane - Bars - Bear Vs Shark - Before Today - Black Cross - Codeseven - Coheed & Cambria - Endicott - Fear Before The March of Flames - The Hope Conspiracy - Liars Academy - Silent Drive - The Snake The Cross The Crown - Time In Malta - Vaux
GENRES — Alternative - Hardcore - Metal - Punk - Rock
SUBMISSION POLICY — Send a CD, photo, band bio and contact information by mail to ATTN: Demo Submission; Will contact if interested

Steve Reddy . . . . .Owner (steve@equalvision.com)
Dan Sandshaw . . . . .General Manager (dan@equalvision.com)
Curtis Tanner . . . . .A&R/Production (curt@equalvision.com)
Jason DeRose . . . . .Publicity/Advertising (jason@equalvision.com)
Tom Mullen . . . . .Marketing (tom@equalvision.com)
Bill Scoville . . . . .Art Director (bill@equalvision.com)
Greg Sieme . . . . .New Media (greg@equalvision.com)

EQUITY MUSIC GROUP
1222 16th Ave. South
Nashville, TN 37212
PHONE 615-695-2350/866-273-4433
FAX 615-695-2359
EMAIL .info@equitymusicgroup.com
WEB SITE . . . . .www.equitymusicgroup.com
DISTRIBUTOR — Navarre Corporation
ARTIST ROSTER — Little Big Town - Kevin Fowler - Clint Black - Carolina Rain - Laura Bryna
GENRES — Country
SUBMISSION POLICY — Only material submitted by managers or music attorneys will be accepted

Mike Kraski . . . . .President/Partner
Clint Black . . . . .Partner
Charles Sussman . . . . .Partner
Tim Wipperman . . . . .Chief Creative Officer
Tara Austin . . . . .A&R/Projects Manager
David Haley . . . . .VP, Promotion
Joe Carroll . . . . .Promotion Manager, Midwest
Jeff Davis . . . . .Promotion Manager, Southeast
Gary Greenberg . . . . .Promotion Manager, West Coast
Brad Helton . . . . .Promotion Manager, Southwest
Bob Reeves . . . . .Promotion Manager, Northwest
Kristen Strean . . . . .Promotion Coordinator
Sylvia "Pepper" Meiler . . . . .Executive Assistant/Office Manager

*ESP DISK
PO Box 1261
New York, NY 10009
PHONE 212-979-0590
FAX 212-995-5422
EMAIL . . . . .info@espdisk.com
SECOND EMAIL . . . . .sales@espdisk.com
WEB SITE . . . . .www.espdisk.com
GENRES — Jazz - Rock

Bernard Stollman . . . . .Owner

ESSENTIAL RECORDS
741 Cool Springs Blvd.
Franklin, TN 37067
PHONE 615-261-6500
FAX 615-261-5907
EMAIL . . . . .info@essentialrecords.com
WEB SITE . . . . .www.essentialrecords.com
DISTRIBUTORS — Provident Music Group - Sony BMG Sales Enterprise
ARTIST ROSTER — Bebo Norman - Caedman's Call - FFH - Third Day - Jars of Clay - City on a Hill - Day of Fire - Overflow - Olivia the Band
GENRES — Christian - Pop - Rock

Terry A. Hemmings . . . . .President/CEO
Robert Beeson . . . . .Sr. VP, A&R, Provident Label Group (rbeeson@providentmusicgroup.com)
Skip Bishop . . . . .VP, Mainstream Promotion & Marketing
Dean Diehl . . . . .Sr. VP, Marketing, Provident Label Group
Andrew Patton . . . . .VP, National Promotions, Provident Label Group
Jacquelyn Marushka Smith . .VP, Public Relations, Provident Music Group (615-261-6439)
Nina Williams . . . . .VP, Label Operations, Provident Label Group

EVERLOVING, INC.
3165 Los Feliz Blvd.
Los Angeles, CA 90039
PHONE 323-953-0075
FAX 323-410-0467
WEB SITE . . . . .www.everloving.com
DISTRIBUTOR — Alternative Distribution Alliance (ADA)
ARTIST ROSTER — Michael Andrews (aka Elgin Park) - Inara George - Wan Santo Condo - Ritmo Y Canto - Culver City Dub Collective - Piers Faccini
SUBMISSION POLICY — No unsolicited demos

Andy Factor . . . . .Partner (andy@everloving.com)
J.P. Plunier .Partner (jp@everloving.com)
Cathy Duncan . . . . .Marketing (cathy@everloving.com)
Wayne Greene . . . . .Marketing (wayne@everloving.com)

FACE TO FACE
21421 Hilltop St., Ste. 20
Southfield, MI 48034-4009
PHONE 248-354-5151
FAX 248-354-5153
GENRES — Christian

Fred Hammond . . . . .President (x12, fwham@aol.com)
Darius Fentris . . . . .A&R
Kevin Wilson . . . . .Manager

FANTASY RECORDS
2600 10th St.
Berkeley, CA 94710
PHONE 510-549-2500
FAX 510-486-2015
EMAIL . . . . .info@fantasyjazz.com
WEB SITE . . . . .www.fantasyjazz.com
ARTIST ROSTER — John Fogerty
GENRES — Jazz - Rock - Roots

Bill Belmont . . . . .Label Manager
Terri Hinte . . . . .Publicist

FAT POSSUM RECORDS

PO Box 1923
Oxford, MS 38655-1923
PHONE 662-473-9994
FAX 662-473-9090
EMAIL . . . . .firstname_lastinitial@fatpossum.com
WEB SITE . . . . .www.fatpossum.com
ARTIST ROSTER   Hasil Adkins - Robert Belfour - The Black
                       Keys - Kenny Brown - Solomon Burke -
                       R.L. Burnside - Robert Cage - Country
                       Teasers - Cedell Davis - Scott Dunbar -
                       Johnny Farmer - T-Model Ford -
                       Grandpaboy - John Hermann - Paul
                       Jones - Junior Kimbrough - Jelly Roll
                       Kings - Little Axe - Bob Log III - Fred
                       McDowell - The Neckbones - Asie
                       Payton - Super Chikan - Dave Thompson
                       - Twenty Miles - Elmo Williams - Robert
                       Pete Williams
GENRES   Blues

Matthew Johnson . . . . .President
Bruce Watson . . . . .Label Manager
Justin McGuirk . . . . .Director, A&R

FAT WRECK CHORDS

PO Box 193690
San Francisco, CA 94119
PHONE 415-284-1790
EMAIL . . . . .mailbag@fatwreck.com
WEB SITE . . . . .www.fatwreck.com
DISTRIBUTOR   RED Music Distribution
ARTIST ROSTER   Against Me! - Consumed - Good
                       Riddance - The Lawrence Arms - NOFX -
                       Propagandhi - Sick of It All - Swingin'
                       Utters - Tilt - Snuff - Rise Against - None
                       More Black - Anti-Flag - Avail - The
                       Dickies - Frenzal Rhomb - Caddies - No
                       Use for a Name - Screeching Weasel -
                       Strung Out - Wizo - Zero Down -
                       Subhumans - Only Crime - Me First &
                       the Gimme Gimmes - Lagwagon -
                       Dillinger Four - Bracket - The Epoxies -
                       Smoke or Fire - The Soviettes - Love =
                       Death - Western Addiction - The Real
                       McKenzies - Bad Astronaut - Chixdiggit -
                       Descendents - Lawrence Arms - None
                       More Black
GENRES   Alternative - Punk - Rock

Mike Burkett . . . . .Owner
Erin Burkett . . . . .Owner
Vanessa Burt . . . . .Publicist
Jason Hall . . . . .Radio & Retail

FAVORED NATIONS, LLC

17328 Ventura Blvd., Ste. 165
Encino, CA 91316
PHONE 818-385-1989
FAX 818-385-1070
EMAIL . . . . .fn@favorednations.com
SECOND EMAIL . . . . .press@favorednations.com
WEB SITE .www.favorednations.com
DISTRIBUTOR   RED Music Distribution
ARTIST ROSTER   Mike Keneally - Bob Carpenter - Johnny
                       Hiland - Novecento feat. Stanley Jordan
                       - Robin DiMaggio - Mattias "IA" Eklundh
                       - Ellis - Marty Friedman - Frank
                       Gambale - Mimi Fox - Stuart Hamm -
                       Allan Holdsworth - Johnny A. - Eric
                       Johnson & Alien Love Child - Tak
                       Matsumoto - Greg Koch - Steve Vai -
                       Ark - Neil Citron - Pierre Bensusan -
                       Dweezil Zappa - Greg Bissonette - Chad
                       Wackerman - Larry Carlton - Steve
                       Lukather - Billy Sheehan - Andy Tmmons
                       - Banned From Utopia - Eric Sardinas -
                       The Yardbirds - Al Kooper - Terry Bozzio
                       - Steve Lukather - Neal Schon - Stef
                       Burns
GENRES   Adult Contemporary - Blues - Classical -
                       Jazz - Metal - New Age - Rock
SUBMISSION POLICY   Does not accept unsolicited material

Steve Vai . . . . .President/Sr. VP, A&R
Karen Hogan . . . . .General Manager
David Ferraria . . . . .Product Manager
Kevin Richards . . . . .Product Management
Celeste Moses . . . . .International Product Manager
Jason Scherr . . . . .Production Manager
Jason Feinberg . . . . .Web Design/Online Marketing
Dawn Clegg . . . . .Office Manager

FEARLESS RECORDS

13772 Goldenwest St., #545
Westminster, CA 92683
PHONE 714-638-7090
FAX 714-638-7120
EMAIL . . . . .adam@fearlessrecords.com
SECOND EMAIL . . . . .other@fearlessrecords.com
WEB SITE . . . . .www.fearlessrecords.com
DISTRIBUTOR   Alternative Distribution Alliance (ADA)
ARTIST ROSTER   Dynamite Boy - Bigwig - Plain White T's
                       - Brazil - Sugarcult - Rock Kills Kid -
                       Yesterdays Rising - Gatsbys American
                       Dream - At The Drive-In - So They Say -
                       The Fully Down
GENRES   Punk - Rock
SUBMISSION POLICY   Accepts demos

Bob Becker . . . . .President
Kevin Knight . . . . .Director, A&R

FEDORA RECORDS
106 W. 71st St.
New York, NY 10023
PHONE 212-873-2020
FAX 212-877-0407
WEB SITE . . . . .www.jazzdepot.com
DISTRIBUTOR   Ryko Distribution
ARTIST ROSTER   Johnnie Bassett - Mojo Buford - Little
                    Buster - Jimmy Dawkins - Big Al Dupree
                    - Fillmore Slim - Al Garrett - Hosea
                    Hargrove - Harmonica Slim - Homesick
                    James - Hosea Leavy - J.J. Malone -
                    Dave Riley - Iceman Robinson - Matthew
                    Robinson - Bennie Smith - Robert "Bilbo"
                    Walker - Arthur Williams
GENRES   Blues

Barney Fields . . . . .President
Chris Millar . . . . .A&R

FENWAY RECORDINGS
PO Box 15709, Kenmore Station
Boston, MA 02215-0015
PHONE 617-497-2012
EMAIL . . . . .info@fenwayrecordings.com
WEB SITE . . . . .www.fenwayrecordings.com
SECOND WEB SITE . . . . .www.fenwayrecordings.co.uk
DISTRIBUTOR   Alternative Distribution Alliance (ADA)
ARTIST ROSTER   Read Yellow - The Love Scene -
                    Consonant - Gerling - longwave - State
                    Radio - The Kickovers - Robbers on High
                    Street - Guster
GENRES   Alternative - Pop - Rock
SUBMISSION POLICY   Send Attn: A&R; No follow-ups

Mark Kates . . . . .CEO (mark@fenwayrecordings.com)
Priya Dewan . . . . .General Manager (priya@fenwayrecordings.com)

FILE 13
2348 W. Cortez Ave.
Chicago, IL 60622
PHONE 773-489-0851
EMAIL . . . . .info@file-13.com
WEB SITE www.file-13.com
DISTRIBUTOR   Lumberjack Mordam Music Group

Stephen Schmidt . .Distribution, Ordering, Manufacturing, Radio, Retail
                                              (stephen@file-13.com)
Justin Sinkovich . . .Business, Licensing & Production (justin@file-13.com)

*FLAGSHIP RECORDINGS
11054 Ventura Blvd., #484
Studio City, CA 91604
PHONE 818-487-3811
FAX 818-487-9211
EMAIL . . . . .info@flagshiprecordings.com
DISTRIBUTOR   Fontana Distribution
ARTIST ROSTER   The Vanity Project (Steven Page) - Brett
                    Dennen - Tremolo - Eugene Edwards

Marc Nathan . . . . .President

FLAMESHOVEL RECORDS
1658 N. Milwaukee Ave., Ste. 276
Chicago, IL 60647
PHONE 773-489-1107
FAX 773-489-1124
EMAIL . . . . .info@flameshovel.com
WEB SITE . . . . .www.flameshovel.com
DISTRIBUTOR   Southern Records, Inc.
ARTIST ROSTER   Ancient Greeks - Che Arthur - The
                    Duddley Corporation - Joan of Arse -
                    The Joggers - Judah Johnson - Low Skies
                    - Lying in States - Make Believe - The
                    Narrator - The Natural History - The
                    Race - Viza-Noir - Chin Up Chin Up -
                    Sybris - Bound Stems - Voltage
LABELS   Pretty Activity Records - Flameshovel
                    Records
GENRES   Pop - Rock
SUBMISSION POLICY   Open

James Kenler . . . . .Partner (james@flameshovel.com)
Jesse Woghin . . . . .Partner (jesse@flameshovel.com)

FLAWLESS RECORDS
2220 Colorado Ave.
Santa Monica, CA 90404
PHONE 310-865-1000
FAX 310-865-8055
EMAIL . . . . .flawless@umusic.com
WEB SITE . . . . .www.flawless-records.com
DISTRIBUTOR   Universal Music & Video Distribution
ARTIST ROSTER   She Wants Revenge - Puddle of Mudd -
                    The Revolution Smile - Ringside
GENRES   Rock
SUBMISSION POLICY   All submissions accepted

Fred Durst .Owner/President (310-865-7671)
David Levy . . . . .VP, A&R
Lobo Hong . . . . .No Title

FOODCHAIN RECORDS
6525 Sunset Blvd., 4th Fl.
Hollywood, CA 90028
PHONE 323-957-7900
FAX 323-957-7911
EMAIL . . . . .info@foodchainrecords.com
WEB SITE . . . . .www.foodchainrecords.com
DISTRIBUTOR   Navarre Corporation
ARTIST ROSTER   Supagroup - Minibar - Coyote Shivers -
                    Betty Blowtorch - Dear John Letters - The
                    Januaries - Iffy - Liars Inc. - Garageland
GENRES   Alternative - Pop - Rock

Scott Milano . . . . .Chairman
Kelly Spencer . . . . .Sr. Director, A&R
Dave Bagley . . . . .Sales & Marketing

FORE REEL ENTERTAINMENT
201 E. 87th St., Ste. 370
New York, NY 10128
PHONE 212-410-9055
FAX 212-831-0823
EMAIL . . . . .forereelent@aol.com
SECOND EMAIL . . . . .itsabouteve@aol.com
WEB SITE . . . . .www.forereelent.com
SECOND WEB SITE . . . . .www.itsabouteve.org
ARTIST ROSTER   Deena Miller - It's About Eve
GENRES   Adult Contemporary - Alternative - Blues
                    - Country - Folk - Jazz - Latin - New Age
                    - Pop - Rock - World
SUBMISSION POLICY   Call first; Indie female artists/groups only
COMMENTS   Distributed by Rock Bottom

Hernando Courtright . . . . .President

FREDDIE RECORDS, INC.
5979 S. Staples St.
Corpus Christi, TX 78413
PHONE 361-992-8411
FAX 361-992-8428
EMAIL . . . . .info@freddierecords.com
WEB SITE . . . . .www.freddierecords.com
GENRES   Latin
COMMENTS   Tejano

Freddie Martinez Sr. . . . . .Owner
Freddie Martinez Jr. . . . . .VP

FRENCHKISS RECORDS
111 East 14th St., Ste. 229
New York, NY 10003
PHONE 212-414-4533
EMAIL . . . . .info@frenchkissrecords.com
WEB SITE . . . . .www.frenchkissrecords.com
DISTRIBUTOR   Caroline Distribution
ARTIST ROSTER   Les Savy Fav - The Apes - Sean Na Na -
                                Lifter Puller - S PRCSS - Ex Models - The
                                BloodThirstylovers - Enon - Thunderbirds
                                Are Now! - Rahim - The Hold Steady -
                                The Plastic Constellations - Tangiers
GENRES   Rock
SUBMISSION POLICY   Mail photo and personal note; Must
                                have information about the band on the
                                CD and a Web site

Syd Butler . . . . .President
Steve Hahnel . . . . .Head, Operations

FUEL 2000 RECORDS
6607 Sunset Blvd., 2nd Fl.
Los Angeles, CA 90028
PHONE 323-464-7984
FAX 323-465-8926
EMAIL . . . . .info@fuel2000.com
WEB SITE www.fuel2000.com
DISTRIBUTOR   Universal Music & Video Distribution
GENRES   Blues - Jazz - Reggae - Rock - World
SUBMISSION POLICY   Accepts submissions

Len Fico .President (ficol@yahoo.com)
Martin Schwartz . . . . .Sr. VP
Maurice De Noble . . . . .A&R
Bob Copeland . . . . .Assistant

FUTURE FARMER RECORDINGS
PO Box 225128
San Francisco, CA 94122
PHONE 415-503-1091/415-495-0851
EMAIL . . . . .lowdown@futurefarmer.com
SECOND EMAIL . . . . .radio@futurefarmer.com
WEB SITE . . . . .www.futurefarmer.com
LABELS   Devil in the Woods

Dennis Mitchell . . . . .CEO (dennis@futurefarmer.com)
Dana Lazarovitz . . . . .Publicist (dana@drunkdatepr.com)

GEARHEAD RECORDS
PO Box 421219
San Francisco, CA 94142
PHONE 530-758-7967
FAX 530-758-5724
EMAIL . . . . .michelle@gearheadrecords.com
WEB SITE . . . . .www.gearheadrecords.com
DISTRIBUTORS   Carrot Top Distribution, Ltd. - Choke
                                Distribution - Crystal Clear Distribution -
                                Get Hip Records - Revolver USA
                                Distribution
ARTIST ROSTER   The Hellacopters - The Hives - Mensen -
                                New Bomb Turks - Red Planet - The
                                Riverboat Gamblers - The Turbo A.C.'s -
                                The Wildhearts - The Dragons - The
                                Bluck Furies - Electric Eel Shock - The
                                Pink Swords - Gitogito Hustler - The
                                Million Dollar Marxists
GENRES   Punk - Rock
SUBMISSION POLICY   Email before sending demos
COMMENTS   Publishes *Gearhead Magazine*

Michelle Haunold . . . . .President
Mike LaVella . . . . .CEO
Carrie Goodeill . . . . .Mail Order
Heather Klinger . . . . .Radio & Street Teams
Jen Malone . . . . .Publicity
Ralph Miller . . . . .Artwork

GEFFEN RECORDS
2220 Colorado Ave., 4th Fl.
Santa Monica, CA 90404-3506
PHONE 310-865-4500
FAX 310-865-1610
EMAIL . . . . .firstname.lastname@umusic.com
WEB SITE . . . . .www.geffen.com
DISTRIBUTOR   Universal Music & Video Distribution
GENRES   All Genres - Alternative - Electronica -
                                Pop - R&B - Rap/Hip-Hop - Rock -
                                Urban
COMMENTS   See also Interscope Geffen A&M

Jordan Schur . . . . .President (310-865-7966)
Jim Merlis . . . . .Head, Press
Eric Hunter .A&R (310-865-7058)
Joel Mark . . . . .A&R
James Mormile . . . . .A&R
Thom Panunzio . . . . .A&R
Evan Peters . . . . .A&R
Michael Chavez . . . . .A&R, Urban
Jaha Johnson . . . . .A&R, Urban
Shawn Suggs . . . . .A&R, Urban
Mike Woglom . . . . .Assistant to President
Zane Smythe . . . . .Assistant to President

GET HIP RECORDS
Columbus & Preble Aves.
Pittsburgh, PA 15233
PHONE 412-231-4766
FAX 412-231-4777
EMAIL . . . . .gethip@gethip.com
WEB SITE . . . . .www.gethip.com
GENRES   Folk - Punk - Rock
COMMENTS   Also a distributor

Gregg Kostelich . . . . .Owner
Barbara Garcia-Bernado . . . . .VP (barbara@gethip.com)

GHOSTLY INTERNATIONAL
416 E. Huron St., Ste. 1B
Ann Arbor, MI 48104
PHONE 734-623-0077
FAX 734-623-7906
EMAIL . . . . .dado@ghostly.com
WEB SITE . . . . .www.ghostly.com
DISTRIBUTOR   Caroline Distribution
ARTIST ROSTER   Tadd Mullinix - Matthew Dear - Midwest
                              Product - Twine - Dykehouse - Aeroc -
                              Kill Memory Crash - KILN - James T.
                              Cotton - Dabrye - Audion - Mobius
                              Band - Skeletons & the Girl Faced Boys
LABELS   Ghostly International - Spectral Sound
GENRES   Alternative - Electronica - Pop - Rap/Hip-
                              Hop - Rock
SUBMISSION POLICY   Demos accepted by mail, Attn: A&R,
                              with contact info clearly marked on CD,
                              DAT or cassette
COMMENTS   Publishing controlled by The Ghostly
                              International Company (ASCAP);
                              Represented for North American com-
                              mercial advertising by Ten Music;
                              Contact licensing@ghostly.com for all
                              other usages

Sam Valenti IV . . . . .Principal (dado@ghostly.com)
Jeremy Peters . . . . .Manager, Licensing/Publishing/Distribution
                                    (jeremy@ghostly.com)

GLOBAL CREATIVE GROUP
11664 National Blvd., PMB 361
Los Angeles, CA 90064
PHONE 310-837-5011
FAX 310-837-5010
EMAIL . . . . .info@gcgmusic.com
WEB SITE . . . . .www.gcgmusic.com
GENRES   Pop - Rock - World

Ian Faith . . . . .CEO

GNP CRESCENDO RECORDS
8271 Melrose Ave., Ste. 104
Los Angeles, CA 90046
PHONE 323-655-5006
FAX 323-655-5233
EMAIL . . . . .gnp@pacificnet.net
WEB SITE . . . . .www.gnpcrescendo.com

Gene Norman . . . . .President
Neil Norman . . . . .VP
Linda Anderson . . . . .Comptroller
Mary Lou Burns . . . . .Administrator

THE GOLD LABEL
9229 Sunset Blvd., Ste. 220
Los Angeles, CA 90069
PHONE 310-858-1181/877-728-7453
EMAIL . . . . .info@patsgold.com
WEB SITE . . . . .www.patsgold.com
DISTRIBUTOR   Universal Music & Video Distribution
LABELS   Pat's Gold
GENRES   Christian - Country - Gospel - Pop

Holly Zoley . . . . .VP
Zack Shaw . . . . .A&R/Promotions

GOLD STANDARD LABORATORIES (GSL)
PO Box 65091
Los Angeles, CA 90065
PHONE 562-923-0535
FAX 562-923-0430
EMAIL . . . . .info@goldstandardlabs.com
WEB SITE . . . . .www.goldstandardlabs.com
DISTRIBUTOR   Lumberjack Mordam Music Group
GENRES   Punk - Rap/Hip-Hop - Rock
SUBMISSION POLICY   Demos accepted

Sonny Kay . . . . .Founder
Omar Rodriguez . . . . .Co-Owner
Charlotte Kay . . . . .Street Teams
Tim Jones . . . . .Office Manager

GOODFELLOW RECORDS
22 Wilson St.
Hamilton, ON L8R 1C5 Canada
PHONE 905-777-1223
FAX 905-777-1161
EMAIL . . . . .xchrisx@goodfellowrecords.com
WEB SITE . . . . .www.goodfellowrecords.com
DISTRIBUTOR   Lumberjack Mordam Music Group
ARTIST ROSTER   Blessing the Hogs - Bloodjinn - Cursed -
                              Purity's Failure - Quell - Smackdown -
                              Taken - The Good Fight - The Secret -
                              The Spirit That Guides Us
GENRES   Hardcore - Metal
COMMENTS   Partnered with Sonic Unyon Records

Chris Logan . . . . .Owner
Sean Palmerston . . . . .Press, Radio & Promotions (Canada)
                                        (sean@sonicunyon.com)
Sean Rhorer . . . . .Press, Radio & Promotions (US) (863-686-8990,
                                        sean@invisibleyouthpr.com)

GOTHAM RECORDS
PO Box 237067
New York, NY 10023
PHONE 212-799-5513
EMAIL . . . . .info@gothamrecords.com
WEB SITE . . . . .www.gothamrecords.com
DISTRIBUTORS   KOCH Entertainment Distribution - RED
                              Music Distribution
ARTIST ROSTER   Slant - Supafuzz - Liquid Gang - Tony
                              Justice - Loose Nuts - The Booda Velvets
                              - Wired - Rip Dizzy - Frybanger - Tom
                              Gillam - The Love Huskies
GENRES   Punk - Rock - Roots
RECENT SOUNDTRACKS   American Pie - Laguna Beach -
                              Smallville - The Osbournes
SUBMISSION POLICY   Accepts demos; Materials will not be
                              returned

Patrick Arn . . . . .Owner

THE GRANDA GROUP
2644 NW 97th Ave.
Miami, FL 33172-1400
PHONE 305-599-1837
FAX 305-599-8511
EMAIL . . . . .info@grandaent.com
WEB SITE . . . . .www.grandaent.com
LABELS | Angel Eyes Records
GENRES | Alternative - Electronica - Latin - Pop
SUBMISSION POLICY | No unsolicited material accepted
COMMENTS | Eyes Of An Angel Music (BMI); Joey-Joe Music (ASCAP); Playroom Recording Studios

Joe Granda . . . . .President/COO
Aldo Gonzalez . . . . .Creative/Promotion Coordinator
Eduardo Acosta . . . . .Artist Relations/Bookings
Dennis Niaves . . . . .Studio Producer/Engineer
Dorita Rodriguez . . . . .Publicity & Promotion
Joe Blanco . . . . .Production Assistant/Stage Manager
Anabel Mesa . . . . .Executive Assistant

GRATEFUL DEAD PRODUCTIONS
PO Box X
Novato, CA 94948
PHONE 415-492-5500
FAX 415-507-0750
WEB SITE . . . . .www.dead.net
DISTRIBUTOR | Rhino Entertainment
GENRES | Rock

Cameron Sears . . . . .President

GREEN LINNET RECORDS
PO Box 1905
Danbury, CT 06813
PHONE 203-730-0333
FAX 203-730-0345/203-778-4443
EMAIL . . . . .comments@greenlinnet.com
WEB SITE . . . . .www.greenlinnet.com
DISTRIBUTOR | Ryko Distribution
LABELS | Xenophile - Celtophile
SUBMISSION POLICY | By mail or email

Wendy Newton . . . . .Owner

G Unit

G-UNIT RECORDS
c/o Interscope Records
PO Box 1500
New York, NY 10116
PHONE 212-359-3000
FAX 212-359-3019
WEB SITE . . . . .www.gunitsoldier.com
DISTRIBUTOR | Universal Music & Video Distribution
ARTIST ROSTER | 50 Cent - Lloyd Banks - Young Buck - Tony Yayo - Olivia - Mobb Deep - M.O.P. - Spider Loc - DJ Whoo Kid
GENRES | R&B - Rap/Hip-Hop

50 Cent . . . . .President
Sha Money XL . . . . .VP
Jay Johnson . . . . .A&R

*HACKTONE RECORDS
12517 Venice Blvd.
Mar Vista, CA 90066
PHONE 310-572-9999
FAX 310-572-9996
EMAIL . . . . .david@hacktone.com
WEB SITE . . . . .www.hacktone.com
DISTRIBUTOR | Shout! Factory
ARTIST ROSTER | David Allan Coe - Lewis Taylor
GENRES | Blues - Country

David Gorman . . . . .Co-President
Michael Nieves . . . . .Co-President
Aleeta Mayo . . . . .Product Manager

HAIRBALL8 RECORDS
6306 Forest Village
San Antonio, TX 78250
PHONE 210-520-8749
FAX 530-689-6407
EMAIL .ryan@hairball8.com
WEB SITE www.hairball8.com
ARTIST ROSTER | Asmodeus - Barnyard Ballers - Bloody Hollys - Captain Bringdown & the Buzzkillers - The Casketeers - Concombre Zombi - The Deadutantes - Demon City Wreckers - Flesh - The Formaldehydes - Hayride to Hell - Kevin Goes 2 College - The Koffin Kats - Mad Marge & the Stonecutters - Pagan Dead - The Rocketz - Skunk All Stars - Uncle Focker - Uptown Creepers
GENRES | Country - Punk - Rock
COMMENTS | Psychobilly - Ska

Ryan Davis . . . . .Director, Operations (ryan@hairball8.com)
Paige Lester . . . . .Interns/Street Teams (paige@hairball8.com)

*HARMONIZED RECORDS
6520 Oak Grove Church Rd.
Mebane, NC 27302
PHONE 828-252-3686
FAX 828-252-3906
WEB SITE . . . . .www.harmonizedrecords.com
ARTIST ROSTER | Lotus - Perpetual Groove - Garaj Mahal - New Monsoon - The Motet - The Recipe - ulu - Mecca Bodega - DJ Williams Projekt - Big Fuzz - Modereko - Infradig - Cadillac Jones
GENRES | Jazz - Rock
SUBMISSION POLICY | No unsolicited submissions

Brian Asplin . . . . . .A&R/Marketing/Sales (brian@homegrownmusic.net)
Lee Crumpton . . . . .A&R/Accounting (lee@homegrownmusic.net)
Chris Robie . . . . .Radio/Press (robie@homegrownmusic.net)
Bryan Rodgers .Publicity/Fullfillment

HEADS UP INTERNATIONAL
23309 Commerce Park Rd.
Cleveland, OH 44122
PHONE 216-765-7381
FAX 216-464-6037
EMAIL .headsup@headsup.com
WEB SITE . . . . .www.headsup.com

Dave Love . . . . .President (dave@headsup.com)
Lynne Hoffman-Engel . . . . .VP, Domestic Sales (lhoffman@headsup.com)
Rob Saslow . . . . .VP, Marketing
Mike Wilpizeski . . . . .VP, Publicity (mikew@headsup.com)
Doug Ashland . . . . .Marketing Manager (sales@headsup.com)
Jason Linder . . . . .Marketing Director (jlinder@headsup.com)
David Newsom . . . . .Technical Support (x 333, support@headsup.com)

HEAVYWEIGHT RECORDS
160 E. Tamarack Ave.
Inglewood, CA 90301-3378
PHONE 310-673-9113
FAX 310-673-1665
EMAIL . . . . .heavyweightr@aol.com
WEB SITE . . . . .www.heavyweightrecords.com
ARTIST ROSTER   Mr. Short Khop - Anthony "A.K." King - Problem Chyld - DeJai
GENRES   Rap/Hip-Hop - Urban

Terry Carter . . . . .President

HEFTY RECORDS
1658 N. Milwaukee Ave., Ste. 287
Chicago, IL 60647
PHONE 312-633-9100
FAX 312-633-9127
EMAIL . . . . .info@heftyrecords.com
WEB SITE . . . . .www.heftyrecords.com
ARTIST ROSTER   Telefon Tel Aviv - Slicker - Samadha - Eliot Lipp - L'Altra - Some Water & Sun
GENRES   Jazz - Rock
COMMENTS   Electronic

John Hughes III . . . . .Owner
Jon Schultz . . . . . .Head, Business Affairs (jon.schultz@heftyrecords.com)

HIDDEN BEACH RECORDINGS
3030 Nebraska Ave., PH
Santa Monica, CA 90404
PHONE 310-453-1400
FAX 310-453-6760
EMAIL . . . . .info@hiddenbeach.com
WEB SITE . . . . .www.hiddenbeach.com
ARTIST ROSTER   Jill Scott - Kindred - Bebe Winans - Lina - Darius Rucker - Michael Phillips - Jeff Bradshaw - Brenda Russell - Karen Briggs - Peter Black - Keite Young - Onitsha Shaw
GENRES   Rap/Hip-Hop

Steve McKeever . . . . .President (steve@hiddenbeach.com)
Roger Patton . . . . .General Manager (roger@hiddenbeach.com)
Alex Kesicbasian . . . . .CFO (alex@hiddenbeach.com)
Charles Whitfield . . . . .A&R/Sales (charles@hiddenbeach.com)
Jerrold Thompson . . . . .A&R (jerrold@hiddenbeach.com)
Jeryl Busbey . . . . .Head, Promotions (bruce@hiddenbeach.com)

HIFI RECORDINGS
580 Broadway, Ste. 200
New York, NY 10012-3223
PHONE 212-226-4580
FAX 212-226-6726

John Hecker . . . . .President
Mike Read . . . . .A&R

HIGH WIRE RECORDS
1971 Western Ave., Ste. 194
Albany, NY 12203-5071
PHONE 518-453-3469
FAX 518-453-2441
EMAIL . . . . .hwprod2743@aol.com
SECOND EMAIL . . . . .infohighwire@aol.com
WEB SITE . . . . .www.highwirerecords.com
ARTIST ROSTER   TriFe - DoMOB - GRAMZ - Gangsta Slim - Officer Bolo - Landlord - Raw Tim - Cee J - Tarzan
GENRES   R&B - Rap/Hip-Hop - Urban
RECENT SOUNDTRACKS   Made (MTV)
SUBMISSION POLICY   Send three songs, photo and bio to A&R, c/o Peter Nesbit
COMMENTS   Member of Heelan Publishers (ASCAP)

Edward J. Heelan . . . . .Owner
Peter Nesbit . . . . .A&R
Michael Corts . . . . .Booking

HIGHER OCTAVE MUSIC, INC.
4650 N. Port Washington Rd.
Milwaukee, WI 53212
PHONE 414-961-8350
FAX 414-961-8351
EMAIL . . . . .info@higheroctave.com
SECOND EMAIL . . . . .baileym@narada.com
WEB SITE . . . . .www.higheroctave.com
SECOND WEB SITE . . . . .www.omtown.com
DISTRIBUTOR   EMI Music Marketing
LABELS   Higher Octave - Cyber Octave - Om Town
GENRES   World
RECENT SOUNDTRACKS   The Constant Gardner - Playing for Change - The Triplets of Belleville
SUBMISSION POLICY   No unsolicited demos

David Neidhart . . . . .Sr. VP, Sales & Marketing
Anne Aufderheide . . . . .VP, Operations
Greg Jansen . . . . .VP, Business/Legal Affairs
Jill Weindorf . . . . .Director, Media Relations
Michael Bailey . . . . .A&R
Bruce Sullivan . . . . .Product Manager, Higher Octave
Steve Pedo . . . . .Finance Director

HIGHNOTE RECORDS
106 W. 71st St.
New York, NY 10023
PHONE 212-873-2020
FAX 212-877-0407
EMAIL . . . . .jazzdepo@ix.netcom.com
WEB SITE . . . . .www.jazzdepot.com
DISTRIBUTOR   Ryko Distribution
ARTIST ROSTER   Houston Person - Larry Coryell - Chris Connor - Cedar Walton - David "Fathead" Newman - Mark Murphy - Joey DeFrancesco - Wesla Whitfield - Carol Sloane - Vincent Herring - Sheila Jordan - John Hicks - Dave Valenti - Frank Morgan - Freddy Cole
LABELS   HighNote - Savant
GENRES   Jazz

Barney Fields . . . . .President

HIGHTONE RECORDS
220 Fourth St., Ste. 101
Oakland, CA 94607
PHONE 510-763-8500
FAX 510-763-8558
EMAIL . . . . .hightone@hightone.com
WEB SITE . . . . .www.hightone.com
DISTRIBUTOR   WEA Corp.
LABELS   HMG
GENRES   Folk - Roots
COMMENTS   Americana

Larry Sloven .Owner (larry@hightone.com)
Darrell Anderson . . . . .Operations Manager (dba@hightone.com)

HOLLYWOOD RECORDS
500 S. Buena Vista St.
Burbank, CA 91521
PHONE 818-560-5670/212-925-0331
FAX 818-560-3230/212-925-9126
EMAIL . . . . .firstname.lastname@disney.com
WEB SITE . . . . .www.hollywoodrecords.com
DISTRIBUTOR   Universal Music & Video Distribution
GENRES   All Genres
COMMENTS   East Coast office: 99 Hudson St., 8th
                    Fl., New York, NY 10013

Bob Cavallo . . . . .Chairman, BVMG (818-560-1800)
Mitchell Leib . . . . .President, Music & Soundtracks, Walt Disney Pictures/
                    Television & Buena Vista Music Group (818-560-5124)
David Agnew . .Executive VP/General Manager, BVMG (818-560-6406)
Justin Fontaine . . . . .Sr. VP, Promotion (818-560-5521)
Abbey Konowitch . . . . .Sr. VP/General Manager (818-560-5787)
Jon Lind . . . . .Sr. VP, A&R (818-560-2595)
Geoffrey Weiss . . . . .Sr. VP, A&R (818-560-4600)
Ken Bunt . . . . .Sr. VP, Marketing, BVMG (818-560-6161)
Curt Eddy . . . . .VP, Sales (818-560-7415)
Kris Ferraro . . . . .VP, Publicity (818-560-6197)
Geordie Gillespie . . . . .VP, Promotion (818-560-6014)
Allison Hamamura . . . . .VP, A&R (818-560-2809)
Jason Jordon . . . . .VP, A&R (212-925-0331)
Lillian Matulic . . . . .VP, Publicity (818-560-6197)
Dave Snow . . . . .VP, Creative Services (818-560-5795)
Rob Souriall . . . . .VP, Strategic Marketing (818-560-7380)
J. Scavo . . . . . .Executive Director, Artist Management (818-560-1305)
Sharrin Summers . . . . .Executive Director, Publicity (818-560-5787)
Dominic Griffin . . . . .Director, Music Placement (818-560-1483)
Eric Clinger . . . . .Manager, A&R (818-560-1745)
Deseree Craig Ramos . .Manager, Soundtracks, BVMG (818-560-5129)
Eric Ferris . . . . .Marketing (818-560-2220)
Matt Brant . . . . .Publicity Coordinator (818-560-2793)
Lori Lerner . . . . .Assistant to Chairman (818-560-7505)
Matt Harris . . . . .A&R Assistant (818-560-4210)

HOPELESS RECORDS
PO Box 7495
Van Nuys, CA 91409
PHONE 818-997-0444
FAX 818-997-6445
EMAIL . . . . .info@hopelessrecords.com
WEB SITE . . . . .www.hopelessrecords.com
DISTRIBUTOR   KOCH Entertainment Distribution
ARTIST ROSTER   Avenged Sevenfold - Break the Silence -
                    Thrice - Melee - Kaddisfly - Nural - Mike
                    Park - Mustard Plug - Against All
                    Authority
LABELS   Hopeless - Sub City -
                    Downloadpunk.com - Take Action!
GENRES   Alternative - Hardcore - Metal - Punk -
                    Rock
SUBMISSION POLICY   Accepts demos

Louis Posen . . . . .President
Al Person . . . . .GM
Jake Bright . . . . .Director, Sales
Ian Harrison . . . . .Publicity, Radio & Video
Gerardo "G" Cueva . . . . . .Retail & New Media Advertising Coordinator

HYBRID RECORDINGS
1515 Broadway, 36th Fl.
New York, NY 10036
PHONE 212-277-7171
EMAIL . . . . .info@hybridrecordings.com
WEB SITE . . . . .www.hybridrecordings.com
DISTRIBUTOR   RED Music Distribution
ARTIST ROSTER   Jen Chapin - Mathew Ryan - Pepper's
                    Ghost - Sarah Bettens - Vertical Horizon
                    - The Sound of Urchin - Assembly of
                    Dust
GENRES   Folk - Pop - Rock
RECENT SOUNDTRACKS   Hedwig & the Angry Inch - Casa de Los
                    Babys - Prey for Rock & Roll
SUBMISSION POLICY   No unsolicited submissions
COMMENTS   Associated with Metropolitan Talent

John Scher . . . . .Co-CEO (x7155)
Al Cafaro . . . . .Co-CEO (x7166)
Joe Augustine . . . . .A&R (x7169)
Chuck Bliziotis . . . . .Radio (x7170)
Howard Brooks . . . . .New Media (x7185)
Eric Levine . . . . .Legal (x7158)
Colleen Hendricks . . . . .New Media Assistant (x7172)
Dana Wise . . . . .Radio/Production Assistant (x7182)
Diana Guthey .Assistant (x7157)

HYENA
156 12th St., Ste. 4R
Brooklyn, NY 11215
PHONE 718-369-6567
EMAIL . . . . .hyenarecords@aol.com
WEB SITE . . . . .www.hyenarecords.com
ARTIST ROSTER   Grayson Capps - Jacob Fred Jazz
                    Odyssey - James Blood Ulmer - John
                    Ellis - Lafayette Gilchrist - Iswhat?! -
                    Mocean Worker - Dr. John - Don
                    McLean
GENRES   Blues - Jazz - Rock
SUBMISSION POLICY   No unsolicited material

Kevin Calabro . . . . .No Title

I AM
27783 Hidden Trail Rd.
Laguna Hills, CA 92653-7821
PHONE 949-305-5570
FAX 949-305-5574
EMAIL . . . . .harmonfreeze@aol.com
DISTRIBUTOR   EMI Music Marketing
GENRES   Alternative - Rock

Ross Robinson . . . . .President
John Reese . . . . .Manager (jreese3067@aol.com)
Scott Harmon . . . . .Assistant

IDOL RECORDS
PO Box 720043
Dallas, TX 75372
PHONE 214-321-8890
FAX 214-321-8889
EMAIL . . . . .info@idolrecords.com
WEB SITE . . . . .www.idolrecords.com
DISTRIBUTOR   Navarre Corporation
ARTIST ROSTER   Black Tie Dynasty - Sponge - The Fags -
                        Centro-Matic - [Daryl] - The Deathray
                        Davies - Watershed - Old 97's -
                        Flickerstick - The Skeemin' - No Goods -
                        GBH - Cold Cash Machine
GENRES   Alternative - Pop - Punk - Rock
COMMENTS   Publisher

Erv Karwelis . . . . .President

IGO RECORDS
1100 18th Ave. South
Nashville, TN 37212
PHONE 615-321-0033
FAX 615-321-2244
EMAIL . . . . .igorecords@aol.com
WEB SITE . . . . .www.igorecords.com
DISTRIBUTOR   Select-O-Hits
ARTIST ROSTER   Kacey Jones - Jesse Goldberg - Michael
                       Snow - Chris Ramey
GENRES   Alternative - Blues - Country - Folk

Kacey Jones . . . . .President/CEO
Erle Mulligan . . . . .General Manager

IMMORTAL RECORDS
12200 Olympic Blvd., Ste. 400
West Los Angeles, CA 90064
PHONE 310-481-1800
FAX 310-481-1444
EMAIL . . . . .contact@immortalrecords.com
WEB SITE . . . . .www.immortalrecords.com
DISTRIBUTOR   RED Music Distribution
GENRES   Alternative - Urban

Happy Walters . . . . .CEO (hwalters@immortalent.com)
Harvey Finkel . . . . .CFO (hfinkel@immortalent.com)
Dominica Johnson . . . . .COO (djohnson@immortalent.com)
Daniel Sena . . . . .VP, Marketing (dsena@immortalent.com)
Jason Markey . . . . .Sr. Director, A&R (jmarkey@immortalent.com)
Jamie Talbot . . . . .Sr. Director, A&R (jtalbot@immortalent.com)
Yuri Dutton . . . . .Director, Sales (ydutton@immortalent.com)
Greg Deutelbaum . . . . .Manager, Operations
                                          (gdeutelbaum@immortalent.com)

INNERHYTHMIC
133 W. 25th St., 5th Fl.
New York, NY 10001-7206
PHONE 212-414-0505
FAX 212-414-0525
EMAIL . . . . .info@innerhythmic.com
WEB SITE . . . . .www.innerhythmic.com
DISTRIBUTOR   Caroline Distribution
ARTIST ROSTER   Bill Laswell - Praxis
GENRES   Blues - Electronica - Jazz - Rap/Hip-Hop
                      - World
SUBMISSION POLICY   No unsolicited submissions

Peter Casperson . . . . .Co-President (x106)
Steven Saporta . . . . .Co-President (x102)
Steve Dalmer . . . .General Manager (x118, dalmer@innerhythmic.com)
Bill Laswell . . . . .A&R (x100)
Etty Glenn . . . . .Assistant

INO RECORDS
210 Jamestown Park, Ste. 100
Brentwood, TN 37027-2805
PHONE 615-777-2500
FAX 615-376-0532
EMAIL . . . . .susanz@inorecords.com
WEB SITE . . . . .www.inorecords.com
DISTRIBUTORS   Integrity - Provident Music Group
ARTIST ROSTER   The Afters - Bart Millard - Disciple -
                      Todd Agnew - Skillet - Jonah 33 - Sandi
                      Patty - Phillips, Craig & Dean - MercyMe
                      - CeCe Winans - Darlene Zschech -
                      Sonicflood - Sara Groves - Derek Webb
                      - Brooklyn Tabernacle Choir - Kara -
                      Anthony Evans - Mark Harris
GENRES   Adult Contemporary - Christian - Pop -
                      Rock

Jeff Moseley . . . . .President/CEO
Dan Michaels . . . . .VP, Promotions
Chris Erlanson . . . . .Director, Marketing Operations
James Rueger . . . . .A&R
John van der Veen . . . . .Director, Retail Sales
Susan Zaffiro . . . . .A&R Assistant

INPOP RECORDS
1820 Charleston Ln.
Franklin, TN 37067
PHONE 615-778-8897
FAX 615-377-7860
EMAIL . . . . .info@inpop.com
WEB SITE . . . . .www.inpop.com
GENRES   Christian - Rock

Wes Campbell . . . . .President
Bruno Pirecki . . . . .VP, Sales & Distribution
Rob Poznanski . . . . .VP, Marketing/Artist Development
Lizza Connor . . . . .Publicity Director
Breeon Phillips . . . . .Director, Sales & Distribution
Shara Katerberg . . . . .Regional & Online Marketing Coordinator
Ryan Longnecker . . . . .National Promotions Coordinator
Lauren Froggatte . . . . .Project Coordinator/Church Marketing
Claire Indie . . . . .Office Manager
Chanel Campbell . . . . .Publicity Assistant

INRADIO
PO Box 6882
Minneapolis, MN 55406
PHONE 612-332-9606
FAX 612-338-6043
WEB SITE . . . . .www.inradio.net
COMMENTS   Subscription-based compilation CDs

Dan Carroll . . . . .President

LABELS

INTEGRITY
1000 Cody Rd.
Mobile, AL 36695-3499
PHONE 251-633-9000
FAX 251-776-5117
WEB SITE . . . . .www.integritymusic.com

Danny McGuffey . . . . .Chief Marketing Officer (dannym@integinc.com)
Craig Dunnigan . . . . .VP, Church Resources (craigd@integinc.com)
Jackie Patillo   General Manager, Integrity Gospel (jackiep@integinc.com)
Chris Springer . . . . .Director, A&R/Producer (chriss@integinc.com)
Steve Merkel . . . . .Manager, A&R (stevem@integinc.com)

INTERSCOPE GEFFEN A&M
2220 Colorado Ave.
Santa Monica, CA 90404
PHONE 310-865-1000/212-333-8000
EMAIL . . . . .feedback@igamail.com
WEB SITE . . . . .www.interscope.com
DISTRIBUTOR   Universal Music & Video Distribution
GENRES   Alternative - Pop - Rap/Hip-Hop - Rock
COMMENTS   East Coast office: 1755 Broadway, 8th
                          Fl., New York, NY 10019

Jimmy Iovine . . . . .Chairman
David Cohen . . . . .Vice Chairman
Ron Fair . . . . .President, A&M
Steve Berman . . . . .Co-President, Interscope
Brenda Romano . . . . .Co-President, Interscope
Polly Anthony . . . . .Co-President, Geffen
Jordan Schur . . . . .Co-President, Geffen
Jurgen Grebner .VP, International
Michelle Thomas . . . . .General Manager, A&M Records
Dennis Dennehy . . . . .Head, Publicity
Rand Hoffman . . . . .Head, Business Affairs
Courtney Holt . . . . .Head, New Media
M. Kierszenbaum . . . . .Head, International
Christina Meloche . . . . .Head, Marketing, Interscope
Deb Fenstermacher .Marketing
Julie Hovsepian . . . . .Marketing
Dyana Kass . . . . .Marketing
Paul Kremen . . . . .Marketing
Cyndy Villano . . . . .Marketing (NY)
Tom Williams . . . . .Marketing
Scott Enright . . . . .A&R
Tony Ferguson . . . . .A&R
Ben Gordon . . . . .A&R
Marcus Heisser . . . . .A&R
Wendy Higgs . . . . .A&R
Eric Hunter . . . . .A&R, Geffen
DJ Mormile . . . . .A&R
Chuck Reed . . . . .A&R
Justin Siegel . . . . .A&R
Debbie Southwood-Smith . . . . .A&R (NY)
Mark Williams . . . . .A&R
Luke Wood . . . . .A&R
Erica Grayson .Urban A&R
Jennie Boddy .Publicity (NY)
Greg Miller . . . . .Publicity
Step Johnson . . . . .Urban Promotion
David Saslow . . . . .Video Promotion (NY)
Gretchen Anderson . . . . .Production
Cindy Cooper . . . . .Production
Fred Durst . . . .(LA)
Karen Rait . . . .(NY)
Candy Berry . . . . .Sales
Ingrid Erickson . . . . .New Media
Ryan O'Donnell . . . . .A&R Assistant to Chairman
Ginger Ramsey . . . . .Assistant to Chairman
Crystal Riley . . . . .Assistant to Chairman

IPECAC RECORDINGS
PO Box 1778
Orinda, CA 94563
PHONE 212-228-4868
EMAIL . . . . .info@ipecac.com
WEB SITE . . . . .www.ipecac.com
DISTRIBUTOR   Caroline Distribution
ARTIST ROSTER   Bohren & Der Club of Gore - Desert
                        Sessions - Dälek - End - Eyvind Kang -
                        Fantômas - Isis - Kaada - kid606 -
                        Maldoror - Melvins - Melvins/Lustmord -
                        Moistboyz - Mondo Generator -
                        Phantomsmasher - Pink Anvil - Ruins -
                        Sensational - Skeleton Key - Steroid
                        Maximus - The Curse of the Golden
                        Vampire - The Kids of Widney High -
                        The Lucky Stars - The Young Gods -
                        Tomahawk - Trevor Dunn's Trio
                        Convulsant - Venomous Concept -
                        Vincent & Mr. Green - Yoshimi & Yuka
GENRES   Rock

Mike Patton . . . . .Co-Owner
Greg Werckman . . . . .Co-Owner
Rai Sandow . . . . .Label Manager
Shaun MacDonald .Production

THE ISLAND DEF JAM MUSIC GROUP (LOS ANGELES)
8920 Sunset Blvd., 2nd Fl.
Los Angeles, CA 90069
PHONE 310-276-4500
FAX 310-860-9245
EMAIL . . . . .firstname.lastname@umusic.com
WEB SITE . . . . .www.islanddefjam.com
DISTRIBUTOR   Universal Music & Video Distribution
ARTIST ROSTER   Jay-Z - Mariah Carey - Bon Jovi - Ja
                        Rule - Ashanti - Sum 41 - The Killers - PJ
                        Harvey - LL Cool J - Saliva - Method
                        Man - Redman - Marc Broussard - 112 -
                        Ludacris - Christina Milian - Lloyd - Patti
                        LaBelle - Lionel Richie - Blue Merle -
                        N.O.R.E. - Shawna - Cam'Ron -
                        Ghostface - Letter Kills - Shyne - Musiq -
                        Hoobastank - Fefe Dobson - Teairra
                        Mari - Rihanna - Ne-Yo - The Bravery -
                        Bobby Valentino - Fall Out Boy - Kanye
                        West - Foxy Brown - Ron Isley - Utada -
                        Thrice
LABELS   Def Jam - Def Jam South - Def Soul -
                        Island - The Inc. - Roc-A-Fella -
                        American Recordings - Damon Dash
                        Music Group - Russell Simmons Music
                        Group - Lost Highway - Roc La Familia
GENRES   Adult Contemporary - Alternative - Metal
                        - Pop - Punk - R&B - Rap/Hip-Hop -
                        Rock - Urban

Paul Pontius . . . . . . .Executive VP, A&R, Island Def Jam (310-288-5381)
Spring Aspers . . . .VP, Soundtracks & Music Supervision (310-288-5362)
Christine Chiappetta . . . . . .VP, Modern-Rock Promotion, Island Records
Howie Miura . . . . .VP, Promotion, Island Records
Amy Bloebaum . . .Sr. Director, Media & Artist Relations (310-288-5386)
Noah Sheer . . . . .Sr. Director, Rhythm/Crossover & Promotion
Bronwen Boyan . . . . .Manager, Soundtracks & Music Supervision
                                                            (310-288-5347)
Daniel Schulman . . . . . .A&R Executive, Island Records (310-288-5312)
Will Westfall . . . . .A&R Rep, Island Records (310-288-5337)
Angela Vredenburg . . . . .A&R Assistant, Island Def Jam (310-288-5363)
Aishah White . . . . .Media & Artists Relations (310-288-5347)
Mark Nieto . . . . .Promotion Assistant (310-288-5323)

THE ISLAND DEF JAM MUSIC GROUP (NEW YORK)

825 Eighth Ave., 28th Fl.
New York, NY 10019
PHONE 212-333-8000
FAX 212-603-7931
EMAIL .firstname.lastname@umusic.com
WEB SITE . . . . .www.islanddefjam.com

DISTRIBUTOR	Universal Music & Video Distribution
ARTIST ROSTER	Jay-Z - Mariah Carey - Bon Jovi - Ja Rule - Ashanti - Sum 41 - The Killers - PJ Harvey - LL Cool J - Saliva - Method Man - Redman - Marc Broussard - 112 - Ludacris - Christina Milian - Lloyd - Patti LaBelle - Lionel Richie - Blue Merle - N.O.R.E. - Shawna - Cam'Ron - Ghostface - Letter Kills - Shyne - Musiq - Hoobastank - Fefe Dobson - Teairra Mari - Rihanna - Ne-Yo - The Bravery - Bobby Valentino - Fall Out Boy - Kanye West - Foxy Brown - Ron Isley - Utada - Thrice
LABELS	Def Jam - Def Jam South - Def Soul - Island - The Inc. - Roc-A-Fella - American Recordings - Damon Dash Music Group - Russell Simmons Music Group - Lost Highway - Roc La Familia
GENRES	Adult Contemporary - Alternative - Metal - Pop - Punk - R&B - Rap/Hip-Hop - Rock - Urban

Antonio "LA" Reid . . . . .Chairman, Island Def Jam
Steve Bartels . . . . .President, Island Records
Shawn "Jay-Z" Carter . . . . .President, Def Jam Recordings
Matt Signore . . . . .CFO/Co-General Manager (212-333-8474)
Jay Brown . . . . .Executive VP, A&R, Def Jam
Karen Kwak . . . . .Executive VP, A&R (212-333-1332)
Greg Thompson . . . . .Executive VP, Promotion (212-333-8001)
Steve Gawley . . . . .Sr. VP, Business & Legal Affairs (212 333 8534)
Mitchell Imber . . . . .Sr. VP, Sales & Marketing (212-333-1408)
Benny Pough . . . . .Sr. VP, Promotion
Marthe Reynolds . . . . .Sr. VP, Rhythm & Crossover Promotion
Laura Swanson . . . . .Sr. VP, Publicity & Artist Relations
Alli Truch . . . . .Sr. VP, Creative Services
Matt Voss . . . . .Sr. VP, International (212-333-8085)
Larry Mattera . . . . .Sr. VP, New Media
Joe Calitri . . . . .VP, Field Marketing
Shawn "Pecas" Costner . . . . .VP, Lifestyle Promotion
Jana Fleishman . . . . .VP, Publicity
Ross Grierson . . . . .VP, Promotion
Heath Kudler .VP, Legal & Business Affairs
Linda Lee . . . . .VP, A&R Administration (212-445-3631)
David McGilvray . . . . .VP, Rock Promotion
Josh Sarubin . . . . .VP, A&R (212-445 3518)
Shakir Stewart . . . . .VP, A&R (Atlanta)
Jeff Straughn . . . . .VP, Strategic Marketing
Rich Westover . . . . .VP, Promotion/Research & Information Systems
Karen Wiessen . . . . .VP, Media & Artist Relations (212-603-7950)
Diana Fragnito . . . . .Sr. Director, A&R (212-333-8521)
Bridgett Germroth . . . . .Sr. National Director, Adult Promotion
Vol Stephen Davis III   Director, Recording Administration (212-603-7950)
Ben Lazar . . . . .Director, A&R/Research (212-333-8509)
Skane . . . . .Director, A&R, Def Jam/Def Soul
Rob Stevenson . . . . .Director, A&R (212-445-3664)
Jimmel Keaton . . . . .A&R, Def Jam
Tyran Smith . . . . .A&R, Def Jam
Ian Allen . . . . .Manager, A&R Administration/Clearance (212-333-8190)
Jonathan Benedict . . . . .Manager, A&R (212-333-6727)
Leesa Brunson . . . . .Manager, A&R, Def Jam/Def Soul (212-445-3646)
Tara Podolsky . . . . .Manager, A&R Administration (212-445-3611)
Donna Fetchko . . . . .A&R Administration (212-333-8351)
Rob Mitchell . . . . .A&R Administration (212-603-7782)
Erica Novich . . . . .A&R Administration (212-445-3639)

J RECORDS/ARISTA RECORDS

745 Fifth Ave., 6th Fl.
New York, NY 10151
PHONE 646-840-5600
EMAIL .firstname.lastname@sonybmg.com
WEB SITE . . . . .www.jrecords.com

ARTIST ROSTER	Alicia Keys - Angie Stone - Annie Lennox - Cassidy - Faithless - Fantasia - Gavin Degraw - Luther Vandross - Mario - Maroon 5 - Monica - Shells - Silvertide - Rod Stewart - Tyrese - Wyclef Jean - Babyface - Jamie Foxx - Kenny G - Sarah McLachlan - Whitney Houston - Santana - Rhymefest - Smitty - Dido - Faithless - I Nine - Say Anything - Mashonda - Carrie Underwood
LABELS	Def Squad - Flipmode - Swizz Beatz - Y Clef Records - Octone Records
GENRES	Pop - R&B - Rap/Hip-Hop - Rock - Roots - Urban

Clive Davis . . . . .Chairman/CEO, BMG US
Charles Goldstuck . . . . .President/COO, BMG US
Tom Corson . . . . .Executive VP/General Manager, Arista/J Records
Peter Edge . . . . .Executive VP, A&R, Arista/J Records
Richard Palmese .Executive VP, Promotion
Julie Swidler . . . . .Executive VP, Legal & Business Affairs
Mike Bergin . . . . .Sr. VP, Top 40 Promotion
Jeff Burroughs . . . . .Sr. VP, Urban Marketing & Artist Development, Arista/J Records
James Diener . . . . .Sr. VP, A&R/Marketing
Mika El-Baz . . . . .Sr. VP, Publicity
Jeff Fenster . . . . .Sr. VP, A&R, Arista
Lou Robinson . . . . .Sr. VP, Video Promotion & Artist Development
Ken Wilson . . . . .Sr. VP, Urban Promotion, Arista/J Records
Kevin Beisler . . . . .VP, TV Publicity, Arista/J Records
Theola Borden . . . . .VP, Urban Publicity
Bill Burrs . . . . .VP, Rock Music
Donna Clower . . . . .VP, Strategic Marketing & Artist Development
Sarah Weinstein Dennison . . . . .VP, Publicity, Arista/J Records
Randy Franklin . . . . .VP, Urban Promotion, Arista/J Records
Peter Gray . . . . .VP, Top 40 Promotion, RCA Music Group
Hosh Gureli . . . . .VP, A&R, Arista/J Records
Rani Hancock . . . . .VP, A&R Administration
Larry Jackson . . . . .VP, A&R, Arista/J Records
Sam Lecca . . . . .VP, Video Production
Rob Love . . . . .VP, Urban Promotion, Arista/J Records
Adrian Moreira . . . . .VP, Adult Promotion
Liz Morentin . . . . .VP, Publicity, West Coast, Arista/J Records
Victor Murgatroyd . . . . .VP, A&R, Arista/J Records
Scott Seviour . . . . .VP, Marketing & Artist Development, Arista/J Records
Matt Shay . . . . .VP, A&R Marketing, Arista/J Records
Carolyn Williams . . . . .VP, Urban Marketing, Arista/J Records
Michael Williams . . . . .VP, Crossover/Rhythm Promotion
Trevor Jerideau .Sr. Director, A&R, J Records
Russ Jones . . . . . .Sr. Director, Rap/Street Marketing, Arista/J Records
Dontay Thompson . . . . .Director, National Crossover Promotion
Mark Springer . . . . .Manager, A&R Administration
Paula Chaltas . . . . .Executive Assistant to CEO
Deana Smart . . . . .Executive Assistant to President

LABELS

*JACK RECORDS
c/o Warner Bros. Records Nashville
20 Music Square East, 3rd Fl.
Nashville, TN 37203-4344
PHONE 615-748-8000/615-214-1567
FAX 615-214-1537
EMAIL . . . . .firstname.lastname@wbr.com
WEB SITE . . . . .www.wbrnashville.com
DISTRIBUTOR   WEA Corp.
ARTIST ROSTER   Bill Engvall - Jeff Foxworthy - Lisa
                         Lampanelli - Larry the Cable Guy -
                         Naked Trucker
GENRES   Comedy

Peter Strickland . . . . .VP, Sales & A&R
Eric Mansfield . . . . .Director, Creative Services
Jeremy Witt . . . . .Manager, A&R (615-214-1464)

JADE TREE
2310 Kennwynn Rd.
Wilmington, DE 19810
PHONE 302-661-2099
FAX 302-661-1848
EMAIL . . . . .jadetree@jadetree.com
WEB SITE . . . . .www.jadetree.com
ARTIST ROSTER   Lords - Statistics - Pedro the Lion - Paint
                         It Black - The Lovedones
GENRES   Hardcore - Pop - Punk - Rock

Tim Owen . . . . .Co-Owner/Marketing & Promotion
                                   (timowen@jadetree.com)
Darren Walters . . . . .Co-Owner/Business Affairs & Licensing
                                   (dwalters@jadetree.com)
Mehron Mitchell Moqtaderi . . . . .Art Department/Tech Guru
                                   (mehron@jadetree.com)
Charlie Warren Kaericher II . . . . .Retail & Tour Promotion
                                   (charles@jadetree.com)
David L. Wagenschutz . . . . .Office/Production Manager
                                   (david@jadetree.com)

JARGON RECORDS
1237 E. Main St.
Rochester, NY 14609
PHONE 585-288-3150
FAX 585-288-7720
EMAIL . . . . .danderson@jargonrecords.com
WEB SITE .www.jargonrecords.com
GENRES   Rock
COMMENTS   '60s garage rock 'n' roll

Dave Anderson . . . . .Owner

JELLYBEAN RECORDINGS, INC.
235 Park Ave. South, 10th Fl.
New York, NY 10003
PHONE 212-777-5678
FAX 212-777-7788
EMAIL . . . . .info@jellybeanrecordings.com
SECOND EMAIL . . . . .promo@jellybeanrecordings.com
WEB SITE . . . . .www.jellybean-recordings.com
ARTIST ROSTER   Jaque - Maxine Inniss - Bang the Party -
                         Mena Keys - Marlon D - Quentin Harris
                         - Treen Rose
LABELS   Jellybean Soul - Fuego
GENRES   Electronica - Latin - World
RECENT SOUNDTRACKS   Anime Toons Vols. 3 - Puro Sabor - Asi
                         Lo Hacemos
SUBMISSION POLICY   No unsolicited submissions

Jellybean Benitez . . . . .President/CEO (x117)
John Gambuzza . . . . .General Manager (x103)
Jason Chin . . . . .Director, Business Affairs (x129)
Phil D. . . . . .Sales (x122)

JUSTIN TIME RECORDS
5455 Paré, Ste. 101
Montréal, PQ H4P 1P7 Canada
PHONE 514-738-9533
FAX 514-737-9780
EMAIL . . . . .info@justin-time.com
WEB SITE . . . . .www.justin-time.com
LABELS   Just A Memory Records - Just A Minute
                         Records
GENRES   Blues - Folk - Gospel - Jazz - World

Jim West . . . . .Founder

K RECORDS
PO Box 7154
Olympia, WA 98507
PHONE 360-786-1594/360-786-5020
FAX 360-786-5024
EMAIL . . . . .info@krecs.com
SECOND EMAIL .promo@krecs.com
WEB SITE . . . . .www.krecs.com
DISTRIBUTOR   Secretly Canadian
ARTIST ROSTER   The Microphones - Mirah - The Blow -
                         Little Wings - Kimya Dawson - Jason
                         Anderson - Old Time Relijun - Calvin
                         Johnson - Landing - The Beakers -
                         Blackouts - C.O.C.O. - Dub Narcotic
                         Sound System - All Girl Summer Fun
                         Band - Tender Forever - Karl Blau
SUBMISSION POLICY   No demos accepted

Calvin Johnson . . . . .K Ring Leader (k@krecs.com)
Mariella Luz . . . . .Label Manager/Mail Order & Distribution
                                   (mariella@krecs.com)
Rhett Nelson . . . . .Production Manager (production@krecs.com)
Amber Bua . . . . .General Promotions (promo@krecs.com)
Joel Brazzel . . . . .Mail Order (mailorder@krecs.com)
Susie Noble . . . . .Bookkeeping (books@krecs.com)

K2B2 RECORDS
1748 Roosevelt Ave.
Los Angeles, CA 90006
PHONE 323-732-1602
FAX 323-731-2758
EMAIL . . . . .marty@k2b2.com
WEB SITE www.k2b2.com
GENRES   Bluegrass - Children's - Classical -
                         Country - Jazz - World

Marty Krystall . . . . .No Title
Marv Moses . . . . .No Title

KANINE RECORDS
204 Power St., #1
Brooklyn, NY 11211
PHONE 718-609-2490
FAX 718-609-2490
EMAIL . . . . .info@kaninerecords.com
WEB SITE . . . . .www.kaninerecords.com
DISTRIBUTOR   Fontana Distribution
ARTIST ROSTER   The Flesh - Four Volts - Grizzly Bear -
                         The Izzys - Mommy & Daddy - Oxford
                         Collapse - Rockethouse - Mixel Pixel
GENRES   Pop - Punk - Rock

Kay Quartararo . . . . .Owner

KEMADO RECORDS
601 W. 26th St., 11th Fl.
New York, NY 10001
PHONE 212-242-8883
EMAIL . . . . .info@kemado.com
WEB SITE . . . . .www.kemado.com
DISTRIBUTOR   Hollywood Records
ARTIST ROSTER   Elefant - The Fever - Shout! - Lansing-
                     Dreiden - Diamond Nights - Dungen -
                     The Sword - Turantula A.D. -
                     Cheeseburger
GENRES   Rock
SUBMISSION POLICY   Will respond to radical demos; Do not
                     call

Tom Clapp . . . . .Founder
Andres Santo Domingo . . . . .Founder
Jeff Kaye . . . . .Marketing
Keith Abrahamsson . . . . .A&R
Megan La Slanme . . . . .Sales

KILL ROCK STARS
120 NE State Ave., PMB 418
Olympia, WA 98501
PHONE 360-357-9732
FAX 360-357-6408
EMAIL . . . . .slim@killrockstars.com
WEB SITE . . . . .www.killrockstars.com
ARTIST ROSTER   5 Rue Christine: Nervous Cop - Hella -
                     Amps for Christ - The Advantage - Xiu
                     Xiu - Deerhoof - The Planet The -
                     Woonden Wand & the Vanishing Voice -
                     Punks - Excepter - No Neck Blues Band -
                     The Mae Shi - Metalux - BARR - The
                     Robot Ate Me; Kill Rock Stars: The
                     Makers - Linda Perry - Gold Chains &
                     Sue Cie - The Decemberists - Gravy
                     Train!!!! - Nedelle & Thom - the pAper
                     chAse - John Wilkes Booze - Stereo Total
                     - Jeff Hanson - Nedelle - Two Ton Boa -
                     Anna Oxygen - Numbers - Gossip -
                     Laura Veirs - Harvey Danger - Comet
                     Gain - Delta 5 - Imaad Wasif
LABELS   5 Rue Christine - Kill Rock Stars
GENRES   Alternative

Slim Moon . . . . .Owner (x13)
Aaron Tuller . . . . .Chief Information Officer
Ingrid Renan . . . . .Production Manager (x15)
Maggie Vail . . . . .VP (x11, maggie@killrockstars.com)
Audrey Faine . . . . .Director, Marketing (x15)
Nard Mullan . . . . .Accounting (x16)
Tobi Vail . . . . .Mail Order Manager (x17)
Marissa Young . . . . .Executive Assistant/Advertising (x10)
Lauren Ross . . . . .Assistant to Slim Moon (x13)

KIMCHEE RECORDS
6 Sagamore Rd.
Ipswich, MA 01938
PHONE 978-356-0093
FAX 978-356-1783
EMAIL . . . . .info@kimcheerecords.com
WEB SITE . . . . .www.kimcheerecords.com
DISTRIBUTOR   Redeye Distribution
ARTIST ROSTER   Willard Grant Conspiracy - Chris
                     Colbourn & Hilken Mancini - Paula
                     Kelley - Seekonk - Tiger Saw - Skating
                     Club
GENRES   Alternative - Pop - Rock
SUBMISSION POLICY   Listens to all submissions, but does not
                     respond unless interested

Robert Dubrow . . . . .Most Things (bob@kimcheerecords.com)
Andy Hong . . . . .Some Things

KING STREET SOUNDS
115 W. 30th St., Ste. 306-308
New York, NY 10001-4010
PHONE 212-594-3737
FAX 212-594-3636
EMAIL . . . . .info@kingstreetsounds.com
WEB SITE . . . . .www.kingstreetsounds.com
DISTRIBUTOR   Studio Distribution
GENRES   Electronica

Hisa Ishioka . . . . .President
Joe Berinato . . . . . . .Office Director/A&R (joeb@kingstreetsounds.com)
Rob Wunderman . . . . .Consultant (917-744-1000,
                                          robw@kingstreetsounds.com)

KLEPTO RECORDS
3470 19th St.
San Francisco, CA 94110
PHONE 415-864-1967
FAX 415-864-1966
EMAIL . . . . .kcosta@kleptorecords.com
SECOND EMAIL . . . . .recording@kleptorecords.com
ARTIST ROSTER   Ride the Blinds
SUBMISSION POLICY   Send promotional packages to Attn: A&R

Jeromy Smith . . . . .Owner (recording@kleptorecords.com)
Duane Ramos . . . . .Recording Engineer (dr@duaneramos.com)
Kevin Costa . . . . .Web Maintenance (kcosta@kleptorecords.com)

KNITTING FACTORY ENTERTAINMENT
81 Franklin St., 3rd Fl.
New York, NY 10013
PHONE 212-219-3006
FAX 212-219-3401
EMAIL . . . . .info@knittingfactory.com
WEB SITE . . . . .www.knittingfactory.com
DISTRIBUTOR   RED Music Distribution
LABELS   Instinct Records - Shadow Records -
                     Evolver Entertainment
GENRES   Adult Contemporary - Alternative -
                     Bluegrass - Country - Electronica - Folk -
                     Jazz - Metal - Punk - Rock - World

Jared Hoffman . . . . .President
Peter Wright . . . . .GM, Label Group
Shay Vishawadia . . . . .GM, New York Club
Morgan Margolis . . . . .GM, Los Angeles Club

KOCH RECORDS
740 Broadway, 7th Fl.
New York, NY 10003
PHONE 212-353-8800, x209
EMAIL . . . . .firstname.lastname@kochent.com
SECOND EMAIL . . . . .michelle.bayer@kochent.com
WEB SITE . . . . .www.kochent.com
SECOND WEB SITE .www.sugaroo.com
ARTIST ROSTER　　　　The Kinks - Master P - Goodie Mab -
　　　　　　　　　　　Abra Moore - Ringo Starr - William
　　　　　　　　　　　Hung - The Wiggles - C Murder
LABELS　　　　　　　　KOCH Records - DRG Records
GENRES　　　　　　　　All Genres
SUBMISSION POLICY　　No unsolicited material
COMMENTS　　　　　　Publisher; Distributor

Michael Koch . . . . .CEO
Bob Frank . . . . .President (x216)
Larry Offsey . . . . .COO/CFO
Alan Grunblatt .Executive VP (x211)
Cliff Cultreri . . . . .Sr. VP, A&R (x229)
Ed Franke . . . . .Sr. VP, Sales
Chris Calahan . . . . .VP, Distribution
John Franck . . . . .VP, Marketing
Gio Melchiore . . . . .VP, Media Relations
Rick Meuser . . . . .VP, Business Affairs
Chuck Oliner . . . . .VP, Promotion
Susan Del Giorno . . . . .Director, Classics
Catania Whalen . . . . .Director, International
Veronica Villarreal . . . . .Director, Children's Marketing
Kim Frizza . . . . .Label Manager
Dave Howlett . . . . .Label Manager
Chris Isidori . . . . .Urban Label Manager
Scott Kuchler . . . . .Label Manager
Michelle Bayer . . . . .Publishing Administrator, TV/Film Licensing
Heidi Peborde . . . . .Manager, Royalties
Courtney Adams .Product Manager
Michael Healy . . . . .Controller
Christian Mariano . . . . .Publicity Coordinator
Marleny Dominguez .Assistant, A&R

*KUNG FU RECORDS
PO Box 38009
Hollywood, CA 90038
PHONE 323-822-3939
EMAIL . . . . .questions@kungfurecords.com
WEB SITE . . . . .www.kungfurecords.com
DISTRIBUTOR　　　　　Fontana Distribution
ARTIST ROSTER　　　　Underminded - Godawfuls - Useless ID -
　　　　　　　　　　　The Ataris - Tsunami Bomb - The
　　　　　　　　　　　Vandals - Ozma - Assorted Jellybeans -
　　　　　　　　　　　Bigwig
GENRES　　　　　　　　Hardcore - Pop - Punk - Rock

Joe Escalante . . . . .President

LAKESHORE RECORDS
9268 W. Third St.
Beverly Hills, CA 90210
PHONE 310-867-8000
FAX 310-300-3038
EMAIL . . . . .firstnamelastname@lakeshoreentertainment.com
WEB SITE . . . . .www.lakeshore-records.com
SECOND WEB SITE . . . . .www.lakeshoreentertainment.com
DISTRIBUTOR　　　　　RED Music Distribution
ARTIST ROSTER　　　　The Legends - Tweaker - Davey Ray
　　　　　　　　　　　Moor - Kinnie Starr - The Belles
LABELS　　　　　　　　Lakeshore - RUN Recordings -
　　　　　　　　　　　Waxploitation - Reverberations - WIL
　　　　　　　　　　　Records
GENRES　　　　　　　　Alternative - Electronica - Pop - Rock
RECENT SOUNDTRACKS　Napoleon Dynamite - Mr. & Mrs. Smith -
　　　　　　　　　　　Daltry Calhoun - Lord of War
SUBMISSION POLICY　　Accepts mail submissions; No calls

Skip Williamson . . . . .President
Brian McNelis . . . . .VP/General Manager (310-867-8044)
Christine Buckley .VP, Music Legal
Eric Craig . . . . .A&R (310-867-8045)
Lynn Hobensack . . . . .Director, Music Administration
Stephanie Mente . . . . .Product Manager (310-867-8059)

LAMON RECORDS
PO Box 23625
Charlotte, NC 28227
PHONE 704-282-9910
FAX 704-282-0505
EMAIL . . . . .info@lamonrecords.com
WEB SITE . . . . .www.lamonrecords.com
LABELS　　　　　　　　Lamon - Americana Street - Pearse Street
　　　　　　　　　　　- Bluegrass Boulevard - Acoustic Allee -
　　　　　　　　　　　Kids Club Avenue
GENRES　　　　　　　　Adult Contemporary - Bluegrass - Blues -
　　　　　　　　　　　Children's - Christian - Country - Folk -
　　　　　　　　　　　Gospel - R&B - Rock - Roots
SUBMISSION POLICY　　Email first
COMMENTS　　　　　　Nashville office: 9005 Overlook Blvd.,
　　　　　　　　　　　Brentwood, TN 37027

Dave Moody . . . . .President
Nelson McSwain . . . . .VP, A&R
Bridget McSwain . . . . .Artist Relations & Promotions
Susan Moody . . . . .Music Publishing & Accounting

LANDSLIDE RECORDS
PO Box 20387
Atlanta, GA 30325
PHONE 404-239-5441
EMAIL . . . . .mrland@mindspring.com
ARTIST ROSTER　　　　Webb Wilder - King Johnson - Sean
　　　　　　　　　　　Costello - Sector 9 - The Lost
　　　　　　　　　　　Continentals - The Derek Trucks Band -
　　　　　　　　　　　The Steam Donkeys - Cigar Store
　　　　　　　　　　　Indians - Colonel Bruce Hampton -
　　　　　　　　　　　Dave Bartholomew - Paul McCandless
GENRES　　　　　　　　Blues

Michael Rothschild . . . . .President

LAVA RECORDS
See Atlantic Records Group

LEFTWING RECORDINGS

1162 N. Stone St., #102
Los Angeles, CA 90063
PHONE 323-397-3460
FAX 323-262-3399
EMAIL . . . . .leftwinger@leftwingrecordings.com
SECOND EMAIL . . . . .steven@leftwingrecordings.com
WEB SITE . . . . .www.leftwingrecordings.com
ARTIST ROSTER   Midnight Movies - Laytun - Richard Swift
                         - Tinpaco - Giant Drag - Jessica Dobson
                         - West Indian Girl
GENRES   Rock

Steven Melrose . . . . .GM/A&R

LIGHTYEAR

434 Avenue of the Americas, 6th Fl.
New York, NY 10011-8411
PHONE 212-353-5084
FAX 212-353-5083
EMAIL . . . . .mail@lightyear.com
WEB SITE . . . . .www.lightyear.com
DISTRIBUTOR   WEA Corp.

Arnie Holland . . . . .CEO/President
Joel Kaplan . . . . .VP, Finance
Don Spielvogel . . . . .VP, Sales & Marketing
Victoria Rose . . . . .Publicity
Peter Cascio .Director, Operations
Pam Daniel . . . . .Director, Creative Services
Norman "Dore" Spivey . . . . .Director, Retail Marketing

LIQUIDCITY RECORDS

PO Box 4418
Seattle, WA 98194
PHONE 206-853-8433/877-547-2489
WEB SITE . . . . .www.liquidcity.com
ARTIST ROSTER   Jovino Santos Neto - Scott Law Band -
                         Around the Fire - Living Daylights - Zony
                         Mash - Tough Mama - Jim Page - Annie
                         O'Neill - Souls of the Sound
GENRES   Folk - Jazz - Rock

Chris Chappell . . . . .President
Ric Vaughan . . . . .VP

LIQUOR & POKER MUSIC

2323 W. El Segundo Blvd.
Hawthorne, CA 90250
PHONE 323-418-1400
FAX 323-418-0118
WEB SITE . . . . .www.liquorandpokermusic.com
DISTRIBUTOR   Caroline Distribution
ARTIST ROSTER   Backyard Babies - Black Halos - Thieves
                         - Nebula - The Hellacopters - Fireball
                         Ministry - Crash Kelly - Dirty Americans
GENRES   Rock

Brandon Stratton . . . . .Label Manager/A&R (x126)
Clay Marshall . . . . .A&R (x241)

LITTLE DOG RECORDS

2219 W. Olive Ave., Ste. 150
Burbank, CA 91506
PHONE 818-557-1595
FAX 818-557-0524
EMAIL . . . . .info@littledogrecords.com
WEB SITE .www.littledogrecords.com
DISTRIBUTOR   Fontana Distribution
ARTIST ROSTER   Curt Kirkwood - Moot Davis - The
                         Blazers - Pete Anderson - Cisco - Scott
                         Joss
GENRES   Country - Rock - Roots
SUBMISSION POLICY   Email first; No calls

Pete Anderson . . . . .President
Bob Bernstein . . . . .GM
Judy Cocuzza . . . . .Director, A&R/Office & Studio Manager
Kevin Sepriano . . . . .Retail Manager
Leon Luiz . . . . .Publicity
Sally Browder . . . . .Staff Producer

LML MUSIC

PO Box 48081
Los Angeles, CA 90048
PHONE 323-856-9202
FAX 323-856-9204
EMAIL . . . . .lee@lmlmusic.com
WEB SITE . . . . .www.lmlmusic.com
DISTRIBUTOR   Allegro Corporation
ARTIST ROSTER   'Nita Whitaker - Brian Lane Green -
                         Stephen Schwartz - Joan Ryan - Anne
                         Kerry Ford - Barbara Brussell - Stacy
                         Sullivan - Joanne O'Brien - Franc
                         D'Ambrosio - Stephen Schwartz - Cory
                         Jamison - Corky Hale - Babbie Green -
                         Jim Caruso - Lee Lessack - Betsyann
                         Faiella - Heather Mac Rae - Pamela
                         Myers - Gloria Loring - Ted Keegan -
                         D.C. Anderson - Jack Donahue -
                         Charles Cermele - Linda Purl - Susan
                         Egan
GENRES   Adult Contemporary - Pop
SUBMISSION POLICY   Send press kit and CD
COMMENTS   Traditional Pop Vocals

Lee Lessack .Owner (lee@lmlmusic.com)
Lori Donato . . . . .Concerts Division
David Franklin . . . . .Administration, Licensing & Royalties

LOOKOUT! RECORDS

3264 Adeline St.
Berkeley, CA 94703
PHONE 510-450-8310
FAX 510-450-8311
EMAIL . . . . .information@lookoutrecords.com
WEB SITE .www.lookoutrecords.com
DISTRIBUTOR   RED Music Distribution
GENRES   Punk - Rock

Cathy Bauer . . . . .No Title (lucky@lookoutrecords.com)

LABELS

LABELS

LOST HIGHWAY RECORDS
54 Music Square East
Nashville, TN 37203
PHONE 615-524-7500
FAX 615-524-7600
WEB SITE . . . . .www.losthighwayrecords.com
SECOND WEB SITE . . . . .www.umusic.com
DISTRIBUTOR — Universal Music & Video Distribution
ARTIST ROSTER — Ryan Adams - Elvis Costello - Mary Gauthier - Tift Merritt - Sam Roberts - Willie Nelson - Glen Phillips - Lucinda Williams - Lyle Lovett (Curb/Lost Highway) - Johnny Cash (American/Lost Highway) - Jayhawks (American/Lost Highway) - Sam Roberts
GENRES — Country - Roots

Luke Lewis . . . . .Chairman
Andy Nelson . . . . .VP, Marketing & Artist Development
Ray Di Pietro . . . . . . .National Sr. Director, Adult Alternative Promotions
Eric Dout . . . . .Coordinator, A&R
Parker Nusbickel . . . . .Coordinator, Marketing

LOUISIANA RED HOT RECORDS
2001 Gentilly Blvd.
New Orleans, LA 70119-1711
PHONE 504-948-4600
FAX 504-948-4422
EMAIL . . . . .info@louisianaredhot.com
WEB SITE . . . . .www.louisianaredhot.com
LABELS — Louisiana Red Hot - Blue Jay - Black Dog - Kole - Rec'd - Endangered Species - 2EZ
GENRES — Blues - Jazz - New Age - R&B - Roots - World
SUBMISSION POLICY — Accepts finished products of established artists

Harris Rea . . . . .President (harrisr@louisianaredhot.com)
Harris Green Lee Rea IV . .Sales Coordinator (leer@louisianaredhot.com)
Tonia Taffaro . . . . .Art Director/Production Manager (tonia@louisianaredhot.com)

LOVELESS RECORDS
1122 E. Pike St., Ste. 1361
Seattle, WA 98122
PHONE 206-373-4070
FAX 206-373-4035
EMAIL . . . . .pete@lovelessrecords.com
WEB SITE . . . . .www.lovelessrecords.com
DISTRIBUTORS — Allegro Corporation - NAIL Distribution
ARTIST ROSTER — Tom Brosseau - Vendetta Red - Jonny Polonsky - Los Halos - Voyager One - Pris - The Ruby Doe - The Drop - Orbiter - Bundle of Hiss - The Mellors - Tuffy - Man of the Year
GENRES — Rock
SUBMISSION POLICY — Send it, but only if it's good

Pete Nordstrom . . . . .No Title
Erin Kurtz . . . . .No Title
John Richards . . . . .No Title
Eric Richards . . . . .No Title
Kate Weber . . . . .Director, Marketing & Promotions
Amy Bauer . . . . .Marketing Assistant

LOVESLAP RECORDINGS
1177 Polk St., Ste. 304
San Francisco, CA 94109
PHONE 415-929-5237
FAX 718-504-3759
EMAIL . . . . .info@loveslap.com
WEB SITE .www.loveslap.com
DISTRIBUTOR — Studio Distribution
ARTIST ROSTER — Charles Spencer - Goapele - DJ Spinna - Migvel Migs - Julius Papp - Jay-J - David Hurness - Chris Lum

Jesse Singer . . . . .No Title

LOVITT RECORDS
PO Box 100248
Arlington, VA 22041
PHONE 703-824-0510
FAX 703-824-0511
EMAIL . . . . .info@lovitt.com
WEB SITE . . . . .www.lovitt.com
ARTIST ROSTER — The Grey - Denali - Engine Down - Bats & Mice - Decahedron - Del Cielo - Division of Laura Lee - Ben Davis - Pinebender - Supine to Sit - Sleepytime Trio - Four Hundred Years - Rah Bras - The Cassettes - Maximillain Colby
GENRES — Alternative - Rock
COMMENTS — Distributed by Dischord Direct

Brian Lowit . . . . .President
Keeley Davis . . . . .Art
Nathan Tsoi . . . . .Press/Radio

LUAKA BOP
14 E. Fourth St.
New York, NY 10012
PHONE 212-320-8500
WEB SITE .www.luakabop.com
DISTRIBUTOR — EMI Music Marketing
GENRES — World
SUBMISSION POLICY — No unsolicited submissions accepted

David Byrne . . . . .CEO
Yale Evelev . . . . .President
Monica Vasquez . . . . .Label Manager

LYRIC STREET RECORDS

1100 Demonbreun St., Ste. 100
Nashville, TN 37203
PHONE 615-963-4848
FAX 615-963-4846
EMAIL . . . . .webmaster@lyricstreet.com
SECOND EMAIL . . . . .firstname.lastname@disney.com
WEB SITE . . . . .www.lyricstreet.com
DISTRIBUTOR   Universal Music & Video Distribution
ARTIST ROSTER   Rascal Flatts - SHeDAISY - Josh Gracin -
                     Aaron Tippin - Kerry Harvick - Ragsdale
                     - Trent Tomlinson - Sarah Buxton
GENRES   Country

Randy Goodman . . . . .President
Douglas Howard . . . . .Sr. VP, A&R
Kevin Herring . . . . .VP, National Promotion
Dale Turner . . . . .VP, Promotion Administration
Greg McCarn . . . . .VP, Marketing
Renee Leymon . . . . .Sr. Director, Promotion
Kirk Boyer . . . . .Director, A&R
Robin Gordon . . . . .Sr. Manager, A&R Administration
Teresa Russell . . . . .Sr. Manager, Artist & Label Relations
Ashley Heron . . . . .Manager, Marketing
Tonya Stroud . . . . .Coordinator, A&R

MAILBOAT RECORDS

9200 Sunset Blvd., Ste. 530
West Hollywood, CA 90069
PHONE 310-550-5245
FAX 310-550-5246
EMAIL . . . . .info@mailboatrecords.com
WEB SITE . . . . .www.mailboatrecords.com
ARTIST ROSTER   Jimmy Buffett - Boz Scaggs - Dan
                     Fogelberg - Maria McKee - Bret
                     Michaels - Marilyn Scott - Mac McAnally
GENRES   Country - Folk - Pop - Rock

Jimmy Buffett . . . . .Owner
Harold Sulman . . . . .President
Mindy Espy . . . . .Marketing Director

MANHATTAN RECORDS

150 Fifth Ave., 6th Fl.
New York, NY 10011
PHONE 212-786-8600
WEB SITE . . . . .www.manhattanrecords.com
ARTIST ROSTER   Richard Marx - Angela McCluskey - Keri
                     Noble - Low Millions - Raúl Midón
GENRES   Adult Contemporary - Pop - Rock
SUBMISSION POLICY   No unsolicited material accepted

Bruce Lundvall . . . . .CEO, EMI Jazz & Classics
Ian Ralfini . . . . .Sr. VP/General Manager, Manhattan
Kevin Carroll . . . . .Sr. VP, Radio Promotion, EMI Music Collective
Zach Hochkeppel . . . . .VP, Marketing, EMI Jazz & Classics
Dennis Reese . . . . .VP, Pop Promotion, EMI Music Collective
Saul Shapiro .VP, Sales, EMI Jazz & Classics
Josh Gold . . . . .Director, Product Management, EMI Jazz & Classics
Gordon Jee . . . . .Director, Creative, EMI Jazz & Classics
Eli Wolf . . . . .Director, A&R, EMI Jazz & Classics
Sharon Russell . . .Manager, International Marketing, EMI Jazz & Classics

MANIFESTO

740 N. La Brea Ave.
Los Angeles, CA 90038-3339
PHONE 323-954-1555
FAX 323-936-6354
EMAIL . . . . .info@manifesto.com
WEB SITE . . . . .www.manifesto.com
DISTRIBUTOR   Navarre Corporation
ARTIST ROSTER   Dead Kennedys - Cinerama - Tom Waits
                     - Tim Buckley - Lilys - The Wedding
                     Present - Cranes
GENRES   Alternative - Hardcore - Pop - Rock

Evan S. Cohen . . . . .President (ecohen@manifesto.com)
Vanessa Gill . . . . .Product Management

MARSALIS MUSIC

323 Broadway
Cambridge, MA 02139
PHONE 617-354-2736
FAX 617-354-2396
EMAIL . . . . .info@marsalismusic.com
WEB SITE . . . . .www.marsalismusic.com
DISTRIBUTOR   Rounder Records
ARTIST ROSTER   Branford Marsalis - Doug Wamble -
                     Miguel Zenon - Joey Calderazzo
GENRES   Jazz
SUBMISSION POLICY   Copyright material only to A&R

Branford Marsalis . . . . .CEO
Sherry McAdams . . . . .President
Bob Blumenthal . . . . .A&R

MATADOR RECORDS

625 Broadway, 12th Fl.
New York, NY 10012
PHONE 212-995-5882
FAX 212-995-5883
EMAIL . . . . .info@matadorrecords.com
WEB SITE . . . . .www.matadorrecords.com
ARTIST ROSTER   Cat Power - Cornelius - Dead Meadow -
                     Guided by Voices - Interpol - Stephen
                     Malkmus - Matmos - Mission of Burma -
                     Mogwai - A.C. Newman - The New
                     Pornographers - Pavement - Preston
                     School of Industry - Pretty Girls Make
                     Graves - Prosaics - Seachange - M.
                     Ward - Yo La Tengo
GENRES   Alternative

Gerard Cosloy . . . . .Co-President (gerard@matadorrecords.com)
Chris Lombardi . . .Co-President/Owner (lombardi@matadorrecords.com)
Patrick Amory . . . . .General Manager (patrick@matadorrecords.com)
Nils Bernstein . . . . .Director, Publicity (nils@matadorrecords.com)
Rusty Clarke . . . . .Director, National Sales
Lucy Hurst . . . . .Publicist (lucyhurst@beggars.com)
Jesper Eklow . . . . . . .Director, Production (jesper@beggars.com)
Jeremy Goldstein . . . . .Director, Radio Promotion
                     (jeremygoldstein@beggars.com)
Jennifer Lanchart . . . . . . .Film & TV Music (jennlanchart@beggars.com)

LABELS

MAVERICK RECORDING COMPANY

3300 Warner Blvd.
Burbank, CA 91505
PHONE 818-953-4360
EMAIL . . . . .firstname.lastname@maverick.com
WEB SITE . . . . .www.maverick.com
DISTRIBUTOR   WEA Corp.
ARTIST ROSTER   Michelle Branch - Deftones - Iyler Hilton
                     - Lillix - Mest - Alanis Morissette -
                     MoZella - Paul Oakenfold - Prodigy -
                     The Shore - Story of the Year - Tantric -
                     Team Sleep - John Stevens - The
                     Wreckers (Michelle Branch & Jessica
                     Harp) - Goldfinger - Jack's Mannequin -
                     Candice - Stutterfly - Clear Static -
                     Family Force 5
GENRES   All Genres - Pop - Rock
RECENT SOUNDTRACKS   Kill Bill Vols. 1&2 - 50 First Dates - The
                     Matrix: Reloaded - One Tree Hill
SUBMISSION POLICY   Industry referral only; No unsolicited
                     material of any kind

Guy Oseary .Partner/CEO (818-953-4380)
Sara Zambreno . .Executive Coordinator to Guy Oseary (818-953-4362)
Lizabeth Zindel . .Executive Coordinator to Guy Oseary (818-953-4380)
Scott Austin . . . . .A&R (818-953-4370)
Shawn Keohen .A&R (818-953-4366)
Kevin Williamson . . . . .A&R (818-953-4369)
Holly Adams . . . . .Marketing (818-953-4362)
David Grant . . . . .Marketing (818-953-4367)
Robbie Snow . . . . .Marketing (818-953-4363)
Kelly Fogel . . . . .Marketing (818-953-4371)
Jill Augusto . . . . .Marketing (818-953-4368)
Esther Somlo . . . . .Marketing (818-953-4364)
Emily Fife . . . . .New Media (818-953-4378)
Frank Maddocks . . . . .Creative (818-953-4375)
Shane Cosme . . . . .Creative (818-953-4377)
Nick Spanos . . . . .Production (818-953-4376)

MAXJAZZ

115 W. Lockwood Ave.
St. Louis, MO 63119
PHONE 800-875-8331
FAX 314-961-6074
EMAIL . . . . .info@maxjazz.com
WEB SITE . . . . .www.maxjazz.com
DISTRIBUTOR   Ryko Distribution
ARTIST ROSTER   Russell Malone - René Marie - Jeremy
                     Pelt - Carla Cook - Rebecca Martin -
                     Erin Bode - Jessica Williams - Bruce
                     Barth
GENRES   Jazz

Richard McDonnell . . . . .President
Clayton McDonnell . . . . .Executive VP

MCA NASHVILLE

60 Music Square East
Nashville, TN 37203
PHONE 615-524-7500
FAX 615-524-7600
WEB SITE . . . . .www.mca-nashville.com
ARTIST ROSTER   Gary Allan - Vince Gill - Hanna/McEuen
                     - Hot Apple Pie - Reba McEntire -
                     George Strait - Josh Turner - Lee Ann
                     Womack - Trisha Yearwood
GENRES   Country

James Stroud . . . . .Co-Chairman, UMG Nashville
Luke Lewis . . . . .Co-Chairman, UMG Nashville
Bill Catino . . . . .Executive VP, Promotions
Jason Owen . . . . .Sr. VP, Media, Artist Relations & Creative Services
Allison Jones . . . . .VP, A&R
Regina Stephens Stuve . . . . .Director, Artist & Media Relations
Amber Williams . . . . .Director, Artist & Media Relations
Brian Wright . . . . .Director, A&R
Doug Rich . . . . .Manager, A&R Administration
Stephanie Wright . . . . .Manager, A&R Administration

MEMPHIS INTERNATIONAL RECORDS

2240 Union Ave., #39
Memphis, TN 38104
PHONE 901-276-6661
FAX 901-276-5867
EMAIL . . . . .info@memphisinternational.com
WEB SITE . . . . .www.memphisinternational.com
ARTIST ROSTER   Philipp Fankhauser - Louise Hoffsten -
                     The Mighty Echoes - The Red Stick
                     Ramblers - Tracy Nelson - Gene Pistilli
                     the Hoboken Saddle Tramp - The Gypsy
                     Hombres - Harmonica Frank Floyd -
                     Alvin Youngblood Hart - Carla Thomas
LABELS   Memphis International Records -
                     Brooklyn International Records
GENRES   Adult Contemporary - Blues - Country -
                     Folk - Jazz - R&B - Roots

David Less . . . . .Principal
Bob Merlis . . . . .Principal
Jonathan Campbell . . . . .Assistant

MERCURY NASHVILLE

60 Music Square East
Nashville, TN 37203
PHONE 615-524-7500
FAX 615-524-7600
WEB SITE . . . . .www.mercurynashville.com
ARTIST ROSTER   Terri Clark - Billy Currington - Calaisa -
                     Tracy Lawrence - Julie Roberts - Shania
                     Twain - Sugarland
GENRES   Country

James Stroud . . . . .Co-Chairman, UMG Nashville
Luke Lewis . . . . .Co-Chairman, UMG Nashville
Jason Owen . . . . .Sr. VP, Media, Artist Relations & Creative Services
Allison Jones . . . . .VP, A&R
Regina Stephens Stuve . . . . .Director, Artist & Media Relations
Amber Williams . . . . .Director, Artist & Media Relations
Brian Wright . . . . .Director, A&R
Doug Rich . . . . .Manager, A&R Administration
Stephanie Wright . . . . .Manager, A&R Administration

MERGE RECORDS
PO Box 1235
Chapel Hill, NC 27514
PHONE 919-688-9969
FAX 919-688-9970
WEB SITE . . . . .www.mergerecords.com
ARTIST ROSTER   Tenement Halls - Dinosaur Jr - ...And
                         You Will Know Us By The Trail Of Dead
                         - Ashley Stove - Paul Burch - Buzzcocks -
                         The Clean - The Clientele - Crooked
                         Fingers - Destroyer - The Essex Green -
                         Imperial Teen - The Ladybug Transistor -
                         Lambchop - The Magnetic Fields -
                         Neutral Milk Hotel - Portastatic - Radar
                         Bros. - The Rosebuds - Shark Quest -
                         Spaceheads - Spoon - Matt Suggs -
                         Superchunk - Versus - M. Ward - 3Ds -
                         The 6ths - American Music Club - Lou
                         Barlow - The Arcade Fire - Beatnik
                         Filmstars - Breadwinner - Richard
                         Buckner - Butterglory - Camera Obscura
                         - East River Pipe - Matt Elliott - Future
                         Bible Heroes - Ganger - Guv'ner -
                         Annie Hayden - The Karl Hendricks Trio -
                         David Kilgour - The Mad Scene - The
                         Music Tapes - Pipe - Polvo - Pram - The
                         Rock*A*Teens - Seaweed - Spent - Matt
                         Suggs - Superchunk - The Third Eye
                         Foundation
GENRES   Rock

Paul Cardillo . . . . .Film, TV Licensing & Retail
Martin Hall . . . . .National Publicity & Promotions
Christina Rentz . . . . .Regional Publicity & Promotions

MESSENGER RECORDS
PO Box 1607
New York, NY 10113-1607
PHONE 212-675-6164
FAX 212-675-8676
WEB SITE .www.messengerrecords.com
DISTRIBUTOR   RED Music Distribution
ARTIST ROSTER   Chris Whitley - Johnny Society - Dan
                         Bern - Anne McCue
GENRES   Folk - Rock
SUBMISSION POLICY   No unsolicited demos

Brandon Kessler . . . . .President (brandon@messengerrecords.com)

METAL BLADE RECORDS
2828 Cochran St., Ste. 302
Simi Valley, CA 93065
PHONE 805-522-9111
FAX 805-522-9380
EMAIL . . . . .metalblade@metalblade.com
WEB SITE . . . . .www.metalblade.com
DISTRIBUTOR   RED Music Distribution
ARTIST ROSTER   Amon Amarth - Ancient - Armored Saint
                         - As I Lay Dying - Beyond the Embrace -
                         The Black Dahlia Murder - Bolt Thrower
                         - Brainstorm - Cannibal Corpse -
                         Cataract - Cattle Decapitation - The
                         Crown - Demericous - Disillusion -
                         Falconer - Fates Warning - Fleshcrawl -
                         Fragments of Unbecoming - Goatwhore
                         - God Dethroned - Gorerotted - The
                         Heavils - Impious - Into the Moat - King
                         Diamond - King's X - Lizzy Borden - Losa
                         - Mercyful Fate - Neal Morse - The Red
                         Chord - Rival - Shining Fury - Six Feet
                         Under - Starwood - Symphorce -
                         Torchbearer - Unearth - Vader -
                         Vehemence - Vision Divine - Vomitory -
                         Winter Solstice - Yob
GENRES   Hardcore - Metal - Rock
SUBMISSION POLICY   Accepts unsolicited demos

Brian Slagel . . . . .CEO/Chairman
Michael Faley . . . . .President
Tracy Vera . . . . .Sr. VP/General Manager
Brian Ames .VP, Creative Services
Andy Bedrosian .VP, Distribution
Dan Fitzgerald . . . . .VP, Sales & Marketing
Kelli Mallela . . . . .Publicity
Heather Parsons . . . . .Office Manager/Licensing

*METROPOLIS RECORDS
PO Box 54307
Philadelphia, PA 19105
PHONE 610-595-9940
FAX 610-595-9944
EMAIL .label@metropolis-records.com
ARTIST ROSTER   Mindless Self Indulgence - KMFDM -
                         VNV Nation - Covenant - The Birthday
                         Massacre
GENRES   Rock

Jim Smith . . . . .Buying & Import/Export Distribution (610-595-0103,
                              buyer@metropolis-records.com)
Jerry Bennett . . . . .Distribution (610-595-9940,
                              distro1@metropolis-records.com)
Dave Heckman . . . . .Film & Licensing (415-474-1149,
                              daveh@metropolis-records.com)
Shannon Ludwig . . . . .Publicity & Promotions (610-595-0356,
                              promotions@metropolis-records.com)
Jim Sewell . . . .Mail Order (610-595-0429, info@industrial-music.com)

LABELS

MILAN ENTERTAINMENT
3500 W. Olive Ave., Ste. 750
Burbank, CA 91505
PHONE 818-953-7800
FAX 818-953-7801
EMAIL . . . . .firstname.lastname@milanrecords.com
WEB SITE . . . . .www.milanrecords.com
DISTRIBUTOR   WEA Corp.
LABELS   Chicooligan - Milan Records - Jade
                                Records
GENRES   Blues - Electronica - Gospel - Jazz -
                                World
RECENT SOUNDTRACKS   The Island - Millions - Melinda &
                                Melinda - My Summer of Love - March
                                of the Penguins - The Baxter - I Heart
                                Huckabees - Brothers Grimm - Before
                                Sunset - Once Upon a Time in Mexico -
                                Bend It Like Beckham - Talk to Her - City
                                of God - Riding Giants
COMMENTS   Soundtracks, electronic music

Ian Hierons . . . . . . .Sr. VP, Acquisitions (ian.hierons@milanrecords.com)
Russell Aiello . . .VP, Sales & Marketing (russell.aiello@milanrecords.com)
Roya Hekmat . . . . .VP, Business & Legal Affairs
                                (roya.hekmat@milanrecords.com)
Jodi Tack . . . . . . .VP, Production & Design (jodi.tack@milanrecords.com)
Nick Bobetsky . . . . .Director, Special Markets
                                (nick.bobetsky@milanrecords.com)

THE MILITIA GROUP
13892 Harbor Blvd., Ste. 4-A
Garden Grove, CA 92843
PHONE 714-554-4477
FAX 714-554-6152
EMAIL . . . . .contact@themilitiagroup.com
WEB SITE . . . . .www.themilitiagroup.com
DISTRIBUTOR   RED Music Distribution
ARTIST ROSTER   Umbrellas - The Rocket Summer -
                                Copeland - Brandtson - Lovedrug -
                                Denison Witmer - Cartel - The Jealous
                                Sound - Man Alive - Let Go - fielding -
                                The Panic Division
GENRES   Alternative - Folk - Pop - Punk - Rock
SUBMISSION POLICY   Open

Rory Christopher Felton . . . . .Owner
Chad Pearson . . . . .Owner
Chris Donohue . . . . .Label Manager
Paul Mazier . . . . .Publicity/Advertising/Marketing
Eugene Kim . . . . .Tour Promotions
Mason Long . . . . .Street Team/New Media
Mikey Bernard . . . . .Office Manager
Randall Jenkins . . . . .Art Director
Wyatt Miller . . . . .Sales Manager

MIMICRY RECORDINGS
PO Box 229
Felton, CA 95018
EMAIL . . . . .wom@webofmimicry.com
WEB SITE . . . . .www.webofmimicry.com
DISTRIBUTOR   Revolver USA Distribution
ARTIST ROSTER   Secret Chiefs 3 - Sleepytime Gorilla
                                Museum - Asva - Estradasphere -
                                Brazzaville - Dengue Fever - The Tuna
                                Helpers - Faxed Head - Danubius

Trey Spruance . . . . .President
Timb Harris . . . . .Mailroom

MINTY FRESH RECORDS
PO Box 577400
Chicago, IL 60657-7400
PHONE 773-665-0289
FAX 773-665-0215
EMAIL . . . . .info@mintyfresh.com
WEB SITE . . . . .www.mintyfresh.com
SECOND WEB SITE . . . . .www.minifresh.com
DISTRIBUTOR   Alternative Distribution Alliance (ADA)
ARTIST ROSTER   The Living Blue - Husky Rescue - Viva
                                Voce - Komeda - Tahiti 80 - Ralph's
                                World - Papas Fritas - The Waterboys -
                                Ivy
LABELS   Minty Fresh - Mini Fresh
GENRES   Adult Contemporary - Alternative - Rock
SUBMISSION POLICY   Responds to submissions only if interest-
                                ed
COMMENTS   Mini Fresh Productions: Video production
                                company putting out music/educational
                                videos

Jim Powers . . . . .President (jpmf@mintyfresh.com)
Anthony Musiala . . . . .VP, A&R (musiala@mintyfresh.com)

*MORAINE MUSIC GROUP
437 E. Iris Dr.
Nashville, TN 37204
PHONE 615-383-0400
FAX 615-383-2375
WEB SITE . . . . .www.morainemusic.com
GENRES   Country

Nina Rossman . . . . .National Director, Promotion
John Vick . . . . .Director, Artist Development

MRK RECORDS
701 Seventh Ave., 6th Fl.
New York, NY 10036-1505
PHONE 212-575-4660
FAX 212-575-4799
EMAIL . . . . .kamen@kamen.com
WEB SITE . . . . .www.mrkrecords.com
GENRES   Electronica - Pop
COMMENTS   Producer; Publisher;
                                Licensing/Clearance; Recording
                                Studio/Soundstage; Podcasting

Roy Kamen . . . . .President (roy@kamen.com)
Marina Kamen . . . . .Creative Director (marina@kamen.com)

MSC MUSIC ENTERTAINMENT
6430 Sunset Blvd., Ste. 1506
Hollywood, CA 90028
PHONE 323-769-8340
FAX 323-769-8350
EMAIL . . . . .webmaster@mscmusic.com
WEB SITE . . . . .www.mscmusic.com
DISTRIBUTOR   RED Music Distribution
ARTIST ROSTER   Tech N9ne - Skatterman & Snug Brim -
                                Kutt Calhoun - Project Deadman - Los
                                Temerarios
GENRES   Latin - Rap/Hip-Hop

Mark Cerami . . . . .CEO
Talin Kouyoumdjian . . . . .Sr. VP, Production & Operations
Manny Arredando . . . . .Marketing Director
Jennifer Castille . . . . .Sr. Financial Analyst

MUGHAL ENTERTAINMENT GROUP, INC.
4325 Steeles Ave. West, Ste. 913
North York, ON M3N 1V7 Canada
PHONE 416-885-5656
FAX 905-738-8901
EMAIL . . . . .info@mughalentertainment.com
SECOND EMAIL . . . . .demos@mughalentertainment.com
WEB SITE . . . . .www.mughalentertainment.com
RECENT RELEASES | The Future - My Word
GENRES | R&B - Rap/Hip-Hop
SUBMISSION POLICY | Accepts unsolicited material
COMMENTS | Production company and music producer

Nadeem Mughal . . . . .CEO
N. Shandell . . . . .VP, Marketing & Operations
JoJo Brim . . . . .Sr. Director, A&R
Zee Aslam . . . . .Director, Marketing
Pak Man . . . . .A&R
Muhammad Javed . . . . .Sr. Audio Engineer
Len Gaik . . . . .Corporate Legal Affairs
Tie Aslam . . . . .Head, Security

MUSCLETONE RECORDS
842 N. Fairfax Ave.
Los Angeles, CA 90046
PHONE 323-852-0457
FAX 323-651-2946
EMAIL . . . . .muscletone@muscletonerecords.com
WEB SITE . . . . .www.muscletonerecords.com
DISTRIBUTOR | Image Entertainment, Inc.
ARTIST ROSTER | Wayne Kramer - Cobra Verde - Mother Superior - Mad for the Racket - MC5 - DKT/MC5
GENRES | Rock
SUBMISSION POLICY | No unsolicited demos accepted

Wayne Kramer . . . . .Partner
Margaret Saadi Kramer . . . . .Partner

MUSIC FOR LITTLE PEOPLE
PO Box 1460
Redway, CA 95560
PHONE 800-346-4445
FAX 707-923-3241
WEB SITE . . . . .www.mflp.com
GENRES | Children's

Sheron Sherman . . . . .VP, Sales/COO (sheron@mflp.com)
Marianne McCormick . . . . .VP, Operations (marianne@mflp.com)
Aimee Frank . .Alternative Marketing & Sales (aimeefrank@earthlink.net)
Gina Guinn .Accounting (gina@mflp.com)

MUTE RECORDS
140 W. 22nd St., Ste. 10A
New York, NY 10011
PHONE 212-255-7670
FAX 212-255-6056
EMAIL . . . . .mute@mute.com
WEB SITE . . . . .www.mute.com
DISTRIBUTOR | Caroline Distribution
ARTIST ROSTER | M83 - Diamonda - Laibach - Goldfrapp - Erasure - Client
GENRES | Alternative - Electronica
SUBMISSION POLICY | No unsolicited material

Mark Fotiadis . . . . .General Manager (x234)
Nicole Blonder . . . . .Director, Marketing (x235)
Susan McDonald . . . . .Director, Creative Services (x238)
Roberta Moore . . . . .Director, Publicity (x241)
Adrian Janssens . . . . .Operations (x233)
Ellena Osis . . . . .Manager, Promotion (x230)

MY PAL GOD RECORDS
47 Hardy Dr.
Princeton, NJ 08540
PHONE 609-924-0244
FAX 609-924-6459
EMAIL . . . . .info@mypalgodrecords.com
WEB SITE . . . . .www.mypalgodrecords.com
DISTRIBUTOR | Southern Records, Inc.
GENRES | Alternative - Folk - Hardcore - Metal - Punk - Rock

Jon Solomon . . . . .Owner

NAKED JAIN RECORDS
1301 N. Palm Canyon Dr., Ste. 208
Palm Springs, CA 92262-4425
PHONE 760-325-8663/866-597-6787
FAX 760-320-4305
EMAIL . . . . .info@nakedjainrecords.com
WEB SITE . . . . .www.nakedjainrecords.com
ARTIST ROSTER | Lewinski - Lung Cookie - Furious IV - Fallback - The Strap-Ons
GENRES | Alternative - Pop - Punk

Dey Martin . . . . .President
Dena Banes . . . . .Director, A&R
Christina Putnam . . . . .Director, A&R

NARADA PRODUCTIONS, INC.
4650 N. Port Washington Rd.
Milwaukee, WI 53212
PHONE 414-961-8350
FAX 414-961-8351
EMAIL . . . . .friends@narada.com
WEB SITE . . . . .www.narada.com
SECOND WEB SITE . . . . .www.naradajazz.com
DISTRIBUTOR   Music Design
GENRES   Jazz - New Age - World
COMMENTS   Electronica - Americana - Celtic

Steve Pedo . . . . .CFO
David Neidhart . . . . .Sr. VP, Sales & Marketing
Anne Aufderheide .VP, Operations
Greg Jansen . . . . .VP, Business/Legal Affairs
Jill Weindorf . . . . .Director, Media Relations
Michael Bailey . . . . .A&R Representative
Dan Harjung .A&R Representative
Rich Denhart . . . . .A&R Director

NARNACK RECORDS
381 Broadway, 4th Fl., #3
New York, NY 10013
PHONE 212-871-6661
FAX 212-871-6668
EMAIL . . . . .camille@narnackrecords.com
SECOND EMAIL . . . . .info@narnackrecords.com
WEB SITE . . . . .www.narnackrecords.com
DISTRIBUTOR   Caroline Distribution
ARTIST ROSTER   Lee "Scratch" Perry - Cairo Gang - The
                     Fall - Friends of Dean Martinez - Guitar
                     Wolf - Coachwhips - Langhorne Slim -
                     Tyondai Braxton - Parts & Labor - X27 -
                     Lil Pocketknife - Vaz - OCS - Aa
GENRES   Alternative - Rock
SUBMISSION POLICY   Accepts unsolicited material

Shahin Ewalt . . . . .Owner, President, A&R (shahin@narnackrecords.com)
Camille Sciara . . . . . .General Manager (camille@narnackrecords.com)
Billy Nord . . . . .Press (billy@narnackrecords.com)

NAXOS
416 Mary Lindsay Polk Dr., Ste 509
Franklin, TN 37067
PHONE 615-771-9393
FAX 615-771-6747 x11
EMAIL . . . . .jbaker@naxosusa.com
SECOND EMAIL . . . . .llange@naxosusa.com
WEB SITE . . . . .www.naxos.com
LABELS   Distributes: CBC - CPO - Dacapo -
                     Analekta - Arthouse - BBC/Opusarte -
                     TDK - Naive - Naxos
GENRES   Classical - Jazz - World
SUBMISSION POLICY   Email proposals

Jim Selby . . . . .General Manager, Operations
Justyn Baker . . . . .Licensing Manager
Mark Berry . . . . .Publicity & Promotions
Peter Wolff . . . . .Sales

NERVOUS RECORDS NYC
575 Lexington Ave., Ste. 2840
New York, NY 10022
PHONE 212-410-7567
FAX 212-888-3182
EMAIL .info@nervousnyc.com
WEB SITE .www.nervousnyc.com
GENRES   Electronica - Rap/Hip-Hop
SUBMISSION POLICY   Accepts submissions by mail

Michael Weiss . . . . .President
Sam Weiss . . . . .VP, Licensing
Kasem Coleman . . . . .VP
Kevin Williams . . . . .VP, A&R
Julie Weiss .Creative Director
Jason Hayer . . . . .Publicity
Stewart Upchurch . . . . .Retail Promotions
Linda Williams . . . . .Office Manager
Michelle Verley . . . . .Bookkeeper

NETTWERK AMERICA
8730 Wilshire Blvd., Ste. 304
Beverly Hills, CA 90211-2710
PHONE 310-855-0643/212-629-0004
FAX 310-855-0658/212-629-9079
EMAIL . . . . .info@nettwerk.com
WEB SITE . . . . .www.nettwerk.com
DISTRIBUTOR   EMI Music Marketing
ARTIST ROSTER   See Web site for full list
GENRES   All Genres
COMMENTS   East Coast office: 345 Seventh Ave.,
                     24th Fl., New York, NY 1000; Canada
                     office: 1650 W. Second Ave., Vancouver,
                     BC V6J 4R3 Canada

Brent Muhle . . . . .Operations
Maria Alonte McCoy . . . . .VP, Film & TV Soundtracks
Rae Cline .Head, Promotion
John Meadows .Head, Sales
Ianthe Zevos . . . . .Director, Production & Creative
Jenny Oppenheimer . . . . .Product Manager
Bernadette Walsh . . . . .Product Manager
David Nedorezov . . . . .Staff Accountant

NEURODISC RECORDS
3801 N. University Dr., Ste. 403
Ft. Lauderdale, FL 33351
PHONE 954-572-0289
FAX 954-572-2874
EMAIL . . . . .info@neurodisc.com
WEB SITE . . . . .www.neurodisc.com
DISTRIBUTOR   Navarre Corporation
ARTIST ROSTER   Ryan Farish - Amethystium - Etro Anime -
                     Peplab - Tastexperience - Eric Hanser -
                     Nu Sound - Bass Hit
GENRES   Classical - Electronica - New Age -
                     Urban - World
SUBMISSION POLICY   Accepts unsolicited demos

Tom O'Keefe . . . . .President, A&R
Troy Kelley . . . . .Office Manager, A&R

NEW LINE RECORDS
116 N. Robertson Blvd., Ste. 705
Los Angeles, CA 90048
PHONE 310-967-6953
EMAIL . . . . .newlinerecords@newline.com
WEB SITE . . . . .www.newlinerecords.com
DISTRIBUTOR   Alternative Distribution Alliance (ADA)
ARTIST ROSTER   The Sounds - Robbers on High Street -
                     The Sights - Paris, Texas
LABELS   Scratchie Records
GENRES   All Genres
RECENT SOUNDTRACKS   Wedding Crashers - The Notebook -
                     Monster-in-Law - Elf - Secondhand Lions
                     - About Schmidt

Jason Linn . . . . .Executive VP, New Line Records (310-967-6486)
Kevin Kertes . . . . .VP, Promotions (310-967-6569, radio@newline.com)
Genevieve Morris . . . . .VP, Sales (310-967-6487)
Pete Axelrad . . . . .Manager, Finance (310-967-6549)
Sandeep Sriram .No Title (310-967-6466)
Karin Sung . . . . .No Title (310-967-6414)

NEW WEST RECORDS LLC
9215 Olympic Blvd.
Beverly Hills, CA 90212
PHONE .310-246-5766/512-472-4200
FAX 310-246-5767/512-472-0900
EMAIL . . . . .info@newwestrecords.com
WEB SITE .www.newwestrecords.com
DISTRIBUTOR   RED Music Distribution
ARTIST ROSTER   The Flatlanders - Dwight Yoakam -
                     Drive-By Truckers - Old 97's - Buddy &
                     Julie Miller - Delbert McClinton - Tim
                     Easton - Chuck Prophet - Randall
                     Bramblett - Stephen Bruton - Vic
                     Chesnutt - Slobberbone - John Hiatt -
                     Sarah Lee Guthrie & Johnny Irion - Alice
                     Cooper - Nic Armstrong & the Thieves -
                     Patterson Hood - Ben Lee
GENRES   Alternative - Blues - Country - Folk -
                     Rock - Roots
SUBMISSION POLICY   Currently not accepting unsolicited mate-
                     rial
COMMENTS   Texas office: 608 W. Monroe St., Ste. C
                     Austin, TX 78704

Cameron Strang .President (310-246-5766)
Jay Woods . . . . . . .Sr. VP, Sales (Austin) (jwoods@newwestrecords.com)
Peter Jesperson .VP, A&R (310-246-5766)
Kat Delaney . . . . .Director
Gary Briggs . . . . .A&R
Jeff Cook . . . . .Promotion
Steve Nice . . . . .Promotion
Steve Rosenblatt . . . . .Marketing Director
Traci Thomas . . . . .Media Relations
Clare Surgeson . . . . .Office Manager/Promotions (Austin)
Mary Jurey . . . . . .Office Manager/Manufacturing/International Business
J.R. Wilson . . . . .Executive Assistant
Chris Fagot . . . . .New Media
George Fontaine Jr. . . . . .Marketing Assistant/Licensing
Jacob Green .Shipping/Recieving (Austin)

NITRO RECORDS
7071 Warner Ave., Ste. F736
Huntington Beach, CA 92647
PHONE 714-842-8897
FAX 714-842-8609
EMAIL . . . . .nitrorec@nitrorecords.com
WEB SITE . . . . .www.nitrorecords.com
DISTRIBUTOR   Fontana Distribution
ARTIST ROSTER   Rufio - The Aquabats - A Wilhelm
                     Scream - The Start - Don't Look Down -
                     Original Sinners - The Letters Organize -
                     Crime in Stereo - No Trigger - Bullet
                     Train to Vegas - Enemy You
GENRES   Punk - Rock
SUBMISSION POLICY   Accepts CDs addressed to Demo Man

Dexter Holland . . . . .Owner
Brad Pollack . . . . .General Manager
Mitch Townsend . . . . .A&R
Sean Ziebarth . . . . .A&R/Radio
Chris Fenn . . . . .Production
Jerod Gunsberg . . . . .Head, Sales & Marketing
Dave Reece . . . . .Accounts Payable
Lexie Weber . . . . .Publicity

NOISE FACTORY RECORDS
675 Annette St., Ste. 001
Toronto, ON M6S 2C9 Canada
PHONE 416-761-0099
FAX 416-907-5451
EMAIL .info@noisefactoryrecords.com
WEB SITE . . . . .www.noisefactoryrecords.com
DISTRIBUTOR   Carrot Top Distribution, Ltd.
ARTIST ROSTER   K.C. Accidental - Sparrow Orange - V/A
                     Beautiful Noise - Beef Terminal - Broken
                     Social Scene - Naw - Tinkertoy - Hexes
                     & Ohs - Nybbl
SUBMISSION POLICY   Accepts demos

Joe English . . . . .Owner (joe@noisefactoryrecords.com)
Sean English . . . . .A&R (sean@noisefactoryrecords.com)
Zenia Horoszko . . . . .Marketing (zenia@noisefactoryrecords.com)

NONESUCH RECORDS
1290 Avenue of the Americas, 24th Fl.
New York, NY 10104
PHONE 212-707-2900
FAX 212-707-3205
EMAIL . . . . .info@nonesuch.com
SECOND EMAIL . . . . .firstname.lastname@nonesuch.com
WEB SITE . . . . .www.nonesuch.com
DISTRIBUTOR   WEA Corp.
ARTIST ROSTER   John Adams - Laurie Anderson - Buena
                     Vista Social Club - David Byrne - Ry
                     Cooder & Manuel Galbán - Bill Frisell -
                     Gipsy Kings - Philip Glass - Richard
                     Goode - Michael Gordon - Adam
                     Guettel - Emmylou Harris - Gidon
                     Kremer - k.d. lang - Lorraine Hunt
                     Lieberson - Kronos Quartet - The
                     Magnetic Fields - Audra McDonald -
                     Brad Mehldau - Joni Mitchell - Youssou
                     N'Dour - Randy Newman - Mandy
                     Patinkin - Sam Phillips - Omara
                     Portuondo - Orchestra Baobab - Steve
                     Reich - Stephen Sondheim - Rokia
                     Terrace - Dawn Upshaw - Laura Veirs -
                     Caetano Veloso - Wilco - Brian Wilson
GENRES   Classical - Jazz - Pop - Rock - World

Robert Hurwitz . . . . .President (212-707-2901)
David Bither . . . . .Sr. VP (212-707-2920)
Peter Clancy . . . . .VP, Associated Labels
Melissa Cusick . . . . .Director, Publicity
Josh Berman .Marketing Coordinator

NORTH STAR MUSIC
22 London St.
East Greenwich, RI 02818
PHONE 800-346-2706
FAX 401-886-8880/401-886-8888
EMAIL . . . . .info@northstarmusic.com
WEB SITE . . . . .www.northstarmusic.com
DISTRIBUTOR   Goldenrod Music, Inc.
ARTIST ROSTER   David Osborne - Bruce Abbott & the
                          North Star Jazz Ensemble - Robin
                          Spielberg - David Tolk - Cheryl Wheeler
                          - Dennis Hysom - Emilio Kauderer -
                          Calido - Bruce Foulke - Steve Schuch &
                          the Night Heron Consort - Peter Calo -
                          Judith Lynn Stillman
GENRES   Christian - Classical - Folk - Jazz - World
SUBMISSION POLICY   Email for permission to send CD demo
                          package
COMMENTS   Mostly instrumental; Concentrates on the
                          gift store/bookstore market

Richard R. Waterman . . . . .President
Susan Waterman . . . . .Executive VP, A&R/Promotions
Paul Mason . . . . .VP, Music Licensing & Private Label
Jean Robinson . . . . .Sales Manager

NORTHERNBLUES MUSIC INC.
225 Sterling Rd., Unit 19
Toronto, ON M6R 2B2 Canada
PHONE .416-536-4892/866-540-0003
FAX 416-536-1494
EMAIL . . . . .info@northernblues.com
WEB SITE . . . . .www.northernblues.com
DISTRIBUTOR   Big Daddy Music Distribution
ARTIST ROSTER   Carlos del Junco - Eddie Turner - Chris
                          Beard - Mem Shannon - Douc Cox &
                          Sam Hurrie - Watermelon Slim - Janiva
                          Magness - Dan Treanor & Frankie Lee -
                          Kevin Breit - Paul Reddick - Taxi Chain -
                          Glamour Puss - Otis Taylor - Harry Manx
                          - Toni Lynn Washington - David Jacobs-
                          Strain - James Cohen - JW Jones Blues
                          Band - Rita Chiarelli - NB Gospel
                          Allstars
GENRES   Blues - Gospel - World
RECENT SOUNDTRACKS   The Badge - Mail Order Bride

Fred Litwin . . . . .President
Pamela Brennan . . . . .General Manager

NOT LAME RECORDING COMPANY
PO Box 2266
Fort Collins, CO 80522
PHONE 970-407-0250
FAX 970-407-0256
EMAIL . . . . .popmusic@notlame.com
WEB SITE . . . . .www.notlame.com
GENRES   Rock

Bruce Brodeen . . . . .Founder
Ryan Gaudie . . . . .No Title
Marlene Palumbo . . . . .No Title

NUCLEAR BLAST AMERICA
2323 W. El Segundo Blvd.
Hawthorno, CA 90250
PHONE 323-418-1400
FAX 323-418-0118
EMAIL .mail@nuclearblastusa.com
SECOND EMAIL . . . . .name@nuclearblastusa.com
DISTRIBUTOR   Caroline Distribution
ARTIST ROSTER   Soilwork - In Flames - Hammerfall -
                          Meshuggah - Dimmu Borgir - Death
                          Angel - Exodus - Edguy
GENRES   Metal - Rock
SUBMISSION POLICY   Listens to mailed demos on cassette or
                          CD; Will contact if interested

Marco Barbieri . . . . .GM (x113)
Gerardo Martinez . . . . .Product Manager (x136)
Hannah Raymond .Publicity (x139)
Andrew Sample . . . . .Director, Radio Promotions (x112)
Steve Aschenbrenner . . . . . . .Manager, Sales & Distribution (x106)
Kurt Briggs .Radio Promotions (x105)
Loana Valencia . . . . .Publicity (x124)

NYC/EXIT NINE
PO Box 230877
New York, NY 10023-0877
PHONE 212-496-1625
FAX 212-496-1608
EMAIL . . . . .mmvibe@aol.com
SECOND EMAIL . . . . .info@nycrecords.com
WEB SITE . . . . .www.nycrecords.com
SECOND WEB SITE . . . . .www.deecarstensen.com
LABELS   NYC Records Inc. - Exit Nine Records
GENRES   Folk - Jazz
RECENT SOUNDTRACKS   Beautiful - Goodbye Girl

Michael Mainieri . . . . .President
Steve White . . . . .CFO

OCTONE RECORDS
560 Broadway, Ste. 500
New York, NY 10012
PHONE 646-613-0200
FAX 646-613-9096
EMAIL . . . . .info@octonerecords.com
WEB SITE . . . . .www.octonerecords.com
DISTRIBUTOR   Sony BMG Sales Enterprise
ARTIST ROSTER   Maroon 5 - Michael Tolcher - Flyleaf -
                          Dropping Daylight - As Fast As
GENRES   Alternative - Pop - Rock

James Diener .President (646-840-5604)
David Boxenbaum . . . . . . .General Manager (box@octonerecords.com)
Ben Berkman . . . . .Executive VP (bberkman@octonerecords.com)
Yu-Ting Lin . . . . .Label Manager

LABELS

OGLIO ENTERTAINMENT
PO Box 404
Redondo Beach, CA 90277
PHONE 310-791-8600
FAX 310-791-8670
EMAIL . . . . .getinfo4@oglio.com
WEB SITE . . . . .www.oglio.com
DISTRIBUTOR   Alternative Distribution Alliance (ADA)
LABELS   Oglio Records - Glue Factory Records -
                         DMAFT Records
GENRES   Alternative - Electronica - Rock
SUBMISSION POLICY   Unsolicited materials not accepted

Carl Caprioglio . . . . .Owner

OH BOY RECORDS
33 Music Square West, Ste. 102B
Nashville, TN 37203
PHONE 615-742-1250
FAX 615-742-1360
EMAIL . . . . .ohboy@ohboy.com
WEB SITE . . . . .www.ohboy.com
DISTRIBUTOR   Ryko Distribution
ARTIST ROSTER   John Prine - Kris Kristofferson - Shawn
                         Camp - Slick Ballinger - Dan Reeder
LABELS   Oh Boy - Red Pajamas - Blue Plate
GENRES   Folk - Roots
SUBMISSION POLICY   Call for permission to submit

Al Bunetta . . . . .President
Josh Preston . . . . .Director, Business & Legal Affairs
Doug Johnson . . . . .Accounting
Josh Swann . . . . .Assistant to Al Bunetta

OM RECORDS
665 Third St., Ste. 425
San Francisco, CA 94107
PHONE 415-904-1800
FAX 415-904-1807
WEB SITE . . . . .www.om-records.com
ARTIST ROSTER   Mark Farina - Kaskade - Marques Wyatt
                         - Afro Mysik - King Kooba - Rithma - J
                         Boogie - People Under the Stairs -
                         Colette - JT Donaldson & Land Desardi -
                         Colossus - Miguel Migs - Greenskeepers
                         - Fred Everything - DJ Sneak - King Britt
                         - Groove Junkies
GENRES   Electronica - Jazz - World

John Cornett . . . . .Commercial Licensing & Digital Distribution
                         (john@om-records.com)
Ramiro Garcia . . . . . .Compilation Licensing (ramiro@om-records.com)
Gunnar Hissam . . . . .Press & Advertising (gunnar@om-records.com)

OMNITONE
98 Fourth St., Ste. 211
Brooklyn, NY 11231-4821
PHONE 718-622-1989
FAX 718-504-3645
EMAIL . . . . .jazz@omnitone.com
WEB SITE . . . . .www.omnitone.com
DISTRIBUTOR   Allegro Corporation
LABELS   OmniTone - ToneScience - Songlines -
                         Love Slave
GENRES   Jazz
SUBMISSION POLICY   Unsolicited submissions must include full
                         contact information; Will contact submit-
                         ter if interested

Frank Tafuri . . . . .President (frank@omnitone.com)
Alicia Krueger . . . . . .Administrative Coordinator (alicia@omnitone.com)

ONE LITTLE INDIAN RECORDS US
119 W. 23rd St.
New York, NY 10011
PHONE 212-206-1233
FAX 212-206-1375
EMAIL . . . . .info@onelittleindian-us.com
WEB SITE . . . . .www.onelittleindian-us.com
DISTRIBUTOR   Navarre Corporation
ARTIST ROSTER   Björk - Sigur Rós - The Twilight Singers -
                         Lloyd Cole
GENRES   All Genres
RECENT SOUNDTRACKS   Chasing Dora - One Last Thing
SUBMISSION POLICY   Accepts unsolicited submissions

Jennifer George . . . . .No Title
Kevin King . . . . .No Title
Celia Hirschman . . . . .Directing Manager, North America

*OPEN ROAD RECORDINGS
c/o Maplecore
30 St. Clair West, Unit 103
Toronto, ON M4V 3A1 Canada
PHONE 416-961-1040
FAX 416-343-9986
EMAIL . . . . .ron.kitchener@openroadrecordings.com
WEB SITE . . . . .www.openroadrecordings.com
DISTRIBUTOR   Universal Music Canada
ARTIST ROSTER   Jason McCoy - Dac Walker - Road
                         Hammers
GENRES   Country

Ron Kitchener . . . . .Label Director

OR MUSIC
37 W. 17th St., Ste. 5W
New York, NY 10011
PHONE 212-675-8200
FAX 212-675-8222
EMAIL . . . . .info@ormusic.com
WEB SITE . . . . .www.ormusic.com
DISTRIBUTOR   RED Music Distribution
ARTIST ROSTER   Pure Reason Revolution - Matisyahu -
                         Los Lonely Boys - John Cale - Particle -
                         Pitty Sing - Adam Richman - Phil Roy
GENRES   All Genres
SUBMISSION POLICY   See Web site

Larry Miller . . . . .CEO
Michael Caplan . . . . .President
Dan Mackta .VP/General Manager
Angelo Montrone . . . . .Director, A&R

ORANGE PEAL RECORDS, INC.
12 S. First St., Ste. 318
San Jose, CA 95113
PHONE 408-998-1630
FAX 408-998-1633
EMAIL . . . . .info@orangepeal.com
WEB SITE . . . . .www.orangepeal.com
SUBMISSION POLICY   Accepts unsolicited demos Attn: A&R

Robert J. Trisler . . . . .CEO/President
Joe Eick . . . . .Director, Operations
Glen Schwartz . . . . .A&R
Curtis Smith . . . . .Publicity
Eddie Echols Jr. . . . . .Webmaster
Nick Schuneman . . . . .Sales & Distribution

LABELS

ORANGE RECORDINGS
801 S. Wells St., #401
Chicago, IL 60607
FAX 312-922-2884
EMAIL . . . . .info@orangerecordings.com
WEB SITE .www.orangerecordings.com

DISTRIBUTORS	Allegro Corporation - Cargo Music, Inc. - Carrot Top Distribution, Ltd. - NAIL Distribution
ARTIST ROSTER	White Hassle - The Mother Hips - Ultrababyfat - Cash Audio - The Drapes - The Peelers
GENRES	Alternative - Pop - Punk - Rock
SUBMISSION POLICY	Email request for shipping address and submission guidelines
COMMENTS	Also distributed by eMusic, iTunes and DRA

Ron Sievers . . . . .President
Joe Muran . . . . .VP
Valerie Aiello . . . . .Publicity

BARBARA ORBISON PRODUCTIONS
1625 Broadway, Ste. 200
Nashville, TN 37203-3137
PHONE 615-242-4201
FAX 615-242-0942
EMAIL . . . . .info@orbison.com
WEB SITE . . . . .www.orbison.com

GENRES	Blues - Country - Pop - R&B - Rock - Roots
RECENT SOUNDTRACKS	Taken
COMMENTS	Publisher

Barbara Orbison . . . . .President

PALM PICTURES
76 9th Ave., Ste. 1110
New York, NY 10011
PHONE 212-320-3600
FAX 212-320-3609
WEB SITE . . . . .www.palmpictures.com

Chris Blackwell . . . . .Chairman
Steven Lehrhoff . . . . .President
Ramon Villa . . . . .CFO
Jake Hurn . . . . .Director, A&R

PALMETTO RECORDS, INC.
443 Greenwich St., 6th Fl.
New York, NY 10013
PHONE 212-274-1500
FAX 212-334-4630
EMAIL . . . . .info@palmetto-records.com
WEB SITE .www.palmetto-records.com

SUBMISSION POLICY	No unsolicited material

Matt Balitsaris . . . . .President
Pat Rustici . . . .Executive VP/General Manager (pat.palmetto@thorn.net)
Terry Coen . . . . .VP, Promotion (terry.palmetto@thorn.net)
Meg Cortright . . .Director, Retail & Marketing (meg.palmetto@thorn.net)

PANDISC/STREETBEAT
15982 NW 48th Ave.
Miami, FL 33014
PHONE 305-557-1914
FAX 305-557-9262
EMAIL . . . . .bocrane@pandisc.com
WEB SITE . . . . .www.pandisc.com

DISTRIBUTOR	KOCH Entertainment Distribution
LABELS	Pandisc - Streetbeat
GENRES	Alternative - Electronica - Jazz - Rap/Hip-Hop
SUBMISSION POLICY	Submissions welcome
COMMENTS	Online Distributor; Publisher: Whooping Crane Music (BMI)

Bo Crane . . . . .President (x128, bocrane@pandisc.com)
Beth Sereni . . . . .Label Manager (x125, beth@pandisc.com)
Sheldon Goldberg . . . . .Business Affairs (x132, goldberg@pandisc.com)
Stacey Taylor . . . . .Sales & Marketing (x131, stacey@pandisc.com)

PARAGON SOUNDTRACKS
4111 W. Alameda Ave., Ste. 501
Burbank, CA 91505
PHONE 818-972-1112
FAX 818-972-9011

DISTRIBUTOR	Universal Music & Video Distribution
LABELS	Bungalo Records
GENRES	Rap/Hip-Hop - Urban
RECENT SOUNDTRACKS	My Baby's Daddy (Miramax)
SUBMISSION POLICY	No unsolicited material accepted
COMMENTS	An exclusively urban soundtrack label

Art Ford . . . . .President/Owner
Brooke Lizotte . . . . .VP
Robyn Haizlip . . . . .Office Manager
Lachlan McLean . . . . .Online Catalog Manager

PARASOL
303 W. Griggs St.
Urbana, IL 61801
PHONE 217-344-8609
FAX 217-344-8652
EMAIL . . . . .promo@parasol.com
WEB SITE . . . . .www.parasol.com

DISTRIBUTOR	Redeye Distribution
ARTIST ROSTER	Jose Gonzalez - Kevin Tihista's Red Terror - Moonbabies - Bettie Serveert
LABELS	Mud - Spur - Hidden Agenda - Reaction
GENRES	Alternative - Pop - Rock - Roots

Geoff Merritt . . . . .Owner
Jim Kelly . . . . .A&R
Michael Roux . . . . .A&R

PARLIAMENT
449 N. Vista St.
Los Angeles, CA 90036-5742
PHONE 818-362-9853
FAX 323-653-7670
EMAIL . . . . .parlirec@aol.com
WEB SITE . . . . .www.parliamentrecords.com
ARTIST ROSTER   Jewel With Love - E'Morey - Tré - Sister
                       Maxine West - Chosen Gospel Recovery
                       - Ruby Hayes - Winds of Faith - Rapture
                       7 - Wisdom Gospel Singers - Dean
                       Givens - Kenneth Williams - Dave Shirley
                       - Lil Winnie - Kre-Shen-Do - Bishop Joe
                       Simon - The Co.Mission - Rain
LABELS   Parliament - Princess House
GENRES   Gospel - Pop - R&B - Rap/Hip-Hop -
                       Urban
SUBMISSION POLICY   Does not respond to demos unless there
                       is interest; Prefers CD; Include SASE to
                       have material returned; Track producers
                       may submit their productions

Ben Weisman . . . . .President
Jewel Rowe . . . . .Director, Gospel Music A&R

PEAK RECORDS
100 N. Crescent Dr., Ste. 275
Beverly Hills, CA 90210
PHONE 310-385-4040
FAX 310-385-4050
EMAIL . . . . .peakrecords@aol.com
WEB SITE . . . . .www.peakrecords.com
DISTRIBUTOR   Concord Records
ARTIST ROSTER   Latoya London - Gerald Albright - Lee
                      Ritenour - The Rippingtons feat. Russ
                      Freeman - Regina Belle - Cassandra
                      Reed - Eric Marienthal - Paul Taylor -
                      O'2L - The House of Urban Grooves -
                      David Pack - David Benoit - The Braxton
                      Brothers
GENRES   Jazz - Latin - Pop - R&B - Urban
SUBMISSION POLICY   No unsolicited material

Russ Freeman . . . . .CEO
Andi Howard . . . . .President

PEHR
6546 Hollywood Blvd., Ste. 201
Los Angeles, CA 90028
PHONE 323-466-7347/323-304-5684
EMAIL . . . . .press@pehrlabel.com
SECOND EMAIL . . . . .demos@pehrlabel.com
WEB SITE .www.pehrlabel.com
ARTIST ROSTER   Timonium - Grimble Grumble - Empress
                      - Arco - Sir - Languis - Mus - Tse Tse Fly
                      - Transitional - Mount Analog - Delaney
                      - Giardini Di Miro - The Relict - [the]
                      Caseworker
SUBMISSION POLICY   Accepts demos

Adam Hervey . . . . .No Title (adam@pehrlabel.com)
Darren King . . . . .No Title (darren@pehrlabel.com)

PI RECORDINGS
PO Box 1849, Cathedral Station
New York, NY 10025
PHONE 646-872-7072
FAX 212-222-1270
EMAIL . . . . .info@pirecordings.com
WEB SITE . . . . .www.pirecordings.com
DISTRIBUTOR   NAIL Distribution
ARTIST ROSTER   Henry Threadgill - The Art Ensemble of
                      Chicago - Vijay Iyer - Wadada Leo Smith
                      - Rudresh Mahanthappa - Liberty
                      Ellman - Marc Ribot - James "Blood"
                      Ulmer - Steve Lehman - The
                      Revolutionary Ensemble
GENRES   Classical - Jazz

Seth Rosner . . . . .No Title

PISSED OFF RECORDS
410 N. Maple Dr., Ste. 300
Beverly Hills, CA 90210-3833
PHONE 310-278-2272
FAX 310-278-2272
EMAIL . . . . .pissedoffrecords@aol.com
ARTIST ROSTER   The Buzzz... - Hell on Wheels - Grinnin'
                      Moon - Superthrive - Livid - Bone Jar -
                      Niya - If Man Is Five - Redezra - Others -
                      Leap Hole - Deafness - One Hitters -
                      Born Again Rebels - Suture Self -
                      Nightmare
GENRES   Punk - Rock
SUBMISSION POLICY   Send submissions to PO Box 16133,
                      Beverly Hills, CA 90209

Brent Lee Kendall JD, CPA . . . . .President
Valerie Diane . . . . .Director, A&R
Ian Paige . . . . .Scout

PLANET EARTH RECORDS
1120 Westchester Pl.
Los Angeles, CA 90019
PHONE 323-373-1537
FAX 323-373-1583
EMAIL . . . . .onfilm1@pacbell.net
WEB SITE . . . . .www.planetearthrecords.com
ARTIST ROSTER   Joseph Emont - Jody English - 40oz. -
                      Kirlian Process - Eric Lange - Eric Whited
                      - Lil' Jess
LABELS   Artificial Intelligence - Off World Records
                      - Metropolis Rekkord - Off World Digital
                      - On Film 1 - Treehouse Toys - HD Films
                      - Groovetech
GENRES   Alternative - Electronica - Jazz - Pop -
                      Rap/Hip-Hop - Rock
SUBMISSION POLICY   Accepts unsolicited material
COMMENTS   Distributed by Neon Soldier Music/Ghost
                      Werks

John Gocha . . . . .CEO/Owner

PLATANO RECORDS
3081 NW 24th St.
Miami, FL 33142
PHONE 305-633-9963/212-582-4546
FAX .305-634-3775/212-977-7581
WEB SITE . . . . .www.platanorecords.com
GENRES   Children's - Christian - Electronica -
                      Latin - Pop - Rap/Hip-Hop - Reggae -
                      World
COMMENTS   East Coast office: 661 10th Ave., New
                      York, NY 10036

Mercy Rivero .Director, Marketing
Carmen Silvera . . . . .Director, Promotion
Gregorio Sjogreen . . . . .Promotions

LABELS

PLATINUM RECORDS
3695 Cascade Rd., Ste. F190
Atlanta, GA 30331
PHONE 404-344-8238
FAX 404-349-4544
EMAIL . . . . .info@realplatinumrecords.com
WEB SITE . . . . .www.realplatinumrecords.com
ARTIST ROSTER   Johnny Sanders - The Preacher's Kid - Lori Perry - Danielle Roberson
GENRES   Gospel - Jazz
SUBMISSION POLICY   Submit bio, CD demo, head shot package

Kathryn Yanceey . . . . .A&R

PLUG RESEARCH
4519 Santa Monica Blvd.
Los Angeles, CA 90029
PHONE 323-662-1435
FAX 818-773-1754
EMAIL . . . . .info@plugresearch.com
DISTRIBUTOR   Caroline Distribution
ARTIST ROSTER   Adventure Time - AmmonContact - Calamalka - Camping - Chessie - Daedelus - Damon Aaron - Dntel - Headset - John Tejada - Languis - Mia Doi Todd - Milosh - Soulo - Thomas Fehlmann

Allen Avanessian . . . . .Label Manager/A&R
Ryan Gamsby . . . . .Sales & Marketing
Cameron Porter . . . . .Music Supervision/Promotion

POLYVINYL RECORD CO.
PO Box 7140
Champaign, IL 61826-7140
PHONE 217-403-1752/217-403-1754
FAX 217-403-1753
EMAIL . . . . .info@polyvinylrecords.com
WEB SITE . . . . .www.polyvinylrecords.com
DISTRIBUTOR   Alternative Distribution Alliance (ADA)
ARTIST ROSTER   31Knots - Aloha - Audible - Collections of Colonies of Bees - Decibully - Hail Social - Ida - Joan of Arc - Mates of State - Of Montreal - Owen - Picastro - Rainer Maria - Saturday Looks Good To Me - Volcano, I'm Still Excited!! - xbxrx - ZZZZ
GENRES   Rock
SUBMISSION POLICY   Does not accept unsolicited demos

Matt Lunsford . . . . .Owner

POP SWEATSHOP
PO Box 460954
Denver, CO 80246
PHONE 303-525-5840
EMAIL . . . . .chris@popsweatshop.com
WEB SITE . . . . .www.popsweatshop.com
SECOND WEB SITE . . . . .www.bdcdistribution.com
DISTRIBUTOR   Burnside Distribution Corp.
ARTIST ROSTER   Hemi Cuda - Spiv - Sam Densmore - Migas - Riddlehouse - Riveroots - Magstatic - Christopher Jon - Soylint Green - New Monkey - Velvet Elvis
GENRES   Pop - Punk - Rock - World
SUBMISSION POLICY   Accepts unsolicited demos

Chris Barber . . . . .President
Anistacia Barber . . . . .Marketing
Jon Freisland . . . . .Management/Booking

POST-PARLO RECORDS
PO Box 852
Chapel Hill, NC 27514
PHONE 919-932-9601
FAX 919-932-9166
EMAIL . . . . .info@postparlo.com
SECOND EMAIL . . . . .orders@postparlo.com
WEB SITE . . . . .www.postparlo.com
DISTRIBUTOR   Revolver USA Distribution
ARTIST ROSTER   Actionslacks - Ann Arbor Canasta Fix - Eskimo Kisses - John Vanderslice - Kapsize - Subset - Super XX Man - The Fall on Deaf Ears - The Olive Group - Those Peabodys - Western Keys - Zykos
SUBMISSION POLICY   No unsolicited demos

Ben Dickey . . . . .President (ben@postparlo.com)
Dana West . . . . .Promotion & Marketing (dana@postparlo.com)

PRA RECORDS
1255 Fifth Ave., #7K
New York, NY 10029
PHONE 212-860-3233
FAX 212-860-5556
EMAIL . . . . .pra@prarecords.com
WEB SITE . . . . .www.prarecords.com
DISTRIBUTORS   Ryko Distribution - Universal Music & Video Distribution
SUBMISSION POLICY   No unsolicited material

Patrick Rains . . . . .President

LABELS

PRESERVATION HALL RECORDINGS
726 Saint Peter St.
New Orleans, LA 70116
PHONE 504-522-2841
FAX 504-558-9192
EMAIL . . . . .contact@preservationhall.com
SECOND EMAIL . . . . .music@preservationhall.com
WEB SITE . . . . .www.preservationhall.com
SECOND WEB SITE . . . . .www.imnworld.com
DISTRIBUTOR   RED Music Distribution
ARTIST ROSTER   Preservation Hall Jazz Band - Sweet
                        Emma Barrett - Sister Gertrude Morgan
GENRES   Jazz

Ben Jaffe . . . . .President/Label Co-Manager
Sandra Jaffe . . . . .Label Co-Manager
Lee Frank . . . . .Label VP
Daniel Skarbek . . . . .Label Assistant

PSYCHOPATHIC RECORDS
32575 Folsom Rd.
Farmington Hills, MI 48336
PHONE 248-426-0800
FAX 248-426-6765
WEB SITE . . . . .www.psychopathicrecords.com
DISTRIBUTOR   RED Music Distribution
ARTIST ROSTER   Insane Clown Posse - Twiztid - Blaze ya
                        Dead Homie - Anybody Killa - Esham -
                        Zug Island - Psychopathic Rydas -
                        Double 0 Gangstaz

Nathan Richard . . . . .Office Manager

PUTUMAYO
411 Lafayette St., 4th Fl.
New York, NY 10003
PHONE 212-625-1400
FAX 212-460-0095
EMAIL . . . . .info@putumayo.com
WEB SITE . . . . .www.putumayo.com
GENRES   World
SUBMISSION POLICY   Mail demo CD to Attn: Jacob Edgar

Dan Storper . . . . .President (x216)
Jacob Edgar . . . . .No Title

PYRAMID RECORDS
11077 Biscayne Blvd., Ste. 200
Miami, FL 33161
PHONE 305-893-2007
FAX 305-893-0059
EMAIL . . . . .info@pyramidrecords.com
SECOND EMAIL . . . . .jbd@pyramidrecords.com
WEB SITE . . . . .www.pyramidrecords.com
DISTRIBUTOR   Universal Music & Video Distribution
ARTIST ROSTER   Bridge to Havana - Layla Hathaway -
                        Stephen Stills
GENRES   All Genres

Allen Jacobi . . . . .President
Josh Danoff . . . . .VP, Production
Christian Unruh . . . . .VP, Promotion

Q DIVISION RECORDS
363 Highland Ave.
Somerville, MA 02144-2574
PHONE 617-623-3500/617-625-9900
FAX 617-625-2224
EMAIL . . . . .info@qdivision.com
WEB SITE . . . . .www.qdivision.com
DISTRIBUTOR   Redeye Distribution
ARTIST ROSTER   Anne Heaton - Bill Janovitz & Crown
                        Victoria - Francine - The Gravel Pit
GENRES   Alternative - Pop - Rock
COMMENTS   Producer; Recording Studio

Michael Denneen . . . . .Owner (mike.denneen@qdivision.com)
Jon Lupfer .Owner (jlupfer@qdivision.com)
Ed Valauskas . . . . .Label Manager/Studio Manager (ed@qdivision.com)
Andrea Kramer . . . . . .Assistant Label Manager (andrea@qdivision.com)

QUARK RECORDS
357 Buena Vista Rd.
New York, NY 10956
PHONE 917-687-9988
FAX 845-708-0113
EMAIL . . . . .quarkent@aol.com
GENRES   Electronica - Pop
RECENT SOUNDTRACKS   Uncommon Scents - Xenchaos

Curtis Urbina . . . . .President

RADICAL RECORDS
77 Bleecker St., #C2-21
New York, NY 10012-1549
PHONE 212-475-1111
FAX 212-475-3676
EMAIL . . . . .bryan@radicalrecords.com
SECOND EMAIL . . . . .chiba@radicalrecords.com
WEB SITE . . . . .www.radicalrecords.com
DISTRIBUTORS   The Orchard - Select-O-Hits
ARTIST ROSTER   The Agents - Blanks 77 - The Booked -
                        Clocked In - The Cuffs - 5 Cent Deposit
                        - From Safety To Where - I.C.U. -
                        Inspector 7 - Road Rage - Social Scare -
                        Speedealer - Sturgeon General -
                        Submachine - Sex Slaves
GENRES   Alternative - Hardcore - Punk - Rock

Keith Masco . . . . .President
Bryan Mechutan . . . . .General Manager/Sales/A&R
Johnny Chiba . . . . .Public Relations/A&R/Advertising
Andy Perez . . . . .Radio & Internet
James Glayat . . . . .Retail

LABELS

RAINMAN RECORDS
315 S. Beverly Dr., Ste. 407
Beverly Hills, CA 90212
PHONE 310-277-3020
FAX 310-557-8421
WEB SITE . . . . .www.rainmanrecords.com
DISTRIBUTOR   RED Music Distribution
ARTIST ROSTER   Alvin Lee - John Kay - John Kay &
                         Steppenwolf - The Fixx - Melvin Seals -
                         Danny Johnson - The Mix - Kid Creole &
                         the Coconuts - The Blasters
GENRES   Adult Contemporary - Blues - Pop - Rock
SUBMISSION POLICY   Referrals or finished product only

Ron Rainey . . . . .President
Greg Lewerke . . . . .GM
Kevin Moorehouse . . . . .Director, Business Affairs

RANDOM CHANCE RECORDS
Box 208, 200 E. 10th St.
New York, NY 10003
PHONE 212-353-2140
FAX 212-460-5850
EMAIL . . . . .info@randomchancerecords.com
WEB SITE . . . . .www.randomchancerecords.com
DISTRIBUTOR   City Hall Records
ARTIST ROSTER   AFROdysia - Bill O'Connel - Charles
                        Fambrough - Chet Baker - Chief
                        Schabutte Gilliame - Eric Dolphy -
                        Harmonica Blues Orgy - Jimmy Lee
                        Robinson - Little Arthur Duncan - Lotz of
                        Music - Pyeng Threadgill - Robert Jospé
                        - Sam Lay - Ya Ya Fournier - Jerry
                        Gonzales & Fort Apache Band - Khan
                        Jamal
GENRES   Blues - Jazz - Latin - World
SUBMISSION POLICY   Send demos to PO Box

Rick Congress . . . . .CEO

RAP-A-LOT RECORDS
2141 W. Governors Circle
Houston, TX 77092-8727
PHONE 713-680-8588
FAX 713-680-1879
EMAIL . . . . .info@rapalotrecords.com
WEB SITE .www.rapalotrecords.com
ARTIST ROSTER   Geto Boys - Do or Die - Scarface - Dirty
                        - Devin, the Dude - Yuckmouth - Tela -
                        Z-Ro - UTP - Bun-B - Pimp C - Partners-
                        N-Crime
GENRES   Rap/Hip-Hop - Urban

James Prince . . . . .President
Rhonda Prince . . . . .COO
Thomas Randall . . . . .Director, A&R
Anzel Jennings . . . . .Manager, A&R
Carlton Joshua . . . . .Director, Marketing & Promotions
Omar Wilson . . . . .Publicity
Kerry Roy . . . . .Video Promotion
Alvin Stafford . . . . .Director, Street & Rap Promotion
Mike Mack . . . . .Director, Sales & Crossover Promotions
Xavier James . . . . .College & Record Pools Promotion

RASA MUSIC
120 Fifth Ave., 7th Fl.
New York, NY 10011
PHONE 212-253-1567
FAX 212-253-1521
EMAIL . . . . .info@rasamusic.com
WEB SITE . . . . .www.rasamusic.com
GENRES   World
SUBMISSION POLICY   By mail

Donna D'Cruz . . . . .Founder

RATTLESNAKE VENOM RECORDS, INC.
PO Box 1475
Burbank, CA 91507-1475
PHONE 818 842 5800
FAX 818-842-7974
EMAIL . . . . .steve@selakentertainment.com
WEB SITE . . . . .www.selakeentertainment.com
DISTRIBUTOR   City Hall Records
ARTIST ROSTER   The Bus Boys - 96 Decibel Freaks - It's
                        Me Margaret
GENRES   Alternative - Pop - Rock
RECENT SOUNDTRACKS   The Haunted Mansion - Bam Bam &
                        Celeste
SUBMISSION POLICY   No unsolicited submissions; Call first
COMMENTS   Licensing, Music Supervision, DVD pro-
                        duction

Steve Selak . . . . .President
Brian O'Neal . . . . .Producer

*RAYBAW RECORDS
c/o Warner Bros. Records Nashville
20 Music Square East, 3rd Fl.
Nashville, TN 37203-4344
PHONE 615-748-8000/615-214-1567
FAX 615-214-1537
EMAIL . . . . .firstname.lastname@wbr.com
WEB SITE . . . . .www.wbrnashville.com
DISTRIBUTOR   WEA Corp.
ARTIST ROSTER   Cowboy Troy - James Otto
GENRES   Country

Paul Worley . . . . .Chief Creative Officer/A&R
Bill Bennett . . . . .Executive VP
Cory Gierman . . . . .General Manager/A&R
Gator Michaels . . . . .Sr. VP, Promotions
Jules Wortman . . . . .Sr. VP, Publicity & Artist Development
Jim Malito .VP, National Promotion
Peter Strickland . . . . .VP, Sales
Lynette Garbonola . . . . .Director, New Media
Eric Mansfield . . . . .Director, Creative Services
Jennie Smythe . . . . .Director, New Media
Kristen Doyscher . . . . .Manager, Midwest Promotion
George Meeker . . . . .Manager, Secondary Promotion
Maura Mooney . . . . .Manager, Publicity (615-214-1500)
Glenn Noblit . . . . .Manager, Southwest Promotion
Brooks Quigley . . . . .Manager, Southeast Promotion
Joe Redmond . . . . .Manager, Northeast Promotion
Jeremy Witt . . . . .Manager, A&R (615-214-1464)
Rick Young . . . . .Manager, West Coast Promotion
Brian Horner . . . . .Sales & Marketing Coordinator (615-214-1550)
Danielle Taylor . . . . .Promotion Coordinator (615-214-1555)
Paige Connors . . . . .Executive Assistant to Paul Worley (615-214-1553)
Christy Hathcock . . . .Executive Assistant to Bill Bennett (615-214-1433)
Bill Moore . . . . .Assistant to Cory Gierman
Kelli Cashiola . . . . .Promotion Assistant

LABELS

RAZOR & TIE
214 Sullivan St., Ste. 4A
New York, NY 10012-1354
PHONE 212-473-9173
FAX 212-473-9174
EMAIL . . . . .info@razorandtie.com
SECOND EMAIL . . . . .firstinitiallastname@razorandtie.com
WEB SITE .www.razorandtie.com
DISTRIBUTOR   Sony BMG Sales Enterprise
GENRES   Alternative - Folk - Pop - R&B - Rap/Hip-
                    Hop - Reggae - Rock - World

Craig Balsam . . . . .Co-Owner
Cliff Chenfeld . . . . .Co-Owner
Sebouh Yegparian . . . . .Sr. VP, Sales
Victor Zaraya . . . . .Sr. VP, Finance & Operations
Michael Krumper . . . . .Sr. VP, Marketing
Gerard Babbits . . . . .VP, A&R
Paul Butler . . . . .VP, Business Development
Kurt Steffek . . . . .VP, Promotion
Carise Yatter . . . . .VP, Media & Artist Relations
Aaron Brotherton .Sr. Producer
Tony Bruno . . . . .Sr. Director, Sales
Kevin O'Connor . . . . .Director, Children's Entertainment
Sandi Hemmerlein . . . . .Director, Marketing
Jeremy Kramer . . . . .Product Manager
Tim Foisset . . . . .New Media Marketing Manager

RCA LABEL GROUP (NASHVILLE)
1400 18th Ave. South
Nashville, TN 37212
PHONE 615-301-4300
FAX 615-301-4347
EMAIL . . . . .firstname.lastname@sonybmg.com
WEB SITE .www.rcalabelgroup.com
DISTRIBUTOR   Sony BMG Sales Enterprise
LABELS   RCA - BNA - Arista Nashville
GENRES   Country

Joe Galante . . . . .Chairman
Butch Waugh . . . . .Executive VP
Paul Barnabee . . . . .Sr. VP, Finance & Administration
Renee Bell . . . . .Sr. VP, A&R
Allen Brown . . . . .VP, Media
Jon Elliot . . . . .VP, Artist Development/Marketing
Wade Hunt .VP, Creative Services
Jim Saliby . . . . .VP, Sales
Kathy Woods . . . . .VP, Legal/Business Affairs
Lori Genes . . . . .Director, Media
Brian Foyster . . . . .Manager, Online Marketing
Donna Duarte . . . . .Assistant to Mr. Galante
Tiffany Swinea . . . . .Assistant to Ms. Bell

RCA RECORDS (LOS ANGELES)
2100 Colorado Ave.
Santa Monica, CA 90404
PHONE 310-449-2100
FAX 310-449-2230
EMAIL . . . . .firstname.lastname@sonybmg.com
WEB SITE . . . . .www.rcarecords.com
DISTRIBUTOR   Sony BMG Sales Enterprise
GENRES   Alternative - New Age - Pop - R&B -
                    Rap/Hip-Hop - Rock

Matt Marshall . . . . .VP, A&R, RCA Records
Liz Morentin . . . . .VP, Publicity, West Coast, Arista/J Records
Roger Widynowski . . .VP, Publicity, RCA Records (rogerw@sonybmg.com)
Antero Fail . . . . . .West Coast Regional Director, Urban Radio Promotion
Dennis Blair . . . . .Sr. Director, Rock & Alternative Promotion
Tom Smith . . . . .Sr. Director, Sales, RCA Music Group
Wendy Goodman . . . . .Director, National Adult Promotion
Megan Youngblood . . . . . . .Associate Director, Promotion, West Coast
Sara Langerman . . . . .Publicity Assistant, RCA/Arista/J Records
Matt Walsh . . . . .Assistant to Matt Marshall, RCA Records
Shih Ko-Fung . . . . .Assistant, Promotion

RCA RECORDS (NEW YORK)
1540 Broadway
New York, NY 10036
PHONE 212-930-4936
EMAIL . . . . .firstname.lastname@sonybmg.com
WEB SITE . . . . .www.rcarecords.com
DISTRIBUTOR   Sony BMG Sales Enterprise
ARTIST ROSTER   Anti-Flag - Avril Lavigne - American Idol
                    - Ben Kweller - Black Rebel Motorcycle
                    Club - Bo Bice - Bullets & Octane -
                    Christina Aguilera - Citizen Cope - Clay
                    Aiken - The Cooper Temple Clause -
                    Dave Matthews Band - David Gray -
                    Elvis Presley - Foo Fighters - Heather
                    Headley - Jem - Kelly Clarkson -
                    Kasabian - Kings of Leon - Landon Pigg
                    - Longwave - Mylo - My Morning Jacket
                    - Natalie Imbruglia - Rachael Yamagata
                    - Ray LaMontagne - Rooster - stellastarr*
                    - The Strokes - The Kills - Velvet Revolver
                    - ZZ Top
LABELS   Dirty Martini - Windham Hill - Roswell
GENRES   Pop - Rock

Richard Sanders . . . . .Executive VP/General Manager
Ashley Newton . . . . .Executive VP, A&R
Steve Ralbovsky . . . . .Sr. VP, A&R
Hugh Surratt . . . . .Sr. VP, Artist Development & Creative Services
Steve Ferrera . . . . .Sr. VP, A&R (J Records Office) (646-840-5600)
Sherry Ring . . . . .Sr. VP, Publicity
Eamon Sherlock . . . . .Sr. VP, International Marketing
Aaron Borns . . . . .VP, Marketing
Sam Lecca . . . . .VP, Video Production
Scott Givens . . . . .Sr. Director, Marketing
Caron Veazey . . . . .Sr. Director, Marketing
Tamra Wilson . . . . .Director, Publicity
Sarah Takenaga . . . . .Manager, Publicity

RCA VICTOR GROUP
1540 Broadway
New York, NY 10036
PHONE 212-930-4000
FAX 212-930-4070
WEB SITE . . . . .www.rcavictorgroup.com
ARTIST ROSTER   Bebo & Cigala - Etta James - The
                    Chieftains - Eliane Elias - Rachael
                    Yamagata - George Winston - Leo
                    Kottke - Cesaria Evora - Amici Forever -
                    Jim Brickman - Fourplay - Judd &
                    Maggie - Cook, Dixon & Young
LABELS   RCA Victor - Windham Hill - Bluebird
GENRES   Blues - Jazz - New Age - World
COMMENTS   Classical Crossover - Singer/Songwriter

Jeb Hart . . . . .Sr. VP/General Manager
Larry Hamby . . . . .Sr. VP, A&R
David Einstein . . . . .VP, Promotion
Bob Hoch . . . . .Sr. Director, Marketing
Stacie Negas . . . . .Director, Marketing
Greg Repicci . . . . .Marketing Coordinator
Malkia Garrett . . . . .Executive Assistant

REBEL RECORDS
PO Box 7405
Charlottesville, VA 22906
PHONE 434-973-5151
FAX 434-973-6655
EMAIL . . . . .questions@rebelrecords.com
SECOND EMAIL . . . . .radio@rebelrecords.com
WEB SITE . . . . .www.rebelrecords.com
ARTIST ROSTER   David Davis - Dave Evans - Chris Jones
                             - King Wilkie - Longview - Lost & Found
                             - Mark Newton - Perfect Strangers - Rock
                             County - Karl Shiflett - Kenny & Amanda
                             Smith - Valerie Smith - Larry Sparks -
                             Ralph Stanley - Ralph Stanley II - Steep
                             Canyon Rangers - Cliff Waldron -
                             Wildwood Valley Boys - Paul Williams
GENRES   Bluegrass - Country - Folk - Roots
Dave Freeman . . . . .Owner
Mark Freeman . . . . .No Title

RED HOUSE RECORDS
501 W. Lynnhurst Ave.
St. Paul, MN 55104
PHONE 651-644-4161
FAX 651-644-4248
WEB SITE . . . . .www.redhouserecords.com
DISTRIBUTOR   KOCH Entertainment Distribution
GENRES   Folk - Roots
Robert M. Feldman . . . . .President
C.W. Frymire . . . . .VP, Operations
Eric Peltoniemi . . . . .VP, Production/A&R
Alex Seitz . . . . .Marketing

RELAPSE RECORDS
PO Box 2060
Upper Darby, PA 19082
PHONE 610-734-1000
FAX 610-734-3719
EMAIL . . . . .relapse@relapse.com
WEB SITE . . . . .www.relapse.com
DISTRIBUTOR   Ryko Distribution
ARTIST ROSTER   The Dillinger Escape Plan - Nile -
                             Mastodon - High on Fire - Pig Destroyer
                             - Zombi - Exhumed - Gadget - Cephalic
                             Carnage - Soilent Green - Buried Inside
                             - Neurosis - Skinless
GENRES   Alternative - Metal - Rock
RECENT SOUNDTRACKS   The Cave
COMMENTS   European office: PO Box 6818, 5975
                             ZG Sevenum, The Netherlands
Matt Jacobson . . . . .President
Gordon Conrad . . . . .Label Manager
Carl Schultz . . . . .Promotions
Reynold Jaffe . . . . .Business Affairs

RENDEZVOUS ENTERTAINMENT
100 N. Crescent Dr., Ste. G-100
Beverly Hills, CA 90210
PHONE 310-305-4377
FAX 310-305-4378
WEB SITE . . . . .www.rendezvousmusic.com
SECOND WEB SITE . . . . .www.davekoz.com
DISTRIBUTOR   RED Music Distribution
ARTIST ROSTER   Jonathan Butler - Brian Simpson - Tom
                             Braxton - Kirk Whalum - Adani & Wolf -
                             Camiel - Kyle Eastwood - Marc Antoine -
                             Michael Lington - Praful - Wayman
                             Tisdale
GENRES   Adult Contemporary - Jazz
COMMENTS   Smooth Jazz
Dave Koz . . . . .Founder
Hyman Katz . . . . .Co-Founder
Frank Cody . . . . .Co-Founder
Mark Gorbelow . . . . .A&R
Julie Gorov . . . . .Director, Strategic Marketing
Susan Levin . . . . .Director, Promotions
Ryan Conlon . . . . .New Media
Mitch Shannon .Artists Relations
Jeff Chiang . . . . .Product Manager
Janice Dela Cruz . . . . .Executive Assistant/Office Manager

REPRISE RECORDS
3300 Warner Blvd.
Burbank, CA 91505
PHONE 818-846-9090/212-275-4500
FAX 818-840-2409/212-275-3526
WEB SITE . . . . .www.repriserec.com
DISTRIBUTOR   WEA Corp.
ARTIST ROSTER   Eric Benet - Built to Spill - Kasey
                             Chambers - Cher - Claudia Church -
                             Eric Clapton - Cut Chemist - Deftones -
                             Disturbed - DJ Quik - Enya - The
                             Flaming Lips - Fleetwood Mac - Filter -
                             Jeff Foxworthy - John Frusciante - Goo
                             Goo Dolls - Green Day - Josh Groban -
                             Guster - Hot Hot Heat - Faith Hill - Chris
                             Isaak - Mark Knopfler - Linkin Park - k.d.
                             lang - Madonna - Brad Mehldau -
                             Metallica - Pat Metheny - Mandy Moore
                             - My Chemical Romance - Stevie Nicks -
                             Tom Petty & the Heartbreakers - R.E.M. -
                             Robert Randolph & the Family Band -
                             Red Hot Chili Peppers - Joshua Redman
                             - Lou Reed - Adam Sandler - Seal - The
                             Secret Machines - Sixpence None the
                             Richer - Steely Dan - The Distillers - The
                             Walkmen - Von Bondies - Neil Young
GENRES   Alternative - Blues - Country -
                             Electronica - Jazz - Metal - Pop - R&B -
                             Rap/Hip-Hop - Rock - Urban
SUBMISSION POLICY   No unsolicited submissions
COMMENTS   East Coast address: 75 Rockefeller
                             Plaza, New York, NY 10019
Tom Whalley . . . . .Chairman/CEO, Warner Bros. Records, Inc.
Phil Costello . . . . .Sr. VP, Promotion
Alex Coronfly . . . . .VP, Promotion, Adult Formats
Lynn McDonnell . . . . .VP, Alternative
Raymond McGlamery . . . . .VP, Rock/Album Promotion
Bob Weil . . . . .VP, Pop Promotion
Tommy Page . . . . .VP, Top 40

REPUBLIC RECORDS
1755 Broadway
New York, NY 10019
PHONE 212-841-5100
FAX 212-841-8012
EMAIL . . . . .republic@umusic.com
WEB SITE . . . . .www.republicrecords.com
DISTRIBUTOR   Universal Music & Video Distribution
ARTIST ROSTER   3 Doors Down - Bloodhound Gang -
                     Flaw - Godsmack - The Lost Trailers -
                     Pat Green - Waylon Payne - Rammstein -
                     The Soundtrack of Our Lives
GENRES   Alternative - Country - Pop - Rock

Avery Lipman . . . . .President
Tom MacKay . . . . .A&R
Julia Mannes . . . . .A&R
Anthony Rollo . . . . .A&R

RESERVOIR MUSIC
276 Pearl St.
Kingston, NY 12401
PHONE 845-338-1834
FAX 845-338-4266
EMAIL .mfeldmanmd@hvc.rr.com
WEB SITE . . . . .www.reservoirmusic.com
SECOND WEB SITE .www.rsrjazz.com
DISTRIBUTOR   City Hall Records
ARTIST ROSTER   Nick Brignola - Kenny Barron - Peter
                     Leitch - John Hicks - Steve Kuhn
GENRES   Jazz

Mark Feldman . . . . .Owner

REUNION RECORDS
741 Cool Springs Blvd.
Franklin, TN 37067
PHONE 615-261-6350
FAX 615-261-5916
EMAIL . . . . .info@reunionrecordes.com
WEB SITE . . . . .www.reunionrecords.com
DISTRIBUTOR   Provident Music Group
ARTIST ROSTER   Casting Crowns - Joy Williams - Michael
                     W. Smith
GENRES   Christian - Pop - Rock

Terry A. Hemmings . . . . .President/CEO
Dean Diehl . . . . .Sr. VP, Marketing, Provident Label Group
Robert Beeson . . . . .Sr. VP, A&R, Provident Label Group
Skip Bishop . . . . .VP, Mainstream Promotion & Marketing
Andrew Patton . . . . .VP, National Promotions, Provident Label Group
Jacquelyn Marushka Smith . .VP, Public Relations, Provident Music Group
                                                   (615-261-6439)
Nina Williams . . . . .VP, Label Operations, Provident Label Group

REVELATION RECORDS
PO Box 5232
Huntington Beach, CA 92615-5232
PHONE 714-842-4264
FAX 714-375-4266
WEB SITE . . . . .www.revelationrecords.com
SECOND WEB SITE . . . . .www.revhq.com
GENRES   Hardcore - Punk - Rock

Vique Martin . . . . .No Title

RHINO ENTERTAINMENT
3400 W. Olive Ave.
Burbank, CA 91505
PHONE 818-238-6200
FAX 818-562-9236
EMAIL .firstname.lastname@wmg.com
WEB SITE . . . . .www.rhino.com
DISTRIBUTOR   WEA Corp.
GENRES   All Genres

Scott Pascucci . . . . .President
Jim Hliboki . . . . .CFO/Sr. VP
Kevin Gore . . . . .Executive VP, Sales & Marketing
John Beug . . . . .Sr. VP, Video
David Dorn . . . . .Sr. VP, New Media
Malia Doss . . . . .Sr. VP, Business Affairs & Administration
Jimmy Edwards . . . . .Sr. VP, Business Development
Greg Goldman . . . . .Sr. VP, Business Development
Robin Hurley . . . . .Sr. VP, A&R
Mark Pinkus . . . . .Sr. VP, Strategic Marketing, Custom Products &
                                                   Synch Licensing
Colin Reef . . . . .Sr. VP, Business Development
Karen Ahmed . . . . .VP, A&R
James Austin . . . . .VP, A&R/Special Products
Rachel Bickerton . . . . .VP, Business Affairs
Hugh Brown . . . . .VP, Creative
Paul DeGooyer . . . . .VP, Marketing & Sales, Video
Mike Engstrom . . . . .VP, Marketing
Alan Fletcher . . . . .VP, TV Marketing
Maria McKenna .VP, Creative Services
Dee Murphy . . . . .VP, Sales
Laura Kayser . . . . .Sr. Director, New Media/Marketing
John Adams . . . . .National Promotions/Sports Director
Niki Gascon . . . . .Creative Director, WMG Film/Soundtracks

LABELS

RHOMBUS RECORDS

PO Box 7938
Van Nuys, CA 91409
PHONE 818-709-8480
FAX 818-709-8480
EMAIL . . . . .thomteresi@rhombus-records.com
WEB SITE . . . . .www.rhombus-records.com
ARTIST ROSTER   Affirmation - Alessandro - Anthony - Benny Velarde - Bill Fultonmore - Bob Leatherbarrow - Chris Bennett - Christiaan Mostert - Charlie Taylor - Chris Ho - Dan Carlin - Danny Pucillo Quartet - Deambra - Dick Weller - Donald Rubinstein - Eldad Tarmu - Fred Horn - Jazzy Devils - Jeff Babko Group - Jimbo Ross - Joe Gaeta - Karen Hammack/Paul Kreibich Quartet - John F. Hammond - Kerry Strayer Septet - Lanny Aplanalp - Lenny Smith & Friends - Lisa Madison - Lori Barth - Lorraine Feather - Los Gordos - Mark Winkler - Michael Geraci - Mike Bardash Trio - Moses & the Guys with Jobs - Nicky DePaola - Rastus - Reggae Dreams - Rick Holland - Kerry Strayer Quartet - Sam Rivers Trio - Steady Fready - Steve & Iqua Colson - Steve Blackwood - Stu Goldberg - Suburban Alphabet - Terri & the T-Bones - Thom Teresi - Tom Schuman - Tony Adamo - Trans Atlantic Cool Down - Tres-Dos - Tish Oney - Vick Silva - Willie Waldman - Judy Wexler
GENRES   Blues - Jazz - Latin - Reggae - World
Thom Teresi . . . . .Owner

RHYMESAYERS ENTERTAINMENT

2411 Hennepin Ave. South
Minneapolis, MN 55405
PHONE 612-977-9870
FAX 612-977-9871
EMAIL . . . . .info@rhymesayers.com
WEB SITE . . . . .www.rhymesayers.com
ARTIST ROSTER   Atmosphere - Brother Ali - Eyedea & Abilities - Musab - Soul Position - Mr. Dibbs - Micranots - Semi.Official - Los Nativos - DJ K-Salaam - Dynospectrum - Mass Hysteria - MF Doom - Oliver Hart - Vitamin D
GENRES   Rap/Hip-Hop
Brent Sayers . . . . .CEO
Jason Cook . . . . .Marketing

RIGHTEOUS BABE RECORDS

PO Box 95, Ellicott Station
Buffalo, NY 14205-0095
PHONE 716-852-8020
FAX 716-852-2741
EMAIL . . . . .info@righteousbabe.com
SECOND EMAIL . . . . .firstname@righteousbabe.com
WEB SITE . . . . .www.righteousbabe.com
DISTRIBUTOR   KOCH Entertainment Distribution
ARTIST ROSTER   Ani DiFranco - Hamell on Trial - Andrew Bird - Bitch & Animal - Sara Lee - Arto Lindsay - Sekou Sundiata - Kurt Swinghammer - Drums & Tuba - Utah Phillips - Toshi Reagon
GENRES   Alternative - Folk - Jazz - Latin - Pop - Rock
SUBMISSION POLICY   No unsolicited submissions
COMMENTS   UK office: 50A Stroud Green Rd., London, N4 3ES UK, phone: 44-20-7561-1620, fax: 44-20-7263-7979

Ani DiFranco . . . . .Founder
Scot Fisher . . . . .President
Mary Begley . . . . .Label Manager
Sarah Collins . . . . .Store Manager
Susan Tanner . . . . .Retail Marketing
Anna Kapechuk . . . . .Promotions
Sean O'Connell .Radio Promotions
Sara Otto . . . . .Licensing

*RM RECORDS

10713 Burbank Blvd.
North Hollywood, CA 91601
PHONE 818-753-9300
FAX 818-753-9966
EMAIL . . . . .info@rmrecords.com
SECOND EMAIL .brad@rmrecords.com
WEB SITE . . . . .www.rmrecords.com

Peter Rafelson . . . . .President/COO
Yongbae Cho . . . . .VP, International A&R
Brad Houshour . . . . .Label Manager

R.O.A.D. RECORDS

PO Box 68096
Nashville, TN 37206
PHONE 615-227-1947
EMAIL . . . . .fred@blueslandproductions.com
WEB SITE . . . . .www.blueslandproductions.com
DISTRIBUTOR   City Hall Records
ARTIST ROSTER   Frank Frost - Sam Carr's Delta Jukes - Mary-Ann Brandon - The Excello Legends - Fred James
GENRES   Blues
SUBMISSION POLICY   Contact by email before submitting
COMMENTS   Owns the catalogs of Champion, Poncello, Ref-O-Ree, Bullet/Sur-Speed, Rogana, Rich, IFJM and Cascade Records for licensing

Fred James . . . . .Publishing, Production & Licensing

ROADRUNNER RECORDS

902 Broadway, 8th Fl.
New York, NY 10010
PHONE 212-274-7500
FAX 212-505-7469
EMAIL . . . . .roadrunner@roadrunnerrecords.com
SECOND EMAIL . . . . .lastname@roadrunnerrecords.com
WEB SITE . . . . .www.roadrunnerrecords.com
DISTRIBUTOR   Universal Music & Video Distribution
GENRES   Alternative - Rock

Jonas Nachsin . . . . .President
Doug Keogh . . . . .Executive VP
Ron Burman . . . . .Sr. VP, A&R
Monte Conner . . . . .Sr. VP, A&R
Dave Loncao . . . . .Sr. VP, Promotion
Mark Abramson . . . . .VP, Promotion
Michael Canter . . . . .VP, Sales
Michelle Van Arendonk . . . .Sr. Director, A&R - Film, TV Music & Lifestyle
Jeff Chenault . . . . .Sr. Director/Creative Services/Video Production
Harlan Frey . . . . .Sr. Director, Touring/Artist Development
Ray Garcia . . . . .Sr. Director, Business Affairs
Bob Johnsen . . . . .Sr. Director, Marketing
Jamie Roberts . . . . .Sr. Director, Media/Artist Relations
David Bason . . . . .Director, A&R/R2 Publishing
Michael Gitter . . . . .Director, A&R
Dave Rath . . . . .Director, A&R Administration
Amy Sciarretto . . . . . . .Director, Metal Radio/Regional Video Promotion
Jeffery Kish . . . . .Assistant to Mr. Nachsin

ROBBINS ENTERTAINMENT

159 W. 25th St., 4th Fl.
New York, NY 10001
PHONE 212-675-4321
FAX 212-675-4441
EMAIL . . . . .info@robbinsent.com
WEB SITE . . . . .www.robbinsent.com
DISTRIBUTOR   Sony BMG Sales Enterprise
GENRES   Electronica

Cory Robbins . . . . .President
Paul Mislov . . . . .Sr. VP, Finance
Lisa Levy . . . . .VP, Sales/Production
Frank Murray . . . . .VP, Promotion
John Parker . . . . .VP, A&R/Promotion
Anne Amann . . . . .Director, Business Affairs
Stephanie Karten . . . . .Promoter/A&R Rep.

ROC-A-FELLA RECORDS

825 Eighth Ave., 29th Fl.
New York, NY 10019-7472
PHONE 212-333-8000
EMAIL . . . . .firstname.lastname@umusic.com
WEB SITE . . . . .www.rocafellarecords.com
DISTRIBUTOR   Universal Music & Video Distribution
ARTIST ROSTER   Allen Anthony - Beanie Sigel - Biggs -
                                Cam'ron - Dame Dash - Denim - The
                                Diplomats - DJ Clue - Freekey Zeekey -
                                Freeway - Jay-Z - Jim Jones - Julez
                                Santana - Kanye West - M.O.P. -
                                Memphis Bleek - N.O.R.E. - Nicole Wray
                                - Oschino & Sparks - Peedi Crakk - Rell
                                - Sas - Samantha Ronson - State
                                Property - Young Gunz - Young Steff
GENRES   Rap/Hip-Hop - Urban

Damon Dash . . . . .CEO (212-445-3613)

ROCKETSTAR RECORDINGS

PO Box 54108
Redondo, WA 98054-0108
PHONE 253-850-9119
FAX 253-854-7836
EMAIL . . . . .darrick@rocketstar.com
WEB SITE . . . . .www.rocketstar.com
ARTIST ROSTER   Long Since Forgotten - Gatsby's
                                American Dream - Time to Fly - The
                                Home Team - Acceptance - Surrounded
                                by Lions - The Providence
GENRES   Alternative - Punk
SUBMISSION POLICY   Open to submissions by mail or email

Darrick Bourgeois . . . . .President (darrick@rocketstar.com)
Eric Slagle . . . . .Label Manager (eric@rocketstar.com)
Lizzie Kozar . . . . .Publicity (lizzie@rocketstar.com)

ROIR

PO Box 501
Prince Street Station
New York, NY 10012
PHONE 212-477-0563
FAX 212-505-9908
EMAIL . . . . .info@roir-usa.com
WEB SITE . . . . .www.roir-usa.com
DISTRIBUTORS   Bayside Entertainment Distribution -
                                Revolver USA Distribution - Select-O-Hits
                                - Southern Records, Inc.
GENRES   Electronica - Punk - Reggae - Rock

Lucas Cooper . . . . .President
Adam Silverman . . . . .Press

ROUGH TRADE RECORDS UK

66 Golborne Rd.
London W10 5PS United Kingdom
PHONE 44-20-8960-9888
FAX 44-20-8968-6715
WEB SITE . . . . .www.sanctuarygroup.com
ARTIST ROSTER   Aberfeldy - A.R.E. Weapons - Virginia
                                Astley - Babyshambles - Beachwood
                                Sparks - Belle & Sebastian - British Sea
                                Power - Delays - The Detroit Cobras -
                                Cara Dillon - Baxter Dury - Eastern Lane
                                - Equation - The Fiery Furnaces - Adam
                                Green - Hal - The Hidden Cameras -
                                Jeffrey Lewis - The Libertines - Low -
                                Cerys Matthews - The Moldy Peaches -
                                Oneida - Queen Adreena - Eddi Reader
                                - Relaxed Muscle - Alasdair Roberts -
                                Royal City - Hope Sandoval & The Warm
                                Inventions - The Strokes - Sufjan Stevens
                                - The Sun - The Tyde - The Unicorns -
                                The Veils
GENRES   Alternative - Punk - Rock

Geoff Travis . . . . .Managing Director
Jeannette Lee . . . . .Managing Director
James Endeacott . . . . .A&R
Kelly Kiley . . . . .A&R Coordinator

LABELS

ROUGH TRADE RECORDS US

75 Ninth Ave.
New York, NY 10011
PHONE 212-599-2757
FAX 212-599-2747
EMAIL .info@roughtradeamerica.com
WEB SITE . . . . .www.sanctuarygroup.com
ARTIST ROSTER   Aberfeldy - Adam Green - Baxter Dury -
                             Belle & Sebastian - Brakes -
                             Babyshambles - Bell Orchestre - British
                             Sea Power - Cara Dillon - Cerys
                             Mathews - Cornershop - Delays -
                             Eastern Lane - Hal - The Hidden
                             Cameras - Royal City - Scritti Politti - The
                             Fiery Furnaces - The Kills - The Libertines
                             - The Tyde - Mystic Chords of Memory -
                             The Veils - Virginia Astley
GENRES   Alternative - Rock

Richard Priest . . . . .General Manager
Sean Maxson . . . . .Manager, Rough Trade Marketing
Alex Moss . . . . . . .Rough Trade Marketing & Administrative Coordinator

ROUNDER RECORDS

One Camp St.
Cambridge, MA 02140
PHONE 617-354-0700
FAX 617-354-4840
EMAIL . . . . .info@rounder.com
SECOND EMAIL . . . . .firstinitiallastname@rounder.com
WEB SITE . . . . .www.rounder.com
DISTRIBUTOR   Universal Music & Video Distribution
LABELS   Flying Fish - Heartbeat - Philo - Zoe -
                             Bullseye
GENRES   Bluegrass - Blues - Folk - Jazz - Rock

Ken Irwin . . . . .Owner/A&R (617-218-4448)
Marian Leighton-Levy . . . . .Owner/A&R (617-218-4409)
Bill Nowlin . . . . .Owner (617-218-4411)
John Virant . . . . .President (617-218-4426)
Jeff Grady . . . . .COO
Paul Foley . . . .General Manager (617-218-4425, pfoley@rounder.com)
Scott Billington . . . . .A&R (617-218-4428)
Troy Hansbrough . . . . .A&R (617-218-4436)
Paul Langton . . . . .VP, Radio Promotion
Brad Paul . . . . .VP, Promotion
Sheri Sands . . . . .VP, Sales & Marketing
Lauren Calista . . . . . . .Publicist (617-218-4483, lcalista@rounder.com)
Dave Godowsky . . . . .Publicity Coordinator (617-218-4480,
                                          dgodowsky@rounder.com)

RUBRIC LABEL GROUP

356 Bowery, 2nd Fl.
New York, NY 10012
PHONE 212-253-1110
FAX 212-253-1422
WEB SITE . . . . .www.rubricrecords.com
DISTRIBUTOR   Caroline Distribution
LABELS   Rubric - Tee Pee
GENRES   Rock

Fernando Martinez . . . . .No Title
Tony Presedo . . . . .No Title

RYKODISC/RYKO LABEL GROUP

Oddfellows Hall, 3 Broadway
Beverly, MA 01915
PHONE 978-921-4699
FAX 978-921-4610
EMAIL . . . . .info@rykodisc.com
WEB SITE . . . . .www.rykodisc.com
DISTRIBUTOR   Ryko Distribution
ARTIST ROSTER   Misfits - Frank Zappa - Big Star - The
                             Fire Theft - Alishaheed Muhammad -
                             Felix Da Housecat - Josh Rouse -
                             Morphine - Joe Jackson - Mission of
                             Burma - The Replacements - Ladytron -
                             Bruce Campbell
LABELS   Hannibal - Tradition - Rykodisc - Penalty
                             Recordings
SUBMISSION POLICY   No unsolicited submissions

William Hein . . . . .President
Neil Levine . . . . .COO
Jeff Rougvie .VP, A&R & Special Projects
Thomas Enright . . . . .VP, National Sales
Evan Jahn . . . . .Director, Marketing
Ilana Mondschein . . . . .Master Licensing

SADDLE CREEK

PO Box 8554
Omaha, NE 68108-8554
PHONE 402-558-8208
EMAIL . . . . .info@saddle-creek.com
WEB SITE . . . . .www.saddle-creek.com
DISTRIBUTOR   Alternative Distribution Alliance (ADA)
ARTIST ROSTER   Azure Ray - Bright Eyes - Cursive -
                             Desaparecidos - The Faint - The Good
                             Life - Mayday - Now It's Overhead -
                             Son, Ambulance - Sorry About Dresden
DISTRIBUTOR   ADA
SUBMISSION POLICY   Listens to mailed tapes & CDs

Robb Nansel . . . . .Owner

SANCTUARY RECORDS GROUP NORTH AMERICA

75 Ninth Ave.
New York, NY 10011
PHONE 212-599-2757
FAX 212-599-2747
EMAIL . . . . .info@sanctuaryrecordsgroup.com
SECOND EMAIL . . . . .info@sanctuarygroup.com (LA office)
WEB SITE . . . . .www.sanctuaryrecordsgroup.com
SECOND WEB SITE . . . . .www.sanctuarygroup.com (LA office)

DISTRIBUTORS	EMI Music Marketing - Sony BMG Sales Enterprise
ARTIST ROSTER	.38 Special - The Allman Brothers Band - Anthrax - Bad Company - Paul Rodgers - Big Head Todd & the Monsters - Billy Idol - Bruce Dickinson - Buddahead - Corrosion of Conformity - Craig Armstrong - Crosby/Nash - Dokken - The Doobie Brothers - Earth Wind & Fire - Gene Simmons - The Hiss - Kelly Osbourne - King Crimson - Kiss - Lynyrd Skynyrd - Morrissey - Motörhead - Nancy Sinatra - Paul Stanley - Ray J - Tegan & Sara - Tesla - Widespread Panic
LABELS	Attack Records - CMC - Indigo - Metal-Is - Noise - Rough Trade - T&T - Trojan - Vertical - Fantastic Plastic
GENRES	Alternative - Rock
COMMENTS	Los Angeles office: 9255 Sunset Blvd., #200, Los Angeles, CA 90069, phone: 310-205-3000, fax: 310-205-5001; North Carolina office: 5226 Greens Dairy Rd., Raleigh, NC 27616-4612, phone: 919-875-3500, fax: 919-875-3550; Canada office: 3109 American Dr., Mississauga, ON L4V 1B2, phone: 905-364-3238, fax: 905-677-1651

Merck Mercuriadis . . . . .CEO, Sanctuary Group Worldwide (NY)
Joe Cockell . . . . .CEO, Sanctuary Recorded Music Worldwide (UK)
Tom Lipsky . . . .CEO, Sanctuary Records Group North America (Raleigh)
Bob Cahill . . . . .Sr. VP, Sales (NY)
Drew Murray . . . . .Sr. VP, National Promotion (NY)
Madelyn Scarpulla . . . . .Sr. VP, Marketing (NY)
Katy Krassner . . . . .VP, Publicity (NY)
Kenny Ochoa . . . . .VP, Film & TV Licensing (NY)

SANCTUARY RECORDS GROUP UK

c/o Sanctuary House
45-53 Sinclair Rd.
London England W14 0NS UK
PHONE 44-20-7602-6351
FAX 44-20-7603-5941
WEB SITE .www.sanctuarygroup.com
SECOND WEB SITE . . . . .www.sanctuaryrecordsgroup.co.uk

ARTIST ROSTER	Alison Moyet - Allman Brothers Band - Anthrax - Blondie - The Blue Nile - Brides of Destruction - Chaka Khan - Crosby & Nash - De La Soul - Fun Lovin' Criminals - Gary Jules - Hurricane Party - Kiss - Gene Simmons - Lynyrd Skynrd - Morrissey - Megadeth - Nancy Sinatra - New York Dolls - RZA - South - Spiritualized - St. Etienne - Superjoint Ritual - Tesla - The Ga*Ga*s - Tim Booth - Widespread Panic - Wu-Tang Clan - The Beat Up - HelpSheCan'tSwim - Jason Nevins - Oxide & Neutrino - The Aspects - Europe - DJ Yoda - Prince Paul
GENRES	Alternative - Hardcore - Punk - Rap/Hip-Hop - Rock

Joe Cokell . . . . .CEO, Sanctuary Recorded Music Worldwide
Roger Semon . . . . .Chief Operating Officer
John Williams . . . . .Sr. VP, A&R
Giles Green . . . . .Head, UK Marketing
Julian Wall . . . . .Head, International Marketing

SANCTUARY URBAN RECORDS

75 Ninth Ave.
New York, NY 10011
PHONE 212-599-2757
FAX 212-599-2747
WEB SITE . . . . .www.sanctuarygroup.com
SECOND WEB SITE . . . . .www.sanctuaryrecords.com

ARTIST ROSTER	De La Soul - Earth Wind & Fire - Glenn Lewis - Jon B - Keith Sweat - Mason Road - Michelle Williams - Papa Reu - The O'Jays - Ray J - Solange
GENRES	Urban

Mathew Knowles . . . . .President, Sanctuary Urban Records Group

SAVOY LABEL GROUP

429 Santa Monica Blvd., Ste. 330
Santa Monica, CA 90405
PHONE 310-451-0451
FAX 310-451-3162
WEB SITE . . . . .www.slgmusic.com
SECOND WEB SITE .www.429records.com

DISTRIBUTOR	WEA Corp.
ARTIST ROSTER	Andy Bey - James Moody - Hubert Laws - Ravi Coltrane - Warren Brothers - Cosmic Rough Riders - Joan Armatrading - Steve Reynolds - Saucy Monky - Milton Nascimento - Andreas Vollenweider
LABELS	Savoy Jazz - 429 Records - Denon - Kin Kou
GENRES	Adult Contemporary - Alternative - Classical - Jazz - New Age - Pop - World
RECENT SOUNDTRACKS	Veronica Mars - Catch Me If You Can - Zoey 101 - Lakawana Blues
SUBMISSION POLICY	Solicited only

Steve Vining . . . . .President (x221, steve@slgmusicus.com)
Sheila Volpe . . . . .Sr. Director, Marketing (sheila@slgmusicus.com)
Josh Sherman . . . . .Sr. Director, Marketing (josh@slgmusicus.com)
Dave Wiese . . . . .Director, Sales (dave@slgmusicus.com)
Dan Marx . . . . .Production (dan@slgmusicus.com)
Christine Ayres . . . . . . .Marketing Assistant (christine@slgmusicus.com)

SCI FIDELITY RECORDS
4760 Walnut St., Ste. 106
Boulder, CO 80301
PHONE 303-544-1818
FAX 303-544-1919
WEB SITE .www.scifidelity.com
ARTIST ROSTER   String Cheese Incident - Umphrey's
                         McGee - Keller Williams - DJ Harry -
                         Brothers Past - Steve Kimock Band
GENRES   Rock

Kevin Morris . . . . .President (kevin@scifidelity.com)
Matt Hogan . . . . .Director, Marketing (hogan@scifidelity.com)
Reis Baron . . . . .Director, Radio Promotions, Internet Development
                         (reis@scifidelity.com)
Katie Sorenson . . . . .Director, Retail/Director, Administration
                         (katie@scifidelity.com)
Val Harris . . . . .Street Marketing (val@scifidelity.com)
Jack Mento . . . . .Bookkeeper (kaimana@stringcheeseincident.com)

SCRATCHIE
239 11th Ave.
New York, NY 10001-1206
PHONE 212-924-2193
EMAIL . . . . .webmaster@scratchie.com
WEB SITE . . . . .www.scratchie.com
ARTIST ROSTER   The Sights - The Sounds - Robbers on
                         High Street
GENRES   Alternative - Rock

James Iha . . . . .A&R
Adam Schlesinger . . . . .A&R

SECRETLY CANADIAN
1499 W. Second St.
Bloomington, IN 47403
PHONE 812-335-1572
FAX 812-323-8494
EMAIL .info@secretlycanadian.com
WEB SITE .www.secretlycanadian.com
SUBMISSION POLICY   Accepts demos
COMMENTS   Distributor

Jonathan Cargill . . . . . .Label Owner (jonathan@secretlycanadian.com)
Chris Welz . . . . .Label Manager (info@secretlycanadian.com)

SEGUE RECORDS
15 Kemble Ave.
Cold Spring, NY 10516
PHONE 845-265-2944
FAX 914-764-0138
EMAIL . . . . .info@seguerecords.com
WEB SITE . . . . .www.seguerecords.com
DISTRIBUTOR   Sumthing Else Music Works
ARTIST ROSTER   Vaneese Thomas - Nine Men's Morris -
                         Dana Edelman
GENRES   Adult Contemporary - Pop
SUBMISSION POLICY   No unsolicited material; Email or call
                         Steven Goff with a description before
                         submitting material
COMMENTS   Singer-Songwriter; State-of-the-art
                         recording facility; Album production,
                         soundtrack production, music publishing

Wayne Warnecke . . . . .Executive VP
Steven Goff . . . . .VP/Label Manager (steven@seguerecords.com)

SEQUOIA RECORDS, INC.
1106 Second St., Ste. 119
Encinitas, CA 92024
PHONE 800-524-5513
FAX 541-488-7870
EMAIL . . . . .merrill@sequoiarecords.com
SECOND EMAIL . . . . .customerservice@sequoiarecords.com
WEB SITE .www.sequoiarecords.com
DISTRIBUTORS   Allegro Corporation - Music Design
ARTIST ROSTER   Artemesia - David & Steve Gordon -
                         Gary Stadler - Zingaia - Jaya Lakshmi -
                         Sophia - EverStar - Shajan - TYA
GENRES   New Age - World
SUBMISSION POLICY   Submit links by email only; No physical
                         demos accepted
COMMENTS   Also distributed by BSC Music and New
                         Leaf

David Gordon . . . . .President/Comptroller (760-942-7574)
Steve Gordon . . . . .VP/Art & Promotions Director (707-829-8449)
Merrill Ward Operations Manager/National Distribution (541-301-6570)
Lita-Luise Chappell International Distribution & Licensing (949-830-8635)
Tanya Aziere . . . . .Customer Service (541-488-7880, x100)
Phyllis Hammon . . . . .A/R & A/P (phyllis@sequoiarecords.com)

SESSIONS RECORDS
60 Old El Pueblo Rd.
Scotts Valley, CA 95066
PHONE 831-461-5080
FAX 831-461-4680
WEB SITE .www.sessionsrecords.com
GENRES   Alternative - Punk - Rock

Joe Clements . . . . .Label Manager
Jon C. . . . . .Marketing/Design
Josh D. . . . . .Street Team Coordinator

SHADY RECORDS
151 Lafayette St., 6th Fl.
New York, NY 10013
PHONE 212-324-2410
FAX 212-324-2415
WEB SITE . . . . .www.shadyrecords.com
DISTRIBUTOR   Universal Music & Video Distribution
ARTIST ROSTER   Eminem - 50 Cent - D12 - Obie Trice -
                         Stat Quo - Bobby Creekwater
GENRES   Rap/Hip-Hop - Urban
RECENT SOUNDTRACKS   8 Mile

Eminem . . . . .CEO
Paul Rosenberg . . . . .President
Tracy McNew . . . . .General Manager
Marc Labelle . . . . .VP, A&R & Marketing
Riggs Morales . . . . .Sr. Director, A&R
Dart La . . . . .Director, A&R

*SHAMAN WORK RECORDINGS
PO Box 9522
Atlanta, GA 22304
EMAIL . . . . .info@shamanwork.com
WEB SITE . . . . .www.shamanwork.com
ARTIST ROSTER   Sol Uprising - Emanon - Wale Oyejide -
                         Ta'Raach - Scienz of Life - Finale - MF
                         Doom - C.L. Smooth
GENRES   R&B - Rap/Hip-Hop - Urban

Chris Craft . . . . .CEO (chris@shamanwork.com)
John Robinson . . . . .President (john@shamanwork.com)
Lamar Gilliam . . . . .COO (lamar@shamanwork.com)
Mark Cremins . . . . . .General Manager, UK (mark@shamanwork.com)
Marquis Williams . .General Manager, US (mikchek@shamanwork.com)
Jennifer Calloway Director, Communications (jennifer@shamanwork.com)

SHANACHIE ENTERTAINMENT

37 E. Clinton St.
Newton, NJ 07860
PHONE 973-579-7763
FAX 973-579-7083
WEB SITE . . . . .www.shanachie.com
GENRES   Blues - Christian - Country - Folk -
                          Gospel - Jazz - Latin   Pop   R&B -
                          Reggae - Rock - Roots - World
RECENT SOUNDTRACKS   Ghost World

Richard Nevins . . . . .President
Monifa Brown . . . . .VP, Publicity
Bill Cason .VP, Media/Artist Relations
Rick Rosenberg . . . . .VP, Sales/Marketing
Randall Grass . . . . .General Manager/A&R (rfgrass@aol.com)
Frank Ritchie . . . . .National Director, Promotions
Sherwin Dunner . . . . .Video/Yazoo Records/International Manager
Danny Weiss . . . . .Jazz, A&R

SHOCKLEE ENTERTAINMENT

244 Fifth Ave., Ste. A260
New York, NY 10001-7604
PHONE 212-909-2707
FAX 212-909-2707
EMAIL . . . . .info@shocklee.com
WEB SITE . . . . .www.shocklee.com
GENRES   Alternative - Electronica - Rap/Hip-Hop
COMMENTS   Also Progressive music

Hank Shocklee . . . . .President/CEO
Jo-Ann Nina . . . . .General Manager (jo-ann@shocklee.com)

SHOUT! FACTORY

2042-A Armacost Ave.
Los Angeles, CA 90025
PHONE 310-979-5000
FAX 310-979-5899
EMAIL . . . . .info@shoutfactory.com
WEB SITE . . . . .www.shoutfactory.com
DISTRIBUTOR   SONY BMG MUSIC ENTERTAINMENT
LABELS   HackTone Records
GENRES   Adult Contemporary - Alternative - Blues
                          - Folk - Jazz - Pop - Rock - Roots -
                          Urban
RECENT SOUNDTRACKS   The 40 Year Old Virgin - Mayor of the
                          Sunset Strip
SUBMISSION POLICY   No unsolicited material
COMMENTS   DVDs & CDs

Richard Foos . . . . .CEO
Bob Emmer . . . . .COO
Garson Foos . . . . .President/General Manager
John Rotella . . . . .VP, Sales
Shawn Amos . . . . .A&R
Melissa Boag . . . . .Marketing Director
Lorrie Shapiro . . . . .Video Acquisition
Stacey Studebaker . . . . .Publicity

SICKROOM RECORDS

PO Box 47830
Chicago, IL 60647
PHONE 312-493-0474
WEB SITE .www.sickroomrecords.com
DISTRIBUTOR   Southern Records, Inc.

Mitch Cheney . . . . .No Title (mitch@sickroomrecords.com)
Ryan Duncan . . . . .No Title (ryan@sickroomrecords.com)
Steve Sostak . . . . .No Title (steve@sickroomrecords.com)

SIDECHO RECORDS

13892 Harbor Blvd., Ste. 4A
Garden Grove, CA 92843
PHONE 714-554-4499
FAX 714-554-6152
WEB SITE . . . . .www.sidecho.com
DISTRIBUTOR   RED Music Distribution
ARTIST ROSTER   Neva Dinova - Charlemagne - The Pale
                          Pacific - Sherwood - Tokyo Rose - Some
                          by Sea

James Cho . . . . .Owner (james@sidecho.com)

SIDEONEDUMMY RECORDS

1944 N. Cahuenga Blvd.
Los Angeles, CA 90068
PHONE 323-790-0990
FAX 323-790-0988
EMAIL . . . . .dummy2@sideonedummy.com
WEB SITE .www.sideonedummy.com
DISTRIBUTOR   Alternative Distribution Alliance (ADA)
ARTIST ROSTER   7 Seconds - Avoid One Thing - Flogging
                          Molly - Go Betty Go - Kill Your Idols -
                          Maxeen - Piebald - Slick Shoes - The
                          Briggs - The Casualties - The Mighty
                          Mighty Bosstones - The Suicide
                          Machines - The Dan Band - MXPX -
                          Gogol Bordello - Bedouin Soundclash -
                          VCR - American Eyes
GENRES   Punk
SUBMISSION POLICY   Mail demos to PO Box 2350, Los
                          Angeles, CA 90078

Bill Armstrong . . . . .Owner
Joe Sib . . . . .Owner
Kevin Ames . . . . .Executive Assistant (kevin@sideonedummy.com)

SIGNATURE SOUND RECORDINGS

PO Box 106
Whately, MA 01093
PHONE . . . . .413-665-4036/860-974-2016 (Studio)
FAX 509-691-0457
EMAIL . . . . .info@signaturesounds.com
WEB SITE .www.signaturesounds.com
DISTRIBUTOR   KOCH Entertainment Distribution
ARTIST ROSTER   Amy Rigby - Kris Delmhorst - Peter
                          Mulvey - Jeffrey Foucault - The
                          Mammals - Mark Erelli - Winterpills
GENRES   Folk - Pop - Rock - Roots
COMMENTS   Signature Studio: 227 Peterson Rd.,
                          Pomfret, CT 06259

Jim Olsen . . . . .President
Mark Thayer . . . . .VP & Chief Engineer (mthayer814@aol.com)
Flora Reed . . . . .Tour Publicity
Biff Kennedy . . . . .Radio Promotion
Leah Kunkel . . . . .Legal

LABELS

SILVERLINE RECORDS
2231 S. Carmelina Ave.
Los Angeles, CA 90064
PHONE 310-207-5181
FAX 310-207-5331
EMAIL . . . . .info@silverlinerecords.com
WEB SITE . . . . .www.silverlinerecords.com
ARTIST ROSTER   Gordon Goodwin's Big Phat Band - Josh
        One - Lauren Ellis
GENRES   Alternative - Blues - Classical -
        Electronica - Jazz - Pop - Reggae - Rock
        - World
RECENT SOUNDTRACKS   The Wild Thornberrys - Abandon
COMMENTS   Creates and distributes DualDiscs

John Trickett . . . . .CEO
Jeff Dean . . . . .President
Bob Michaels . . . . .President, Production
Phil Blume .VP, Sales & Marketing
Sandi Taylor . . . . .VP, Production

SIRE RECORDS
75 Rockefeller Plaza
New York, NY 10019
PHONE 212-275-4646

Seymour Stein . . . . .CEO
Michael Goldstone . . . . .President (michael.goldstone@wbr.com)
Craig Winkler . . . . .Director, A&R
Brie Greenberg .Executive Assistant
Ed Romaine . . . . .Executive Assistant

SIX DEGREES RECORDS
PO Box 411347
San Francisco, CA 94141-1347
PHONE 415-626-6334
FAX 415-626-6167
EMAIL . . . . .info@sixdegreesrecords.com
WEB SITE .www.sixdegreesrecords.com
DISTRIBUTOR   Bayside Entertainment Distribution
ARTIST ROSTER   Issa Bagayogo - Banco de Gaia -
        Batidos - Bossacucanova - Bobi
        Cespedes - Cibelle - dj Cheb i Sabbah -
        dZihah & Kamien - Ekova - Euphoria -
        Bebel Gilberto - Bob Holroyd - Karsh
        Kale - Los Mocosos - MIDIval PunditZ -
        Ben Neill - Patato - Willy Porter - Suba -
        Trio Mocoto - Zuco 103
GENRES   Electronica - World
SUBMISSION POLICY   No unsolicited demos accepted

Patrick Berry . . . . .CEO (x11, pat@sixdegreesrecords.com)
Robert Duskis . . . . .President (x12, bobd@sixdegreesrecords.com)
Robert Appel . . . . .VP, A&R (x14, boba@sixdegreesrecords.com)
Kathy Barobs . . . . .National Sales Manager (x26,
        kathy@sixdegreesrecords.com)
Louisa Spier . . . .Director, Publicity (x15, louisa@sixdegreesrecords.com)

SIX GUN LOVER RECORDS
1029 Reinli St., Ste. 1
Austin, TX 78723
PHONE 512-452-1197, x2
FAX 512-452-7565
EMAIL . . . . .jason@sixgunlover.com
WEB SITE . . . . .www.sixgunlover.com
DISTRIBUTOR   Carrot Top Distribution, Ltd.
ARTIST ROSTER   An Automotive - Adolfo's Reversal -
        Bosco and Jorge - Ghosts & Vodka -
        Jeweled Handles - Meadowlark - Rhythm
        of Black Lines - Slave One - Victor
        Villarreal + Ryan Rapsys - Les Messieurs
        du Rock - Joan of Arc - Will Johnson
GENRES   Folk - Pop - Rock

Jason Butler . . . . .Owner

SKAGGS FAMILY RECORDS
PO Box 2478
Hendersonville, TN 37077
PHONE 615-264-8877
FAX 615-264-8899
EMAIL . . . . .info@skaggsfamilyrecords.com
WEB SITE . . . . .www.skaggsfamilyrecords.com
DISTRIBUTORS   Hollywood Records - Universal Music &
        Video Distribution
GENRES   Bluegrass - Country - Roots
SUBMISSION POLICY   Call for permission

Ricky Skaggs . . . . .President
Stephen Day . . . . .GM

SLAMJAMZ
PO Box 310
Roosevelt, NY 11575-0310
PHONE 770-997-9124/516-378-4876
WEB SITE . . . . .www.slamjamz.com
GENRES   Urban
COMMENTS   SLAMjamz South: 7139 Highway 85,
        Ste. 293, Riverdale, GA 30274-2900

Chuck D . . . . .GM (mrchuck@rapstation.com)
Dan Lugo . . . . .President (danlugo@aol.com)
DJ Johnny Juice . . . . .Director, A&R (juice@slamjamz.com)
C Doc . . . . .Product Manager & Video (cdoc@slamjamz.com)
Triniti . . . .Engineer/Production, SLAMsouth (triniticoclough@yahoo.com)

SLIP-N-SLIDE
919 Fourth St.
Miami, FL 33169-4559
PHONE 305-535-7595/305-770-0771
FAX 305-535-1535
WEB SITE . . . . .www.slipnsliderecords.net
DISTRIBUTOR   WEA Corp.
ARTIST ROSTER   Trick Daddy - Trina - Don Yute - Duece
        Poppi - Lost Tribe - Plies
GENRES   Rap/Hip-Hop - Reggae - Urban

Ted Lucas . . . . .President
Fernando Watkins . . . . .Public Relations/President
Roc Valdes . . . . .General Manager
Jullian Boothe . . . . .VP
Alex Martin . . . . .Director, Public Relations
Byron Trice . . . . .Director, A&R
Philly Smith .Public Relations/A&R

SMALL STONE
PO Box 02007
Detroit, MI 48202
PHONE 248-546-1206
FAX 248-541-6536
EMAIL . . . . .sstone@smallstone.com
WEB SITE . . . . .www.smallstone.com
DISTRIBUTORS   Allegro Corporation - NAIL Distribution
ARTIST ROSTER   Antler - Dozer - The Brought Low - A
        Thousand Knives Of Fire - Acid King -
        Axehandle - Dixie Witch - Five Horse
        Johnson - Erik Larson - Gideon Smith &
        the Dixie Damned - Greenleaf - Halfway
        To Gone - Lord Sterling - Los Natas -
        Medusa Cyclone - Milligram - Morsel -
        Novadriver - Perplexa - Porn (The Men
        Of) - Puny Human - Red Giant -
        Sasquatch - Slot - Soul Clique - The
        Glasspack - Throttlerod - Tummler - Valis
GENRES   Alternative - Metal - Rock
RECENT SOUNDTRACKS   2K5 NHL Hockey (Video Game)
SUBMISSION POLICY   Accepts demos; Will contact if interested

Scott Hamilton .President/Owner
Mike Saputo . . . . .Art Director
David Adamski .Legal Department

SMOG VEIL RECORDS

1658 N. Milwaukee Ave., #284
Chicago, IL 60647
PHONE 773-706-0450
FAX 312-276-8519
EMAIL . . . . .info@smogveil.com
WEB SITE . . . . .www.smogveil.com
DISTRIBUTORS   Revolver USA Distribution - Super D
ARTIST ROSTER   Rocket from the Tombs - Rubber City
    Rebels - New Christs - David Thomas
    and the 2paleboys
RECENT SOUNDTRACKS   Tony Hawk Underground
SUBMISSION POLICY   Email before sending demo

Frank Mauceri . . . . .President (franklisa@aol.com)

SONANCE RECORDS

PO Box 130338
Carlsbad, CA 92013
PHONE 866-227-9595
FAX 760-804-5817
EMAIL . . . . .customerservice@sonancerecords.com
SECOND EMAIL . . . . .fanclub@sonancerecords.com
WEB SITE . . . . .www.sonancerecords.com
DISTRIBUTOR   Select-O-Hits
ARTIST ROSTER   Salty the Pocketknife - The Breakfast -
    Children on the Corner - SGR - Zen
    Dog - Silicon Monk - A Better Way
GENRES   Alternative - Electronica - Gospel - Jazz -
    Pop - Rap/Hip-Hop - Rock
SUBMISSION POLICY   Send submissions Attn: Ben Frimmer

Rick Frimmer . . . . .President/CEO (ceo@sonancerecords.com)
Andrea Frimmer . . . . .Executive VP (andi@sonancerecords.com)
Ben Frimmer . . . . .VP/Chief Engineer/Audio & Artist Development
    (ben@sonancerecords.com)
Alex DeFelice . . . . . .Licensing & Distribution (adeflice@mindspring.com)

SONIC UNYON RECORDS

22 Wilson St.
Hamilton, ON L8R 1C5 Canada
PHONE 905-777-1223
FAX 905-777-1161
EMAIL . . . . .jerks@sonicunyon.com
WEB SITE . . . . .www.sonicunyon.com
ARTIST ROSTER   A Northern Chorus - A. Graham & the
    Moment Band - Andre Ethier - Frank
    Black - Jens Lekman - Manishevitz -
    Raising the Fawn - Sianspheric - Simply
    Saucer - Tangiers - The Nein
GENRES   Alternative - Rock
COMMENTS   Partnered with Goodfellow Records

Tim Potocic . . . .President/VP, Sales & Purchasing (tim@sonicunyon.com)
Mark Milne . . . . .CFO/VP, Operations (mark@sonicunyon.com)
Chris Logan . . . . . . .Advertising & Marketing (tiffany@sonicunyon.com)
Sean Palmerston . . . . .Promo (sean@sonicunyon.com)

SONY BMG LEGACY RECORDINGS

550 Madison Ave., 17th Fl.
New York, NY 10022-3211
PHONE 212-833-8000
FAX 212-833-4646
EMAIL . . . . .feedback@legacyrecordings.com
WEB SITE .www.legacyrecordings.com
GENRES   Adult Contemporary - Bluegrass - Blues -
    Country - Folk - Jazz - Pop - R&B -
    Reggae - Rock
SUBMISSION POLICY   No unsolicited material
COMMENTS   Reissues and box sets from the Sony
    BMG catalog

Jeff Jones .Executive VP, Legacy Recordings,
    Sony BMG Catalog Worldwide
Steve Berkowitz . . . . .Sr. VP, A&R (212-833-8610,
    steve_berkowitz@sonymusic.com)
Adam Block . . . . .VP, Marketing
Vicki Petrella . . . . .Office Manager & Assistant to Jeff Jones

SONY BMG MASTERWORKS

550 Madison Ave., 16th Fl.
New York, NY 10022-3211
PHONE 212-833-8692
FAX 212-833-8318
EMAIL . . . . .paul.cremo@sonybmg.com
WEB SITE . . . . .www.sonyclassical.com
ARTIST ROSTER   Yo-Yo Ma - Joshua Bell - Murray Perahia
    - Kristin Chenoweth
LABELS   Sony Classical - RCA Red Seal -
    Deutsche Harmonia Mundi - Arte Nova
GENRES   Classical
RECENT SOUNDTRACKS   Alexander - Phantom of the Opera -
    Hero - Lemony Snicket's A Series of
    Unfortunate Events
COMMENTS   Soundtracks; Cast Albums

Gilbert Hetherwick . . . . .President (212-833-7255)
David Lai .Sr. VP, A&R (212-833-4431)
Paul Cremo . . . . .VP, Soundtracks/Cast Albums (212-833-8692)
Deborah Surdi . . . . .Sr. Director, A&R

SONY BMG MUSIC CANADA

190 Liberty St., Ste. 100
Toronto, ON M6K 3L5 Canada
PHONE 416-589-3000
FAX 416-589-3003
WEB SITE . . . . .www.sonybmg.ca
LABELS   Epic - Columbia - Arista - Jive - J - Sony
    Urban - BMG Classics - LaFace - Legacy
    - RCA - So So Def - Verity
GENRES   All Genres

Lisa Zbitnew . . . . .President
Neil Foster . . . . .General Manager
Vito Luprano . . . . .Sr. VP, Quebec A&R
Shane Carter . . . . .VP, International Marketing
Norman Miller . . . . . . .VP, Digital Business, IS&T & Marketing Services
Christine Prudham . . . . .VP, Legal & Business Affairs
Steve Simon . . . . .VP, Sales
David Toomey . . . . .VP, Domestic Marketing (416-589-3016)
Liew Wong . . . . .VP, Finance & Administration
Ken Bain . . . . .Director, Country/AC/Video
Warren Copnick . . . . .Director, CHR/AHC/Rock
Jonathan Ramos . . . . .Director, A&R
Sonia Watkins . . . . .Director, Human Resources

LABELS

SONY BMG MUSIC ENTERTAINMENT

550 Madison Ave.
New York, NY 10022
PHONE 212-833-8000/310-449-2100
WEB SITE . . . . .www.sonybmg.com
LABELS   Arista - Columbia Records - Epic
                           Records - Jive - J Records - Legacy
                           Recordings - Masterworks - RCA - Sony
                           Classical - Sony Nashville - Sony Urban
                           Music - Sony Wonder - Zomba
COMMENTS   West Coast office: 2100 Colorado Ave.,
                           Santa Monica, CA 90404

Andrew Lack . . . . .CEO
Rolf Schmidt Holtz . . . . .Chairman of the Board of Directors
Kevin Kelleher . . . . .Executive VP/CFO
Don Ienner . . . . .President/CEO, Sony Music Label Group
Clive Davis . . . . .Chairman/CEO, BMG Label Group, US
Charles Goldstuck . . . . .President/COO, BMG Label Group, US
Gilbert Hetherwick . . . . .President, Sony BMG Masterworks
Kevin Lawrie . . . . .President, Sony BMG Norte
Michael Smellie . . . . .COO, SONY BMG MUSIC ENTERTAINMENT
Michele Anthony . . .Executive VP, SONY BMG MUSIC ENTERTAINMENT/
                           COO, Sony Music Label Group, US
Daniel Mandil . . . . . .Executive VP/Global General Counsel & Secretary
Tim Prescott . . . . .Executive VP/Chief Marketing Officer
Thomas Hesse . . . . .President, Global Digital Business
Tim Bowen   Sony BMG UK/Canada/Australia/New Zealand/South Africa
Maarten Steinkamp . . . . .Sony BMG Continental Europe
Jim Wilson . . . . .Executive VP/General Manager, Sony Wonder
Ira Sallen . . . . .Executive VP, Human Resources
Cory Shields . . . . .Sr. VP, Communications
Sofia Sondervan . . . . .Sr. VP, Feature Films
Ron Wilcox . . . . . .Executive VP/Chief Business & Legal Affairs Officer
Joe DiMuro . . . . .Executive VP, Sony BMG Strategic Marketing
Jeremiah Bosgang . . . . .Executive VP, Television
Jeff Jones . . . . .Executive VP, Sony BMG Catalog
John McKay .VP, Communications

SONY BMG MUSIC ENTERTAINMENT - US LATIN (LOS ANGELES)

2100 Colorado Ave.
Santa Monica, CA 90404
PHONE 310-449-2200/212-833-8000
FAX 310-449-2215/212-833-8233
WEB SITE . . . . .www.sonymusic.com
SECOND WEB SITE . . . . .www.sonydiscos.com
ARTIST ROSTER   Pop Artists: Kalimba - Ha-ash - La Oreja
                           de Van Gogh - Sin Bandera - Franco de
                           Vita - Kevin Johansen - Pandora - Gian
                           Marco - Gloria Estefan - Celia Cruz -
                           Gilberto Santa Rosa - Reyli - Marc
                           Anthony - Robi Rosa; Regional Mexican
                           Artists: Alejandro Fernández - Vicente
                           Fernandez - Pepe Aguilar - Ana Gabriel
                           - Víctor García - Los Razos de
                           Sacramento y Reynaldo - Beto Terrazas -
                           Julio Preciado - Ulises Quintera - La
                           Firma - Sergio Vega - La Chío
GENRES   Latin
COMMENTS   East Coast office: 550 Madison Ave.,
                           19th Fl., New York, NY 10022-3211

Nir Seroussi . . . . .VP, A&R & Marketing
Miguel Trujillo . . . . .General Manager/VP, Regional Mexican Norte
Mayra Vasquez . . . . .Sr. Director, West Coast Sales
Jean Gavinet . . . . .Director, Sales
Samuel Lopez .Special Marketing
Linda Crespo .Marketing Manager
Miguel Garrocho . . . . .Marketing Manager, Pop
Jose Marquez . . . . .Manager, Pop Promotions
Manuel Prado .Promotion Manager
Karina Puente .Promotion Manager
Erika Nuño . . . . .Executive & A&R Coordinator
Oscar Correa . . . . .Promotion Representative
Veronica Maldonado . . . . .Promotion Representative, East Coast
Rocio Gutierrez . . . . .Publicity
Cindy Baez . . . . .Assistant to Mayra Vasquez

SONY BMG MUSIC ENTERTAINMENT - US LATIN (MIAMI)

605 Lincoln Rd., 7th Fl.
Miami Beach, FL 33139
PHONE 305-695-3500
WEB SITE . . . . .www.sonymusic.com
SECOND WEB SITE . . . . .www.sonydiscos.com
DISTRIBUTOR   Sony BMG Sales Enterprise
ARTIST ROSTER   Alexandre Pires - Jose Jose - Jerry Rivera
                           - Camilo Sesto - Aterciopelados - Los
                           Razos - Julio Preciado - Juan Gabriel -
                           Alejandro Fernandez - Vicente Fernandez
                           - Ricardo Arjona - Sin Bandera - Reyli
                           Barba - Ha*Ash - Chayanne - Ricky
                           Martin - Shakira - Vicente Fernandez -
                           Reik - Ednita Nazario - Beto Terrazas -
                           La 5ta. Estacion - M.R.P. - Johnny Prez -
                           Ulises Quintero
LABELS   Ariola - RCA - Sony
GENRES   Latin

Kevin Lawrie . . . . .President, Latin Region
Angel Carrasco . . . . .Sr. VP, A&R (305-695-3540)
Teresa de la Concha . . . . .Sr. Director, Marketing
Cindy Becerra .Product Manager
Lorenzo Braun . . . . .Marketing
Paula Kaminsky . . . . .Marketing
Socorro Cadena . . . . .Assistant to Kevin Lawrie

SONY BMG MUSIC INTERNATIONAL

10 Great Marlborough St., 7th Fl.
London W1F 7LP United Kingdom
PHONE 44-207-911-8200
FAX 44-207-911-8742
EMAIL . . . . .firstname.lastname@sonybmg.com
WEB SITE . . . . .www.sonymusic.com
GENRES   All Genres

Nick Feldman . . . . .Director, A&R (44-207-911-8836)
Ricardo Fernandez . . . . .Director, A&R (44-207-911-8566)

SONY MUSIC LABEL GROUP, US

550 Madison Ave.
New York, NY 10022
PHONE 212-833-8000
WEB SITE . . . . .www.sonybmg.com
LABELS   Columbia Records - Epic Records - Sony
                           Music Nashville - Sony Urban Music
GENRES   All Genres
COMMENTS   West Coast office: 2100 Colorado Ave.,
                           Santa Monica, CA 90404, phone: 310-
                           449-2100

Don Ienner . . . . .CEO, Sony Music Label Group, US
Michele Anthony . . . . .President/COO, Sony Music Label Group
Steve Barnett . . . . .Chairman, Columbia Records Group
Steve Greenberg . . . . .President, Columbia Records
Lisa Ellis . . . . .General Manager, Sony Urban Music
John Grady . . . . .President, Sony Music Nashville
David Massey . . . . . . .Executive VP, A&R, Sony Music Label Group, US/
                           President, Daylight Records
Jeff Walker . . . . .Executive VP, Business & Legal Affairs
Keith Naftaly . . . . .Sr. VP, A&R, Sony Music Label Group, US
Tracy Nurse . . . .Sr. VP, International Marketing, Sony Music Label Group

SONY MUSIC NASHVILLE
1400 18th Avenue South
Nashville, TN 37212
PHONE 615-858-1300
EMAIL . . . . .firstname.lastname@sonybmg.com
WEB SITE . . . . .www.sonynashville.com
GENRES   Country

John Grady . . . . .President
Mark Wright . . . . .Executive VP, A&R
Kay Smith . . . . .VP, A&R Administration (615-742-4321)
Tracy Baskette-Fleaner . . . . .Sr. Art Director
Amy Willis .Associate Director, Press & Publicity
Tonya Derry . . . . .Manager, A&R Administration (615-742-4328)
Lauren Stephens . . . . .Media Department Coordinator
Joe Simpson . . . . .A&R Administration (615-742-4386)
Sarah Brosmer .Assistant to Mark Wright
Susan Myers . . . . .Assistant to John Grady
Brooke Sommer . . . . .Assistant to Kay Smith, Joe Simpson & Tonya Derry

SONY MUSIC SOUNDTRAX
2100 Colorado Ave., 2nd Fl.
Santa Monica, CA 90404-3504
PHONE 310-449-2100
FAX 310-449-2259
EMAIL . . . . .firstname.lastname@sonybmg.com
WEB SITE . . . . .www.sony.com
GENRES   All Genres

Glen Brunman . . . . .President, Soundtracks (310-449-2249)
Debbie Patton . . . . .Sr. Director, Soundtracks (310-449-2252)
Archie Castillo . . . . .Assistant to Debbie Patton
Fran Salafia .Assistant to Glen Brunman

SONY URBAN
550 Madison Ave.
New York, NY 10022
PHONE 212-833-8000
WEB SITE . . . . .www.sonyurban.com
ARTIST ROSTER   Nas - Beyoncé - Destiny's Child - Three
                         6 Mafia - Bow Wow - Maxwell - Jennifer
                         Lopez - Amerie - John Legend -
                         Ginuwine - Goapele - Vivian Green -
                         Jagged Edge - Omarion
GENRES   Electronica - R&B - Rap/Hip-Hop -
                         Urban
COMMENTS   West Coast office: 2100 Colorado Ave.,
                         Santa Monica, CA 90404, Phone: 310-
                         449-2100

Lisa Ellis . . . . .President
"KP" Kawan Prather . . .Executive VP/Head, Urban A&R (212-833-7795)
Gary Beech . . . . . .Sr. VP/Head, Sony Urban Marketing (212-833-4748)
Dino Delvaille . . . . .Sr. VP, Urban A&R (212-833-4496)
Stephanie Gayle . . . . .Sr. VP, Urban Marketing (212-833-8381)
C.C. McClendon   Sr. VP/Head, Sony Urban Promotions (212-833-8958)
Yvette Noel-Schure . . . . .Sr. VP, Media (212-833-4483)
David Belgrave . . . . .VP, Product Marketing (212-833-4166)
James Brown . . . . .VP, Urban Promotions (212-833-8008)
Joseph Burney . . . . .VP, Gospel A&R
Chad Elliot . . . . .VP, Urban A&R (212-833-8008)
Bilal Hill . . . . .VP, Finance & Operations (212-833-7163)
Malcolm Miles . . . .National Director, Street Promotions (212-833-6811)
Sherri Warren . . . .National Director, Urban Promotions (212-833-8895)
James White . . . . .National Director, Crossover Mixshow Promotions (LA)
                         (310-449-2476)
Juli Knapp . . . . .Sr. Director, A&R Operations (212-833-7248)
David Goldfrach . . . . .Director, Tour Marketing (212-833-8578)
Liz Hausle . . . . .Director, Product Marketing (212-833-5648)
Quincy Jackson . . . . .Director, Product Marketing (212-833-7467)
Anton Marchand . . . . .Director, A&R (212-833-7116)
Ampora Perez . . . . .Director, A&R (212-833-8684)
Jennifer Gray . . . . .Associate Director, A&R (212-833-4926)
Chris Green . . . . .Manager, Mixshow (212-833-4956)
Amberdawn Mickle . . . . .Manager, Product Marketing (212-833-6981)
Celessa Batchan . . . . .Promotions/Regional Promotion Manager,
                         West Coast (310-449-2426)
                                                     (Continued)

SONY URBAN (Continued)
Charita Brittenum-Carter . . . .Promotions/Regional Promotion Manager,
                         Southeast (770-673-5835)
Michelle Burden . . . . .Promotions/Regional Promotion Manager,
                         Midwest (847-640-4308)
Luther Clark . . . . .Promotions/Regional Promotion Manager,
                         Mid-Atlantic (704-752-7818)
Beverlee Garvin . . . . .Promotions/Regional Product Manager,
                         Northeast (201-498-1127)
Jerome Kemp . . . . .Promotions/Regional Product Manager, Ohio
                         (847-640-4349)
Demetrius Lloyd . . . . .Promotions/Regional Product Manager,
                         Southwest (972-602-3781)
Nick Mossberg . . . . .Promotions/Assistant to Baby Paul & Malcolm Miles
                         (212-833-6811)
Sean Robinson   Promotions/Assistant to David Lawrence & Sherri Warren
                         (212-833-5127)
Darryl Smith . . . . .Promotions/Regional Product Manager, Memphis
                         (770-673-5830)
Jennifer Turner   . . .Promotions/Assistant to James Brown & Sherri Warren
                         (212-833-4990)
Miranda Hawkins . . . . .Promotions Coordinator (212-833-7542)
Ian Holder   A&R Coordinator/Assistant to Ampora Perez & Jennifer Gray
                         (212-833-7598)
Andre McKenzie . . . . . . .A&R Coordinator/Assistant to Dino Delvaille &
                         Juli Knapp (212-833-6206)
David Wright . . . . . . .A&R Coordinator/Assistant to *KP* Kawan Prather
                         (212-833-7079)
Mary Beth McArdle . . . . .A&R Administration, Sony Urban Artists
                         (212-833-4731)
Kathy Baker . . . . .Online Consultant (212-833-8861)
Devronya Brathwaite . . . . .Strategic Marketing (212-833-7115)
Nate Johnson . . . . . . .Marketing Coordinator/Assistant to Gary Beech
                         (212-833-8663)
Lisa Wiggins . . . . . . .Marketing/Assistant to David Belgrave & Liz Hausle
                         (212-833-4139)
Joseph O'Connell . . . . .Urban Scheduling (212-833-5574)
Simon Perez . . . . .Finance/Assistant to Bilal Hill (212-833-4294)
Tanya Lawson . . . . .Assistant to David Goldfrach & Kathy Baker
                         (212-833-5151)

SONY WONDER
2100 Colorado Ave.
Santa Monica, CA 90404-3504
PHONE 310-449-2100/212-833-8000
FAX 310-449-2089
WEB SITE . . . . .www.sonywonder.com
GENRES   Children's
SUBMISSION POLICY   No unsolicited material
COMMENTS   Family Entertainment

Jim Wilson . . . . .Executive VP/General Manager
Rynda Laurel . . . . .A&R/Project Development
Annemarie Gatti . . . . .Sr. Director, Marketing (NY)

SOUND FEELINGS RECORDS
18375 Ventura Blvd., Ste. 8000
Tarzana, CA 91356
PHONE 818-757-0600
WEB SITE . . . . .www.soundfeelings.com
GENRES   Adult Contemporary - Children's -
                         Classical - Country - New Age - Pop -
                         R&B

Howard Richman . . . . .President

LABELS

SOUTHERN LORD RECORDINGS
5653 Hollywood Blvd.
Los Angeles, CA 90028
PHONE 323-467-6076
FAX 323-467-6314
EMAIL . . . . .info@southernlord.com
SECOND EMAIL . . . . .southernlord@yahoo.com
WEB SITE . . . . .www.southernlord.com
DISTRIBUTOR   Caroline Distribution
ARTIST ROSTER   Thrones - Urgehal - Saint Vitus - Lair of
                     the Minotaur - Tangorodrim - Goatsnake
                     - WarHorse - Khanate - Probot - Place of
                     Skulls - Outlaw Order - Attila Csihar -
                     Teeth of Lions Rule the Divine - Church
                     of Misery - Boris - Grief - Pentagram -
                     Earthride - Thorr's Hammer
GENRES   Metal

Greg Anderson . . . . .Owner
Eddie Solis . . . . .Manager, Sales & Distribution

SOVEREIGN ARTISTS, INC.
2601 Ocean Park Blvd., Ste. 110
Santa Monica, CA 90405
PHONE 310-314-4137
FAX 310-314-4132
WEB SITE . . . . .www.sovereignartists.com
ARTIST ROSTER   Heart - Don Grusin - The Crickets -
                     Chris Hillman - Loudon Wainwright III
GENRES   Folk - Jazz - Rock

Ken Lemunyon . . . . . .CFO (310-314-4135, ken@sovereignartists.com)
Charlie Springer . . . . .Sales & Marketing (310-314-4137,
                                        charlie@sovereignartists.com)
Geoff Cline . . . . .Business Affairs (310-314-4136,
                                        geoff@sovereignartists.com)
Tommy Funderburk . . . . .Artist Relations (310-314-4133,
                                        tommy@sovereignartists.com)
Chip Schutzman . . . . . . .Internet Marketing Strategist (310-314-4134,
                                        chip@sovereignartists.com)

SPINART RECORDS
PO Box 1798
New York, NY 10156
PHONE 718-852-3294
FAX 718-852-4166
EMAIL . . . . .info@spinartrecords.com
SECOND EMAIL . . . . .anr@spinartrecords.com
WEB SITE . . . . .www.spinartrecords.com
DISTRIBUTOR   Ryko Distribution
ARTIST ROSTER   The Apples in Stereo - Frank Black & the
                     Catholics - The Dears
GENRES   Alternative - Rock - Roots
SUBMISSION POLICY   Accepts unsolicited submissions
COMMENTS   Americana

Jeff Price . . . . .President
Chris Mooney . . . . .Director, Marketing

SPINOUT RECORDS
PO Box 3341
Duluth, MN 55803
PHONE 218-724-7433
EMAIL . . . . .biz@spinoutrecords.com
WEB SITE . . . . .www.spinoutrecords.com
GENRES   Blues - Folk - R&B - Reggae - Roots
SUBMISSION POLICY   No unsolicited material

Bernie Larsen . . . . .Owner
Tim Nelson . . . . .Owner

SPIRITUS RECORDS
24280 Junpier Flats Rd.
Homeland, CA 92548
PHONE 310-699-3898/951-926-3640
FAX 951-926-3640
EMAIL . . . . .maxxvaxx@spiritusrecords.com
WEB SITE . . . . .www.spiritusrecords.com

Jake Maguire . . . . .President
Max Vasquez . . . . .Producer

SPUN OUT
1525 S. Winchester Blvd.
San Jose, CA 95128-4335
PHONE 408-871-8829
FAX 408-871-8831
EMAIL . . . . .robert@soundmgt.com
WEB SITE . . . . .www.spunoutrecords.com
ARTIST ROSTER   Drist - Summer - Triple Seven
GENRES   Alternative - Pop - Rock

Robert Hayes . . . . .CEO
Steve Harwell . . . . .A&R

SST RECORDS
441 E. Fourth St.
Long Beach, CA 90802
PHONE 562-590-8853
FAX 562-590-8513
EMAIL . . . . .ginn@sstsuperstore.com
WEB SITE . . . . .www.sstsuperstore.com
GENRES   Alternative - Electronica - Reggae - Rock
SUBMISSION POLICY   Submissions accepted

Greg Ginn . . . . .Owner/President

*STARTIME INTERNATIONAL RECORDS
328 Flatbush Ave., PMB 297
Brooklyn, NY 11238
PHONE 718-636-9755
FAX 718-636-1292
EMAIL . . . . .info@startimerecords.com
WEB SITE . . . . .www.startimerecords.com
ARTIST ROSTER   Foreign Born - The Futureheads - The
                     Walkmen - The Joggers - Tom Vek - dios
                     (malos)

Isaac Green . . . . .Owner

STONY PLAIN RECORDS
PO Box 861
Edmonton, AB T5J 2L8 Canada
PHONE 780-468-6423
FAX 780-465-8941
EMAIL . . . . .info@stonyplainrecords.com
WEB SITE . . . . .www.stonyplainrecords.com/Web
DISTRIBUTOR   Navarre Corporation
ARTIST ROSTER   Maria Muldaur - Duke Robillard -
                     Ronnie Earl - Jay Geils
GENRES   Blues - Roots
SUBMISSION POLICY   Open policy; Submit to Chris Martin

Holger Petersen . . . . .President (holger@stonyplainrecords.com)
Chris Martin . . . . .A&R (chris@stonyplainrecords.com)

STORYVILLE RECORDS
Esplanaden 8 D
1263 Copenhagen K Denmark
PHONE 45-38198590
FAX 45-38190110
EMAIL . . . . .storyvil@post8.tele.dk
WEB SITE . . . . .www.storyville-records.com
GENRES   Blues - Jazz

Mona Granager .Managing Director

STUDIO DISTRIBUTION
150 W. 22nd St., 12th Fl.
New York, NY 10011
PHONE 212-685-7161
FAX 212-685-8731
WEB SITE . . . . .www.studiodistribution.com
GENRES   Electronica - Rap/Hip-Hop - Reggae

Thomas Ryan . . . . .Director, Sales
Doug Smiley . . . . .Director, Marketing
Matthew Sporlock . . . . .Production Manager

SUB POP
2013 4th Ave., 3rd Fl.
Seattle, WA 98121
PHONE 206-441-8441
FAX 206-448-7420/206-441-8245
EMAIL . . . . .info@subpop.com
SECOND EMAIL . . . . .firstnamelastinitial@subpop.com
WEB SITE . . . . .www.subpop.com
DISTRIBUTOR   Alternative Distribution Alliance (ADA)
GENRES   Alternative

Jonathan Poneman . . . . .CEO
Megan Jasper . . . . .General Manager
Eric Brown . . . . .VP, Business Affairs
Chris Jacobs . . . . .Marketing Director
Jeff Kleinsmith . . . . .Art Director
Andy Kotowicz . . . . .Director, Sales
Steve Manning . . . . .Publicity Director
Carly Starr . . . . .International Licensing
Jennifer Czeisler . . . . .International Licensing
Tony Kiewel . . . . .A&R
Stuart Meyer . . . . .A&R

SUBLIMINAL
199 Hackensack Plank Rd.
Weehawken, NJ 07087
PHONE 201-866-5340
FAX 201-866-5444
EMAIL . . . . .info@subliminalrecords.com
WEB SITE . . . . .www.subliminalrecords.com
SECOND WEB SITE . . . . .www.erickmorillo.com
LABELS   Double Platinum Productions
GENRES   Electronica
SUBMISSION POLICY   Accepts unsolicited submissions

Erick Morillo . . . . .President (eric@subliminalrecords.com)
Steve Hulme . . . . .International Director (steve@subliminalrecords.com)
Aggie Chavez . . . . . . .Office Manager (aggie@subliminalrecords.com)

SUGAR HILL RECORDS
PO Box 55300
Durham, NC 27717 5300
PHONE 919-489-4349
FAX 919-489-6080
EMAIL . . . . .info@sugarhillrecords.com
WEB SITE . . . . .www.sugarhillrecords.com
GENRES   Bluegrass - Roots

Barry Poss . . . . .Chairman
Kevin Welk . . . . .President, Welk Music (LA)
Bev Paul . . . . .General Manager
Dan Sell . . . . .VP, National Sales (LA)
Kim Fowler . . . . .VP, Artist & Media Relations (Nashville)
Steve Fishell . . . . .A&R (Nashville)
Tasha Thomas .Art Director (Durham)
Lynn Lancaster . . . . .International Sales & Marketing (Durham)
Lindsay Reid . . . . .Radio Promotions (Durham)
Holly Lowman . . . . .Marketing Manager (Durham)

SUNDAZED MUSIC, INC.
PO Box 85
Coxsackie, NY 12051
PHONE 518-731-6262
FAX 518-731-9492
EMAIL . . . . .info@sundazed.com
WEB SITE . . . . .www.sundazed.com
GENRES   Blues - Country - Jazz - Pop - Punk -
                       R&B - Rock

Tim Livingston . . . . .No Title
Bob Irwin . . . . .No Title
Jud Cost . . . . .No Title
Jeff Smith . . . . .No Title
Stephanie Kennedy . . . . .No Title
Jayme Pieruzzi . . . . .No Title
Kip Smith . . . . .No Title
Ric Zannitto . . . . .No Title
Jeff Jarema . . . . .No Title
Bill Dhalle . . . . .No Title
Mary Irwin . . . . .No Title
Suellen Cary . . . . .No Title

SUPEREGO RECORDS
511 Avenue of the Americas, Ste. 197
New York, NY 10011
PHONE 212-505-1943
FAX 212-505-1127
EMAIL . . . . .management@aimeemann.com
SECOND EMAIL . . . . .press@aimeemann.com
WEB SITE . . . . .www.aimeemann.com
DISTRIBUTOR   RED Music Distribution
ARTIST ROSTER   Aimee Mann
GENRES   Adult Contemporary - Alternative
SUBMISSION POLICY   No unsolicited material

Michael Hausman . . . . .President
Karen Malluk . . . . .Marketing
William Simon . . . . .Marketing
Michael Johnson . . . . .Assistant

*SUPERLATONE RECORDS
c/o Universal South
40 Music Square West
Nashville, TN 37203
PHONE 615-259-5300
FAX 615-259-5301
ARTIST ROSTER   Marty Stuart
GENRES   Bluegrass - Country - Gospel

Marty Stuart . . . . .Principal

SURFDOG RECORDS
1126 South Coast Hwy. 101
Encinitas, CA 92024
PHONE 760-944-7873
FAX 760-944-7808
EMAIL . . . . .promo@surfdog.com
WEB SITE . . . . .www.surfdog.com
DISTRIBUTOR   Alternative Distribution Alliance (ADA)
ARTIST ROSTER   Brian Setzer - Gary Hoey - Dan Hicks -
                       Echobrain - Voivod - Slightly Stoopid -
                       Agent 51 - Pato Banton - Gibby Haynes
                       & His Problem - Stray Cats - Richard
                       Cheese & Lounge Against the Machine
SUBMISSION POLICY   Accepts general submissions

Dave Kaplan . . . . .President
Niels Schroeter . . . . .General Manager
Nola Schoder . . . . .Production
Pierce Flynn . . . . .Surfdog Entertainment
Scott Seine . . . . .Program Manager
Anita Strine .Assistant to Mr. Kaplan

LABELS

SYMPATHY FOR THE RECORD INDUSTRY
4450 California Pl., Ste. 303
Long Beach, CA 90807-2229
PHONE 562-989-9387
EMAIL ....sympathy13@aol.com
WEB SITE ....www.sympathyrecords.com
DISTRIBUTOR   Lumberjack Mordam Music Group
ARTIST ROSTER   The Dwarves - Suicide - Scarling - The
                    Gun Club - The Willowz - The A-Lines -
                    The Muffs - Jack-O & the Tearjerkers -
                    Katastrophy Wife - The Geraldine
                    Fibbers
GENRES   Alternative - Blues - Rock
SUBMISSION POLICY   No unsolicited material

Long Gone John ....Owner

TAANG! RECORDS
706 Pismo Court
San Diego, CA 92109
PHONE 858-488-5950
FAX 858-488-5156
EMAIL ....orders@taang.com
WEB SITE ....www.taang.com
GENRES   Alternative - Hardcore - Metal - Pop -
                    Punk - Rock
COMMENTS   Ska

Miggz ....Group Events, Press
Curtis Taang ....A&R
Tara Taang ....Administrative

TEE PEE RECORDS
PO Box 20307
New York, NY 10009-9991
PHONE 212-253-1110
FAX 212-253-1422
EMAIL ....contact@teepeerecords.com
WEB SITE ....www.teepeerecords.com
DISTRIBUTOR   Caroline Distribution
GENRES   Rock

Tony Presedo ....President

TELARC RECORDS
23307 Commerce Park Way
Cleveland, OH 44122
PHONE 216-464-2313
FAX 216-464-4108
EMAIL ....vrzepka@telarc.com
WEB SITE ....www.telarc.com

Jack Renner ....Chairman/CEO
Robert Woods ....President/COO
Elaine Martone ....VP, Production
Evelyn Mowbray ....VP, Business Affairs
Vikki Rzepka ....Manager, National Radio Promotions/Artist &
                                Tour Information (x228)

TEXAS MUSIC GROUP
805 West Ave., Ste. 1
Austin, TX 78701-2207
PHONE 512-322-0617/800-962-5827
FAX 512-477-2930
EMAIL ....info@txmusicgroup.com
WEB SITE ....www.txmusicgroup.com
LABELS   Antone's Records - Lonestar Records -
                    TMG Records
GENRES   Blues - Country - Folk - Roots

Randolph Clendenen ....CEO (randolph@txmusicgroup.com)
Heinz Geissler ....Label Manager (heinz@txmusicgroup.com)

THE END RECORDS
331 Rio Grande, Ste. 58
Salt Lake City, UT 84101
PHONE 801-355-0963
FAX 801-355-3091
EMAIL ....theend@theendrecords.com
SECOND EMAIL ....orders@theendrecords.com
WEB SITE ....www.theendrecords.com
GENRES   Metal - Rock
SUBMISSION POLICY   Accepts demos by mail

Jacob H. Christ ....No Title

THICK RECORDS
PO Box 351899
Los Angeles, CA 90035-1899
PHONE 323-931-1303
EMAIL ....info@thickrecords.com
WEB SITE ....www.thickrecords.com
DISTRIBUTOR   Lumberjack Mordam Music Group
ARTIST ROSTER   New Black - Horace Pinker - Lasalle -
                   Fingers Cut - Megamachine - The
                   Tossers - The Methadones - The Arrivals
                   - Calliope - Haymarket Riot - Hanalei -
                   The Bomb

Zak Einstein ....Owner (zak@thickrecords.com)

THIRSTY EAR RECORDINGS, INC.
22 Knight St.
Norwalk, CT 06851
PHONE 203-838-0099
FAX 203-838-0006
EMAIL ....info@thirstyear.com
WEB SITE ....www.thirstyear.com
DISTRIBUTOR   Alternative Distribution Alliance (ADA)
ARTIST ROSTER   Matthew Shipp - Antipop Consortium -
                   DJ Spooky - Albert King - William Parker
                   - EL-P - Mark Eitzel - Spring Heel Jack -
                   Tim Berne - David S. Ware - DJ Wally -
                   Craig Taborn - Mike Ladd - Dave
                   Lombardo - Meat Beat Manifesto -
                   Groundtruther - KTU
GENRES   Alternative - Blues - Hardcore - Jazz -
                   Metal - Rock
SUBMISSION POLICY No unsolicited material

Peter Gordon ....President
Hope Kramer ....A&R
Rob Beam ....Radio Promotions/Creative Director
Michael Puccio ....Publicist

THORP RECORDS
PO Box 6786
Toledo, OH 43612
PHONE 419-255-3555
FAX 419-255-3555
EMAIL ....info@thorprecords.com
WEB SITE ....www.thorprecords.com
DISTRIBUTORS   Lumberjack Mordam Music Group -
                    Sonic Unyon Records
GENRES   Hardcore - Metal - Punk

Chris Hnat ......Publicity, Press, & Promotion (chris@thorprecords.com)

THRILL JOCKEY RECORDS, INC.
PO Box 08038
Chicago, IL 60608
PHONE 312-492-9634
FAX 312-492-9640
EMAIL .info@thrilljockey.com
WEB SITE .www.thrilljockey.com
DISTRIBUTOR   Alternative Distribution Alliance (ADA)
ARTIST ROSTER   Tortoise - Bobby Conn - Freakwater -
                     Trans Am - The Sea & Cake - Chicago
                     Underground - Califone - Oval
GENRES   Country - Electronica - Jazz - Pop - Rock
RECENT SOUNDTRACKS   Young Adam
SUBMISSION POLICY   No unsolicited demos

Erik Keldsen . . . . .Director, Licensing
Jon Brown . . . . .Sales
Jamie Proctor . . . . .Publicity

THRIVE MUSIC/THRIVE PICTURES
1024 N. Orange Dr., Ste. 100
Los Angeles, CA 90038
PHONE 323-308-3555
FAX 323-308-3556
EMAIL .info@thrivemusic.com
WEB SITE .www.thrivemusic.com
DISTRIBUTOR   RED Music Distribution
ARTIST ROSTER   Deep Dish - Roni Size - Infusion - Paul
                     Oakenfold - Hyper - Sander Kleinenberg
                     - Taylor Hawkins & The Coattail Riders
LABELS   Perfecto Records - Renaissance Records
GENRES   Alternative - Electronica - Rock
RECENT SOUNDTRACKS   Pi - Memento - Irreversible - Confidence
                     - Shattered Glass - Swordfish - XX/XY -
                     The Real Cancun - Requiem for a Dream
SUBMISSION POLICY   Submissions accepted via US Mail, Attn:
                     A&R Department
COMMENTS   Music Licensing/Clearance; Manager;
                     Soundtracks

Ricardo Vinas . . . . .President
Lee Kurisu . . . . .General Manager
Peter Torres . . . . .A&R
Jared Barboza .Director, Marketing
Natalie Pappas . . . . .Licensing Manager
Austin Beltran . . . . .Assistant/Office Manager

THUMP RECORDS
PO Box 445
Walnut, CA 91788-0445
PHONE 909-595-2144
FAX 909-598-7028
EMAIL .info@thumprecords.com
WEB SITE .www.thumprecords.com
DISTRIBUTOR   Universal Music & Video Distribution
ARTIST ROSTER   Mr. Capone-E - Tierra - Lenny Williams -
                     Frost - Weeto - Troy Cash - Rocky Padilla
LABELS   Thump - Thump Street - B-Dub
GENRES   Electronica - Latin - Pop - R&B -
                     Rap/Hip-Hop - Urban

Bill Walker . . . . .President (bwalker@thumprecords.com)
Pebo Rodriguez . . . . .Executive VP, A&R (prodriguez@thumprecords.com)
Jim Cowan . . . . . . .VP, Sales & Marketing (jcowan@thumprecords.com)
Diana Villalobos . . . . .Business Affairs (dvillalobos@thumprecords.com)

TIGHT SPOT RECORDS
PO Box 49543
Austin, TX 78765
PHONE 512-947-8077
EMAIL .info@tightspotrecords.com
SECOND EMAIL . . . . .chris@tightspotrecords.com
WEB SITE .www.tightspotrecords.com
DISTRIBUTORS   Carrot Top Distribution, Ltd. - Choke
                     Distribution - Revolver USA Distribution -
                     Southern Records, Inc.
ARTIST ROSTER   bedbug - Fivehead - Masonic - Subset -
                     This Microwave World

Chuck Stephens . . . . .Owner
Chris Hillen . . . . .Label Manager

TIME BOMB RECORDINGS
31652 Second Ave.
Laguna Beach, CA 92651
PHONE 949-499-4497
FAX 949-499-4496
WEB SITE . . . . .www.timebombrecordings.com
DISTRIBUTOR   Sony BMG Sales Enterprise

Jim Guerinot . . . . .Owner/A&R
Greg Gallardo . . . . .Finance

TIMES BEACH RECORDS
118 E. Seventh St.
Royal Oak, MI 48067
PHONE 248-548-2000
FAX 248-548-1091
EMAIL .info@timesbeachrecords.com
WEB SITE .timesbeachrecords.com
DISTRIBUTOR   NAIL Distribution
ARTIST ROSTER   Black Moses - The Ribeye Brothers -
                     Audra Kubat - Deadstring Brothers -
                     Ethan Daniel Davidson - Gold Cash
                     Gold - Man Incorporated - The
                     Hentchmen - The Muggs - Mark Dignam
GENRES   Blues - Country - Folk - Punk - Rock -
                     Roots

Dave Allison . . . . .President (dave@timesbeachrecords.com)
Philip Durr . . . . .A&R (phild@timesbeachrecords.com)
Becki Carr . . . . .Publicist (becki@timesbeachrecords.com)
Melanie Authier . . . .Office Manager (melanie@timesbeachrecords.com)

TOMBSTONE RECORDS
16631 SE 82nd Dr.
Clackamas, OR 97015
PHONE 503-657-0929
WEB SITE .www.deadmoonusa.com
ARTIST ROSTER   Dead Moon
GENRES   Rock

Fred Cole . . . . .Owner
Toody Cole . . . . .Owner

LABELS

LABELS (side tab)

TOMMY BOY ENTERTAINMENT
120 5th Ave., 7th Fl.
New York, NY 10011
PHONE 212-388-8300
FAX 212-388-8431
EMAIL . . . . .firstname.lastname@tommyboy.com
WEB SITE . . . . .www.tommyboy.com
DISTRIBUTOR   Alternative Distribution Alliance (ADA)
ARTIST ROSTER   Biz Markie - Kristine W - The Roc Project
    - Disco D - Murk - Fannypack
GENRES   Electronica - Rap/Hip-Hop - Urban

Tom Silverman . . . . .Chairman (212-388-8301)
Victor Lee . . . . .General Manager (212-388-8307)
Tom Sladek . . . . .Head, Sales (212-388-8346)
Hazel Zoleta . . . . .Radio Promotions (212-388-8485)
Mike Gomez . . . . .Production (212-388-8325)
Rosie Lopez . . . . .International Marketing (212-388-8475)

TONE CASUALTY RECORDS
c/o Klasky Csupo, Inc.
6353 Sunset Blvd.
Los Angeles, CA 90028
PHONE 323-468-2600
EMAIL .tko@tonecasualties.com
WEB SITE . . . . .www.tonecasualties.com
SECOND WEB SITE . . . . .www.klaskycsupo.com

Gabor Csupo . . . . .Co-Chairman
Arlene Klasky . . . . .Co-Chairman

TONE-COOL RECORDS
831 Beacon St., #335
Newton, MA 02459
PHONE 617-250-0828
FAX 617-250-0828
EMAIL . . . . .info@tonecool.com
WEB SITE . . . . .www.tonecool.com
DISTRIBUTOR   Artemis Records
ARTIST ROSTER   Bernard Allison - Kid Bangham & Amyl
    Justin - John Brim - Rick Holmstrom -
    Johnny Hoy - Mark Hummel - Little
    Anthony & Sugar Ray - The Love Dogs -
    David Maxwell - James Montgomery -
    North Mississippi Allstars - Rod Piazza &
    the Mighty Flyers - Paul Rishell & Annie
    Raines - Terrance Simien - Susan
    Tedeschi - Toni Lynn Washington - Mike
    Welch - Tony Z
GENRES   Blues - Pop - Rock

Richard Rosenblatt . . . . .President

TOOTH AND NAIL RECORDS
3522 W. Government Way
Seattle, WA 98199-1323
PHONE 206-691-9782
FAX 206-691-9776
EMAIL . . . . .webmaster@toothandnail.com
WEB SITE . . . . .www.toothandnail.com
DISTRIBUTOR   EMI Music Marketing
LABELS   Solid State Records - BEC Recordings -
    Uprok Records
GENRES   Alternative - Rock

Brandon Ebel . . . . .President/CEO
Jim Worthen . . . . .VP/CFO
Tyson Paoletti . . . . .Director, Marketing/A&R
John Frazier . . . .Director, Marketing, General Market, New Media, A&R
Chad Johnson . . . . .Director, A&R
Amanda MacKinnon . . . . .Director, Publicity, A&R
Allison Stipe . . . . .Director, Promotions
Derek Tenbusch . . . . .Director, Sales
Scott Carlton . . . . .Marketing Manager/Tour Marketing
Ryan Clark .Art Director, Designer
Jonathan Dunn . . . . .Manager, Licensing & Publishing Manager/A&R
Josh Jeter .Marketing Coordinator/A&R
Kevin H. Sheppard . . . . .Sales & Distribution Coordinator
Brad Davis . . . . .Designer
Jason Powers . . . . .Designer
Zaine Tarpo . . . . .Webmaster, A&R
Anneka Winters . . . . .Accounting Assistant

TOUCH AND GO/QUARTERSTICK
PO Box 25342
Chicago, IL 60625-0520
PHONE 773-388-8888
FAX 773-388-3888
EMAIL . . . . .info@tgrec.com
WEB SITE . . . . .www.touchandgorecords.com
DISTRIBUTOR   Alternative Distribution Alliance (ADA)
RECENT RELEASES   !!! - Calexico - Enon - Mekons - TV on
    the Radio - Coco Rosie - Nina Nastastia
    - Black Heart Procession - The New Year
    - Pinback
LABELS   Touch and Go Records - Quarterstick
    Records - Merge - Jade Tree - Suicide
    Squeeze - Kill Rock Stars - Overcoat -
    Estrus - Atavistic
GENRES   Alternative - Punk - Rock
RECENT SOUNDTRACKS   Happy Endings - Collateral - The O.C.
SUBMISSION POLICY   Accepts unsolicited submissions

Corey Rusk . . . . .President (corey@tgrec.com)
Ed Roche . . . . .Film/TV Licensing (edr@tgrec.com)
Miranda Lange . . . . .Publicity (miranda@tgrec.com)
John Londas . . . . .Publicity (john@tgrec.com)

TRANSMIT SOUND
PO Box 3141
Jersey City, NJ 07303
PHONE 201-963-6030
FAX 201-963-6530
EMAIL .sharon@transmitsound.com
WEB SITE . . . . .www.transmitsound.com
SECOND WEB SITE .www.jayfarrar.net
ARTIST ROSTER   Jay Farrar
SUBMISSION POLICY   No unsolicited submissions

Sharon Agnello . . . . .Label Manager

TRAVELER ENTERPRISES
PO Box 3234
Wichita Falls, TX 76301-0234
PHONE 940-855-6710
EMAIL . . . . .mudcoot@excite.com
WEB SITE . . . . .www.travelerrecordsonline.com
GENRES   Country

Harold Crosby . . . . .President

TRILOKA RECORDS
23852 Pacific Coast Hwy., Ste. 745
Malibu, CA 90265
PHONE 310-589-1760
EMAIL . . . . .info@triloka.com
WEB SITE . . . . .www.triloka.com
DISTRIBUTOR   Musicrama
ARTIST ROSTER   Krishna Das - Samite - M Path - Hassan
                               Hakmoun - Tarika - Walela - Spirit
                               Nation - Ziroq - Bhagavan Das - Vieux
                               Diop - Charanga Cakewalk - Les
                               Nubians
GENRES   Folk - Latin - New Age - Roots - World
SUBMISSION POLICY   Attn: A&R; No follow up phone calls
COMMENTS   Native American - Trance-Chant

Mitchell Markus . . . . .President

TRUE NORTH RECORDS
260 Richmond St. West, Ste. 501
Toronto, ON M5V 1W5 Canada
PHONE 416-596-8696
FAX 416-596-6861
EMAIL . . . . .general_inquiries@truenorthrecords.com.
WEB SITE . . . . .www.truenorthrecords.com
DISTRIBUTOR   Universal Music Canada
ARTIST ROSTER   The Golden Dogs - Bruce Cockburn -
                               Colin Linden - Howie Beck - Rheostatics
GENRES   All Genres

Bernie Finkelstein . . . . .President
Dan Broome . . . . .VP, Operations & Administration
Stewart Duncan . . . . .VP, Sales & Marketing
Elizabeth Blomme . . . . .Director, Publishing & Licensing
Julian Tuck . . . . .National Promotions Manager
James Grimes . . . . .Product & Production Manager
Sue McCallum . . . . .Public Relations
Paul Gagnon .Financial Administration
Sarah Scott . . . . .Office Manager

TRUSTKILL RECORDS
23 Farm Edge Ln.
Tinton Falls, NJ 07724
PHONE 732-542-7956
FAX 732-542-7957
EMAIL . . . . .info@trustkill.com
SECOND EMAIL .press@trustkill.com
WEB SITE . . . . .www.trustkill.com
DISTRIBUTOR   RED Music Distribution
ARTIST ROSTER   Fight Paris - Bedlight for Blue Eyes -
                               Bullet for My Valentine - Bleeding
                               Through - Eighteen Visions - Hopesfall -
                               Most Precious Blood - Nora - Open
                               Hand - Poison the Well - Throwdown -
                               Walls of Jericho - It Dies Today - Roses
                               Are Red - Terror
GENRES   Hardcore - Metal - Rock
RECENT SOUNDTRACKS   The Cave - Masters of Horror
SUBMISSION POLICY   Always open to demo submissions

Josh Grabelle . . . . .President
Kyle White . . . . .Office Manager
Dave Comeau . . . . .CIO
Robert Dippold . . . . .GM
Joel Jordan . . . . .Creative Director

TVT RECORDS
23 E. Fourth St., 3rd Fl.
New York, NY 10003
PHONE 212-979-6410/323-769-3501
FAX 212-979-6489/323-769-3507
EMAIL . . . . .info@tvtrecords.com
WEB SITE . . . . .www.tvtrecords.com
ARTIST ROSTER   Teedra Moses - Just Jack - 213 - Lil Jon
                               & the Eastside Boyz - Ying Tang Twins -
                               Pitbull - Jacki-O - The Eastsidaz -
                               Ambulance - Baldwin Bros. - Blue Epic -
                               Default - Sevendust - The Blue Van - The
                               Kicks
GENRES   All Genres
COMMENTS   Publisher; West Coast office: 1680 N.
                               Vine St., Ste. 806, Hollywood, CA
                               90028

Steve Gottlieb . . . . .President (steve@tvtrecords.com)
Paul Burgess . . . . .Executive VP, Marketing
Vera Savcic . . . . .General Manager
Joey Carvello . . . . .Sr. VP, Promotion
Leonard B. Johnson . . . . .VP, A&R (lbj@tvtrecords.com)
Patricia Joseph . . . . .VP, Soundtracks/A&R (pjoseph@tvtrecords.com)
Bryan Leach . . . . .VP, A&R Urban (bryan@tvtrecords.com)
Marvyn Mack .VP, Urban Promotion
Paul Raimer . . . . .VP, Production
Jason Consoli . . . . .Sr. Director, Publicity
Gary Jay . . . . .Sr. Director, National Alternative/Adult Promotion
John Perrone . . . . .Sr. Director, National Alternative/Adult Promotion
Sean Roberts . . . . .Sr. Director, A&R (sean@tvtrecords.com)
Christina Zafiris . . . . .Sr. Director, New Media & Strategic Marketing
Josh Freni . . . . .Director, A&R
Michelle Oakes . . . . .Director, A&R
Joe Wiggins . . . . .Manager, Urban Publicity

UBIQUITY RECORDS
1010 W. 17th St.
Costa Mesa, CA 92627
PHONE 949-764-9012
FAX 949-764-9013
EMAIL . . . . .mail@ubiquityrecords.com
WEB SITE . . . . .www.ubiquityrecords.com
DISTRIBUTOR   Alternative Distribution Alliance (ADA)
ARTIST ROSTER   Radio City - Owusu & Hannibal -
                               Greyboy - Platinum Pied Pipers - Sa-Ra
                               Creative Partners - Quantic - Roy Davis
                               Jr. - As One - Jeremy Ellis
LABELS   Ubiquity - Cubop - Luv 'N Haight
GENRES   Electronica - Jazz - Rap/Hip-Hop

Jody McFadin . . . . .Co-Founder
Michae McFadin . . . . .Co-Founder
Andrew Jervis . . . . .Director, A&R (andrew@ubiquityrecords.com)

ULTRA RECORDS
150 Lafayette St., Ste. 11R
New York, NY 10013
PHONE 212-343-2200
FAX 212-343-9429
EMAIL . . . . .info@ultrarecords.com
SECOND EMAIL . . . . .info@sequencerecords.com
WEB SITE . . . . .www.ultrarecords.com
SECOND WEB SITE . . . . .www.sequencerecords.com
LABELS   Ultra - Sequence - Escondida Music -
                               YOU Records
GENRES   Electronica - World
SUBMISSION POLICY   Address demos Attn: A&R

Patrick Moxey . . . . .President

UNDERTOW RECORDS

PO Box 300553
St. Louis, MO 63130
FAX 314-306-4091
EMAIL . . . . .chris@undertowmusic.com
WEB SITE . . . . .www.undertowmusic.com
DISTRIBUTOR   Redeye Distribution
ARTIST ROSTER   Jay Bennett - Bennett-Burch - Magnolia
                     Summer - Waterloo - The Redwalls -
                     Anna Fermin's Trigger Gospel - Glossary
                     - The Dreadful Yawns - Milton Mapes -
                     The Amazing Pilots - South San Gabriel -
                     Will Johnson - Dolly Varden - Steve
                     Dawson & Diane Christiansen - The Love
                     Experts
GENRES   Alternative - Blues - Rock - Roots
SUBMISSION POLICY   Not taking submissions at this time

Chris Grabau . . . . .Operations (chris@undertowmusic.com)
Rene Saller . . . . .Promotions (rene@undertowmusic.com)
Mark Ray . . . . .Creative Director (mark@undertowmusic.com)

UNION ENTERTAINMENT GROUP, INC.

1323 Newbury Rd., Ste. 104
Thousand Oaks, CA 91320
PHONE 805-375-5647
FAX 805-375-5649

Bryan Coleman . . . . .Partner (bryan@ueginc.com)
John Greenberg . . . . .Partner (jcgreenpad@aol.com)
Tim Heyne . . . . .Partner (tpkoone@aol.com)

UNITED MUSICIANS

511 Avenue of the Americas, Ste. 197
New York, NY 10011
PHONE 212-505-1943
FAX 212-505-1127
WEB SITE .www.unitedmusicians.com
DISTRIBUTOR   RED Music Distribution
ARTIST ROSTER   Aimee Mann - Michael Penn - Bob
                     Mould - Julian Coryell - Pete Droge -
                     Patton Oswalt
GENRES   Adult Contemporary - Alternative
SUBMISSION POLICY   No unsolicited material

Michael Hausman . . . . .Co-Founder
Aimee Mann . . . . .Co-Founder
Michael Penn . . . . .Co-Founder
Karen Malluk . . . . .Director
William Simon . . . . .Marketing
Michael Johnson . . . . .Assistant

UNIVERSAL CLASSICS GROUP

825 Eighth Ave., 19th Fl.
New York, NY 10019
PHONE 212-333-8000
FAX 212-333-8060
EMAIL . . . . .firstname.lastname@umusic.com
WEB SITE . . . . .www.iclassics.com
DISTRIBUTOR   Universal Music & Video Distribution
GENRES   Classical - Jazz

Chris Roberts . . .Chairman, UCG/President Classics & Jazz International
                                                          (212-333-8153)
Pat Clancy . . . . .COO, UCG/CFO , Classics & Jazz Worldwide
                                                          (212-333-8228)
Marc Johnston . . . . .Sr. VP/General Manager
Gerry Kopecky . . . . .Sr. VP, Sales (212-603-3948)
David Novik . . . . .Sr. VP, A&R
Randy Dry . . . . .VP, Marketing (212-333-8314)
Olga Makrias . . . . .VP, Publicity
Steve Singer . . . .VP, New Media/Internet/E-Commerce (212-333-8472)
Patricia Barry . . . . .Sr. Director, Creative Services & Production
Sarah Humphries . . . . . . .Sr. Director, ECM Marketing (212-333-8449)
Rebecca Pyle Davis . . . . .Director, Publicity
Bob Kranes . . . . .Director, Marketing, Classical Crossover
Elizabeth Baisley . . . . .Marketing Manager, Core Classics

UNIVERSAL MOTOWN RECORDS GROUP

1755 Broadway
New York, NY 10019
PHONE 212-373-0600
EMAIL . . . . .firstname.lastname@umusic.com
WEB SITE . . . . .www.motown.com
SECOND WEB SITE . . . . .www.universalrecords.com
DISTRIBUTOR   Universal Music & Video Distribution
GENRES   Country - Pop - R&B - Rap/Hip-Hop -
                     Rock

Mel Lewinter . . . . .President, Universal Motown Records Group
Sylvia Rhone   President, Motown Records/Executive VP, Universal Records
Jolene Cherry . . . . . .President, Cherry Entertainment/Sr. Executive, A&R
Monte Lipman . . . . .President, Universal Records
Avery Lipman . . . . .President, Republic Records/Sr. VP, Universal Records
Steve Rifkind .President, SRC Records
Andrew Kronfeld . .General Manager, Universal Motown Records Group
Samuel "Tone" Barnes . . . . .Executive VP, A&R
Bruce Carbone .Executive VP, A&R
Shanti Das . . . . .Sr. VP, Marketing & Artist Development
David Ellner . . . . .Sr. VP/CFO, Universal Motown Records Group
Serena Gallagher . . . . .Sr. VP, Pop/Rock Publicity
Kim Garner . . . . .Sr. VP, Marketing & Artist Development
Kevin Law . . . . .Sr. VP, A&R
Pat Monaco . . . . .Sr. VP, Sales
Eric Nicks . . . . .Sr. VP, A&R
Michael Reinert . . . . . .Sr. VP, Business & Legal Affairs, Universal Motown
                                                          Records Group
Wendy Washington . . . . .Sr. VP, Urban Publicity
Larry Baach . . . . .VP, New Media & Digital Strategies
Lori Lambert . . . . .VP, Strategic Alliances
Tom Mackay . . . . .VP, A&R, Republic/Universal

UNIVERSAL MUSIC CANADA

2450 Victoria Park Ave., Ste. 1
Toronto, ON M2J 5H3 Canada
PHONE 416-718-4000
FAX 416-718-4230
EMAIL . . . . .firstname.lastname@umusic.com
WEB SITE . . . . .www.umusic.ca
DISTRIBUTOR   Universal Music & Video Distribution
ARTIST ROSTER   Direct Signed: Jann Arden - Naida Cole
                     - Matthew Good - Sam Roberts - Remy
                     Shand - The Tragically Hip - Hawksley
                     Workman; US Signed: Bryan Adams -
                     Broken Social Scene - Nelly Furtado -
                     Diana Krall - Shania Twain - Rufus
                     Wainwright - Fefe Dobson - Matt Dusk
GENRES   All Genres
SUBMISSION POLICY   Send demo CD with bio and photo to
                     Attn: A&R
COMMENTS   Publisher; Licensing/Clearance;
                     Distributor

Randy Lennox . . . . .President/CEO (416-718-4188)
Steve Cranwell Sr. VP, Universal/Island/Def Jam Records (416-718-4090)
Wesley Hayden . . . . .Sr. VP, Sales (416-718-4020)
Bruce Hooey . . . . .Sr. VP, Finance/Administration (416-718-4010)
Les Houston . . . . .Sr. VP, Operations (416-718-4040)
Sarah Norris . . . . .Sr. VP, Interscope (416-718-4033)
Allan Reid .Sr. VP, A&R (416-718-4070)
Sarah Scott . . . . .VP, Business Affairs (416-718-4033)
Jodie Ferneyhough . . . . .Director, Music Publishing Creative Operations
                                                          (416-718-4110)
Tyson Parker . . . . . . .Director, Media & Artist Relations (416-718-4065)
Dave Porter . . . . .Director, A&R (416-718-4045)
Voula Vagdatis . . . . .Director, Human Resources (416-718-4155)
David Cox . . . . .A&R Representative (416-718-4239)
Susan Brearton . . . . .Manager, A&R Administration (416-718-4072)
Chris Corless . . . . .Creative Manager, Publishing (416-718-4112)
Catherine Jones . . . . .Manager, Licensing (416-718-4033)
Shawn Marino . . . . .International Marketing Manager (416-718-4066)
Darlene Gilliland . . . . .Contract Administrator (416-718-4135)
Ted Seto .A&R Assistant (416-718-4048)
Brenda Brown . . . . .Executive Assistant (416-718-4202)

UNIVERSAL MUSIC ENTERPRISES
2220 Colorado Ave., 1st Fl.
Santa Monica, CA 90404
PHONE 310-865-5000/212-373-0600
WEB SITE . . . . .www.umusic.com
GENRES   All Genres

Bruce Resnikoff . . . . .President
Lori Froeling . . . . .Sr. VP, Business & Legal Affairs
Richie Gallo . . . . .Sr. VP, Sales & Marketing
Kathy Hale . . . . .Sr. VP, Special Markets
Pat Lawrence . . . . .Sr. VP, Product Development
Bill Levenson . . . . .Sr. VP, A&R (NY)
Andy McKaie .Sr. VP, A&R (LA)
Bob Mercer . . . . .Sr. VP, New Business & Artist Development
Glen Sanatar . . . . .Sr. VP, Finance & Operations
Terry Ash . . . . .VP, Premium Sales
Chris Butler . . . . .VP, Finance/Controller
Felicia Gearhart . . . . .VP, Premium Sales
Vartan Kurjian . . . . .VP, Creative Services
Jeff Moskow . . . . .VP, Consumer Marketing & Product Management
Sujata Murthy . . . . .VP, Publicity
Ken Patrick . . . . .VP, Marketing & Sales
Tom Rowland . . . . .VP, Film & TV Music
Thane Tierney . . . . .VP, Hip-O Select
Harry Weinger . . . . .VP, A&R (NY)
Bob Zipkin . . . . .VP, Sales, Special Products
Ashley Culp . . . . .Sr. Director, New Media/Strategic Marketing
Antone DeSantis . . . . .Sr. Director, Catalog Analysis
Jay Gilbert . . . . .Sr. Director, New Media
Robin Kirby . . . . .Sr. Director, Merchandising/Consumer Marketing
Rhonda Malmlund . . . . .Sr. Director, Licensing
Mike Ragogna . . . . .Sr. Director, A&R
Jerry Stine . . . . .Sr. Director, Production
Don Terbush . . . . .Sr. Director, Film & TV Music
Bill Waddell . . . . .Sr. Director, Business Affairs
Steve Heldt . . . . .Director, Sales & Marketing, Midwest Region
Tom Lopinski . . . . .Director, Film & TV Music
Mike Rosenberg . . . . .Director, Sales & Marketing, Eastern Region
Cameron Smith . . . . .Director, Sales & Marketing, Western Region
Adam Starr . . . . .Director, Consumer Marketing & Product Management
Ramon Galbert . . . . .Associate Director, Consumer Marketing &
                                        Product Management
Robert Kelley . . . . .Associate Director, Film & TV Music
Elliot Kendall . . . . .Associate Director, Radio Promotions
Kelly Martinez . . . . .Associate Director, Licensing
Todd Nakamine . . . . .Associate Director, Publicity
Scott Ravine . . . . .Associate Director, Licensing
Dana Smart . . . . .Associate Director, A&R

UNIVERSAL MUSIC GROUP
2220 Colorado Ave.
Santa Monica, CA 90404
PHONE 310-865-5000/212-841-8000
WEB SITE . . . . .www.universalmusic.com
DISTRIBUTOR   Universal Music & Video Distribution
GENRES   All Genres
COMMENTS   East Coast office: 1755 Broadway, New
                         York, NY 10019

Doug Morris . . . . .Chairman/CEO
Nick Henny . . . . .Vice Chairman
Zach Horowitz . . . . .President/COO
Charles Ciongoli . . . . .Executive VP/CFO, North America
Scott Belmont .Executive VP/CIO
Michael Ostroff . . . . .Executive VP, Business & Legal Affairs
Vinnie Freda . . . . .Executive VP, Digital Logistics & Business Services
Peter LoFrumento . . . . .Sr. VP, Corporate Communications
Gayle Moore . . . . .Sr. VP, Human Resources, North America
Marjorie Fieldman . . . . .Sr. VP, Global Royalties
                                                        (Continued)

UNIVERSAL MUSIC GROUP (Continued)
Christine Grbelja . . . . .Sr. VP, Royalties
Harvey Geller . . . . .Sr. VP, Business & Legal Affairs
Maria Ho . . . . .VP, Corporate Communications (NY)
Grant Pavolka . . . . .Sr. Director, Corporate Communications (NY)
Margaret Wilhelm . . . .Sr. Director, Consumer Relationship Management
Renee Nahabedian . . . . .Director, Corporate Communications (LA)

UNIVERSAL MUSIC GROUP - ELABS
2220 Colorado Ave.
Santa Monica, CA 90404
PHONE 310-865-5000
FAX 310-865-1236
WEB SITE . . . . .www.umusic.com
COMMENTS   Focuses on new technologies and digital
                         distribution

Larry Kenswil . . . . .President
Amanda Marks . . . . .Executive VP
David Ring . . . . .Sr. VP, Business Affairs & Business Development
Chris Horton . . . . .VP, Advanced Technology
Susan Povich . . . . .VP, Business & Legal Affairs

UNIVERSAL MUSIC GROUP NASHVILLE
60 Music Square East
Nashville, TN 37203-4315
PHONE 615-524-7500
FAX 615-524-7600
EMAIL . . . . .firstname.lastname@umusic.com
WEB SITE . . . . .www.umusic.com
SECOND WEB SITE .www.losthighway.com
DISTRIBUTOR   Universal Music & Video Distribution
ARTIST ROSTER   **Mercury:** Terri Clark - Billy Currington -
                         Calaisa - Tracy Lawrence - Julie Roberts
                         - Shania Twain - Sugarland; **MCA**
                         Nashville: Gary Allan - Vince Gill -
                         Hanna-McEuen - Hot Apple Pie - Reba
                         McEntire - George Strait - Josh Turner -
                         Lee Ann Womack - Trisha Yearwood;
                         DreamWorks Records: Jessica
                         Andrews - Gary Nichols - Richie Jones -
                         Toby Keith - Jimmy Wayne - Darryl
                         Worley; **Lost Highway:** Ryan Adams -
                         Elvis Costello - Mary Gauthier - Tift
                         Merritt - Willie Nelson - Glen Phillips -
                         Lucinda Williams - Lyle Lovett (Curb/Lost
                         Highway) - Johnny Cash (American/Lost
                         Highway) - The Jayhawks (American/Lost
                         Highway) - Sam Roberts
LABELS   DreamWorks - Mercury - MCA Nashville
                         - Lost Highway
GENRES   Country - Rock

Luke Lewis . . . . .Co-Chairman, Mercury, MCA, DreamWorks/
                                        Chairman, Lost Highway
James Stroud . . . . .Co-Chairman, Mercury, MCA, DreamWorks
Jason Owen . . . . .Sr. VP, Media, Artist Relations & Creative Services,
                                        Mercury, MCA, DreamWorks
Ben Kline . . . . .Sr. VP, Sales & Marketing
Allison Jones . . . . .VP, A&R, Mercury, MCA, DreamWorks
Andy Nelson . . . . .VP, Marketing & Artist Development, Lost Highway
Bill Catino . . . . .Executive VP, Promotions
Ray Dipietro . . . . . . .National Sr. Director, Adult Alternative Promotions,
                                        Lost Highway
Brian Wright . . . . .Director, A&R, Mercury, MCA, DreamWorks
Doug Rich . . . . .Manager, A&R, Mercury, MCA, DreamWorks
Stephanie Wright . . . . . . .Manager, A&R, Mercury, MCA, DreamWorks
Eric Dout . . . . .Coordinator, A&R, Lost Highway
Parker Nusbickel . . . . .Coordinator, Marketing, Lost Highway
Tammy Luker . . . . . . .Executive Assistant to Co-Chairman, James Stroud
Erin Mason . . . . .Executive Assistant to Co-Chairman, Luke Lewis

UNIVERSAL MUSIC LATINO
420 Lincoln Rd., Ste. 200
Miami Beach, FL 33139
PHONE 305-938-1300/305-604-1300
FAX 305-938-1369/305-604-1340
EMAIL . . . . .firstname.lastname@umusic.com
WEB SITE .www.universalmusica.com
DISTRIBUTOR   Universal Music & Video Distribution
GENRES   Latin
COMMENTS   West Coast office: 303 N. Glenoaks
                    Blvd., Ste. 300, Burbank, CA 91502

John Echeverria . . . . .President, US & Puerto Rico (305-938-1351)
Ivan Alvarez . . . .Sr. VP, Music Publishing, Latin America (305-938-1310)
Walter Kolm . . . . .Sr. VP, Marketing/A&R (305-938-1355)
Gilberto Moreno . . . . .VP, Mexican Regional (281-772-9233)
Eddy Laca . . . . .National Sales Director (305-938-1345)
Luis Estrada . . . . .Sr. Label Manager (305-938-1309)
Patricia Flores . . . . . . .West Coast Media & Promotions Manager
                    (818-972-5698)
Elena Rodrigo . . . . . . .Rock/Alternative Label Manager (818-972-5673)
Nedy Maya . . . . .Assistant, Music Publishing (305-938-1310)
Mireya Flores . . . . . . .Assistant to VP, Mexican Regional (713-961-5430)
Marlene Martinez . . . . .Assistant to President (305-938-1375)

UNIVERSAL RECORDS
1755 Broadway, 7th Fl.
New York, NY 10019
PHONE .212-373-0600/310-865-2700
FAX 212-373-0660
EMAIL . . . . .firstname.lastname@umusic.com
WEB SITE . . . . .www.universalrecords.com
DISTRIBUTOR   Universal Music & Video Distribution
ARTIST ROSTER   Toni Braxton - Damian Marley - David
                    Banner - Lil Wayne - Chamillionaire -
                    Jack Johnson - 10 Years - Hinder - Blue
                    October - Kaiser Chiefs - Ra -
                    Abandoned Pools - Crazy Frog - Cherry
                    Monroe - Tami Chynn - BodyRockers - 3
                    Doors Down - Marques Houston - Akon
                    - Kem - Jamie Cullum - Lindsay Lohan -
                    India.Arie
GENRES   All Genres
COMMENTS   West Coast office: 2200 Colorado Ave.,
                    Santa Monica, CA 90404

Mel Lewinter . . . . .Chairman (212-373-0775)
Monte Lipman . . . . .President (212-373-0717)
Avery Lipman . . . . .President, Republic Records (212-841-8168)
David Ellner . . . . .Sr. VP/CFO (212-373-0620)
Samuel "Tone" Barnes . . . . . .Executive VP, Urban A&R (212-373-0642)
Bruce Carbone . . . . .Executive VP, A&R (212-841-8677)
Gary Gersh . . . . .Executive VP, West Coast A&R (310-865-2711)
Jolene Cherry . . . . .Sr. VP, A&R (310-865-2717)
Cynthia Cochrane   Sr. VP, Production & Creative Services (212-373-0761)
Shanti Das . . . . .Sr. VP, Urban Marketing (212-373-0623)
Valerie DeLong . . . . .Sr. VP, Promotions (310-865-2720)
Kim Garner . . . . . .Sr. VP, Marketing/Artist Development/Media Relations
                    (212-373-0741)
Michael Horton . . . . .Sr. VP, Urban Promotions (212-373-0714)
Pat Monaco . . . . .Sr. VP, Sales (212-841-8626)
Jeff Panzer . . . . .Sr. VP, Music Video Production (310-865-2728)
Michael Reinert . . . .Sr. VP, Business & Legal Affairs, Universal & Motown
                    (212-841-8609)
Wendy Washington . . . . .Sr. VP, Urban Media Relations (212-373-0702)
Eloise Bryan . . . . .VP, A&R Administration (212-373-0742)
Douglas Koch . . . . .VP, Marketing Administration (212-373-0745)
Tom MacKay . . . . .VP, A&R, Republic Records (212-841-8212)
George Marolda . . . . .VP, Financial Analysis (212-331-2774)
Tony Novia . . . . .VP, International (212-841-8777)
Jay Wilson . . . . .Sr. Director, Media Relations (212-373-0684)
Beth Bogdan . . . . .Director, Artist Relations, Pop/Rock
Dave Downey . . . . .Director, Rock Promotion
Phylicia Fant .Director, Publicity
Kevin Law .A&R (212-841-8647)
Sue Vellanti . . . . .Assistant to Mel Lewinter

UNIVERSAL SOUTH
40 Music Square West
Nashville, TN 37203
PHONE 615-259-5300
FAX 615-259-5301
EMAIL . . . . .firstname.lastname@umusic.com
WEB SITE . . . . .www.universal-south.com
DISTRIBUTOR   Universal Music & Video Distribution
ARTIST ROSTER   Rockie Lynne - The Elms - Marty Stuart -
                    Erika Jo - Joe Nichols - Bering Strait -
                    Cross Canadian Ragweed - Matt Jenkins
                    - Matthew West - Amanda Wilkinson -
                    Katrina Elam - The Notorious Cherry
                    Bombs - George Canyon - Holly
                    Williams - Shooter Jennings - Lee Roy
                    Parnell
LABELS   Superlatone Records
GENRES   Christian - Country - Pop

Tony Brown . . . . .Sr. Partner
Tim DuBois . . . . .Sr. Partner
Van Fletcher . . . . .Sr. VP/General Manager
Michael Pavers .Sr. VP, Promotion
Susan Levy . . . . .VP, Artist Development
Mike Owens . . . . .Director, A&R
Marty Craighead . . . . . . .Manager, Administration/Executive Assistant to
                    Tim DuBois
Amy Russell   Manager, A&R Production/Executive Assistant to Tony Brown

UP ABOVE RECORDS, LLC
130 Pine Ave., Ste. 200
Long Beach, CA 90802
PHONE 562-983-9999
FAX 562-590-2277
EMAIL . . . . .contact@upabove.com
WEB SITE . . . . .www.upabove.com
GENRES   Rap/Hip-Hop

Doug Kato . . . . .President
Key-Kool . . . . .VP
Kenny Ong . . . . .Art Director
Darrell Powe Jr. . . . . .A&R Director
Jonny Park . . . . .Production Manager
Alan Ward . . . . .Sales Manager
Jeff Gilbert .Marketing/Promotions
Samantha Sayon . . . . .Marketing/Promotions

*UPSTAIRS RECORDS, INC.
15814 Champion Forest Dr.
Spring, TX 77379
PHONE 281-655-8727
WEB SITE . . . . .www.upstairsrecordsinc.com

George Garcia . . . . .A&R
Jo Lopez . . . . .Radio Promotions
Jose Melendez . . . . .Operations
Joey Peralta . . . . .Retail

LABELS

V2 RECORDS

14 E. Fourth St., 3rd Fl.
New York, NY 10012
PHONE 212-320-8500/310-358-4000
FAX 212-320-8600
EMAIL . . . . .firstname.lastname@v2music.com
WEB SITE www.v2music.com
GENRES   All Genres

Andy Gershon . . . . .President (212-320-8550)
Matt Pollack . . . . .Sr. VP, Promotion
Dave Yeskel . . . . .Sr. VP, Sales
Scott Graves . . . . .VP, A&R (212-320-8532)
David Calderley . . . . .Head, Art & Design
Scott Hueston . . . . .Head, Sales
Jon Sidel . . . . .A&R (LA) (323-512-0060)
Samantha Tillman . . . . .Head, Publicity (212-320-8502)
Dan Cohen . . . . .Director, Marketing (212-320-8519)
Karen Durkot . . . . .National Promotion Director
Ted Hoekstra . . . . .National Promotion Director
Lisa Klipsic . . . . .Marketing Director (212-320-8635)
Jon Sidel . . . . .Director, A&R (LA) (323-512-0060)
Jeff Wooding . . . . . .Director, Marketing & New Media (212-320-8564)
Aimee Saiger . . . . .Southeast Promotion Director
Kristie Vogel . . . . .West Coast Promotion Director
Scott Graves . . . . .A&R Coordinator (212-320-8532)
Jane Grodd . . . . .A&R Administration (212-320-8642)
Keith Morris . . . . .A&R (LA) (323-512-0060)
Rebecca Lane . . . . .Publicity (212-320-8638)
Christina Tisone . . . . .Sales
Jon Lipman . . . . .Assistant to Andy Gershon (212-320-8557)

VAGRANT RECORDS

2118 Wilshire Blvd., Ste. 361
Santa Monica, CA 90403
PHONE 323-302-0100/212-331-2912
FAX 323-302-0111/212-331-2970
EMAIL . . . . .info@vagrant.com
SECOND EMAIL . . . . .publicity@vagrant.com
WEB SITE . . . . .www.vagrant.com
DISTRIBUTOR   Fontana Distribution
ARTIST ROSTER   Dashboard Confessional - Saves the Day
                      - Alkaline Trio - Senses Fail - From
                      Autumn to Ashes - Paul Westerberg
SUBMISSION POLICY   Accepts demos by US Mail
COMMENTS   East Coast office: 1755 Broadway, 3rd
                      Fl., New York, NY 10019

Richard Egan . . . . .Partner/President
Jon Cohen . . . . .Partner
Fernando Aguilar . . . . .Publicist (NY)

VANGUARD RECORDS

2700 Pennsylvania Ave.
Santa Monica, CA 90404
PHONE 310-829-9355/615-297-2588
FAX 310-315-9306/615-297-2510
EMAIL . . . . .info@vanguardrecords.com
WEB SITE . . . . .www.vanguardrecords.com
ARTIST ROSTER   Hootie & the Blowfish - Blues Traveler -
                      Deana Carter - Carbon Leaf - Bob
                      Schneider - Victor Wooten - Shurman -
                      Mindy Smith - Big Bad Voodoo Daddy -
                      Garrison Starr - Peter Case - Beau Soleil
GENRES   Adult Contemporary - Alternative -
                      Bluegrass - Blues - Christian - Country -
                      Folk - Gospel - Jazz - Rock - World
RECENT SOUNDTRACKS   Lackawanna Blues (HBO)
COMMENTS   Singer/Songwriters; Nashville office: PO
                      Box 159159, Nashville, TN 37215

Kevin Welk . . . . .President (LA)
Steve Buckingham . . . . .Sr. VP, A&R (Nashville)
Dan Sell . . . . .Sr. VP, Sales & Marketing
Lellie Capwell . . . . .VP, Publicity
Bob Kirsch . . . . .VP, Music Publishing (Nashville)
Art Phillips . . . . .VP, Promotions
(Continued)

VANGUARD RECORDS (Continued)

Patty Morris-Capers . . . . .National Director, Promotions
Steve Fishell . . . . .A&R, Sugar Hill Records (Nashville)
Vince Hans . . . . .Director, Sales & Catalog Marketing
Tricia Rice .Director, New Media
Ken Hauptman . . . . .Film & TV Music Consultant
Stephen Brower . . . . . . .Sales & Marketing Manager, A&R Development
Lauren Gaffney . . . . .Publicity Coordinator
Patricia Maduke . . . . .Business Affairs Coordinator
Mary Mahn . . . . .Promotion Manager
Ayappa Biddanda . . . . . . .Coordinator, Street Teams & Tour Marketing
Jo Bohannan . . . . .Contracts Administrator
Candice Smart . . . . .Publicity Assistant
Kim DeFranco . . . . .Marketing Assistant
Morgana Kennedy . . . . .Assistant to Kevin Welk

VAPOR RECORDS

1460 Fourth St., Ste. 300
Santa Monica, CA 90401-3414
PHONE 310-393-8442
FAX 310-393-6512
EMAIL . . . . .webstar@vaporrecords.com
WEB SITE . . . . .www.vaporrecords.com
ARTIST ROSTER   Tracy Lyons - Jonathan Richman - Tegan
                      & Sara - Cake Like - Catatonia -
                      Customers
GENRES   Rock
RECENT SOUNDTRACKS   Dead Man
SUBMISSION POLICY   Accepts submissions by mail; No calls

Elliot Roberts . . . . .Owner
Bonnie Levetin . . . . .General Manager

VARÈSE SARABANDE RECORDS

11846 Ventura Blvd., Ste. 130
Studio City, CA 91604
PHONE 818-753-4143
FAX 818-753-7596
EMAIL . . . . .info@varesesarabande.com
SECOND EMAIL . . . . .sales@varesesarabande.com
WEB SITE . . . . .www.varesesarabande.com
LABELS   Fuel 2000 - Water Music - Sunswept -
                      Varèse Vintage
GENRES   Bluegrass - Blues - Classical - Country -
                      Folk - Jazz - Pop - R&B - Rock
SUBMISSION POLICY   No unsolicited submissions
COMMENTS   Soundtracks - Oldies

Bryon Davis . . . . .Director, Sales & Marketing
Marian Cordry . . . . .Publicity

VEE-JAY LTD. PARTNERSHIP

43 Chestnut Woods Rd.
Redding, CT 06896
PHONE 203-938-2404
FAX 203-938-5533
EMAIL . . . . .info@veejay.mu
WEB SITE . . . . .www.veejay.mu
ARTIST ROSTER   Jimmy Reed - John Lee Hooker - Betty
                      Everett - The Spaniels - Gene Chandler -
                      Little Richard
GENRES   Blues - Country - Gospel - Jazz - R&B -
                      Rock
RECENT SOUNDTRACKS   Martin Scorsese Presents The Blues

Brayton Fogerty . . . . .No Title
Michele Tayler . . . . .No Title

LABELS

LABELS

THE VERVE MUSIC GROUP
1755 Broadway, 3rd Fl.
New York, NY 10019
PHONE 212-331-2000/818-729-4804
FAX 212-331-2064/818-729-4904
EMAIL .firstname.lastname@umusic.com
WEB SITE . . . . .www.vervemusicgroup.com
SECOND WEB SITE . . . . .www.ververecords.com
DISTRIBUTOR   Universal Music & Video Distribution
GENRES   Jazz
COMMENTS   West Coast office: 100 N. First St., 4th
                               Fl., Burbank, CA 91502-1845

Ron Goldstein . . . . .President/CEO (212-331-2002)
Tommy Lipuma . . . . .Chairman Emeritus (212-331-2001)
Michael Goldberg . . . . .CFO (212-331-2012)
Nate Herr . . . . .General Manager/Sr. VP, Marketing & Production
                                                           (212-331-2024)
Suzanne Berg . . . . .Sr. VP, Promotion (212-331-2009)
Michael Kauffman . . . . .Sr. VP, Sales & Catalog (212-331-2028)
David McDonagh . . . . .Sr. VP, International (212-331-2036)
Ken Druker . . . . .VP, Catalog Development (212-331-2083)
Bud Harner . . . . .VP, A&R (LA) (818-729-4805)
Regina Joskow .VP, Publicity (212-331-2053)
Hollis King . . . . .VP, Creative (212-331-2029)
Joe McEwen . . . . .VP, A&R (212-331-2034)
Jon Vanhala . . . .VP, New Media & Strategic Marketing (212-331-2050)
John Newcott . . . . .Sr. Director, Marketing (212-331-2038)
Dahlia Ambach Caplin . . . . .Director, A&R (212-331-2007)
Thedora Kuslan . . . . .Director, Marketing (212-331-2032)
J'ai St. Laurent-Smyth . . . . .Director, Publicity (212-331-2047)
Jamie Krents .Manager, International
Erin Whelan . . . . .Associate Manager, Marketing (212-331-2054)
Jesse Frye . . . . . .Coordinator, A&R/A&R Administration (212-331-2016)
Samantha White . . . . .Assistant to Ron Goldstein (221-331-2004)

VICE RECORDINGS
97 N. 10th St., Ste. 202
Brooklyn, NY 11211
PHONE 718-599-3101
FAX 718-599-1769
EMAIL . . . . .wassup@vice-recordings.com
WEB SITE . . . . .vice-recordings.com
DISTRIBUTOR   Alternative Distribution Alliance (ADA)
ARTIST ROSTER   Bloc Party - Death From Above 1979 -
                               Chromeo - The Stills - Yes New York -
                               The Streets - Panthers - Run the Road -
                               Boredoms
GENRES   Rap/Hip-Hop - Rock

Adam Shore . . . . .General Manager/A&R
Pat Riley .Director, Sales & Marketing
Jamie Farkas . . . . .Marketing Manager
Ghazal Sheei .Marketing Coordinator

VICTORY RECORDS
346 N. Justine St., Ste. 504
Chicago, IL 60607
PHONE 312-666-8661/44-0207-4247896
FAX 312-666-8665/44-0207-4247897
EMAIL . . . . .info@victoryrecords.com
WEB SITE .www.victoryrecords.com
DISTRIBUTOR   RED Music Distribution
ARTIST ROSTER   A Perfect Murder - A18 - Action Action -
                               Aiden - Atreyu - Bayside - Between the
                               Buried & Me - Bury Your Dead - Catch-
                               22 - Comeback Kid - Darkest Hour -
                               Dead to Fall - Freya - Giles - Glasseater
                               - Hawthorne Heights - June - Madcap -
                               Minus - Premonitions of War - Ringworm
                               - Scars of Tomorrow - Silverstein - Sinai
                               Beach - Snapcase - Spitalfield -
                               Straylight Run - Streetlight Manifesto -
                               Taking Back Sunday - The Black Maria -
                               The Forecast - The Hurt Process - The
                               Junior Varsity - The Tossers -
                               theAUDITION - Voodoo Glow Skulls -
                               Waterdown - With Honor
GENRES   Hardcore - Metal - Punk - Rock
COMMENTS   UK office: 85-87 Bayham St., Camden
                               Town, London NW1 0AG United
                               Kingdom

Anthony Brummel . . . . .CEO (x113)
Ramsey Dean . . . . .VP, Sales (x107)
Clint Billington . . . . .Production (x101)
Tim Binder . . . . .Director, Radio Promotions (x105)
Heather West . . . . .Director, US Publicity (x111)
Paul Friemel .New Media Desgner (x123)
Rick Linus . . . . .Sales (x121)
Stephanie Marlow . . . . .Tour & Video Promotions (x110)

VIRGIN ENTERTAINMENT GROUP NORTH AMERICA
5757 Wilshire Blvd., Ste. 300
Los Angeles, CA 90036
PHONE 323-935-1500
FAX 323-937-9110
WEB SITE . . . . .www.virgin.com
GENRES   All Genres

Simon Wright . . . . .CEO
Ravi Ahuja . . . . .CFO
David Alder . . . . .CMO
Sean Magee . . . . .VP, Operations
Kevin Milligan . . . . .VP, Product
Maureen Ferguson . . . . .Divisional Merchandise Manager,
                                           Books Merchandise, Accessories
Bart Saunt . .Divisional Merchandise Manager, Movies, Interactive Media
Jerry Suarez . . . . .Divisional Merchandise Manager, Music
Scott Leibow . . . . .Manager, Replenishment

VIRGIN RECORDS AMERICA, INC.

150 Fifth Ave.
New York, NY 10011
PHONE .212-786-8300/212-786-8370
WEB SITE . . . . .www.virginrecords.com
DISTRIBUTOR   EMI Music Marketing
GENRES   Alternative - Electronica - New Age - Pop
                     - R&B - Rock - Urban
COMMENTS   West Coast office: 5750 Wilshire Blvd.,
                     Los Angeles, CA 90036, phone: 323-
                     692-1100

Jason Flom .Chairman/CEO, Virgin Records
Mike Harris . . . . .CFO, Virgin Records
Lee Trink . . . . .General Manager
Jermaine Dupri .President, Urban Music
Jeffrey Kempler . . . . .Executive VP, Business Affairs & Development
Randy Miller . . . . .Executive VP, Marketing
Lionel Ridenour . . . . .Executive VP, Urban Music
Hilary Shaev . . . . .Executive VP, Promotion
Patti Conte . . . . .Sr. VP, Communications
Adam Lowenberg . . . . .Sr. VP, Marketing
Brian Postelle . . . . .Sr. VP, A&R
Rodney Shealey . . . . .Sr. VP, Urban Promotion
Phillip Wild . . . . .Sr. VP, Business Affairs
Bill Carroll . . . . .VP, Alternative Promotion
Danny Cooper . . . . .VP, Pop Promotion (LA)
Glenn Delgado . . . . .VP, Business Affairs
Amani Duncan . . . . .VP, Video Promotion
Jennifer Frommer . . . . .VP, Strategic Marketing
Ray Gmeiner . . . . .VP, Promotion (LA)
Andrea Kline . . . . .VP, Crossover Promotion
Doneen Lombardi . . . . .VP, Marketing (212-786-8358)
Jennifer McDaniels . . . . .VP, Urban Marketing
Jason McFadden .VP, Pop Promotion
Dominic Pandiscia . . . . .VP, Sales
Jonathan Rice . . . . .VP, International Marketing
Michelle Ryang . . . . .VP, A&R Administration
Syd Schwartz . . . . .VP, New Media
Randy Skinner . . . . .VP, Video Production
Sean Mosher Smith . . . . .VP, Creative Services
Eddie Weathers . . . . .VP, A&R
David Wolter . . . . .VP, A&R
Tracy Zamot . . . . .VP, Publicity (212-786-8370)
Michael Howe . . . . .Director, A&R (LA) (323-692-1204)
Julie Lichtenstein . . . . .Director, Publicity (212-786-8375)
Mak Niederhauser . . . . .Regional Promotions (Austin) (512 342 1942)

VIVATON RECORDS

702 18th Ave. South
Nashville, TN 37203
PHONE 615-255-5233
FAX 615-255-9133/615-255-5994
EMAIL . . . . .info@vivatonrecords.com
WEB SITE . . . . .www.vivatonrecords.com
DISTRIBUTOR   RED Music Distribution
ARTIST ROSTER   Chely Wright - Angela Wolf - Mark
                     Chesnutt
GENRES   Country

Jeff Huskins . . . . .President/CEO
Amy Stevens . . . . .VP, Legal Affairs & International Licensing
Dave Weigand . . . . .VP, Sales & Marketing
Darrell Vanzant . . . . .Director, A&R
Ronna Reeves . . . . .Manager, A&R
Tracy Long . . . . .Manager, Promotions
Mandy McCormack . . . . .Director, Regional Promotions/Midwest
Trudie Richardson . . . .Director, Regional Promotions/Southeast (Atlanta)
Larry Santiago . . . . .Director, Regional Promotions/West Coast
Brian Thiele . . . . .Director, Regional Promotions/Northeast

VOLCOM ENTERTAINMENT

1740 Monrovia Ave.
Costa Mesa, CA 92627
PHONE 949-646-2175
FAX 949-645-1101
EMAIL . . . . .volcoment@volcom.com
WEB SITE . . . . .www.volcoment.com
ARTIST ROSTER   Guttermouth - Pepper - ASG - Vaux - A
                     Faith Called Chaos - Single Frame -
                     Another Damn Disappointment - theLINE
                     - Dorothy Sanchez - Arkham -
                     Con$umer$ - Goons of Doom - Valient
                     Thorr - Riverboat Gamblers
GENRES   Hardcore - Punk - Rock

Ryan Immegart . . . . .No Title
Mark Gardner . . . . .No Title
Mike Nobrega . . . . .No Title
Reid Sheldon . . . . .No Title

WARNER BROS. RECORDS

3300 Warner Blvd.
Burbank, CA 91505
PHONE 818-846-9090/212-275-4500
WEB SITE . . . . .www.wbr.com
DISTRIBUTOR   WEA Corp.
LABELS   Reprise Records - Nonesuch - WBR
                     Nashville - WB Jazz - Maverick - Word
                     Records - Sire Records
COMMENTS   East Coast office: 75 Rockefeller Plaza,
                     New York, NY 10019

Tom Whalley . . . . .Chairman/CEO (818-953-3456)
Susan Genco . . . . .Sr. VP, Business & Legal Affairs (818-953-3221)
Hildi Snodgrass . . . . .CFO (818-953-3362)
Craig Aaronson .A&R (818-953-3544)
Jeff Aldrich . . . . .A&R (818-953-3782)
Naim Ali . . . . .A&R (818-953-3593)
Damon Booth . . . . .A&R (818-953-3508)
Rob Cavallo . . . . .A&R (818-953-3303)
James Dowdall .A&R (212-275-4816)
Rachel Howard .A&R (818-953-3227)
Andy Olyphant .A&R (818-953-3783)
Perry Watts-Russell . . . . .A&R (818-953-3553)
(Continued)

LABELS

WARNER BROS. RECORDS (Continued)

Rochelle Staab . . . . .Advertising (818-953-3487)
Nick Light . . . . .Artist Relations/Development (818-953-3733)
Steve Margo . . . . .International (818-953-3445)
Alex Levy . . . . .International (818-953-3368)
Diarmuid Quinn . . . . .Marketing (818-953-3242)
Mitra Darab . . . . .Marketing (818-953-3268)
Eric Fritschi . . . . .Marketing (818-953-3618)
Rob Gordon . . . . .Marketing (818-953-3461)
Azizi Murray . . . . .Marketing (818-953-3534)
Xavier Ramos . . . . .Marketing (818-953-3433)
Tami Rittberg . . . . .Marketing (818-953-3559)
Andie Simon . . . . .Marketing (212-275-4855)
Peter Standish . . . . .Marketing (818-953-3236)
Brant Weil . . . . .Marketing (818-953-3386)
Denise Williams . . . . .Marketing (818-953-3708)
Lori Feldman . . . . .TV Marketing (212-275-4871)
Luke Burland . . . . .Media Relations (818-953-3626)
Jim Baltutis . . . . .Media Relations (818-953-3375)
Bill Bentley . . . . .Media Relations (818-953-3671)
Brian Bumbery .Media Relations (818-953-3203)
Rick Gershon . . . . .Media Relations (818-953-3473)
Liz Rosenberg .Media Relations (212-275-4616)
Dave Burke . . . . .Merchandising (818-953-3702)
Robin Bechtel . . . . .New Media (818-953-3555)
Jennifer Bird . . . . .New Media (818-953-3551)
Phil Costello .Reprise Promotion (818-953-3777)
Brent Battles .Reprise Promotion (818-953-3754)
Alex Coronfly .Reprise Promotion (818-953-3744)
Anne Marie Foley . . . . .Reprise Promotion (212-275-4571)
Jeff Gillis . . . . .Reprise Promotion (212-275-4682)
Lynn McDonnell . . . . .Reprise Promotion (818-953-3549)
Raymond McGlamery . . . . .Reprise Promotion (818-953-3785)
Tommy Page . . . . .Reprise Promotion (212-275-4652)
Bob Weil . . . . .Reprise Promotion (818-953-3751)
Dave Stein . . . . .Sales (818-953-3498)
Judy Neubauer . . . . .Sales (818-953-3633)
Amy Zaret . . . . .Sales (818-953-3629)
Yvette Ziraldo . . . . .Sales (818-953-3584)
Wendy Griffiths . . . . .Video (212-275-4550)
Liz Lewis . . . . .Video (212-275-4512)
Andy Manning . . . . .Video (212-275-4580)
Tom Biery . . . . .WB Promotion (818-953-3715)
Debra Cerchione . . . . .WB Promotion (212-275-4601)
Dale Connone . . . . .WB Promotion (212-275-4558)
Robert Goldklang . . . . .WB Promotion (818-953-3366)
Franco Iemmello .WB Promotion (212-275-4614)
Heather Luke . . . . .WB Promotion (818-953-3742)
Julie Muncy . . . . .WB Promotion (818-953-3567)
Mike Rittberg . . . . .WB Promotion (818-953-3723)
Myra Simpson . . . . .WB Promotion (818-953-3709)
Felicia Swerling . . . . .WB Promotion (818-953-3611)

WARNER BROS. RECORDS NASHVILLE

20 Music Square East, 3rd Fl.
Nashville, TN 37203-4344
PHONE 615-748-8000
FAX .615-214-1567/615-214-1537
EMAIL . . . . .firstname.lastname@wbr.com
WEB SITE . . . . .www.wbrnashville.com
DISTRIBUTOR   WEA Corp.
ARTIST ROSTER   Alexis - Big & Rich - Shannon Brown -
                     Joanna Cotton - Faith Hill - Lauren
                     Lucas - Lance Miller - Jon Nicholson -
                     Anna Owens - Ray Scott - Blake Shelton
                     - Jimmy Stewart - Brad Stein - Rick
                     Trevino - Lane Turner
GENRES   Country

Paul Worley . . . . .CCO
Bill Bennett . . . . .Executive VP
Tracy Gershon . . . . .Sr. VP, A&R
Gator Michaels . . . . .Sr. VP, Promotions
Jules Wortman . . . . .Sr. VP, Publicity & Artist Development
Jim Malito . . . . .VP, National Promotion
Peter Strickland . . . . .VP, Sales
Lynette Garbonola .Director, New Media
Scott Heuerman . . . . .Director, Marketing
(Continued)

WARNER BROS. RECORDS NASHVILLE (Continued)

Danny Kee . . . . .Director, A&R (615-214-1464)
Eric Mansfield . . . . .Director, Creative Services
Jennie Smythe . . . . .Director, New Media
Kristen Doyscher . . . . .Manager, Midwest Promotion
George Meeker . . . . .Manager, Secondary Promotion
Maura Mooney . . . . .Manager, Publicity (615-214-1500)
Glenn Noblit . . . . .Manager, Southwest Promotion
Brooks Quigley . . . . .Manager, Southeast Promotion
Joe Redmond . . . . .Manager, Northeast Promotion
Jeremy Witt . . . . .Manager, A&R (615-214-1464)
Rick Young . . . . .Manager, West Coast Promotion
Brian Horner . . . . .Sales & Marketing Coordinator (615-214-1550)
Danielle Taylor . . . . .Promotion Coordinator (615-214-1555)
Paige Connors . . . . .Executive Assistant to CCO (615-214-1553)
Christy Hathcock . . .Executive Assistant to Executive VP (615-214-1433)
Kelli Cashiola . . . . .Promotion Assistant

WARNER BROS. RECORDS URBAN

3300 Warner Blvd.
Burbank, CA 91505
PHONE 818-846-9090/212-275-4500
FAX .818-846-8474/212-275-4595
EMAIL . . . . .urbanmusic@wbr.com
WEB SITE . . . . .www.wbr.com
DISTRIBUTOR   WEA Corp.
ARTIST ROSTER   Jaheim - Mike Jones - Eric Benet -
                     Trillville - Lil Scrappy - Cruna - J. Spears
                     - Jody Breeze - Leela James - Bohagon -
                     E-40
GENRES   Urban
COMMENTS   East Coast office: 75 Rockefeller Plaza,
                     New York, NY 10019

Cynthia Johnson . . . . .Sr. VP, Promotion (Bi-Coastal)
Naim Ali . . . . .VP, A&R (LA, Bi-Coastal)
Denise Williams . . . . .Sr. Director, Marketing (LA, Bi-Coastal)

WARNER MUSIC GROUP (WMG)

75 Rockefeller Plaza
New York, NY 10019
PHONE 212-275-4500
WEB SITE . . . . .www.wmg.com
LABELS   Asylum - The Atlantic Records Group
                     (Atlantic Records - Lava Records - Bad
                     Boy Records - Elektra Records) - East
                     West - Warner Bros. Records Inc.
                     (Warner Bros. Records - WBR Nashville -
                     Sire Records - Reprise Records -
                     Maverick Records - Word Records -
                     Nonesuch) - Warner Music International
                     - Rhino Entertainment - Word
                     Entertainment (Word Label Group -
                     Squint Entertainment - Word Distribution)

Edgar Bronfman Jr. . . . . .Chairman/CEO, Warner Music Group
Lyor Cohen   Chairman/CEO, US Recorded Music, Warner Music Group
Paul-René Albertini . . . . . . .Chairman/CEO, Warner Music International
Richard Blackstone . . . . . . .Chairman/CEO, Warner/Chappell Music, Inc.
Michael D. Fleisher . . . . .Executive VP/CFO, Warner Music Group
Dave Johnson . . . .Executive VP, General Counsel, Warner Music Group
Kevin Liles . . . . .Executive VP
Caroline Stockdale . . . . .Executive VP, Global Human Resources
Jill Krutick . . . . .Sr. VP, Investor Relations & Corporate Development
Paul Robinson . . . . .Sr. VP, Deputy General Counsel
Will Tanous . . . . .Sr. VP, Corporate Communications
George White . . . . .Sr. VP, Strategy & Product Development

WARNER SUNSET SOUNDTRACKS
4000 Warner Blvd., Bldg. 3, Rm. 175
Burbank, CA 91522-0001
PHONE 818-954-3456
FAX 818-954-3418
WEB SITE . . . . .www.wbr.com
DISTRIBUTOR   WEA Corp.
GENRES   All Genres

Gary LeMel . . . . .President
Doug Frank . . . . .Co-President
Keith Zajic . . . . .Executive VP, Business & Legal Affairs

WATER MUSIC RECORDS
PO Box 261640
Encino, CA 91426
PHONE 818-808-0800
FAX 818-808-0844
EMAIL . . . . .releases@watermusicrecords.com
WEB SITE . . . . .www.watermusicrecords.com
DISTRIBUTOR   Universal Music & Video Distribution
ARTIST ROSTER   ATB - Blank & Jones - Fragma - Matt
                          Darcy - Kate Ryan - Ashley Jade
GENRES   Electronica

Brad Pressman . . . . .President
Mara Pressman . . . . .VP/CFO
Rod Linnum . . . . .VP, National Sales/A&R
Mary Dolezal . . . . .Marketing & Promotion

WATERDOG MUSIC
329 W. 18th St., Ste. 313
Chicago, IL 60616
PHONE 312-421-7499
FAX 312-421-1848
EMAIL . . . . .waterdog@waterdogmusic.com
WEB SITE . . . . .www.waterdogmusic.com
SECOND WEB SITE . . . . .www.ralphsworld.com
DISTRIBUTOR   Big Daddy Music Distribution
ARTIST ROSTER   Ralph Covert - The Bad Examples -
                         Ralph's World - Middle8 - Suzy Brack &
                         the New Jack Lords
LABELS   Waterdog Records - Whitehouse Records
GENRES   Children's - Rock
RECENT SOUNDTRACKS   The Last Road
SUBMISSION POLICY   No unsolicited submissions accepted

Ralph Covert . . . . .Founder
Rob Gillis . . . . .Record Guy

WAXPLOITATION
201 S. Santa Fe Ave., #100
Los Angeles, CA 90012
PHONE 213-687-9563
FAX 213-687-9569
EMAIL . . . . .info@waxploitation.com
WEB SITE .www.waxploitation.com
ARTIST ROSTER   Tweaker - Danger Mouse - J Wells
GENRES   Alternative - Electronica - Rap/Hip-Hop -
                         Reggae - Rock

Jeff Antebi . . . . .Co-President

WELK MUSIC GROUP
2700 Pennsylvania Ave.
Santa Monica, CA 90404
PHONE 310-829-9355/615-297-2588
FAX 310-315-9306/615-297-2510
EMAIL . . . . .info@welkmg.com
ARTIST ROSTER   Dolly Parton - Nickel Creek - Hootie &
                         the Blowfish - Blues Traveler - Big Bad
                         Voodoo Daddy - George Jones - Mindy
                         Smith - Carbon Leaf - Deana Carter -
                         Julia Fordham - Bob Schneider - Peter
                         Case
LABELS   Sugar Hill - Vanguard - Ranwood
GENRES   Adult Contemporary - Alternative -
                         Bluegrass - Blues - Christian - Country -
                         Folk - Gospel - Jazz - Rock - World
COMMENTS   Distributor; Publisher; Nashville office:
                         PO Box 159159, Nashville, TN 37215

Larry Welk . . . . .CEO
Kevin Welk . . . . .President
Steve Buckingham . . . . .Sr. VP, A&R
Dan Sell . . . . .Sr. VP, Sales & Marketing
Lellie Capwell . . . . .VP, Publicity (Vanguard)
Kim Fowler . . . . .VP, Artist & Media Relations (Sugar Hill)
Bob Kirsch . . . . .VP, Music Publishing
Art Phillips . . . . .VP, Promotions
Ken Hauptman . . . . .Film/TV Consultant
Tricia Rice . . . . .Director, New Media
Patricia Maduke . . . . .Business Affairs Coordinator
Jo Bohannan . . . . .Contracts Administrator

WHAT ARE RECORDS?
2401 Broadway
Boulder, CO 80304
PHONE 303-440-0666
FAX 303-447-2484/303-817-3839
EMAIL . . . . .info@whatarerecords.com
WEB SITE . . . . .www.whatarerecords.com
SECOND WEB SITE . . . . .www.haharecords.com
DISTRIBUTOR   Select-O-Hits
ARTIST ROSTER   Maceo Parker - Stephen Lynch - David
                        Wilcox - The Innocence Mission - The
                        Samples - Glenn Tilbrook - Tim Finn -
                        The Radiators - Frank Black & the
                        Catholics - House of Large Sizes - Lloyd
                        Cole - Melissa Ferrick - The Ocean Blue
                        - Sally Taylor - Munly - Joseph Brenna -
                        Tony Furtado - Yazbek - Felicia Michaels
                        - The Poppy Family - 24-7 Spyz - Jeep
                        Cycomotogoat - Primitive Radio Gods -
                        Lir - Reggae on the Rocks - Stuart
                        Matthewman - Daniel Mackenzie
GENRES   Alternative - Blues - Folk - Jazz - Pop -
                        Reggae - Rock - Roots
COMMENTS   Licensing/Clearance

Rob Gordon . . . . .President/A&R
Rebecca Gordon .Executive VP
Dan Booth . . . . .Director, Sales (dan@whatarerecords.com)
Jillian Reitsma   Director, Radio/Publicity/Art (jillian@whatarerecords.com)
F.X. Wallace . . . . .Director, Licensing (fx@whatarerecords.com)
Mathew Wilkening . . . . .Director, Fan/Tour/Online Marketing
                        (mw@whatarerecords.com)

LABELS

LABELS

WILD OATS RECORDS
PO Box 210982
Nashville, TN 37221
PHONE 615-662-1677
FAX 615-673-2860
EMAIL . . . . .info@wildoatsrecords.com
SECOND EMAIL . . . . .production@wildoatsrecords.com
WEB SITE . . . . .www.wildoatsrecords.com
ARTIST ROSTER   Steve Haggard - Pat DiNizio - Mark
                       Brine - Gail & the Tricksters - Joel Alan
                       Lehman
GENRES   Blues - Country - Folk - Rock - Roots
SUBMISSION POLICY   Open policy, but email first
COMMENTS   Americana

Steve Haggard . . . . .Producer
Otis Kay . . . . .Label Manager
Glen Edwards . . . . .Director, Operations
Randall Merryman . . . . .Chief Recording Engineer

WILDCATTER RECORDS
PO Box 1210, 616 Fifth St.
Graham, TX 76450
PHONE .940-549-3292/940-550-5439
FAX 940-549-5162
WEB SITE . . . . .www.wildcatterrecords.com
DISTRIBUTOR   RED Music Distribution
ARTIST ROSTER   Red Steagall - Joni Harms - David Ball
GENRES   Country
COMMENTS   Specializes in contemporary Western and
                       classic Country music

Mickey Dawes . . . . .CEO (mickey@wildcatterrecords.com)

WIND-UP RECORDS
72 Madison Ave., 8th Fl.
New York, NY 10016
PHONE .212-895-3100/212-251-9665
EMAIL . . . . .windup@winduprecords.com
SECOND EMAIL . . . . .firstinitiallastname@winduprecords.com
WEB SITE . . . . .www.wind-upent.com
SECOND WEB SITE . . . . .www.winduprecords.com
DISTRIBUTOR   Sony BMG Sales Enterprise
ARTIST ROSTER   12 Stones - Alter Bridge - Atomship -
                       Ben Moody - Big Dismal - Breaking Point
                       - Drowning Pool - Evanescence - Finger
                       Eleven - Megan McCauley - People in
                       Planes - Seether - Scott Stapp - Strata -
                       Submersed
GENRES   Alternative - Pop - Rock

Alan Meltzer . . . . .CEO
Steve Lerner . . . . .President
Edward Vetri . . . . .COO/CFO
Diana Meltzer . . . . .Executive VP, A&R
Shanna Fischer . . . . .Sr. VP, Promotions
Steve Karas . . . . .Sr. VP, Publicity & Video (212-895-3140)

WORD ENTERTAINMENT
25 Music Square West
Nashville, TN 37203
PHONE 615-251-0600
FAX 615-726-7886
EMAIL . . . . .firstname.lastname@wbr.com
WEB SITE . . . . .www.wordlabelgroup.com
DISTRIBUTOR   WEA Corp.
ARTIST ROSTER   Word Label Group Roster: Amy Grant -
                       Jaci Velasquez - BarlowGirl - Randy
                       Travis - Big Daddy Weave - By the Tree -
                       Point of Grace - Nicole C. Mullen -
                       Mark Schultz - Salvador - Rachael
                       Lampa - David Phelps - Mute Math -
                       Building 429 - Stellar Kart - Karen Clark
                       Sheard - George Huff - Inhabited
LABELS   Word Records - Myrrh Records - Fervent
                       Records - Elektra - Big Idea - Curb -
                       SHELTERecords - Daywind - Floodgate -
                       Garden City - Metro1 - Praise Gathering
                       - Spring Hill - Spindust - Toonacious -
                       Word Music - A'postrophe Records - BHT
                       Entertainment - Brash Music - Doxology
                       Records - 20th Century Fox Home
                       Entertainment - Lightyear Entertainment -
                       Lions Gate Entertainment - Maranatha!
                       Music - Taseis Media Group - Warner
                       Home Video - Wet Cement Productions -
                       SideOneDummy Records
GENRES   Adult Contemporary - Christian -
                       Country - Rock
SUBMISSION POLICY   No unsolicited material

Jim Van Hook . . . . .CEO, Word Entertainment
Don Cason . . . . .President/General Manager, Word Music
Mark Funderburg . . . . .President, Word Distribution
Tim Marshall . . . . .Sr. VP, A&R, Word Label Group
Rod Riley . . . . .Sr. VP, Marketing, Word Label Group

YELLOW DOG RECORDS
99 S. Second St., Ste. A-277
Memphis, TN 38103
PHONE 901-452-4087
EMAIL . . . . .info@yellowdogrecords.com
WEB SITE . . . . .yellowdogrecords.com
DISTRIBUTOR   Burnside Distribution Corp.
ARTIST ROSTER   Mark Lemhouse - The Bo-Keys - Bluff
                       City Backsliders - Big Joe Duskin - Chris
                       Cotton - Calvin Newborn - Terry Robb
GENRES   Blues - Folk - Jazz - Roots
SUBMISSION POLICY   Email with description of music

Michael Powers . . . . .President

YEP ROC RECORDS
449-A Trollingwood Rd.
Haw River, NC 27515-4821
PHONE 336-578-7300/877-733-3931
FAX 336-578-7388
EMAIL . . . . .info@yeproc.com
WEB SITE . . . . .www.yeproc.com
DISTRIBUTORS   Outside Music Inc. - Redeye Distribution
ARTIST ROSTER   Dave Alvin - Thad Cockrell - John Doe -
                     Robbie Fulks - Robyn Hitchcock - The
                     Iguanas - The Kingsbury Manx - Los
                     Straitjackets - Marah - Bob Mould - The
                     Reverend Horton Heat - The Sadies -
                     Laika & the Cosmonauts - Paul Weller -
                     Nick Lowe - The Go-Betweens - The
                     Comas - Jason Ringenberg - Chris
                     Stamey - Forty-Fives - C.C. Adcock -
                     Doyle Bramhall - Big Sandy - Robert
                     Skoro - The Legendary Shack Shakers -
                     Minus 5 - The Fleshtones - Caitlin Cary -
                     Tres Chicas - Dolorean - The Standard -
                     Southern Culture on the Skids - Ken
                     Stringfellow - Heavy Trash - Ian Moore -
                     Chatham County Line - The Moaners -
                     American Princes - Cities
GENRES   Blues - Country - Folk - Pop - Rock -
                     Roots
SUBMISSION POLICY   Accepts demos by mail
COMMENTS   Also distributed by Shellshock (UK),
                     Cargo (Germany) and I.R.D. (Italy)

Glenn Dicker . . . . .Label Manager/A&R (x205, glenn@yeproc.com)
Tor Hansen   Sales & Marketing Director/A&R (x203, tor@redeyeusa.com)
Angie Carlson . . . . .Director, Publicity (x209, angie@yeproc.com)
Lily Olive . . . . .Advertising/Tour Press (x244, lily@yeproc.com)
Hank Stockard . . . . .Promotions/Street Team (x201, hank@yeproc.com)
Steve Gardner . .Director, Radio Promotions (x242, steveg@yeproc.com)
Joe Swank . . . . .Radio (x223, joe.swank@yeproc.com)
Jill Sweeney . . . . .Retail Marketing & Promotions (215-923-4644,
                                              jill@redeyeusa.com)
Dave Thomas . . . . . . .Director, New Media (x213, davet@yeproc.com)

ZEBRA RECORDS
PO Box 9178
Calabasas, CA 91372-9178
PHONE 818-988-6285
FAX 818-988-6282
EMAIL . . . . .zebradisc@aol.com
DISTRIBUTOR   WEA Corp.
ARTIST ROSTER   Kevin Mahogany - BeatleJazz - Jazz Is
                     Dead
GENRES   Adult Contemporary - Jazz
SUBMISSION POLICY   Artists with established sales and release
                     history

Ricky Schultz . . . . .President
Sean Green . . . . .Associate

ZOMBA LABEL GROUP
137-139 W. 25th St.
New York, NY 10001
PHONE 212-727-0016/310-449-2100
FAX 212-645-3783
EMAIL . . . . .firstname.lastname@sonybmg.com
DISTRIBUTOR   SONY BMG MUSIC ENTERTAINMENT
LABELS   Jive - LaFace - So So Def - Verity -
                     Violator - Volcano - Silvertone - Gospo
                     Centric
GENRES   Gospel - Pop - Rock - Urban
COMMENTS   West Coast office: 2100 Colorado Ave.,
                     Santa Monica, CA 90404, phone: 310-
                     449-2100; Verity Records: phone: 212-
                     824-1872, fax: 212-229-5846;
                     Silvertone: phone: 212-824-1730, fax:
                     212-337-0990

Barry Weiss . . . . .President
Max Siegel . . . . .President, Verity/VP, Zomba Music
Tom Carrabba .Sr. VP/General Manager
Jazzy Jordan . . . .Sr. VP, Black Music Marketing/General Manager, Verity
Larry Khan . . . . .Sr. VP, R&B Promotion & Marketing
Janet Kleinbaum . . . . .Sr. VP, Artist Marketing
Chris Lighty . . . . .Sr. VP, Urban A&R
Julia Lipari . . . . .Sr. VP, Marketing
Deane Marcus . . . . .Sr. VP, Operations
Sonia Muckle . . . . .Sr. VP, Publicity, Jive
Mark Pitts . . . . .Sr. VP, A&R, Jive
Joe Riccitelli . . . . .Sr. VP, CHR Promotion
Cliff Silver . . . . .Sr. VP, Finance
Peter Thea . . . . .Sr. VP, Zomba Label Group
Daniel Zucker . . . . .Sr. VP, Business Affairs
Bob Anderson . . . . .VP, National Sales
Julie Bruzzone-Goldstein . . . . .VP, Marketing/Special Projects
Lisa Cambridge . . . . .VP, Urban Marketing
Julia Dillon . . . . .VP, Sales
Jeff Dodes . . . . .VP, New Media
Jeff Grant . . . . .VP, Verity Promotion
JoAnn Kaeding . . . . .VP, International
Gerry Kuster . . . . .VP, Production
Teresa LaBarbera-Whites . . . . .VP, A&R, Jive
Debra Lucarello . . . . .VP, Human Resources
Steve Lunt . . . . .VP, A&R
Jimmy Maynes . . . . .VP, Creative A&R
Jon McHugh . . . . .VP, Creative Developments
Shannah Miller . . . . .VP, Video/Adult Promotion
Jackie Murphy . . . . .VP, Art Department
Gina Orr . . . . .VP, Publicity
Rick Sackheim . . . . .VP, Rhythm/Crossover
Daniel Sassoon .VP, Business Affairs
Roger Skelton . . . . .VP, Business Affairs
John Strazza . . . . .VP, Top 40 Promotion
Michael Tedesco . . . . .VP, A&R, Rock
Stephanie Tudor . . . . .VP, A&R Administration
Wayne Williams . . . . .VP, A&R, Jive (Chicago)
Lorraine Caruso . . . . .Sr. Director, Rock Promotion
Joanne Grand . . . . .Sr. Director, Rock Promotion
Roberta Magrini . . . . .Sr. Director, Publicity
Tice Merriweather . . . . .Sr. Director, Publicity
Nancy Roof . . . . .Sr. Director, A&R Administration
Jeff Sledge . . . . .Sr. Director, Zomba Label Group
H.M. Wollman . . . . .Q Prime/Volcano (212-302-3790)

LABELS

WORKSHEET

DATE	PROJECT	CONTACT	NOTES

SECTION **B**

REPRESENTATION

- **Agents**
- Managers
- Attorneys

Asterisks (*) next to companies denote new listings.

ABOUT ARTIST AGENCY
1650 Broadway, Ste. 1406
New York, NY 10019
PHONE 212-581-1857
TYPES OF CLIENTS   Musical Artists - Variety Artists - Comedians
SUBMISSION POLICY   By mail only
COMMENTS   Represents actors over 18

Renee Glicker . . . . .President/Agent
Phil Cassese . . . . .Associate
Chase Jennings . . . . .Assistant

ABRAMS ARTISTS AGENCY
275 Seventh Ave., 26th Fl.
New York, NY 10001
PHONE 646-486-4600/310-859-0625
FAX 646-486-0100/310-276-6193
TYPES OF CLIENTS   Musical Artists - Film/TV Composers
COMMENTS   West Coast office: 9200 Sunset Blvd., 11th Fl., Los Angeles, CA 90069

Harry Abrams . . . . .President
Neal Altman . . . . .Sr. VP/Voice-Over
Robert Atterman . . . . .VP, Theatrical/Motion Pictures/TV
Tracey Goldblum . . . . .VP, Commericals

ACTS NASHVILLE
1103 Bell Grimes Lane
Nashville, TN 37207
PHONE 615-254-8600
FAX 615-254-8667
EMAIL . . . . .info@actsnashville.com
WEB SITE . . . . .www.actsnashville.com
TYPES OF CLIENTS   Musical Artists
MUSICAL ARTIST TYPES   Country - Rock

Eddie Rhines . . . . .President (eddie@actsnashville.com)
Tracy Jones . . . . .VP (tracy@actsnashville.com)
Dave Schuder . . . . .Agent (dave@actsnashville.com)
Scott Hogue . . . . .Agent (scott@actsnashville.com)
Marty Martel . . . . .Agent (marty@actsnashville.com)

AGENCY FOR THE PERFORMING ARTS, INC.
(LOS ANGELES)
9200 Sunset Blvd., Ste. 900
Los Angeles, CA 90069
PHONE 310-888-4200
FAX 310-888-4242
EMAIL . . . . .firstinitiallastname@apa-agency.com
TYPES OF CLIENTS   Musical Artists - Music Producers - Film/TV Composers - Lyricists - Songwriters - Variety Artists - Comedians
MUSICAL ARTIST TYPES   All Genres

Roger Vorce .Chairman Emeritus
Jim Gosnell . . . . .President/CEO
Troy Blakely . . . . .Sr. VP, Concert Department
Josh Humiston . . . . .VP, Concert Department
Andrew Simon . . . . .VP, Concert Department
Jaime Kelsall .Concert Department
Craig Newman . . . . .Concert Department
Shane Shuhart . . . . .Concert Department
Jason Zell . . . . .Concert Department
Danny Robinson . . . . .Sr. VP, Comedy
Jackie Miller-Knobbe . . . . .Comedy Department
Tim Scally . . . . .Comedy Department
Joanna Scott . . . . .Comedy Department

AGENCY FOR THE PERFORMING ARTS, INC. (NASHVILLE)
3017 Poston Ave.
Nashville, TN 37203
PHONE 615-297-0100
FAX 615-297-5434
EMAIL . . . . .firstinitiallastname@apanashville.com
TYPES OF CLIENTS   Musical Artists - Comedians
MUSICAL ARTIST TYPES   All Genres
COMMENTS   Nashville office books musical talent only; Christian affiliation with Jeff Roberts & Associates

Bonnie Sugarman . . . . .Sr. VP, Personal Appearance/Agent/Co-Head
Steve Lassiter . . . . .Sr. VP, Personal Appearance/Agent/Co-Head
Rob Battle .Personal Appearance/Agent
John Dotson . . . . .Personal Appearance/Agent
Jeff Howard . . . . .Personal Appearance/Agent
Ryan Small .Personal Appearance/Agent
Frank Wing .Personal Appearance/Agent

THE AGENCY GROUP LTD. (LOS ANGELES)
9348 Civic Center Dr., Ste. 200
Beverly Hills, CA 90210
PHONE 310-385-2800
FAX 310-385-1220
WEB SITE .www.theagencygroup.com
TYPES OF CLIENTS   Musical Artists - Music Producers - Music Supervisors - Film/TV Composers - Lyricists - Songwriters - Studio Musicians - Studio Vocalists - Variety Artists - Comedians
MUSICAL ARTIST TYPES   All Genres
CLIENT LIST   The White Stripes - 3 Doors Down - De La Soul - George Clinton & Parliament/Funkadelic - Rickie Lee Jones - Sandra Bernhard
SUBMISSION POLICY   No unsolicited submissions
COMMENTS   See Web site for full client list

Andy Somers . . . . .Sr. VP
Bruce Solar . . . . .VP
Linda Kordek . . . . .TV & Film Licensing
Paul Buck . . . . .Agent
Corrie Christopher . . . . .Agent
Donovan Hebard . . . . .Agent
Melody King . . . . .Agent
John Pantle . . . . .Agent
Val Wolfe . . . . .Agent
Mike Galt . . . . .Assistant to Corrie Christopher
Courtney Hyatt . . . . .Assistant to Andy Somers
Jenny McPhee . . . . .Assistant to Val Wolfe
Tawny Mitchell . . . . .Assistant to Linda Kordek
Lanell Rumion . . . . .Assistant to Melody King & John Pantle
David Strunk . . . . .Assistant to Bruce Solar

THE AGENCY GROUP LTD. (TORONTO)
2 Berkeley St., Ste. 202
Toronto, ON M5A 4J5 Canada
PHONE 416-368-5599
FAX 416-368-4655
WEB SITE .www.theagencygroup.com
MUSICAL ARTIST TYPES   All Genres

Steve Herman . . . . .North American CEO
Ralph James . . . . .VP/Co-Head, Toronto office
Jack Ross . . . . .VP/Co-Head, Toronto office
Omar Al-Joulani . . . . .Agent
Paul Gourlie . . . . .Agent
Colin Lewis . . . . .Agent
Rob Zifarelli . . . . .Agent
Adam Countryman . . . . .Assistant
Greg Henderson . . . . .Assistant
Heather Rolph . . . . .Assistant
Ben Waldman . . . . .Assistant
Lorraine Webb . . . . .Assistant
Jean Wilkinson . . . . .Assistant
Christina Miller . . . . .Reception

THE AGENCY GROUP USA LTD. (NEW YORK)
1775 Broadway, Ste. 515
New York, NY 10019
PHONE 212-581-3100
FAX 212-581-0015
WEB SITE . . . . .www.theagencygroup.com
TYPES OF CLIENTS | Musical Artists - Music Producers - Music Supervisors - Film/TV Composers - Lyricists - Songwriters - Studio Musicians - Studio Vocalists
MUSICAL ARTIST TYPES | All Genres
CLIENT LIST | See Web site for full client list
SUBMISSION POLICY | No unsolicited submissions

Neil Warnock . . . . .Chairman/Worldwide CEO
Steve Martin . . . . .President, North America/Head, Film & TV/
                                                    Literary & Comedy
Ken Fermaglich . . . . .Sr. VP
Peter Schwartz . . . . .VP
Tim Borror . . . . .Agent
Jordan Burger . . . . .Agent
Nick Caris . . . . .Agent
Jeremy Holgersen . . . . .Agent
David Kaplan . . . . .Agent
Steve Kaul . . . . .Agent
Mike Mori . . . . .Agent
Seth Rappaport . . . . .Agent
Marc Bauer . . . . .Assistant to Dave Kaplan
Kelly Di Stefano . . . . .Assistant to Seth Rappaport
Joshua Dick . . . . .Assistant to Steve Martin
David Galea . . . . .Assistant to Ken Fermaglich
Megan Kesler . . . . .Assistant to Mike Mori & Jordan Burger
Josh Kline .Assistant to Tim Borror
Bryan Nye . . . . .Assistant to Jeremy Holgersen
Anthony Paolercio . . . . .Assistant to Steve Kaul
Leah Peterson . . . . .Assistant to Tim Borror
Zach Quillen . . . . .Assistant to Peter Schwartz

*AGENT M BOOKING
401 20th St., 3rd Fl.
Brooklyn, NY 11215
PHONE 718-360-3878
EMAIL . . . . .m@agentmbooking.com
SECOND EMAIL . . . . .ralph@agentmbooking.com
WEB SITE . . . . .www.agentmbooking.com
TYPES OF CLIENTS | Musical Artists - Lyricists
CLIENT LIST | The Giraffes - Apsci - Seems So Bright - A.D.M. - Apollo Heights

Maya Contreras . . . . .President
Ralph Cutler . . . . .Agent
Mike Quinn . . . . .Agent
Adam Phillips . . . . .Publicist

AGENTS FOR THE ARTS, INC.
203 W. 23rd St., 3rd Fl.
New York, NY 10011
PHONE 212-229-2562
TYPES OF CLIENTS | Musical Artists - Variety Artists - Comedians
SUBMISSION POLICY | Demos by request only; No drop-ins
COMMENTS | Musical Theater performers

Carole J. Russo . . . . .Agent

*AIR-EDEL (LONDON)
18 Rodmarton St.
London W1U 8BJ United Kingdom
PHONE 44-207-486-6466
FAX 44-207-224-0344
EMAIL .air-edel@air-edel.co.uk
WEB SITE . . . . .www.air-edel.co.uk

Maggie Radford . . . . .Managing Director
Mark Lo . . . . .Film, Television, Theatre
Alison Wright . . . . .Film, Television, Theatre
Matt Biffa . . . . .Film, Television, Theatre
Lucy Evans . . . . .Commercials

AIR-EDEL (LOS ANGELES)
9255 Sunset Blvd., Ste. 200
Los Angeles, CA 90069
PHONE 310-205-5079/44-207-486-6466
FAX 310-205-5001/44-207-224-0344
EMAIL . . . . .info@air-edel.co.uk
SECOND EMAIL . . . . .info@airedel.com
WEB SITE . . . . .www.air-edel.com
SECOND WEB SITE . . . . .www.air-edel.co.uk
TYPES OF CLIENTS | Music Supervisors - Film/TV Composers - Lyricists
SUBMISSION POLICY | No unsolicited material

Maggie Rodford . . . . .Managing Director
Mark Thomas . . . . .Film & TV Music

*J. ALBERT & SON (U.K.) LTD.
Unit 29, Cygnus Business Center, Dalmeyer
London NW10 2XA United Kingdom
PHONE 44-208-830-0330
FAX 44-208-830-0220
EMAIL .info@albertmusic.co.uk
WEB SITE .www.albertmusic.co.uk

James Cassidy . . . . .No Title

ALPHAFEMALE (M.T.) BOOKING
PO Box 20702
Seattle, WA 98102
PHONE 206-325-6246
FAX 206-323-0635
EMAIL .julianne@alphafemale.net
WEB SITE . . . . .www.alphafemale.net
TYPES OF CLIENTS | Musical Artists

Julianne Andersen . . . . .Agent

AMERICAN ARTISTS
315 S. Beverly Dr., Ste. 407
Beverly Hills, CA 90212
PHONE 310-277-7877
FAX 310-277-9697
EMAIL . . . . .infoaa@aol.com
WEB SITE . . . . .www.americanartists.net
TYPES OF CLIENTS | Musical Artists
MUSICAL ARTIST TYPES | Adult Contemporary - Alternative - Bluegrass - Blues - Country - Jazz - Pop - Rock
CLIENT LIST | Alvin Lee Band - Atlanta Rhythm Section - Banyan - The Blasters - Buckethead - Feel - Fred Wilson - The Georgia Satellites - Kid Creole & The Coconuts - The Marshall Tucker Band - Marty Balin - Melvin Seals & JGB - Melvin Seals' Melting Pot

Philip Hache . . . . .Agent (x107)
Mike Weinstein . . . . .Agent (x113)
Cris Busam . . . . .Assistant

AMERICAN PROGRAM BUREAU

36 Crafts St.
Newton, MA 02458
PHONE 617-965-6600
FAX 617-965-6610
EMAIL . . . . .apb@apbspeakers.com
SECOND EMAIL . . . . .firstinitiallastname@apbspeakers.com
WEB SITE . . . . .www.apbspeakers.com
TYPES OF CLIENTS   Musical Artists - Film/TV Composers - Comedians
MUSICAL ARTIST TYPES   Jazz - Rap/Hip-Hop

Tammy Choquette . . . . .Agent (617-614-1608)
Heather Colburn . . . . .Agent (617-614-1626)
Bob Davis . . . . .Agent (617-614-1618)
Ken Eisenstein . . . . .Agent (617-614-1612)
Nancy Eisenstein . . . . .Agent (617-614-1616)
Brenda Kane . . . . .Agent (617-614-1607)
Kathleen Larsen . . . . .Agent (617-614-1625)
Flip Porter . . . . .Agent (617-614-1624)
Trinity Ray . . . . .Agent (617-614-1614)
Michael Rosenberg . . . . .Agent (617-614-1607)
Harry Sandler . . . . .Agent (617-614-1626)
Dan Schlossberg . . . . .Agent (617-614-1631)
Andrew Walker . . . . .Agent (617-614-1611)
Jan Tavitian . . . . .Sr. VP (617-614-1631)
Caroline Campo . . . . .Marketing Coordinator (617-614-1632)
Susan Yurof . . . . .Marketing Coordinator (617-614-1622)

ARTISTS INTERNATIONAL

9850 Sandalfoot Blvd., Ste. 458
Boca Raton, FL 33428
PHONE 561-498-1300
FAX 561-498-2004
EMAIL . . . . .aiminc1@aol.com
TYPES OF CLIENTS   Musical Artists
MUSICAL ARTIST TYPES   Metal - Pop - Rap/Hip-Hop - Rock
CLIENT LIST   Twisted Sister - Little River Band - BTO - Brian Howe - Jerry Lee Lewis - Molly Hatchet - Atlanta Rhythm Section - Nazareth - Percy Sledge - Baha Men - Starship - Dr. Hook - Blessid Union of Souls - Player - Poco - Firefall - Rick Derringer - Pat Travers Band - Black Oak Arkansas - Vanilla Ice - A Flock of Seagulls

Steve Green . . . . .President
Mark Lyman . . . . .Agent
Magaly Newcomb . . . . .Agent

ARTISTS WORLDWIDE

3921 Wilshire Blvd., Ste. 619
Los Angeles, CA 90010
PHONE 213-368-2112
FAX 213-368-2110
EMAIL . . . . .artistsworldwide@aol.com
WEB SITE . . . . .www.artists-worldwide.com
TYPES OF CLIENTS   Musical Artists
CLIENT LIST   45 Grave - Adler's Appetite - Agent Orange - Bang Tango - Beautiful Creatures - Blackmore's Night - Brides of Destruction - Briggs - Channel 3 - Destruction - D.I. - Dickies - Discharge - Enuff Z' Nuff - Exploited - Faster Pussycat - Flotsam & Jetsam - Genitorturers - George Lynch - Gilby Clarke - Guilt by Association - Kingdom Come - LA Guns - Marduk - Marky Ramone - Mayhem - Metal Church - Michael Schenker Group - Misfits - Nina Hagen - Pretty Boy Floyd - Real McKenzies - Stephen Pearcy - Total Chaos - Tramp's White Lion - Union - Vice Squad - W.A.S.P. - Wednesday 13 - Y&T

Chuck Bernal . . . . .Booking Agent
Chris Maggiore . . . . .Booking Agent
Charlie Overby . . . . .Booking Agent

ASA TALENT & MODELING

4430 Fountain Ave., Ste. A
Hollywood, CA 90029
PHONE 323-662-9787
EMAIL . . . . .asatalent@asatalent.com
WEB SITE . . . . .www.asatalent.com/models
TYPES OF CLIENTS   Musical Artists
SUBMISSION POLICY   Mail only; Include email address

Mike Bujko . . . . .Owner/Agent
George Markoski . . . . .Agent

ASSOCIATED BOOKING CORPORATION (ABC)

545 Madison Ave., 8th Fl.
New York, NY 10022
PHONE 212-874-2400
FAX 212-769-3649
EMAIL . . . . .musicbiz@mindspring.com
WEB SITE . . . . .www.abcbooking.com
TYPES OF CLIENTS   Musical Artists
MUSICAL ARTIST TYPES   Blues - Gospel - Jazz - Pop - R&B - Reggae - Urban - World
CLIENT LIST   Chuck Berry - The O'Jays - Keith Sweat - Johnny Gill - Duke Ellington Orchestra - Maynard Ferguson - The Gap Band - Roberta Flack - Chante Moore & Kenny Lattimore - Gerald Levert - Regina Belle - The Whispers - Angela Bofill - Yolanda Adams - The Manhattans feat. Gerald Alston & Blue Lovett - The Dells - Beres Hammond - Jay Black & the Americans - Morris Day & the Time - Freddie Jackson - The Dramatics - Chubby Checker - George Shearing - John Hendricks - Pieces of a Dream - Kid Creole & the Coconuts - Millie Jackson - Third World - Jordan Knight - Jeff Timmons - Ashford & Simpson - Najee - Alexander O'Neal - Shaggy - Maxi Priest - Diana King - Ben E. King - Vesta - Teddy Pendergrass - Friars Folics - Gloria Gaynor - Black Uhuru - Freddie McGregor - Jeffrey Osbourne - George Duke - Keith Washington
COMMENTS   Represents estates of Louis Armstrong and Duke Ellington

Oscar Cohen . . . . .President
Lisa Cohen .Agent/Director, Marketing

BACKSTREET BOOKING
5658 Kirby Ave.
Cincinnati, OH 45239-7260
PHONE 513-542-9544
FAX 513-542-9545
EMAIL . . . . .info@backstreetbooking.com
WEB SITE . . . . .www.backstreetbooking.com
TYPES OF CLIENTS   Musical Artists
MUSICAL ARTIST TYPES   Alternative - Jazz - Rock - World
CLIENT LIST   Acumen - Adrian Legg - Alex Skolnick
                          Trio - Attention Deficit - Bill Connors -
                          CAB - Dave LaRue - DeMania Trio -
                          Derek Sherinian - The Flower Kings -
                          Frank Gambale - Greg Howard - Greg
                          Howe - Happy The Man - Joe Stump -
                          John Novello - Mads Eriksen - McGill-
                          Manring-Stevens - Michael Manring -
                          Mike Keneally Band - Moth - Neal
                          Morse - Nektar - Niacin - Nick D'Virgilio
                          (NDV) - O2'L - Ohm - Oz Noy - Proto-
                          Kaw - Reign Of Terror - Ryo Okumoto -
                          Spock's Beard - Stu Hamm - Tunnels -
                          ZO2

Jim Sfarnas . . . . .President (x1, jimbb@backstreetbooking.com)
Brooks Jordan . . . . .VP (x3, brooks@backstreetbooking.com)
Chris Lee . . . . .Agent (x2, hrislee@backstreetbooking.com)
Brandon Wheeler . . . . . .Office Manager (bjw@backstreetbooking.com)

BARON ENTERTAINMENT
5757 Wilshire Blvd., Ste 659
Los Angeles, CA 90036-3600
PHONE 323-936-7600
FAX 323-936-8600
EMAIL . . . . .rod@baronentertainment.com
WEB SITE . . . . .www.baronentertainment.com
TYPES OF CLIENTS   Musical Artists - Music Producers -
                          Variety Artists - Comedians
SUBMISSION POLICY   Mail only

Rod Baron . . . . .Agent
April Hennie . . . . .Assistant
Julie Kopalson . . . . .Assistant
Mike Sacks . . . . .Assistant
Michael Sutton . . . . .Assistant

BASKOW & ASSOCIATES, INC.
2948 E. Russell Rd.
Las Vegas, NV 89120
PHONE 702-733-7818
FAX 702-733-2052
EMAIL . . . . .info@baskow.com
WEB SITE . . . . .www.baskow.com
TYPES OF CLIENTS   Musical Artists - Songwriters - Variety
                          Artists - Comedians

Jaki Baskow . . . . .Owner/Agent
Jennifer Patino . . . . .President

BASS/SCHULER ENTERTAINMENT
4001 W. Devon Ave., Ste. 510
Chicago, IL 60646
PHONE 773-481-2600
FAX 773-481-2601
EMAIL . . . . .info@bass-schuler.com
WEB SITE . . . . .www.bass-schuler.com
TYPES OF CLIENTS   Musical Artists - Variety Artists -
                          Comedians
MUSICAL ARTIST TYPES   Alternative - Blues - Classical - Country -
                          Electronica - Folk - Jazz - Latin - Pop -
                          R&B - Rap/Hip-Hop - Reggae - Rock -
                          Urban - World
SUBMISSION POLICY   Fill out online submission form on Web
                          site

Scott Bass . . . . .Agent
Bec Hunter . . . . .Agent
Chris Schuler . . . . .Agent
Mia Bass . . . . .CFO
Carolyn Riehl . . . . .Office Manager

BEACHFRONT BOOKINGS
PO Box 13218
Portland, OR 97213-0218
PHONE 503-281-3874
FAX 503-281-3881
EMAIL . . . . .tammartin@aol.com
WEB SITE . . . . .www.beachfrontbookings.com
TYPES OF CLIENTS   Musical Artists - Songwriters -
                          Comedians
CLIENT LIST   Suzanne Westenhoefer - Holly Near -
                          Kate Clinton - Marga Gomez - Teresa
                          Trull - Barbara Higbie

Tam Martin . . . . .Owner/Agent

BEACON ARTISTS AGENCY
208 W. 30th St., Ste. 401
New York, NY 10001
PHONE 212-736-6630
FAX 212-868-1052
TYPES OF CLIENTS   Film/TV Composers - Lyricists -
                          Songwriters
SUBMISSION POLICY   By referral only

Patricia McLaughlin . . . . .President

THE BERKELEY AGENCY
2608 Ninth St., Ste. 301
Berkeley, CA 94710
PHONE 510-843-4902
FAX 510-843-7271
EMAIL . . . . .mail@berkeleyagency.com
WEB SITE . . . . .www.berkeleyagency.com
TYPES OF CLIENTS   Musical Artists
MUSICAL ARTIST TYPES   Blues - Gospel - Jazz - Latin - World
CLIENT LIST   Pancho Sanchez - Eddie Palmieri - Flora
                          Purim & Airto - Claudia Villela - Marlena
                          Shaw - The Brubeck Brothers - James
                          Moody - Eddie Daniels - Lavay Smith
                          and Her Red Hot Skillet Lickers - James
                          Cotton - The Persuasions - The Gospel
                          Hummingbirds
SUBMISSION POLICY   No unsolicited material accepted

Jim Cassell . . . . .Agent
Connie Laventurier . . . . .Agent

BIGSHOT TOURING ARTISTS
828 SW First Ave., Ste. 210
Portland, OR 97204
PHONE 503-731-8700
FAX 503-731-0920
EMAIL . . . . .kevin@bigshottouring.com
WEB SITE . . . . .www.bigshottouring.com
TYPES OF CLIENTS   Musical Artists
MUSICAL ARTIST TYPES   Alternative
CLIENT LIST   Apollo Sunshine - Lou Barlow - Bobby
                          Bare, Jr. - Brian Jonestown Massacre -
                          Clearlake - Deathray Davies - The
                          Decemberists - Dressy Bessy - Earlimart -
                          Film School - French Kicks - Jason
                          Lowenstein - Kaito - Kid Dakota - The
                          Kingdom - Mazarin - The National - The
                          Natural History - The Posies - The Rogers
                          Sisters - Richard Swift & Sons of National
                          Freedom - The Ruby Doe - Sebodah -
                          Sound Team - The Sun - Swords - Tom
                          Heinl - The Tyde - Talkdemonic - The
                          Walkmen - You Am I
SUBMISSION POLICY   No unsolicited material accepted without
                          a telephone call first

Kevin French . . . . .Owner/Agent (kevin@bigshottouring.com)
Rachel Demy . . . . .Agent/Assistant (rachel@bigshottouring.com)

THE BILLIONS CORPORATION
833 W. Chicago Ave., Ste. 101
Chicago, IL 60622-5497
PHONE 312-997-9999
FAX 312-997-2287
EMAIL . . . . .lastname@billions.com
WEB SITE . . . . .www.billions.com
CLIENT LIST   The Black Keys - Blues Explosion - Neko
                          Case - Freakwater - Idlewild - Marah -
                          Mekons - Nick Cave & the Bad Seeds -
                          Southern Culture on the Skids - The
                          Waco Brothers
SUBMISSION POLICY   No unsolicited material of any kind
                          accepted

David T. Viecelli . . . . . .President/Agent/Manager (boche@billions.com)
Ali Giampino . . . . .Agent
Rachael Finn . . . . .Sr. Agency Associate
Amy Butterer . . . . .Management Associate/Agent
Beth Shafer . . . . .Office Administrator
Shannin Cartdright . . . . .Agency Associate

BLUE MOUNTAIN ARTISTS (BMA)
818 Tyvola Rd., Ste. 109
Charlotte, NC 28217
PHONE 704-525-1559
FAX 704-525-1561
WEB SITE . . . . .www.bluemountainartists.com
TYPES OF CLIENTS   Musical Artists
MUSICAL ARTIST TYPES   Bluegrass - Blues - Jazz - World
CLIENT LIST   Tab Benoit - Big Daddy's Bluegrass Band
                          - Elvin Bishop - Michael Burks - The
                          Codetalkers - Garaj Mahal - Corey
                          Harris - Larry Keel & Natural Bridge -
                          E.G. Kight - Steady Rollin' Bob Margolin
                          - Cyril Neville - The Nighthawks -
                          Pinetop Perkins - Willie 'Big Eyes' Smith -
                          Hubert Sumlin - Jimmy Thackery - Tony
                          Trischka - Rev. Billy C. Wirtz - Bernie
                          Worrell & the WOO Warriors - Grease
                          Factor - Drums & Tuba - Gongzilla -
                          Janiva Magness - Bluerunners - Anthony
                          Gomes - Tim Reynolds - Porter, Batiste &
                          Stoltz - Terrance Simien & the Zydeco
                          Experience - The Recipe - James Cotton
                          - Steep Canyon Rangers - Maria
                          Muldaur - Rod Piazza & the Mighty
                          Flyers

Hugh Southard . . . . .President/Agent (hugh@bluemountainartists.com)
Derek Smith . . . . .Agent (derek@bluemountainartists.com)
Page Stallings . . . . .Agent (page@bluemountainartists.com)
Allison Beck . . . . . . .Office Manager (allison@bluemountainartists.com)

BOBBY BALL TALENT AGENCY
4342 Lankershim Blvd.
Universal City, CA 91602
PHONE 818-506-8188
FAX 818-506-8588
WEB SITE . . . . .www.bobbyballagency.com
TYPES OF CLIENTS   Musical Artists - Music Producers -
                          Studio Vocalists
MUSICAL ARTIST TYPES   Children's - Dance/DJ - Rap/Hip-Hop -
                          Urban

Patty Grana-Miller .Owner/Agent, Commercial
Michelle Zeitlin . . . . .Agent, Dance Department

THE BRODER • WEBB • CHERVIN • SILBERMANN AGENCY
9242 Beverly Blvd., Ste. 200
Beverly Hills, CA 90210
PHONE 310-281-3400
FAX 310-276-3207
TYPES OF CLIENTS   Music Supervisors - Film/TV Composers
CLIENT LIST   Unsolicited queries and material not
                          accepted; Industry referral only

Bob Broder . . . . .Partner, Literary
Elliot Webb . . . . .Partner, Literary
Ted Chervin . . . . .Partner, Literary
Chris Silbermann . . . . .Partner, Literary
Dan Donahue . . . . .COO
Brice Gaeta . . . . .Below-the-Line, Composers
Jay Gilbert . . . . .Below-the-Line
Hilarie Roope . . . . .Below-the-Line
Lesley Feinstein .Department Coordinator

AGENTS

*BRUCK TALENT
12 W. Ninth St., Ste. 2D
New York, NY 10011
PHONE 212-614-1606
FAX 646-330-4513
EMAIL . . . . .craig@brucktalent.com
TYPES OF CLIENTS   Musical Artists
CLIENT LIST   Aaron Carter - Florez - Jonas Brothers -
Jump5 - Lil' Romeo - Socialburn - Stevie
Brock - Sugar Hill Gang - Teddy Geiger

Craig Bruck . . . . .Agent

CARMICHAEL TALENT
PO Box 884, 337 N. Railroad Ave.
Johnsonville, SC 29555
PHONE 843-386-3320
FAX 843-386-3893
EMAIL . . . . .sherman@acmenet.net
WEB SITE . . . . .carmichaelsc.tripod.com
TYPES OF CLIENTS   Musical Artists - Film/TV Composers -
Lyricists - Studio Musicians - Studio
Vocalists
MUSICAL ARTIST TYPES   All Genres
SUBMISSION POLICY   Mail only
COMMENTS   Nationwide talent representation

Sherman Carmichael . . . . .Owner

THE CARSON ORGANIZATION, LTD.
419 Park Ave. South, Ste. 606
New York, NY 10016
PHONE 212-221-1517
TYPES OF CLIENTS   Musical Artists
SUBMISSION POLICY   Mail only

Barry Kolker . . . . .Agent/President
Jenevieve Brewer . . . . .Agent, Commercial/Print
Alice Skiba .Office Assistant

KEITH CASE & ASSOCIATES
1025 17th Ave., 2nd Fl.
Nashville, TN 37212
PHONE 615-327-4646
FAX 615-327-4949
EMAIL . . . . .keith@keithcase.com
SECOND EMAIL . . . . .lesley@keithcase.com
WEB SITE .www.keithcase.com
TYPES OF CLIENTS   Musical Artists - Songwriters
MUSICAL ARTIST TYPES   Adult Contemporary - Bluegrass -
Country - Folk - Roots
CLIENT LIST   Alison Krauss & Union Station - Blue
Highway - Bryn Bright - Charivari - Chris
Hillman - Dan Tyminski - Fairfield Four -
Gurf Morlix - Guy Clark - Hot Rize -
Jeannie Kendall - Jerry Douglas - Jesse
Winchester - Jimmy Rankin - Kami Lyle -
King Wilkie - Lonesome River Band -
Nashville Bluegrass Band - Peter Rowan
- Ralph Stanley - Ramblin' Jack Elliott -
Red Clay Ramblers - Slaid Cleaves - The
Seldom Scene - Sierra Hull & Highway
111 - Tony Rice - Verlon Thompson -
Angel Band - David Bromberg
SUBMISSION POLICY   Musical acts with national distribution

Keith Case . . . . .Owner
Lee Olsen . . . . .VP/Agent
Kevin Howell . . . . .Agent
Randy Pitts . . . . .Agent
Lesley Cuttler . . . . .Administrative Manager
Marilee Chipoletti . . . . .Contract Administration
Bobbi Hoffman . . . . .Publicity Support
Kristy Jo Steinmetz . . . . .Publicity Support
Emilee Warner . . . . .Publicity Support

CASTLE HILL TALENT AGENCY
1101 S. Orlando Ave.
Los Angeles, CA 90035
PHONE 323-653-3535
EMAIL . . . . .leigh@castlehill.net
WEB SITE . . . . .www.castlehill.net
TYPES OF CLIENTS   Musical Artists - Comedians
COMMENTS   Legitimate theater

Leigh Castle . . . . .Owner/Agent

CAVALERI & ASSOCIATES
178 S. Victory Blvd., Ste. 205
Burbank, CA 91502
PHONE 818-955-9300
FAX 818-955-9399
EMAIL . . . . .cavaleri@hotmail.com
SECOND EMAIL . . . . .cavaleri@usfilm.com
TYPES OF CLIENTS   Musical Artists - Variety Artists -
Comedians
SUBMISSION POLICY   Mail only; No drop-ins

Ray Cavaleri .Owner/Agent
Cinthia Becks . . . . .Children/Young Adults

CELEBRITY DIRECT ENTERTAINMENT
PO Box 494314
Port Charlotte, FL 33949
PHONE 941-624-2254/239-939-7001
FAX 309-218-1426
EMAIL . . . . .cde@celebritydirect.net
WEB SITE . . . . .www.celebritydirect.net
TYPES OF CLIENTS   Musical Artists - Music Producers -
Film/TV Composers - Lyricists -
Songwriters - Studio Musicians -
Comedians
MUSICAL ARTIST TYPES   Bluegrass - Blues - Country - Gospel -
Jazz - Rock
CLIENT LIST   Big Al Downing - The Marvelettes Revue
feat. Pam Darden - Al Holland - The
Platters - Monroe Powell - Leon Hughes
- Ali Woodson - The Calvanes - Joey
Arminio & The Family - The Original
Fireballs - The Reflections - Terry
Johnson's Flamingos - Bill Godwin's Ink
Spots - Linwood Peel - Harriet Schock -
Stevie Marie - Jamie Leigh - Rio Drive -
Marty Davis & The Legend of the
Pioneers - Gary Ray Harvey - Wilson
Williams - Verceal Whitaker - David
Johnson - The Winstons - The Surf City
All-Stars - Jim Morris & The Big Bamboo
Band - LoLo and Harold Moore - Barbra
Streisand - Vonzell Soloman
SUBMISSION POLICY   Promo packs welcome

Cord Coslor . . . . .Owner/Agent
Jim Osburn . . . . .Owner/Agent
Ted Osburn . . . . .Agent

CENTRAL ENTERTAINMENT GROUP
166 Fifth Ave., 4th Fl.
New York, NY 10010
PHONE 212-921-2100
FAX 212-921-8761
EMAIL . . . . .name@cegtalent.com
WEB SITE . . . . .www.cegtalent.com
TYPES OF CLIENTS   Musical Artists
MUSICAL ARTIST TYPES   Dance/DJ - Jazz - Pop - R&B - Rap/Hip-Hop - Rock
CLIENT LIST   Ying Yang Twins - Tommy Lee with DJ Aero - Crooklyn Clan feat. DR Riz & Sizzahands - Wayman Tisdale - Grace Jones - RuPaul - Foxy Brown - Sugar Hill Gang - Patti Austin - DJ Hurricane - DJ Skribble - Ivy Queen - Ryan Dunn & Don Vito
COMMENTS   Celebrity Hosts

Michael Schweiger . . . . .CEO
Ricky Greenstein . . . . .President
Johnny Falcones . . . . .VP
Vicki Baradi . . . . .Agent
Al Bentel . . . . .Agent
Albert Beutel . . . . .Agent
Kirk Ceballos . . . . .Agent
Fred Hansen . . . . .Agent
John Maroney . . . . .Agent
Tom Riveria . . . . .Agent

NANCY CHAIDEZ AGENCY & ASSOCIATES
1555 N. Vine St., Ste. 223
Hollywood, CA 90028
PHONE 323-467-8954
FAX 323-462-6613
TYPES OF CLIENTS   Musical Artists - Music Producers - Songwriters - Variety Artists - Comedians

Nancy Chaidez . . . . .Agent
Maria Chaidez . . . . .Director, General Talent

CHAOTICA
32 E. 31st St., 9th Fl.
New York, NY 10016
PHONE 212-725-5588
FAX 212-725-6868
EMAIL .inquire@chaotica.com
WEB SITE . . . . .www.chaotica.com
TYPES OF CLIENTS   Musical Artists
MUSICAL ARTIST TYPES   Alternative - Electronica - Rock
CLIENT LIST   Perry Farrell - The Chemical Brothers - DJ Krush - Prodigy - Underworld - Creamer & K - The Avalanches - Daft Punk - Orb - Paul Oakenfold - Pete Tong - Reprazent - Roni Size - The Streets

Gerry Gerrard . . . . .Agent
Steve Goodgold . . . . .Agent
Emma Hoser . . . . .Agent
Merideth Fisher . . . . .Assistant

CHL ARTISTS
864 S. Robertson Blvd., Ste. 205
Los Angeles, CA 90035
PHONE 310-360-6666
FAX 310-360-6667
EMAIL . . . . .info@chlartists.com
WEB SITE . . . . .www.chlartists.com
TYPES OF CLIENTS   Musical Artists - Music Supervisors - Film/TV Composers
MUSICAL ARTIST TYPES   Classical
CLIENT LIST   Bruce Broughton - Ed Kalnins
SUBMISSION POLICY   Send credits and reel by mail or email

Christopher Ling . . . . .No Title
Jet Carole . . . . .No Title

JOEL CHRISS & COMPANY
300 Mercer St., Ste. 3J
New York, NY 10003
PHONE 212-353-0855
FAX 212-353-0094
EMAIL . . . . .jchriss@aol.com
WEB SITE . . . . .www.jchriss.com
TYPES OF CLIENTS   Musical Artists - Film/TV Composers - Lyricists - Studio Musicians
MUSICAL ARTIST TYPES   Blues - Jazz
COMMENTS   Focus on jazz talent

Joel Chriss . . . . .President
Eric Addeo . . . . .Agent
James Eiteljorg . . . . .Agent
Jamie Ziefert . . . . .Agent

COLBERT ARTISTS MANAGEMENT
111 W. 57th St.
New York, NY 10019
PHONE 212-757-0782
FAX 212-541-5179
EMAIL . . . . .nycolbert@colbertartists.com
TYPES OF CLIENTS   Musical Artists
COMMENTS   Classical musicians only

Charlotte Schroeder . . . . .President
Christina Putnam . . . . .VP

THE COLLECTIVE AGENCY
443 Greenwich St., Ste. 4B
New York, NY 10013
PHONE 212-431-4740
FAX 212-431-4714
EMAIL . . . . .info@tca-web.com
WEB SITE . . . . .www.thecollectiveagency.com
TYPES OF CLIENTS   Musical Artists - Music Producers
MUSICAL ARTIST TYPES   Dance/DJ
CLIENT LIST   Chris Fortier - Hype - James Zabiela - Jimmy Van M - John Digweed - John Graham - Junkie XL - Lee Burridge - Nick Warren - Oliver Lieb - Randall Jones - Sander Kleinenberg - Sasha - Sean Cusick - Steve Lawler - Steve Porter - Three - Dieselboy - Colette - Dave Seaman - Desyn Masiello - DJ Rap - Infusion - James Holden - James Lavelle - U.N.K.L.E. - Luke Fair - Phil K - Richard Vission - Tom Stephan - Superchumbo

Jimmy Van M . . . . .Manager
Joel Zimmerman . . . . .Manager
Kristopher Krasewski . . . . .Agent
Emily Smith . . . . .Business & Marketing Consultant (UK)

CONCERT IDEAS, INC.
73 Ratterman Rd.
Woodstock, NY 12498
PHONE 845-679-6000/513-631-5365
FAX 845-679-9022/513-631-5374
EMAIL . . . . .harrisg@concertideas.com
WEB SITE . . . . .www.concertideas.com
TYPES OF CLIENTS   Musical Artists
COMMENTS   Books both signed and unsigned bands; Ohio office: 3358 Arrow Ave., Cincinnati, OH 45213

Harris Goldberg . . . . .President
Adam Tobey . . . . .Sr. VP
Brian Brady . . . . .Agent
Lindsay Brown . . . . .Agent
Mike Russo . . . . .Agent
Dave Stevens . . . . .Agent (Ohio)

AGENTS

*COOL MUSIC LTD.
62A Warwick Gardens
Kensington, London W14 8PP United Kingdom
PHONE 44-207-565-2665
FAX 44-207-603-8431
EMAIL . . . . .enquiries@coolmusicltd.com

Darrell Alexander . . . . .No Title
Richard Nelson . . . . .No Title

CORALIE JR. THEATRICAL AGENCY
4789 Vineland Ave., Ste. 100
North Hollywood, CA 91602
PHONE 818-766-9501
EMAIL .coraliejr@earthlink.net
TYPES OF CLIENTS   Musical Artists - Variety Artists
COMMENTS   Dancers - Legitimate Theater

Coralie Jr. . . . . .Owner/Agent
Stuart Edward . . . . .Commercial/Theatrical Agent

CREATIVE ARTISTS AGENCY - CAA (LOS ANGELES)
9830 Wilshire Blvd.
Beverly Hills, CA 90212
PHONE 310-288-4545
FAX 310-288-4800
TYPES OF CLIENTS   Musical Artists - Music Producers -
                       Film/TV Composers

Richard Lovett . . . . .President
Rob Light . . . . .Managing Director/Head of Music Department
Lee Gabler . . . . .Co-Chairman
Kevin Huvane . . . . .Managing Director
Bryan Lourd . . . . .Managing Director
Rick Nicita . . . . .Co-Chairman
David O'Connor . . . . .Managing Director
Jenna Adler . . . . .Music
Dennis Ashley . . . . .Music
Erin Culley . . . . .Music
Christopher Dalston .Music
Darryl Eaton . . . . .Music
Jeffrey Frasco . . . . .Music
Kevin Gelbard .Sponsorship
Robert Gibbs II . . . . .Music
Ruth Gonzalez . . . . .Music
Brian Greenbaum . . . . .Music
Carole Kinzel . . . . .Music
Jim Lewi . . . . .Music
Brian Loucks . . . . .Music
Brian Manning . . . . .Music
Allison McGregor . . . . .Marketing
Jason Miller . . . . .Music
Don Muller . . . . .Music
Candy Nguyen . . . . .Music, Artist Relations
Robert Norman . . . . .Corporate Booking
Carrie Phillips . . . . .Music
Jon Pleeter . . . . .Music
Angie Rho . . . . .Music, Business Affairs
Mitch Rose . . . . .Music
Rick Roskin . . . . .Music
LaPrial Runkel . . . . .Music
Susan Simpson . . . . .Music
Brett Steinberg . . . . .Music
Marlene Tsuchii . . . . .Music
Allison Winkler . . . . .Music

CREATIVE ARTISTS AGENCY - CAA (NASHVILLE)
3310 West End Ave., 5th Fl.
Nashville, TN 37203
PHONE 615-383-8787
TYPES OF CLIENTS   Musical Artists - Music Producers

Stan Barnett . . . . .Music
Tim Beeding . . . . .Music
Brad Bissell . . . . .Music
Scott Clayton . . . . .Music
Marc Dennis . . . . .Music
Rodney Essig . . . . .Music
Nancy Gent . . . . .Music
Jeff Gregg . . . . .Music
Jeff Hill . . . . .Music
John Huie . . . . .Music
Tony Johnsen . . . . .Music
Darin Murphy . . . . .Music
Bryan Myers . . . . .Music
Risha Rodgers . . . . .Music

CREATIVE ARTISTS AGENCY - CAA (NEW YORK)
162 Fifth Ave., 6th Fl.
New York, NY 10010
PHONE 212-277-9000
TYPES OF CLIENTS   Musical Artists - Music Producers -
                       Songwriters
MUSICAL ARTIST TYPES   Pop - R&B - Rap/Hip-Hop - Rock

Joe Brauner . . . . .Music
Nat Farnham . . . . .Music
Mario Tirado . . . . .Music
David Zedeck . . . . .Music

DATTNER DISPOTO AND ASSOCIATES
10635 Santa Monica Blvd., Ste. 165
Los Angeles, CA 90025
PHONE 310-474-4585
FAX 310-474-6411
EMAIL . . . . .talent@dattnerdispoto.com
WEB SITE . . . . .www.dattnerdispoto.com
COMMENTS   DPs for film, TV and music videos

Fay Dattner . . . . .Partner/Agent
Bill Dispoto . . . . .Partner/Agent, Commercials/Music Videos
Dan Burnside . . . . .Agent, Commercials/Music Videos
Lisa Holguin . . . . .Agent, Commercials/Music Videos
Juanita Tiangco . . . . .Agent, Commercials/Music Videos

DOWN THE ROAD ENTERTAINMENT
1121 Sprucewood Lane
Glenwood Springs, CO 81601
PHONE 970-945-7930
EMAIL .downroad@sopris.net
WEB SITE . . . . .www.downtheroadentertainment.com

Tony Grifasi .Booking Agent
Judith King . . . . .Assistant

ENTERTAINMENT ARTISTS NASHVILLE
2409 21st Ave. South, Ste. 100
Nashville, TN 37212
PHONE 615-320-7041
FAX 615-320-0856
EMAIL . . . . .entartnash@aol.com
TYPES OF CLIENTS   Musical Artists - Film/TV Composers
MUSICAL ARTIST TYPES   Adult Contemporary - Bluegrass -
                           Children's - Electronica - Metal - Pop -
                           R&B - Reggae - Rock - Urban
CLIENT LIST   Lil Jon & The East Side Boyz - Ying Yang
                           Twins - David Banner - Twista - Trillville -
                           Lil Flip - 112 - Flavor Flav - Tweet - Stat
                           Quo - Nappy Roots - Slim Thugg -
                           Digital Underground - Tone-Loc - Coolio
                           - Sir Mix-A-Lot - Naughty by Nature -
                           Slick Rick - Young MC - Rob Base & DJ
                           EZ Rock - Sugar Hill Gang - Cee-Lo

Bobby Bessone .Co-Owner/President
Margaret Bessone . . . . .Co-Owner/Sr. VP
Micky Bessone . . . . .Agent

ENTOURAGE TALENT ASSOCIATES
236 W. 27th St., 8th Fl.
New York, NY 10001
PHONE 212-633-2600
FAX 212-633-1818
EMAIL . . . . .administration@entouragetalent.com
WEB SITE . . . . .www.entouragetalent.com
TYPES OF CLIENTS   Musical Artists - Film/TV Composers -
                           Lyricists - Songwriters - Studio Musicians
                           - Studio Vocalists
MUSICAL ARTIST TYPES   Adult Contemporary - Alternative -
                           Bluegrass - Blues - Children's - Folk -
                           Jazz - Metal - Pop - Rock - Roots
CLIENT LIST   Joan Armatrading - Al Di Meola - Gord
                           Downie - Candy Dulfer - Tony Furtado -
                           G3 - Eric Johnson - Howard Jones -
                           Ozric Tentacles - Rockapella - Joe
                           Satriani - The Derek Trucks Band - The
                           Pink Floyd Experience - Jai Uttal
COMMENTS   AFM

Wayne Forte . . . . .President
Jennifer Lasker .Director, Operations
Mark Dinerstein . . . . .Agent
Ben Shprits . . . . .Agent
Adi Riesenberg .Executive Assistant
Jill Tuthill . . . . .Administrative Assistant

EVOLUTION MUSIC PARTNERS, LLC
9100 Wilshire Blvd., Ste. 201, East Tower
Los Angeles, CA 90212
PHONE 310-623-3388
FAX 310-623-1897
EMAIL . . . . .firstname@evolutionmusicpartners.com
WEB SITE . . . . .www.evolutionmusicpartners.com
TYPES OF CLIENTS   Musical Artists - Music Producers - Music
                           Supervisors - Film/TV Composers
COMMENTS   Music Publishing catalogs; Copyright
                           holders; Licensing

Seth Kaplan . . . . .Partner
Christine Russell . . . . .Partner
Jennifer Fowler . . . . .No Title
Michael Levine . . . . .No Title

FANTASMA TOURS INTERNATIONAL
2000 S. Dixie Hwy.
West Palm Beach, FL 33401
PHONE 561-832-6397
FAX 561-832-2043
EMAIL .fantasma@fantasma.com
WEB SITE . . . . .www.fantasma.com
TYPES OF CLIENTS   Musical Artists
CLIENT LIST   ABC - Al Jardine - Ambrosia - Animotion
                           - Birtles Shorrock Goble - Bob Welch -
                           Boys from Beatlemania - Canned Heat -
                           Ricci Martin - Edgar Winter - Family
                           Stone Experience - Gallagher - Gary
                           Wright - Gator Country - Gene Pitney -
                           Herman's Hermits - Honeymoon Suite -
                           It's A Beautiful Day - John Cafferty & the
                           Beaver Brown Band - Mason Proffit -
                           Montrose - Mountain - Naked Eyes -
                           Orleans - Pablo Cruise - Paul Williams -
                           Poco - Pure Prairie League - Rick
                           Derringer - Ronnie Spector - Gregg Rolie
                           - Sauce Boss - Show Suede Blues -
                           Simon Kirke - Spooky Tooth - Starship -
                           Ten Years After - The Fixx - The Knack -
                           The Lovin' Spoonful - The Producers -
                           Tommy Tutone - Trent Carlini

Steve Peck . . . . .Agent (speck@fantasma.com)
Belle Forino . . . . .Agent (bforino@fantasma.com)
Scott Gartner . . . . .Agent (sgartner@fantasma.com)
Rich Rees . . . . .Agent (rrees1@aol.com)

FIRST ARTISTS MANAGEMENT
16000 Ventura Blvd., Ste. 605
Encino, CA 91436
PHONE 818-377-7750
FAX 818-377-7760
EMAIL . . . . .fam-info@firstartistsmgmt.com
SECOND EMAIL . . . . .firstinitiallastname@firstartistsmgmt.com
WEB SITE .www.firstartistsmgmt.com
TYPES OF CLIENTS   Music Supervisors - Film/TV Composers
SUBMISSION POLICY   No unsolicited material of any kind;
                           Industry referral only

Vasi Vangelos . . . . .Owner/Agent
Randy Gerston . . . . .Agent
Rich Jaocobellis . . . . .Agent
Robert Messinger . . . . .Agent
Dan Davis . . . . .Operations

FLEMING & ASSOCIATES
167 Little Lake Dr.
Ann Arbor, MI 48103
PHONE 734-995-9066
FAX 734-662-6502
EMAIL . . . . .contact@flemingartists.com
SECOND EMAIL . . . . .firstname@flemingartists.com
WEB SITE . . . . .www.flemingartists.com

TYPES OF CLIENTS	Musical Artists
MUSICAL ARTIST TYPES	Alternative - Country - Folk - Pop - Rock - Roots
CLIENT LIST	Suzy Bogguss - Dan Bern - Craig Cardiff - Jeff Daniels - Ani DiFranco - Utah Phillips - Eric Bogle - Capitol Steps - Clumsy Lovers - Rachael Davis - Eddie from Ohio - Melissa Ferrick - Fruit - Hammell on Trial - Martyn Joseph - Connie Kaldor - Lucy Kaplansky - Stephen Kellogg & The Sixers - Dougie MacLean - Ellis Paul - Tom Paxton - Kelly Joe Phelps - Glen Phillips - Willy Porter - Garnet Rogers - Xavier Rudd - Richard Shindell - Jane Siberry - Ember Swift - Cheryl Wheeler - Adrienne Young & Little Sadie
SUBMISSION POLICY	Must have established national touring history for consideration

Jim Fleming . . . . .CEO/Agent
Adam Bauer . . . . .Agent
Susan Giang . . . . .Agent
Amy Nesbitt . . . . .Agent
Kim Szuma .Contract & Promotional Support
Cynthia Dunitz . . . . .Business Manager
Karla Rice . . . . .Office Manager

FLOWERBOOKING, INC.
1532 N. Milwaukee Ave., Ste. 201
Chicago, IL 60622
PHONE 773-289-3400
FAX 773-289-3434
EMAIL . . . . .info@flowerbooking.com
SECOND EMAIL . . . . .firstname@flowerbooking.com
WEB SITE . . . . .www.flowerbooking.com

TYPES OF CLIENTS	Musical Artists
MUSICAL ARTIST TYPES	Alternative - Country - Dance/DJ - Pop - Rock - World
SUBMISSION POLICY	Submit a package that includes latest material on CD, with photo and bio/press clippings

Susanne Dawursk . . . . .President
Tim Edwards . . . . .Agent
Mahmood Shaikh . . . . .Agent

FONTAINE MUSIC
205 S. Beverly Dr., Ste. 212
Beverly Hills, CA 90212
PHONE 310-471-8631
FAX 310-471-8630
EMAIL . . . . .fontainetalent@aol.com
WEB SITE . . . . .www.fontainetalent.com

TYPES OF CLIENTS	Musical Artists - Lyricists - Studio Vocalists
MUSICAL ARTIST TYPES	Adult Contemporary - Alternative - Country - Latin - Pop - Punk - R&B - Reggae - Rock - Urban
SUBMISSION POLICY	By mail
COMMENTS	Specializes in representing young musicians, bands and singers seeking major label deals

Judith Fontaine . . . . .President
Debbie Fontaine . . . . .Agent

FORMAN BROS. RECORDINGS
12711 Ventura Blvd., Ste. 320
Studio City, CA 91604
PHONE .818-782-4692/917-887-8505
FAX 818-782-5474/973-882-1559
EMAIL . . . . .david@musictrademark.com
SECOND EMAIL . . . . .michael@musictrademark.com

COMMENTS	Source Music: International Pop, Rock & Ethnic; Management; Representatives for Movie Tunes; U.S. Representative (Film & TV) for DKD/Aquarius Records; East Coast office: 20 Dogwood Circle, Pine Brook, NJ 07058

David Forman . . . . .President, Forman Bros. Holdings, Inc.
Michael Abramson . . . . .President, Forman Bros. Recordings

*FOUR BARS INTERTAINMENT (FBI)
1390 Saddle Rack St.
San Jose, CA 95126
PHONE 408-294-3488
EMAIL .bobrice@fourbarsintertainment.com
WEB SITE .www.fourbarsintertainment.com

COMMENTS	Composers and sound design for video games

Bob Rice . . . . .CEO

GORFAINE/SCHWARTZ AGENCY
4111 W. Alameda Ave., Ste. 509
Burbank, CA 91505
PHONE 818-260-8500
FAX 818-260-8522
EMAIL . . . . .clusey@gsamusic.com
WEB SITE . . . . .www.gsamusic.com

TYPES OF CLIENTS	Musical Artists - Music Producers - Music Supervisors - Film/TV Composers - Songwriters

Michael Gorfaine . . . . .Partner/Agent
Samuel H. Schwartz . . . . .Partner/Agent
Maria Machado . . . . .Agent
Cheryl Tiano . . . . .Agent

*THE GRANATA AGENCY
39 Cooper Rd.
Oak Ridge, NJ 07438
PHONE 973-208-7291
FAX 973-208-8567
EMAIL . . . . .mary@granataagency.com
WEB SITE . . . . .www.granataagency.com

CLIENT LIST	Jesse Colin Young - Lowen and Navarro - The Jeff and Vida Band - Sloan Wainwright - Cliff Eberhardt - Jeff Black - The Kennedys - Liz Queler

Mary Granata . . . . .Agent

GREAT AMERICAN TALENT
PO Box 2476
Hendersonville, TN 37077
PHONE 615-452-7878
FAX 615-452-7887
WEB SITE . . . . .www.gatalent.com

MUSICAL ARTIST TYPES	Alternative - Country
CLIENT LIST	Eddy Raven - Johnny Lee - Joe Stampley - Moe Bandy - Jo-El Sonnier - Johnny Rodriguez - Webb Wilder - Billy "Crash" Craddock

Sheila Futch . . . . .President

*LIZ GREGORY TALENT

9 Music Square South, Ste. 357
Nashville, TN 37203
PHONE 615-312-7058/888-455-7549
FAX 615-312-7059
EMAIL .lizgregtal@aol.com
WEB SITE . . . . .www.lizgregorytalent.com

Liz Grogory . . . . .Agent

GROUND CONTROL TOURING

190 N. 10th St., Ste. 301
Brooklyn, NY 11211
PHONE 718-218-8203/919-932-9165
FAX 718-218-8205/919-932-9166
EMAIL . . . . .eric@groundcontroltouring.com
SECOND EMAIL . . . . .jim@groundcontroltouring.com
WEB SITE . . . . .www.groundcontroltouring.com
TYPES OF CLIENTS | Musical Artists
MUSICAL ARTIST TYPES | All Genres
SUBMISSION POLICY | No unsolicited material
COMMENTS | North Carolina office: 104 Jones Ferry Rd., Ste. E, Carrboro, NC 27510

Eric Dimenstein .Agent (NY)
Jim Romeo . . . . .Agent (NC)
Ben Dickey . . . . .Agent (NC)
Tom McCabe . . . . .Assistant/Agent (NY)
Dana West . . . . .Assistant (NC)

HARMONY ARTISTS

8455 Beverly Blvd., Ste. 400
Los Angeles, CA 90048
PHONE 323-655-5007
FAX 323-655-5154
EMAIL . . . . .contact_us@harmonyartists.com
WEB SITE . . . . .www.harmonyartists.com
TYPES OF CLIENTS | Musical Artists - Variety Artists

Mike Dixon . . . . .Agent/President
Jerry Ross . . . . .Agent/VP
Mike Berton . . . . .Agent
Adrienne Crane . . . . .Agent

HELLO! BOOKING

11623 E. Laketowne Dr.
Albertville, MN 55301
PHONE 651-647-4464
FAX 763-463-1264
EMAIL . . . . .info@hellobooking.com
WEB SITE . . . . .www.hellobooking.com
TYPES OF CLIENTS | Musical Artists
MUSICAL ARTIST TYPES | Alternative - Rock
CLIENT LIST | Asylum Street Spankers - Cigar Store Indians - Dazy Head Mazy - Deke Dickerson - Dolly Varden - Giant Step - Heiruspecs - Judith Owen - Martin Zellar - Red Elvises - Skywynd - Slobberbone - That 1 Guy - The Kissers - The Nadas - Wayne Hancock

Eric Roberts . . . . .Eastern US
Michael McGregor . . . . .Western US
Kris Meyer Christensen . . . . .College Bookings

HIGH ROAD TOURING

751 Bridgeway, 3rd Fl.
Sausalito, CA 94965
PHONE 415-332-9292
FAX 415-332-4692
EMAIL . . . . .info@highroadtouring.com
WEB SITE . . . . .www.highroadtouring.com
TYPES OF CLIENTS | Musical Artists
MUSICAL ARTIST TYPES | Adult Contemporary - Alternative - Bluegrass - Blues - Children's - Classical - Country - Folk - Gospel - Jazz - Latin - New Age - Pop - Rock - Roots - World

Jackson Haring . . . . .Agent
Matt Hickey . . . . .Agent
Frank Riley . . . . .Agent
Lisa O'Hara . . . . .Agent

INLAND EMPIRE TOURING

48 Laight St., 1st Fl.
New York, NY 10013
PHONE 212-965-9149
FAX 212-219-9073
EMAIL . . . . .info@inlandempiretouring.com
WEB SITE . . . . .www.inlandempiretouring.com
TYPES OF CLIENTS | Musical Artists
CLIENT LIST | !!! - The Album Leaf - AZITA - Beehive and the Barracudas - The Bevis Frond - The Bloodthirsty Lovers - The Boggs - Dub Narcotic Sound System - Fruit Bats - The Glands - The Helio Sequence - Holopaw - Iron & Wine - Jenny Toomey - Les Savy Fav - The Magic Magicians - Modest Mouse - Need New Body - Rogue Wave - Sam Jayne - The Shins - The Thermals - Ugly Casanova - White Hassle - The Hold Steady - Travis Morrison - Love As Laughter - Eugene Mirman

Robin Taylor .Booking Agent

INTERNATIONAL CREATIVE MANAGEMENT, INC. - ICM (LOS ANGELES)

8942 Wilshire Blvd.
Beverly Hills, CA 90211
PHONE 310-550-4000
FAX 310-550-4100
WEB SITE . . . . .www.icmtalent.com
TYPES OF CLIENTS | Musical Artists - Music Producers - Music Supervisors - Film/TV Composers - Lyricists - Songwriters - Studio Musicians - Studio Engineers/Technicians
MUSICAL ARTIST TYPES | Adult Contemporary - Pop - R&B - Rap/Hip-Hop - Rock - Urban
COMMENTS | Dancers, Legitimate Theater

Jeffrey Berg .Chairman/CEO
Ed Limato . . . . .Vice Chairman/Co-President
Nancy Josephson . . . . .Co-President
Robert Murphy . . . . .CFO/Treasurer
Richard B. Levy, Esq. . . . . .COO/General Counsel
Steve Levine   Executive VP/Head, Comedy & West Coast Music/Concerts
David Shane . . . . .Sr. VP, Corporate Communications
Keith Naisbitt . . . . .VP, International Concerts
Chris Smith . . . . .VP, Concerts
Marty Beck . . . . .Concerts
Chyna Chuan . . . . .Concerts
Rick Farrell . . . . .Concerts
Scott Mantell . . . . .Concerts
Scott Pang . . . . .Concerts
Hal Ray . . . . .Concerts
Michelle Scarbrough . . . . .Concerts

AGENTS

INTERNATIONAL CREATIVE MANAGEMENT, INC. - ICM (NEW YORK)
40 W. 57th St.
New York, NY 10019
PHONE 212-556-5600
FAX 212-556-5665
WEB SITE . . . . .www.icmtalent.com
TYPES OF CLIENTS   Musical Artists - Songwriters
MUSICAL ARTIST TYPES   Adult Contemporary - Pop - R&B - Rap/Hip-Hop - Rock - Urban
COMMENTS   Dancers - Legitimate Theater Performers; London office: 4-6 Soho Square, London, W1D 3PZ, UK, phone: 44-207-432-0800

Jeffrey Berg . . . . .Chairman/CEO
Ed Limato . . . . .Vice Chairman/Co-President
Nancy Josephson . . . . .Co-President
Robert Murphy . . . . .CFO/Treasurer
Richard B. Levy, Esq. . . . . .COO/General Counsel
Mark Cheatham . . . . .VP, Urban Contemporary Music
Terry Rhodes . . . . .VP/Head, East Coast Music/Concerts
Lucia Chang . . . . .Concerts
Kristine Marshall . . . . .Concerts
Scott Morris . . . . .Concerts
Rich Murphy . . . . .Urban Contemporary Music
Roger Paul . . . . .Concerts
Mark Siegel . . . . .Concerts
Christianne Weiss . . . . .Concerts
Bob Zievers . . . . .Concerts

INTERNATIONAL MUSIC NETWORK (IMN)
278 Main St.
Gloucester, MA 01930
PHONE 978-283-2883
FAX 978-283-2330
WEB SITE . . . . .www.imnworld.com
TYPES OF CLIENTS   Musical Artists

Deborah Cohen . . . . .European Agent
Jeanna Disney . . . . .East Coast Agent
David Lloyd . . . . .Midwest Agent
Katherine McVicker . . . . .European Agent
Scott Southard . . . . .International Agent
Todd Walker . . . . .West Coast Agent
Michael Garron . . . . .Controller
Tom Korkidis . . . . .Artist Relations/Domestic Tour Coordinator
Alycia Mack . . . . .Domestic Tour Coordinator (East Coast)
Kristen Teixeira . . . . .International Coordinator
Holly Brennock . . . . .Contract Administrator

THE KAUFMAN AGENCY
12007 Laurel Terrace Dr.
Studio City, CA 91604-3617
PHONE 818-506-6013
FAX 818-506-7270
EMAIL . . . . .jhk@pacbell.net
WEB SITE . . . . .www.kaufmanagency.net
TYPES OF CLIENTS   Musical Artists - Music Producers - Film/TV Composers - Lyricists - Songwriters
CLIENT LIST   Carl Davis - Barry Goldberg - Dick Hyman - Mark McKenzie - Peter Melnick - Rob Lane - Hummie Mann - Sheldon Mirowitz - Andy Bush - David Gale - Alan Williams - Michael Wahlen - Ron Jones
COMMENTS   Handles talent worldwide with a focus on film and TV composers

Jeff H. Kaufman . . . . .Film Music Agent/Consultant
Debi Kaufman . . . . .Associate

THE JOYCE KETAY AGENCY
630 Ninth Ave., Ste. 706
New York, NY 10036-5653
PHONE 212-354-6825
FAX 212-354-6732
TYPES OF CLIENTS   Film/TV Composers - Lyricists - Songwriters
COMMENTS   Legitimate Theater

Joyce P. Ketay . . . . .Partner/Agent
Carl Mulert . . . . .Partner/Agent
Seth Glewen . . . . .Assistant to Carl Mulert
Jessica Sarbo . . . . .Assistant to Joyce P. Ketay

KORK AGENCY
1501 Powell, Ste. H
Emeryville, CA 94608
PHONE 510-658-4455/510-658-4459
FAX 510-658-4456
EMAIL . . . . .info@korkagency.com
WEB SITE . . . . .www.korkagency.com
TYPES OF CLIENTS   Musical Artists - Comedians
MUSICAL ARTIST TYPES   Rock
CLIENT LIST   ...And You Will Know Us by the Trail of Dead - Peaches - Atmosphere - Aesop Rock - Jello Biafra - Lifesavas - Lyrics Born - MF Doom - Mr. Dibbs - Pilot to Gunner

Christian Bernhardt . . . . .Owner/Agent
BKZ . . . . .Agent
Erik Carter . . . . .Agent
Ryan Craven . . . . .Agent
Andrew Skikne . . . . .Agent/Assistant
Molly Fitzgerald . . . . .Assistant
Tal Tahir . . . . .Web Designer

KRAFT-ENGEL MANAGEMENT
15233 Ventura Blvd., Ste. 200
Sherman Oaks, CA 91403
PHONE 818-380-1918
FAX 818-380-2609
EMAIL . . . . .info@kraftengel.com
TYPES OF CLIENTS   Musical Artists - Music Supervisors - Film/TV Composers - Lyricists - Songwriters
SUBMISSION POLICY   Referral only

Richard Kraft . . . . .Agent
Laura Engel . . . . .Agent
Adriana Getz . . . . .VP, Special Projects
David Klane . . . . .VP, Operations
Julie Michaels . . . . .Executive Coordinator
Dawna Shinkle . . . . .Executive Coordinator

TED KURLAND ASSOCIATES

173 Brighton Ave.
Boston, MA 02134
PHONE 617-254-0007
FAX 617-782-3577
EMAIL . . . . .agents@tedkurland.com
WEB SITE . . . . .www.tedkurland.com

TYPES OF CLIENTS	Musical Artists - Film/TV Composers - Lyricists - Songwriters
MUSICAL ARTIST TYPES	Blues - Jazz - New Age - World
CLIENT LIST	Pat Metheny - Kevin Eubanks - Pat Martino - Ralph Towner - Vernon Reid - Chick Corea - Ellis Marsalis - Ramsey Lewis - Danilo Perez - Marian McPartland - Keiko Matsui - Bill Charlap - Carla Bley - Lyle Mays - Makoto Ozone - Wynton Marsalis - Christian McBride - John Patitucci - Bill Laswell - Patricia Barber - Dee Dee Bridgewater - Ann Hampton Callaway - Kurt Elling - Stacey Kent - Steve Tyrell - Sonny Rollins - Branford Marsalis - Jimmy Heath - Joshua Redman - Kenny Garrett - Roy Haynes - Bill Bruford - Gary Burton - Delfeayo Marsalis - The Original Blues Brothers Band - Yellowjackets - Oregon - Lincoln Center Jazz Orchestra with Wynton Marsalis
SUBMISSION POLICY	No unsolicited material

Ted Kurland . . . . .President
David Sholemson . . . . .VP/Managing Director
Laurel J. Wicks . . . . .VP, Domestic Division
David Greenberg . . . . .Director, Marketing
Eric Hanson . . . . .Agent
Jack Randall . . . . .Agent
Denis Sullivan . . . . .International Agent
Marilyn Rosen . . . . .International Agent
Gunter Schroeder . . . . . . .Director, Licensing/Associate Artist Manager
Gille Amaral . . . . .Associate, Manager Division

*EDDIE LAMBERT/RILEX ENTERTAINMENT

7601 Graystone Dr.
West Hills, CA 91304
PHONE 818-406-1251
FAX 818-346-1717
EMAIL . . . . .rilex2@aol.com

Eddie Lambert . . . . .President

BUDDY LEE ATTRACTIONS, INC.

38 Music Square East, Ste. 300
Nashville, TN 37203-4396
PHONE 615-244-4336
FAX 615-726-0429
EMAIL . . . . .tconway@blanash.com
WEB SITE . . . . .www.buddyleeattractions.com

TYPES OF CLIENTS	Musical Artists - Film/TV Composers - Songwriters - Studio Musicians - Studio Vocalists
MUSICAL ARTIST TYPES	Bluegrass - Christian - Country
CLIENT LIST	David Allen Coe - Jeff Foxworthy - Lee Ann Womack - Mark Chesnutt - Marty Stuart - Ricky Van Shelton - Ronnie Milsap & Crystal Gayle
COMMENTS	AFM; Affiliated with Endeavor Agency, LLC

Joey Lee . . . . .CEO
Tony Conway . . . . .President
Joan Saltel . . . . .Executive VP
Kevin Neal . . . . .Sr. VP
Bob Kinkead . . . . .Jr. VP
Jon Folk . . . . .Agent
Gary Kirves . . . . .Agent
David Kiswiney . . . . .Agent
Tony Lee . . . . .Agent

LITTLE BIG MAN BOOKING

155 Avenue of the Americas, 6th Fl.
New York, NY 10013
PHONE 646-336-8520
FAX 646-336-8522
EMAIL . . . . .info@littlebigman.com
WEB SITE . . . . .www.littlebigman.com

TYPES OF CLIENTS	Musical Artists
MUSICAL ARTIST TYPES	Adult Contemporary - Alternative - Dance/DJ - Folk - Metal - Pop - Punk - R&B - Rap/Hip-Hop - Rock - Roots
CLIENT LIST	Badly Drawn Boy - Barenaked Ladies - Blue Man Group - The Cardigans - Neneh Cherry - Coldplay - Dido - Franz Ferdinand - Five for Fighting - Joe Jackson - Avril Lavigne - Sarah McLachlan - Joni Mitchell - Jason Mraz - N*E*R*D - William Orbit - Liz Phair - P.O.D. - The Polyphonic Spree - Damien Rice - Supergrass
SUBMISSION POLICY	No unsolicited music; Email for permission to send

Jonathan Adelman . . . . .Agent
Marty Diamond . . . . .Agent
Steve Ferguson . . . . .Agent
Larry Webman . . . . .Agent
Heather Kolker . . . . .Office Manager, Contracts
Andy Adelewitz .Public Relations
Andrea Milier . . . . .General Assistant/Receptionist

LUCKY ARTIST BOOKING

745 W. Katella Ave.
Orange, CA 92867-4630
PHONE 714-997-9141
FAX 714-997-0961
EMAIL . . . . .firstname@luckyartistbooking.com
WEB SITE . . . . .www.luckyartistbooking.com

TYPES OF CLIENTS	Musical Artists
MUSICAL ARTIST TYPES	Alternative - Christian - Hardcore - Metal - Pop - Punk - Rock
CLIENT LIST	Big D and the Kids Table - The Matches - Voodoo Glow Skulls - Streetlight Manifesto - Minutes Too Far - Terminal - Punchline - Underminded - Whole Wheat Bread - Zolof the Rock and Roll Destroyer - Falling Up - El Pus - June - Pillar Controlling the Famous
SUBMISSION POLICY	Solicited music only

Vince Pileggi . . . . .Co-Owner
Angie Dunn . . . . .Agent/Co-Owner
Kevin Gunther . . . . .Agent
Josh Lacey . . . . .Agent
Lindsey Murrell . . . . .Agent

MAD BOOKING & EVENTS, INC.

644 Antone St., Ste. 3
Atlanta, GA 30318
PHONE 404-355-7710
FAX 404-355-7712
EMAIL . . . . .info@madbooking.com
WEB SITE . . . . .www.madbooking.com

TYPES OF CLIENTS	Musical Artists

Laura Valente . . . . .President
Sheila Merritt .Sponsorship Director
Andria Towne . . . . .Director, Business Development/Project Manager
Dacia Moore . . . . .Talent Buyer/Project Manager
Andi Hill . . . . .Marketing Coordinator

AGENTS

MARIS AGENCY
17620 Sherman Way, Ste. 213
Van Nuys, CA 91406-3511
PHONE 818-708-2493
FAX 818-708-2165
TYPES OF CLIENTS   Musical Artists
MUSICAL ARTIST TYPES   Adult Contemporary - Pop - Rock

Stephen Mariscal . . . . .President

MAXIMUS ENTERTAINMENT
PO Box 27517
Austin, TX 78755
PHONE 512-343-6299
FAX 512-338-2209
EMAIL . . . . .tammy@maximustalent.com
WEB SITE . . . . .www.maximustalent.com
TYPES OF CLIENTS   Musical Artists
MUSICAL ARTIST TYPES   Alternative - Blues - Country - Metal -
                          Rock

Robert Devine . . . . .Agent
Tammy Taylor . . . . .Agent

DAVIS MCLARTY AGENCY
708-D S. Lamar Blvd.
Austin, TX 78704
PHONE 512-444-8750
FAX 512-416-7531
EMAIL . . . . .davis@davismclarty.com
SECOND WEB SITE . . . . .www.davismclarty.com
TYPES OF CLIENTS   Musical Artists
MUSICAL ARTIST TYPES   Bluegrass - Blues - Country - Roots
CLIENT LIST   Bruce Robison - Dale Watson - Derailers
                          - Doyle Branhall - The Gourds - Reckless
                          Kelly - Terry Allen - Chris Knight - Kelly
                          Willis
SUBMISSION POLICY   By referral only

Davis McLarty . . . . .Agent
Bonnie McManners . . . . .Assistant

METRO TALENT GROUP
83 Walton St., 3rd Fl.
Atlanta, GA 30303
PHONE 404-954-6620
FAX 404-954-6681
EMAIL . . . . .mail@metrotalentgroup.com
WEB SITE . . . . .www.metrotalentgroup.com
TYPES OF CLIENTS   Musical Artists
MUSICAL ARTIST TYPES   Pop - Rock
CLIENT LIST   Sister Hazel - Edwin McCain - Jump
                          Little Children - Stroke 9 - Drivin' N'
                          Cryin'

Cass B. Scripps . . . . .Owner/Booking Agent
Rodney Stammel .Booking Agent
Tanner Smith . . . . .Assistant

THE M.O.B. AGENCY
6404 Wilshire Blvd., Ste. 505
Los Angeles, CA 90048
PHONE 323-653-0427
FAX 323-653-0428
EMAIL . . . . .mobster411@aol.com
SECOND EMAIL . . . . .yorkshirejoy@gmail.com
WEB SITE . . . . .www.mobagency.com
TYPES OF CLIENTS   Musical Artists
CLIENT LIST   Berlin - Bow Wow Wow - Brookville -
                          The Creatures - Dread Zeppelin -
                          Fireball Ministry - Fountains of Wayne -
                          Gwen Stefani - Ivy - Komeda - Matt
                          Costa - Minnie Driver - No Doubt -
                          Oslo - Paco - Peter Himmelman - The
                          Randies - Red House Painters - Siouxsie
                          and the Banshees - The Start - Sun Kil
                          Moon - Tahiti 80

Mitch Okmin . . . . .President

MONTEREY INTERNATIONAL
200 W. Superior, Ste. 202
Chicago, IL 60610
PHONE 312-640-7500/831-625-6300
FAX 312-640-7515/831-625-6335
WEB SITE . . . . .www.montereyinternational.net
TYPES OF CLIENTS   Musical Artists
MUSICAL ARTIST TYPES   All Genres
CLIENT LIST   Acoustic Alchemy - Adrian Belew - Arc
                          Angels - Assembly of Dust - Better Than
                          Ezra - Big Bad Voodoo Daddy - Blue
                          October - Bob Schneider - BoDeans -
                          Bonnie Raitt - Bob James - Brendan
                          James - Buddy Guy - Camper Van
                          Beethoven - Cesaria Evora - Cesar
                          Rosas - Cheap Trick - Cowboy Mouth -
                          Cracker - Dave Grusin - Double Trouble
                          - DJ Logic and Project Logic - Eric
                          Hutchinson - Eric Johnson - E.S.T. - The
                          Flatlanders - The Freddy Jones Band -
                          Experience Hendrix - Fourplay - George
                          Thorogood & the Destroyers - Geoff Tate
                          - Indigenous - Ingram Hill - Iris DeMent
                          - Jimmie Vaughan - Jackie Greene - Joe
                          Ely - The Johnny Clegg Band - John
                          Mayall & The Bluesbreakers - The John
                          Popper Project - Jonny Lang - Joss Stone
                          - Jorge Drexler - Josh Dion Band - Keb'
                          Mo' - Keri Noble - King Sunny Ade &
                          His African Beats - Kill Hannah - Koko
                          Taylor & Her Blues Machine - Latin
                          Playboys - Larry Carlton - Ledisi - Lila
                          Downs - Lee Ritenour - Little Feat - Los
                          Lobos - Los Van Van - Los Lonely Boys -
                          Madeleine Peyroux - Martin Sexton - olu
                          dara - Queensrÿche - Robben Ford -
                          Samantha Moore - Sonya Kitchell -
                          Soulive - Shannon Curfman - Shemekia
                          Copeland - Spyro Gyra - Suffrajett -
                          Susie Suh - Toto - Taj Mahal - Susan
                          Tedeschi - Tuck & Patti - Yohimbe
                          Brothers
COMMENTS   West Coast office: PO Box 297, Carmel-
                          by-the-Sea, CA 93921

Brodie Becker . . . . .Agent (brodie@montereyinternational.net)
Garry Buck . . . . .Agent (garry@montereyinternational.net)
Kevin Daly . . . . .Agent (Carmel) (kevin@montereyinternational.net)
Paul Goldman . . . . . . .Agent (Carmel) (paul@montereyinternational.net)
Ron Kaplan . . . . .Agent (ron@montereyinternational.net)
Maria Matias . . . . . .Agent (Carmel) (maria@montereyinternational.net)
Ryan Owens . . . . .Agent (ryan@montereyinternational.net)
Josh Brinkman . . . . .Agent/Assistant to Ron Kaplan
                          (josh@montereyinternational.net)

(Continued)

MONTEREY INTERNATIONAL (Continued)

Joshua Knight . . . . .Agent/Assistant to Paul Goldman
(joshua@montereyinternational.net)
Michael A. Kazda . . . . .Controller/Business Manager
(mike@montereyinternational.net)
Jerry Lima . . . . .Assistant to Kevin Daly (Carmel)
(jerry@montereyinternational.net)
Patrick McAuliff . . . . . . .Assistant to Garry Buck/Administrative Assistant,
Contracts (patrick@montereyinternational.net)
Erica Deiters . . . . .Administrative Assistant, Contracts
(erica@montereyinternational.net)
Katie Farver . . . . .Administrative Assistant, Promotions
(katie@montereyinternational.net)
Joanne Graham . . . . .Administrative Assistant, Contracts
(joanne@montereyinternational.net)
Trevor McSpadden . . . . .Administrative Assistant, Deposits
(trevor@montereyinternational.net)
Colleen Gubbins . . . . .Administrative Assistant/Receptionist
(colleen@montereyinternational.net)

MONTEREY PENINSULA ARTISTS/PARADIGM

509 Hartnell St.
Monterey, CA 93940
PHONE 831-375-4889
FAX 831-375-2623
WEB SITE . . . . .www.montereypeninsulaartists.com
TYPES OF CLIENTS   Musical Artists
MUSICAL ARTIST TYPES   All Genres
CLIENT LIST   Aerosmith - The B-52's - The Black
                         Crowes - Black Eyed Peas - Carole King
                         - Cowboy Junkies - Dave Matthews Band
                         - Jem - Joan Osborne - k.d. lang - Lyle
                         Lovett - Randy Newman - Steve Miller
                         Band - Wyclef Jean - The Bacon
                         Brothers - Chris Isaak - The Corrs -
                         Fiona Apple - Shawn Colvin
COMMENTS   See Web site for full artist roster and
                         agent territories

Fred Bohlander . . . . .Agent
Lynn Cingari . . . . .Agent
Chip Hooper . . . . .Agent
Jonathan Levine . . . . .Agent
Duffy McSwiggin . . . . .Agent
Jackie Nalpant . . . . .Agent
Hank Sacks . . . . .Agent
Brian Swanson . . . . .Agent
Dan Weiner . . . . .Agent

MONTEREY PENINSULA ARTISTS/PARADIGM (NASHVILLE)

124 12th Ave. South, Ste. 410
Nashville, TN 37203
PHONE 615-251-4400
FAX 615-251-4401
WEB SITE . . . . .www.montereypeninsulaartists.com
TYPES OF CLIENTS   Musical Artists
CLIENT LIST   Montgomery Gentry - Ricky Skaggs -
                         Robert Earl Keen - Toby Keith - Travis Tritt
COMMENTS   See Web site for full artist roster and
                         agent territories

Bobby Cudd . . . . .Agent
Steve Dahl . . . . .Agent
Brian Hill . . . . .Agent
Greg Janese . . . . .Agent
Curt Motley . . . . .Agent
Ray Shelide . . . . .Agent
James Yelich . . . . .Agent

MONTEREY PENINSULA ARTISTS/PARADIGM (NEW YORK)

19 W. 44th St., Ste. 1410
New York, NY 10036
PHONE 212-391-1112
FAX 212-398-9677
WEB SITE . . . . .www.montereypeninsulaartists.com
TYPES OF CLIENTS   Musical Artists
CLIENT LIST   Kem - Keyshia Cole - Lil Wayne - T.I. -
                         Twista
COMMENTS   See Web site for full artist roster and
                         agent territories

Stephanie Mahler . . . . .Agent
Fleurette Vincent . . . . .Agent

M.P.I. TALENT AGENCY

9255 Sunset Blvd., Ste. 407
Los Angeles, CA 90069
PHONE 310-859-7300
FAX 310-275-7437
EMAIL . . . . .mpiinc@earthlink.net
TYPES OF CLIENTS   Musical Artists - Variety Artists

Michael Pick . . . . .President/CEO/Agent
Todd Bartleson . . . . .Agent
Lana Meier . . . . .Director, Business Affairs
Merrian Malubay . . . . .Junior Agent
Jamie E. Goldberg . . . . .Agent Assistant

*MUSIC FOR FILMS

34 Batchelor St.
London N1 0EG United Kingdom
PHONE 44-207-278-4288/323-850-4470
EMAIL . . . . .robgoldmusic@aol.com

Rob Gold . . . . .No Title

NASH-ANGELES, INC.

PO Box 363
Hendersonville, TN 37077-0363
PHONE 615-347-8258
EMAIL . . . . .nafilm1@aol.com
TYPES OF CLIENTS   Musical Artists - Music Producers -
                         Film/TV Composers - Songwriters

Eddie Reasoner . . . . .CEO
Jack Edwards . . . . .General Manager

NENE MUSIK TALENT AGENCY, LLC

3577 Wiles Rd., #106
Coconut Creek, FL 33073
PHONE 954-360-6820
FAX 954-360-6847
EMAIL . . . . .nenemusik@hotmail.com
WEB SITE . . . . .www.nenemusik.com
TYPES OF CLIENTS   Musical Artists - Music Producers -
                         Songwriters
MUSICAL ARTIST TYPES   Dance/DJ - Latin - Pop - R&B - Rap/Hip-
                         Hop - Rock - Urban
CLIENT LIST   Elvis Crespo - Aventura - Fulanito - DHT
                         - Lasgo - Ian Van Dahl - Lucas Prata -
                         Adassa - Dan Balan of O-Zone - La
                         Bouche - Kevin Ceballo - Dana Rayne -
                         Vic Latino - The Riddler - Kristy Kay - Fall
                         as Well - Michael Buffer - David Hodo
                         of The Village People

Rubin Martinez . . . . .Agent

PARADISE ARTISTS
PO Box 1821
Ojai, CA 93024-1821
PHONE 805-646-8433/212-879-5900/734-477-6677
FAX 805-646-3367/212-879-0668/734-477-0272
WEB SITE . . . . .www.paradiseartists.com
TYPES OF CLIENTS   Musical Artists - Variety Artists -
                         Comedians
MUSICAL ARTIST TYPES   Pop - Rock
CLIENT LIST   Blue Öyster Cult - Taylor Dayne - Foghat
                         - Stephen Bishop - Micky Dolenz - Davy
                         Jones - Gary Puckett - Bobby Sherman -
                         Esteban - A.J. Jamal - Weird Al Yankovic
                         - Chubby Checker - Sheena Easton -
                         Rare Earth
COMMENTS   Formerly Ashley Talent; East Coast office:
                         216 E. 75th St., New York, NY 10021;
                         Michigan office: 2002 Hogback Rd.,
                         Ste. 20, Ann Arbor, MI 48105

Robert Birk . . . . .Agent
Charlie Davis . . . . .Agent
Jay Frey . . . . .Agent (NY)
Mark Hyman . . . . .Agent (MI)
Bobby Lee . . . . .Agent
Jim Lenz . . . . .Agent
Bill Monot . . . . .Agent
Michael Rand . . . . .Agent (MI)
Steve Schenck . . . . .Agent (NY)
Howard Silverman . . . . .Agent
John Lappen . . . . .Music Licensing/Paradise MusicWerks

PARK AVENUE WEST ENTERTAINMENT
611 Mound Ave., Ste. C
South Pasadena, CA 91030
PHONE 866-236-4729/626-441-2716
FAX 626-441-0742
EMAIL . . . . .mjmiddleman@murraymiddleman.com
WEB SITE . . . . .www.murraymiddleman.com
TYPES OF CLIENTS   Musical Artists
MUSICAL ARTIST TYPES   Classical - Jazz - Latin - Pop - World
CLIENT LIST   Hal Ketchum - Leon Russell - Doug
                         Supernaw - Mindy Ellis - Russell Ray - Pat
                         Travers - Alan Haynes - Vallejo - Canvas
                         - Rick Derringer - Joe King Carrasco -
                         The Georgia Satellites - Jake Andrews -
                         Foghat - Bugs Henderson - Mountain -
                         Brian Auger
COMMENTS   Provides complete live music services
                         from any style for events

Murray Middleman . . . . .Musical Director

PIEDMONT TALENT INC.
PO Box 680006
Charlotte, NC 28216
PHONE 704-399-2210
FAX 704-399-2261
EMAIL . . . . .info@piedmonttalent.com
WEB SITE .www.piedmonttalent.com
TYPES OF CLIENTS   Musical Artists
MUSICAL ARTIST TYPES   Blues
CLIENT LIST   Albert Cummings - Alvin Youngblood
                         Hart - Alvin Youngblood Hart's Muscle
                         Theory - Ana Popovic Band - Anders
                         Osborne - Anson Funderburgh & the
                         Rockets feat. Sam Myers - Bobby Rush -
                         Candye Kane - Carey & Lurrie Bell -
                         Cephas & Wiggins - Cyril Lance - Dave
                         Hole - Debbie Davies Band - Deborah
                         Coleman - Eddy "The Chief" Clearwater
                         - Guitar Shorty - James Blood Ulmer -
                         Jody Williams - Johnny Winter - Little
                         Charlie & the Nightcats - Lonnie Brooks
                         - Michael Hill's Blues Mob - Nora Jean
                         Bruso - Papa Grows Funk - Robert
                         Gordon - Robert Lockwood, Jr. - Rory
                         Block - Rosie Ledet & The Zydeco
                         Playboys - Roy Rogers & the Delta
                         Rhythm Kings - Smokin' Joe Kubek Band
                         feat. Bnois King - Too Slim & The
                         Taildraggers - W.C. Clark - Walter
                         "Wolfman" Washington

Steve Hecht . . . . .Director/Agent (steve@piedmonttalent.com)
Tina Terry . . . . .Agent (tina@piedmonttalent.com)
Michelle Kaplan . . . . .Agent Assistant/IT Officer
                                 (michelle@piedmonttalent.com)
Emily Berger . . . . .Office Manager (emily@piedmonttalent.com)

PODELL TALENT AGENCY
22 W. 21st St., 9th Fl.
New York, NY 10010
PHONE 212-941-9390
FAX 212-941-9391
WEB SITE . . . . .www.podelltalent.com
TYPES OF CLIENTS   Musical Artists

Jonny Podell . . . . .Owner
C.J. Strock . . . . .Agent
Noah Perabo . . . . .Agent
Brian Hosey . . . . .Assistant

THE PROGRESSIVE GLOBAL AGENCY (PGA)
PO Box 50294
Nashville, TN 37205
PHONE 615-354-9100
FAX 615-354-9101
EMAIL . . . . .info@pgamusic.com
WEB SITE . . . . .www.pgamusic.com
TYPES OF CLIENTS   Musical Artists
MUSICAL ARTIST TYPES   All Genres
CLIENT LIST   Barbara Cue - Caitlin Cary - Cary Pierce
                         - The Connells - Chuck Leavell - deSol -
                         Jackopierce - Jerry Joseph &
                         Jackmormons - The Legendary Wailers -
                         R.E.M. - Signal Path - Smiling Assassins -
                         Stockholm Syndrome - Topaz - Tortured
                         Soul - Trent Dabbs - Tres Chicas -
                         Tuatara - Waylandsphere - Widespread
                         Panic - Caitlin Cary & Thad Cockrell -
                         Jerry Joseph - JoJo & His Mojo Mardi
                         Gras Band - Outformation - Ten Out Of
                         Tennessee - Steve Tibbetts & Choying
                         Drolma

Buck Williams . . . . .President
Jason Pitzer . . . . .Agent (East Coast) (jason@pgamusic.com)

(Continued)

THE PROGRESSIVE GLOBAL AGENCY (PGA) (Continued)

Hunter Williams . . . . .Agent (CA, Northwest, Midwest)
(hunter@pgamusic.com)
Dan Titcomb . . . . .Agent (Midwest) (dan@pgamusic.com)
Patti Williams . . . . .Accounting (patti@pgamusic.com)
Beth Barnett . . . . . . .Assistant to Buck Williams (beth@pgamusic.com)
Jennifer Fowler . . . . .Assistant (jennifer@pgamusic.com)

PYRAMID ENTERTAINMENT GROUP

377 Rector Pl., Ste. 21A
New York, NY 10280
PHONE 212-242-7274
FAX 212-242-6932
EMAIL . . . . .info@pyramid-ent.com
WEB SITE . . . . .www.pyramid-ent.com

TYPES OF CLIENTS	Musical Artists
MUSICAL ARTIST TYPES	Gospel - Jazz - Pop - R&B - Rap/Hip-Hop - Urban
CLIENT LIST	Kool & the Gang - Gladys Knight - Commodores - The Whispers - Isley Brothers - Jeffrey Osborne - Peabo Bryson - New Edition - EnVogue - O'Jays - Freddie Jackson - Patti LaBelle - Dennis Edwards' Temptations Review - Gerald Levert - Maze feat. Frankie Beverly - Teena Marie - Jack Ashford of The Funk Brothers feat. Joe Hunter - Mary Jane Girls feat. Val Young and the Stone City Family - Gap Band - Lakeside - SOS Band - Klymaxx - Ohio Players - Dazz Band - Rose Royce - Con Funk Shun - Midnight Star - Atlantic Starr - BarKays - Omarion - O'Ryan - Juvenile - Johnny Gill - Young Rome - Houston - Marques Houston - Pitbull - Ashanti - Mobb Deep - Cam'ron & The Diplomats - Memphis Bleek - Freeway - Slick Rick - Lil Jon & The East Side Boyz - Beanie Man - Jagged Edge - Avant - Keith Sweat - 112 - Young Bloodz - Silk - Chante Moore & Kenny Lattimore - Trina - Lil' Romeo - Jadakiss - JS - Eve - Ying Yang Twins - Fat Joe & Terror Squad - Angie Stone - Yolanda Adams - Patti Austin - Shirley Caesar - Fred Hammond - Jennifer Holiday - Najee - Ann Nesby - Take 6 - Hezekhia Walker - Angela Winbush - Kelly Price - KRS-One - Martha Reeves & the Vandellas - David Banner - Howard Hewett - Fabolous - ATL - Doug E. Fresh - Beanie Sigel - War - Gloria Gaynor - Peaches & Herb - All4One - Free Sol - Village People - Thelma Houston - Michael Bolton - Switch - James Ingram - Three 6 Mafia - Will Downing - MC Lyte - Regina Bell - The Whispers - Ruff Endz - Sister Sledge - Styles P - Too Short - Trick Daddy

E'lyse Murray . . . . .Agent (x3)
Stacey Sussman . . . . .Agent (x5)
Seth Cohen . . . . .Assistant (x2)
Matt Santo . . . . .Assistant (x6)

*REAL ARTISTS

29 Hurricane St., Ste. 2
Marina Del Rey, CA 90292
PHONE 310-710-4622
FAX 310-301-4070
EMAIL . . . . .tammyco@comcast.net

Tammy Krutchkoff . . . . .Agent

RED ENTERTAINMENT GROUP

16 Penn Plaza, Ste. 1750
New York, NY 10001
PHONE 212-563-7575
FAX 212-563-9393
EMAIL . . . . .info@redentertainment.com
WEB SITE . . . . .www.redentertainment.com

TYPES OF CLIENTS	Musical Artists
CLIENT LIST	Dionne Warwick - Gloria Gaynor - Charlie Wilson - Cameo - Gap Band - JT Taylor formerly of Kool & The Gang - O'Jays - Whispers - Peabo Bryson - Jeffrey Osborne - James Ingram - Freddie Jackson

Carlos Keyes . . . . .President
Wesley Goodman . . . . .Agent
Ivelisse Fernandez . . . . .Agent
Michael Elder . . . . .Agent

RITMO ARTISTS

Box 684705
Austin, TX 78768-4705
PHONE 512-447-5661
FAX 512-447-5886
EMAIL . . . . .info@ritmoartists.com
WEB SITE . . . . .www.ritmoartists.com

TYPES OF CLIENTS	Musical Artists
MUSICAL ARTIST TYPES	Blues - Country - Folk - Jazz - Latin - Reggae - Roots - World
CLIENT LIST	Emeline Michel - Ex-Centric Sound System - Geno Delafose - Kékélé - Lágbájá - Mahotella Queens - Mariza - Mory Kante - Oliver Mtukudzi - Plena Libre - Ricardo Lemvo - Sandra Luna - Värttinä - Waldemar Bastos - Hugh Masakela
SUBMISSION POLICY	No unsolicited materials

David Gaar . . . . .Agent

JEFF ROBERTS & ASSOCIATES

206 Bluebird Dr.
Goodlettsville, TN 37072
PHONE 615-859-7040
FAX 615-859-6504
EMAIL . . . . .jeff@jeffroberts.com
WEB SITE . . . . .www.jeffroberts.com

TYPES OF CLIENTS	Musical Artists
MUSICAL ARTIST TYPES	Christian
CLIENT LIST	Anointed - Avalon - Jeff Deyo - Twila Paris - Rebecca St. James - Skillet - Tree 63 - Casting Crowns - Everyday Sunday - Fusebox - Jeff Anderson - Jonah33 - Josh Bates - Joyce Martin - Jump5 - Kids in the Way - KJ-52 - Overflow - Seventh Day Slumber - The Katinas - ZOEgirl

Jeff Roberts . . . . .President
Ron Cantrell . . . . .Sr. Agent
Randy Humphries . . . . .Sr. Agent
Mike Roberts . . . . .Sr. Agent
Tom DeKorne . . . . .Agent
Michele Gocking . . . . .Marketing Director
Rhonda Hunt . . . . .Administration
Ann Sprouse . . . . .Administration

THE BOBBY ROBERTS COMPANY, INC.
PO Box 1547
Goodlettsville, TN 37070-1547
PHONE 615-859-8899
FAX 615-859-2200
EMAIL . . . . .info@bobbyroberts.com
WEB SITE . . . . .www.bobbyroberts.com
TYPES OF CLIENTS   Musical Artists
MUSICAL ARTIST TYPES   Adult Contemporary - Country - Rock
CLIENT LIST   John Anderson - Merle Haggard -
                          Sammy Kershaw - Pam Tillis - Classic
                          Rock All Stars

Bobby Roberts . . . . .Owner
Tim Bowers . . . . .Agent
Coby Futch . . . . .Agent
Travis James . . . . .Agent
Brian Jones . . . . .Agent
Lance Roberts . . . . .Agent
Bob Younts . . . . .Agent
Tara Shore . . . . .Marketing & Information Systems

THE ROOTS AGENCY
177 Woodland Ave.
Westwood, NJ 07675
PHONE 201-263-9200
FAX 201-358-8784
EMAIL . . . . .info@therootsagency.com
WEB SITE . . . . .www.therootsagency.com
TYPES OF CLIENTS   Musical Artists
MUSICAL ARTIST TYPES   Adult Contemporary - Bluegrass - Blues -
                          Children's - Folk - Jazz - Latin - Rock -
                          Roots - World
CLIENT LIST   Dee Carstensen - Janis Ian - Jess Klein -
                          John Gorka - Mustard's Retreat - Richie
                          Havens - Vance Gilbert - Susan Werner -
                          Crooked Still - Guy Davis - Peru Negro -
                          Tierra Tango - Hothouse Flowers - Sol y
                          Canto - The Barra MacNeils - Ashley
                          MacIsaac - Eileen Ivers & Immigrant
                          Soul - Gandalf Murphy & the
                          Slambovian Circus of Dreams - The
                          Glengarry Bhoys - The Saw Doctors -
                          Ann Rabson
COMMENTS   Boston office: 199 Pemberton St.,
                          Cambridge, MA 02140, phone: 617-
                          492-1515, fax: 617-649-0299;
                          Midwest office: 408 Westwood Ave.,
                          Ann Arbor, MI 48103, phone: 734-622-
                          8337, fax: 734-622-8463

Tim Drake . . . . .Agent/President (tim@therootsagency.com)
Rosi Amador . . . . .VP, Performing Arts & Latin Music (Boston)
                          (rosi@therootsagency.com)
David Tamulevich . . . . .Agent/VP Artist Development (Ann Arbor)
                          (david@therootsagency.com)
Kathy Drake . . . . . .Contract Administrator (kathy@therootsagency.com)
Regina Mullen . . . . . . .Financial Manager (regina@therootsagency.com)
Nancy Ambrose . . Assistant to Tim Drake (nancy@therootsagency.com)
Jan Krist . . . . . . .Office Assistant (Ann Arbor) (jan@therootsagency.com)

THE HOWARD ROSE AGENCY, LTD.
9460 Wilshire Blvd., Ste. 310
Beverly Hills, CA 90212
PHONE 310-858-3838
FAX 310-858-1995
TYPES OF CLIENTS   Musical Artists
MUSICAL ARTIST TYPES   Folk - Pop - Rock
CLIENT LIST   Elton John - Jimmy Buffett - Chicago -
                          Stevie Nicks - Boz Scaggs - Dan
                          Fogelberg
SUBMISSION POLICY   No unsolicited material

Howard Rose . . . . .Agent
Steve Smith . . . . .Agent

ROSEBUD AGENCY
PO Box 170429
San Francisco, CA 94117
PHONE 415-386-3456
FAX 415-386-0599
EMAIL .info@rosebudus.com
WEB SITE .www.rosebudus.com
MUSICAL ARTIST TYPES   Blues - Gospel - Latin - R&B - Roots -
                          World
CLIENT LIST   Bill Frisell - Daby Toure - Booker T. Jones
                          - John Hammond - W.C. Handy All Stars
                          - Charlie Musselwhite - Mavis Staples -
                          Johnny A. - Marcia Ball - Beau Soleil -
                          Robert Cray Band - Cubanismo - Dirty
                          Dozen Brass Band - Fiddlers 4 - Kaki
                          King - David Lindley - Coco Montoya -
                          Blind Boys of Alabama - JJ Cale -
                          Tommy Castro Band - Bettye LaVette -
                          Duke Robillard Band - Loudon
                          Wainwright III - Savoy Doucet Cajun
                          Band - Charlie Watts and the Tentet
SUBMISSION POLICY   Currently accepting submissions, but not
                          looking to add to roster

Mike Kappus . . . . .President
Tom Gold . . . . .Agent
John Lochen . . . . .Agent
Michael Morris . . . . .Agent
Drew Palmer . . . . .Agent

*THE MICHAEL ROSEN AGENCY
An Affiliate of Montana Artists
7715 Sunset Blvd., 3rd Fl.
Los Angeles, CA 90046
PHONE 323-845-4144, x237
FAX 323-845-4155
EMAIL . . . . .mrosen@montanartists.com
WEB SITE .www.montanartists.com

Michael Rosen . . . . .Principal
Toriono Mayek .Executive Assistant

*S.L. FELDMAN & ASSOCIATES (EASTERN DIVISION)
8 Elm St.
Toronto, ON M5G 1G7 Canada
PHONE 416-598-0067
FAX 416-598-1226
WEB SITE . . . . .www.slfa.com

Amy Fritz . . . . .No Title
Stacey Horricks . . . . .No Title

*S.L. FELDMAN & ASSOCIATES (WESTERN DIVISION)
1505 W. Second Ave., #200
Vancouver, BC V6H 3Y4 Canada
PHONE 604-734-5945
FAX 604-732-0922
EMAIL . . . . .webster@slfa.com
WEB SITE . . . . .www.slfa.com

Sarah Webster . . . . .No Title

SEC MANAGEMENT & TALENT
40707 John Mosby Hwy.
Aldie, VA 20105
PHONE 617-308-6984
FAX 617-663-6096
EMAIL . . . . .talent@sectalentgroup.net
WEB SITE . . . . .www.sectalentgroup.net
TYPES OF CLIENTS   Musical Artists
MUSICAL ARTIST TYPES   Adult Contemporary - Folk
CLIENT LIST   Larry Coryell - Flynn - Edie Carey - Anne
                         Heaton - Sam Shaber - Teddy Goldstein
                         - Pamela Means - Rachael Sage - Kyler
                         England - Ben Arnold
SUBMISSION POLICY   Currently not accepting submissions

Elizabeth Cromer . . . . .Manager/Agent

SHOUT BOOKING
419 Lafayette St., 4th Fl.
New York, NY 10003
PHONE 646-723-0668
FAX 212-228-3557
EMAIL . . . . .info@shoutbooking.com
WEB SITE .www.shoutbooking.com
TYPES OF CLIENTS   Musical Artists
MUSICAL ARTIST TYPES   Alternative - Christian - Folk - Pop - Punk
                          - Rock - Roots
CLIENT LIST   Hayes Carll - Richard Buckner - Anders
                          Parker - Tim Easton - The Silos - The
                          High Strung - David Mead - Mary Lou
                          Lord - Patterson Hood - Jason Isbell -
                          Kevn Kinney - The Capitol Years
SUBMISSION POLICY   No unsolicited submissions

Andrew Colvin . . . . .Agent

BRAD SIMON ORGANIZATION
122 E. 57th St.
New York, NY 10022
PHONE 212-980-5920
FAX 212-980-3193
EMAIL . . . . .info@bsoinc.com
SECOND EMAIL . . . . .artistinquiry@bsoinc.com
WEB SITE . . . . .www.bsoinc.com
TYPES OF CLIENTS   Musical Artists
MUSICAL ARTIST TYPES   Adult Contemporary - Jazz - New Age -
                          World
CLIENT LIST   Jennifer Holliday - Lionel Hampton
                          Orchestra - Jon Hendricks - Cassandra
                          Wilson - Women of Windham Hill - Geri
                          Allen - Secret Garden - Rene Marie -
                          Klezmer Conservatory Band - Odean
                          Pope - Abbey Lincoln - Jaco Pastorius
                          Big Band - Nestor Torres - Lalo Schifrin -
                          Abdullah Ibrahim
COMMENTS   Family Entertainment; Theatrical
                          Productions

Brad Simon . . . . .President
Barbara Simon . . . . .President
Keith Ghion . . . . .Agent
Amanda DeMeester .Office Manager

SKYLINE MUSIC, LLC
PO Box 31
Lancaster, NH 03584
PHONE 603-586-7171/213-291-1590
FAX 603-586-7068
EMAIL . . . . .firstname@skylineonline.com
WEB SITE . . . . .www.skylineonline.com
TYPES OF CLIENTS   Musical Artists - Songwriters
MUSICAL ARTIST TYPES   All Genres
CLIENT LIST   Al Stewart - Clarence Clemons - The
                          Commitments - Dave Edmunds - Drew
                          Emmitt - Dr. Demento - Gaelic Storm -
                          Garaj Mahal - George Winston - John
                          Sebastian - Marcus Eaton & The Lobby -
                          Nancy Sinatra - Oteil Burbridge & The
                          Peacemakers - Roger McGuinn -
                          Solomon Burke - Sophie B. Hawkins -
                          Tom Rush - The Ventures - Victor Wooten
                          - The Von Trapp Children - The Machine
                          - The Musical Box - Black 47
SUBMISSION POLICY   Email first

Bruce Houghton . . . . .President (LA) (213-291-1590)
Mark Lourie . . . . . . .VP, Development, Mountain/West (207-878-2330)
Barney Kilpatrick . . . . .Symphony (770-518-6434)
Patrick May .Northeast (802-864-6120)
Barron Ruth . . . . .South/Midwest (404-378-9299)
Andrea Sabata . . . . .ARTS, East/Midwest/South
Kelly Shuttleworth . . . . .ARTS Mountain/West
Erin Smith . . . . .Director, Tour Marketing
Marilyn Delozier . . . . .Administration
Kate Phelps . . . . .Administration
Jenica Johnson . . . . .Assistant (404-378-9299)

*SMA TALENT
The Cottage, Church St.
Fressingfield, Suffolk IP21 5PA United Kingdom
PHONE 44-1379-586-734
FAX 44-1379-586-131
EMAIL . . . . .olav@smatalent.com
SECOND EMAIL . . . . .carolynne@smatalent.com
WEB SITE . . . . .www.smatalent.com

Olav Wyper . . . . .No Title
Carolynne Wyper . . . . .No Title

SMC ARTISTS
4400 Coldwater Canyon Ave., Ste. 127
Studio City, CA 91604-5038
PHONE 818-505-9600
FAX 818-505-0909
TYPES OF CLIENTS   Music Supervisors - Film/TV Composers
                          - Lyricists - Songwriters
MUSICAL ARTIST TYPES   All Genres

Otto Vavrin II . . . . .President

THE SOHL AGENCY
669 N. Berendo St.
Los Angeles, CA 90004
PHONE 323-644-0500
FAX 323-644-0544
TYPES OF CLIENTS   Musical Artists
SUBMISSION POLICY   Currently not accepting submissions

Sohl . . . . .Owner/Agent
Carolyn Mace . . . . .Assistant

AGENTS

SOUNDTRACK MUSIC ASSOCIATES
15760 Ventura Blvd., Ste. 2021
Encino, CA 91436
PHONE 818-382-3300
FAX 818-382-3312
EMAIL . . . . .info@soundtrk.com
WEB SITE . . . . .www.soundtrk.com
TYPES OF CLIENTS   Music Supervisors - Film/TV Composers
                         - Lyricists - Songwriters
SUBMISSION POLICY   No unsolicited material

Cathy Schleussner . . . . .Sr. Partner/Agent
John Tempereau . . . . .Sr. Partner/Agent
Michael Horner . . . . .Business Affairs
Teresa Mackey . . . . .Office Manager
Robin Philips . . . . .Jr. Agent/Assistant
Michael Bajrami . . . . .Assistant

SRO ARTISTS, INC.
6629 University Ave., Ste. 206
Middleton, WI 53562
PHONE 608-664-8160
FAX 608-664-8161
EMAIL . . . . .gigs@sroartists.com
WEB SITE . . . . .www.sroartists.com
TYPES OF CLIENTS   Musical Artists - Songwriters
MUSICAL ARTIST TYPES   Adult Contemporary - Blues - Folk - Jazz
                         - Latin - World
CLIENT LIST   A Winter's Eve - Alison Brown - Ballet
                         Folklorico "Quetzalli" - Barbarito Torres -
                         bohola - California Guitar Trio - Catie
                         Curtis - Corky Siegel's Chamber Blues -
                         Dark Star Orchestra - Drum Drum -
                         Fiamma Fumana - Four Bitchin' Babes -
                         From Mother to Daughter - Hormonal
                         Imbalance...A Mood Swinging Musical
                         Revue! - JIGU! Thunder Drums of China
                         - Jimmy Johnson - Karla Bonoff - Ladies
                         Must Swing - La Guitara - Los
                         Folkloristas - Moscow Boys Choir® -
                         Nollaig - Patty Larkin - Peking Acrobats®
                         - Randy Sabien - Samite - Shangri-La
                         Chinese Acrobats® - Shooglenifty -
                         Simon Shaheen - Smithsonian Jazz
                         Orchestra - Stars of the Peking
                         Acrobats® - Tlen-Huicani - Tribute to
                         Stephane Grappelli
SUBMISSION POLICY   Established talent only

Jeff Laramie . . . . .President
Steve Heath . . . . .Artist Representative
Michael Wolke . . . . .Artist Representative
Toni Ziemer . . . . .Office Manager/Contract Administrator
Jef Pertzborn . . . . .Special Projects Coordinator
Ann Schmidt . . . . .Bookkeeper

SCOTT STANDER & ASSOCIATES
13701 Riverside Dr., Ste. 201
Sherman Oaks, CA 91423
PHONE 818-905-7000
FAX 818-990-0582
EMAIL . . . . .standrman2@aol.com
WEB SITE . . . . .www.scottstander.com
TYPES OF CLIENTS   Musical Artists
MUSICAL ARTIST TYPES   All Genres
CLIENT LIST   Charo - Debbie Reynolds - Larry Elgart -
                         Thelma Houston - Jeff Trachta - Lauren
                         Wood - Rita McKenzie - Freda Payne
COMMENTS   Also represents Broadway music

Scott Stander . . . . .President
Jacqueline Stander . . . . .Agent
Tama Kennemer . . . . .Agent
Eric Beck . . . . .Assistant

*STARS AND ARTISTS ENTERTAINMENT
99 S. Cameron St.
Harrisburg, PA 17101
PHONE 717-236-4500
FAX 717-236-4600
EMAIL .starsandartists@msn.com
WEB SITE . . . . .www.starsandartists.com
TYPES OF CLIENTS   Musical Artists
MUSICAL ARTIST TYPES   Alternative - Blues - Gospel - Jazz - Pop
                         - R&B - Rap/Hip-Hop - Rock

Annamaria Grabski . . . . .President, Urban Music

SUPREME ENTERTAINMENT
PO Box 35425
Boston, MA 02135
PHONE 617-782-7179
FAX 617-249-1735
EMAIL . . . . .alex@supremeentertainment.net
WEB SITE . . . . .www.supremeentertainment.net
TYPES OF CLIENTS   Musical Artists

Alex Ross . . . . .President

TALENT BUYERS NETWORK
700 S. Ninth St.
Las Vegas, NV 89101
PHONE 702-256-9811
FAX 702-256-9818
EMAIL . . . . .khouston@tbn.net
WEB SITE . . . . .www.tbn.net
TYPES OF CLIENTS   Musical Artists
MUSICAL ARTIST TYPES   All Genres

Kell Houston . . . . .VP

TALENT CONSULTANTS INTERNATIONAL (TCI)
1560 Broadway, Ste. 1308
New York, NY 10036
PHONE 212-730-2701
FAX 212-730-2706
EMAIL . . . . .email@tciartists.com
WEB SITE . . . . .www.tciartists.com
TYPES OF CLIENTS   Musical Artists
MUSICAL ARTIST TYPES   Blues - Electronica - Folk - Pop - R&B -
                         Rock - Roots
CLIENT LIST   Asia - Belinda Carlisle - Billy J. Kramer
                         and The Dakotas - Bo Diddley - Bonnie
                         Bramlett - Comedy You Can't Refuse -
                         Darlene Love - Dave Davies of The Kinks
                         - Deney Terrio - Denny Lane - Dion -
                         Donovan - Evelyn "Champagne" King -
                         Gary "US" Bonds - Genya Ravan - The
                         Hollies - The Human League - Jack
                         Jones - The Jones Gang - Lesley Gore -
                         Midge Ure - Mike Smith of Dave Clark
                         Five - Musique - Neil Innes - Ronnie
                         Spector - The Searchers - Steve Hackett -
                         Tavares - Thelma Houston - The
                         Trammps feat. Earl Young - Wilson
                         Pickett - The Zombies

Margo Lewis . . . . .President
Mitchell Karduna . . . . .VP/Director, Talent Representative
Mike Oberman . . . . .Agent
Robert Rowland . . . . .Agent
Chris Tuthill . . . . .Agent

THAT'S ENTERTAINMENT INTERNATIONAL
PO Box 2230
Folsom, CA 95763-2230
PHONE 916-294-0800/714-693-9300
FAX 916-294-0022/714-693-7963
EMAIL . . . . .thatentsac@sbcglobal.com
WEB SITE . . . . .www.teisacramento.com
TYPES OF CLIENTS   Musical Artists
MUSICAL ARTIST TYPES   All Genres
CLIENT LIST   Common Sense - Flying Blind - Freddy
                         Fender - John Cafferty & the Beaver
                         Brown Band - Starship feat. Mickey
                         Thomas - The Nelsons - Toto
COMMENTS   Anaheim office: 3820 E. La Palma Ave.,
                         Anaheim, CA 92807; Nashville office:
                         1711 Lawrence Rd., Franklin, TN
                         37069, phone: 615-646-1800, fax:
                         615-329-4918

Scott Mason . . . . .Agent (Northern California)
Tina Sexton . . . . .Agent (Northern California)
Scott Thomas .Agent (Northern California)
John McEntee . . . . .Agent (Anaheim)
Lynne Schula . . . . .Agent (Anaheim)
Buddy Emmer .Agent (Northern Nevada)
Mike Furlong . . . . .Agent (Northern Nevada)
Frank Garrett . . . . .Agent (Northern Nevada)
Rick Ricketts . . . . .Agent (Northern Nevada)

THIRD COAST ARTISTS AGENCY
2021 21st Ave. South, Ste. 220
Nashville, TN 37212
PHONE 615-297-2021
FAX 615-297-2776
EMAIL . . . . .info@tcaa.biz
WEB SITE . . . . .www.tcaa.biz
TYPES OF CLIENTS   Musical Artists

Lisa Snider . . . . .President/Agent
Mike Snider . . . . .VP/Agent
Chris Blaney . . . . .Agent
Dan Rauter . . . . .Agent
Keith Shackleford . . . . .Agent

UNITED TALENT AGENCY - UTA
9560 Wilshire Blvd.
Beverly Hills, CA 90212
PHONE 310-273-6700
FAX 310-247-1111
TYPES OF CLIENTS   Musical Artists - Comedians
SUBMISSION POLICY   Referral only

Rob Prinz . . . . .Head, Music/Agent
Steve Seidel . . . . .Agent, Music
Nikki Wheeler . . . . .Agent, Music
Mark Winkler . . . . .Agent, Music
Preston Gaspar . . . . .Assistant to Nikki Wheeler
Caitlin Roffman . . . . .Assistant to Rob Prinz
Carlos Shaw . . . . .Assistant to Steve Seidel

*ROBERT M. URBAND & ASSOCIATES
8981 Sunset Blvd., Ste. 311
West Hollywood, CA 90069
PHONE 310-858-3000
FAX 310-858-3002
EMAIL . . . . .rurband@aol.com

Robert M. Urband . . . . .Owner/President
Keith Anderson . . . . .No Title
Sasha Mitchell . . . . .No Title

VARIETY ARTISTS INTERNATIONAL
1924 Spring St.
Paso Robles, CA 93446-1620
PHONE 805-237-4275
FAX 805-237-4283
EMAIL . . . . .zach@varietyart.com
TYPES OF CLIENTS   Musical Artists
CLIENT LIST   311 - A Change of Pace - Gerald
                         Albright - Marc Antoine - Michael
                         Cavanaugh - Daphne Loves Derby -
                         Dixie Dregs - Down to the Bone - Kyle
                         Eastwood - Richard Elliot - Jeff Golub -
                         Graham Central Station feat. Larry
                         Graham - Euge Groove - Warren Hill -
                         Hiroshima - Incubus - June Kuramoto -
                         Jeff Lorber - Steve Morse Band -
                         Ordinary Peoples - Otis Day and the
                         Knights - Quietdrive - Sherwood - Strunz
                         & Farah - Robin Trower - Kirk Whalum -
                         Willie & Lobo
COMMENTS   Musicians on major labels with major
                         distribution only

Bob Engel . . . . .Agent
John Harrington . . . . .Agent
Carey Jones . . . . .Agent
Zach Mullinax . . . . .Agent
Lloyd St. Martin . . . . .Agent

MARSHA VLASIC ORGANIZATION (MVO)
307 Seventh Ave., Ste. 907
New York, NY 10001
PHONE 212-414-9380
FAX 212-414-9886
EMAIL . . . . .mvoltd@earthlink.net
TYPES OF CLIENTS   Musical Artists
CLIENT LIST   Neil Young - Elvis Costello - Van
                         Morrison - Lou Reed - Moby - The
                         Strokes - Courtney Love - The Exit - Le
                         Tigre

Marsha Vlasic . . . . .Owner

WENIG-LAMONICA ASSOCIATES (WLA)
580 White Plains Rd., Ste. 130
Tarrytown, NY 10591
PHONE 914-631-6500
FAX 914-631-0101
WEB SITE . . . . .www.wlatalent.com
TYPES OF CLIENTS   Musical Artists
MUSICAL ARTIST TYPES   Adult Contemporary - Blues - Jazz - Pop
                         - R&B - Reggae - Urban
CLIENT LIST   Ashford & Simpson - B.B. King - Bernie
                         Mac - Beres Hammond - Bobby "Blue"
                         Bland - Dr. John - Isaac Hayes - The
                         Manhattans - Roberta Flack - Stephanie
                         Mills - Teddy Pendergrass - Third World -
                         The Whispers - Yellowman - Ahmad
                         Jamal - Hiromi
SUBMISSION POLICY   Open

Paul LaMonica . . . . .Agent/Principal
Jody Wenig . . . . .Agent/Principal
Ari Bernstein . . . . .Agent
Mitch Blackman . . . . .Agent
Vincent Piazza . . . . .Agent

WHATEVER...TALENT AGENCY

3125 Lorraine Dr.
Missoula, MT 59803
PHONE 818-360-4843
FAX 888-226-8567
WEB SITE . . . . .www.whateveragency.com
TYPES OF CLIENTS   Musical Artists - Music Producers -
                          Film/TV Composers - Songwriters
MUSICAL ARTIST TYPES   All Genres
CLIENT LIST   Pete Yorn - Paul Buckmaster - Jim
                          Latham - Conrad Pope - Beck - Foo
                          Fighters - Ryan Adams - Sonic Youth
SUBMISSION POLICY   No unsolicited material accepted

Lesley Lotto . . . . .Agent

THE WILD AGENCY

7400 Hollywood Blvd., Ste. 409
Los Angeles, CA 90046
PHONE 323-578-4777
FAX 323-874-2105
EMAIL .info@filmmusichollywood.com
WEB SITE . . . . .www.filmmusichollywood.com
TYPES OF CLIENTS   Music Producers - Film/TV Composers
SUBMISSION POLICY   Email queries preferred
COMMENTS   Associated with Robert Light Agency

Helga Wild . . . . .President/Agent

WILLIAM MORRIS AGENCY - WMA (LOS ANGELES)

One William Morris Pl.
Beverly Hills, CA 90212
PHONE 310-859-4000
FAX 310-859-4462
WEB SITE . . . . .www.wma.com
TYPES OF CLIENTS   Musical Artists
MUSICAL ARTIST TYPES   Adult Contemporary - Alternative -
                          Bluegrass - Blues - Christian - Country -
                          Dance/DJ - Folk - Gospel - Hardcore -
                          Jazz - Latin - Metal - New Age - Pop -
                          Punk - R&B - Rap/Hip-Hop - Reggae -
                          Rock - Roots - Urban - World
COMMENTS   See Web site for full artist roster

Norman Brokaw . . . . .Chairman of the Board
Walter Zifkin . . . . .CEO
Jim Wiatt . . . . .President/Co-CEO
David Wirtschafter . . . . .President
Irv Weintraub . . . . .COO
Peter Grosslight . . . . . . .Worldwide Head, Personal Appearance
David Snyder . . . . .Head, Adult Contemporary Music
Marc Geiger . . . . .Head, Contemporary Music
Tony Goldring .Head, International
Benjamin Scales . . . . .Music Administrative Manager
Brian Ahern . . . . .Music
Dick Alen . . . . .Music
Ben Bernstein . . . . .Music
Michele Bernstein . . . . .Music
John Branigan . . . . .Music
Chris Burke . . . . .Music
Brian Edelman . . . . .Music
Heidi Feigin . . . . .Music
Amy Flax . . . . .Music
Robby Fraser . . . . .Music
Bradley Goodman . . . . .Music
Rob Heller . . . . .Music
Gayle Holcomb . . . . .Music
Tom Illius . . . . .Music
Andrew Lanoie . . . . .Music
David Levine . . . . .Music
Stacy Mark . . . . .Music
Rob Markus . . . . .Music
John Marx . . . . .Music
Stephanie Miles . . . . .Music
Clint Mitchell . . . . .Music
Craig Mogil . . . . .Music
Ron Opaleski . . . . .Music

(Continued)

WILLIAM MORRIS AGENCY - WMA (LOS ANGELES)

(Continued)
Aaron Pinkus . . . . .Music
Marshall Reznick . . . . .Music
Guy Richard . . . . .Music
Akiko Rogers . . . . .Music
Joel Roman . . . . .Music
Keith Sarkisian . . . . .Music
Brent Smith . . . . .Music
Kirk Sommer . . . . .Music
Nanci Stevens . . . . .Music

WILLIAM MORRIS AGENCY - WMA (MIAMI)

119 Washington Ave., Ste. 400
Miami Beach, FL 33139
PHONE 305-938-2000
FAX 305-938-2002
WEB SITE . . . . .www.wma.com
TYPES OF CLIENTS   Musical Artists

Raul Mateu . . . . .Agent/Sr. VP
Eric Rovner . . . . .Agent, TV
Pedro Bonilla . . . . .Agent, Commercials/Sponsorships
Michel Vega .Agent, Music, VP
Albert Garcia Jr. . . . . .Assistant to Raul Mateu
Jeremy Norkin . . . . .Assistant to Michel Vega
Gabriella Sosa . . . . .Assistant
Margarita Montilla . . . . .Trainee

WILLIAM MORRIS AGENCY - WMA (NASHVILLE)

1600 Division St., Ste. 300
Nashville, TN 37202
PHONE 615-963-3000
FAX .615-963-3090/615-963-3091
WEB SITE . . . . .www.wmanashville.com
TYPES OF CLIENTS   Musical Artists
MUSICAL ARTIST TYPES   Christian - Country - Rock
COMMENTS   See Web site for full artist roster

Paul Moore . . . . .Co-COO
Rick Shipp . . . . .Co-COO
Greg Oswald . . . . .Sr. VP, Country Department
Keith Miller . . . . .Sr. VP, Country Department
Charles Dorris . . . . .VP, Christian Department
Valerie Summers . . . . .VP, Christian Department
Ginger Anderson . . . . .VP, Country Department
Rob Beckham . . . . .VP, Country Department
Steve Hauser . . . . .VP, Country Department
Barry Jeffrey .VP, Fair Department
Mark Roeder . . . . .VP, Country Department
Lane Wilson . . . . .VP, Country Department
Kathy Armistead . . . . .Agent, Sponsorships
Carey Nelson Burch .Agent, TV
Scott Galloway . . . . .Club Agent, Country Department
John Gimenez . . . . .Agent, Fair Department
Gloria Green . . . . .Agent, Christian Department
Mark Guynn . . . . .Agent, Christian Department
Tinti Moffat . . . . .Club Agent & Canada, Country Department
Barrett Sellers . . . . .Club Agent, Country Department
Abby Wells . . . . .Club Agent, Country Department
Jay Williams . . . . .Agent, Country Department
Mark Claassen . . . . .Christian Department Coordinator
Dana Burwell . . . . .Executive Assistant to Rick Shipp
Graham Abell . . . . .Assistant to Paul Moore
Eric Arnold . . . . .Assistant to Barry Jeffrey
Becky Baughman . . . . .Assistant to Greg Oswald
Drew Birchfield . . . . .Assistant to Mark Guynn
Christie Blackburn . . . . .Assistant to John Gimenez
Ryan Gardenhire . . . . .Assistant to Ginger Anderson
Anne Marie Gebel . . . . .Assistant to Paul Moore
Amy Grace . . . . .Assistant to Steve Hauser
Denise Tschida Hailey . . . . .Assistant to Rob Beckham
Beth Hamilton . . . . .Assistant to Keith Miller
Matthew Miller . . . . .Assistant to Lane Wilson
Tammy Nichols . . . . .Assistant to Rick Shipp
Pete Olson . . . . .Assistant to Jay Williams
Leigh Parr . . . . .Assistant to Mark Roeder
Erin Pauling . . . . .Assistant to Carey Nelson Burch

(Continued)

WILLIAM MORRIS AGENCY - WMA (NASHVILLE)
(Continued)
Kristen Pridgen . . . . .Assistant to Greg Oswald
Christy Reeves . . . . .Assistant to Rob Beckham
Ember Rigsby . . . . .Assistant to Gloria Green
Erin Taylor . . . . .Assistant to Abby Wells
Gabby Turner . . . . .Assistant to Tinti Moffat
Lisa Whitaker . . . . .Assistant to Barrett Sellers
Ruthanne White .Assistant to Valerie Summers
Anthony Wozniak . . . . .Assistant to Charles Dorris

WILLIAM MORRIS AGENCY - WMA (NEW YORK)
1325 Avenue of the Americas
New York, NY 10019
PHONE 212-586-5100
FAX 212-246-3583
WEB SITE . . . . .www.wma.com
TYPES OF CLIENTS   Musical Artists - Music Producers - Music Supervisors - Film/TV Composers - Lyricists - Songwriters
COMMENTS   Legitimate Theater, Celebrities; See Web site for full artist roster

Lou Weiss . . . . .Chairman Emeritus
Wayne S. Kabak .Co-COO, New York
Cara Stein . . . . .Co-COO, New York
Ken DiCamillo . . . . .Personal Appearance
Sam Kirby . . . . .Personal Appearance
Cara Lewis . . . . .Personal Appearance
Barbara Skydel . . . . .Personal Appearance
Peter Franklin . . . . .Theatre
Biff Liff . . . . .Theater
Roland Scahill . . . . .Theatre
Jack Tantleff . . . . .Theatre
Susan Weaving . . . . .Theatre
David Kalodner . . . . .Theatre Talent
Jeremy Katz . . . . .Theatre Talent
Patti Kim . . . . .Corporate Consulting
Don Aslan . . . . .Business Affairs
Catherine Bennett . . . . .Business Affairs
David Berlin . . . . .Business Affairs
Richard Charnoff .Business Affairs
Eric Zohn . . . . .Business Affairs

WORD OF MOUTH ENTERTAINMENT
2305 Medinah Court
Palos Heights, IL 60463
PHONE 708-371-9900
FAX 708-371-9921
EMAIL . . . . .wominc@mindspring.com
WEB SITE . . . . .www.wordofmouthentertain.com
TYPES OF CLIENTS   Musical Artists - Variety Artists - Comedians

Marie Lewis . . . . .No Title

WORKSHEET

DATE	PROJECT	CONTACT	NOTES

SECTION **B**

REPRESENTATION

- Agents
- **Managers**
- Attorneys

Asterisks (*) next to companies denote new listings.

10TH STREET ENTERTAINMENT
700 San Vicente Blvd., Ste. G410
West Hollywood, CA 90069
PHONE 310-385-4700/212-334-3160
FAX 310-385-4742/212-334-3285
EMAIL . . . . .info@10thst.com
WEB SITE www.10thst.com
TYPES OF CLIENTS   Musical Artists
MUSICAL ARTIST TYPES   Adult Contemporary - Alternative - Metal
                         - Pop - Punk - Rock
CLIENT LIST   Blondie - Buckcherry - The Cars -
                         Everclear - Hanson - Hemigod - Marion
                         Raven - Meat Loaf - Motor Ace - Mötley
                         Crüe - Jonny Lives - Yes - The Years
COMMENTS   FKA Left Bank Organization; East Coast
                         office: 568 Broadway, Ste. 608, New
                         York, NY 10012

Allen Kovac . . . . .CEO (NY, LA)
Jordan Berliant . . . . .Manager & International Marketing (LA)
Jeff Varner . . . . .Manager & Merchandising (LA)
Frank Cimler .Checkmate CEO (LA, NY)
Tom Scarillo . . . . .CFO (NY)
Alisa Berg . . . . .Touring (NY)
Matt D'Amico . . . . .Manager & Retail (LA)
Steve Kline . . . . .Promotion (NY)
Martin Leahy . . . . .Tour Marketing (NY)
Katie McNeil . . . . .Manager, Media (LA)
Josh Scheiner . . . . .New Media (NY)
Jodi Emond .Product Manager (LA)
Beverly Lund .Office Manager (LA)

19 ENTERTAINMENT, INC. (LOS ANGELES)
9440 Santa Monica Blvd., Ste. 705
Beverly Hills, CA 90210
PHONE 310-777-1940
FAX 310-777-1949
WEB SITE www.19.co.uk
TYPES OF CLIENTS   Musical Artists
MUSICAL ARTIST TYPES   Pop
CLIENT LIST   Annie Lennox - Cathy Dennis -
                         Eurythmics - Victoria Beckham - Will
                         Young - Gareth Gates - Emma Bunton -
                         Fantasia Barrino - Christina Christian -
                         Carrie Underwood - Rachel Stevens

Iain Pirie . . . . .No Title

19 ENTERTAINMENT, INC. (NEW YORK)
140 W. 57th St., Ste. 5B
New York, NY 10019
PHONE 212-262-1347
FAX 212-262-1547
WEB SITE www.19.co.uk
TYPES OF CLIENTS   Musical Artists
MUSICAL ARTIST TYPES   Pop
CLIENT LIST   Christina Christian - Carrie Underwood -
                         Rachel Stevens - Annie Lennox - Cathy
                         Dennis - Eurythmics - S Club - Paul
                         Hardcastle - Victoria Beckham - Will
                         Young - Gareth Gates - Emma Bunton -
                         Fantasia Barrino
COMMENTS   UK Main office: Unit 32 Ransomes Dock
                         Business Centre, 35-37 Parkgate Rd.,
                         London, SW11 4NP UK

Tom Ennis . . . . .No Title

2 GENERATIONS SPA MUSIC MANAGEMENT INC.
300 E. 34th St., Ste. 28B
New York, NY 10016
PHONE 212-842-8478
FAX 212-735-6862
EMAIL . . . . .management@2generations.com
WEB SITE www.2generations.com
TYPES OF CLIENTS   Musical Artists - Music Producers -
                         Songwriters - Studio
                         Engineers/Technicians
MUSICAL ARTIST TYPES   Alternative - Metal - Rap/Hip-Hop -
                         Rock
CLIENT LIST   Fifth Year Crush - Squeezetoy - Paulo
                         Gregoletto of Metal Militia & Trivium -
                         Tammany Hall - Dave Pittenger Band -
                         Russ Desalvo - Dug McGuirk - Glen
                         Robinson - The Churchills - Full Force -
                         Manifest

Aimee Berger . . . . .President
Jeremy Williams . . . . .Sr. VP, Southern Regional Division
Ellen Parnett . . . . .Promotions & Marketing Representative
Derek Williams . . . . .Promotions & Marketing Representative

21ST CENTURY ARTIST INCORPORATED
853 Broadway, Ste. 1711
New York, NY 10003
PHONE 212-254-5500
FAX 212-254-4800
MUSICAL ARTIST TYPES   Adult Contemporary - Folk - Pop - R&B -
                         Reggae - Roots - World

Linda Birkenfeld . . . . .Manager
Marc Farrand . . . . .Manager
Toby Ludwig . . . . .Manager

55 ENTERTAINMENT
8680 Melrose Ave.
Los Angeles, CA 90069-5023
PHONE 310-855-0557
FAX 310-855-0549
TYPES OF CLIENTS   Musical Artists - Music Producers -
                         Songwriters
MUSICAL ARTIST TYPES   R&B - Rap/Hip-Hop - Urban
CLIENT LIST   Metro - Dro - Phaedra - Dani
SUBMISSION POLICY   Accepts submissions; No calls
COMMENTS   Seeking producers, songwriters who sing,
                         and male or female singing groups

Bob Francis . . . . .President (BF55ent@aol.com)
Walter Coulter . . . . .GM
Kareem Marshall . . . . .A&R, Rap
Mike B . . . . .A&R, R&B

777 ENTERTAINMENT GROUP
1015 Gayley Ave., Ste. 1128
Los Angeles, CA 90024
PHONE 310-824-0664
FAX 775-251-2583
EMAIL .admin@777entgroup.com
WEB SITE .www.777entgroup.com
TYPES OF CLIENTS   Musical Artists - Music Producers

Marcello Robinson .President/CEO
Onie Rivers . . . . .Producer

MANAGERS

A² MANAGEMENT
2336 W. Belmont Ave.
Chicago, IL 60618
PHONE 773-248-4210
FAX 773-248-4211
WEB SITE . . . . .www.asquaredmgmt.com
MUSICAL ARTIST TYPES   Alternative - Pop - Rock
CLIENT LIST   Liz Phair - Motion City Soundtrack - The Working Title - Mae - Abdel Wright - Jackopierce - Mat Kearney
SUBMISSION POLICY   No unsolicited material
COMMENTS   Division of Aware Records

Gregg Latterman . . . . .Manager (gregg@awardrecords.com)
Mark Cunningham . . . . .Manager (mark@awarerecords.com)
Steve Smith . . . . .Manager (steve@asquaredmgmt.com)
Jason Rio . . . . .Manager (jason@asquaredmgmt.com)
Jason Ienner . . . . .Manger (jienner@awarerecords.com)
Tyler Hagenbuch . . . . .Assistant (tyler@awardrecords.com)
Caroline Linder . . . . .Assistant (caroline@awaredmgmt.com)
Brenden Mulligan . . . . .Assistant (brenden@awarerecords.com)
Jenn Uhen . . . . .Assistant (jenn@asquaredmgmt.com)
Scott Burton . . . . .No Title (scott@awarerecords.com)

ADVANCED ALTERNATIVE MEDIA, INC.
7 W. 22nd St., 4th Fl.
New York, NY 10010
PHONE 212-924-2929
FAX 212-929-6305
EMAIL . . . . .info@aaminc.com
TYPES OF CLIENTS   Music Producers - Film/TV Composers - Lyricists - Songwriters - Studio Engineers/Technicians
MUSICAL ARTIST TYPES   All Genres
CLIENT LIST   Lords of Acid - Praga Khan - The Dust Brothers - William Orbit - Matt Pond PA

Mark Beaven . . . . .Manager/Co-President
Andrew Kipnes . . . . .Manager/Co-President
Heather Hawkins . . . . .Manager/VP
Renee Crowley . . . . .Coordinator
Tara Kelly . . . . .Assistant/Project Coordinator
Becky Scott . . . . .Assistant/Project Coordinator

ALABASTER ARTS
315 10th Ave. South, Ste. 116
Nashville, TN 37203
PHONE 615-662-7400/310-625-6245
FAX 615-662-7879
EMAIL .music@alabaster.com
WEB SITE .www.alabaster.com
TYPES OF CLIENTS   Musical Artists
MUSICAL ARTIST TYPES   Metal - Pop - Rock
CLIENT LIST   Relient K - OC Supertones - The Wedding - House of Heroes - John Davis - Cameron Jaymes - Maylene & the Sons of Disaster
COMMENTS   West Coast office: 4307 Coldwater Canyon Ave., Studio City, CA 91604-1435

Steven Thomas . . . . .President
Milam Byers . . . . .Manager
Jeff Risden . . . . .Manager
Anne Marie Tucker . . . . .Manager
Lucas Boto . . . . .Manager (Los Angeles)

ALIVE ENTERPRISES
3264 S. Kihei Rd.
Kihei, Maui, HI 96753
PHONE 808-891-0022/435-658-1505
FAX 808-879-2734/435-658-2696
EMAIL . . . . .alivewow@maui.net
SECOND EMAIL . . . . .famoustm@aol.com
TYPES OF CLIENTS   Musical Artists
CLIENT LIST   Alice Cooper
COMMENTS   Second office: PO Box 684384, Park City, UT 84068

Toby Mamis .Manager (Park City)
Shep Gordon . . . . .Owner (Maui)

BRUCE ALLEN TALENT
500-425 Carrall St.
Vancouver, BC V6B 6E3 Canada
PHONE 604-688-7274
FAX 604-688-7118
EMAIL .info@bruceallen.com
WEB SITE . . . . .www.bruceallen.com
TYPES OF CLIENTS   Musical Artists - Music Producers
MUSICAL ARTIST TYPES   All Genres
CLIENT LIST   Anne Murray - Bryan Adams - Martina McBride - Michael Bublé - Bob Rock
SUBMISSION POLICY   No unsolicited material accepted

Bruce Allen . . . . .President (bruce@bruceallen.com)
Randy Berswick . . . . .Tour Coordinator (berswick@bruceallen.com)
Sandee Bathgate . . . . .Licensing (sandeeb@bruceallen.com)
Jo Faloona . . . . .Media Relations (jo@bruceallen.com)

ALLIANCE ARTISTS
1111 Alderman Dr., Ste. 285
Alpharetta, GA 30005
PHONE 770-663-4240
FAX 770-663-8757
TYPES OF CLIENTS   Musical Artists
MUSICAL ARTIST TYPES   All Genres
CLIENT LIST   Crazy Anglos - Sam Moore - Red 37 - Styx - Funk Bros. - Outlaws - Dickey Betts

Charlie Brusco . . . . .President
Phyllis McLay . . . . .CFO
Sandy Miller . . . . .Director, Marketing
Cindy Brusco . . . . .Artist Manager
Julie Anderson . . . . .Assistant
Justin Dixon . . . . .Assistant

AMP MANAGEMENT
3201 W. Cahuenga Blvd.
Los Angeles, CA 90068
PHONE 323-851-3267
FAX 323-785-7101
EMAIL . . . . .ampmgmt@aol.com
TYPES OF CLIENTS   Musical Artists
MUSICAL ARTIST TYPES   Alternative - Rock
CLIENT LIST   Taking Back Sunday - Recover - The Honorary Title
SUBMISSION POLICY   No unsolicited submissions accepted

Larry Weintraub . . . . .Manager
Terry Dry . . . . .Manager
Jillian Newman . . . . .Manager

MANAGERS

ANDON ENTERTAINMENT
PO Box 2397
25 Cliff Dr.
Sag Harbor, NY 11963
PHONE 631-725-2506
FAX 631-725-2565
EMAIL . . . . .andonartists@aol.com
SECOND EMAIL . . . . .andonartists3@aol.com
WEB SITE .www.andonartists.com
TYPES OF CLIENTS   Musical Artists
MUSICAL ARTIST TYPES   Alternative - Dance/DJ - New Age - Pop
                         - Rock
CLIENT LIST   Donna Lewis - RA - Edison - Lyza Wilson
                         - FONZIE
SUBMISSION POLICY   No unsolicited material

Avery Andon . . . . .Owner
Arma Andon . . . . .President

ANGELUS ENTERTAINMENT
16000 Ventura Blvd., Ste. 600
Encino, CA 91436
PHONE 310-274-3449
TYPES OF CLIENTS   Musical Artists
MUSICAL ARTIST TYPES   Rock
CLIENT LIST   The Black Crowes - Franky Perez

Peter Angelus . . . . .President
Amy Finkle . . . . .Manager

ARNOLD & ASSOCIATES
280 S. Beverly Dr., Ste. 206
Beverly Hills, CA 90212
PHONE 310-858-4560
FAX 310-858-3803
EMAIL . . . . .arnold.associates@worldnet.att.net
TYPES OF CLIENTS   Musical Artists

Larkin Arnold . . . . .CEO/Attorney

ARTIST IN MIND
14625 Dickens St., Ste. 207
Sherman Oaks, CA 91403
PHONE 818-752-8020
FAX 818-752-8026
EMAIL . . . . .info@artistinmind.com
TYPES OF CLIENTS   Musical Artists - Film/TV Composers -
                         Songwriters - Studio Vocalists
MUSICAL ARTIST TYPES   Alternative - Pop - Rock
CLIENT LIST   Remy Zero - Will Hoge - Sanders Bohlke
                         - Brian Vander Ark - The Verve Pipe -
                         Marc Bonilla - James Hall
SUBMISSION POLICY   No unsolicited material

Doug Buttleman . . . . .Manager

ASSEMBLY ENTERTAINMENT
8033 Sunset Blvd., Ste. 2000
Los Angeles, CA 90046
PHONE 310-888-4040
EMAIL . . . . .aec@assemblyentertainment.com
WEB SITE . . . . .www.assemblyentertainment.com
TYPES OF CLIENTS   Musical Artists - Music Producers - Music
                         Supervisors - Film/TV Composers -
                         Lyricists - Songwriters - Variety Artists
MUSICAL ARTIST TYPES   All Genres
SUBMISSION POLICY   Accepts unsolicited demos

Marty O'Toole . . . . .Manager/Attorney

TOM ATENCIO & ASSOCIATES
5517 Green Oak Dr.
Los Angeles, CA 90068
PHONE 323-468-0105
EMAIL . . . . .noregret1@aol.com
TYPES OF CLIENTS   Musical Artists
SUBMISSION POLICY   No unsolicited material

Tom Atencio . . . . .CEO

*ATMOSPHERE ARTIST MANAGEMENT
6523 California Ave. SW, Ste. 348
Seattle, WA 98136
PHONE 206-935-5400
FAX 206-935-5208
EMAIL . . . . .info@atmospheremanagement.com
WEB SITE . . . . .www.atmospheremanagement.com
TYPES OF CLIENTS   Musical Artists
MUSICAL ARTIST TYPES   Latin - Pop - Rock - World
CLIENT LIST   Children of the Revolution -
                         Soundgarden - Alice In Chains

Deborah Semer . . . . .Manager
Susan Silver . . . . .Manager (ssmanage@msn.com)
Jennifer Kern . . . . .Assistant

AVENUE MANAGEMENT GROUP
276 Fifth Ave., Ste. 507
New York, NY 10001
PHONE 646-424-1600
FAX 646-424-1680
EMAIL . . . . .peter@avenuemusicgroup.com
SECOND EMAIL . . . . .garfbru@aol.com
WEB SITE . . . . .www.avenuemusicgroup.com
TYPES OF CLIENTS   Musical Artists - Music Producers -
                         Film/TV Composers
MUSICAL ARTIST TYPES   All Genres
CLIENT LIST   Claire Toomey - Ten Feet Deep - WAR -
                         Jonathan Elias - Sly Stone
SUBMISSION POLICY   No unsolicited material
COMMENTS   Hardcore - Punk - Metal

Bruce Garfield . . . . .Manager
Glenn Stone . . . . .Manager
Peter Durando . . . . .Manager

BARBARA BAKER MANAGEMENT
1346 Masselin Ave.
Los Angeles, CA 90019
PHONE 323-939-9964
FAX 323-931-3273
EMAIL . . . . .barbra.baker@comcast.net
TYPES OF CLIENTS   Musical Artists - Music Producers -
                         Film/TV Composers - Lyricists -
                         Songwriters
MUSICAL ARTIST TYPES   Adult Contemporary - Alternative -
                         Country - Pop - Punk - R&B - Rap/Hip-
                         Hop - Reggae - Rock - Roots - Urban -
                         World
CLIENT LIST   Nina Hagen - Mark Bryson - Lorraine
                         Lewis
SUBMISSION POLICY   Unsolicited submissions accepted

Barbara Baker . . . . .Owner/Manager

MANAGERS

DAVID BELENZON MANAGEMENT, INC.
PO Box 3819
La Mesa, CA 91944-3819
PHONE 619-462-6400
FAX 619-462-2244
EMAIL . . . . .info@belenzon.com
WEB SITE . . . . .www.belenzon.com
TYPES OF CLIENTS   Musical Artists - Variety Artists
CLIENT LIST   Franz Harary - Michael Moschen - Max Maven - Mark Wenzel - Jon "Bowzer" Bauman
COMMENTS   Also represents Production Shows

David Belenzon . . . . .President
Sherrill Kinsler . . . . .Director, Special Events

BIGGJAY MANAGEMENT
8306 Wilshire Blvd., Ste. 487
Beverly Hills, CA 90211
PHONE 310-358-2773
FAX 323-852-4926
EMAIL . . . . .jay@concreterecordings.com
WEB SITE . . . . .www.concreterecordingsinc.com
TYPES OF CLIENTS   Musical Artists - Music Producers - Lyricists - Songwriters - Studio Vocalists
MUSICAL ARTIST TYPES   Gospel - Jazz - Latin - R&B - Rap/Hip-Hop - World
CLIENT LIST   Young Spook - Knee-Hi - Rudy - St. James - Hypnotik - Ice Blag - The Renegades - Rachel Murray - Indojah
SUBMISSION POLICY   Call before sending a submission

Jay Atkins . . . . .CEO
Kayanta Culbert . . . . .Manager
Mitchell Graham .Creative Director
Marco Durham . . . . .Talent Scout
Conrad Williams . . . . .Talent Scout
Darnell Davis . . . . .Creative Assistant
Brent Hoover . . . . .Assistant to CEO
Ronald Milligan .Creative Assistant
J. Waggoner . . . . .Assistant to CEO

BLACK DOT MANAGEMENT
6820 La Tijera Blvd., Ste. 117
Los Angeles, CA 90045
PHONE 310-568-9091
FAX 310-568-0491
TYPES OF CLIENTS   Musical Artists - Music Producers
MUSICAL ARTIST TYPES   Jazz - R&B - Urban
CLIENT LIST   Lalah Hathaway
SUBMISSION POLICY   No unsolicited material

Raymond A. Shields II . . . . .Partner
Patricia Shields . . . . .Partner
John Turpin . . . . .Associate

BLACK SHEEP MANAGEMENT
6255 Sunset Blvd., Ste. 910
Los Angeles, CA 90028
PHONE 323-769-7211
FAX 323-860-0850
EMAIL . . . . .lindsey@blacksheepfellowship.com
TYPES OF CLIENTS   Musical Artists
CLIENT LIST   Sparta - TSOL - Coheed & Cambria - Brazil - mewithoutYou
SUBMISSION POLICY   Submissions accepted

Blaze James . . . . .Manager
Pete Stahl . . . . .Tour Production
Lindsey Nutter . . . . .Assistant

BLACKGROUND RECORDS
155 W. 19th St., 2nd Fl.
New York, NY 10011
PHONE 646-638-2585
FAX 646-638-2595
WEB SITE . . . . .www.blackground.com
SECOND WEB SITE . . . . .www.universalrecords.com
TYPES OF CLIENTS   Musical Artists - Music Producers - Songwriters
CLIENT LIST   Toni Braxton - Tank - Playa - Key Beats - Bud'da - Ft. Knoxx - Timbaland and Magoo - JoJo

Jomo Hankerson . . . . .President
Barry Hankerson . . . . .CEO

BLACKHEART RECORDS GROUP
636 Broadway, Ste. 1210
New York, NY 10012
PHONE 212-353-9600
FAX 212-353-8300
EMAIL . . . . .bhrecords@aol.com
WEB SITE . . . . .www.blackheart.com
TYPES OF CLIENTS   Musical Artists - Music Producers - Film/TV Composers - Songwriters
MUSICAL ARTIST TYPES   Punk - Rock
CLIENT LIST   Joan Jett & the Blackhearts - The Eyeliners - The Vacancies
COMMENTS   AFM

Kenny Laguna . . . . .President
Lauren Varga . . . . .Office Manager
Karol Kamin .Licensing & Masters
Carianne Laguna .Creative Director
Elliot Saltzman . . . . .Tour Manager
Julie Rader .Radio Promotion, Media

VICTORIA BLAKE MANAGEMENT
23622 Calabasas Rd., Ste. 230
Calabasas, CA 91302
PHONE 818-876-8489
FAX 818-876-8486
EMAIL . . . . .missmgmt@aol.com
TYPES OF CLIENTS   Musical Artists - Music Producers - Music Supervisors - Lyricists - Songwriters - Studio Musicians - Studio Vocalists - Studio Engineers/Technicians
MUSICAL ARTIST TYPES   Folk - Metal - New Age - Pop - Rock
CLIENT LIST   Martyn Le Noble - Tyler Hilton - Kat Parsons - Curtis Peoples - Geza X - Larry Bagby - Romina Arena - Katie Cassidy
SUBMISSION POLICY   No unsolicited material

Victoria Blake . . . . .Manager
Christine Kim . . . . .Manager
Ryan Flamm . . . . .Assistant

MANAGERS

BLANTON, HARRELL, COOKE & CORZINE
5300 Virginia Way, Ste. 100
Brentwood, TN 37027
PHONE 615-627-0444
FAX 615-627-0449
WEB SITE . . . . .www.bhccmgt.com
TYPES OF CLIENTS   Musical Artists
MUSICAL ARTIST TYPES   Christian - Pop
CLIENT LIST   Amy Grant - Michael W. Smith - Frank
                          Peretti - Point of Grace - Joy Williams -
                          Bebo Norman - Kara Williamson -
                          Aaron Shust - Stephanie Bloom
SUBMISSION POLICY   No unsolicited material

Mike Blanton . . . . .Partner
Jennifer Cooke . . . . .Partner
Chaz Corzine . . . . .Partner
Dan Harrell . . . . .Partner
Keith Thomas . . . . .VP, Finances
Mitch White . . . . .VP, Artist Development
Cheri Kaufman .Artist Manager
Traci Bishir . . . . .Executive Assistant
Cami Knott . . . . .Executive Assistant
Amanda McCaslin . . . . .Executive Assistant
Bethany Roe .Executive Assistant

BLEU JEAN MANAGEMENT
2657 33rd St., Ste. B
Santa Monica, CA 90405
PHONE 310-314-3613/310-314-3614
FAX 310-314-3615
EMAIL . . . . .info@bleujean.com
WEB SITE .www.bleujean.com
TYPES OF CLIENTS   Musical Artists - Film/TV Composers
CLIENT LIST   Douglas Romayne Stevens - Peter
                          Senchuk - Costa Kotselas - Michael
                          Sean Colin
SUBMISSION POLICY   By referral or invitation only

Karrie J. Vickery . . . . .Composer Manager, Co-Owner

*BLIND AMBITION MANAGEMENT, LTD.
6 Courthouse Way
Jonesboro, GA 30236
PHONE 770-478-8894
FAX 770-478-9606
WEB SITE . . . . .www.blindambitionmgt
TYPES OF CLIENTS   Musical Artists
CLIENT LIST   Blind Boys of Alabama - Charlie
                          Musselwhite

Charles Driebe . . . . .CEO
Hardy McBee . . . . .Manager
Sue Schrader . . . . .Publicity

*BLUE CAVE ENTERTAINMENT GROUP, LLC (BCEG)
2700 Kingsway Dr., 2nd Fl.
Burbank, CA 91504
PHONE 818-843-6778
FAX 818-841-1787
EMAIL . . . . .info@bceg.net
WEB SITE . . . . .www.bceg.net
TYPES OF CLIENTS   Musical Artists - Music Producers
CLIENT LIST   Jag Star - The Distants - Lindsay -
                          Madisonprep

Eric Fowler . . . . .Partner
Scott LeDuke . . . . .Partner

BLUETREE ARTISTS
PO Box 458
Bellingham, WA 98227
PHONE 360-303-4303/206-297-6221
EMAIL . . . . .booking@bluetreeartists.com
SECOND EMAIL . . . . .info@bluetreerecords.com
WEB SITE . . . . .www.bluetreeartists.com
SECOND WEB SITE . . . . .www.bluetreerecords.com
TYPES OF CLIENTS   Musical Artists - Songwriters
MUSICAL ARTIST TYPES   Alternative - Rock
CLIENT LIST   Late Tuesday - Mindhead - John Van
                          Deusen - Farewell Addison -

Nathan Marion . . . . .Owner/Agent
Seanna Benjamin . . . . .Booking Agent
Isaac Marion . . . . .Writer
Jonathan Warman .Promotions
Alisha S. . . . . .Assistant

BNB ASSOCIATES, LTD. & BSE ENTERTAINMENT, LTD.
8688 E. Corrine Dr.
Scottsdale, AZ 85260-5305
PHONE 480-391-9118
FAX 480-391-9737
TYPES OF CLIENTS   Musical Artists
MUSICAL ARTIST TYPES   Adult Contemporary - Pop - R&B

Sherwin Bash . . . . .No Title
Randy Bash . . . . .No Title
Ricki Sellner . . . . .No Title

B.O.C. MUSIC, INC.
216 E. 75th St.
New York, NY 10021
PHONE 212-879-5900
FAX 212-879-0668
TYPES OF CLIENTS   Musical Artists
CLIENT LIST   Blue Öyster Cult

Steve Schenck . . . . .Manager

BARRY BOOKIN MANAGEMENT
4545 San Feliciano Dr.
Woodland Hills, CA 91364
PHONE 818-999-0622
FAX 818-999-6817
EMAIL . . . . .bbookin@bigfoot.com
TYPES OF CLIENTS   Musical Artists - Film/TV Composers
SUBMISSION POLICY   Referral only

Barry Bookin . . . . .Owner

BORMAN ENTERTAINMENT
1250 Sixth St., Ste. 410
Santa Monica, CA 90401
PHONE 310-656-3150/615-320-3000
FAX 310-656-3160/615-320-3001
EMAIL . . . . .bormanent@aol.com
TYPES OF CLIENTS   Musical Artists
MUSICAL ARTIST TYPES   Adult Contemporary - Country
CLIENT LIST   Faith Hill - James Taylor - Keith Urban -
                          Lonestar - Jimmy Wayne - Natalie Cole -
                          Eliot Morris - Katrina Elam
COMMENTS   Nashville office: 1222 16th Ave. South,
                          Ste. 23, Nashville, TN 37212

Gary Borman .Owner/President
Joni Foraker . . . . .VP (Nashville)
Betsy Cook . . . . .Associate Manager (Nashville)
Lisa Giglio . . . . .Associate Manager (LA)
Donna Jean Kisshauer . . . . .Associate Manager (Nashville)
Barbara Rose . . . . .Associate Manager (LA)
Sandra Westerman . . . . .Associate Manager (Nashville)
Patty McGuire . . . . .No Title (LA)
Daniel Miller . . . . .No Title (Nashville)
Randy Miller . . . . .No Title (Nashville)

MANAGERS

MANAGERS

BOULDER CREEK ENTERTAINMENT
PO Box 910002
San Diego, CA 92191-0002
PHONE 858-793-4141
FAX 858-793-4145
EMAIL . . . . .elott@pacbell.net
TYPES OF CLIENTS   Musical Artists
MUSICAL ARTIST TYPES   Pop
CLIENT LIST   The Beach Boys

Elliott Lott . . . . .President

BRAND X MANAGEMENT
2828 Waverly Dr.
Los Angeles, CA 90039
PHONE 323-660-8230
FAX 323-660-8233
EMAIL . . . . .brandxmgmt@aol.com
TYPES OF CLIENTS   Musical Artists - Music Producers -
                         Film/TV Composers - Lyricists -
                         Songwriters
CLIENT LIST   Kane - Jeehun Hwang - Cory Tenbrink

Charley Chartoff . . . . .Partner
Eric M. Griffin . . . . .Partner
Ian Faith . . . . .Assistant

BRICK WALL MANAGEMENT
648 Amsterdam Ave., Ste. 4A
New York, NY 10025
PHONE 212-501-0748
FAX 212-724-0849
EMAIL . . . . .bwmgmt@brickwallmgmt.com
TYPES OF CLIENTS   Musical Artists - Music Producers -
                         Film/TV Composers - Songwriters -
                         Studio Engineers/Technicians
MUSICAL ARTIST TYPES   All Genres
CLIENT LIST   The Clarks - Citizen Cope - Marc
                         Broussard
SUBMISSION POLICY   Contact before submitting

Rishon Blumberg . . . . .Manager, Principal
Michael Solomon . . . . .Manager, Principal
Hillary Zuckerberg . . . . .Manager
Jennifer O'Reilly . . . . .Office Manager

BOB BROWN MANAGEMENT
PO Box 779
Mill Valley, CA 94942
PHONE 415-381-0181
TYPES OF CLIENTS   Musical Artists
CLIENT LIST   Huey Lewis and the News
SUBMISSION POLICY   No unsolicited material

Bob Brown . . . . .Manager

RON BROWN MANAGEMENT
PO Box 15375
Pittsburgh, PA 15237
PHONE 412-486-8158
FAX 412-486-4894
EMAIL . . . . .ronbrown2@att.net
TYPES OF CLIENTS   Musical Artists - Music Producers -
                         Lyricists - Songwriters - Studio Musicians
                         - Studio Vocalists
MUSICAL ARTIST TYPES   All Genres
CLIENT LIST   Joe Patrick - Kevin Morgan - Allison
                         Gillis - Larry Lee Jones - Davisson
                         Brothers Band - Chris Chambers -
                         Poverty Neck Hillbillies
SUBMISSION POLICY   Send non-returnable CDs

Ron Brown . . . . .Owner/Manager
Larry Garber . . . . .Manager
Nick Romac . . . . .Manager
Kathy Tate . . . . .Manager

AL BUNETTA MANAGEMENT, INC.
33 Music Square West, Ste. 102B
Nashville, TN 37203
PHONE 615-742-1250
FAX 615-742-1360
EMAIL . . . . .ohboy@ohboy.com
WEB SITE . . . . .www.ohboy.com
TYPES OF CLIENTS   Musical Artists
CLIENT LIST   John Prine - Todd Snider - Kris
                         Kristofferson - Janis Ian
COMMENTS   Catalog for Steve Goodman

Al Bunetta . . . . .President/Manager
Ric Taylor . . . . .VP, Finance
Mary Leanderts . . . . .Marketing Director

BURRIS MANAGEMENT GROUP
11990 Beach Blvd., Ste. 34
Jacksonville, FL 32246
PHONE 904-998-8469
FAX 904-998-7758
EMAIL . . . . .burrisentertain@gmail.com
WEB SITE . . . . .www.burrisentertainment-events.com
TYPES OF CLIENTS   Musical Artists
MUSICAL ARTIST TYPES   All Genres
COMMENTS   Events planner

Michael J. Burris . . . . .President
Ruthanna Smith . . . . .VP
Stella Lewis . . . . .Office Manager

PAUL CANTOR ENTERPRISES, LTD.
33042 Ocean Ridge
Dana Point, CA 92629-1078
PHONE 949-240-4400
FAX 949-240-2208
EMAIL . . . . .paulcantor@cox.net
TYPES OF CLIENTS   Musical Artists - Studio Vocalists
MUSICAL ARTIST TYPES   Jazz - Pop
CLIENT LIST   Diane Schuur
SUBMISSION POLICY   By mail only

Paul Cantor . . . . .President/Manager

RUSSELL CARTER ARTIST MANAGEMENT
315 W. Ponce de Leon Ave., Ste. 755
Decatur, GA 30030
PHONE 404-377-9900
FAX 404-377-5131
EMAIL .russell@rcam.com
SECOND EMAIL . . . . .cathy@rcam.com
TYPES OF CLIENTS   Musical Artists
CLIENT LIST   Indigo Girls - Shawn Mullins - The
                          Jayhawks - Matthew Sweet - Tift Merritt -
                          The Thorns - Courtney Jaye - Fastball -
                          Roman Candle - Sarah Lee Guthrie -
                          The Brilliant Inventions

Russell Carter . . . . .Manager
Cathy Lyons . . . . .Office Manager
Beth Hurley . . . . .Assistant
Taryn Kaufman . . . . .Assistant

CEC MANAGEMENT
1123 Broadway, Ste. 317
New York, NY 10010
PHONE 212-206-6765
FAX 212-807-9288
TYPES OF CLIENTS   Musical Artists - Music Producers
MUSICAL ARTIST TYPES   Alternative - Pop - Rock - World
CLIENT LIST   Ben Folds - Darren Jesse - Fleming &
                          John - John Alagia (Producer) - The
                          Screaming Orphans - The Rocket
                          Summer - David Berkeley - The Eighties
                          Matchbox B-Line Disaster - Natasha
                          Atlas

Alan Wolmark . . . . .President/Manager (NY)
Peter Felstead . . . . .Manager (London)
Melissa Sabo . . . . .Manager (NY)
Debbie Tirone .Manager (NY)
Matt Willis .Manager (London)

CENTURY ARTISTS MANAGEMENT AGENCY LLC
140 Riverside Blvd. @ Trump Place, Ste. 620
New York, NY 10069
PHONE 212-724-4160
FAX 212-724-2375
EMAIL . . . . .phorton@centuryartists.com
WEB SITE . . . . .www.centuryartists.com
TYPES OF CLIENTS   Musical Artists - Music Producers -
                          Songwriters
MUSICAL ARTIST TYPES   All Genres
CLIENT LIST   Chuck Berry - The Miracles - Yolanda
                          Adams - Bobby Womack - Duke
                          Ellington Orchestra - Marco Joachim -
                          Tito Puente Jr. and His Orchestra - My
                          Sinatra feat. Cary Hoffman

Paul E. Horton . . . . .President

CHANCELLOR ENTERTAINMENT
10600 Holman Ave., Ste. 1
Los Angeles, CA 90024
PHONE 310-474-4521
FAX 310-470-9273
WEB SITE . . . . .www.chancellorentertainment.com
MUSICAL ARTIST TYPES   Adult Contemporary - Christian -
                          Country - Dance/DJ - Gospel - Latin -
                          Pop - Punk - R&B - Rap/Hip-Hop - Rock
SUBMISSION POLICY   Send demo and picture

Robert P. Marcucci . . . . .President
Benjamin Scantlin . . . . .First VP
Larissa Douglas . . . . .VP, Talent Development

CLARK MANAGEMENT COMPANY
3156 Foothill Blvd.
Glendale, CA 91214
PHONE 818-240-5808
FAX 818-790-8997
EMAIL . . . . .iampuresuccess@hotmail.com
TYPES OF CLIENTS   Musical Artists - Songwriters
MUSICAL ARTIST TYPES   Country
CLIENT LIST   Eddie Cunningham - Rick Ellis
SUBMISSION POLICY   Query by mail or email

Vicki Clark . . . . .Manager
Sara Muriello . . . . .Administrative Assistant

DAN CLEARY MANAGEMENT ASSOCIATES
6399 Wilshire Blvd., Ste. 1019
Los Angeles, CA 90048
PHONE 323-951-1016
EMAIL . . . . .danclearymgmt@earthlink.net
TYPES OF CLIENTS   Musical Artists
MUSICAL ARTIST TYPES   All Genres

Dan Cleary . . . . .Manager
Christi DeClercq . . . . .Associate

CMO MANAGEMENT INTERNATIONAL LTD.
Studio 2.6
Shepherds East, Richmond Way
London W14 0DQ UK
PHONE 44-20-7316-6969
FAX 44-20-7316-6970
EMAIL . . . . .info@cmomanagement.co.uk
WEB SITE . . . . .www.cmomanagement.co.uk
TYPES OF CLIENTS   Musical Artists
CLIENT LIST   Blur - Turin Brakes - Matty Benbrook -
                          Graham Coxon - Siobhan Donaghy -
                          Justine Frischmann - Gorillaz - M.I.A. -
                          Morcheeba - Skye - Pauline Taylor -
                          Grand Transmitter - Tom Vek

Chris Morrison . . . . .Managing Director

COLE CLASSIC MANAGEMENT
PO Box 231
Canoga Park, CA 91305
PHONE 818-222-3790
FAX 818-876-1808
EMAIL . . . . .ecole1247@msn.com
TYPES OF CLIENTS   Musical Artists - Music Producers -
                          Songwriters

Earl Cole . . . . .Manager
Philip Myles . . . . .Manager

MANAGERS

COLUMBIA ARTISTS MANAGEMENT LLC

1790 Broadway
New York, NY 10019-1412
PHONE 212-841-9500
FAX 212-841-9744
EMAIL . . . . .info@cami.com
WEB SITE . . . . .www.cami.com

TYPES OF CLIENTS	Musical Artists - Film/TV Composers - Lyricists - Variety Artists
MUSICAL ARTIST TYPES	Adult Contemporary - Alternative - Blues - Classical - Country - Folk - Jazz - Latin - Pop - R&B - World
COMMENTS	Dance Companies; Offices in New York and Berlin

Ronald A. Wilford . . . . .CEO (212-841-9502)
Tim Fox . . . . .President/COO (212-841-9571)
Jean-Jacques Cesbron . . . . .CAMI Music (212-841-9564)
Margaret Selby . . . . .President, CAMI Spectrum (212-841-9554)
Andrew S. Grossman . . . . .Sr. VP (212-841-9558)
Mark Z. Alpert . . . . .Booking (212-841-9568)
Andrea Anson . . . . .Manager (212-844-9549)
Anna Bacon-Silveira . . . . .Booking (212-841-9533)
Christine Barkley . . . . .Booking (212-841-9566)
Michael Benchetrit . . . . .Manager (212-844-9559)
Ken Benson .Manager (212-841-9545)
Elizabeth Crittenden . . . . .Manager (212-841-9682)
William G. Guerri . . . . .Manager (212-841-9680)
Judie Janowski . . . . .Manager (212-841-9507)
Michaela Kurz . . . . .Manager (212-841-9539)
Ron Merlino .Manager (212-841-9560)
David Neway . . . . .Booking (212-841-9503)
Denise A. Pineau . . . . .Manager (212-841-9527)
Pamela Ramsey McKean . . . . .Booking (415-252-5705)
Robert Scott .Manager (212-841-9540)
R. Douglas Sheldon . . . . .Manager (212-841-9512)
Tobias Tumarkin . . . . .Manager (212-841-9563)
W. Seton Ijams . . . . .Associate Manager (212-841-9752)
Josh Sherman . . . . .Music Theatre Associates (212-841-9741)
Jann Simpson . . . . .Music Theatre Associates (212-841-9690)

CONSERVATIVE MANAGEMENT

635 W. Lakeside Ave., Ste. 204
Cleveland, OH 44113
PHONE 216-523-1361
FAX 216-523-1371
EMAIL . . . . .jmalm@conservative-mgmt.com

TYPES OF CLIENTS	Musical Artists - Film/TV Composers - Songwriters
MUSICAL ARTIST TYPES	Alternative - Country - Rap/Hip-Hop - Rock
CLIENT LIST	Alabama 3 - Spiritualized - Vincenzo
SUBMISSION POLICY	No unsolicited submissions

John A. Malm Jr. . . . . .President/Co-Owner
Bonnie Angotti . . . . .Assistant to President

CORE ENTERTAINMENT ORGANIZATION

A Siddons Lapides Company
14724 Ventura Blvd., PH
Sherman Oaks, CA 91403
PHONE 818-986-8040
FAX 818-986-8041
EMAIL . . . . .core@coreentertainment.biz

TYPES OF CLIENTS	Musical Artists - Film/TV Composers - Songwriters - Comedians
MUSICAL ARTIST TYPES	Adult Contemporary - Alternative - Christian - Classical - Folk - Jazz - New Age - Pop - Rap/Hip-Hop - Rock - World
CLIENT LIST	Elayne Boosler - Jerry Cantrell - Kurt Bestor - USCR - D-Sisive - Jason Dudek - Tom Green - Dave Holmes - Kennedy - Steve Langford - Jennifer Lothrop - Mike McDonald
SUBMISSION POLICY	Demos/press kits by mail; Include sales and performance numbers

Bill Siddons . . . . .President
Howard Lapides . . . . .Partner
Andrew Leow . . . . .VP, Comedic Development
Julia Mays . . . . .VP/Manager
Jackie Stern . . . . .VP/Manager
Kesila Childers . . . . .Executive Assistant

COUNTDOWN ENTERTAINMENT

110 W. 26th St.
New York, NY 10001-6805
PHONE 212-645-3068
FAX 212-989-6459
EMAIL . . . . .countdownent@netzero.net
WEB SITE . . . . .www.countdownentertainment.com

TYPES OF CLIENTS	Musical Artists - Music Producers - Film/TV Composers - Lyricists - Songwriters - Studio Vocalists
MUSICAL ARTIST TYPES	All Genres
CLIENT LIST	Ken Tamplin - Chris Conway - Kickin' Daisies
SUBMISSION POLICY	Email first
COMMENTS	Intellectual properties; Affiliated with International Managers Forum, England

James Citkovic . . . . .President
Lovie Jones . . . . .Sr. Director, A&R
Brenda Starr . . . . .Director, Music Publishing
Ezra Cook . . . . .A&R
John Overland . . . . .A&R

COURAGE ARTISTS & TOURING

17 Polsom St.
Toronto, ON M5A 1A4 Canada
PHONE 416-598-3330
FAX 416-598-5428
EMAIL . . . . .info@courageartists.com

TYPES OF CLIENTS	Musical Artists
MUSICAL ARTIST TYPES	Hardcore - Metal - Punk - Rock - Roots
CLIENT LIST	Voivod - Nashville Pussy - Nebula - Ashley MacIsaac
SUBMISSION POLICY	No unsolicited material

James MacLean . . . . .No Title
David Bluestein . . . . .No Title

MANAGERS

COURTRIGHT MANAGEMENT, INC.
201 E. 87th St., #307
New York, NY 10128

PHONE	212-410-9055
FAX	212-831-0823
EMAIL	courtrightmgmt@aol.com
WEB SITE	www.courtrightmgmt.com
TYPES OF CLIENTS	Musical Artists - Music Producers - Film/TV Composers - Songwriters
MUSICAL ARTIST TYPES	Adult Contemporary - Alternative - Blues - Country - Folk - Jazz - New Age - Rock - Roots - World
SUBMISSION POLICY	Call in advance
COMMENTS	Female artists only

Hernando Courtright . . . . .Owner

COURTYARD MANAGEMENT
21 The Nursery
Sutton Courtenay
Abingdon 0X14 4UA UK

PHONE	44-1235-845-800
FAX	44-870-051-0183
WEB SITE	www.courtyardmanagement.com
TYPES OF CLIENTS	Musical Artists
MUSICAL ARTIST TYPES	Alternative - Dance/DJ - Pop - Rock
CLIENT LIST	awayTEAM - Radiohead - Supergrass

Bryce Edge . . . . .Director/Partner
Chris Hufford . . . . .Director/Partner
Brian Message . . . . .Director/Partner
Craig Newman . . . . .Director/Partner
Julie Calland . . . . .Manager
Kate Cotter . . . . .Personal Assistant
Pippa Mole . . . . .Personal Assistant

CREATIVE CONTENT MANAGEMENT
110 W. 26th St., 3rd Fl. South
New York, NY 10001-6805

PHONE	212-645-3068
FAX	212-989-6459
EMAIL	creativecontentm@aol.com
TYPES OF CLIENTS	Musical Artists - Music Producers - Film/TV Composers - Songwriters - Studio Vocalists
MUSICAL ARTIST TYPES	All Genres
SUBMISSION POLICY	Email queries preferred
COMMENTS	Affiliated with International Managers Forum, London

David Brodie . . . . .Partner
Al Brodie . . . . .Partner
James Citkovic . . . . .Partner

*CROSSWORLDS ENTERTAINMENT INTERNATIONAL, INC.
PO Box 220447
Newhall, CA 91322-0447

PHONE	661-904-3375/661-904-3376
EMAIL	email@crossworldsentertainment.com
WEB SITE	www.crossworldsentertainment.com
TYPES OF CLIENTS	Musical Artists - Music Producers - Film/TV Composers - Lyricists
CLIENT LIST	Desvelo - Max Calo' - Natasha Ponticelli - Susan Toney - Limore Twena

Jay Jaworski . . . . .President/Artist Manager
Lisa Jaworski . . . . .VP/Artist Manager
Karen Almond .Publicist (KBC Media)
Michael Mancini . . . . .Producer

CUE11 ENTERTAINMENT
1622 W. Pinehill Rd.
Spokane, WA 99218

PHONE	509-464-0062
FAX	509-468-0622
EMAIL	shawnwest@cue11.com
WEB SITE	www.cue11.com
TYPES OF CLIENTS	Musical Artists - Music Supervisors - Film/TV Composers - Lyricists - Songwriters
MUSICAL ARTIST TYPES	All Genres
CLIENT LIST	Nathan Wang - Charles David Denler - Peter Rivera - Jamie Rowe - Janie Cribbs - Joe Reggiatore - Flyreal - Finnlux Tuna - Digital Beat - Blake Althen - Paula Rellenoit - Shkirman Miush - John Hughes - Melissa Ferrick - London Calling

David Cebert . . . . .President
Shawn West . . . . .Executive VP
Joe Brasch . . . . .Producer/Composer
John Hartis . . . . .Managing Director (Cuell Media Group)
Brent Oty . . . . .Accounting
Kevin Dodson . . . . .Marketing Assistant/New Project Development

CURTIS MANAGEMENT
969 Thomas St.
Seattle, WA 98109

PHONE	206-447-1819/206-329-4200
FAX	206-447-1848
EMAIL	curtismgmt@aol.com
TYPES OF CLIENTS	Musical Artists
MUSICAL ARTIST TYPES	Rock
CLIENT LIST	Pearl Jam - Brad

Kelly Curtis . . . . .Manager/Owner
Liz Burns . . . . .Assistant

CZAR ENTERTAINMENT
11 W. 25th St., Ste. 300
New York, NY 10010-2001

PHONE	212-414-2483
FAX	212-414-9666
WEB SITE	www.czar-ent.com
TYPES OF CLIENTS	Musical Artists - Music Producers - Songwriters
MUSICAL ARTIST TYPES	Pop - R&B - Rap/Hip-Hop - Reggae - Urban
CLIENT LIST	The Game (Interscope) - Guerilla Black (Virgin) - Mario Winans (Bad Boy) - Black Rob (Bad Boy) - Sharissa (Czar) - Spot (Czar) - Beloved (Czar) - Big Gipp (Dirrty Entertainment) - Smitty (J Records)
COMMENTS	FKA Henchmen Entertainment

Jimmy Henchmen . . . . .CEO/Co-Founder
Bryce Wilson . . . . .President/Co-Founder
Griff . . . . .General Manager
Tony Martin . . . . .Assistant Manager

MANAGERS

MANAGERS

DAS COMMUNICATIONS
83 Riverside Dr.
New York, NY 10024
PHONE 212-877-0400
FAX 212-595-0176
EMAIL .firstname@dasgroup.com

TYPES OF CLIENTS	Musical Artists - Music Producers - Film/TV Composers - Lyricists - Songwriters
MUSICAL ARTIST TYPES	Alternative - Dance/DJ - Folk - Pop - R&B - Rap/Hip-Hop - Reggae - Rock - Urban
CLIENT LIST	Andy Marvel - Black Eyed Peas - Diana King - Wyclef Jean - Joan Osborne - Spin Doctors - The Bacon Brothers - Papa Dee - Bone Thugs-N-Harmony - Dan Dyer - High Speed Scene - Split Shift - John Legend - Meleni Smith - Kaet Brown - The Twenty-Twos - Jim Steinman - Nitty
SUBMISSION POLICY	Material accepted by request only

David Sonenberg . . . . .President
William Derella . . . . .Executive VP
Andrea Timpone . . . . .VP, Business Affairs
Seth Friedman . . . . .Manager
Jason Richardson . . . . .Manager
Anthony Demby . . . . .Manager
Scott Meszaros . . . . .Manager
Rachel Cox . . . . .Coordinator

DDB PRODUCTIONS
13428 Maxella Ave., #632
Marina del Rey, CA 90292
PHONE 310-494-4008
FAX 310-494-4014
EMAIL . . . . .ddbprods@ddbprods.com
WEB SITE . . . . .www.ddbprods.com
SECOND WEB SITE . . . . .www.deedeebridgewater.com

TYPES OF CLIENTS	Musical Artists - Music Producers - Lyricists - Songwriters
SUBMISSION POLICY	No unsolicited material

Dee Dee Bridgewater .Producer
Tulani Bridgewater-Kowalski . . . . .VP/Manager
Jean-Marie Durand . . . . .Co-Producer
Tsia Moses-Anderson . . . . .Associate Manager

DEEP SOUTH ENTERTAINMENT
PO Box 17737
Raleigh, NC 27619
PHONE 919-844-1515
FAX 919-847-5922
EMAIL . . . . .info@deepsouthentertainment.com
SECOND EMAIL . . . . .firstname@deepsouthentertainment.com
WEB SITE . . . . .www.deepsouthentertainment.com

TYPES OF CLIENTS	Musical Artists
CLIENT LIST	Little Feat - Michael Sweet - Stryper - The Warren Brothers - Parmalee - Allison Moorer - Vienna Teng

Andy Martin . . . . .Co-Owner/Manager
Dave Rose .Co-Owner/Manager
Amy Cox . . . . .Associate Manager
Chip Taylor . . . . .Product & Office Manager
Erik Aagaard . . . . .Assistant Product Manager
Greg Gallo . . . . .Nashville Office Manager
Steve Williams . . . . .A&R
Mark Paris . . . . .Web/Internet

DELTA GROOVE PRODUCTIONS, INC.
6442 Coldwater Canyon Ave.
North Hollywood, CA 91606
PHONE 818-755-4460
EMAIL . . . . .deltagroovemusic@earthlink.net
WEB SITE . . . . .www.deltagrooveproductions.com

TYPES OF CLIENTS	Musical Artists - Music Producers - Music Supervisors - Film/TV Composers - Lyricists - Songwriters - Studio Musicians - Studio Vocalists - Studio Engineers/Technicians
MUSICAL ARTIST TYPES	Blues - Roots

Rand Chortkoff .CEO/Producer
Joshua Temkin . . . .Co-Producer/Co-Executive in Charge of Production/
                                  Sr. Art Director & Designer
Jeff Fleenor . . . . .Director, Retail
Frank Roszak . . . . .Director, Radio Promotions/
                                  Co-Executive in Charge of Production
Elizabeth Montes de Oca . . . . .Production Assistant
Malcolm Wiseman . . . . .Business & Legal Representation
Scott Dirks . . . . .Creative Services, Production, Staff Writer
Zelda Bell .Executive Secretary

DEPTH OF FIELD MANAGEMENT
1501 Broadway, Ste. 1304
New York, NY 10036
PHONE 212-302-9200
FAX 212-382-1639

TYPES OF CLIENTS	Musical Artists
MUSICAL ARTIST TYPES	Jazz - Rock
CLIENT LIST	Michael Brecker - Dianne Reeves - The Bad Plus - Happy Apple

Darryl Pitt . . . . .President
Marie-Theres Franke . . . . .Associate
Chris Hinderaker . . . . .Associate

BILL DETKO MANAGEMENT
378 Palomares Ave.
Ventura, CA 93003
PHONE 805-644-0447
FAX 805-644-0469
EMAIL . . . . .brmc@pacbell.net

TYPES OF CLIENTS	Musical Artists - Film/TV Composers - Songwriters - Studio Musicians
MUSICAL ARTIST TYPES	Alternative - Blues - Jazz - Rock
CLIENT LIST	Darwin's Radio - Terry Michael Huud - Cedric Samson
SUBMISSION POLICY	3-4 song CD with bio and photo

Bill Detko . . . . .No Title

DIGGIT ENTERTAINMENT
6 W. 18th St., 8th Fl.
New York, NY 10011
PHONE 212-399-6070
FAX 212-399-6112
EMAIL . . . . .info@diggit.com
WEB SITE . . . . .www.diggit.com

TYPES OF CLIENTS	Musical Artists
MUSICAL ARTIST TYPES	R&B
CLIENT LIST	TLC - Chilli - T-Boz

Bill Diggins . . . . .President/CEO
Aaron E. Kohn . . . . .VP, Business Development

DIRECT MANAGEMENT GROUP
947 N. La Cienega Blvd., Ste. G
Los Angeles, CA 90069
PHONE 310-854-3535
FAX 310-854-0810
WEB SITE . . . . .www.directmgmt.com
TYPES OF CLIENTS   Musical Artists
CLIENT LIST   Lizz Wright - Katy Perry - k.d. lang -
                       Tracy Chapman - Boney James - The
                       Gabe Dixon Band - Go-Go's - Randi
                       Laubek

Steve Jensen . . . . .No Title
Martin Kirkup . . . . .No Title
Bradford Cobb . . . . .No Title
Dana Collins . . . . .No Title
Mandi Davis . . . . .No Title
Ngoc Hoang . . . . .No Title

DOMO MUSIC GROUP
11340 W. Olympic Blvd., Ste. 270
Los Angeles, CA 90064
PHONE 310-966-4414
FAX 310-966-4420
EMAIL . . . . .domo@domo.com
WEB SITE . . . . .www.domo.com
TYPES OF CLIENTS   Musical Artists - Music Producers -
                       Film/TV Composers - Songwriters -
                       Studio Musicians
MUSICAL ARTIST TYPES   Alternative - Classical - Dance/DJ - Jazz
                       - New Age - Pop - Rock - World
CLIENT LIST   Twelve Girls Band - Test Shot Starfish -
                       Appogee - Little Plastic Pilots -
                       Prototokyo - Indicia - Kitaro - Benedetti
                       & Svoboda - Dave Eggar - Chuck Barris
                       - Uma - Randy Armstrong - Agatsuma -
                       The Yoshida Brothers - Peas - Fumio -
                       Hoppy Kamiyama
SUBMISSION POLICY   Send to Dino Malito's attention

Eiichi Naito . . . . .President (eiichi@domo.com)
Dino Malito . . . . .VP, A&R Operations (dino@domo.com)
Howard Sapper . . . . .VP, Business & Legal

THE DOORS MUSIC COMPANY
9000 Sunset Blvd., Ste. 1410
West Hollywood, CA 90069
PHONE 310-274-8471
FAX 310-274-9856
EMAIL .jeff.jampol@thedoors.com
TYPES OF CLIENTS   Musical Artists

Jeff Jampol . . . . .Manager

BONNY DORE MANAGEMENT
10940 Wilshire Blvd., Ste. 1600
Los Angeles, CA 90024
PHONE 310-443-4189
FAX 310-443-4190
EMAIL . . . . .bonnyinc@aol.com
TYPES OF CLIENTS   Musical Artists - Music Producers -
                       Film/TV Composers - Lyricists -
                       Songwriters
MUSICAL ARTIST TYPES   All Genres
CLIENT LIST   Allison Wilke - Rob MacMullen

Bonny Dore . . . . .Manager

DOYLE-KOS ENTERTAINMENT
494 Eighth Ave., 24th Fl.
New York, NY 10001
PHONE 646-674-1500
FAX 646-674-1513
EMAIL . . . . .info@doylekos.com
MUSICAL ARTIST TYPES   Blues - Pop - Rock
CLIENT LIST   Daryl Hall & John Oates - Rusted Root -
                       Jazz Mandolin Project - Shep & Kenny -
                       Rick Springfield - Thalia
SUBMISSION POLICY   No unsolicited submissions

Brian Doyle . . . . .No Title
Rob Kos . . . . .No Title
Jacqueline Kotler . . . . .No Title
Alana Sarratore . . . . .No Title

DREAMAKERS INC.
PO Box 5359
Crestline, CA 92325
PHONE 818-292-3090
FAX 909-338-8560
TYPES OF CLIENTS   Musical Artists - Music Producers

Richard Burkhart . . . . .Personal Manager

DREAMCATCHER ARTIST MANAGEMENT
2910 Poston Ave.
Nashville, TN 37203
PHONE 615-329-2303
FAX 615-329-2350
WEB SITE . . . . .www.dreamcatcherenter.com
TYPES OF CLIENTS   Musical Artists
MUSICAL ARTIST TYPES   Country
CLIENT LIST   Kenny Rogers - Rebecca Lynn Howard -
                       Jo Dee Messina - Jared Ashley

Jim Mazza . . . . .President/CEO (jmazza@dreamcatcherenter.com)
Bob Burwell . . . . .GM/Sr. VP (bburwell@dreamcatcherenter.com)
Kelly Junkerman . . . . . .Sr. VP, Film & Television (kjunkerman@aol.com)
Claire Cook . . . . .VP, Media & Artist Relations
                       (ccook@dreamcatcherenter.com)
Howard Fields . .VP, Artist Management (hfields@dreamcatcherenter.com)
Don Kamerer . . . . .VP, Sales (dkamerer@dreamcatcherenter.com)
Josh Fulmer . . . . .Manager, Tour Coordination
                       (jfulmer@dreamcatcherenter.com)
Debbie Loring . . . . .Manager (dloring@dreamcatcherenter.com)
Melissa Fuller . . . . .Executive Assistant (mfuller@dreamcatcherenter.com)

EAST END MANAGEMENT
12441 Ventura Court
Studio City, CA 91604
PHONE 818-985-5060
FAX 818-985-5069
TYPES OF CLIENTS   Musical Artists
MUSICAL ARTIST TYPES   Rock
CLIENT LIST   Billy Idol - Lindsey Buckingham - Tom
                       Petty and the Heartbreakers - Bill Laswell
SUBMISSION POLICY   No unsolicited material

Tony Dimitriades . . . . .Owner/Manager
Robert Richards . . . . .Manager
Tiffany Goble . . . . .Assistant
Brynne Millrany . . . . .Assistant

EC PRODUCTIONS
36 Old Church St.
London SW3 5BY UK
PHONE 44-20-7351-5529
FAX 44-20-7376-5625
TYPES OF CLIENTS   Musical Artists
CLIENT LIST   Eric Clapton

Graham Court . . . . .General Manager
Vivien Gibson . . . . .Personal Assistant

MANAGERS

MANAGERS

*EDGE MANAGEMENT INC.
10850 Wilshire Blvd., Ste. 380
Los Angeles, CA 90024
PHONE 310-470-4034
FAX 310-234-2770
EMAIL . . . . .hooker@edgemgtinc.com
WEB SITE .www.edgemgtinc.com
TYPES OF CLIENTS   Musical Artists
MUSICAL ARTIST TYPES   Rock
CLIENT LIST   Edgar Winter - Tommy Tutone - The
                        Knack - Orleans - Al Jardine

Jake Hooker . . . . .President
Jonathan Fink . . . . .CEO
Clive Marc Fox . . . . .Chairman
Joel Margulies .Sr. VP, Marketing

EGM
1040 Mariposa St., Ste. 200
San Francisco, CA 94107
PHONE 415-522-5292
FAX 415-522-5293
EMAIL . . . . .james@egminc.com
SECOND EMAIL . . . . .firstname@egminc.com
TYPES OF CLIENTS   Musical Artists
MUSICAL ARTIST TYPES   All Genres
CLIENT LIST   Dakona - Denny Porter - The K.G.B. -
                        Third Eye Blind - Honestly - Retrograde

David Glynn . . . . .Manager
Eric Godtland . . . . .Manager
Wayne Ledbetter . . . . .Manager
James Huxtable . . . . .Administrator

THE EICHNER ENTERTAINMENT COMPANY
381 Broadway
Westwood, NJ 07675-2239
PHONE 201-664-6666
FAX 201-664-6799
EMAIL . . . . .eichent@aol.com
TYPES OF CLIENTS   Musical Artists - Music Producers -
                        Studio Engineers/Technicians

Mickey Eichner . . . . .President
Mark Eichner . . . . .Sr. VP
Randy Eichner . . . . .Manager

EJH ENTERTAINMENT INC.
7331 W. Charleston Blvd., Ste. 150
Las Vegas, NV 89117
PHONE 702-228-1138
FAX 702-228-2488
EMAIL . . . . .info@ejhinc.com
WEB SITE . . . . .www.ejhinc.com
TYPES OF CLIENTS   Musical Artists - Music Producers -
                        Songwriters - Variety Artists - Comedians

Edward Haddad . . . . .President

ELEVATION GROUP INC.
360 17th St., Ste. 200
Oakland, CA 94612
PHONE 510-834-2600
FAX 510-834-1250
EMAIL . . . . .info@elevationgroup.net
WEB SITE . . . . .www.elevationgroup.net
TYPES OF CLIENTS   Musical Artists
CLIENT LIST   Aaron Neville - Funky Meters - The
                        Neville Brothers - Pat McGee Band -
                        Ivan Neville - Michael Tolcher
SUBMISSION POLICY   No unsolicited submissions

Kent Sorrell . . . . .Manager
Jay Wilson . . . . .Manager
Amy Turner . . . . .Manager

EMMIS MANAGEMENT
18136 Califa St.
Tarzana, CA 90356
PHONE 818-345-0910
FAX 818-345-0996
EMAIL . . . . .amazngh@earthlink.net
TYPES OF CLIENTS   Musical Artists
MUSICAL ARTIST TYPES   Pop
CLIENT LIST   Sheena Easton - Loudon Wainwright III

Harriet Wasserman . . . . .Owner/Manager

ENDURE MANAGEMENT
12335 Santa Monica Blvd., Ste. 106
Los Angeles, CA 90025
PHONE 310-281-6859
TYPES OF CLIENTS   Musical Artists - Music Producers
MUSICAL ARTIST TYPES   Alternative - Dance/DJ - Latin - Pop -
                        R&B - Rock
CLIENT LIST   Baby Paul - BPZy - Capone - Tek N
                        Steele - Raydon - Omega Redd - Angie
                        Crowell - Anthony Adams
SUBMISSION POLICY   No unsolicited material accepted
COMMENTS   Commericals, scoring, soundtracks

Taminika Outlaw .President/CEO

ENLIGHT ENTERTAINMENT
2135 Defoor Hills Rd., Ste. 1
Atlanta, GA 30318
PHONE 404-355-2570
FAX 404-355-2670
EMAIL . . . . .emailenlight@enlight-entertainment.com
WEB SITE . . . . .www.enlight-entertainment.com
TYPES OF CLIENTS   Musical Artists
CLIENT LIST   Babygirl - Granjoor Ent. - Nate Butler -
                        Carlus Houston - Chris Flournoy -
                        Deleon - Dent - Script Squad -
                        Shekspere - T. Kura

Tashia Stafford . . . . .CEO (tashial@aol.com)
Stone Stafford . . . . .VP, A&R

ENTERTAINMENT SERVICES UNLIMITED
Main St. Plaza 1000, Ste. 303
Voorhees, NJ 08043
PHONE 856-751-2223
FAX 856-751-1486
EMAIL . . . . .entserv@aol.com
MUSICAL ARTIST TYPES   Rock
CLIENT LIST   Amanda Latona - Lamb of God -
                        Breaking Benjamin - Stone Sour -
                        Everytime I Die - Unearth - Atreyu - A
                        Life Once Lost - From First to Last -
                        Norma Jean

John Daley . . . . .Manager
Larry Mazer . . . . .Manager
Tim Smith . . . . .Manager
Dave Taylor . . . . .Manager
Tamra Feldman . . . . .Assistant
Jody Mazer . . . . .Assistant

MARTIN ERLICHMAN ASSOCIATES
5670 Wilshire Blvd., Ste. 2400
Los Angeles, CA 90036
PHONE 323-653-1555
FAX 323-653-1593
TYPES OF CLIENTS   Musical Artists
CLIENT LIST   Barbra Streisand

Marty Erlichman . . . . .President

ESSENTIAL ARTS MANAGEMENT, LTD.
3500 W. Olive Ave., Ste. 300
Burbank, CA 91505
PHONE 818-623-9999
EMAIL . . . . .essentialartsmanagement@earthlink.net
TYPES OF CLIENTS   Music Producers - Film/TV Composers -
                       Songwriters

Jack Colman . . . . .CEO/President

ESTEFAN ENTERPRISES INC.
420 Jefferson Ave.
Miami Beach, FL 33139
PHONE 305-534-4330
FAX 305-534-5220
TYPES OF CLIENTS   Musical Artists
CLIENT LIST   Carlos Ponce - Gloria Estefan - Jon
                       Secada

Emilio Estefan . . . . .Chairman
Frank Amadeo . . . . .President

*F SHARP PRODS. LTD.
35 W. 81st St., Ste. 11C
New York, NY 10024
PHONE 917-403-1001
FAX 646-505-0508
EMAIL . . . . .jjosie157@aol.com
TYPES OF CLIENTS   Musical Artists

Jim Di Giovanni . . . . .No Title

FEELING PRODUCTIONS INC.
2540 Daniel-Johnson, Ste. 755
Laval, PQ H7T 2S3 Canada
PHONE 450-978-9555/416-445-0555
FAX 450-978-1055
EMAIL . . . . .info@feelingprod.com
WEB SITE . . . . .www.celinedion.com
SECOND WEB SITE . . . . .www.garouland.com
TYPES OF CLIENTS   Musical Artists
CLIENT LIST   Celine Dion - Garou - Marilou
COMMENTS   Toronto office: 1131A Leslie St., PH 5,
                       Toronto, ON, M3C 3L8 Canada

Rene Angelil . . . . .Manager
Dave Platel . . . . .Manager
Mario Lefebvre . . . . .Manager

FEINSTEIN MANAGEMENT
420 Lexington Ave., Ste. 2150
New York, NY 10170
PHONE 212-684-0830
FAX 212-889-0105
EMAIL .mark@feinsteinmgmt.com
TYPES OF CLIENTS   Musical Artists - Music Producers -
                       Songwriters
MUSICAL ARTIST TYPES   Metal - Pop - Rock
CLIENT LIST   Chris Whitley - Genesis P'Orridge -
                       Judas Priest - Patti Smith - Sarah
                       Brightman - Rammstein - Radio 4

Mark Donenfeld . . . . .Management

THE FIRM, INC.
9465 Wilshire Blvd.
Beverly Hills, CA 90212
PHONE 310-860-8000
FAX 310-860-8100
TYPES OF CLIENTS   Musical Artists - Music Producers -
                       Film/TV Composers - Songwriters -
                       Variety Artists

Jeff Kwatinetz . . . . .Co-Chairman/CEO/Manager
Rich Frank . . . . .Chairman
Rick Yorn . . . . .Co-Chairman

FIRSTARS
14724 Ventura Blvd., PH
Sherman Oaks, CA 91403
PHONE 818-461-1701
FAX 818-461-1739/44-171-267-7071
TYPES OF CLIENTS   Musical Artists
CLIENT LIST   Brianna Sage - Carly Hennessy - Emma
                       Shapplin - Gala - I Muvrini - Mario
                       Frangoulis - Oysterhead - Shabaz -
                       Shani - Simon Shaheen - Soraya -
                       Stewart Copeland - Zucchero - The
                       Human League (London)

Miles Copeland III . . . . .Manager

DAVID FISHOF PRESENTS
424 West End Ave., Ste. 22F
New York, NY 10023
PHONE 212-721-0359
FAX 212-265-4234
EMAIL . . . . .dfishof@aol.com
WEB SITE . . . . .www.davidfishofpresents.com
SECOND WEB SITE . . . . .www.rockandrollfantasycamp.com
TYPES OF CLIENTS   Musical Artists
MUSICAL ARTIST TYPES   Rock
CLIENT LIST   Ringo Starr and His All Starr Band - Rock
                       N' Roll Fantasy Camp - The Monkees

David Fishof . . . . .President/CEO

THE FITZGERALD HARTLEY COMPANY
34 N. Palm St., Ste. 100
Ventura, CA 93001
PHONE 805-641-6441/615-322-9493
FAX 805-641-6444/615-322-9582
WEB SITE . . . . .www.fitzhart.com
TYPES OF CLIENTS   Musical Artists - Music Producers - Music
                       Supervisors - Film/TV Composers -
                       Lyricists - Songwriters
SUBMISSION POLICY   No unsolicited material
COMMENTS   Nashville office. 1908 Wedgewood
                       Ave., Nashville, TN 37212

Larry Fitzgerald . . . . .Manager (Nashville)
Tim Bernett . . . . .Manager (Ventura)
Nick Hartley . . . . .Manager (Ventura)
Mark Hartley . . . . .Manager (Ventura)
Anita Heilig . . . . .Manager (Ventura)
Chad Jensen . . . . .Manager (Ventura)
Bill Simmons . . . . .Manager (Nashville)
Kimiko Tokita . . . . .Manager (Ventura)

MANAGERS

FLUTIE ENTERTAINMENT
9300 Wilshire Blvd., Ste. 333
Beverly Hills, CA 90212
PHONE 310-247-1100/212-226-9190
FAX 310-247-1122/212-226-9791
WEB SITE . . . . .www.flutieent.com
TYPES OF CLIENTS   Musical Artists - Film/TV Composers
SUBMISSION POLICY   Mail or appointment only
COMMENTS   East Coast office: 17 Little W. 12th St.,
                         Ste. 333, New York, NY 10014

Robert A. Flutie . . . . .Manager
Vicki McCarty . . . . .Manager
Harley Bauer . . . . .Manager
Paul M. Brown . . . . .Manager
Erin Seem . . . . .Assistant to Robert Flutie
Teri Vargas . . . . .Assistant to Paul M. Brown

FOCUS THREE ENTERTAINMENT
4108 Riverside Dr., Ste. 3
Burbank, CA 91505
PHONE 818-558-1700
FAX 818-558-1055
EMAIL . . . . .firstinitiallastname@focusthree.com
TYPES OF CLIENTS   Musical Artists - Music Producers
MUSICAL ARTIST TYPES   Alternative - Metal - Pop - Punk -
                         Rap/Hip-Hop - Rock
CLIENT LIST   Papa Roach - Type O Negative - Static-X
                         - Hollywood Undead - Wicked Wisdom -
                         Full Scale Band
SUBMISSION POLICY   No unsolicited material

Mike Renault . . . . .Artist Manager
Ivory Daniel . . . . .Artist Manager
Jeff Peters . . . . .Artist Manager
Dennis Sanders . . . . .Artist Manager

FRED LAWRENCE & ASSOCIATES
11603 Addison St.
North Hollywood, CA 91601
PHONE 818-509-8833
FAX 818-769-8312
TYPES OF CLIENTS   Musical Artists
CLIENT LIST   The Everly Brothers - Paul Revere & The
                         Raiders - Samantha Cole - Cleto & The
                         Cletones

Fred Lawrence . . . . .Manager

FREEZE ARTIST MANAGEMENT
27783 Hidden Trail Rd.
Laguna Hills, CA 92653
PHONE 949-305-5570/323-852-1993
FAX 949-305-5574/323-313-0102
WEB SITE . . . . .www.freezemanagement.com
TYPES OF CLIENTS   Musical Artists - Music Producers
COMMENTS   Los Angeles office: 454 N. Gardner St.,
                         Los Angeles, CA 90036

John Reese . . . . .Manager
Paul Gomez . . . . .Manager
Scott Harmon . . . . .Manager

KEN FRITZ ENTERTAINMENT
431 Howland Canal
Venice, CA 90291-4619
PHONE 310-301-9891
FAX 310-301-9893
EMAIL . . . . .thecat88@aol.com
TYPES OF CLIENTS   Musical Artists - Songwriters
MUSICAL ARTIST TYPES   Adult Contemporary - Alternative - Folk -
                         Jazz - Latin - New Age - Pop - R&B
CLIENT LIST   Jose Feliciano
SUBMISSION POLICY   No unsolicited material

Ken Fritz . . . . .Manager

FRONT LINE MANAGEMENT
1100 Glendon Ave., Ste. 2000
Los Angeles, CA 90024
PHONE 310-209-3100
FAX 310-209-3101
TYPES OF CLIENTS   Musical Artists
MUSICAL ARTIST TYPES   Country - R&B - Rock
COMMENTS   Additional Offices:; 9200 Sunset Blvd.,
                         Ste. 530, Los Angeles, CA 90069,
                         Phone: 310-550-5240, Fax: 310-550-
                         5241; 1025 16th Ave. South, Ste. 303,
                         Nashville, TN 37212, Phone: 615-324-
                         2380, Fax: 615-324-2381

Irving Azoff . . . . .No Title (Glendon)
Howard Kaufman .No Title (Sunset)
Alejandro Aseni .No Title (Glendon)
Nina Avrimides . . . . .No Title (Sunset)
Allison Azoff . . . . .No Title (Glendon)
John Baruck . . . . .No Title (Glendon)
David Codikow . . . . .No Title (Glendon)
Tom Consolo . . . . .No Title (Glendon)
Dana Dufine . . . . .No Title (Glendon)
Craig Fruin . . . . .No Title (San Francisco) (415-485-1444)
Lil Gary . . . . .No Title (Glendon)
Paul Geary . . . . .No Title (Glendon)
Trudy Green . . . . .No Title (Sunset)
Brooke Kaufman .No Title (Sunset)
Sheryl Lewis . . . . .No Title (Sunset)
Susan Markheim .No Title (Glendon)
Jared Paul . . . . .No Title (Glendon)
Clarence Spalding . . . . .No Title (Nashville)
Camy Swafford .No Title (Nashville)

FUNZALO MUSIC
PO Box 35880
Tucson, AZ 85740-5880
PHONE 520-628-8655
FAX 520-628-9072
EMAIL . . . . .mikespoop@aol.com
WEB SITE . . . . .www.funzalorecords.com
SECOND WEB SITE . . . . .www.mikesmanagement.com
MUSICAL ARTIST TYPES   All Genres
CLIENT LIST   Tony Furtado - Spookie Daly Pride - Jim
                         Dickinson - Luca - Sean Slade - Paul
                         Kolderie - The Steepwater Band - Nick
                         Raskulinecz - Dusty Wakeman - Jeremy
                         du Bois - Andrew Weiss - Steve
                         Gallagher - Stuart Sikes - Mike Terry
SUBMISSION POLICY   Accepts unsolicited submissions and
                         does respond

Michael J. Lembo . . . . .President
Karen Dumont . . . . .Personal Manager (Bands)
Jessica Oseran . . . . .Associate Manager (Producers)
Adam Oseran . . . . .Artist Contact
Lee Gutowski . . . . .Press

*FUZED MUSIC
PO Box 19436
Seattle, WA 98109
PHONE 206-352-6892
FAX 206-374-2429
EMAIL . . . . .info@fuzedmusic.com
WEB SITE . . . . .www.fuzedmusic.com
MUSICAL ARTIST TYPES   Pop - Rock
CLIENT LIST   The Presidents of the United States of
                            America - Mountain Con - The Village
                            Green - Reggie Watts - Martin Feveyear

Grady Chapman . . . . .No Title
David Meinert . . . . .No Title

GAILFORCE MANAGEMENT LIMITED
55 Fulham High St.
London SW6 3JJ UK
PHONE .44-20-7384-8989
FAX 44-20-7384-8988
TYPES OF CLIENTS   Musical Artists
CLIENT LIST   Chrissie Hynde/The Pretenders - Stephen
                            Street - Mike Edwards/Jesus Jones -
                            Peter Hammill/Van Der Graaf Generator
                            - The Subways

Gail Colson . . . . .Manager

MICHAEL GARDNER COMPANY
PO Box 5359
Crestline, CA 92325
PHONE 818-292-3090
FAX 909-338-8560
EMAIL . . . . .michaelgardnerm@aol.com
TYPES OF CLIENTS   Musical Artists
CLIENT LIST   Bobby Womack - Freddie Jackson -
                            Howard Hewett - Keith Washington - The
                            Whispers - The Dells - Miki Howard -
                            Confunkshun - Glenn Jones - Vesta
                            Williams

Michael Gardner .President
Richard Burkhart . . . . .Personal Manager

GARVAN MEDIA, MANAGEMENT & MARKETING
7919 Fairfax Court
Niwot, CO 80503
PHONE 303-652-3489
FAX 303-652-3610
EMAIL . . . . .steve@garvanmanagement.com
TYPES OF CLIENTS   Musical Artists - Music Producers -
                            Songwriters
MUSICAL ARTIST TYPES   Adult Contemporary - Country - Rock -
                            Roots
CLIENT LIST   Big Wide Grin - Cindy Bullens - Cari
                            Cole - Chris Daniels - Cliff Eberhardt -
                            Mickey Harte (US only) - Katoorah Jayne
                            - Michael Kelsh - Casey Neill - Tom
                            Roznowski - Rye Hollow - Suzanna
                            Spring - Walt Wilkins - Patti Witten
SUBMISSION POLICY   Seeking nationally-established acts;
                            Contact before submitting
COMMENTS   Also manages Americana bands and
                            songwriters; Affiliated with MMF,
                            American Roots Publishing, IMMF, CMA,
                            AMA NARAS and Folk Alliance

Stephen Bond Garvan . . . . .CEO/Expediter

GAYLE ENTERPRISES, INC.
51 Music Square East
Nashville, TN 37203
PHONE 615-327-2651
FAX 615-327-2657
EMAIL . . . . .bg44@aol.com
WEB SITE . . . . .www.crystalgayle.com
TYPES OF CLIENTS   Musical Artists
CLIENT LIST   Manages Crystal Gayle only

Bill Gatzimos . . . . .President
John Donegan . . . . .VP, Operations
Darrell Beatty . . . . .Executive Assistant

GENERATION-X ENTERTAINMENT INTERNATIONAL, INC. (GEN-X)
PO Box 140
Cedar, MN 55011
PHONE 763-413-9611
FAX 763-413-9610
EMAIL . . . . .genxinc@aol.com
WEB SITE . . . . .www.genxentertainment.us
TYPES OF CLIENTS   Musical Artists - Songwriters - Studio
                            Musicians
MUSICAL ARTIST TYPES   Adult Contemporary - Blues - Rock
CLIENT LIST   The Amazing Rhythm Aces - Randy
                            Bachman - Black Oak Arkansas -
                            Bonepony - Bowzer's Rock 'n' Roll Party -
                            Brewer & Shipley - British Invasion - The
                            Byrds Collection - The Contours - Corey
                            Stevens - The DeVilles - Goose Creek
                            Symphony - Head East - Honeymoon
                            Suite - I.R.S. - Kozmic Blues Band -
                            Lester Chambers & Friends - Nick Gilder
                            & Sweeny Todd - Otis Day & the Knights
                            - Pat Travers - Poco - Randy Hansen -
                            The Rembrandts - Rick Derringer -
                            Southern Rock Allstars - Spencer Davis -
                            The Stampeders - Superstar Voices of
                            Rock - Badfinger - Big Brother & the
                            Holding Company - Canned Heat - The
                            Five Man Electrical Band - Full Tilt
                            Boogie Band - The Original Guess Who
                            - Lovin' Spoonful - Manfred Mann's
                            Earth Band - Pure Prairie League - The
                            Troggs - Vanity Fare - Wavy Gravy

Tim Murphy . . . . .Manager

GENUINE ARTISTS
236 W. 27th St., 8th Fl.
New York, NY 10001
PHONE 212-929-5488
FAX 212-929-5489
EMAIL . . . . .info@genuineartists.com
WEB SITE . . . . .www.genuineartists.com
TYPES OF CLIENTS   Musical Artists - Music Producers
CLIENT LIST   BC Camplight - Hail Social - Jay Joyce -
                            Brian McTear - Toshi Yoshioka

Jennifer Lasker .Manager

DAN GILLIS MANAGEMENT
1305 Clinton St., Ste. 120
Nashville, TN 37203
PHONE 615-320-8730
FAX 615-320-8766
TYPES OF CLIENTS   Musical Artists
CLIENT LIST   Steve Earle - Jessi Colter - Mark
                            McGuinn - East Village Opera Company

Dan Gillis . . . . .Manager
Sarah Brown . . . . .Associate Manager

MANAGERS

GMS MANAGEMENT
585 Ellsworth St., Ste. 2G
Bridgeport, CT 06605
PHONE 203-334-9285
FAX 203-371-0656
TYPES OF CLIENTS   Musical Artists
COMMENTS   NCOPM

Dick Grass . . . . .President
Danny Scarpone . . . . .VP

GOLD MOUNTAIN ENTERTAINMENT
3940 Laurel Canyon Blvd., Ste. 444
Studio City, CA 91604
PHONE 323-845-4166/615-255-9000
FAX 818-506-9587/615-255 9001
EMAIL . . . . .info@gmemusic.com
WEB SITE . . . . .www.gmemusic.com
TYPES OF CLIENTS   Musical Artists - Film/TV Composers - Lyricists
CLIENT LIST   Bonnie Raitt - Lisa Loeb - Baha Men - Ronnie Milsap - Nanci Griffith - The Crickets
SUBMISSION POLICY   No unsolicited material
COMMENTS   Nashville office: 2 Music Circle South, Ste. 212, Nashville, TN 37203

Ron Stone . . . . .President
Burt Stein . . . . .Co-President (Nashville)
Alan Koenig . . . . .Associate Manager (Nashville)
Al McManus . . . . .Associate Manager (Nashville)
Tarryn Smith .Assistant (Nashville)

GREENSPAN ARTIST MANAGEMENT
8748 Holloway Dr., 2nd Fl.
Los Angeles, CA 90069
PHONE 310-289-3990
FAX 310-289-8007
EMAIL . . . . .mail@greenartman.com
WEB SITE . . . . .www.greenartman.com
TYPES OF CLIENTS   Musical Artists - Music Supervisors - Film/TV Composers - Studio Engineers/Technicians
MUSICAL ARTIST TYPES   All Genres
CLIENT LIST   Marco Beltrami - Mark Mothersbaugh - Teddy Castellicci - Joel McNeely - Tom Heil - Stuart Matthewman - Philip Steer - Jeff Sudakin - Charlie Mole - Liz Gallagher - Liza Richardson - Michell Norcell - Chris McGeary - Ernie Mannix - Richard Henderson - Edmund Choi - Adam Berry - Chad Fischer - Jan Kaczmarek

Anita Greenspan . . . . .President
Stacey Kelsey . . . . .No Title
Neil Kohan . . . . .No Title

HALLMARK DIRECTION COMPANY
713 18th Ave. South
Nashville, TN 37203
PHONE 615-320-7714
FAX 615-320-5799
TYPES OF CLIENTS   Musical Artists - Film/TV Composers
MUSICAL ARTIST TYPES   Country
CLIENT LIST   Montgomery Gentry - Blake Shelton - Trent Willmon - The Whites - Jeff Bates - Ray Scott
SUBMISSION POLICY   No unsolicited material

John Dorris . . . . .Sr. President/Manager
Ed Blount . . . . .Manager
Johnny Dorris Jr. . . . . .Manager
Shelia Shipley Biddy . . . . .Co-Manager
Pam Harbert . . . . .Artists Coordinator
Jenell Parker . . . . .Accounting
E.J. Butler . . . . .Administrative Assistant

HANDPRINT ENTERTAINMENT
1100 Glendon Ave., Ste. 1000
Los Angeles, CA 90024
PHONE 310-481-4400
FAX 310-481-4419
TYPES OF CLIENTS   Musical Artists - Variety Artists
MUSICAL ARTIST TYPES   All Genres
CLIENT LIST   Mariah Carey

Benny Medina . . . . .Partner
Jeff Pollack . . . . .Partner
Jean Kwolek . . . . .Jr. Music Manager

*HARBOR ARTISTS
21132 Crealock Pl.
Cornelius, NC 28031
PHONE 704-895-8686
FAX 297-937-5381
EMAIL .jim@harborartists.com
WEB SITE . . . . .www.harborartists.com
TYPES OF CLIENTS   Musical Artists
CLIENT LIST   Mandorico

Jim English . . . . .Manager

MICHAEL HAUSMAN ARTIST MANAGEMENT, INC.
511 Avenue of the Americas, #197
New York, NY 10011
PHONE 212-505-1943
FAX 212-505-1127
EMAIL . . . . .michaelhausman@earthlink.net
TYPES OF CLIENTS   Musical Artists
CLIENT LIST   Aimee Mann - Suzanne Vega - Marc Cohn - Angie Mattson

Michael Hausman . . . . .Manager

HEAVY HARMONY MANAGEMENT CORP.
6433 Topanga Canyon Blvd., Ste. 445
Canoga Park, CA 91303-2621
PHONE 818-887-7073
FAX 818-887-4614
WEB SITE . . . . .www.heavyharmonymusic.com
TYPES OF CLIENTS   Musical Artists - Music Producers
CLIENT LIST   Battlecat - Broodeva - C-4 - Ralph Johnson

Rhonda C. Bedikian . . . . .CEO
Dwayne Cornelius . . . . .President
Brett Miller . . . . .Director, Creative Services
Denise Bedikian . . . . .Director, Administration

MANAGERS

GREG HILL MANAGEMENT
PO Box 159310
Nashville, TN 37215
PHONE 615-248-7866
FAX 615-248-7868
WEB SITE . . . . .www.greghillmanagement.com
TYPES OF CLIENTS   Musical Artists - Music Producers - Songwriters
MUSICAL ARTIST TYPES   Christian - Country
CLIENT LIST   Phil Vassar - Rodney Atkins - Cledus T. Judd - Sarah Kelly - Foreign Oren

Greg Hill . . . . .Manager
Jennifer Poppe . . . . .No Title

HMX MANAGEMENT
4658 Wortser Ave.
Sherman Oaks, CA 91423
PHONE 818-789-4483
FAX 818-789-4489
EMAIL . . . . .grumpom@aol.com
WEB SITE . . . . .www.bigdealrecords.com
TYPES OF CLIENTS   Musical Artists - Music Producers - Songwriters
MUSICAL ARTIST TYPES   Adult Contemporary - Alternative - Folk - Jazz - Rock
CLIENT LIST   Bobby Caldwell - The Frank & Joe Show

Henry Marx . . . . .Manager

HOFFMAN ENTERTAINMENT
362 Fifth Ave., Ste. 804
New York, NY 10001
PHONE 212-765-2525
FAX 212-765-2888
EMAIL . . . . .info@hoffmanentertainment.com
MUSICAL ARTIST TYPES   Pop - Rock
CLIENT LIST   John Mellencamp - Thalia - Heather Headley - CKY

Randy Hoffman . . . . .President
Rich Schaefer . . . . .No Title
Miranda Hafford . . . . .No Title
Laura O'Neill . . . . .No Title

HORNBLOW GROUP USA, INC.
PO Box 176
Palisades, NY 10964
PHONE 845-358-7270
FAX 845-358-8041
TYPES OF CLIENTS   Musical Artists - Music Producers - Film/TV Composers - Songwriters
MUSICAL ARTIST TYPES   Alternative - Children's - Pop - Rock
CLIENT LIST   Eric Drew Feldman - OK Go - They Might Be Giants - Spiraling
SUBMISSION POLICY   Accepts press kits

Jamie Kitman . . . . .President
Michael Kahn . . . . .Manager
Brigitta Copple . . . . .Associate
Peter Smolin . . . . .Associate

ANDI HOWARD ENTERTAINMENT
30765 Pacific Coast Hwy., Ste. 134
Malibu, CA 90265
PHONE 310-385-4299
FAX 310-385-4050
EMAIL . . . . .ahowardent@aol.com
TYPES OF CLIENTS   Musical Artists
MUSICAL ARTIST TYPES   Jazz
CLIENT LIST   The Rippingtons - Eric Marienthal - Paul Taylor

Andi Howard . . . . .Owner

ICM ARTISTS, LTD.
1700 Broadway, 26th Fl.
New York, NY 10019
PHONE 212-556-5600/310-550-4000
FAX 212-556-5677/310-550-4100
EMAIL .classical@icmtalent.com
WEB SITE . . . . .www.icmtalent.com
TYPES OF CLIENTS   Musical Artists
MUSICAL ARTIST TYPES   Classical - Jazz
SUBMISSION POLICY   No unsolicited material
COMMENTS   Conductors - Classical Soloists - Chamber Ensembles - Jazz Ensembles - Choral & Vocal Ensembles - New Music Ensembles - Special Attractions - Opera Singers & Composers; London office: 4-6 Soho Square, London, W1D 3PZ, UK, Phone: 011-44-207-432-0800

David V. Foster . . . . .CEO/President
Byron Gustafson . . . . .Executive VP/Manager, Artists & Attractions
Jenny Vogel . . . .Executive VP/Manager, Artists & Conductors (LA, x4477)
Richard Corrado . . . . .Sr. VP/Manager, Artists & Conductors
Patricia A. Winter . . . . .Sr. VP/National Booking Director/Manager, Artists & Attractions
Elaine Lipcan . . . . .Booking Representative
Robert Berretta . . . . .Booking Representative
Seth Malasky . . . . .Booking Representative
Christina Baker .Booking Representative
Andrea Johnson . . . . .Booking Representative
Jason Bagdade . . . . .VP/Manager, Artists & Conductors
Neil Benson   VP/National Booking Director/Manager, Artists & Attractions
Earl Blackburn . . . . .VP/Manager, Artists & Attractions
Rachel Bowron . . . . .VP/Manager, Artists & Conductors
Jonathan Brill . . . . .VP/Manager, Artists & Conductors
Mary Pat Buerkle . . . . .VP/Manager, Artists & Attractions
Risë Kern . . . . .VP/Manager, Artists & Attractions
Leonard Stein . . . . .VP/Director, Tour Administration
Caroline Woodfield . . . . .VP/Manager, Artists
David Baldwin . . . . .Director/ICM Artists (London)
Paul C. Bongiorno . . . . .Manager, Artists & Attractions
Nicole Borrelli Hearn . . . . .Manager, Artists & Attractions/ Booking Representative
Laura Hong . . . . .Manager, Artists & Conductors (LA, x4477)
William Bowler . . . . .Associate Manager, Artists & Attractions
Ira D. Pedlikin . . . . .Associate Manager, Attractions
Deborah-Rose Andrews . . . . .Associate, Program & Travel/ Associate Manager, Chamber Music
James Barry . . . . .Associate, Program & Travel
Miriam Biolek . . . . .Associate, Artists & Attractions
Caroline Cuss . . . . .Associate, ICM Artists (London)
Scott DeLello . . . . .Associate, Program & Travel
Annette DiPerno . . . . .Associate, Dance Division
Jennifer Flores . . . . .Associate, ICM Artists (London)
Jeanine Hoff . . . . .Associate, Artists & Conductors
Liesl Kundert . . . . .Associate
Jane Hermann . . . . .Consultant
Stewart Warkow . . . . .Consultant

IDOL MANAGEMENT
PO Box 1453
Tacoma, WA 98401-1453
PHONE 253-383-6382/253-759-1038
FAX 253-276-0127
EMAIL . . . . .donrobertson@idolmanagement.com
WEB SITE .www.idolmanagement.com
TYPES OF CLIENTS   Musical Artists - Music Producers - Music Supervisors - Studio Musicians
MUSICAL ARTIST TYPES   Adult Contemporary - Alternative - Country - Metal - Punk - Rock
CLIENT LIST   3 Inches of Blood - Zeke - River City Rebels - Post Stardom Depression - Kane Hodder - Burning Armada - The Yo-Yo's - The Golden Gods - Top Heavy Crush - Bob Wayne - Blank Generation

Donny Hales . . . . .Manager (donnyhales@idolmanagement.com)
Don Robertson . . . . . . .Manager (donrobertson@idolmanagement.com)
Pat Brown . . .Radio/Music Supervisor (patbrown@idolmanagement.com)

MANAGERS

IMPACT ARTIST MANAGEMENT
121 W. 27th St., Ste. 1004
New York, NY 10001
PHONE 212-645-3627
FAX 212-367-8315
EMAIL . . . . .info@impactartist.com
WEB SITE . . . . .www.impactartist.com

TYPES OF CLIENTS	Musical Artists - Music Supervisors
MUSICAL ARTIST TYPES	Adult Contemporary - Alternative - Blues - Jazz - Latin - R&B - Rock - World
CLIENT LIST	Dr. John - Gipsy Kings (co-manage) - Tom Wopat - Eliane Elias
SUBMISSION POLICY	No unsolicited material

Ed Gerrard . . . . .Manager, Principal
Peter Himberger . . . . .Manager, Principal
Aki Oduola . . . . .Associate Manager

IN DE GOOT ENTERTAINMENT INC.
119 W. 23rd St., Ste. 609
New York, NY 10011
PHONE 212-924-7775
FAX 212-691-8303
EMAIL . . . . .tcouch@indegoot.com
SECOND EMAIL . . . . .submissions@indegoot.com
WEB SITE . . . . .www.indegoot.com

TYPES OF CLIENTS	Musical Artists
CLIENT LIST	3 Doors Down - Chevelle - Earshot - Fingertight - Future Leaders of the World - Life of Agony - Exit The King - Puddle of Mudd - Saliva - Shinedown - Theory of a Deadman - Black Stone Cherry - Halestorm

Bill McGathy . . . . .Owner/Manager
Corey Sheridan . . . . .Manager
Tony Couch . . . . .Manager
Elizabeth Hahn . . . . .Manager
Vincent Hartong . . . . .Manager
Gwyther Bultman . . . . .Manager

INVASION GROUP, LTD.
133 W. 25th St., 5th Fl.
New York, NY 10001
PHONE 212-414-0505
FAX 212-414-0525
EMAIL . . . . .info@invasiongroup.com
WEB SITE . . . . .www.invasiongroup.com

TYPES OF CLIENTS	Musical Artists - Music Producers - Music Supervisors - Film/TV Composers - Lyricists - Songwriters - Studio Musicians - Studio Vocalists - Studio Engineers/Technicians
MUSICAL ARTIST TYPES	All Genres
CLIENT LIST	Christopher Bjork - Marc Copely - Neil Dorfsman - Mary Fahl - Enter the Haggis - Scott Jacoby - Irvin Johnson - Karsh Kale - Jess Klein - Dan Metreyeon - Limblifter - Ludo - Wayne Sharpe - Maiysha Simpson - Jai Uttal - David Werner

Peter Casperson . . . . .Co-Owner
Steven Saporta . . . . .Co-Owner
Steve Dalmer . . . . .Manager
Noah Dinkin . . . . .Manager
Ali Sachedina . . . . .Manager
Jesse Roman . . . . .Assistant Manager
Etty Glenn . . . . .Assistant, International

JGM
155 Avenue of the Americas, 6th Fl.
New York, NY 10013
PHONE 646-336-8520
FAX 646-336-8522
EMAIL . . . . .jgm@littlebigman.com
SECOND EMAIL . . . . .mat@littlebigman.com

TYPES OF CLIENTS	Musical Artists - Music Producers - Songwriters
MUSICAL ARTIST TYPES	Adult Contemporary - Alternative - Pop
CLIENT LIST	Dan Wilson - Five for Fighting - John Ondrasik - Mike Doughty (co-manage) - Semisonic - Pitty Sing

Jim Grant . . . . .Manager
Mat Hall . . . . .Manager

JH MANAGEMENT & BOOKING
9350 SPID #32
Corpus Christi, TX 78418
PHONE 512-921-5111
FAX 314-228-5111
EMAIL . . . . .jhmanagement@hotmail.com

TYPES OF CLIENTS	Musical Artists
SUBMISSION POLICY	Email prior to submitting

Jessica Hernandez . . . . .President

KAB AMERICA INC.
302-A W. 12th St., #181
New York, NY 10014
PHONE 212-741-1960
FAX 212-741-1916
EMAIL . . . . .evan@kab.com
WEB SITE . . . . .www.sitesakamoto.com
SECOND WEB SITE . . . . .www.kab.com

TYPES OF CLIENTS	Musical Artists - Music Producers - Music Supervisors - Film/TV Composers - Songwriters - Studio Engineers/Technicians
MUSICAL ARTIST TYPES	All Genres
CLIENT LIST	Exclusive management for composer/musician Ryuichi Sakamoto
SUBMISSION POLICY	Submissions accepted

Norika Sora . . . . .President
Evan Balmer . . . . .Manager

*KANE ENTERTAINMENT
1024C 18th Ave. South
Nashville, TN 37212
PHONE 615-695-5260
FAX 615-695-5270
EMAIL . . . . .ksanson@kaneentertainment.com
WEB SITE .www.kaneentertainment.com

TYPES OF CLIENTS	Musical Artists

Karen Kane . . . . .President
Lamar Raley . . . . .VP
Travis Wolf . . . . .Associate Manager
Kelly Sanson . . . . .Executive Assistant

DAVE KAPLAN MANAGEMENT
1126 South Coast Hwy. 101
Encinitas, CA 92024
PHONE 760-944-8800
FAX 760-944-7808
WEB SITE . . . . .www.surfdog.com
TYPES OF CLIENTS   Musical Artists
CLIENT LIST   Brian Setzer - Gary Hoey - Rusty
                        Anderson - Dan Hicks - Richard Cheese
                        - Gibby Haynes
SUBMISSION POLICY   Accepts general submissions

Dave Kaplan . . . . .President
Keith Emrick . . . . .No Title
Pierce Flynn . . . . .No Title
Nola Schoder . . . . .No Title
Niels Schroeter . . . . .No Title
Scott Seine . . . . .No Title

CATHY KERR MANAGEMENT
9079 Nemo St.
Los Angeles, CA 90069
PHONE 310-273-9437
FAX 310-273-2859
TYPES OF CLIENTS   Musical Artists
CLIENT LIST   Randy Newman - Mary Chapin
                        Carpenter

Cathy Kerr . . . . .Manager

KRAGEN & COMPANY
14039 Aubrey Rd.
Beverly Hills, CA 90210
PHONE 310-854-4400
FAX 310-854-0238
EMAIL . . . . .kenkragen@aol.com
WEB SITE . . . . .www.kenkragen.com
TYPES OF CLIENTS   Musical Artists - Songwriters - Variety
                        Artists - Comedians
CLIENT LIST   The Smothers Brothers - Tonic Sol Fa -
                        Ronn Lucas - Suzanne Whang - Jake
                        Simpson - Alisha Mullally - Skip Ewing
SUBMISSION POLICY   No unsolicited submissions

Ken Kragen . . . . .President
Amanda Martin . . . . .Assistant to Ken Kragen

KREBS COMMUNICATION CORPORATION
19 W. 44th St., Ste. 606
New York, NY 10036
PHONE 212-997-5900
FAX 212-997-8522
EMAIL . . . . .david@krebscommunications.com
TYPES OF CLIENTS   Musical Artists - Music Producers
MUSICAL ARTIST TYPES   Adult Contemporary - Metal - Pop -
                        Rock
CLIENT LIST   Hanoi Rocks - Michael Monroe - Marina
                        V - Secret Mind

Tim Baker . . . . .No Title
Debby Diamond . . . . .No Title
David Krebs . . . . .No Title
Tony Zachariadis . . . . .No Title

KSM, INC.
826 Broadway, Ste. 411
New York, NY 10003
PHONE 212-777-5110
FAX 212-777-5145
EMAIL . . . . .kschenker@ksmgmt.com
TYPES OF CLIENTS   Musical Artists
MUSICAL ARTIST TYPES   Rock
CLIENT LIST   Sting

Kathryn Schenker .President/Manager
Dave Sandford . . . . .General Manager (daves@ksmgmt.com)
Tracy Bufferd . . . . .International Media (tracy@tracybufferd.com)
Terence Keegan . . . . .Management (tkeegan@ksmgmt.com)

KURFIRST-BLACKWELL ENTERTAINMENT (LOS ANGELES)
8570 Hedges Pl.
Los Angeles, CA 90069
PHONE 310-659-6598
FAX 310-659-1679
EMAIL . . . . .management@kurfirst-blackwellentertainment.com
SECOND EMAIL . . . . .info@radioactive.com
WEB SITE . . . . .www.kurfirst-blackwellentertainment.com
SECOND WEB SITE . . . . .www.radioactive.net
TYPES OF CLIENTS   Musical Artists
MUSICAL ARTIST TYPES   All Genres
CLIENT LIST   Live - Indigenous - Skinny Puppy -
                        Gosling - Ambulance Ltd. - Yerba Buena
                        - Los Amigos Invisibles - Roger Clyne &
                        the Peacemakers - Johnny Boy - Lake
                        Trout
COMMENTS   RX Records

Gary Kurfirst . . . . .Co-Founder
Chris Hardin . . . . .Manager
Jeff Jacquin . . . . .Manager, A&R

KURFIRST-BLACKWELL ENTERTAINMENT (NEW YORK)
601 W. 26th St., Ste. 1150
New York, NY 10001
PHONE 212-320-3680
FAX 212-320-3689
EMAIL . . . . .management@kurfirst-blackwellentertainment.com
SECOND EMAIL . . . . .info@radioactive.com
WEB SITE . . . . .www.kurfirst-blackwellentertainment.com
TYPES OF CLIENTS   Musical Artists
MUSICAL ARTIST TYPES   Rock
CLIENT LIST   Live - Indigenous - Skinny Puppy -
                        Gosling - Ambulance Ltd. - Yerba Buena
                        - Los Amigos Invisibles - Roger Clyne &
                        the Peacemakers - Johnny Boy - Lake
                        Trout

Gary Kurfirst . . . . .Co-Founder
Chris Blackwell . . . . .Co-Founder
Katie Elliott . . . . .Manager
Veronica Gretton . . . . .Manager
Chris Hardin . . . . .Manager
Jeff Jacquin . . . . .Manager
Josh Kurfirst . . . . .Manager

KUSHNICK ENTERTAINMENT
1779 Wells Branch Parkway, #110B-316
Austin, TX 78728
PHONE 512-255-7700
EMAIL . . . . .kushnickent@sbcglobal.net
TYPES OF CLIENTS   Musical Artists - Music Producers -
                        Film/TV Composers - Lyricists -
                        Songwriters
CLIENT LIST   Lisa Hayes - Ashley Ingram - Jamshied
                        Sharifi - Mark Feist - Laythan Armor -
                        Evan Olson

Ken Kushnick . . . . .Owner/Manager

MANAGERS

L.A. PERSONAL DEVELOPMENT
16130 Ventura Blvd., #540
Encino, CA 91436
PHONE 818-783-7372
FAX 818-783-7350
EMAIL . . . . .lapersdev@yahoo.com
TYPES OF CLIENTS   Musical Artists
CLIENT LIST   Anne McCue - Paul Schwartz - Ronny
                        Cox - Lisbeth Scott

Mike Gormley . . . . .Manager

JON LANDAU MANAGEMENT
80 Mason St.
Greenwich, CT 06830
PHONE 203-625-2636
FAX 203-625-2634
TYPES OF CLIENTS   Musical Artists
CLIENT LIST   Bruce Springsteen - Train

Jon Landau . . . . .No Title
Barbara Carr . . . . .No Title
Jan Stabile . . . . .No Title
Alison Oscar . . . . .No Title
Tammy Comstock . . . . .No Title
Sue Berger . . . . .No Title

*DAVID LEFKOWITZ MANAGEMENT
3470 19th St.
San Francisco, CA 94110
PHONE 415-777-1715
FAX 415-255-0220
TYPES OF CLIENTS   Musical Artists

David Lefkowitz . . . . .Manager

JERRY LEMBO ENTERTAINMENT GROUP
742 Bergen Blvd.
Ridgefield, NJ 07657
PHONE 201-840-9980
FAX 201-840-9921
EMAIL . . . . .jerry@lemboentertainment.com
WEB SITE . . . . .www.lemboentertainment.com
TYPES OF CLIENTS   Musical Artists - Music Producers -
                        Songwriters
MUSICAL ARTIST TYPES   Adult Contemporary - Alternative - Jazz -
                        Pop - Rock
SUBMISSION POLICY   Unsolicited CDs accepted

Jerry Lembo . . . . .Manager

W.F. LEOPOLD MANAGEMENT
4425 Riverside Dr., Ste. 102
Burbank, CA 91505
PHONE 818-955-8511
FAX 818-955-9602
TYPES OF CLIENTS   Musical Artists - Music Producers -
                        Songwriters
MUSICAL ARTIST TYPES   Alternative - Jazz - Pop - Rock
CLIENT LIST   Dave Koz - Melissa Etheridge - Adam
                        Cohen - Low Millions

Bill Leopold . . . . .Manager
John Carter . . . . .Manager
Mark Graham . . . . .Manager
Josh Leopold . . . . .Business Affairs/Publishing
Alison Taylor .Sr. VP, Marketing

LOUIS LEVIN MANAGEMENT
130 W. 57th St., Ste. 7-B
New York, NY 10019
PHONE 212-489-5738
FAX 212-489-6319
EMAIL . . . . .louis@llevinmanagement.com
TYPES OF CLIENTS   Musical Artists
MUSICAL ARTIST TYPES   All Genres
CLIENT LIST   The Grand Skeem - Michael Bolton

Louis Levin . . . . .Owner/Manager
Rebecca Brody . . . . .Assistant Manager

LEVIN/NELSON ENTERTAINMENT
130 W. 57th St., Ste. 7-B
New York, NY 10019
PHONE 212-489-5738
FAX 212-489-6319
EMAIL . . . . .info@levinnelson.com
WEB SITE .www.levinnelson.com
TYPES OF CLIENTS   Musical Artists - Music Producers -
                        Songwriters
MUSICAL ARTIST TYPES   All Genres
CLIENT LIST   Val Emmich - Casino - Trent Tomlinson -
                        James Otto - Steven Baggs - Michael
                        Bolton - Shannon Lawson - Chuck Wicks
                        - Ben Sigston - Low Flying Jets - Chantel
                        Upshaw
SUBMISSION POLICY   Accepts unsolicited packages
COMMENTS   Artist management and development;
                        Nashville office: 1517 16th Ave. South,
                        Nashville, TN 37212

Louis Levin . . . . .Partner
Brian Nelson . . . . .Partner
Monty Powell . . . . .Partner, Nashville
Ralph Hanan . . . . .Manager
Rebecca Brody . . . . .Office Manager

JOHN LEVY ENTERPRISES
1828 Coolidge Ave.
Altadena, CA 91001
PHONE 626-398-8179
FAX 626-398-7563
WEB SITE . . . . .www.lushlife.com
TYPES OF CLIENTS   Musical Artists - Variety Artists
MUSICAL ARTIST TYPES   Jazz - Pop
CLIENT LIST   Nancy Wilson - Clair Dee

John Levy . . . . .President/Manager
Devra Hall . . . . .Manager

LIPPMAN ENTERTAINMENT
23586 Calabasas Rd., Ste. 208
Calabasas, CA 91302
PHONE 818-225-7480
FAX 818-225-7483
EMAIL . . . . .music@lippman-ent.com
TYPES OF CLIENTS   Musical Artists - Music Producers -
                        Film/TV Composers - Songwriters -
                        Studio Engineers/Technicians
MUSICAL ARTIST TYPES   Pop - Rock
CLIENT LIST   Rob Thomas - Bernie Taupin - Matchbox
                        Twenty - Joe Firstman - Anna Nalick -
                        George Michael

Michael Lippman . . . . .Manager/President
Kathy Anaya . . . . .Manager
Nick Lippman . . . . .Manager
Gordon Peters . . . . .Manager

LIVINGSTON PRODUCTIONS
31 E. Merrick Rd.
Valley Stream, NY 11580
PHONE 516-568-1343
FAX 516-872-1147
EMAIL . . . . .livbig1@aol.com
TYPES OF CLIENTS   Musical Artists
CLIENT LIST   Shaggy

Robert Livingston . . . . .Manager

LONE WOLF MANAGEMENT
PO Box 163690
Austin, TX 163690
PHONE 512-314-9653
FAX 512-314-9650
EMAIL . . . . .info@lone-wolf.com
WEB SITE . . . . .www.lone-wolf.com
TYPES OF CLIENTS   Musical Artists
MUSICAL ARTIST TYPES   Latin - Rock - World
CLIENT LIST   ZZ Top - Del Castillo

Bill Ham . . . . .President (bill@lone-wolf.com)
Dave Brichler . .Director, Operations & Marketing (dave@lone-wolf.com)
Bob Small . . . . .Director, Media Relations (bob@lone-wolf.com)

LOOKOUT MANAGEMENT
1460 Fourth St., Ste. 300
Santa Monica, CA 90401
PHONE 310-319-1331
FAX 310-319-5331
TYPES OF CLIENTS   Musical Artists
CLIENT LIST   Neil Young - David Crosby - Ric Ocasek

Elliot Roberts . . . . .Manager

MACKLAM FELDMAN MANAGEMENT
1505 W. Second Ave., Ste. 200
Vancouver, BC V6H 3Y4 Canada
PHONE 604-734-5945
FAX 604-732-0922
WEB SITE . . . . .www.slfa.com
SECOND WEB SITE .www.mfmgt.com
TYPES OF CLIENTS   Musical Artists
MUSICAL ARTIST TYPES   Adult Contemporary - Blues - Folk - Jazz
                          - Pop - R&B - Rock - World
CLIENT LIST   Diana Krall - Jesse Cook - Joni Mitchell
                          - Sissel - The Chieftains - The Tragically
                          Hip - Norah Jones - Elvis Costello -
                          Susan Tedeschi - Liam Titcomb - Ry
                          Cooder - Craig Northey - Sondre Lerche
                          - Leonard Cohen - Anjani Thomas -
                          Samantha Moore - Alexz Johnson -
                          Stripper's Union

Sam Feldman .Partner (feldman@sfla.com)
Steve Macklam . . . . .Partner/President (macklam@mfmgt.com)
Darrell Gilmour . . . . .Director of Operations, Project Manager
                          (Diana Krall, Joni Mitchell) (gilmour@mfmgt.com)
Mary Boutette . . . . .Project Manager (Norah Jones, Craig Northey,
                          Samantha Moore) (boutette@mfmgt.com)
Alison Burns . . . . . . .Project Manager (Susan Tedeschi, Sondre Lerche,
                          Liam Titcomb, Sissel) (burns@mfmgt.com)
Michelle Findlay . . . . .Project Manager (The Chieftains, Leonard Cohen,
                          Anjani Thomas) (findlay@mfmgt.com)
Dave Levinson . . .Project Manager (The Tragically Hip), Tour Coordinator
                          (Jesse Cook, Diana Krall) (levinson@mfmgt.com)
Colin Nairne . . .Project Manager (Elvis Costello, Ry Cooder, Jesse Cook)
                          (nairne@mfmgt.com)
Darren Gilmore   Watchdog (Alexz Johnson) (darren@watchdogmgt.com)
Cathy Clarke . . . . .Assistant to Sam Feldman (clarke@slfa.com)
Alexandra Dembicki   Assistant to Steve Macklam (dembicki@mfmgt.com)
Sarah Fenton . . . . .Management Assistant (fenton@mfmgt.com)
Braden Ricketts . . . . .Management Assistant (ricketts@mfmgt.com)

*MAD HEAVEN ENTERTAINMENT
1126 N. Hollywood Way, #203
Burbank, CA 91505
PHONE 818-842-0375
FAX 818-842-0205
EMAIL . . . . .info@madheavenentertainment.com
WEB SITE . . . . .www.madheavenentertainment.com
SECOND WEB SITE . . . . .www.realmusicfan.com
TYPES OF CLIENTS   Musical Artists - Music Producers
CLIENT LIST   Rene Mercury - Curious Primate - Rockin
                          America - Real Music Fan

S.C. Smith . . . . .Founder
Janan Jem . . . . .IMC/Development

MADHOUSE MANAGEMENT
PO Box 130109
Ann Arbor, MI 48113
PHONE 734-434-8200/310-358-9200
FAX 734-434-2140/310-358-9299
TYPES OF CLIENTS   Musical Artists
CLIENT LIST   Damn Yankees - Tata Young - Ted
                          Nugent

Doug Banker . . . . .Manager

MADISON HOUSE INC.
4760 Walnut St., Ste. 106
Boulder, CO 80301
PHONE 303-544-9900/212-777-0922
FAX 303-544-5879/212-777-0622
EMAIL . . . . .office@madisonhouseinc.com
WEB SITE . . . . .www.madisonhouseinc.com
TYPES OF CLIENTS   Musical Artists
CLIENT LIST   Angelique Kidjo - Augie March -
                          Dinosaur Jr - The Dresden Dolls - Drew
                          Emmitt - Drive-By Truckers - Hot Rod
                          Circuit - J Mascis - Jeff Coffin - MOFRO
                          - Secret Machines
COMMENTS   East Coast office: 628 Broadway, Ste.
                          502, New York, NY 10012-2613

Mike Luba . . . . .New York (luba@madison-house.com)
Nadia Prescher . . . . .Boulder (nadia@madison-house.com)
Jeremy Stein . . . . .Boulder (stein@madison-house.com)
Jesse Aratow . . . . .Boulder (jesse@madison-house.com)
Bart Dahl . . . . .New York (bart@madison-house.com)
Kinsey Miller . . . . .Boulder (kinsey@madison-house.com)
Kevin Morris . . . . .New York
Megan O'Leary . . . . .Boulder (megan@madison-house.com)
Jake Schneider . . . . .Boulder (jake@madison-house.com)
Christine Stauder . . . . .New York
Emily White . . . . .New York
Carrie Lombardi . . . . .Director, Publicity (carrie@mhpublicity.com)
Ashley Mutthews . . . . .Publicity (ashley@mhpublicity.com)
Amy Cummins . . . . .Publicity (amy@mhpublicity.com)

MANAGERS

MAGUS ENTERTAINMENT INC.
33 Greene St., Ste. 3
New York, NY 10013
PHONE 212-343-1577
FAX 212-925-4007
EMAIL . . . . .info@magusentertainment.com
WEB SITE . . . . .www.magusentertainment.com
TYPES OF CLIENTS   Musical Artists - Music Producers - Songwriters - Studio Engineers/Technicians
MUSICAL ARTIST TYPES   Adult Contemporary - Alternative - Pop - R&B - Rap/Hip-Hop - Rock - Urban
CLIENT LIST   Fischerspooner - Ferry Corsten - Sweetback - Duran Duran - The Beu Sisters - Jade - Darren Hayes

Wendy Laister . . . . .Manager/CEO
Paul Adams . . . . .Manager (paul@magusentertainment.com)
Sharon Cho . . . . .Manager (sharon@magusentertainment.com)
Cathy Oates . . . . .Manager (cathy@magusentertainment.com)
Alan Stewart . . . . .Manager (alan@magusentertainment.com)
Johanna Williams . . . . .Assistant (johanna@magusentertainment.com)

MAINE ROAD
195 Chrystie St., Ste. 901F
New York, NY 10002
PHONE 212-979-9004
FAX 212-979-0985
EMAIL . . . . .mainermi@aol.com
WEB SITE . . . . .www.maineroadmanagement.com
TYPES OF CLIENTS   Musical Artists
CLIENT LIST   David Byrne - Jim White - Joe Henry - Mimi - Helmet - David Bowie (Label consultant) - Air (North American tour consultants) - The Flatlanders - Dean & Britta - Jimmie Dale Gilmore - Joe Ely

David Whitehead .President/Director
Caroline Alonzo . . . . .Associate
Paul Dalen . . . . .Associate

MAMBO ARTISTS
250 W. 57th St., Ste. 2120
New York, NY 10019
PHONE 212-765-2330
FAX 212-765-2372
TYPES OF CLIENTS   Musical Artists - Film/TV Composers
CLIENT LIST   Kevin Killen - Craig Street - Steven Barber

Karyn Kaplan . . . . .No Title

MANAGEMENT BY JAFFE (MBJ)
68 Ridgewood Ave.
Glen Ridge, NJ 07028
PHONE 973-743-1075
FAX 973-680-4318
EMAIL . . . . .jerjaf@aol.com
TYPES OF CLIENTS   Musical Artists - Songwriters
MUSICAL ARTIST TYPES   Alternative - Pop - Punk - Rock
SUBMISSION POLICY   No unsolicited submissions accepted

Jerry Jaffe . . . . .President

MANAGEMENT NETWORK
17525 Ventura Blvd., Ste. 210
Encino, CA 91316
PHONE 818-783-0707
EMAIL . . . . .metwork@aol.com
TYPES OF CLIENTS   Musical Artists - Music Producers - Film/TV Composers - Lyricists - Songwriters
MUSICAL ARTIST TYPES   All Genres
CLIENT LIST   Crosby, Stills & Nash - Deep Audio - Graham Nash - Heather Bradley - Stephen Stills

Gerry Tolman . . . . .Manager

*MANTA ENTERTAINMENT
10313 W. Jefferson Blvd.
Culver City, CA 90232
PHONE 310-839-9599
EMAIL . . . . .jerrold@mantaent.com
SECOND EMAIL .lou@mantaent.com
WEB SITE . . . . .www.mantaent.com
MUSICAL ARTIST TYPES   All Genres

Lou Bond . . . . .President
Jerrold Thompson . . . . .Head, Music

MARKS MANAGEMENT
1030 Mission Ridge Rd.
Santa Barbara, CA 93103
PHONE 805-882-1116
FAX 805-882-9116
EMAIL .larry@marksmanagement.com
WEB SITE . . . . .www.marksmanagement.com
TYPES OF CLIENTS   Film/TV Composers
CLIENT LIST   Christopher Dedrick - Grant Geissman - Charles Fox - Nic. tenBroek - Stewart Levin

Lawrence B. Marks . . . . .Owner

MARQUEE MANAGEMENT
274 Madison Ave., Ste. 1900
New York, NY 10016
PHONE 212-889-0420
FAX 212-889-0279
TYPES OF CLIENTS   Musical Artists - Music Producers - Lyricists - Songwriters
MUSICAL ARTIST TYPES   Classical - Dance/DJ - Pop
CLIENT LIST   Tina Novak - Jenn Cuneta - Sasha Lazard - Lisa Pure - Heather Schmid

Steve Kurtz . . . . .President
Christine Dennison . . . . .Assistant

DAVID MARTIN MANAGEMENT
13849 Riverside Dr.
Sherman Oaks, CA 91423
PHONE 818-981-8686
FAX 818-981-0839
EMAIL . . . . .davidmartinmgmt@aol.com
TYPES OF CLIENTS   Musical Artists
MUSICAL ARTIST TYPES   Adult Contemporary - Country - Latin - Pop - R&B
SUBMISSION POLICY   No unsolicited submissions
COMMENTS   Established clients only

David Martin . . . . .President

MANAGERS

*MAY ARTIST MANAGEMENT

8491 Sunset Blvd., Ste. 228
West Hollywood, CA 90069
PHONE 877-629-2784
FAX 951-360-5545
EMAIL . . . . .david@mayartist.com

David May . . . . .President/Owner
Andreanna May . . . . .Assistant

MB MANAGEMENT

PO Box 25703
Chicago, IL 60625
PHONE 310-823-0101
FAX 773-561-1515
EMAIL . . . . .mbmanage@aol.com
TYPES OF CLIENTS   Musical Artists - Music Producers - Music
                         Supervisors - Film/TV Composers -
                         Lyricists - Songwriters - Studio Musicians
CLIENT LIST   Coco Montoya - Keb' Mo'

John Boncimino . . . . .Partner/Manager
Kevin Morrow . . . . .Partner/Manager

MBK ENTERTAINMENT

240 W. 35th St., 18th Fl.
New York, NY 10001
PHONE 212-542-3270
FAX 212-542-3286
EMAIL . . . . .info@mbkentertainment.com
WEB SITE . . . . .www.mbkentertainment.com
MUSICAL ARTIST TYPES   Adult Contemporary - Christian - Gospel
                         - Pop - R&B - Rap/Hip-Hop - Reggae -
                         Urban
CLIENT LIST   Alicia Keys - Shawn Kane - Jermaine
                         Paul - Jessica Wilson - Mike Milz - Tonex
SUBMISSION POLICY   Unsolicited material accepted by mail
                         only

Jeff Robinson . . . . .CEO
Jeanine McLean-Griffin . . . . .GM/VP

MBST ENTERTAINMENT

345 N. Maple Dr., Ste. 200
Beverly Hills, CA 90210
PHONE 310-385-1820
FAX 310-385-1834
TYPES OF CLIENTS   Musical Artists
MUSICAL ARTIST TYPES   Jazz - Pop
SUBMISSION POLICY   Referral only

Larry Brezner . . . . .No Title
David Steinberg . . . . .No Title
Stephen Tenenbaum . . . . .No Title
Jonathan Brandstein . . . . .No Title
Meegan Kelso . . . . .No Title
Andrew D. Tenenbaum . . . . .No Title

MCGHEE ENTERTAINMENT

8730 Sunset Blvd., Ste. 200
Los Angeles, CA 90069
PHONE 310-358-9200
FAX 310-358-9299
EMAIL . . . . .info@mcgheela.com
WEB SITE . . . . .www.mcgheela.com
TYPES OF CLIENTS   Musical Artists - Songwriters
MUSICAL ARTIST TYPES   Country - Rock
CLIENT LIST   KISS - Hootie & The Blowfish - Ted
                         Nugent - Tata Young - Randy Coleman -
                         Shurman - Bonnie McKee - The Drew
                         Davis Band - Ron Benise

Doc McGhee . . . . .President
Doug Banker . . . . .Manager, Music
Scott McGhee . . . . .Manager, Music
Frank Rand . . . . .Manager, Music
Melissa Madden .Office Manager

MCPHERSON ARTIST MANAGEMENT

PO Box 50657
Los Angeles, CA 90050-0657
PHONE 213-422-8433
FAX 323-417-4984
EMAIL . . . . .bmcpherson@prodigy.net
TYPES OF CLIENTS   Musical Artists - Music Producers -
                         Songwriters
MUSICAL ARTIST TYPES   Pop - Punk - Rock
CLIENT LIST   The Twilight Singers
SUBMISSION POLICY   No unsolicited CDs

Brian McPherson . . . . .President

*MEDIA CREATURE MUSIC

PO Box 39500
Los Angeles, CA 90039
PHONE 323-468-8888
FAX 323-468-8889
EMAIL . . . . .info@mediacreature.com
WEB SITE . . . . .www.mediacreature.com

Sharal Churchill . . . . .President/CEO
Renee Travis . . . . .VP
J.P. Lacasse .Copyright Coordinator

MEDIA FIVE ENTERTAINMENT

3005 Brodhead Rd., Ste. 170
Bethlehem, PA 18020
PHONE 610-954-8100
FAX 610-954-8118
WEB SITE . . . . .www.mediafiveent.com
TYPES OF CLIENTS   Musical Artists
MUSICAL ARTIST TYPES   Alternative - Pop - Rock
CLIENT LIST   July for Kings - Condition K - Bridges
                         and a Bottle - K8
SUBMISSION POLICY   No unsolicited material

David Sestak . . . . .President
Gregory Epler . . . . .VP

MANAGERS

METROPOLITAN TALENT
1515 Broadway, 36th Fl.
New York, NY 10036
PHONE 212-277-7171
FAX 212-719-9396
TYPES OF CLIENTS Musical Artists
MUSICAL ARTIST TYPES Rock
CLIENT LIST Art Garfunkel - Bob Weir & Ratdog - Vertical Horizon - Bruce Hornsby - Jen Chapin
SUBMISSION POLICY Referral only
COMMENTS Associated with Hybrid Recordings

John Scher . . . . .President
Al Cafaro . . . . .Co-CEO
Doug Thaler . . . . .Sr. VP, Artist Management
Bridget Nolan . . . . .Director, Artist Management
Kristen Hill . . . . .Director, Artist Management

MIXED MEDIA ENTERTAINMENT COMPANY
395 Totten Pond Rd., Ste. 301
Waltham, MA 02154
PHONE 800-647-3404/781-547-0085
FAX 781-547-0109
EMAIL . . . . .showbizmanager@aol.com
TYPES OF CLIENTS Musical Artists - Variety Artists
SUBMISSION POLICY No unsolicited material

Michael Glynn . . . . .Manager

MOGUL ENTERTAINMENT GROUP, INC./
GLOBAL COOLING MUSIC, INC.
PO Box 16665
Beverly Hills, CA 90209
PHONE 310-278-8877/310-395-2386
FAX 310-395-2387
EMAIL . . . . .g@globalcoolingmusic.com
TYPES OF CLIENTS Musical Artists - Music Producers
MUSICAL ARTIST TYPES Alternative - Pop - Rock
CLIENT LIST Chinese Whispers - Submix

George Ghiz . . . . .President
Paul Mitchell . . . . .VP

MOIR/MARIE ENTERTAINMENT
16101 Ventura Blvd., Ste. 325
Encino, CA 91436
PHONE 818-995-8707
FAX 818-995-8705
EMAIL .freaks@moirmarie.com

Lisa Marie . . . . .Owner
Brenda McDowell . . . . .Manager
Nicole Simon . . . . .Manager
Nadia Monet Betkouchar . . . . .Executive Assistant

MONOTONE, INC.
820 Seward St.
Hollywood, CA 90038
PHONE 323-308-1818
FAX 323-308-1819
CLIENT LIST The White Stripes - The Shins - Autolux - The Standard

Ian Montone . . . . .Manager

MOREY MANAGEMENT GROUP
9255 Sunset Blvd., Ste. 600
Los Angeles, CA 90069
PHONE 310-205-6100
FAX 310-205-6199
TYPES OF CLIENTS Musical Artists - Music Producers - Songwriters
MUSICAL ARTIST TYPES All Genres
CLIENT LIST America - Clint Black - Macy Gray - Julio Iglesias - Michael Feinstein - Pointer Sisters - FFH - Joshua Payne
SUBMISSION POLICY No unsolicited submissions
COMMENTS Entertainment consulting

Jim Morey . . . . .President
Jason Morey . . . . .VP
Robert Collin . . . . .Manager
Erin Edwards . . . . .Manager
Andrew Leff . . . . .Manager

MORRIS MANAGEMENT GROUP
181 19th Ave. South
Nashville, TN 37203
PHONE 615-321-5025
FAX 615-327-0312
TYPES OF CLIENTS Musical Artists

Dale Morris . . . . .President
Clint Hyam . . . . .VP

MPL COMMUNICATIONS, INC.
41 W. 54th St.
New York, NY 10019
PHONE 212-246-5881
FAX 212-246-7852
EMAIL . . . . .info@mplcommunications.com
WEB SITE . . . . .www.mplcommunications.com
TYPES OF CLIENTS Musical Artists - Lyricists - Songwriters
MUSICAL ARTIST TYPES All Genres
CLIENT LIST Paul McCartney
SUBMISSION POLICY No unsolicited material
COMMENTS Music Supervisors; A&R Reps

William Porricelli . . . . . . .Sr. VP, Promotions/New Product Development
Peter Silvestri . . . . .VP, Licensing & Royalties
Jessica Bumsted . . . . .Creative Services

*MUSIC GALLERY INTERNATIONAL MANAGEMENT
3400 Montrose Blvd., Ste. 300
Houston, TX 77006
PHONE 713-942-7441/310-954-7571
FAX 713-942-2566/323-655-9889
EMAIL . . . . .maxbrooks@hpmgmt.com
WEB SITE . . . . .www.musicgalleryinternational.com
TYPES OF CLIENTS Musical Artists
CLIENT LIST Twin Method - Eyes of Fire - Platoon 13 - The Numb Ones - Motograter - Santa's Missile - London After Midnight - Porselain - Vladamir
COMMENTS West Coast office: 8391 Beverly Blvd., Ste. 482, Los Angeles, CA 90048

Shawn Barusch . . . . .Rainmaker, Worldwide
Max Brooks . . . . .A&R/GM
Ron Goudie .Producer/A&R, Europe
Mike Peel . . . . .A&R, Europe & USA
Rodger Smith . . . . .Tour Management/Production/A&R/Marketing
Tito Picon .Tour Manager/A&R
Dana Dark . . . . .Office Manager/Group Management
Michael Farrel . . . . .Independent Radio Promotions (Los Angeles)
Peter Herman . . . . .Marketing & Artist Relations (Germany/France)
Andrew Spalding . . . . .Artist Relations/Touring/Promotions
Lindsay Ann Waistell . . . . .Marketing & Artist Management (UK)
Tracy Greene . . . . .Publicity & Marketing (Los Angeles)
Bob Nalbandian . . . . .A&R/Marketing (Los Angeles)
Dave London . . . . .Radio/A&R/Marketing/Webmaster

MUSIC WORLD ENTERTAINMENT/SANCTUARY URBAN ARTIST MANAGEMENT INC.
1505 Hadley St.
Houston, TX 77002
PHONE 713-772-5175
FAX 713-772-3034
EMAIL . . . . .mathew.knowles@sanctuarygroup.com
TYPES OF CLIENTS   Musical Artists - Music Producers
MUSICAL ARTIST TYPES   Gospel - Pop - R&B - Urban
CLIENT LIST   Beyoncé - Destiny's Child - Kelly
                       Rowland - Michelle Williams - PLAY -
                       Solange - Ted & Sheri - Trin-i-tee 5:7 -
                       Mario - Mason Road - L'il J Xavier -
                       Bama Boyz - Project Popstar - Maurice
                       Joshua - Nelly - D-12 - Amerie - Fat Joe
                       - Floetry - Tweet - Bizarre - St. Lunatics

Mathew Knowles . . . . . . .CEO, Music World/President, Sanctuary Urban
                                           Artist Management Inc.
Johnna Lister . . . . .VP/General Manager
Lin Almanza . . . . .Sr. Executive Assistant to Mathew Knowles

MYRACLEWORKS STUDIOS MANAGEMENT AND PHOTOPUBLICITY
PO Box 252084
Los Angeles, CA 90025
PHONE 310-283-7700
EMAIL . . . . .info@myracleworks.com
WEB SITE . . . . .www.myracleworks.com
TYPES OF CLIENTS   Musical Artists
SUBMISSION POLICY   Not accepting new talent
COMMENTS   Also represents WWE Wrestling Talent

Aaron D. Settipane . . . . .Owner, Photographer
Jerry Pena . . . . .Executive VP, Information Services

JACK NELSON & ASSOCIATES
PO Box 3718
Los Angeles, CA 90078
PHONE 818-755-8825
FAX 818-755-1587
TYPES OF CLIENTS   Musical Artists
CLIENT LIST   Jeffrey Osborne

Jack Nelson . . . . .Manager

NETTWERK MANAGEMENT
8730 Wilshire Blvd., Ste. 304
Beverly Hills, CA 90211
PHONE 310-855-0668/310-855-0643
FAX 310-855-0674/310-855-0658
WEB SITE . . . . .www.nettwerk.com
TYPES OF CLIENTS   Musical Artists - Music Producers -
                        Film/TV Composers - Songwriters -
                        Studio Engineers/Technicians
MUSICAL ARTIST TYPES   Adult Contemporary - Alternative -
                        Bluegrass - Christian - Dance/DJ - Folk -
                        Latin - Pop - Punk - Rap/Hip-Hop - Rock
CLIENT LIST   Barenaked Ladies - Chantal Kreviazuk -
                        Chris Fortier - Dayna Manning - Devlins
                        - Dido - Gob - Groove Armada - Jet Set
                        Satellite - Kendall Payne - Maren Ord -
                        Matthew Jay - Moist - Noel Sanger - Poe
                        - Sarah McLachlan - Avril Lavigne -
                        Griffin House - Nathan - Susan Enan -
                        Leigh Nash - Jars of Clay - Butterfly
                        Boucher - Stereophonics - Rachael
                        Yamagata - Kristian Leontiou - Swollen
                        Members - Treble Charger - Tom McRae
SUBMISSION POLICY   Accepts general submissions
COMMENTS   Offices in Vancouver, New York, Boston
                        & London

Terry McBride . . . . .CEO
Dana Childs . . . . .Producer Management
(Continued)

NETTWERK MANAGEMENT (Continued)
Jay Clark . . . . .Artist Management
Alia Fahlborg .Producer Management
Dan Garnett . . . . .Artist Management
Matt Griffin . . . . .Producer Management
Peter Leak . . . . .Artist Management (peterl@nettwerk.com)
Nicole Martin .Artist Management
Martie Muhoberac . . . . .Producer Management
Coleen Novak .Artist Management
Patrick Pocklington . . . . .Artist Management
Janet Weir . . . . .Artist Management
Aaron Wilhelm .Producer Management
Naomi Recania . . . . .Office Manager/Assistant
Hayley Chilton . . . . .Assistant
Carolina Gazzolo . . . . .Assistant
Heidi Rhoades . . . . .Assistant

NEW HEIGHTS ENTERTAINMENT, LLC
PO Box 8489
Calabasas, CA 91372
PHONE 818-992-7910
EMAIL . . . . .alanmelina@newheightsent.com
TYPES OF CLIENTS   Musical Artists - Music Producers -
                        Songwriters
MUSICAL ARTIST TYPES   All Genres
CLIENT LIST   Adam Anders - Amadeus - CedSolo -
                        Jonnie Davis - David Frank - Michael Jay
                        - Ron Lawrence - Joshua Thompson -
                        Reed Vertelney - RoomForTwo
SUBMISSION POLICY   No unsolicited material
COMMENTS   Represents production companies,
                        record labels, publishing companies

Alan Melina . . . . .President
Laurent Besencon . . . . .Partner

NOVI ENTERTAINMENT LLC
201 N. Robertson Blvd., Ste. 205
Beverly Hills, CA 90211
PHONE 310-858-6650
FAX 310-858-6879
EMAIL . . . . .pspriggs@novi-media.com
SECOND EMAIL . . . . .kevinl@novi-media.com
WEB SITE . . . . .www.novi-media.com
CLIENT LIST   Dead Celebrity Status - George Lynch -
                        redlightmusic - Five Foot Thick - Jon
                        Heintz - Adema - Paloalto - Jessic

Paul D. Spriggs . . . . .Manager
Kevin Lee . . . . .Manager
Jessica Davis .Executive Assistant
Sarah Shoup . . . . .Executive Assistant

NSI MANAGEMENT
PO Box 197
Merrimac, MA 01860
PHONE 978-346-4577
FAX 978-346-7608
EMAIL . . . . .info@nsimgmt.com
TYPES OF CLIENTS   Musical Artists
MUSICAL ARTIST TYPES   Folk - Rock
CLIENT LIST   Black Rebel Motorcycle Club (co-man-
                        age) - Sam Phillips

Dan Russell . . . . .President
Tony Wallace . . . . .General Manager

MANAGERS

OK MANAGEMENT
311 N. Robertson Blvd., Ste. 709
Beverly Hills, CA 90211
PHONE 310-535-1647
FAX 310-888-2810
MUSICAL ARTIST TYPES   Rock
CLIENT LIST   Bob Dylan - Paul Simon - Amos Lee
SUBMISSION POLICY   No unsolicited material accepted

Jeff Kramer . . . . .Manager
Cindy Osbourne . . . . .Manager

ONE MOMENT MANAGEMENT, INC.
PO Box 55156
Sherman Oaks, CA 91413
PHONE 818-735-0382
FAX 818-337-2243
WEB SITE . . . . .www.onemomentmgmt.com
TYPES OF CLIENTS   Musical Artists
MUSICAL ARTIST TYPES   Punk - Rock
CLIENT LIST   Matchbook Romance - Name Taken -
                           Roses Are Red - Plain White T's -
                           Millencolin - The Beautiful Mistake -
                           Darren Doane

Lance Brown . . . . .Founder/CEO/Manager
Mike Kamisky . . . . .Manager
Megan MacLeod . . . . .Manager
Aaron "Tex" Finnin . . . . .Endorsements & Special Projects

OPEN ALL NITE ENTERTAINMENT
9636 McLennan Ave.
Northridge, CA 91413
PHONE 818-892-5564
FAX 775-263-3526
EMAIL . . . . .info@openallnite.com
WEB SITE . . . . .www.openallnite.com
TYPES OF CLIENTS   Musical Artists
MUSICAL ARTIST TYPES   Country - Jazz - World
CLIENT LIST   Grant Geissman - Shapes (featuring
                           Roger Burn) - Larry Steen World Jazz
                           Ensemble - Matthew Van Doran -
                           Joanne Tatham - Random Traveler -
                           Hugh James Hardman - Richard Bowden
COMMENTS   Music consultant for artist development;
                           Label development; Marketing

Steve Belkin . . . . .President/Manager

OPEN DOOR MANAGEMENT
865 Via de la Paz, Ste. 365
Pacific Palisades, CA 90272
PHONE 310-459-2559
FAX 310-454-7803
EMAIL . . . . .info@opendoormanagement.com
WEB SITE . . . . .opendoormanagement.com
TYPES OF CLIENTS   Musical Artists - Film/TV Composers
MUSICAL ARTIST TYPES   Jazz - World
SUBMISSION POLICY   No unsolicited material accepted
COMMENTS   Jazz and World musicians and singers
                           only

Bill Traut . . . . .President/Manager

ORIGINAL ARTISTS
826 Broadway, 4th Fl.
New York, NY 10003
PHONE 212-254-1234
FAX 212-254-3121
EMAIL .oa@originalartists.com
TYPES OF CLIENTS   Musical Artists - Music Producers - Music
                           Supervisors - Film/TV Composers -
                           Lyricists - Songwriters - Studio Vocalists -
                           Studio Engineers/Technicians
CLIENT LIST   Bobby McFerrin - Paula Cole

Linda Goldstein . . . . .President

SHARON OSBOURNE MANAGEMENT
9292 Civic Center Dr.
Beverly Hills, CA 90210
PHONE 310-859-7761
FAX 310-859-2897
EMAIL . . . . .info@divinerecordings.com
TYPES OF CLIENTS   Musical Artists
MUSICAL ARTIST TYPES   Metal - Pop - Rock
CLIENT LIST   Ozzy Osbourne - Kelly Osbourne - Black
                           Sabbath - Osbourne Family

Sharon Osbourne . . . . .CEO
Michael Guarracino . . . . .General Manager
John Fenton . . . . .Director, Operations
Dana Kiper . . . . .Accounting

OVERBROOK ENTERTAINMENT
450 N. Roxbury Dr., 4th Fl.
Beverly Hills, CA 90210-4218
PHONE 310-432-2400
FAX 310-432-2401
TYPES OF CLIENTS   Musical Artists
CLIENT LIST   Robin Thicke - Javier - Wicked Wisdom -
                           Will Smith - McKinney

James Lassiter . . . . .President/CEO
Will Smith . . . . .Partner
John Dukakis . . . . .Manager
Miguel Melendez . . . . .Manager

*PALO DURO MANAGEMENT
PO Box 810
Ooltewah, TN 37363
PHONE 423-238-3848/866-725-6387
FAX 423-238-3760
TYPES OF CLIENTS   Musical Artists
MUSICAL ARTIST TYPES   Country
CLIENT LIST   Ed Burleson - Morrison-Williams - Two
                           Tons of Steel

Chris Thomas . . . . .Manager

PANACEA ENTERTAINMENT
13587 Andalusia Dr.
Camarillo, CA 93012
PHONE 805-491-9400
EMAIL . . . . .juno@panacea-ent.com
TYPES OF CLIENTS   Musical Artists - Music Producers -
                           Film/TV Composers - Songwriters
SUBMISSION POLICY   No unsolicited submissions

Eric Gardner . . . . .Chairman/CEO

PARK PLACE MANAGEMENT
922 S. Barrington Ave., Ste. 305
Los Angeles, CA 90049
PHONE 310-826-8126
EMAIL . . . . .info@parkplace99.com
TYPES OF CLIENTS   Musical Artists - Music Producers -
        Lyricists - Songwriters - Variety Artists -
        Comedians

Eric Parkinson . . . . .Owner/Manager

DAVID PASSICK ENTERTAINMENT
162 Fifth Ave., Ste. 1005
New York, NY 10010
PHONE 646-336-6465
FAX 646-336-6865
TYPES OF CLIENTS   Musical Artists - Music Producers -
        Film/TV Composers - Lyricists
CLIENT LIST   Morningwood - Game Rebellion - Jill
        Sobule - Richard Bona - Stephanie
        McKay - Descemer Bueno - Angie Aparo
        - Jim Bogia - Phil Galdston - Balewa
        Muhammad - Salme Dahlstrom

David Passick .President (passick@dpent.net)
Eddie Appelbaum . . . . .Manager
Jack Leitenberg . . . . .Manager (okaybabe@aol.com)
Matthew Morgan . . . . .Manager
Matt Vogel . . . . .Manager (matt@dpent.net)

PAT'S MANAGEMENT COMPANY
5900 Wilshire Blvd., Ste. 1720
Los Angeles, CA 90036
PHONE 310-786-4900
FAX 310-777-2192
MUSICAL ARTIST TYPES   Pop - Rock
CLIENT LIST   All-American Rejects - Charlie Morris -
        Goo Goo Dolls - Green Day - Mars

Pat Magnarella . . . . .Partner, Music
Chris Allen . . . . .Manager
John Dehais . . . . .Manager
Nick Fishbaugh . . . . .Assistant
Tyler Willingham . . . . .Assistant

PHANTOM MANAGEMENT
2500 NW 23rd St.
Boca Raton, FL 33434
PHONE 561-870-3603
FAX 561-482-1867
EMAIL . . . . .talent@phantom-management.com
WEB SITE . . . . .www.phantom-management.com
TYPES OF CLIENTS   Musical Artists - Music Producers -
        Film/TV Composers - Songwriters -
        Studio Musicians - Studio
        Engineers/Technicians
MUSICAL ARTIST TYPES   Adult Contemporary - Alternative - Latin
        - Pop - Rock
CLIENT LIST   Alex Bach - Menudo - Waking Season

Cary Reichbach . . . . .Manager
Barry Solomon . . . . .Manager
Jeff Weiner . . . . .Manager
Jerry Brenner . . . . .Manager
Richard Brusca . . . . .Assistant

THE DEREK POWER COMPANY, INC.
818 N. Doheny Dr., Ste. 1003
Los Angeles, CA 90069
PHONE 310-550-0770
FAX 310-550-6292
EMAIL . . . . .iampower@pacbell.net
SECOND EMAIL . . . . .iampower2003@yahoo.com
WEB SITE www.artists4film.com
TYPES OF CLIENTS   Musical Artists - Film/TV Composers
SUBMISSION POLICY   No unsolicited material

Ilene Kahn Power . . . . .Manager
Derek Power . . . . .Manager
Jeremy Kahn . . . . .VP, New Media

POWER STEERING
2850 Ocean Park Blvd., Ste. 300
Santa Monica, CA 90405
PHONE 818-905-5343/631-324-4821
FAX 631-324-3251
EMAIL .psmgt@optonline.net
WEB SITE . . . . .www.supertramp.com
TYPES OF CLIENTS   Musical Artists
MUSICAL ARTIST TYPES   Adult Contemporary
CLIENT LIST   Rick Davies - Supertramp
SUBMISSION POLICY   No unsolicited material accepted

Susan Davies . . . . .President

PRECISION MANAGEMENT, INC.
110 Coliseum Crossing, Ste. 158
Hampton, VA 23666
PHONE 800-275-5336, x0381042
FAX 757-249-8507
EMAIL . . . . .precisionmanagement@netzero.com
WEB SITE . . . . .www.pmmusicgroup.com
TYPES OF CLIENTS   Musical Artists - Music Producers -
        Songwriters
CLIENT LIST   Nastacia 'Nazz' Kendall - Darius Brooks
        - J-Trend and Ko'sha - David Broom
COMMENTS   Also represents hosts, sports personalities
        and voice-over artists

Cappriccieo M. Scates, MBA . . . . .Director, Operations
Marco Ramsey . . . . .CFO
Eric Daniels .Sr. VP, A&R
Don Lewis .Director, Marketing
Alicia Cooper . . . . .Distribution Coordinator
St. Paul Williams . . . . .Staff Assistant

JOE PRIESNITZ MANAGEMENT
PO Box 5249
Austin, TX 78763
PHONE 512-472-5435
FAX 512-472-5717
EMAIL .jpamaustin@aol.com
TYPES OF CLIENTS   Musical Artists
MUSICAL ARTIST TYPES   Country - Folk - Rock - Roots
SUBMISSION POLICY   No unsolicited material

Joe Priesnitz . . . . .Manager

*PRIMAL SCREAM MUSIC/RUBBERBAND
12200 Olympic Blvd., Ste. 400
Los Angeles, CA 90064
PHONE 310-481-1884
FAX 310-481-9957
WEB SITE . . . . .www.primalscreammusic.com
TYPES OF CLIENTS   Film/TV Composers

Nicole Dionne . . . . .Creative Director
Scott Burton . . . . .Technical Manager
Hans Hitner . . . . .Assistant Producer

MANAGERS

PRINCIPLE MANAGEMENT
250 W. 57th St., Ste. 2120
New York, NY 10019
PHONE 212-765-2330
FAX 212-765-2372
TYPES OF CLIENTS   Musical Artists
MUSICAL ARTIST TYPES   Rock
CLIENT LIST   U2 - PJ Harvey - The Rapture
COMMENTS   Dublin office: 30/32 Sir John Rogerson's Quay, Dublin 2, Ireland

Keryn Kaplan . . . . .Director (New York)
Steve Matthews . . . . .Director (Dublin)
Paul McGuinness .Manager (Dublin)
Shan Lui . . . . .New York

*PROJECT PRODUCERS, LLC
3283 Lawrence St.
Detroit, MI 48206
PHONE 313-883-1118/313-743-7532
EMAIL .toya@projectproducers.com
SECOND EMAIL . . . . .projectproducers@msn.com
WEB SITE . . . . .www.projectproducers.com
SECOND WEB SITE . . . . .www.kemistryrecords.com
TYPES OF CLIENTS   Musical Artists - Music Producers - Lyricists - Songwriters
MUSICAL ARTIST TYPES   R&B - Rap/Hip-Hop - Roots
CLIENT LIST   KEM - Black Bottom Collective
COMMENTS   Also represents photographers including Cybelle Codish

Toya Hankins . . . . .CEO
Andrea Ashford . . . . .Adminstrative & Event Manager
Will Burnett . . . . .Stage Manager/Production Assistant
Dean Watts . . . . .Tour/Production Manager
Carla Rivers . . . . .Public Relations Specialist

PUNCH ENTERPRISES
567 Purdy St.
Birmingham, MI 48009
PHONE 248-642-0910
FAX 248-642-4626
TYPES OF CLIENTS   Musical Artists - Music Producers
MUSICAL ARTIST TYPES   Rap/Hip-Hop - Rock
CLIENT LIST   Kid Rock - Bob Seger & The Silver Bullet Band

Punch Andrews . . . . .President

Q PRIME MANAGEMENT, INC.
729 Seventh Ave., 16th Fl.
New York, NY 10019
PHONE 212-302-9790
FAX 212-302-9589
EMAIL . . . . .info@qprime.com
WEB SITE . . . . .www.qprime.com
TYPES OF CLIENTS   Musical Artists
MUSICAL ARTIST TYPES   Bluegrass - Country - Folk - Pop - Rock
CLIENT LIST   Metallica - Red Hot Chili Peppers - Shania Twain - Garbage - Nina Gordon - Fountains of Wayne - Lostprophets - Nickel Creek - Gillian Welch - The Living Things - Muse - The Dead 60s

Cliff Burnstein . . . . .Co-Founder
Peter Mensch . . . . .Co-Founder
Marc Reiter . . . . .No Title
Michael Caldarella . . . . .No Title
Warren Christensen . . . . .No Title (Los Angeles)
Erica Collins .No Title (Los Angeles)
Tony DiCioccio . . . . .No Title
Gayle Fine . . . . .No Title
Jewly Hight . . . . .No Title (Nashville)
Michelle Munz . . . . .No Title (Los Angeles)
Holland Nix . . . . .No Title (Nashville)
John Peets . . . . .No Title (Nashville)

(Continued)

Q PRIME MANAGEMENT, INC. (Continued)
Randi Seplow . . . . .No Title
Matt Surrena .No Title (Los Angeles)
Sue Tropio . . . . .No Title
H.M. Wollman . . . . .No Title
Christine Zebrowski . . . . .No Title

R.E.M. ATHENS LTD.
PO Box 8032
Athens, GA 30603
PHONE 706-353-6689
FAX 706-546-6069
TYPES OF CLIENTS   Musical Artists
CLIENT LIST   R.E.M.

Bertis Downs . . . . .Manager

RON RAINEY MANAGEMENT
315 S. Beverly Dr., Ste. 407
Beverly Hills, CA 90212
PHONE 310-277-4050/310-557-0661
FAX 310-557-8421
EMAIL . . . . .rrainey425@aol.com
WEB SITE . . . . .www.ronrainey.com
TYPES OF CLIENTS   Musical Artists
MUSICAL ARTIST TYPES   Blues - Pop - Rock - Roots
CLIENT LIST   Melvin Seals - Kid Creole & The Coconuts - Ten Years After - The Fixx - The Marshall Tucker Band - Alvin Lee
SUBMISSION POLICY   Referrals only

Ron Rainey . . . . .President
Greg Lewerke . . . . .Manager
Kevin Moorehouse . . . . .Director, Business Affairs

PATRICK RAINS & ASSOCIATES (PRA)
1255 Fifth Ave., Ste. 7-K
New York, NY 10029
PHONE 212-860-3233
FAX 212-860-5556
EMAIL . . . . .pra@prarecords.com
WEB SITE . . . . .www.prarecords.com
TYPES OF CLIENTS   Musical Artists
MUSICAL ARTIST TYPES   Jazz - Pop - Rock
CLIENT LIST   David Sanborn - Jonatha Brooke - Joe Sample - The Crusaders - Tower of Power - Melissa Errico
SUBMISSION POLICY   No unsolicited material

Patrick Rains . . . . .President

REBEL WALTZ, INC.
31652 Second Ave.
Laguna Beach, CA 92651
PHONE 949-499-4497
FAX 949-499-4496
WEB SITE . . . . .www.rebelwaltz.com
TYPES OF CLIENTS   Musical Artists - Music Producers - Film/TV Composers - Songwriters
MUSICAL ARTIST TYPES   Pop - Rock
CLIENT LIST   Mike Ness - No Doubt - Social Distortion - The Offspring - Hot Hot Heat - Josh Freese - Tim Armstrong - Nine Inch Nails - Gwen Stefani

Jim Guerinot . . . . .Manager
Greg Gallardo . . . . .Accountant
Eric Fermin . . . . .Assistant Manager
Lisa Kidd . . . . .Assistant Manager
Paris Montoya . . . . .Assistant Manager
Shane Trulin .Assistant Manager
Larry Tull . . . . .Assistant Manager

RED LIGHT MANAGEMENT

PO Box 1911
Charlottesville, VA 22903
PHONE 540-456-4900
FAX 540-456-4933
TYPES OF CLIENTS   Musical Artists
MUSICAL ARTIST TYPES   Dance/DJ - Rock - World
CLIENT LIST   Dave Matthews Band - Sasha - North Mississippi Allstars - Blue Merle - Vusi Marhlasela - John Butler Trio (co-manage) - Graham Colton Band (co-manage) - Gomez - Army of Me - Los Lobos - Trey Anastasio - Camper Van Beethoven (co-manage) - Cracker (co-manage) - Jamison Parker - Mike Gordon - Underoath - The Starting Line - UNKLE (co-manage) - James Lavelle (co-manage) - O.A.R. (co-manage) - Robert Randolph & The Family Band (co-manage)

Coran Capshaw . . . . .Manager
Chris Tetzeli . . . . .Manager
Randy Nichols . . . . .Manager
Randy Reed . . . . .Manager
Chris Sampson . . . . .Manager
Adam Foley . . . . .Assistant
Sarah Tucker . . . . .Assistant

REFUGEE MANAGEMENT INTERNATIONAL

209 10th Ave. South, Ste. 347
Nashville, TN 37203
PHONE 615-256-6615
FAX 615-256-6717
WEB SITE . . . . .www.refugeemanagement.com
TYPES OF CLIENTS   Musical Artists
MUSICAL ARTIST TYPES   Country

Stuart Dill . . . . .CEO

RELUCTANT MANAGEMENT

c/o Strike Up the Brand
PO Box 49709
Los Angeles, CA 90049-9998
PHONE 310-472-9121
TYPES OF CLIENTS   Musical Artists
CLIENT LIST   Kate Bush
SUBMISSION POLICY   Not accepting submissions

Brad Gelfond . . . . .Principal

RIGHT SIDE MANAGEMENT

PO Box 250806
New York, NY 10025
PHONE 212-586-1223
FAX 646-390-6360
EMAIL . . . . .leftside@bway.net
TYPES OF CLIENTS   Musical Artists
CLIENT LIST   Claudette Sierra - Chris Botti - Tony Levin

Marc Silag . . . . .President

ERIC ROSEN MANAGEMENT

1 Woodhill Court
Huntington Station, NY 11746
PHONE 917-548-7798
EMAIL . . . . .erosenmusicman@yahoo.com
TYPES OF CLIENTS   Musical Artists
CLIENT LIST   From Safety to Where - Aaron Brady
COMMENTS   Represents up-and-coming musical acts

Eric Rosen . . . . .Manager

ROSEN MUSIC CORP.

717 El Medio Ave.
Pacific Palisades, CA 90272
PHONE 310-230-6040
FAX 310-230-4074
EMAIL .steven@rosenmusiccorp.com
WEB SITE .www.rosenmusiccorp.com
TYPES OF CLIENTS   Music Producers - Music Supervisors Lyricists - Songwriters - Studio Engineers/Technicians
MUSICAL ARTIST TYPES   All Genres
CLIENT LIST   Guy Roche - Rob Chiarelli - Julian Raymond - Hakan Glarte - Exposé - Itchycoo - Bruce Brody - Kevin Kendrick
SUBMISSION POLICY   No unsolicited material

Steven Rosen . . . . .President

MARK ROTHBAUM & ASSOCIATES

PO Box 2689
Danbury, CT 06813
PHONE 203-792-2400
FAX 203-791-9014
EMAIL . . . . .mrai2400@aol.com
TYPES OF CLIENTS   Musical Artists
MUSICAL ARTIST TYPES   Country
CLIENT LIST   Willie Nelson

Mark Rothbaum . . . . .Manager

RPM MANAGEMENT

2214 Elliston Place, Ste. 304
Nashville, TN 37203
PHONE 615-256-1980
FAX 615-256-1134
TYPES OF CLIENTS   Musical Artists
MUSICAL ARTIST TYPES   Adult Contemporary - Country
CLIENT LIST   Tim McGraw - Holly Williams - The Warren Brothers - Brice Long - Hot Apple Pie
SUBMISSION POLICY   No unsolicited material accepted

Scott Siman . . . . .President (ssiman@rpmweb.com)
Kelly Wright .Sr. VP (kwright@rpmweb.com)
Teresa Siman . . . . .VP (tbsiman@rpmweb.com)
Chris Caravacci . . . . . .Assistant to President (ccaravacci@rpmweb.com)
Jaynie Chowning . . . . .Reception (jchowning@rpmweb.com)
Maria Eckhardt . . . . .No Title (meckhardt@rpmweb.com)
Sam Ramage . . . . .No Title (sramage@rpmweb.com)

RPM MUSIC PRODUCTIONS

48 W. 10th St., Ste. B
New York, NY 10011
PHONE 212-246-8126
FAX 212-397-1371
TYPES OF CLIENTS   Musical Artists
CLIENT LIST   Tony Bennett
SUBMISSION POLICY   No unsolicited material accepted

Danny Bennett . . . . .President
Sandi Rogers . . . . .General Manager
Dario Dalla Lasta . . . . .Assistant to Danny Bennett

RZO

250 W. 57th St.
New York, NY 10107
PHONE 212-765-7550
FAX 212-245-2356
TYPES OF CLIENTS   Musical Artists

Joseph Rascoff . . . . .Manager
Bill Zysblat . . . . .Manager

MANAGERS

SAFFYRE MANAGEMENT
23401 Park Sorrento, #38
Calabasas, CA 91302
PHONE 818-842-4368
EMAIL . . . . .ebsaffyre@yahoo.com
TYPES OF CLIENTS   Musical Artists - Songwriters
MUSICAL ARTIST TYPES   Adult Contemporary - Alternative - Rock
SUBMISSION POLICY   Call or email for permission to submit

Esta Bernstein . . . . .President

BILL SAMMETH ORGANIZATION
9255 Sunset Blvd., Ste. 600
Los Angeles, CA 90069
PHONE 310-275-6193
FAX 310-441-5111
EMAIL . . . . .curt@bsorg.com
TYPES OF CLIENTS   Musical Artists - Variety Artists
MUSICAL ARTIST TYPES   Alternative - Blues - Folk - Jazz - Pop -
                         R&B - Rock
CLIENT LIST   KC & the Sunshine Band - Joan Rivers

Bill Sammeth . . . . .Manager
Curt Burich . . . . .Manager

SANCTUARY ARTIST MANAGEMENT/THE SANCTUARY GROUP
9255 Sunset Blvd., Ste. 200
Los Angeles, CA 90069
PHONE 310-205-5000
FAX 310-205-5001
WEB SITE . . . . .www.sanctuarygroup.com
TYPES OF CLIENTS   Musical Artists
MUSICAL ARTIST TYPES   All Genres
CLIENT LIST   A Dozen Furies - Alanis Morissette -
                         Beyoncé - Bizarre - Boston - Brave
                         Captain - Bruce Dickinson - Buddahead
                         - Candice - Chris Neil - Courtney Love -
                         D12 - Danny Rampling - Dave Navarro
                         - Destiny's Child - Ed Harcourt - Elton
                         John - Eve - Fat Joe - Fightstar -
                         Fleetwood Mac - Floetry - From Autumn
                         to Ashes - Fu Manchu - Funeral for a
                         Friend - Gizmachi - Gorkys - Zygotic
                         Mynci - Groove Armada - Guns N'
                         Roses - Hope Sandoval - Iron Maiden -
                         Jack's Mannequin - James Blunt -
                         Jamiroquai (North America Only) -
                         Jane's Addiction - Jazze Pha - Jimmy
                         Chamberlin Complex - Joss Stone - Kelis
                         - Kelly Rowland - Kenna - Kinky - Kurt
                         Cobain Estate - Lil' Wayne - Luna Halo -
                         Manic Street Preachers - Mario - Marti
                         Pellow - Mastodon - Michelle Williams -
                         Mick Fleetwood - Morrissey - Murphy
                         Lee - Ned Sherrin - Nelly - Nirvana (co-
                         managed) - Overseer - Paulina Rubio -
                         Pras Michel - Rachel Fuller - Rob
                         Dickinson - Robert Plant - Scott Stapp -
                         Shapeshifters - Sierra Swan - Slayer -
                         Slipknot - Solange Knowles - Soledad
                         Brothers - Something Corporate - St.
                         Lunatics - Stateless - Super Furry Animals
                         - Teairra Mari - The Cult - The Departure
                         - The Who - Tommy Lee - Trackboyz -
                         Trin-I-Tee 5:7 - Tweet - UB40 - Victor
                         Calderone - Whitesnake -
                         Yourcodenameis: Milo
COMMENTS   New York office: 75 Ninth Ave, New
                         York, NY 10011, Phone: 212-599-
                         2757, Fax: 212-599-2747; London
                         office: Sanctuary House, 45-53 Sinclair
                         Rd., London, W14 0NS, UK, Phone: 44-
                         20-7602-6351, Fax: 44-20-7603-5941

(Continued)

SANCTUARY ARTIST MANAGEMENT/THE SANCTUARY GROUP (Continued)
Deke Arlon . . . . .Manager
Jamie Arlon . . . . .Manager
Peter Asher . . . . .Manager
Keith Bradley . . . . .Manager
Cory Brennan . . . . .Manager
Rick Canny . . . . .Manager
Mitch Clark . . . . .Manager
Blain Clausen . . . . .Manager
Bill Curbishley . . . . .Manager
Larissa Friend . . . . .Manager
Jeremy Geffen . . . . .Manager
Frank Gironda . . . . .Manager
Martin Hall . . . . .Manager
Caresse Henry . . . . .Manager
Todd Interland . . . . .Manager
Craig Jennings . . . . .Manager
Jaison John . . . . .Manager
Nick John . . . . .Manager
Mathew Knowles . . . . .Manager
Alun Llwyd . . . . .Manager
Marty Maidenberg . . . . .Manager
Merck Mercuriadis . . . . .Manager
Kristen Mulderig . . . . .Manager
Frank Presland . . . . .Manager
Irene Richter . . . . .Manager
Robert Rosenberg . . . . .Manager
Rick Sales . . . . .Manager
Rod Smallwood . . . . .Manager
Carl Stubner . . . . .Manager
Amy Touma . . . . .Manager
Corey Wagner . . . . .Manager
Jed Weitzman . . . . .Manager

SANTANA MANAGEMENT
PO Box 10348
San Rafael, CA 94912
PHONE 415-458-8130
FAX 415-458-8145
WEB SITE . . . . .www.santana.com
TYPES OF CLIENTS   Musical Artists - Songwriters
MUSICAL ARTIST TYPES   Pop - Rock
CLIENT LIST   Carlos Santana - Santana
SUBMISSION POLICY   Approval needed in advance of submit-
                         ting

Kevin Chisholm . . . . .Tour Director
Kitsaun King . . . . .Publicity/Merchandising
Adam Fells . . . . .Artist Relations
Peggy Nederlof . . . . .Administrative Assistant

STEVEN SCHARF ENTERTAINMENT
126 E. 38th St.
New York, NY 10016
PHONE 212-779-7977 x3905
FAX 212-725-9681
EMAIL . . . . .sscharf@carlinamerica.com
SECOND EMAIL . . . . .jmizrachi@carlinamerica.com
WEB SITE . . . . .www.stevenscharf.com
TYPES OF CLIENTS | Musical Artists - Music Producers - Music Supervisors - Film/TV Composers
MUSICAL ARTIST TYPES | Alternative - Blues - Folk - Jazz - Pop - Rap/Hip-Hop - Rock - Roots - Urban - World
CLIENT LIST | Barry Goldberg - Michael Vail Blum - Askold Buk - Shane "The Doctor" Faber - Mark Hukezalie - Mark Suozzo - Mark Wilder - Miles Wilkinson - Emily Curtis - Ali & the Electric Insect - Darran Falcone - Chicago Blues Reunion - Intercooler - Julius "Juice" Butty - Gezax - Stirling - Blue Raincoats
SUBMISSION POLICY | Call or email first
COMMENTS | Licensing

Steven Scharf . . . . .President
Jon Mizrachi . . . . .Assistant

CHERYL SCOTT MANAGEMENT
25 Breezy Hill Rd.
Canton, CT 06019
PHONE 860-693-0891
FAX 860-693-8270
TYPES OF CLIENTS | Musical Artists - Film/TV Composers - Songwriters
MUSICAL ARTIST TYPES | Alternative - Children's - Rock
CLIENT LIST | The Tirebiter Band - Abbey Road - The Nifty Fifties Band - Zachary Scott - Phala Tracy
SUBMISSION POLICY | Not taking new clients
COMMENTS | NCOPM

Cheryl A. Scott . . . . .Personal Manager/President

LINDSAY SCOTT MANAGEMENT
8899 Beverly Blvd., Ste. 600
Los Angeles, CA 90048
PHONE 310-860-1040
FAX 310-860-1042
TYPES OF CLIENTS | Musical Artists
MUSICAL ARTIST TYPES | Adult Contemporary - Alternative - Pop - R&B - Rock
CLIENT LIST | Tina Turner - Cher

Lindsay Scott . . . . .President
Zana Benson . . . . .Executive Assistant

RON SHAPIRO MANAGEMENT AND CONSULTING LLC
135 W. 26th St., Ste. 4A
New York, NY 10001
EMAIL . . . . .info@ronshapiro.com
WEB SITE .www.ronshapiro.com
TYPES OF CLIENTS | Musical Artists
COMMENTS | Consults labels and promoters

Ron Shapiro . . . . .Owner
Elliott Baer . . . . .Manager
Joe Hegleman . . . . .Manager

SHARPE ENTERTAINMENT SERVICES, INC.
683 Palmera Ave.
Pacific Palisades, CA 90272
PHONE 310-230-2100
FAX 310-230-2109
TYPES OF CLIENTS | Musical Artists - Music Producers - Film/TV Composers - Songwriters
MUSICAL ARTIST TYPES | Adult Contemporary - Alternative - Pop - Rock
SUBMISSION POLICY | No unsolicited material

Wil Sharpe . . . . .Owner/Manager
Frances Sharpe . . . . .Marketing

SILVA ARTIST MANAGEMENT (SAM)
722 Seward St.
Los Angeles, CA 90038
PHONE 323-856-8222
FAX 323-856-8256
TYPES OF CLIENTS | Musical Artists
MUSICAL ARTIST TYPES | Alternative
CLIENT LIST | Beastie Boys - Foo Fighters - Jimmy Eat World - Tenacious D - The Mars Volta - AFI - Sonic Youth - Beck - Probot - Jackson - Trainwreck

John Silva .Owner/President
John Cutcliffe . . . . .General Manager
David Summers . . . . .VP, Operations
Michele Fleischli . . . . .Manager
Michael Meisel . . . . .Manager
Gaby Skolnek . . . . .Manager
Kristen Welsh . . . . .Manager
Jennifer Carrizo . . . . .Assistant
Jennifer Hall . . . . .Assistant
Chris Kelly . . . . .Assistant
Steve Kohn . . . . .Assistant
Eduardo Trujillo .Messenger

BILL SILVA MANAGEMENT
8981 Sunset Blvd., Ste. 303
West Hollywood, CA 90069
PHONE 310-246-5200/310-246-5220
FAX 310-858-0648
EMAIL . . . . .aya@billsilva.net
WEB SITE . . . . .www.billsilvamanagement.com
TYPES OF CLIENTS | Musical Artists - Film/TV Composers - Lyricists - Songwriters
CLIENT LIST | Margaret Cho - Bruce Daniels - David Pack - Raul Midón - Snowhite - Jason Mraz - John Hogan (Songwriting) - Dropping Daylight

Bill Silva .President/CEO
Matt Cohen . . . . .Manager
Aya Taguchi . . . . .Manager
Kurt Willms . . . . .Manager
Jerry Lindahl . . . . .Music Licensing
Glenn Miller . . . . .New Media & Brand Licensing
Amanda Harrison . . . . .Tour Marketing
Mike Walker . . . . .COO

SUSAN SILVER MANAGEMENT
SEE Atmosphere Artist Management

MANAGERS

SIMMONS AND SCOTT ENTERTAINMENT, LLC/
LAIKA ENTERTAINMENT, LLC

4110 W. Burbank Blvd.
Burbank, CA 91505
PHONE .818-556-3345/818-557-7570
FAX 818-556-3315/818-557-7555
EMAIL . . . . .tucker@nx10-31.com
WEB SITE . . . . .www.simmonsandscott.com
SECOND WEB SITE . . . . .www.laikaentertainment.com

TYPES OF CLIENTS	Musical Artists - Music Producers - Film/TV Composers - Songwriters
MUSICAL ARTIST TYPES	All Genres
CLIENT LIST	Laura Turner - Michelle Stucker - David Lyndow Huff

Carl Scott . . . . .Partner/Manager
Jon Simmons . . . . .Partner/Manager
Tucker Williamson . . . . .Partner/Manager
Molly Sweet . . . . .Manager

PAUL SIMON MUSIC

1619 Broadway, Ste. 500
New York, NY 10019
PHONE 212-541-7571
FAX 212-582-7607

MUSICAL ARTIST TYPES	Adult Contemporary - Folk - Pop
CLIENT LIST	Paul Simon

C. WINSTON SIMONE MANAGEMENT

140 W. 57th St., Ste. 13-B
New York, NY 10019
PHONE 212-974-5322
FAX 212-974-3988
EMAIL .wsimone@destonsongs.com

TYPES OF CLIENTS	Musical Artists
CLIENT LIST	Desmond Child - Michael Beinhorn

C. Winston Simone . . . . .Manager
David Simone . . . . .Manager
Maggie Reinhart . . . . .Manager
Erika Simonelli . . . . .Assistant

SINGERMAN ENTERTAINMENT

1601 Cloverfield Blvd., 2nd Fl., South Tower
Santa Monica, CA 90404
PHONE 310-255-8867
FAX 562-908-7973
EMAIL . . . . .tsingerman@aol.com

TYPES OF CLIENTS	Musical Artists
MUSICAL ARTIST TYPES	Alternative - Metal - Pop - Punk - Rock
CLIENT LIST	Motörhead - Pure Rubbish - Zebrahead - Sepultura
SUBMISSION POLICY	Accepts unsolicited material

Todd Singerman . . . . .Manager
Shelly Berggren . . . . .Manager
Tom Maher . . . . .Manager

CHRIS SMITH MANAGEMENT

21 Camden St., 5th Fl.
Toronto, ON M5V1V2 Canada
PHONE 416-362-7771
FAX 416-362-6648
EMAIL . . . . .info@chrissmithmanagement.com
WEB SITE . . . . .www.chrissmithmanagement.com

TYPES OF CLIENTS	Musical Artists
MUSICAL ARTIST TYPES	Alternative - Dance/DJ - Pop - R&B - Rap/Hip-Hop - Reggae - Rock - Urban
CLIENT LIST	Jacksoul - Jarvis Church - Jelleestone - Nelly Furtado - Simon & Milo - Tamia - Fefe Dobson - The Philosopher Kings - Kris Kelli - K-OS - YOGIE

Chris Smith . . . . .President
Blair Holder . . . . .Lawyer
Ray Hammond . . . . .Manager
Rose Slanic . . . . .Manager

SO WHAT MEDIA & MANAGEMENT

264 W. 91st St.
New York, NY 10024
PHONE 212-877-9631
FAX 212-877-9735
EMAIL . . . . .sowhatinfo@aol.com

TYPES OF CLIENTS	Musical Artists
MUSICAL ARTIST TYPES	Adult Contemporary - Pop - Rock
CLIENT LIST	Cyndi Lauper - Simply Red - The Mooney Suzuki

Lisa Barbaris . . . . .Manager
Cathy Zorgo . . . . .Assistant

SOLID MUSIC COMPANY

2230 Stanley Hills Dr.
Los Angeles, CA 90046
PHONE 323-654-6085
FAX 323-654-6086
EMAIL . . . . .solidmusic@sbcglobal.net
WEB SITE . . . . .www.solidmusic.net

CLIENT LIST	The Dan Band - The Outline - Fielding - Matt Mahassey - Chris Fudurich - Tim Harkins - DJ Kev E Kev

David Surnow . . . . .President

SONIC MANAGEMENT

3112 Washington Blvd.
Marina del Rey, CA 90292
PHONE 310-578-1617
FAX 310-578-1657
EMAIL . . . . .info@sonicmanagement.com
WEB SITE . . . . .www.sonicmanagement.com

TYPES OF CLIENTS	Musical Artists - Music Producers - Songwriters
CLIENT LIST	Chris Pierce - Slow Train Soul - The Yards - AM Radio - Last Day of April
SUBMISSION POLICY	No unsolicited material

Ben Laski . . . . .Founder

SOUND CITY ENTERTAINMENT

15456 Cabrito Rd.
Van Nuys, CA 91406
PHONE 818-787-6436
FAX 818-787-3981

TYPES OF CLIENTS	Musical Artists - Variety Artists

Tom Skeeter . . . . .President

SPOT LIGHT MUSIC, INC.
PO Box 1949
Lawrenceville, GA 30046
PHONE 770-822-1036
FAX 770-822-9902
EMAIL . . . . .info@slcomedy.com
SECOND EMAIL . . . . .mandrews@slcomedy.com
WEB SITE .www.spotlightentertainment.com
SECOND WEB SITE .www.slcomedy.com

TYPES OF CLIENTS	Musical Artists - Music Producers - Songwriters - Comedians
MUSICAL ARTIST TYPES	Adult Contemporary - Gospel - Pop - R&B - Rap/Hip-Hop
CLIENT LIST	Faith 14:29

Michael Andrews . . . . .Talent Manager/Agent
Charles Williams . . . . .Marketing, Sales & Promotions
Larry "Doc" Elliot . . . . .Radio Promotions & Marketing
Charles Jackson . . . . .Promotions & Marketing

SRO MANAGEMENT INC.
189 Carlton St.
Toronto, ON M5A 2K7 Canada
PHONE 416-923-5855
FAX 416-923-1041
EMAIL . . . . .sro-anthem@sro-anthem.com
WEB SITE . . . . .www.sro-anthem.com
SECOND WEB SITE . . . . .www.anthementertainmentgroup.com

TYPES OF CLIENTS	Musical Artists
CLIENT LIST	Rush - The Tea Party

Ray Danniels . . . . .President
Pegi Cecconi . . . . .VP
Shelley Nott . . . . .Publicity/Touring

GARY STAMLER MANAGEMENT
3055 Overland Ave., Ste. 200
Los Angeles, CA 90034
PHONE 310-838-1995
FAX 310-838-9280

TYPES OF CLIENTS	Musical Artists - Music Producers
MUSICAL ARTIST TYPES	All Genres
CLIENT LIST	Daniel Powter - Mitchell Froom - Tchad Blake - Waltham - The Ditty Bops - Lalaine

Gary Stamler . . . . .No Title
Nancy Sefton . . . . .No Title

STARKRAVIN' MANAGEMENT
20501 Ventura Blvd., Ste. 217
Woodland Hills, CA 91364
PHONE 818-587-6801
FAX 818-587-6802
EMAIL . . . . .bcmclane@aol.com
WEB SITE . . . . .www.benmclane.com

TYPES OF CLIENTS	Musical Artists - Music Producers - Songwriters
MUSICAL ARTIST TYPES	All Genres
SUBMISSION POLICY	Accepts unsolicited material

B.C. McLane, Esq. . . . . .No Title

STC ENTERTAINMENT
5627 Sepulveda Blvd., Ste. 205
Van Nuys, CA 91411
PHONE 818-787-4065
FAX 818-787-4194
EMAIL . . . . .stc@stcent.com

TYPES OF CLIENTS	Musical Artists - Music Producers - Songwriters
MUSICAL ARTIST TYPES	All Genres
CLIENT LIST	L.A. Guns - Slaughter - Warrant - Great White - Eric Gales - Morgan Grace - Taylor Hawkins/The Coattail Writers - Corey Feldman - Veruca Salt - Red Letter Print - Nelson
COMMENTS	Also theatrical representation

Obi Steinman . . . . .Manager
Scott Carlson . . . . .Manager

STERLING ARTIST MANAGEMENT
11054 Ventura Blvd., Ste. 285
Studio City, CA 91604
PHONE 818-907-5556
FAX 818-907-5558
EMAIL .mark@sterlingartist.com
WEB SITE . . . . .www.sterlingartist.com

TYPES OF CLIENTS	Musical Artists - Music Producers - Songwriters - Studio Engineers/Technicians
MUSICAL ARTIST TYPES	Adult Contemporary - Country - Folk - Pop - Rock - Roots
CLIENT LIST	Janet Robin - Rebecca Simone - Shelley Campbell - Julie Neumark - Betty Power; Producers: John Dexter - Chris Fuhrman - Dan Marfisi - William Pearson; Mix Engineer: Tony Phillips

Mark Sterling . . . . .Owner/Manager
Kathy Stanton . . . . .Manager

THE STERLING/WINTERS COMPANY
10877 Wilshire Blvd., Ste. 1550
Los Angeles, CA 90006
PHONE 310-557-2700
FAX 310-557-1722

TYPES OF CLIENTS	Musical Artists

Erik Sterling . . . . .COO
Jason Winters . . . . .Vision Strategist
Jon Carrasco . . . . .Executive VP
Stephen Roseberry . . . . .Sr. VP/Head, Talent/Marketing
Steve Rosenblum . . . . .Sr. VP, Corporate
Rocco Ingemi . . . . .VP, Brand Management
Konrad Leh . . . . .VP, Talent Department
Miles Robinson . . . . .VP/Executive Assistant to Jon Carrasco
Tony Carnot . . . . .Art Director
Richard Morales . . . . .Director, Communications
Jim Scalfani . . . . .Director, Project Management
Joel Blitz . . . . .Administration
Georgia DeCaro . . . . .Administration
Dee Rockoff . . . . .Administration
Mitch Sternard .Research & Development
Ruben Torres . . . . .Marketing
Zulma Ponce . . . . .Executive Assistant to Erik Sterling
Yesenia Morales . . . . .Executive Assistant to Stephen Roseberry

HARRIET STERNBERG MANAGEMENT
4530 Gloria Ave.
Encino, CA 91436
PHONE 818-906-9600
FAX 818-906-1723
EMAIL . . . . .mgrbabe@aol.com
TYPES OF CLIENTS   Musical Artists - Film/TV Composers - Songwriters
MUSICAL ARTIST TYPES   Rock
CLIENT LIST   Delbert McClinton - Spinal Tap
SUBMISSION POLICY   No unsolicited material

Harriet Sternberg . . . . .President

STEVLAND MORRIS MUSIC
4616 W. Magnolia Blvd.
Burbank, CA 91505
PHONE 323-877-8383
FAX 818-508-7863
TYPES OF CLIENTS   Musical Artists
CLIENT LIST   Stevie Wonder

Milton Hardaway . . . . .Manager/Publicist

STEVE STEWART MANAGEMENT
10 Universal City Plaza, Ste. 2000
Universal City, CA 91608
PHONE 818-753-2380
FAX 818-753-2303
WEB SITE . . . . .www.stevestewart.com
TYPES OF CLIENTS   Musical Artists
MUSICAL ARTIST TYPES   Alternative - Hardcore - Pop - Rock
CLIENT LIST   Screaming Trees/Mark Lanegan - The Sun - Paige Lewis - 84 National

Steve Stewart . . . . .President
Brian Klein . . . . .Manager

STIEFEL ENTERTAINMENT
21650 Oxnard St., Ste. 1925
Woodland Hills, CA 91367
PHONE 310-275-3377
FAX 310-271-5175
EMAIL . . . . .stiefelent@aol.com
TYPES OF CLIENTS   Musical Artists
CLIENT LIST   Rod Stewart

Arnold Stiefel . . . . .CEO

STILETTO ENTERTAINMENT
PO Box 45348
Los Angeles, CA 90045
PHONE 310-957-5757
FAX 310-957-5758
EMAIL . . . . .firstinitiallastname@stilettoentertainment.com
WEB SITE . . . . .www.stilettoentertainment.com
TYPES OF CLIENTS   Musical Artists - Music Producers - Songwriters
MUSICAL ARTIST TYPES   All Genres
CLIENT LIST   Barry Manilow - Karrin Allyson - Diane Schurr - Kimberly Locke - Sara Gazarek - Jimmy Demers - Matt Dusk - Natalie Loftin - Jim Verraros - Jason & DeMarco - Nemesis - Oliver Future

Garry Kief . . . . .President (x220)
Rob Kief .Executive VP (x226)
Douglas Senecal . . . . .General Manager (x234)
David Britz . . . . .VP, Artist Development (x215)
Jerry Sharell . . . . .VP, Artist Development (x260)
John Adams . . . . .VP, Marketing (x258)
Libby Fabro . . . . .VP, Operations (x252)
Lynn Michelson . . . . .VP, Business Services (x220)
Mark Grove . . . . .VP, Television (x432)
Troy Queen . . . . .VP, Television (x431)
(Continued)

STILETTO ENTERTAINMENT (Continued)
Kenny Pyle . . . . .Director, Business Affairs (x281)
Kirsten Kief . . . . .Director, Business Services (x229)
Chris Walters . . . . .Director, Marketing (x216)
Sara Zickuhr . . . . .Director, Creative Services (x253)
Michael Hattrup . . . . .Manager, International Marketing (x238)
Ruth Bryant . . . . .Manager, Business Services (x222)
Sacha Bambadji . . . . .Manager, Production (x206)
Ken Romero . . . . .Casting Supervisor (x214)
James Nadeau . . . . .Casting Supervisor (x209)
Stephanie Hengstenberg . . . . .Casting Supervisor (x218)
Kim Kvardfordt . . . . .Production Supervisor (x255)
JR White . . . . .Production Supervisor (x221)
Ken Leist . . . . .Production Supervisor (x208)
Sean Bryant . . . . .Warehouse Supervisor (x400)
Adam Kief . . . . .Assistant Production Manager (x238)
Vikki Thomas . . . . .Business Services Representative (x237)
Thami Schorr . . . . .Executive Assistant (x211)
Helena Ngo . . . . .Assistant Manager (x212)

*STRATEGIC ARTIST MANAGEMENT
1100 Glendon Ave., Ste. 1000
Los Angeles, CA 90024
PHONE 310-208-7882
FAX 310-208-7881
TYPES OF CLIENTS   Musical Artists
CLIENT LIST   Anastacia - Clay Aiken - Dixie Chicks - Miranda Lambert

Simon Renshaw . . . . .Principal/Manager
Gayle Boulware . . . . .Manager
Marion Kraft . . . . .Manager
JoAnn Burnside . . . . .Marketing & Promotion Manager
Kat Darnell . . . . .Jr. Manager
Yamile Fernandez . . . . .Jr. Manager
Natalie Miller . . . . .Jr. Manager

TALENT HOUSE
7336 Santa Monica Blvd., Ste. 699
Los Angeles, CA 90046
PHONE 323-938-4692
FAX 323-938-6152
EMAIL . . . . .thetalenthouse@aol.com
TYPES OF CLIENTS   Musical Artists - Film/TV Composers - Lyricists
CLIENT LIST   April March - The Presidents of the United States of America - Bicycle Music - Thick Records - Ultimatum Music - Original Productions - Powerman 5000
SUBMISSION POLICY   No unsolicited material
COMMENTS   Music for film and TV placement only

Staci Slater . . . . .Owner/President
Andrea Becker . . . . .Office Manager/Coordinator

TALENT SOURCE
1560 Broadway, Ste. 1308
New York, NY 10036
PHONE 212-764-2001
FAX 212-730-2706
EMAIL . . . . .talentsource@tciartists.com
TYPES OF CLIENTS   Musical Artists - Variety Artists
MUSICAL ARTIST TYPES   All Genres
CLIENT LIST   Bo Diddley - Wilson Pickett

Margo Lewis . . . . .President
Faith Fusillo . . . . .VP
Chris Tuthill . . . . .Associate

TAXI
5010 N. Parkway Calabasas, Ste. 200
Calabasas, CA 91302-2556
PHONE 818-222-2464/800-458-2111
FAX 818-888-8811
WEB SITE . . . . .www.taxi.com
TYPES OF CLIENTS   Musical Artists - Film/TV Composers -
                         Songwriters
MUSICAL ARTIST TYPES   All Genres
SUBMISSION POLICY   Must be a Taxi member

Michael Laskow . . . . .President
Chris Baptiste . . . . .Director, Film/TV
Cathy Genovese . . . . .Director, A&R
Clint McBay . . . . .Director, A&R

*TEITELL MANAGEMENT
3966 Cochran St., Ste. 76
Simi Valley, CA 93063
PHONE 805-306-9326
FAX 805-306-9326
EMAIL . . . . .teitellmgt@aol.com
SECOND EMAIL . . . . .bruce@spankycheese.com
WEB SITE . . . . .www.spankycheese.com

Bruce A. Teitell . . . . .Owner
Leslie B. Reece . . . . .VP

BILL THOMPSON MANAGEMENT
2051 Third St.
San Francisco, CA 94107
PHONE 415-431-3301
FAX 415-431-2128
EMAIL . . . . .thomps2051@aol.com
TYPES OF CLIENTS   Musical Artists
CLIENT LIST   Hot Tuna - Jefferson Airplane

Bill Thompson . . . . .President
Minda Miseray . . . . .Office Manager

THREE ARTIST MANAGEMENT
14260 Ventura Blvd., Ste. 201
Sherman Oaks, CA 91423
PHONE 818-380-0303
FAX 818-380-0484
EMAIL . . . . .info@threeam.net
WEB SITE . . . . .www.threeam.net
TYPES OF CLIENTS   Musical Artists - Film/TV Composers
CLIENT LIST   Henry Rollins - The Crystal Method - BT
                         - Paul Oakenfold - Grandaddy - The
                         Exies - Lemon Jelly

Richard Bishop . . . . .Manager/Owner
Suzann Brantner . . . . .Manager
Jon Clayden . . . . .Manager
Geoff Barnett . . . . .Day to Day Manager
Susan Ham . . . . .Executive Assistant
Melanie McBride .Executive Assistant

*THREE TWINS ENTERTAINMENT, INC.
PO Box 210
Staten Island, NY 10310
PHONE 888-383-1088
EMAIL . . . . .threetwinsent@aol.com
WEB SITE . . . . .www.threetwinsentertainment.com
TYPES OF CLIENTS   Musical Artists
MUSICAL ARTIST TYPES   All Genres
COMMENTS   Submissions accepted via mail or email;
                         See Web site prior to submitting via
                         email

John Elias . . . . .President/CEO

THRIVE MUSIC/THRIVE PICTURES
1024 N. Orange Dr., Ste. 100
Los Angeles, CA 90038
PHONE 323-308-3555
FAX 323-308-3556
EMAIL . . . . .info@thrivemusic.com
WEB SITE . . . . .www.thrivemusic.com
TYPES OF CLIENTS   Musical Artists
MUSICAL ARTIST TYPES   Alternative - Dance/DJ
CLIENT LIST   Paul Oakenfold - Sandra Collins -
                         Sandra Kleinenberg - Seb Fontaine -
                         Taylor Hawkins - The Coattail Riders
SUBMISSION POLICY   Submissions accepted via US mail
COMMENTS   Record company; Licensing/Clearance

Ricardo Vinas . . . . .President
Lee Kurisu . . . . .General Manager
Adam Merims . . . . .Development
Peter Torres . . . . .A&R
Austin Beltran . . . . .Assistant/Officer Manager

TKO ARTIST MANAGEMENT
1107 17th Ave. South
Nashville, TN 37212
PHONE 615-383-5017
FAX 615-292-3328
EMAIL . . . . .tk@tkoartistmanagement.com
TYPES OF CLIENTS   Musical Artists
MUSICAL ARTIST TYPES   Country
CLIENT LIST   Toby Keith - Chris Le Doux - Mac
                         McAnally - Scotty Emerick - Western
                         Underground
SUBMISSION POLICY   No unsolicited material

T.K. Kimbrell . . . . .Manager
JoAnne Ritchey . . . . .Office Manager/Artist Relations
Taylor Shults . . . . .Artist Relations, Publishing
Mark Sissel . . . . .Artist Relations
Andy Frederick . . . . .Assistant
Amanda Joyner . . . . .Assistant
Cassie Petty . . . . .Assistant
Ali Weber . . . . .Publishing Assistant

TRACTOR BEAM MANAGEMENT & CONSULTING
PO Box 1591
New York, NY 10276-1591
PHONE 212-204-2490
FAX 646-536-4035
EMAIL . . . . .dan@tractor-beam.com
WEB SITE . . . . .www.tractor-beam.com
TYPES OF CLIENTS   Musical Artists - Music Producers - Music
                         Supervisors - Film/TV Composers -
                         Studio Engineers/Technicians
MUSICAL ARTIST TYPES   Alternative - Folk - Jazz - Pop - Punk -
                         Rock - Roots
CLIENT LIST   The Apples in Stereo - Robert Schneider
                         - Ezra Reich - The Klezmatics
SUBMISSION POLICY   No unsolicited materials

Dan Efram . . . . .Manager
Zaby Currie . . . . .Assistant

TRINIFOLD MANAGEMENT
12 Oval Rd.
London NW1 7DH United Kingdom
PHONE 44-20-7734-4480
FAX 44-20-7439-7394
WEB SITE . . . . .www.sanctuarygroup.com
TYPES OF CLIENTS   Musical Artists
MUSICAL ARTIST TYPES   Rock
CLIENT LIST   Judas Priest - Rachel Fuller - Robert Plant
                         - The Who - UB40
COMMENTS   A part of The Sanctuary Group

Bill Curbishley . . . . .Manager
Robert Rosenberg . . . . .Manager

MANAGERS

TRIPLE O PRODUCTIONS
12746 Kling St.
Studio City, CA 91604
PHONE 818-506-8356
FAX 818-980-6888
TYPES OF CLIENTS   Musical Artists
CLIENT LIST   Jackson Browne - Joel Rafael

Corrina Miller . . . . .Manager
Donald Miller . . . . .Manager

TRUE TALENT MANAGEMENT
9663 Santa Monica Blvd., Ste. 320
Beverly Hills, CA 90210
PHONE 310-560-1290
FAX 310-441-2005
EMAIL . . . . .jenniferhcd@truetalentmgmt.com
WEB SITE . . . . .www.truetalentmgmt.com
MUSICAL ARTIST TYPES Adult Contemporary - Alternative - Pop -
                      Rock
CLIENT LIST   Aidan Hawken - Elysia - Highwater
                      Rising - Alucard - Michael Miller
COMMENTS   NARAS - WIF

Jennifer Yeko . . . . .Manager, Music
Neil Forn, Esq. .In-House Counsel
Marianne Burns . . . . .Assistant Manager, Music

TSUNAMI ENTERTAINMENT
2525 Hyperion Ave.
Los Angeles, CA 90027
PHONE 323-210-2525
FAX 323-913-3197
EMAIL . . . . .info@tsunament.com
SECOND EMAIL . . . . .firstnamelastinitial@tsunament.com
WEB SITE . . . . .www.tsunament.com
TYPES OF CLIENTS   Musical Artists - Music Producers
MUSICAL ARTIST TYPES Alternative - Dance/DJ - Latin - Pop -
                      Punk - Rock - World
CLIENT LIST   Artists: The Von Bondies - Billy Corgan -
                      The Dandy Warhols - Sarah Brightman
                      (US) - Goldfrapp (US) - GusGus -
                      Ozomatli - Go Betty Go; Producers:
                      Bernd Burgdorf - Robert Carranza - Ken
                      Casey - Jez Colin/Latin Project - Steve
                      Fisk - Bon Harris - HyLo Productions -
                      Gareth Jones (US) - Linus of Hollywood -
                      John McEntire - Ted Nicely - Jason
                      Roberts - Clark Stiles - Swiss American
                      Federation - Bjorn Thorsrud - David
                      Tickle - Dave Trumfio - Chris Walla
SUBMISSION POLICY   No unsolicited material of any kind;
                      Industry referral only

Bruce Kirkland . . . . .CEO/President
John Babbitt . . . . .Artist Manager
Amy Blackman . . . . .Artist Manager
Adam Katz . . . . .Producer Manager
Matthew Larsen . . . . .Label Group Manager
Cael Kirkland .Touring/Production
Fiona Framey . . . . .Executive Assistant to President
Andy Valdez . . . . .Management Assistant

TURNER MANAGEMENT GROUP
374 Poli St.
Ventura, CA 93001
PHONE 805-585-0080
FAX 805-585-0081
EMAIL . . . . .info@turnermanagementgroup.com
TYPES OF CLIENTS   Musical Artists
MUSICAL ARTIST TYPES Jazz - Pop - R&B - Rock
CLIENT LIST   George Benson - Kirsten Profit

Dennis Turner . . . . .President
Stephanie Gonzalez . . . . .Manager
Lisa Pina . . . . .Executive Assistant

*TWENTY-FIRST ARTISTS
1 Blythe Rd.
London W14 0HG United Kingdom
PHONE 44-20-7348-4800
FAX 44-20-7348-4801
WEB SITE . . . . .www.sanctuarygroup.com
TYPES OF CLIENTS   Musical Artists
MUSICAL ARTIST TYPES Adult Contemporary - Pop
CLIENT LIST   Elton John - James Blunt
COMMENTS   A part of The Sanctuary Group

Keith Bradley . . . . .Manager
Todd Interland . . . . .Manager
Frank Presland . . . . .Manager

UNION ENTERTAINMENT GROUP INC.
PO Box 300
Mustang, OK 73064
PHONE 405-256-0325
FAX 405-256-0329
EMAIL . . . . .fowler@coxinet.net
WEB SITE . . . . .www.fowlerandassociates.com
TYPES OF CLIENTS   Musical Artists - Songwriters
MUSICAL ARTIST TYPES All Genres
CLIENT LIST   Pillar - subseven - Grits
COMMENTS   FKA Fowler & Associates

Jason Fowler . . . . .Manager
Lorraine Isbell . . . . .Assistant

V ENTERTAINMENT
PO Box 1704
Studio City, CA 91604
PHONE 818-761-0300
FAX 818-761-0363
EMAIL . . . . .ventertain@aol.com
TYPES OF CLIENTS   Musical Artists - Music Producers
COMMENTS   International Latin talent

Valentino Fazzari . . . . .CEO/President
Karen Medak . . . . .Manager
Paul Graham . . . . .Manager

VALOR ENTERTAINMENT
3342 Bonnie Hill Dr.
Los Angeles, CA 90068
PHONE 323-876-4046
FAX 866-281-8389
EMAIL . . . . .valorbb@mac.com
SUBMISSION POLICY   No unsolicited materials accepted
COMMENTS   Music management & production

Bruce L. Berman . . . . .President

VAL'S ARTIST MANAGEMENT
259 W. 30th St., 15th Fl.
New York, NY 10001
PHONE 212-760-5500
FAX 212-760-5505
WEB SITE . . . . .www.vamnation.com
TYPES OF CLIENTS   Musical Artists - Studio Vocalists
SUBMISSION POLICY   Mail CDs, photos, bios and/or resumes;
                      No drop-offs or office visits
COMMENTS   Licensing

Valerie Wilson Morris . . . . .Owner/President
Simone Goodwin . . . . .Manager
Michael Bove . . . . .Manager/West Coast Representative

MANAGERS

VECTOR MANAGEMENT

1607 17th Ave. South
Nashville, TN 37212
PHONE 615-269-6600/212-317-2323
FAX 615-269-6002/212-317-5983
EMAIL . . . . .info@vectormgmt.com

TYPES OF CLIENTS	Musical Artists
MUSICAL ARTIST TYPES	All Genres - Blues - Country - Folk - Pop - Rock - Roots
CLIENT LIST	.38 Special - Peter Cincotti - Shawn Colvin - Billy Currington - Emmylou Harris - John Hiatt - Jonny Lang - Kings of Leon - Lyle Lovett - Lynyrd Skynyrd - Michael McDonald - Buddy & Julie Miller - Patty Griffin - Trace Adkins - Van Zant - Old 97's - Rhett Miller - Steve Winwood - Damien Rice - Queen Latifah - Herbie Hancock - Angelique Kidjo - Bon Jovi - Big Fella - Hank Williams, Jr. - Josh Gracin - Matt Jenkins - Peter Cincotti - Secret Machines - Sister Hazel - Trisha Yearwood - Danielia Cotton - Seth James - Peter Frampton
SUBMISSION POLICY	No unsolicited material
COMMENTS	East Coast office: 113 E. 55th St., New York, NY 10022

Ken Levitan . . . . .Co-President
Jack Rovner . . . . .Co-President, Vector Recordings (NY)
Joel Hoffner . . . . .General Manager/Sales & Marketing
Lisa Arzt . . . . .Manager (NY)
John Dennis . . . . .Manager
Michelle Goldsworthy . . . . .Manager
Lisa Jenkins . . . . .Manager
Jake LaGrone . . . . .Manager
Andy Mendelsohn . . . . .Manager (NY)
Ross Schilling . . . . .Manager
Chris Stacey . . . . .Manager
Kathi Whitley . . . . .Manager
Emily Deaderick . . . . .Publicist
Beth Schackne . . . . .Assistant to Ken Levitan
Libby McCord . . . . .Assistant to Jack Rovner
Chris Clapp . . . . .Assistant
Nicole Porter . . . . .Receptionist

VELVET HAMMER MUSIC & MANAGEMENT GROUP

9911 W. Pico Blvd., Ste. 350 West
Los Angeles, CA 90035
PHONE 310-657-6161
FAX 310-659-0310
EMAIL . . . . .vhm@velvethammer.net
WEB SITE . . . . .www.streetwise.com

TYPES OF CLIENTS	Musical Artists
MUSICAL ARTIST TYPES	Rock
CLIENT LIST	Deftones - System of a Down - Rise Against - Taproot - Graditude - Micky Avelon - Republic

David Benveniste . . . . .President/CEO
Mark Wakefield . . . . .VP/Sr. Manager
Missy Worth . . . . .GM/Manager
Braden Asher . . . . .Manager
Graham Martin . . . . .Jr. Manager
Caroline Park . . . . .Publicity Coordinator

VIOLATOR MANAGEMENT

36 W. 25th St., 11th Fl.
New York, NY 10010
PHONE 646-486-8900
FAX 646-486-8929
WEB SITE . . . . .www.violator.com

TYPES OF CLIENTS	Musical Artists
MUSICAL ARTIST TYPES	Rap/Hip-Hop
CLIENT LIST	Busta Rhymes - Capone N Noreaga - Missy Elliott - Parental Advisory - Red Alert - 50 Cent - Clipse - Govenor - Kool DJ Red Alert - Lil Mo - Nore - Seven - Lil Scrappy

Chris Lighty . . . . .CEO
Mona Scott . . . . .President

TOM VITORINO MANAGEMENT, INC.

11606 Vimy Rd.
Granada Hills, CA 91344
PHONE 818-368-9060
FAX 818-368-9061

CLIENT LIST	Riders on the Storm - The Cult - Ian Astbury - Thin Lizzy - Pat Travers - Blue Murder

Tom Vitorino . . . . .Manager

W MANAGEMENT

266 Elizabeth St., Rm. 1A
New York, NY 10012
PHONE 212-274-8952
FAX 212-925-2937
EMAIL . . . . .wmgmt2@aol.com

TYPES OF CLIENTS	Musical Artists
MUSICAL ARTIST TYPES	Pop - Rock
CLIENT LIST	Doyle Bramhall II - Sheryl Crow - Todd Wolfe - Aphonic - Matt White - Antigone Rising
SUBMISSION POLICY	No unsolicited material

Stephen Weintraub . . . . .Manager
Pam Wertheimer . . . . .Manager
Pam Adams . . . . .Associate

THE ROBERT D. WACHS COMPANY

418 E. 59th St., Ste. 16B
New York, NY 10022
PHONE 212-935-9444
FAX 212-935-9229
EMAIL . . . . .wachsmgr@aol.com

TYPES OF CLIENTS	Musical Artists - Comedians
SUBMISSION POLICY	Referral preferred

Robert Wachs . . . . .No Title

WILLIAM F. WAGNER

14343 Addison St., Ste. 221
Sherman Oaks, CA 91423
PHONE 818-905-1033

TYPES OF CLIENTS	Musical Artists - Film/TV Composers - Songwriters
MUSICAL ARTIST TYPES	Country - Jazz - Pop
COMMENTS	Recording producer

William F. Wagner . . . . .Owner

MANAGERS

NORBY WALTERS
1100 Alta Loma Rd.
Los Angeles, CA 90069
PHONE 310-289-8660
FAX 310-289-0227
TYPES OF CLIENTS   Musical Artists - Songwriters
MUSICAL ARTIST TYPES   Pop - R&B - Urban

Norby Walters . . . . .Manager

WILHELMINA ARTIST MANAGEMENT
300 Park Ave. South
New York, NY 10010
PHONE 212-271-1606
FAX 212-271-1641
TYPES OF CLIENTS   Musical Artists
MUSICAL ARTIST TYPES   Pop
CLIENT LIST   Jessica Simpson

Jeff Schock . . . . .Director

WILKINS MANAGEMENT
323 Broadway
Cambridge, MA 02139
PHONE 617-354-2736
FAX 617-354-2396
EMAIL . . . . .info@wilkinsmanagement.com
TYPES OF CLIENTS   Musical Artists
MUSICAL ARTIST TYPES   Jazz
CLIENT LIST   Branford Marsalis - David Sánchez -
                          Harry Connick, Jr. - Joshua Redman

Ann Marie Wilkins . . . . .Owner
Maria Betro . . . . .Associate
Marilynn Davis . . . . .Associate
Sherry McAdams . . . . .Associate
Wayne Sharp . . . . .Associate

THE ERV WOOLSEY COMPANY
1000 18th Ave. South
Nashville, TN 37212
PHONE 615-329-2402
FAX 615-327-4917
TYPES OF CLIENTS   Musical Artists
MUSICAL ARTIST TYPES   Country
CLIENT LIST   George Strait - Lee Ann Womack -
                          Dierks Bentley

Erv Woolsey . . . . .CEO/Chairman
Connie Woolsey . . . . .President
Danny O'Brien . . . . .VP
Tom Cheney . . . . .Manager
Scott Kernhan . . . . .Manager
Dottie Oelhasen . . . . .Executive Assistant

WORLDS END
183 N. Martel Ave., Ste. 270
Los Angeles, CA 90036
PHONE 323-965-1540
FAX 323-965-1547
EMAIL . . . . .info@worldsend.com
WEB SITE . . . . .www.worldsend.com
TYPES OF CLIENTS   Music Producers
CLIENT LIST   Steve Lillywhite - Dave Sardy - The
                          Matrix - Matthew Gerrard - Nick Launay
                          - Tim Palmer - Rick Parker - Lou
                          Giordano

Sandy Robertson . . . . .Manager
Andrew Brightman . . . . .Manager

WRIGHT ENTERTAINMENT GROUP
424 Central Blvd., PMB 189
Orlando, FL 32801
PHONE 407-826-9100
FAX 407-826-9107
WEB SITE . . . . .www.wegmusic.com
TYPES OF CLIENTS   Musical Artists
MUSICAL ARTIST TYPES   Adult Contemporary - Christian - Pop -
                          R&B - Rap/Hip-Hop - Rock

Johnny Wright . . . . .CEO/President

WYNONNA INC.
PO Box 128229
Nashville, TN 37212
PHONE 615-790-8300
FAX 615-790-8222
WEB SITE . . . . .www.wynonna.com
TYPES OF CLIENTS   Musical Artists
MUSICAL ARTIST TYPES   Country
CLIENT LIST   Wynonna

Kerry Hansen . . . . .Manager/VP (kerryhansen@wynonna.com)
Rondal Richardson . . . . .General Manager (rondal@wynonna.com)

SECTION **B**

REPRESENTATION

- Agents
- Managers
- **Attorneys**

Asterisks (*) next to companies denote new listings.

ABRAMS GARFINKEL MARGOLIS BERGSON LLP
9229 Sunset Blvd., Ste. 710
Los Angeles, CA 90069
PHONE 310-300-2900/212-201-1170
FAX 310-300-2901/212-201-1171
EMAIL . . . . .babrams@agmblaw.com
WEB SITE . . . . .www.agmblaw.com
ENTERTAINMENT LAW SERVICES — Full Service Representation - Acquisitions & Mergers - Arbitration & Mediation - Contract Negotiation & Drafting - Copyright & Trademark Matters - Corporate Matters - Employment/Labor Law - Financing - First Amendment Issues - Intellectual Property Law - Libel & Privacy Matters - Licensing - Litigation - Misappropriation of Name, Voice, Likeness - Motion Picture & TV Law - Music Law - Partnerships/Joint Ventures - Right of Publicity - Royalty Law - Tax Law - Transactional Law
COMMENTS — Accounting and Management Services; Long Island office: 425 Broadhollow Rd., Ste. 203, Melville, NY 11747, phone: 631-777-2401, fax: 631-777-2402; Newport Beach office: 4100 Newport Place, Ste. 830, Newport Beach, CA 92660, phone: 949-250-8655, fax: 949-250-8656

William L. Abrams . . . . .Partner
Neil B. Garfinkel . . . . .Partner
Barry Margolis . . . . .Partner
Robert Bergson . . . . .Partner
Deron Colby . . . . .Partner
Michael J. Tulchiner . . . . .Partner
Shannon C. Hensley . . . . .Attorney
John Keating . . . . .Attorney
Caryn Kertzner . . . . .Attorney
Steve Matz . . . . .Attorney
Jonathan Misher . . . . .Attorney
Tina Palazzo-Fairweather . . . . .Attorney
Jaime Solomon . . . . .Attorney
Michael J. Twersky . . . . .Attorney
Michael J. Weiss . . . . .Attorney

IRA ABRAMS, ESQ.
5692B Fox Hollow Dr.
Boca Raton, FL 33486
PHONE .561-362-5212/828-262-9944
FAX 561-362-0245/828-262-9901
EMAIL . . . . .iraabrams@hotmail.com
ENTERTAINMENT LAW SERVICES — Arbitration & Mediation - Contract Negotiation & Drafting - Copyright & Trademark Matters - Intellectual Property Law - Music Law - Talent Representation
COMMENTS — Music industry representation; Mediator in major cases; Internet distribution

Ira Abrams . . . . .Partner

AKIN GUMP STRAUSS HAUER & FELD, LLP
2029 Century Park East, Ste. 2400
Los Angeles, CA 90067
PHONE 310-229-1000
FAX 310-229-1001
EMAIL .losangelesinfo@akingump.com
WEB SITE . . . . .www.akingump.com
ENTERTAINMENT LAW SERVICES — Full Service Representation - Copyright & Trademark Matters - Corporate Matters - Employment/Labor Law - Financing - Licensing - Litigation - Motion Picture & TV Law - Music Law - Partnerships/Joint Ventures - Tax Law
COMMENTS — Electronic games; Film & TV production; Distribution & Finance; Music Industry Live Event Production and Distribution; Sixteen offices worldwide

David A. Braun . . . . .Sr. Counsel (LA)
John Burke . . . . .Partner (LA)
Howard D. Fabrick . . . . .Partner (LA)
Steve Fayne . . . . .Partner (LA)
Channing D. Johnson . . . . .Partner (LA)
Lawrence D. Levien . . . . .Partner (DC)
Scott H. Racine . . . . .Partner (LA)
Marissa Román . . . . .Partner (LA)
Cecil Shenker . . . . .Partner (San Antonio)
James O. Thoma . . . . .Partner (Austin)
Jason Karlov . . . . .Counsel (LA)
Wilhelm E. Liebmann . . . . .Counsel (San Antonio)
Jonathan M. Wight . . . . .Counsel (LA)
Tuneen Chisolm . . . . .Associate (LA)
Alissa L. Morris . . . . .Associate (LA)

ALEXANDER NAU LAWRENCE & FRUMES & LABOWITZ, LLP
1925 Century Park East, Ste. 850
Los Angeles, CA 90067
PHONE 310-552-0035
FAX 310-552-0135
EMAIL . . . . .admin@anlf.com
WEB SITE . . . . .www.anlf.com
ENTERTAINMENT LAW SERVICES — Full Service Representation - Acquisitions & Mergers - Arbitration & Mediation - Contract Negotiation & Drafting - Corporate Matters - Financing - Licensing - Motion Picture & TV Law - Partnerships/Joint Ventures - Talent Representation - Transactional Law
COMMENTS — Financing and distribution matters; Executive employment agreements; Authors/publishing

Wayne Alexander . . . . .Partner
Robert Nau . . . . .Partner
Robert Lawrence . . . . .Partner
Howard Frumes . . . . .Partner
Edward Labowitz . . . . .Partner
Hope Toffel Mastras . . . . .Associate

ATTORNEYS

ALSCHULER GROSSMAN STEIN & KAHAN LLP
1620 26th St., 4th Fl., North Tower
Santa Monica, CA 90404-4060
PHONE 310-907-1000
FAX 310-207-2000
EMAIL . . . . .info@agsk.com
WEB SITE . . . . .www.agsk.com

ENTERTAINMENT LAW SERVICES	Arbitration & Mediation - Corporate Matters - Employment/Labor Law - Intellectual Property Law - Litigation - Talent Representation - Tax Law
COMMENTS	Representation of talent (film, television and music), distributors, production companies, managers and agents; Defamation; Right-of-Privacy and publicity violations; Labor Commission disputes

Stanton L. (Larry) Stein .Partner
Michael J. Plonsker . . . . .Partner, Co-Chair, Entertainment & Media Department
Yakub Hazzard . . .Partner, Co-Chair, Entertainment & Media Department
Melissa A. Addison .Associate
Matthew R. Belloni .Associate
Bennett A. Bigman . . . . .Partner
Tony D. Chen . . . . .Partner
Karen L. Dillon . . . . .Partner
Brooke H. Eisenhart . . . . .Associate
Melissa A. Fein . . . . .Associate
Daniel A. Fiore . . . . .Associate
Chad R. Fitzgerald .Associate
David S. Gubman . . . . .Partner
Marcia J. Harris . . . . .Partner
Stacy Weinstein Harrison . . . . .Of Counsel
Michael R. Heimbold .Partner
Lawrence C. Hinkle II . . . . .Partner
Thomas F. Kennedy . . . . .Associate
Andrew F. Kim . . . . .Partner
Sally S. Liu . . . . .Associate
Ann Loeb . . . . .Partner
Mark A. Neubauer . . . . .Partner
Mark D. Passin . . . . .Partner
Samuel R. Pryor . . . . .Partner
Samuel E. Rogoway . . . . .Associate
David R. Shraga . . . . .Associate
Jonathan E. Stern .Associate
Lauren Sudar . . . . .Associate
Bridgette Taylor . . . . .Partner
Mary Lee Wegner . . . . .Partner
Lee M. Weinberg . . . . .Partner

ALTSCHUL & OLIN, LLP
16133 Ventura Blvd., Ste. 1270
Encino, CA 91436
PHONE 818-990-1800
FAX .818-990-1429/818-479-9787

ENTERTAINMENT LAW SERVICES	Contract Negotiation & Drafting - Copyright & Trademark Matters - Intellectual Property Law - Licensing - Music Law - Partnerships/Joint Ventures - Royalty Law - Talent Representation - Transactional Law

David E. Altschul . . . . .Partner
Milton E. Olin Jr. . . . . .Partner
Jonathan B. Altschul . . . . .Attorney
Esther M. Rubin . . . . .Executive Assistant/Office Manager
Brandi Neeld . . . . .Executive Assistant

DENNIS ARDI, ATTORNEY AT LAW
340 N. Camden Dr., Ste. 300
Beverly Hills, CA 90210
PHONE 310-271-6900
FAX 310-271-6963
EMAIL . . . . .da@dennisardi.com

ENTERTAINMENT LAW SERVICES	Motion Picture & TV Law - Talent Representation

Dennis Ardi . . . . .Attorney at Law

ARNOLD & PORTER
777 S. Figueroa St.
Los Angeles, CA 90017
PHONE 213-243-4000
FAX 213-243-4199
WEB SITE . . . . .www.arnoldporter.com

ENTERTAINMENT LAW SERVICES	Contract Negotiation & Drafting - Copyright & Trademark Matters - Intellectual Property Law - Talent Representation
COMMENTS	New business structuring; Unfair competition matters; Telecommunications; East Coast office: 399 Park Ave., New York, NY 10022-4690, phone: 212-715-1000, fax: 212-715-1399; Offices in Washington DC, Denver, Brussells and London

Ronald L. Blanc . . . . .Partner
Ronald L. Johnston .Partner
Ronald D. Lee .Partner (DC)
Steve Parker . . . . .Partner (Northern VA)
Sol Rosenthal . . . . .Of Counsel

BAKER & HOSTETLER LLP, COUNSELLORS AT LAW
3200 National City Center
1900 E. 9th St.
Cleveland, OH 44114-3485
PHONE 216-621-0200
FAX 216-696-0740
WEB SITE .www.bakerlaw.com

ENTERTAINMENT LAW SERVICES	Acquisitions & Mergers - Arbitration & Mediation - Employment/Labor Law - Financing - First Amendment Issues - Intellectual Property Law - Libel & Privacy Matters - Licensing - Litigation - Motion Picture & TV Law - Music Law - Partnerships/Joint Ventures - Right of Publicity - Royalty Law - Talent Representation - Tax Law - Transactional Law
COMMENTS	For a complete listing of the firm's offices, services and attorneys, please visit Web site; West Coast office: 333 S. Grand Ave., Ste. 1800, Los Angeles, CA 90071-1523, ph: 213-975-1600, fax: 213-975-1740; East Coast office: 666 Fifth Ave., New York, NY 10103, ph: 212-589-4200, fax: 212-589-4201

Angela C. Agrusa . . . . .Partner
Penny M. Costa . . . . .Partner
Lawrence J. Gartner .Partner
Gary L. Gilbert . . . . .Partner
Nigel E. Jacques . . . . .Partner
Peter W. James . . . . .Partner
Helen B. Kim . . . . .Partner
Andrew Lurie . . . . .Partner
David C. Sampson . . . . .Partner
Kimberly M. Talley . . . . .Partner

(Continued)

ATTORNEYS

BAKER & HOSTETLER LLP, COUNSELLORS AT LAW
(Continued)

Teresa R. Tracy	Partner
Kimberly R. Wells	Partner
Cranston J. Williams	Partner
Gary York	Partner
Naomi Young	Partner
Lisa Hinchliffe	Of Counsel
Loura L. Alaverdi	Associate
Sean A. Andrade	Associate
André Y. Bates	Associate
Scott H. Bradford	Associate
Anthony S. Brill	Associate
Stephen Butler	Associate
Lisa I. Carteen	Associate
Gene A. Coppa	Associate
Stefanie M. Gushá	Associate
Carrie M. Hemphill	Associate
Tazamisha H. Imara	Associate
Lydia W. Lee	Associate
Robert W. Lofton	Associate
Devon K. McGranahan	Associate
Barbara B. Thompson	Associate
Shanaira F. Udwadia	Associate
Roger M. Vinayagalingam	Associate
Felicia A. Starr	Staff Attorney

BARNES MORRIS KLEIN MARK YORN BARNES & LEVINE
1424 Second St.
Santa Monica, CA 90401
PHONE 310-319-3900
FAX 310-319-3999
WEB SITE ....www.bmkylaw.com
ENTERTAINMENT LAW SERVICES   Full Service Representation

Michael Barnes	Partner
P. Kevin Morris	Managing Partner
Deborah Klein	Partner
Douglas Mark	Partner
Kevin Yorn	Managing Partner
Stephen Barnes	Partner
Jared Levine	Partner
David Krintzman	Partner
Todd Rubenstein	Partner
Jeff Endlich	Attorney
Corinne Farley	Attorney
David Ferreria	Attorney
Gregg Gellman	Attorney
Pamela Hicks	Attorney
Alexander Kohner	Attorney
Jennifer Massey	Attorney
Derek Reynolds	Attorney
Lawrence Kopeikin	Of Counsel

BELDOCK LEVINE & HOFFMAN, LLP
99 Park Ave., Ste. 1600
New York, NY 10016
PHONE 212-490-0400/800-275-4977
WEB SITE ....www.blhny.com
ENTERTAINMENT LAW SERVICES   Intellectual Property Law
COMMENTS   Ecommerce and computer law; Production, distribution and executive employment matters for film, TV, radio, music, theater and live events

Myron Beldock	Partner
Elliot L. Hoffman	Partner

BERGER KAHN GLADSTONE
4215 Glencoe Ave., 2nd Fl.
Marina del Rey, CA 90292
PHONE 310-821-9000
FAX 310-578-6178
EMAIL ....info@bergerkahn.com
SECOND EMAIL ....entertainment@bergerkahn.com
WEB SITE ....www.bergerkahn.com
ENTERTAINMENT LAW SERVICES   Full Service Representation - Contract Negotiation & Drafting - Copyright & Trademark Matters - Corporate Matters - Employment/Labor Law - Financing - Intellectual Property Law - Licensing - Litigation - Misappropriation of Name, Voice, Likeness - Motion Picture & TV Law - Music Law - Partnerships/Joint Ventures - Royalty Law - Talent Representation - Transactional Law
COMMENTS   Litigation in all entertainment law areas noted above; Packaging; Entertainment Insurance matters; Offices in Orange County and San Francisco Bay Area

Leon Gladstone	Principal/Founding Member
Craig Simon	Principal/Founding Member
Owen Sloane	Principal
Michael Aiken	Partner
Ronald Alberts	Partner
Patricia Campbell	Partner
Stephan Cohn	Partner
David Ezra	Partner
Steven Gentry	Partner
Arthur Grebow	Partner
James Henshall	Partner
Wayne Hersh	Partner
Ann Johnston	Partner
Lance LaBelle	Partner
Melanie Long	Partner
Arthur G. Meneses	Partner
Allen Michel	Partner
Jon Miller	Partner
Timothy Nicholson	Partner
Teresa Ponder	Partner
Janice Ramsay	Partner
Sherman Spitz	Partner
Marcy Tieger	Partner
Jason Wallach	Partner
Gene Weisberg	Partner
Arthur Willner	Partner
William Yee	Partner
Courtney Dillaplain	Attorney

BERLINER, CORCORAN & ROWE
1101 17th St., NW, Ste. 1100
Washington, DC 20036
PHONE 202-293-5555/301-570-1761
FAX 202-293-9035/301-570-4183
EMAIL ....jrose13@aol.com
WEB SITE ....www.bcr-dc.com
ENTERTAINMENT LAW SERVICES   Contract Negotiation & Drafting - Copyright & Trademark Matters - Intellectual Property Law - Music Law - Talent Representation

Thomas G. Corcoran Jr.	Partner
Jay A. Rosenthal	Partner
Bridget Wimbish	Assistant to Mr. Rosenthal

ATTORNEYS

GREG S. BERNSTEIN - A PROFESSIONAL CORPORATION
9601 Wilshire Blvd., Ste. 240
Beverly Hills, CA 90210
PHONE 310-247-2799
FAX 310-247-2798
EMAIL . . . . .greg@thefilmlaw.com
WEB SITE . . . . .www.thefilmlaw.com

ENTERTAINMENT LAW SERVICES	Full Service Representation - Contract Negotiation & Drafting - Corporate Matters - Financing - Intellectual Property Law - Licensing - Motion Picture & TV Law - Partnerships/Joint Ventures - Right of Publicity - Talent Representation - Transactional Law
REPRESENTS	Producers - Distributors - Financiers - Sales Agents - Production Companies
COMMENTS	Legal production matters; Financing and sales matters; Sales representation

Greg S. Bernstein . . . . .President/Attorney
Brenda Pannell . . . . .Attorney

STUART BERTON - A PROFESSIONAL CORPORATION
12400 Ventura Blvd., Ste. 661
Studio City, CA 91604
PHONE 818-509-8113
FAX 818-985-1527
EMAIL . . . . .stuartberton@earthlink.net

ENTERTAINMENT LAW SERVICES	Contract Negotiation & Drafting - Talent Representation
REPRESENTS	Actors - Writers - Directors - Producers - Executives

Stuart Berton . . . . .Attorney

BIENSTOCK & MICHAEL, P.C.
250 W. 57th St., Ste. 1917
New York, NY 10107
PHONE 212-399-0099
FAX 212-399-1278
EMAIL . . . . .ronald.bienstock@musicsq.com
WEB SITE . . . . .www.musicsq.com

ENTERTAINMENT LAW SERVICES	Contract Negotiation & Drafting - Copyright & Trademark Matters - Corporate Matters - Intellectual Property Law - Licensing - Litigation - Music Law - Royalty Law

Ronald S. Bienstock . . . . .Partner
Jill A. Michael . . . . .Partner
Daniel S. Schuman . . . . .Associate
Randall S.D. Jacobs .Of Counsel

LAW OFFICES OF PETER R. BIERSTEDT
2039 N. Gramercy Pl.
Hollywood, CA 90068-3616
PHONE 323-465-4633
FAX 323-465-3511
EMAIL . . . . .peter@bierstedt.com
WEB SITE . . . . .www.bierstedt.com

ENTERTAINMENT LAW SERVICES	Acquisitions & Mergers - Arbitration & Mediation - Contract Negotiation & Drafting - Copyright & Trademark Matters - Corporate Matters - Financing - First Amendment Issues - Intellectual Property Law - Libel & Privacy Matters - Licensing - Motion Picture & TV Law - Music Law - Partnerships/Joint Ventures - Right of Publicity - Transactional Law
COMMENTS	Legal and business consulting

Peter R. Bierstedt . . . . .Principal

LAW OFFICE OF WILLIAM W. BLACKWELL
433 N. Camden Dr., Ste. 970
Beverly Hills, CA 90210
PHONE 310-278-8011/310-888-8711
FAX 310-278-2254
EMAIL . . . . .wwblackwell@sbcglobal.net

ENTERTAINMENT LAW SERVICES	Full Service Representation - Arbitration & Mediation - Contract Negotiation & Drafting - Copyright & Trademark Matters - Corporate Matters - First Amendment Issues - Intellectual Property Law - Libel & Privacy Matters - Licensing - Litigation - Misappropriation of Name, Voice, Likeness - Motion Picture & TV Law - Music Law - Talent Representation - Transactional Law
COMMENTS	DUI representation; Demo tapes from unsigned bands and artists accepted; Screenplays accepted

William W. Blackwell . . . . .Attorney
Angela Black . . . . .Talent Management

LAW OFFICES OF EDWARD BLAU
1901 Avenue of the Stars, Ste. 1900
Los Angeles, CA 90067
PHONE 310-556-8468
FAX 310-282-0579
EMAIL .edblauenlw@aol.com

ENTERTAINMENT LAW SERVICES	Contract Negotiation & Drafting - Licensing - Motion Picture & TV Law - Music Law - Talent Representation - Transactional Law

Edward Blau . . . . .Sole Proprietor
Dalia de la Sota . . . . .Secretary

ATTORNEYS

BLOOM HERGOTT DIEMER ROSENTHAL & LAVIOLETTE, LLP

150 S. Rodeo Dr., 3rd Fl.
Beverly Hills, CA 90212
PHONE 310-859-6800
FAX 310-859-2788
ENTERTAINMENT LAW SERVICES   Full Service Representation

Jacob A. Bloom . . . . .Partner
Alan S. Hergott . . . . .Partner
John D. Diemer . . . . .Partner
Stuart M. Rosenthal . . . . .Partner
John LaViolette . . . . .Partner
Lawrence H. Greaves . . . . .Partner
Candice S. Hanson . . . . .Partner
Tina J. Kahn . . . . .Partner
Leigh C. Brecheen . . . . .Partner
Stephen F. Breimer . . . . .Partner
David B. Feldman . . . . .Partner
Eric M. Brooks . . . . .Partner
Michael L. Schenkman . . . . .Partner
Thomas B. Collier . . . . .Partner
Patrick M. Knapp . . . . .Partner
Carlos Goodman . . . . .Partner
Leif W. Reinstein . . . . .Partner
Brad S. Small . . . . .Partner
Ralph P. Brescia . . . . .Associate
Thomas F. Hunter . . . . .Of Counsel
Richard D. Thompson . . . . .Of Counsel

LAW OFFICES OF KATHLEEN BRAHN

15233 Ventura Blvd., PH 3
Sherman Oaks, CA 91403
PHONE 818-905-6790
FAX 818-905-6791
EMAIL . . . . .kbrahn@msn.com
WEB SITE . . . . .www.brahnlaw.com
ENTERTAINMENT LAW SERVICES   Acquisitions & Mergers -
                                Contract Negotiation & Drafting
                                - Copyright & Trademark Matters
                                - Financing - Libel & Privacy
                                Matters - Licensing -
                                Misappropriation of Name,
                                Voice, Likeness - Motion Picture
                                & TV Law - Music Law - Right of
                                Publicity - Talent Representation -
                                Transactional Law
REPRESENTS   Production companies and
                                established individuals
COMMENTS   Literary Property, Publishing, Fine
                                Arts, Submissions, Independent
                                Productions, Distribution
                                Transactions

Kathleen Brahn .Attorney/Principal

LAW OFFICES OF JEFFREY BRANDSTETTER

One Market, Spear Tower, 36th Fl.
San Francisco, CA 94105
PHONE 415-920-9002
FAX 415-920-9003
EMAIL . . . . .sfentlawyer@aol.com
SECOND EMAIL . . . . .jeff@windlinefilms.com
WEB SITE . . . . .www.windlinefilms.com
ENTERTAINMENT LAW SERVICES   Full Service Representation
COMMENTS   Specializes in film and music
                                law; Production and distribution;
                                Business plans; Entity formation
                                and dissolution; Co-author of
                                *The Music Business (Explained In
                                Plain English)*

Jeffrey D. Brandstetter . . . . .Attorney

LAW OFFICE OF WILLIAM A. BROWN, JR.

3255 Wilshire Blvd., Ste. 1024
Los Angeles, CA 90010-1414
PHONE 213-387-0661/213-910-5550
FAX 213-387-0884
EMAIL . . . . .attywab@aol.com
WEB SITE . . . . .www.wabrownjr-law.net
ENTERTAINMENT LAW SERVICES   Contract Negotiation & Drafting
                                - Corporate Matters - Libel &
                                Privacy Matters - Litigation -
                                Motion Picture & TV Law - Music
                                Law - Partnerships/Joint Ventures
                                - Talent Representation
REPRESENTS   Whitefire Productions, Inc. -
                                Celebrity Entertainment
                                Productions, LLC - The
                                Manifestation, LLC;
                                Screenwriters: Richard M.
                                Johnson - Q. deChambres -
                                David Cobb - Michelle Blackwell
                                - Kay Spencer - David Sheppard
                                - Sandra Payne - Jeffrey Moshier
                                - Julian Aguirre - Marla Cukor -
                                James C. Schlicker - Cindy
                                Boucher
COMMENTS   Screenplay marketing; Business
                                incorporation; Limited liability
                                company (LLC) formation

William A. Brown Jr. . . . . .Principal/Attorney at Law

BROWNE, WOODS & GEORGE, LLP

450 N. Roxbury Dr., 7th Fl.
Beverly Hills, CA 90210-4231
PHONE 310-274-7100
FAX 310-275-5697
EMAIL . . . . .info@brownewoods.com
WEB SITE . . . . .www.brownewoods.com
ENTERTAINMENT LAW SERVICES   Copyright & Trademark Matters -
                                First Amendment Issues -
                                Intellectual Property Law

Allan Browne . . . . .Attorney
Edward A. Woods . . . . .Attorney
Eric M. George . . . . .Attorney
Ira G. Bibbero . . . . .Attorney
Michael A. Bowse . . . . .Attorney
Robert Broadbelt . . . . .Attorney
Hunter R. Eley . . . . .Attorney
N. Kemba Extavour . . . . .Attorney
Miles J. Feldman . . . . .Attorney
Sylvia P. Lardiere . . . . .Attorney
Sonia Y. Lee . . . . .Attorney
Marcy Railsback . . . . .Attorney
Peter Wayne Ross . . . . .Attorney
Benjamin D. Scheibe . . . . .Attorney
Gene F. Williams . . . . .Attorney

ATTORNEYS

CARROLL, GUIDO & GROFFMAN, LLP

9111 Sunset Blvd.
Los Angeles, CA 90069
PHONE 310-271-0241/212-759-2300
FAX .310-271-0775/212-759-9556
WEB SITE . . . . .www.ccgglaw.com
ENTERTAINMENT LAW SERVICES   Music Law
COMMENTS   Legal services for music and new media industries; No unsolicited demos; East Coast office: 660 Madison Ave., 10th Fl., New York, NY 10021

Rosemary Carroll . . . . .Attorney
Michael Guido . . . . .Attorney
Elliot J. Groffman . . . . .Attorney
Rob Cohen . . . . .Attorney
Jennifer L. Justice . . . . .Attorney
Gillian Malken . . . . .Attorney
Michael Rexford . . . . .Attorney
Janine Small . . . . .Attorney

LAW OFFICES OF ROBERT A. CELESTIN, ESQ.

250 W. 57th St., Ste. 2331
New York, NY 10107
PHONE 212-262-1103
FAX 212-262-1173
EMAIL . . . . .johncarlo@nyct.net
ENTERTAINMENT LAW SERVICES   Contract Negotiation & Drafting - Copyright & Trademark Matters - Intellectual Property Law - Licensing - Motion Picture & TV Law - Music Law - Talent Representation - Transactional Law
REPRESENTS   3LW - Petey Pablo - City High - Family Bond (HBO)

Robert A. Celestin Esq. . . . . .Attorney
Joel C. Barnett Esq. . . . . .Attorney
Alicia Ferriabough Esq. . . . . .Attorney
Giancarlo Ciammaichella .Assistant

CHRISTENSEN, MILLER, FINK, JACOBS, GLASER, WEIL & SHAPIRO, LLP

10250 Constellation Blvd., 19th Fl.
Los Angeles, CA 90067
PHONE 310-553-3000
FAX 310-556-2920
WEB SITE . . . . .www.chrismill.com
ENTERTAINMENT LAW SERVICES   Full Service Representation - Acquisitions & Mergers - Arbitration & Mediation - Contract Negotiation & Drafting - Copyright & Trademark Matters - Corporate Matters - Employment/Labor Law - Financing - First Amendment Issues - Intellectual Property Law - Libel & Privacy Matters - Licensing - Litigation - Misappropriation of Name, Voice, Likeness - Motion Picture & TV Law - Partnerships/Joint Ventures - Right of Publicity - Talent Representation - Tax Law - Transactional Law
COMMENTS   Motion picture and TV production; Finance and distribution transactions; Internet content agreements; Purchase, sale and valuation of film libraries; Merchandising; Literary property acquisitions; Litigation in all entertainment areas

(Continued)

CHRISTENSEN, MILLER, FINK, JACOBS, GLASER, WEIL & SHAPIRO, LLP (Continued)

Terry N. Christensen   Managing Partner/Chairman, Mergers & Acquisitions
Louis R. Miller . . . . .Partner/Co-Chair, Litigation
Barry E. Fink . . . . .Partner/Chair, Taxation, International Law
Patricia Glaser . . . . .Partner/Co-Chair, Litigation
Peter M. Weil . . . . .Partner/Chair, Real Estate & Business Law
Robert L. Shapiro . . . . .Partner/Chair, Business Crimes
Nabil L. Abu-Assal . . . . .Partner, Litigation
Terry D. Avchen . . . . .Partner/Chair, Environmental Group
Leslie Lo Baugh . . . . .Partner, Litigation
Mark L. Block . . . . .Partner, Litigation
Brett J. Cohen . . . . .Partner, Real Estate
Eric P. Early . . . . .Partner, Litigation
Joie Marie Gallo .Partner, Litigation
Miriam J. Golbert . . . . .Partner, Estate Planning & Trusts
Roger H. Howard . . . . .Partner, Real Estate
Carolyn C. Jordan . . . . .Partner, Real Estate
Seong H. Kim . . . . .Partner, Litigation
Joel Klevens . . . . .Partner, Litigation
Warren A. Koshofer . . . . .Partner
Mark G. Krum . . . . .Partner, Litigation
Kevin J. Leichter .Partner, Litigation
Alisa Morgenthaler Lever . . . . .Partner, Litigation
Thomas S. Levyn .Partner, Real Estate
Caroline Mankey .Partner, Litigation
Janet S. McCloud . . . . .Partner, Corporate Securities
Sean Riley . . . . .Partner, Litigation
Gregory Rovenger . . . . .Partner, Tax
James S. Schreier .Partner, Litigation
Peter C. Sheridan .Partner, Litigation
Stephen D. Silbert . . . . . . .Partner, Corporate Securities & Business Law
Gary Sommerstein . . . . .Partner/Chair, Entertainment Law Practice
Jeffrey C. Soza . . . . .Partner, Corporate Securities & Business Law
Kerry Garvis Wright . . . . .Partner, Litigation
Dina Appleton . . . . .Of Counsel, Entertainment Law Practice
Gary N. Jacobs . . . . .Of Counsel
Greg Suess . . . . .Of Counsel

COLE, RAYWID & BRAVERMAN, LLP

1919 Pennsylvania Ave., NW
Washington, DC 20006
PHONE 202-659-9750
FAX 202-452-0067
EMAIL . . . . .bbraverman@crblaw.com
WEB SITE . . . . .www.crblaw.com
ENTERTAINMENT LAW SERVICES   Acquisitions & Mergers - Arbitration & Mediation - Contract Negotiation & Drafting - Copyright & Trademark Matters - Corporate Matters - Financing - First Amendment Issues - Intellectual Property Law - Libel & Privacy Matters - Licensing - Litigation - Misappropriation of Name, Voice, Likeness - Motion Picture & TV Law - Music Law - Partnerships/Joint Ventures - Right of Publicity - Talent Representation - Transactional Law
REPRESENTS   Cable TV Networks - Cable Operators - Production Companies - Radio & TV Stations - Entertainment Companies - Artists - Internet & New Media Companies
COMMENTS   Regulatory advice; Over sixty attorneys and legal assistants in Los Angeles and Washington, DC offices

Burt A. Braverman . . . . .Partner
Maurita K. Coley . . . . .Partner
Maria Browne . . . . .Partner
David M. Silverman . . . . .Partner
Jeremy Stern . . . . .Partner
Julian Quattlebaum . . . . .Of Counsel
Debra Holland . . . . .Assistant to Mr. Braverman
Lena Moiley . . . . .Assistant to Ms. Coley

WALLACE COLLINS, ESQ.
254 W. 54th St., 14th Fl.
New York, NY 10019
PHONE 212-245-7300
FAX 212-586-5175
EMAIL . . . . .wallace@wallacecollins.com
WEB SITE . . . . .www.wallacecollins.com
ENTERTAINMENT LAW SERVICES   Full Service Representation - Contract Negotiation & Drafting - Copyright & Trademark Matters - Corporate Matters - Intellectual Property Law - Licensing - Litigation - Motion Picture & TV Law - Music Law - Right of Publicity - Royalty Law - Transactional Law
COMMENTS   Deal structuring and negotiation; Member: NARAS, The Copyright Society of the U.S.A.

Wallace Collins . . . . .Attorney

LAW OFFICE OF KEITH E. COOPER, ESQ.
PO Box 691237
West Hollywood, CA 90069
PHONE 310-657-0829
FAX 310-657-4773
EMAIL . . . . .hcd@productioncounsel.com
WEB SITE . . . . .www.productioncounsel.com
ENTERTAINMENT LAW SERVICES   Arbitration & Mediation - Contract Negotiation & Drafting - Copyright & Trademark Matters - Corporate Matters - Licensing - Motion Picture & TV Law - Transactional Law
COMMENTS   Production counsel for independent feature films, from acquisition of literary property to delivery of completed picture; Represents production companies and established individuals; Mediator for all types of entertainment industry disputes

Keith Cooper . . . . .Attorney

BRIAN LEE CORBER, ATTORNEY AT LAW
PO Box 44212
Panorama City, CA 91412-0212
PHONE 818-786-7133
FAX 818-785-6495
EMAIL . . . . .corberlaw@aol.com
ENTERTAINMENT LAW SERVICES   Full Service Representation - Arbitration & Mediation - Contract Negotiation & Drafting - Copyright & Trademark Matters - Corporate Matters - Intellectual Property Law - Licensing - Litigation - Motion Picture & TV Law - Music Law - Right of Publicity - Royalty Law - Talent Representation - Transactional Law
COMMENTS   Business structuring

Brian Lee Corber . . . . .Owner/Sole Proprietor

DEL, SHAW, MOONVES, TANAKA & FINKELSTEIN
2120 Colorado Ave., Ste. 200
Santa Monica, CA 90404
PHONE 310-979-7900
FAX 310-979-7999
ENTERTAINMENT LAW SERVICES   Full Service Representation - Copyright & Trademark Matters - Intellectual Property Law - Misappropriation of Name, Voice, Likeness - Motion Picture & TV Law - Partnerships/Joint Ventures - Talent Representation - Transactional Law

Ernest Del . . . . .Partner
Nina L. Shaw . . . . .Partner
Jonathan D. Moonves . . . . .Partner
Jean E. Tanaka . . . . .Partner
Jeffrey S. Finkelstein . . . . .Partner
Abel M. Lezcano . . . . .Partner
Jay Goldberg . . . . .Associate
Gordon M. Bobb . . . . .Associate
Loan T. Dang . . . . .Associate
Thomas R. Greenberg . . . . .Associate

DONALDSON & HART
9220 Sunset Blvd., Ste. 224
Los Angeles, CA 90069-3501
PHONE 310-273-8394/310-274-7157
FAX 310-273-5370/310-274-1437
EMAIL . . . . .staff@donaldsonhart.com
WEB SITE . . . . .www.donaldsonhart.com
ENTERTAINMENT LAW SERVICES   Full Service Representation - Copyright & Trademark Matters - Motion Picture & TV Law - Talent Representation
REPRESENTS   Independent Films - Writers - Directors - Producers
COMMENTS   General Counsel to Film Independent (FIND) and the Writers Guild Foundation; Former president of the International Documentary Association; Author, *Clearance and Copyrights, Negotiating for Dummies* and *Do It Yourself! Trademarks & Copyrights*

Michael C. Donaldson . . . . .Attorney
Joseph F. Hart . . . . .Attorney
Larry E. Verbit . . . . .Attorney
Vincent L. Ravine . . . . .Attorney
Katheleen A. Ebora . . . . .Assistant to Michael C. Donaldson
Sylvia Mendoza . . . . .Assistant to Joseph F. Hart
Ryan Gooden . . . . .General Office Assistant

EDELSTEIN, LAIRD & SOBEL
9255 Sunset Blvd., Ste. 800
Los Angeles, CA 90069
PHONE 310-274-6184
FAX 310-274-6185
ENTERTAINMENT LAW SERVICES   Full Service Representation

Peter Laird . . . . .Partner
William Sobel . . . . .Partner
Gerald Edelstein . . . . .Of Counsel

ATTORNEYS

ENGSTROM, LIPSCOMB & LACK
10100 Santa Monica Blvd., 16th Fl.
Los Angeles, CA 90067
PHONE 310-552-3800
FAX 310-552-9434
WEB SITE . . . . .www.elllaw.com
ENTERTAINMENT LAW SERVICES   Contract Negotiation & Drafting - Intellectual Property Law - Litigation - Music Law

Paul W. Engstrom . . . . .Partner
Lee G. Lipscomb . . . . .Partner
Walter J. Lack . . . . .Partner
Jared W. Beilke . . . . .Attorney
Robert T. Bryson . . . . .Attorney
Elizabeth Lane Crooke . . . . .Attorney
Brian D. Depew . . . . .Attorney
Brian J. Heffernan . . . . .Attorney
Elizabeth Hernandez .Attorney
Ann A. Howitt . . . . .Attorney
Richard P. Kinnan . . . . .Attorney
Brian J. Leinbach . . . . .Attorney
Steven J. Lipscomb . . . . .Attorney
Mark E. Millard . . . . .Attorney
Adam D. Miller . . . . .Attorney
Gary A. Praglin . . . . .Attorney
Jerry A. Ramsey . . . . .Attorney
Rahul Ravipudi . . . . .Attorney
Joy L. Robertson . . . . .Attorney
Steven C. Shuman . . . . .Attorney
Stephen R. Terrell . . . . .Attorney
Paul A. Traina . . . . .Attorney
Daniel G. Whalen . . . . .Attorney
Robert J. Wolfe . . . . .Attorney

ENTERTAINMENT LAW CHICAGO, PC
18744 Highland Ave.
Homewood, IL 60430
PHONE 773-882-4912
FAX 708-206-1663
EMAIL . . . . .dsimon@entertainmentlawchicago.com
WEB SITE . . . . .www.entertainmentlawchicago.com
ENTERTAINMENT LAW SERVICES   Contract Negotiation & Drafting - Copyright & Trademark Matters - Corporate Matters - Financing - Intellectual Property Law - Motion Picture & TV Law - Music Law - Partnerships/Joint Ventures
REPRESENTS   Dreamscape Design - Semidivine - Onesti Entertainment - American English - Mimi Productions - Robert Z'Dar
COMMENTS   Special emphasis on TV, film and video; Production and distribution contracts; Host and talent agreements; Music clearance; Screenplay protection and stock footage licenses; Music: Recording and performance agreements, demo shopping assistance

Donald R. Simon Esq. . . . . .Owner/CEO
Ryan S. Alexander Esq. . . . . .Of Counsel

FAGELBAUM & HELLER, LLP
2049 Century Park East, Ste. 2050
Los Angeles, CA 90067
PHONE 310-286-7666
FAX 310-286-7086
ENTERTAINMENT LAW SERVICES   Full Service Representation

Jerald Fagelbaum . . . . .Partner
Philip Heller . . . . .Partner
Debi Ramos . . . . .Attorney

LAW OFFICES OF GORDON P. FIREMARK
468 N. Camden Dr., Ste. 200
Beverly Hills, CA 90210
PHONE 310-860-7465
FAX 310 477 7676
EMAIL . . . . .info@firemark.com
WEB SITE . . . . .www.firemark.com
ENTERTAINMENT LAW SERVICES   Full Service Representation - Contract Negotiation & Drafting - Copyright & Trademark Matters - Corporate Matters - Financing - First Amendment Issues - Intellectual Property Law - Libel & Privacy Matters - Licensing - Litigation - Misappropriation of Name, Voice, Likeness - Motion Picture & TV Law - Music Law - Partnerships/Joint Ventures - Right of Publicity - Royalty Law - Talent Representation - Transactional Law
COMMENTS   Theatre law

Gordon P. Firemark . . . . .Attorney at Law

FRANKFURT KURNIT KLEIN & SELZ
488 Madison Ave.
New York, NY 10022
PHONE 212-980-0120
FAX 212-593-9175
EMAIL . . . . .info@fkks.com
WEB SITE . . . . .www.fkks.com
ENTERTAINMENT LAW SERVICES   Full Service Representation
REPRESENTS   Producers - Distributors - Financiers - Executives - Writers - Directors - Filmmakers - Actors - Models - Musicians - Fine Artists - Athletes

Victoria Cook . . . . .Attorney
Lisa E. Davis . . . . .Attorney
Michael Frankfurt . . . . .Attorney
Salil Gandhi . . . . .Attorney
Richard B. Heller . . . . .Attorney
Richard Hofstetter . . . . .Attorney
Mark A. Merriman . . . . .Attorney
Amy Nickin . . . . .Attorney
Thomas D. Selz . . . . .Attorney
Stuart Silfen . . . . .Attorney
Amy B. Vernick . . . . .Attorney
Helen Wan . . . . .Attorney
S. Jean Ward . . . . .Attorney
Michael R. Williams . . . . .Attorney

FRANKLIN, WEINRIB, RUDELL & VASSALLO, PC

488 Madison Ave.
New York, NY 10022
PHONE 212-935-5500
FAX 212-308-0642
EMAIL . . . . .lawfirm@fwrv.com
WEB SITE . . . . .www.fwrv.com

ENTERTAINMENT LAW SERVICES	Acquisitions & Mergers - Arbitration & Mediation - Contract Negotiation & Drafting - Copyright & Trademark Matters - Corporate Matters - First Amendment Issues - Intellectual Property Law - Libel & Privacy Matters - Licensing - Misappropriation of Name, Voice, Likeness - Motion Picture & TV Law - Music Law - Partnerships/Joint Ventures - Right of Publicity - Royalty Law - Talent Representation - Transactional Law
REPRESENTS	Actors - Authors - Recording Artists - Screenwriters - Directors - Theatrical Producers - Corporate Executives
COMMENTS	Theater, Literary Publishing, Record Distribution and Music Publishing, Merchandising and Trademark Licensing, Defamation, New Technologies

Richard A. Abrams . . . . .Partner
Jason P. Baruch . . . . .Partner
Richard A. Beyman . . . . .Partner
Eric S. Brown . . . . .Partner
Elliot H. Brown . . . . .Partner
Jonathan Director . . . . .Partner
Nicholas Gordon . . . . .Partner
Neil J. Rosini . . . . .Partner
Michael I. Rudell . . . . .Partner
Rose H. Schwartz . . . . .Partner
John A. Vassallo . . . . .Partner
Daniel M. Wasser . . . . .Partner
Kenneth M. Weinrib . . . . .Partner
Camrin L. Crisci . . . . .Attorney
Matthew C. Lefferts . . . . .Attorney
Jonathan A. Lonner . . . . .Attorney
Karen M. Platt . . . . .Attorney
Brian R. Shuford . . . . .Attorney

FRASER - ENTERTAINMENT LAW

9595 Wilshire Blvd., Ste. 900
Beverly Hills, CA 90212
PHONE 310-246-1867/416-967-0080
FAX 310-246-1866/416-967-0090
EMAIL . . . . .info@fraser-elaw.com
WEB SITE . . . . .www.fraser-elaw.com

ENTERTAINMENT LAW SERVICES	Acquisitions & Mergers - Contract Negotiation & Drafting - Copyright & Trademark Matters - Corporate Matters - Employment/Labor Law - Financing - First Amendment Issues - Intellectual Property Law - Libel & Privacy Matters - Licensing - Misappropriation of Name, Voice, Likeness - Motion Picture & TV Law - Music Law - Partnerships/Joint Ventures - Right of Publicity - Royalty Law - Talent Representation - Transactional Law
COMMENTS	Toronto office: 110 Spadina Ave., Ste. 222, Toronto, ON M5V 2K4 Canada

Stephen Fraser . . . . .Entertainment Lawyer

FURGANG & ADWAR, LLP

1230 Avenue of the Americas, 7th Fl.
New York, NY 10020
PHONE 212-725-1818
FAX 212-941-9711
EMAIL .info@furgang.com
WEB SITE . . . . .www.furgang.com

ENTERTAINMENT LAW SERVICES	Contract Negotiation & Drafting - Copyright & Trademark Matters - Intellectual Property Law - Libel & Privacy Matters - Licensing - Litigation - Misappropriation of Name, Voice, Likeness - Motion Picture & TV Law - Music Law - Right of Publicity - Transactional Law

Stephanie Furgang Adwar . . . . .Partner
Philip Furgang . . . . .Partner
Bertrand Lanchner . . . . .Of Counsel
Sheldon Palmer . . . . .Of Counsel
Brian Scanlon . . . . .Associate

GAGE TEEPLE, LLP

9255 Towne Centre Dr., Ste. 500
San Diego, CA 92121
PHONE 858-622-7878
FAX 858-622-0411
EMAIL .info@gageteeple.com
WEB SITE . . . . .www.gageteeple.com

ENTERTAINMENT LAW SERVICES	Acquisitions & Mergers - Contract Negotiation & Drafting - Intellectual Property Law - Licensing - Litigation - Music Law - Royalty Law
COMMENTS	Coordination of royalty and participation audits and settlements; Also provides entity formation, intellectual property protection, asset protection, and international business services

Benjamin Gage . . . . .Partner
Grant Teeple . . . . .Partner
Todd Hall . . . . .Partner
Eric Hart . . . . .Associate

GAINES, SOLOMON LAW GROUP, LLP

1901 Avenue of the Stars, Ste. 1100
Los Angeles, CA 90067
PHONE 310-556-1771
FAX 310-556-7955
ENTERTAINMENT LAW SERVICES   Full Service Representation

Frederic N. Gaines . . . . .Partner (fgaines@mggla.com)
Richard P. Solomon . . . . .Partner (rsolomon@mggla.com)

ATTORNEYS

GARFIELD TEPPER & RASKIN

1801 Century Park East, Ste. 2300
Los Angeles, CA 90067
PHONE 310-277-1981
FAX 310-277-1980
ENTERTAINMENT LAW SERVICES   Arbitration & Mediation - Contract Negotiation & Drafting - Copyright & Trademark Matters - Financing - Intellectual Property Law - Libel & Privacy Matters - Licensing - Litigation - Misappropriation of Name, Voice, Likeness - Motion Picture & TV Law - Music Law - Partnerships/Joint Ventures - Right of Publicity - Talent Representation - Transactional Law

Gary S. Raskin . . . . .Partner
Scott J. Tepper . . . . .Partner
Franklin R. Garfield . . . . .Partner
Jason W. Fandrich . . . . .Attorney
Kyle Stewart . . . . .Attorney
Renee Skinner . . . . .Paralegal

GARVIN & COMPANY

9200 Sunset Blvd., PH 25
Los Angeles, CA 90069
PHONE 310-278-7300
FAX 310-278-7306
ENTERTAINMENT LAW SERVICES   Full Service Representation

Thomas F. R. Garvin . . . . .Member
Carol Lynn Akiyama . . . . .Of Counsel
Peter R. Bierstedt . . . . .Of Counsel
Chris Anthony Gemignani . . . . .Of Counsel

GAULIN GROUP LLP

Carnegie Hall Tower
152 W. 57th St.
New York, NY 10019
PHONE 212-582-9400
FAX 212-582-9440
EMAIL . . . . .info@gaulingroup.com
WEB SITE . . . . .www.gaulingroup.com
ENTERTAINMENT LAW SERVICES   Full Service Representation - Acquisitions & Mergers - Arbitration & Mediation - Contract Negotiation & Drafting - Copyright & Trademark Matters - Corporate Matters - Employment/Labor Law - Financing - Intellectual Property Law - Licensing - Litigation - Misappropriation of Name, Voice, Likeness - Motion Picture & TV Law - Music Law - Partnerships/Joint Ventures - Royalty Law - Talent Representation - Transactional Law

Robert V. Gaulin . . . . .Attorney, TV & Film/Publishing/Copyright/Intellectual Property/Executive Employment/Acquisitions/Contract Negotiation & Drafting/Joint Ventures
Ira S. Berg . . . . .Attorney, Licensing/Contract Negotiation & Drafting
Elliot S. Blair . . . .Attorney, Theatre & Film/Copyright/Intellectual Property
Soren Erdmann . . . . .Attorney, Contract Negotiation & Drafting
George T. Gilbert . . . . .Attorney, Music Law/Talent Representation
George S. Sava . . .Attorney, Litigation, Arbitration, Contract Negotiation & Drafting
Frederick M. Shepperd . . . . .Attorney, Acquisitions & Mergers/Corporate Matters, Financing/Transactional

GENDLER & KELLY, APC

450 N. Roxbury Dr., PH 1000
Beverly Hills, CA 90210
PHONE 310-285-6400
FAX 310-275-7333
WEB SITE . . . . .www.gendler-kelly.com
ENTERTAINMENT LAW SERVICES   Full Service Representation

Michael S. Gendler . . . . .Partner
Kevin M. Kelly . . . . .Partner
Brian E. Fortman . . . . .Attorney
Marc E. Golden . . . . .Attorney

GERDES LAW

8950 W. Olympic Blvd., Ste. 382
Beverly Hills, CA 90211
PHONE 310-385-9501
FAX 310-858-6703
EMAIL . . . . .ted@gerdeslaw.com
WEB SITE . . . . .www.gerdeslaw.com
ENTERTAINMENT LAW SERVICES   Contract Negotiation & Drafting - Copyright & Trademark Matters - Licensing - Motion Picture & TV Law - Music Law - Right of Publicity
REPRESENTS   Wide range of clients from individual artists and small producers to Fortune 500 companies
COMMENTS   Clearance: film, TV, internet and advertising

Ted F. Gerdes . . . . .Principal/Attorney

GIBSON, DUNN & CRUTCHER, LLP

333 S. Grand Ave., Ste. 5100
Los Angeles, CA 90071-3197
PHONE .213-229-7000/310-552-8500
FAX .213-229-7520/310-551-8741
WEB SITE . . . . .www.gibsondunn.com
ENTERTAINMENT LAW SERVICES   Acquisitions & Mergers - Financing - Licensing - Motion Picture & TV Law - Partnerships/Joint Ventures
COMMENTS   Second Los Angeles office: 2029 Century Park East, Ste. 4000, Los Angeles, CA 90067-3026; Offices in Dallas, Denver, Orange County, Palo Alto, New York, San Francisco, Washington DC, London, Munich, Brussells and Paris

James P. Clark .Partner, Entertainment
Scott Edelman .Partner, Entertainment
Ruth Fisher .Partner, Entertainment
Lawrence Ulman .Partner, Entertainment
William Wegner .Partner, Entertainment

ATTORNEYS

GIPSON HOFFMAN & PANCIONE

1901 Avenue of the Stars, Ste. 1100
Los Angeles, CA 90067-6002
PHONE 310-556-4660
FAX 310-556-8945
WEB SITE . . . . .www.ghplaw.com
ENTERTAINMENT LAW SERVICES   Acquisitions & Mergers - Arbitration & Mediation - Contract Negotiation & Drafting - Copyright & Trademark Matters - Corporate Matters - Employment/Labor Law - Financing - First Amendment Issues - Intellectual Property Law - Libel & Privacy Matters - Licensing - Litigation - Misappropriation of Name, Voice, Likeness - Motion Picture & TV Law - Partnerships/Joint Ventures - Right of Publicity - Royalty Law - Tax Law - Transactional Law
COMMENTS   Film and TV distribution, finance, production and development matters

Robert E. Gipson . . . . .Attorney
Lawrence R. Barnett . . . . .Attorney
Jeff M. Boren . . . . .Attorney
G. Raymond F. Gross . . . . .Attorney
Brian M. Hoye . . . . .Attorney
Jonathan J. Panzer . . . . .Attorney
Kenneth I. Sidle . . . . .Attorney
Norm D. Sloan . . . . .Attorney
Corey J. Spivey . . . . .Attorney
Robert H. Steinberg . . . . .Attorney

GLADSTONE BAKER KELLEY

49 Music Square West, Ste. 300
Nashville, TN 37203
PHONE 615-329-0900
FAX 615-329-2148
WEB SITE . . . . .www.rowlawyers.com
ENTERTAINMENT LAW SERVICES   Acquisitions & Mergers - Contract Negotiation & Drafting - Copyright & Trademark Matters - Corporate Matters - Employment/Labor Law - Financing - Intellectual Property Law - Licensing - Motion Picture & TV Law - Music Law - Partnerships/Joint Ventures - Royalty Law - Transactional Law
COMMENTS   Entertainment industry transactions and general business representation in entertainment industry; Business planning and financing of entertainment ventures

Robert L. Baker . . . . .Partner
Steven G. Gladstone . . . . .Partner
Roxann K. Baquie . . . . .Attorney
D. Page Kelley III . . . . .Attorney
Tracey K. Houston . . . . .Office Manager/Executive Assistant

GLASSMAN, BROWNING & SALTSMAN, INC.

360 N. Bedford Dr., Ste. 204
Beverly Hills, CA 90210
PHONE 310-278-5100
FAX 310-271-6041
WEB SITE . . . . .www.gbslaw.com
ENTERTAINMENT LAW SERVICES   First Amendment Issues - Intellectual Property Law - Libel & Privacy Matters - Litigation - Misappropriation of Name, Voice, Likeness

Anthony M. Glassman . . . . .Partner
Amy O. Jacobs . . . . .Partner
Roger A. Browning . . . . .Partner
Jane D. Saltsman . . . . .Partner
Suzanne J. Goulet . . . . .Attorney
Richelle L. Kemler M.S.W. . . . . .Attorney
Alexander Rufas-Isaacs . . . . .Attorney

GOLDRING, HERTZ, & LICHTENSTEIN, LLP

450 N. Roxbury Dr., 8th Fl.
Beverly Hills, CA 90210
PHONE 310-271-8777
FAX 310-276-8310
ENTERTAINMENT LAW SERVICES   Full Service Representation

Fred Goldring . . . . .Partner
Kenneth Hertz . . . . .Partner
Seth Lichtenstein . . . . .Partner
John Mason . . . . .Of Counsel

LAW OFFICES OF DESIREÉ GORDY

7095 Hollywood Blvd., Ste. 600
Hollywood, CA 90028
PHONE 323-874-3918
FAX 323-874-4590
ENTERTAINMENT LAW SERVICES   Contract Negotiation & Drafting - Music Law

Desireé Gordy . . . . .Attorney

LAW OFFICE OF BRUCE V. GRAKAL

1541 Ocean Ave., Ste. 200
Santa Monica, CA 90401
PHONE 310-917-1950
FAX 310-917-1112
ENTERTAINMENT LAW SERVICES   Contract Negotiation & Drafting - Motion Picture & TV Law - Music Law - Transactional Law
COMMENTS   Merchandising matters; Sponsorships

Bruce Grakal . . . . .Partner

ATTORNEYS

LAW OFFICES OF JEFFREY L. GRAUBART

350 W. Colorado Blvd., Ste. 200
Pasadena, CA 91105-1855
PHONE 626-304-2800
FAX 626-304-2807
EMAIL ....info@jlgraubart.com
WEB SITE ....www.lawyers.com/entertainmentlaw
ENTERTAINMENT LAW SERVICES   Full Service Representation -
                              Arbitration & Mediation -
                              Contract Negotiation & Drafting
                              - Copyright & Trademark Matters
                              - Corporate Matters - First
                              Amendment Issues - Intellectual
                              Property Law - Libel & Privacy
                              Matters - Licensing - Litigation -
                              Misappropriation of Name,
                              Voice, Likeness - Motion Picture
                              & TV Law - Music Law -
                              Partnerships/Joint Ventures -
                              Right Of Publicity - Royalty Law -
                              Talent Representation -
                              Transactional Law
COMMENTS   Music publishing; Legitimate
                              stage; Book publishing

Jeffrey L. Graubart ....Attorney

GREEN & GREEN LAW & MEDIATION OFFICES

One Embarcardero Center, Ste. 500
San Francisco, CA 94111
PHONE 415-457-8300
FAX 415-457-8757
EMAIL ....bev@musiclawyer.com
SECOND EMAIL ....bev@entertainmentlegal.com
WEB SITE ....www.musiclawyer.com
SECOND WEB SITE ....www.entertainmentlegal.com
ENTERTAINMENT LAW SERVICES   Full Service Representation -
                              Arbitration & Mediation -
                              Contract Negotiation & Drafting
                              - Copyright & Trademark Matters
                              - Corporate Matters -
                              Employment/Labor Law -
                              Financing - First Amendment
                              Issues - Intellectual Property Law
                              - Libel & Privacy Matters -
                              Licensing - Litigation -
                              Misappropriation of Name,
                              Voice, Likeness - Motion Picture
                              & TV Law - Music Law -
                              Partnerships/Joint Ventures -
                              Right of Publicity - Royalty Law -
                              Talent Representation -
                              Transactional Law
REPRESENTS   Alien Music - The Beautiful
                              Losers - Cheap Thrills Music -
                              Family Dog Productions - Merl
                              Saunders - Zakir Hussain
COMMENTS   Marin County office: Courthouse
                              Square, 1000 Fourth St., Ste.
                              595, San Rafael, CA 94901

Beverly Robin Green ....Entertainment Lawyer
Philip R. Green ....Intellectual Property Law Attorney

GREENBERG GLUSKER FIELDS CLAMAN MACHTINGER & KINSELLA, LLP

1900 Avenue of the Stars, 21st Fl.
Los Angeles, CA 90067
PHONE 310-553-3610
FAX 310-553-0687
EMAIL ....info@ggfirm.com
WEB SITE ....www.ggfirm.com
ENTERTAINMENT LAW SERVICES   Copyright & Trademark Matters -
                              Intellectual Property Law -
                              Litigation - Motion Picture & TV
                              Law - Music Law - Right of
                              Publicity - Transactional Law

Arthur N. Greenberg ....Partner, Litigation
Bertram Fields ....Partner, Entertainment Litigation
Stephen Claman ....Partner, Real Estate, Transactional
Dale F. Kinsella ....Partner, Litigation
Hillary Bibicoff ....Partner, Entertainment, Transactional
Heidi Binford ....Partner, Music Litigation
Paul A. Blechner ....Partner, Entertainment Litigation
Robert S. Chapman ....Partner, Entertainment Litigation
Michelle A. Cooke ....Partner, Intellectual Property & Technology
Bonnie E. Eskenazi ....Partner, Entertainment Litigation
E. Barry Haldeman ....Partner, Entertainment, Transactional
Lawrence Y. Iser ....Partner, Entertainment & Music Litigation/
                              Intellectual Property & Technology
Jeffrey A. Krieger ....Partner, Intellectual Property & Technology
Michael Kump ....Partner, Intellectual Property & Entertainment
Robert F. Marshall ....Partner, Entertainment, Transactional
Patricia A. Millett ....Partner, Entertainment & Music Litigation
Elisabeth A. Moriarty ....Partner, Entertainment Litigation
Richard E. Neff ....Partner, Intellectual Property & Technology
Richard E. Posell ....Partner, Entertainment & Music Litigation
Charles N. Shephard ....Partner, Entertainment Litigation
Stephen Smith ....Partner, Entertainment Litigation
Howard Weitzman ....Partner, Entertainment Litigation
Jonathan B. Sokol ....Partner, Entertainment & Music Litigation/
                              Intellectual Property & Technology
Jeffrey Spitz ....Partner, Entertainment Litigation
Kevin DeBré ....Partner, Intellectual Property & Technology
Aaron Bloom ....Attorney, Entertainment Litigation
Caroline H. Burgos ....Attorney, Entertainment Litigation
Benita Das ....Attorney, Intellectual Property & Technology
Matt Galsor ....Attorney, Entertainment, Transactional
Gregory Korn ....Attorney, Intellectual Property & Technology
Jennifer J. McGrath ....Attorney, Entertainment Litigation
Aaron Moss ....Attorney, Entertainment Litigation
Carla Roberts ....Attorney, Entertainment, Transactional
Kristen Spanier ....Attorney, Entertainment Litigation
David Stanley ....Attorney, Entertainment Litigation
Brenda Tavakoli ....Attorney, Entertainment, Transactional
Herb Williams ....Attorney, Intellectual Property & Technology
James E. Hornstein ....Of Counsel, Entertainment Litigation

ATTORNEYS

GRUBMAN INDURSKY, PC
c/o Carnegie Hall Tower
152 W. 57th St.
New York, NY 10019
PHONE 212-554-0400
FAX 212-554-0444
ENTERTAINMENT LAW SERVICES   Full Service Representation -
Copyright & Trademark Matters -
Intellectual Property Law - Motion
Picture & TV Law - Music Law

Allen J. Grubman . . . . .Partner
Arthur I. Indursky . . . . .Partner
Joseph M. Brenner . . . . .Attorney
Jess H. Drabkin . . . . .Attorney
Jonathan A. Ehrlich . . . . .Attorney
Stuart J. Fried . . . . .Attorney
Donald R. Friedman .Attorney
Martha Georghiou . . . . .Attorney
Michelle Gorove . . . . .Attorney
Karen J. Gottlieb . . . . .Attorney
Peter E. Grant . . . . .Attorney
Bruce G. Grossberg . . . . .Attorney
Sonya W. Guardo . . . . .Attorney
Theodore P. Harris . . . . .Attorney
Jonathan F. Horn . . . . .Attorney
Donald L. Kaplan . . . . .Attorney
Kenneth R. Meiselas .Attorney
Joseph D. Penachio . . . . .Attorney
Paul H. Rothenberg . . . . .Attorney
Eric D. Sacks . . . . .Attorney
Lawrence Shire . . . . .Attorney
Robert A. Strent . . . . .Attorney
David R. Toraya . . . . .Attorney
Howard L. Wattenberg . . . . .Attorney
Debra A. White . . . . .Attorney
Michael K. Goldsmith . . . . .Of Counsel
Gil A. Karson . . . . .Of Counsel
Larry H. Schatz . . . . .Of Counsel

HAHN & BOLSON, LLP
1000 Wilshire Blvd., Ste. 1600
Los Angeles, CA 90017
PHONE 213-630-2600
FAX 213-622-6670
EMAIL . . . . .info@hahnbolsonllp.com
WEB SITE . . . . .www.hahnbolsonllp.com
ENTERTAINMENT LAW SERVICES   Acquisitions & Mergers -
Copyright & Trademark Matters -
Corporate Matters -
Employment/Labor Law - First
Amendment Issues - Intellectual
Property Law - Licensing -
Litigation - Misappropriation of
Name, Voice, Likeness - Motion
Picture & TV Law - Music Law -
Right of Publicity - Transactional
Law

Elliott J. Hahn . . . . .Partner
Jeffrey T. Bolson . . . . .Partner
David R. Denton . . . . .Associate

JONATHAN HANDEL
PO Box 69218
Los Angeles, CA 90069
PHONE 323-650-0060
FAX 323-654-5360
EMAIL . . . . .jhandel@att.net
WEB SITE . . . . .www.jhandel.com
ENTERTAINMENT LAW SERVICES   Full Service Representation -
Acquisitions & Mergers -
Contract Negotiation & Drafting
- Copyright & Trademark Matters
- Intellectual Property Law -
Licensing - Motion Picture & TV
Law - Right of Publicity - Talent
Representation - Transactional
Law
REPRESENTS   Digital Media Companies -
Writers - Producers - Software
Developers - Internet Companies
COMMENTS   Of Counsel to Troy & Gould Law
Firm; Previously WGA Associate
Counsel; Member, Business and
Management Advisory Board of
UCLA Extension Entertainment
Department; Member, Academy
of Television Arts & Sciences

Jonathan Handel . . . . .Attorney

HARRIS MARTIN JONES SHRUM BRADFORD & WOMMACK
49 Music Square West, Ste. 600
Nashville, TN 37203
PHONE 615-321-5400
FAX 615-321-5469
EMAIL . . . . .info@rowlaw.org
WEB SITE . . . . .www.rowlaw.org
ENTERTAINMENT LAW SERVICES   Acquisitions & Mergers -
Contract Negotiation & Drafting
- Copyright & Trademark Matters
- Corporate Matters - Litigation -
Music Law - Partnerships/Joint
Ventures

S. Ralph Gordon . . . . .Of Counsel
Gail S. Bradford . . . . .Attorney
James H. Harris III . . . . .Attorney
Russell A. Jones Jr. . . . . .Attorney
J. Thomas Martin . . . . .Attorney
Barry Neil Shrum . . . . .Attorney
Richard L. Wommack II . . . . .Attorney

JOSEPH F. HART
9220 Sunset Blvd., Ste. 224
Los Angeles, CA 90069-3501
PHONE 310-274-7157
FAX 310-274-1437
EMAIL . . . . .joe@donaldsonhart.com
WEB SITE . . . . .www.donaldsonhart.com
ENTERTAINMENT LAW SERVICES   Arbitration & Mediation -
Contract Negotiation & Drafting
- Copyright & Trademark Matters
- Intellectual Property Law - Libel
& Privacy Matters - Litigation -
Music Law - Right of Publicity

Joseph F. Hart . . . . .Attorney

ATTORNEYS

HERTZ, SCHRAM & SARETSKY, PC
1760 S. Telegraph Rd., Ste. 300
Bloomfield Hills, MI 48302-0183
PHONE 248-335-5000
FAX 248-335-3346
EMAIL . . . . .hhertz@hsspc.com
WEB SITE . . . . .www.hsspc.com
ENTERTAINMENT LAW SERVICES — Full Service Representation
COMMENTS — Entity formation; Estate and tax planning; Member: International Association of Entertainment Lawyers; Board of Directors & President: Motor City Music Foundation (Host of the Detroit Music Awards); Board of Directors: ArtServe Michigan; Member: National Academy of Recording Arts & Sciences, Chicago Chapter, Board of Governors

Howard Hertz . . . . .Partner

HIRSCH WALLERSTEIN HAYUM MATLOF & FISHMAN
10100 Santa Monica Blvd., 23rd Fl.
Los Angeles, CA 90067
PHONE 310-712-6477
FAX 310-712-6199
ENTERTAINMENT LAW SERVICES — Contract Negotiation & Drafting - Motion Picture & TV Law - Talent Representation - Transactional Law

Barry L. Hirsch . . . . .Partner
Robert S. Wallerstein .Partner
George Hayum . . . . .Partner
David J. Matlof . . . . .Partner
Howard A. Fishman . . . . .Partner

HOLLAND & KNIGHT, LLP
633 W. Fifth St., 21st Fl.
Los Angeles, CA 90071
PHONE 213-896-2400/212-513-3200
FAX 213-896-2450/212-385-9010
WEB SITE . . . . .www.hklaw.com
ENTERTAINMENT LAW SERVICES — Acquisitions & Mergers - Contract Negotiation & Drafting - Libel & Privacy Matters - Motion Picture & TV Law - Talent Representation
COMMENTS — Record company acquisitions; Entertainment and sports broadcast; Merchandising; Celebrity sponsorships; Labor relations; Thirty-two locations worldwide; East Coast office: 195 Broadway, 24th Fl., New York, NY 10007

Chad M. Gordon . . . . .Attorney
Robert L. Ivey . . . . .Attorney
Jack S. Sholkoff . . . . .Attorney

*THE HOYT LAW GROUP, LLC
350 Fifth Ave., Ste. 7315
New York, NY 10118
PHONE 212-643-0550
FAX 212-643-0551
EMAIL .choyt@hoytlawgroup.com
WEB SITE .www.hoytlawgroup.com
ENTERTAINMENT LAW SERVICES — Intellectual Property Law - Motion Picture & TV Law - Music Law - Partnerships/Joint Ventures

Christopher Hoyt . . . . .Attorney

IRELL & MANELLA, LLP
1800 Avenue of the Stars, Ste. 900
Los Angeles, CA 90067-4276
PHONE 310-277-1010
FAX 310-203-7199
WEB SITE . . . . .www.irell.com
ENTERTAINMENT LAW SERVICES — Acquisitions & Mergers - Contract Negotiation & Drafting - Copyright & Trademark Matters - Corporate Matters - Intellectual Property Law - Libel & Privacy Matters - Licensing - Litigation - Motion Picture & TV Law - Right of Publicity - Royalty Law - Talent Representation - Tax Law
COMMENTS — Profit participation; Motion picture and TV production

Richard B. Kendall . . . . .Partner
Robert Klieger . . . . .Partner
Joan Lesser . . . . .Partner
Steven A. Marenberg .Partner
Harry A. Mittleman . . . . .Partner
Matthew T. Sant . . . . .Partner
Henry Shields Jr. . . . . .Partner
Clark B. Siegel . . . . .Partner
Jane S. Wald . . . . .Partner
Bruce A. Wessel . . . . .Partner
Juliette Youngblood . . . . .Partner
David Nimmer . . . . .Of Counsel
Peter Shimamoto .Of Counsel
Uri M. Emerson-Fleming . . . . .Associate
Katharine J. Galston . . . . .Associate
Steve Hasegawa . . . . .Associate
Brian E. Jones . . . . .Associate
Philip Kelly . . . . .Associate
Lee M. Liedecke . . . . .Associate
Philip Miller . . . . .Associate
Kenneth J. Weatherwax . . . . .Associate

JACKOWAY TYERMAN WERTHEIMER AUSTEN MANDELBAUM & MORRIS
1888 Century Park East, 18th Fl.
Los Angeles, CA 90067
PHONE 310-553-0305
FAX 310-553-5036
ENTERTAINMENT LAW SERVICES — Full Service Representation

Karl R. Austen . . . . .Attorney
Jeff A. Bernstein . . . . .Attorney
Joseph D'Onofrio . . . . .Attorney
Alan J. Epstein . . . . .Attorney
Andrew L. Galker . . . . .Attorney
Robert S. Getman . . . . .Attorney
Myreon M. Hodur . . . . .Attorney
James R. Jackoway .Attorney
Leon Liu . . . . .Attorney
James C. Mandelbaum . . . . .Attorney
Marcy S. Morris . . . . .Attorney
Michele M. Mulrooney . . . . .Attorney
Geoffry W. Oblath .Attorney
Darren M. Trattner .Attorney
Barry W. Tyerman . . . . .Attorney
Eric C. Weissler . . . . .Attorney
Alan S. Wertheimer .Attorney
Julian Zajfen . . . . .Attorney
Arthur O. Armstrong . . . . .Founder
Ronald J. Bass . . . . .Of Counsel

ATTORNEYS

JACOBSON & COLFIN, PC
60 Madison Avenue, Ste. 1026
New York, NY 10010
PHONE 212-691-5630/516-295-7689
FAX 212-645-5038/516-295-6872
EMAIL . . . . .thefirm@thefirm.com
WEB SITE . . . . .www.thefirm.com
ENTERTAINMENT LAW SERVICES   Full Service Representation -
Contract Negotiation & Drafting
- Copyright & Trademark Matters
- Licensing - Litigation -
Misappropriation of Name,
Voice, Likeness - Motion Picture
& TV Law - Music Law -
Partnerships/Joint Ventures -
Right of Publicity - Royalty Law -
Talent Representation -
Transactional Law
REPRESENTS   Musicians - Record Companies -
Producers - Writers - Directors -
Publishers - Managers

Jeffrey Jacobson . . . . .Partner
Bruce Colfin . . . . .Partner

JEFFER MANGELS BUTLER & MARMARO, LLP
1900 Avenue of the Stars, 7th Fl.
Los Angeles, CA 90067
PHONE 310-203-8080/415-398-8080
FAX 310-203-0567/415-398-5584
EMAIL . . . . .mss@jmbm.com
WEB SITE . . . . .www.jmbm.com
ENTERTAINMENT LAW SERVICES   Full Service Representation -
Acquisitions & Mergers -
Arbitration & Mediation -
Contract Negotiation & Drafting
Copyright & Trademark Matters
- Corporate Matters - Financing
- First Amendment Issues -
Intellectual Property Law - Libel &
Privacy Matters - Licensing -
Litigation - Motion Picture & TV
Law - Music Law -
Partnerships/Joint Ventures -
Right of Publicity - Royalty Law -
Talent Representation - Tax Law -
Transactional Law
REPRESENTS   Actors - Directors - Writers -
Authors - Producers - Production
Companies - Distributors - Banks
- Financiers - Completion
Guarantors - Agents - Managers
- Composers - Musicians
COMMENTS   Music and print publishing law,
Business entity structuring;
Northern California office: Two
Embarcadero Center, San
Francisco, CA 94111

Daniel Grigsby . . . . .Partner
Michael S. Sherman . . . . .Partner
David Lippman . . . . .Associate

JOHNSON & RISHWAIN, LLP
12121 Wilshire Blvd., Ste. 1201
Los Angeles, CA 90025
PHONE 310-826-2410
FAX 310-826-5450
EMAIL . . . . .njohnson@jrllp.com
WEB SITE . . . . .www.jrllp.com
ENTERTAINMENT LAW SERVICES   Copyright & Trademark Matters -
First Amendment Issues - Libel &
Privacy Matters - Litigation -
Misappropriation of Name,
Voice, Likeness - Motion Picture
& TV Law - Music Law - Right of
Publicity - Royalty Law
COMMENTS   Also business litigation

Neville Johnson . . . . .Partner
Brian Rishwain . . . . .Partner
Douglas Johnson . . . . .Associate
Nicholas Kurtz . . . . .Associate
James Ryan . . . . .Associate

LAW OFFICE OF PATRICIA JOHNSON
190 N. Canon Dr., Ste. 403
Beverly Hills, CA 90210
PHONE 310-273-3105
FAX 310-273-3361
EMAIL .pjohnsonlaw@sbcglobal.net
WEB SITE . . . . .www.lawyers.com/pjohnsonlaw
ENTERTAINMENT LAW SERVICES   Contract Negotiation & Drafting
- Copyright & Trademark Matters
- Intellectual Property Law - Libel
& Privacy Matters - Licensing -
Litigation - Misappropriation of
Name, Voice, Likeness - Motion
Picture & TV Law - Music Law -
Right of Publicity - Transactional
Law
COMMENTS   Also a feature film production
counsel

Patricia Johnson Esq. . . . . .Attorney

KATZ, GOLDEN & SULLIVAN, LLP
2001 Wilshire Blvd., Ste. 400
Santa Monica, CA 90403
PHONE 310-998-9200
FAX 310-998-9177
ENTERTAINMENT LAW SERVICES   Full Service Representation -
Contract Negotiation & Drafting
- Financing - Motion Picture &
TV Law - Talent Representation

Steven Katz . . . . .Partner
Diane A. Golden . . . . .Partner
Mary E. Sullivan . . . . .Partner
Shep Rosenman . . . . .Partner
Patricia A. McVerry . . . . .Of Counsel
Suzanne Rosencrans . . . . .Of Counsel
Charles D. Silverberg . . . . .Of Counsel
Lionelle Rosenbaum . . . . .Attorney

ATTORNEYS

KAYE & MILLS
8840 Wilshire Blvd., 2nd Fl.
Beverly Hills, CA 90211
PHONE 310-358-3121
FAX 310-358-3175
EMAIL . . . . .kevinmills@kayemills.com
SECOND EMAIL . . . . .jessicakaye@kayemills.com
WEB SITE . . . . .www.kayemills.com
ENTERTAINMENT LAW SERVICES   Acquisitions & Mergers - Contract Negotiation & Drafting - Copyright & Trademark Matters - Corporate Matters - Financing - First Amendment Issues - Intellectual Property Law - Libel & Privacy Matters - Licensing - Misappropriation of Name, Voice, Likeness - Motion Picture & TV Law - Music Law - Partnerships/Joint Ventures - Right of Publicity - Royalty Law - Talent Representation - Transactional Law
REPRESENTS   Production & Distribution Companies - Writers - Directors - Producers - Actors
COMMENTS   Publishing legal services; General business

Jessica Kaye . . . . .Partner, Publishing & Author Representation
Kevin Mills . . . . .Partner, Film & TV, Business Law
Michael A. Miller . . . . .Of Counsel, Film, TV & Music

KAYE SCHOLER, LLP
1999 Avenue of the Stars, Ste. 1700
Los Angeles, CA 90067
PHONE 310-788-1000
FAX 310-788-1200
WEB SITE . . . . .www.kayescholer.com
ENTERTAINMENT LAW SERVICES   Acquisitions & Mergers - Arbitration & Mediation - Contract Negotiation & Drafting - Copyright & Trademark Matters - Financing - Licensing - Litigation
COMMENTS   Guild arbitration

Robert Barnes . . . . .Partner in Entertainment, Media, Trademark & Copyright Litigation
Julian Brew . . . . .Partner, Entertainment, Media, Trademark & Copyright Litigation
Barry L. Dastin . . . . . .Partner, Entertainment, Media & Communications
Jeffrey S. Gordon . . . . .Partner, Entertainment, Media, Trademark & Copyright Litigation
Peter L. Haviland . . . . .Partner, Entertainment, Media, Trademark & Copyright Litigation
Sheri Jeffrey . . . . . . .Partner, Entertainment, Media & Communications
Ken Lemberger . . . . .Counsel, Entertainment, Media & Communications
Rhonda R. Trotter . . . . . . .Counsel, Entertainment, Media, Trademark & Copyright Litigation
Christopher Reeder . . . . .Associate, Entertainment, Media, Trademark & Copyright Litigation

EDWARD M. KELMAN, ATTORNEY AT LAW
100 Park Ave., 20th Fl.
New York, NY 10017
PHONE 212-371-9490
FAX 212-750-1356
EMAIL . . . . .emknyc@aol.com
ENTERTAINMENT LAW SERVICES   Full Service Representation - Contract Negotiation & Drafting - Copyright & Trademark Matters - Licensing - Motion Picture & TV Law - Music Law

Edward M. Kelman . . . . .Attorney at Law

KIRKPATRICK & LOCKHART NICHOLSON GRAHAM LLP
10100 Santa Monica Blvd., 7th Fl.
Los Angeles, CA 90067
PHONE 310-552-5000
FAX 310-552-5001
EMAIL . . . . .info@klng.com
WEB SITE . . . . .www.klng.com
COMMENTS   Offices in Boston, Dallas, Harrisburg, Miami, Newark, New York, Pittsburgh, San Francisco, Washington, DC and London

Bonnie Berry-LaMon . . . . .Partner, Entertainment
Jill Varon . . . . .Associate, Entertainment

KLEINBERG & LERNER, LLP
2049 Century Park East, Ste. 1080
Los Angeles, CA 90067
PHONE 310-557-1511
FAX 310-557-1540
EMAIL . . . . .mdiliberto@kleinberglerner.com
WEB SITE . . . . .www.kleinberglerner.com
SECOND WEB SITE . . . . .www.mrdmediation.com
ENTERTAINMENT LAW SERVICES   Full Service Representation - Arbitration & Mediation - Contract Negotiation & Drafting - Copyright & Trademark Matters - Intellectual Property Law - Licensing - Litigation - Misappropriation of Name, Voice, Likeness - Motion Picture & TV Law - Music Law
COMMENTS   Internet Law

Michael R. Diliberto . . . . .Partner, Entertainment

KLEINBERG LOPEZ LANGE CUDDY & EDEL, LLP
2049 Century Park East, Ste. 3180
Los Angeles, CA 90067
PHONE 310-286-9696
FAX 310-277-7145
ENTERTAINMENT LAW SERVICES   Contract Negotiation & Drafting - Copyright & Trademark Matters - Motion Picture & TV Law - Music Law - Talent Representation
COMMENTS   Acquisition and sale of film libraries

Kenneth Kleinberg APC . . . . .Partner
Peter Lopez APC . . . . .Partner
Robert Lange APC . . . . .Partner
Christine Cuddy APC . . . . .Partner
Scott Edel APC . . . . .Partner
Elliott Kleinberg APC . . . . .Partner
Ronald Levin . . . . .Attorney
Gary Fine . . . . .Attorney
Stephanie Rosenberg . . . . .Attorney
Mark Kovinsky APC . . . . .Of Counsel

ATTORNEYS

KOPER FIRM
1001 Fourth Ave. Plaza, Ste. 3200
Seattle, WA 98154
PHONE 206-323-9936
FAX 206-350-1706
EMAIL .krys@koperfirm.com
ENTERTAINMENT LAW SERVICES   Full Service Representation - Acquisitions & Mergers - Contract Negotiation & Drafting - Copyright & Trademark Matters - Corporate Matters - Financing - Intellectual Property Law - Libel & Privacy Matters - Licensing - Misappropriation of Name, Voice, Likeness - Motion Picture & TV Law - Music Law - Partnerships/Joint Ventures - Right of Publicity - Royalty Law - Talent Representation - Transactional Law
COMMENTS   Services include international aspects of representation

Krys Koper . . . . .Attorney
Katerina Odra . . . . .Legal Assistant

LAW OFFICES OF BENJAMIN LASKI
3112 Washington Blvd.
Marina del Rey, CA 90292
PHONE 310-578-1617
FAX 310-578-1657
EMAIL . . . . .ben@laskilaw.com
WEB SITE .www.laskilaw.com
ENTERTAINMENT LAW SERVICES   Contract Negotiation & Drafting - Copyright & Trademark Matters - Intellectual Property Law - Libel & Privacy Matters - Misappropriation of Name, Voice, Likeness - Motion Picture & TV Law - Music Law - Talent Representation

Ben Laski . . . . .Attorney

LENARD & KLOTZ LLP
15250 Ventura Blvd., Ste. 411
Sherman Oaks, CA 91403
PHONE .818-990-9869/310-203-8888
ENTERTAINMENT LAW SERVICES   Music Law

Allen D. Lenard . . . . .Partner
Adam M. Klotz . . . . .Partner

LAW OFFICE OF PAUL S. LEVINE
1054 Superba Ave.
Venice, CA 90291-3940
PHONE .310-450-6711/800-742-1819
FAX 310-450-0181
EMAIL . . . . .pslevine@ix.netcom.com
WEB SITE . . . . .www.paulslevine.com
ENTERTAINMENT LAW SERVICES   Arbitration & Mediation - Contract Negotiation & Drafting - Copyright & Trademark Matters - Corporate Matters - Employment/Labor Law - Financing - First Amendment Issues - Intellectual Property Law - Libel & Privacy Matters - Litigation - Misappropriation of Name, Voice, Likeness - Motion Picture & TV Law - Music Law - Partnerships/Joint Ventures - Right of Publicity - Royalty Law - Talent Representation - Transactional Law
REPRESENTS   Writers - Producers - Directors - Musicians - Composers - Animators - Inventors - Production Companies - Distribution Companies
COMMENTS   Document preparation; Literary agent for adult, children, and young adult fiction and non-fiction book authors; Book publishing law

Paul S. Levine . . . . .Attorney

LEWIS BRISBOIS BISGAARD & SMITH, LLP
221 N. Figueroa St., Ste. 1200
Los Angeles, CA 90012-2601
PHONE 213-250-1800
FAX 213-250-7900
WEB SITE . . . . .www.lbbslaw.com
ENTERTAINMENT LAW SERVICES   Copyright & Trademark Matters - Employment/Labor Law - Intellectual Property Law - Litigation - Music Law - Tax Law
COMMENTS   Rights acquisitions and clearances; Offices in Costa Mesa, Sacramento, San Bernardino, San Diego, San Francisco, Las Vegas, Phoenix, Tucson and Chicago; East Coast office: 199 Water St., Ste. 2500, New York, NY 10038

William Archer . . . . .Partner, Entertainment (LA)
Sanford Astor .Associate, Entertainment (LA)
Leo A. Bautista . . . . .Partner, Entertainment (LA)
Dan C. Decarlo . . . . .Partner, Entertainment (LA)
Tom C. Kidde .Partner, Entertainment (LA)
David N. Makous . . . . .Partner, Entertainment (LA)
Gary S. Rattet .Partner, Entertainment (LA)
Deborah F. Sirias . . . . .Partner, Entertainment (LA)
John S. Christopher . . . . .Associate, Entertainment (LA)
Mina F. Hamilton . . . . .Associate, Entertainment (LA)
Isama H. Lee . . . . .Associate, Entertainment (LA)
Michael N. Radparvar . . . . .Associate, Entertainment (LA)

ATTORNEYS

LOEB & LOEB, LLP

10100 Santa Monica Blvd.
Los Angeles, CA 90067-4134
PHONE 310-282-2000/212-407-4000
FAX 310-282-2200/212-407-4990
EMAIL . . . . .firstinitiallastname@loeb.com
WEB SITE . . . . .www.loeb.com

ENTERTAINMENT LAW SERVICES	Full Service Representation - Acquisitions & Mergers - Arbitration & Mediation - Contract Negotiation & Drafting - Copyright & Trademark Matters - Corporate Matters - Employment/Labor Law - Financing - First Amendment Issues - Intellectual Property Law - Libel & Privacy Matters - Licensing - Litigation - Misappropriation of Name, Voice, Likeness - Motion Picture & TV Law - Music Law - Partnerships/Joint Ventures - Right of Publicity - Royalty Law - Talent Representation - Tax Law - Transactional Law
COMMENTS	Securities; Trusts & Estates; Real Estate; East Coast office: 345 Park Ave., New York, NY 10154-0037; Chicago office: 321 N. Clark St., Chicago, IL 60610-4714, ph: 312-464-3100, fax: 312-464-3111; Nashville office: 1906 Acklen Ave., Nashville, TN 37212-3740, ph: 615-749-8300, fax: 615-749-8308

Kenneth B. Anderson . . . . .Attorney, Entertainment (NY)
Leah Antonio-Ketcham . . . . .Attorney, Entertainment (LA)
Roger M. Arar . . . . .Attorney, Entertainment (NY)
Curtis W. Bajak . . . . .Attorney, Entertainment (LA)
John C. Beiter . . . . .Attorney, Entertainment (Nashville)
Marc Chamlin . . . . .Attorney, Entertainment (NY)
John J. Dellaverson . . . . .Attorney, Entertainment (LA)
Alexandra N. DeNeve . . . . .Attorney, Entertainment (NY)
Tiffany Dunn . . . . .Attorney, Entertainment (Nashville)
Craig A. Emanuel . . . . .Attorney, Entertainment (LA)
Keith G. Fleer . . . . .Attorney, Entertainment (LA)
Kenneth R. Florin . . . . .Attorney, Entertainment (NY)
John T. Frankenheimer . . . . .Attorney, Entertainment (LA)
Kevin Garlitz . . . . .Attorney, Entertainment (LA)
Richard E. Garmise . . . . .Attorney, Entertainment (NY)
Seth D. Gelblum .Attorney, Entertainment (NY)
Jim Goodkind . . . . .Attorney, Entertainment (LA)
Carolyn Hunt . . . . .Attorney, Entertainment (LA)
Kenneth L. Kraus . . . . .Attorney, Entertainment (Nashville)
Mickey A. Mayerson . . . . .Attorney, Entertainment (LA)
Douglas E. Mirell . . . . .Attorney, Entertainment (LA)
C. Anthony Mulrain . . . . .Attorney, Entertainment (LA)
Amy B. Ortner . . . . .Attorney, Entertainment (NY)
Nigel Graham Pearson . . . . .Attorney, Entertainment (LA)
Robert S. Reich . . . . .Attorney, Entertainment (NY)
Amanda E. Rykoff . . . . .Attorney, Entertainment (NY)
Stephen Saltzman . . . . .Attorney, Media & Entertainment (LA)
Stefan Schick . . . . .Attorney, Entertainment (NY)
Barry I. Slotnick .Attorney, Entertainment (NY)
Louis Spoto . . . . .Attorney, Entertainment (LA)
Rebel R. Steiner .Attorney, Entertainment (LA)
Denise McIntosh Stevens . . . . .Attorney, Entertainment (Nashville)
Robert L. Sullivan . . . . .Attorney, Entertainment (Nashville)
James D. Taylor .Attorney, Entertainment (NY)
Irwin J. Tenenbaum . . . . .Attorney, Entertainment (LA)
Michael Thurman . . . . .Attorney, Securities Litigation (LA)
Kelly L. Wick . . . . .Attorney, Entertainment (NY)
Susan Z. Williams . . . . .Attorney, Entertainment (LA)
Gavin M. Wise . . . . .Attorney, Entertainment (LA)
Po Yi . . . . .Attorney, Entertainment (NY)
Scott Zolke . . . . .Attorney (LA)

MANATT, PHELPS & PHILLIPS, LLP

11355 W. Olympic Blvd.
Los Angeles, CA 90064
PHONE 310-312-4000/212-541-9090
FAX 310-312-4224/212-541-9250
WEB SITE . . . . .www.manatt.com

ENTERTAINMENT LAW SERVICES	Full Service Representation
COMMENTS	East Coast office: 7 Times Square, New York, NY 10036

Roger L. Armstrong . . . . .Partner, Entertainment (310-312-4263)
Michael Barkow . . . . .Partner, Advertising, Marketing & Media (NY) (212-790-4590)
Fred Bernstein . . . . .Partner, Entertainment (310-312-4166)
Lawrence J. Blake . . . . .Counsel, Entertainment (310-312-4107)
Alan M. Brunswick . . . . . .Partner, Employment & Labor (310-312-4213)
Gregory Clarick . . . . .Partner, Litigation (NY) (212-790-4500)
James S. Cochran . . . . . . .Partner, Bankruptcy & Financial Restructuring (310-312-4131)
Andrew DeVore . . . . .Partner, Litigation (NY) (212-790-4500)
Jeffrey S. Edelstein . . . . . . .Partner, Advertising, Marketing & Media (NY) (212-790-4533)
Beverly Frank . . . . .Partner, Entertainment (310-312-4386)
Linda Goldstein . . . . .Partner, Advertising, Marketing & Media (NY) (212-790-4500)
Steven Hayes . . . . .Partner, Litigation (NY) (212-790-4500)
William M. Heberer . . . . . .Partner, Advertising, Marketing & Media (NY) (212-790-4566)
Susan E. Hollander . . . . .Partner, IP & Internet (650-812-1344)
Johnnie A. James . . . . . . .Partner, Employment & Labor (310-312-4169)
Barry E. Mallen . . . . .Partner, Entertainment (310-312-4339)
Jeffrey A. Mannisto . . . . .Partner, Tax, Employee Benefits & Wealth Management (310-312-4212)
Gerald A. Margolis . . . . .Partner, Entertainment (310-312-4147)
Lawrence M. Marks . . . . .Partner, Entertainment (310-312-4154)
Peter Parcher . . . . .Partner, Litigation (NY) (212-790-4500)
L. Lee Phillips . . . . .Partner, Entertainment (310-312-4111)
Jill M. Pietrini . . . . .Partner, IP & Internet (310-312-4325)
Lisa Rovinsky . . . . .Partner, Advertsing, Marketing & Media (NY) (212-790-4500)
Miwon Yi . . . . .Partner, Employment & Labor (310-312-4344)
Felix H. Kent . . . . .Sr. Counsel, Advertising, Marketing & Media (NY) (212-790-4588)
Eric J. Custer . . . . .Counsel, Entertainment (310-312-4219)
Joseph Horacek III . . . . .Counsel, Entertainment (310-312-4140)
Robert Jacobs . . . . .Counsel, Litigation (NY) (212-790-4500)
Arnold D. Kassoy . . . . .Counsel, Tax, Employee Benefits & Wealth Management (310-312-4314)
Stanley W. Levy . . . . .Counsel, Litigation (310-312-4379)
Alon Markowitz . . . . .Counsel, Litigation (NY) (212-790-4500)
Melissa W. Weaver . . . . .Counsel, Entertainment (310-312-4332)
Shari Mulrooney Wollman . . . . .Counsel, IP & Internet (310-312-4309)
Jennifer N. Deitch . . . . .Associate, Advertising, Marketing & Media (NY) (212-790-4595)
Aaron M. Harrison . . . . .Associate, Entertainment (310-312-4311)
Jennifer V. Koester . . . . . .Associate, Advertising, Marketing & Media (NY) (212-790-4599)
Kimo Peluso . . . . .Associate, Entertainment (NY) (212-790-4500)
Julia Reytblat . . . . .Associate, Advertising, Marketing & Media (NY) (212-790-4554)
Lindsay M. Schoen . . . .Associate, Advertising, Marketing & Media (NY) (212-790-4504)
Daniel K. Stuart . . . . .Associate, Entertainment (310-312-4170)
Joy Teitel . . . . .Associate, Litigation (310-312-4264)
Avi Weitzman . . . . .Associate, Litigation (NY) (212-790-4500)
Monica Youn . . . . .Associate, Litigation (NY) (212-790-4500)

ATTORNEYS

MANNING & MARDER, KASS, ELLROD, RAMIREZ, LLP
660 S. Figueroa St., 23rd Fl.
Los Angeles, CA 90017
PHONE 213-624-6900
FAX 213-624-6999
EMAIL . . . . .info@mmker.com
WEB SITE . . . . .www.mmker.com
ENTERTAINMENT LAW SERVICES   Copyright & Trademark Matters -
Employment/Labor Law -
Intellectual Property Law -
Litigation - Motion Picture & TV
Law - Transactional Law
COMMENTS   Specializes in transactional, litigational and advisory services
for clients in every area of the
entertainment industry

John A. Marder . . . . .Managing Partner
Anthony Ellrod . . . . .Partner
Jeffery M. Lenkov . . . . .Partner

MASURLAW
101 E. 15th St.
New York, NY 10003
PHONE 212-931-8220
FAX 212-931-8221
EMAIL . . . . .info@masurlaw.com
WEB SITE . . . . .www.masurlaw.com
SECOND WEB SITE .www.entmedia.com
ENTERTAINMENT LAW SERVICES   Full Service Representation -
Acquisitions & Mergers -
Contract Negotiation & Drafting
- Copyright & Trademark Matters
- Corporate Matters - Financing
- Intellectual Property Law -
Licensing - Motion Picture & TV
Law - Music Law -
Partnerships/Joint Ventures -
Right of Publicity - Transactional
Law
COMMENTS   Strategic consulting

Steven Masur . . . . .Partner
Mark Anderson . . . . .Associate
Andrew McCormick . . . . .Associate
Cheryl Wickhan . . . . .Associate
Robert Haile . . . . .Business Affairs

MCLANE & WONG
20501 Ventura Blvd., Ste. 217
Woodland Hills, CA 91364
PHONE 818-587-6801
FAX 818-587-6802
EMAIL . . . . .bcmclane@aol.com
WEB SITE . . . . .www.benmclane.com
ENTERTAINMENT LAW SERVICES   Contract Negotiation & Drafting
- Copyright & Trademark Matters
- Intellectual Property Law -
Music Law

Ben McLane . . . . .Partner
Venice Wong . . . . .Partner

THE MIDDLETON LAW GROUP, PC
475 Fifth Ave., Ste. 1516
New York, NY 10017
PHONE 212-573-8100
FAX 212-573-6113
EMAIL . . . . .i.waldon@middletonlawgroup.com
SECOND EMAIL . . . . .iwaldon@waldonlaw.com
WEB SITE . . . . .www.middletonlawgroup.com
ENTERTAINMENT LAW SERVICES   Contract Negotiation & Drafting
- Copyright & Trademark Matters
- Corporate Matters -
Employment/Labor Law -
Licensing - Motion Picture & TV
Law - Music Law -
Partnerships/Joint Ventures -
Royalty Law - Talent
Representation - Transactional
Law
REPRESENTS   Music Artists (Foxy Brown - Mario
- Fabolous - Shyne) - Writers -
Producers - Composers -
Executives - Screenwriters -
Directors - Labels (Blackground
Records) - Production
Companies - Actors
COMMENTS   Executive Compensation;
Endorsement Deals

Matthew J. Middleton . . . . .Partner
Nicole S. George . . . . .Associate
Ian P. Waldon . . . . .Of Counsel

MILLER & PLIAKAS, LLP
9720 Wilshire Blvd., Ste. 700
Beverly Hills, CA 90212
PHONE 310-860-1313
FAX 310-860-1515
EMAIL . . . . .ddm@mp-lawfirm.com
SECOND EMAIL .rap@mp-lawfirm.com
ENTERTAINMENT LAW SERVICES   Full Service Representation -
Contract Negotiation & Drafting
- Corporate Matters - Licensing -
Motion Picture & TV Law - Music
Law - Partnerships/Joint Ventures
- Talent Representation -
Transactional Law

Darrell D. Miller Esq. . . . . .Managing Partner
Roger A. Pliakas Esq. . . . . .Partner
Jesse S. Connors Esq. . . . . .Associate

ATTORNEYS

MITCHELL SILBERBERG & KNUPP, LLP

11377 W. Olympic Blvd.
Los Angeles, CA 90064
PHONE 310-312-2000/202-973-8109
FAX 310-312-3100/202-973-8110
EMAIL . . . . .info@msk.com
WEB SITE . . . . .www.msk.com

ENTERTAINMENT LAW SERVICES Acquisitions & Mergers - Contract Negotiation & Drafting - Copyright & Trademark Matters - Corporate Matters - Employment/Labor Law - Financing - First Amendment Issues - Intellectual Property Law - Licensing - Litigation - Motion Picture & TV Law - Music Law - Partnerships/Joint Ventures

COMMENTS Domain name disputes; Defamation and unfair competition matters; East Coast office: 2300 M St. NW, Ste. 800, Washington, DC 20037

George Borkowski . . . . .Partner
William Cole . . . . .Partner
Philip Davis . . . . .Partner
Ronald DiNicola . . . . .Partner
Russell Frackman . . . . .Partner
Harold Friedman . . . . .Partner
Frida Glucoft . . . . .Partner
Jeffrey Goldman . . . . .Partner
James Guerra . . . . .Partner
Adam Levin . . . . .Partner
Patricia Mayer . . . . .Partner
Alan Pepper . . . . .Partner
Howard Shapiro . . . . .Partner
David Steinberg . . . . .Partner
Joseph Swan . . . . .Partner
Robert Wise . . . . .Partner
Bernard Donnenfeld . . . . .Of Counsel
Robert Dudnik . . . . .Of Counsel
Jocelyn Gutierrez . . . . .Of Counsel
William Kaplan . . . . .Of Counsel
Mark Litvack . . . . .Of Counsel
Jan Powers . . . . .Of Counsel
Kim Swartz . . . . .Of Counsel
Samantha Grant . . . . .Associate
Marc Mayer . . . . .Associate
Guy Roy . . . . .Associate

MORRISON & FOERSTER, LLP

1880 Century Park East, Ste. 1111
Los Angeles, CA 90067-1600
PHONE 310-203-4000/213-892-5200
FAX 310-203-4040/213-892-5454
EMAIL . . . . .info@mofo.com
WEB SITE . . . . .www.mofo.com

ENTERTAINMENT LAW SERVICES Acquisitions & Mergers - Arbitration & Mediation - Contract Negotiation & Drafting - Copyright & Trademark Matters - Corporate Matters - Employment/Labor Law - Financing - First Amendment Issues - Intellectual Property Law - Libel & Privacy Matters - Licensing - Litigation - Misappropriation of Name, Voice, Likeness - Motion Picture & TV Law - Music Law - Partnerships/Joint Ventures - Right of Publicity - Royalty Law - Talent Representation - Tax Law - Transactional Law

COMMENTS International entertainment; Olympic work; Collective bargaining agreements, employment disputes and allegations; Guild and union matters; Additional Los Angeles office: 555 W. Fifth St., Los Angeles, CA 90013; Nineteen offices worldwide

Matthew D. Berger . . . . .Partner, Entertainment & Media (Tokyo)
Ivy Kagan Bierman . . . . . . .Partner, Entertainment & Media (Century City)
Sherri Blount . . . . . .Partner, Entertainment & Media (Washington, D.C.)
Kelly Charles Crabb . . . . .Partner, Entertainment & Media (Century City)
John Delaney . . . . .Partner, Entertainment & Media (NY)
Ed Gray . . . . .Partner, Entertainment & Media (Washington, D.C.)
Douglas L. Hendricks . . .Partner, Entertainment & Media (San Francisco)
Paul E. Jahn . . . . . . .Partner, Entertainment & Media (San Francisco)
Daniel G. McIntosh . . . . .Partner, Entertainment & Media (Century City)
H. Mark Mersel . . . . . .Partner, Entertainment & Media (Orange County)
David Naylor . . . . .Partner, Entertainment & Media (London)
Kate O'Brien . . . . .Partner, Entertainment & Media (Los Angeles)
Jay Ponazecki . . . . .Partner, Entertainment & Media (Tokyo)
Howard Soloway . . . . . . .Partner, Entertainment & Media (Los Angeles)
Pauline M. Stevens . . . . . .Partner, Entertainment & Media (Los Angeles)
Raj Tanden . . . . .Partner, Entertainment & Media (Los Angeles)
Rosemary S. Tarlton . . . . .Partner, Entertainment & Media (San Francisco)
Margaret Tobey . . . . .Partner, Entertainment & Media (Washington, D.C.)
Russell G. Weiss . . . . . . .Partner, Entertainment & Media (Century City)
Kristen Wiggert . . . . .Partner, Entertainment & Media (London)
Robert Woll . . . .Managing Partner, Entertainment & Media (Hong Kong)
M. Kenneth Suddleson . .Sr. Of Counsel, Entertainment & Media (Century City)
Vivian Hanson . . . . .Of Counsel, Entertainment & Media (New York)
Alvaro Pascotto . . . . .Of Counsel, Entertainment & Media (Century City)
Robert D. Cooper . . . . .Associate, Entertainment & Media (Century City)
Bill Gable . . . . .Associate, Entertainment & Media (Century City)
Joseph T. Hahn . . . . . .Associate, Entertainment & Media (Los Angeles)
E. Trey Hatch . . . . .Associate, Entertainment & Media (NY)
Eve D. McCabe . . . . . .Associate, Entertainment & Media (Los Angeles)
Melody N. Torbati . . . . .Associate, Entertainment & Media (Los Angeles)
Brandon Villery . . . . . .Associate, Entertainment & Media (Century City)

ATTORNEYS

MOSES & SINGER, LLP

1301 Avenue of the Americas
New York, NY 10019
PHONE 212-554-7800
FAX 212-554-7700
EMAIL . . . . .entertainmentinfo@mosessinger.com
WEB SITE .www.mosessinger.com

ENTERTAINMENT LAW SERVICES	Full Service Representation - Acquisitions & Mergers - Arbitration & Mediation - Contract Negotiation & Drafting - Copyright & Trademark Matters - Corporate Matters - Employment/Labor Law - Financing - First Amendment Issues - Intellectual Property Law - Libel & Privacy Matters - Licensing - Litigation - Misappropriation of Name, Voice, Likeness - Motion Picture & TV Law - Music Law - Partnerships/Joint Ventures - Right of Publicity - Royalty Law - Tax Law - Transactional Law
COMMENTS	Serving the TV, motion picture, book publishing, recording, and periodical and music publishing industries

Stanley Rothenberg . . . . .Partner, Advertising/Entertainment/
Intellectual Property/Internet/New Media
Cathy J. Frankel . .Partner, Advertising/Entertainment/Intellectual Property/
Internet/New Media
Eric P. Bergner . . .Partner, Entertainment/Intellectual Property/Advertising/
Internet/New Media/Privacy
Mitchell D. Bernstein . . . . . . .Partner, Entertainment/Hotel & Hospitality/
Internet/New Media/Intellectual Property/Litigation
Ross J. Charap . . . . .Partner, Entertainment/Intellectual Property
Elizabeth A. Corradino . . . . .Partner, Advertising/Entertainment/
Intellectual Property/Internet/New Media/Privacy
Jeffrey M. Davis . . . . .Partner, Corporate Securities & Commercial/
Mergers & Acquisitions/Healthcare/Internet/
New Media/Entertainment/Advertising
Howard R. Herman . . . . .Partner, Banking & Finance/Corporate/
Entertainment/Intellectual Property/Internet/New Media/Privacy
David Rabinowitz . . . .Partner, Privacy/Entertainment/Intellectual Property/
Internet/New Media/Litigation
Alvin H. Schulman . . . . . . .Partner, Corporate, Securities & Commercial/
Entertainment/Trusts & Estates
Philippe A. Zimmerman . . . . .Partner, Entertainment/Intellectual Property/
Litigation
Arthur F. Abelman . . . . .Of Counsel, Litigation/Entertainment/
Hotel & Hospitality/Intellectual Property

MYMAN ABELL FINEMAN GREENSPAN LIGHT, LLP

11601 Wilshire Blvd., Ste. 2200
Los Angeles, CA 90025-1758
PHONE 310-231-0800
FAX 310-207-2680

ENTERTAINMENT LAW SERVICES	Contract Negotiation & Drafting - Motion Picture & TV Law - Talent Representation - Transactional Law

Robert Myman . . . . .Partner/Attorney
Leslie Abell . . . . .Partner/Attorney
Tom Fineman . . . . .Partner/Attorney
Eric Greenspan . . . . .Partner/Attorney
Jeffrey T. Light . . . . .Partner/Attorney
David Fox . . . . .Partner/Attorney
Steve Younger . . . . .Partner/Attorney
Glenn Davis . . . . .Attorney
Jennifer Lynn Grega . . . . .Attorney
Laurie Megery . . . . .Attorney
Tamara Milagros-Woeckner .Attorney
Francois Mobasser . . . . .Attorney
Kim Stenton . . . . .Attorney

VALERIE ANN NEMETH

619 S. Vulcan Ave., Ste. 215
Encinitas, CA 92024
PHONE 760-944-4130/310-471-7648
FAX 760-942-6043/760-944-3325
EMAIL . . . . .vanemeth@cs.com
WEB SITE . . . . .www.entlawyer.com

ENTERTAINMENT LAW SERVICES	Contract Negotiation & Drafting - Copyright & Trademark Matters - Intellectual Property Law - Licensing - Motion Picture & TV Law - Music Law - Partnerships/Joint Ventures - Right of Publicity - Transactional Law
COMMENTS	All facets of film, TV, music and publishing

Valerie Ann Nemeth . . . . .Attorney

NOVIAN & NOVIAN

1801 Century Park East, Ste. 1201
Los Angeles, CA 90067
PHONE 310-553-1222
FAX 310-553-0222
WEB SITE . . . . .www.novianlaw.com

ENTERTAINMENT LAW SERVICES	Acquisitions & Mergers - Contract Negotiation & Drafting - Copyright & Trademark Matters - Intellectual Property Law - Libel & Privacy Matters - Licensing - Litigation - Misappropriation of Name, Voice, Likeness - Music Law - Right of Publicity - Royalty Law

Farid Novian . . . . .Partner
Farhad Novian . . . . .Partner
Stephanie Casale . . . . .Attorney
R. Michael Collum . . . . .Attorney
Sam Frankel . . . . .Attorney
Josh Mendelsohn . . . . .Attorney
Susan A. Rodriguez . . . . .Attorney
Lisa Simantub . . . . .Attorney
Vicki Steiner . . . . .Attorney
Aaron J. Weissman . . . . .Attorney

*OBIOHA & ASSOCIATES

5900 Wilshire Blvd., Ste. 2600
Los Angeles, CA 90036
PHONE 323-330-0590
FAX 323-330-0591
EMAIL . . . . .igbo@obiohalaw.com

ENTERTAINMENT LAW SERVICES	Full Service Representation - Contract Negotiation & Drafting - Financing - Licensing - Motion Picture & TV Law - Music Law - Partnerships/Joint Ventures - Talent Representation - Transactional Law
REPRESENTS	Alex Thomas - Claudia Jordan - Okimo Entertainment - Tri Destined Studios - Stepping Stone Productions, LLC
COMMENTS	Artist representation, label formation, licensing and publishing deals; Production counsel for independent film producers; Soundtrack deals

Igbodike G. Obioha . . . . .Attorney

ATTORNEYS

O'BRIEN ZARIAN LLP

445 S. Figueroa St., Ste. 3750
Los Angeles, CA 90071
PHONE 213-629-7400
FAX 213-629-7401
EMAIL .info@obrienzarian.com
WEB SITE .www.obrienzarian.com
ENTERTAINMENT LAW SERVICES   Full Service Representation - Arbitration & Mediation - Contract Negotiation & Drafting - Corporate Matters - First Amendment Issues - Intellectual Property Law - Libel & Privacy Matters - Licensing - Litigation - Misappropriation of Name, Voice, Likeness - Music Law - Right of Publicity
COMMENTS   Second office: 420 Aviation Blvd., Ste. 201, Santa Rosa, CA 95403

Robert C. O'Brien . . . . .Partner, Litigation & Intellectual Property
John N. Zarian . . . . .Partner, Litigation & Intellectual Property
Jerrold Abeles . . . . .Partner, Litigation & Intellectual Property
J. Harrison Colter . . . . . . .Of Counsel, Litigation & Intellectual Property/ Contract Negotiation & Drafting
Bela G. Lugosi . . . . .Of Counsel, Litigation & Intellectual Property/ Contract Negotiation & Drafting
Roy Z. Silva . . . . .Counsel, Litigation & Intellectual Property
David G. Bayles . . . . .Associate, Litigation & Intellectual Property
Amy I. Borlund . . . . .Associate, Litigation & Intellectual Property
Jennifer C. Terry . . . . .Associate, Litigation & Intellectual Property

O'MELVENY & MYERS LLP

400 S. Hope St.
Los Angeles, CA 90071-2899
PHONE 213-430-6000/212-326-2000
FAX .213-430-6407/212-326-2061
EMAIL .omminfo@omm.com
WEB SITE . . . . .www.omm.com
ENTERTAINMENT LAW SERVICES   Full Service Representation - Acquisitions & Mergers - Arbitration & Mediation - Contract Negotiation & Drafting - Copyright & Trademark Matters - Corporate Matters - Employment/Labor Law - Financing - First Amendment Issues - Intellectual Property Law - Libel & Privacy Matters - Licensing - Litigation - Misappropriation of Name, Voice, Likeness - Motion Picture & TV Law - Music Law - Partnerships/Joint Ventures - Right of Publicity - Royalty Law - Talent Representation - Tax Law - Transactional Law
COMMENTS   Century City office: 1999 Avenue of the Stars, Los Angeles, CA 90067-6035, phone: 310-553-6700, fax: 310-246-6779; New York office: Times Square Tower, 7 Times Square, New York, NY 10036-6537, phone: 212-326-2000, fax: 212-326-2061; DC office: 1625 Eye St. NW, Washington, DC 20006-4001; phone: 202-383-5300, fax: 202-383-5414

Brian M. Berliner . . . . .Partner (LA)
Joseph A. Calabrese . . . . .Chair, Entertainment & Media Practice Group (Century City)
Dale M. Cendali . . . . .Partner (NY)
Scott H. Dunham . . . .Chair, Labor and Employment Practice Group (LA)
(Continued)

O'MELVENY & MYERS LLP (Continued)

David P. Enzminger . . . . .Partner (LA)
David A. Krinsky . . . . .Co-Chair, Transactions Department (Newport Beach/Menlo Park)
Mark E. Miller . . . . .Partner (SF)
David B. Murphy . . . . .Partner (Newport Beach)
Christopher C. Murray . . . . .Partner (Century City)
Kenneth R. O'Rourke .Partner (LA)
William J. Peters . . . . .Partner (LA)
Daniel M. Petrocelli . . . . .Partner (Century City)
Claudia E. Ray . . . . .Partner (NY)
George A. Riley . . . . .Partner (SF)
Robert A. Rizzi . .Chair, Tax Practice Group (Washington, DC/Menlo Park)
Richard R. Ross . . . . .Of Counsel (Century City)
Mark A. Samuels . . . . .Chair, Intellectual Property & Technology Practice Group (LA)
Stephen Scharf . . . . .Partner (Century City)
Robert M. Schwartz . . . . .Partner (Century City)
Robert A. Siegel . . . . .Co-Chair, Litigation Department (LA)
Darin W. Snyder . . . . .Partner (SF)
John J. Suydam . . . . .Co-Chair, Transactions Department (NY)
David I. Weil .Partner (Century City)
Brett J. Williamson . . . . .Partner (Newport Beach)
W. Mark Wood . . . . .Co-Chair, Litigation Department (LA)

THE LAW OFFICES OF MARTY O'TOOLE

1999 Avenue of the Stars, Ste. 1100
Los Angeles, CA 90046
PHONE 310-888-4000
EMAIL . . . . .mx@lawofficesofmartyotoole.com
WEB SITE . . . . .www.lawofficesofmartyotoole.com
ENTERTAINMENT LAW SERVICES   Full Service Representation - Arbitration & Mediation - Contract Negotiation & Drafting - Copyright & Trademark Matters - Corporate Matters - First Amendment Issues - Intellectual Property Law - Libel & Privacy Matters - Licensing - Litigation - Misappropriation of Name, Voice, Likeness - Motion Picture & TV Law - Music Law - Partnerships/Joint Ventures - Right of Publicity - Royalty Law - Transactional Law
REPRESENTS   Musicians - Filmmakers - Screenwriters - Authors
COMMENTS   Music shopping; Film packaging and pitching

Marty O'Toole . . . . .Attorney at Law
Adrienne Dameron . . . . .Assistant
Eric Larson . . . . .Assistant
Connor McPherson . . . . .Assistant

PADGETT LAW FIRM

22260 Highway 6
Batesville, MS 38606
PHONE 662-563-9625
FAX 662-578-2473
EMAIL . . . . .jeffpadgett@justice.com
WEB SITE . . . . .www.padgettlawfirmpllc.com
ENTERTAINMENT LAW SERVICES   Full Service Representation - Contract Negotiation & Drafting - Copyright & Trademark Matters - Licensing - Music Law - Partnerships/Joint Ventures - Royalty Law - Talent Representation
REPRESENTS   Cole Point Records - Harpo - Wayne Garrett - Under the Gun - Gary White

Jeff Padgett . . . . .Owner

PAUL, WEISS, RIFKIND, WHARTON & GARRISON, LLP

1285 Avenue of the Americas
New York, NY 10019-6064
PHONE 212-373-3000/212-373-3391
FAX 212-757-3990/212-373-2092
EMAIL . . . . .jbreglio@paulweiss.com
SECOND EMAIL . . . . .mailbox@paulweiss.com
WEB SITE . . . . .www.paulweiss.com

ENTERTAINMENT LAW SERVICES	Full Service Representation - Acquisitions & Mergers - Arbitration & Mediation - Contract Negotiation & Drafting - Copyright & Trademark Matters - Corporate Matters - Financing - First Amendment Issues - Intellectual Property Law - Libel & Privacy Matters - Licensing - Litigation - Misappropriation of Name, Voice, Likeness - Motion Picture & TV Law - Music Law - Partnerships/Joint Ventures - Right Of Publicity - Royalty Law - Talent Representation - Tax Law - Transactional Law
REPRESENTS	A vast array of clients, both personal and institutional, involved in all aspects of the entertainment industry
COMMENTS	Offices in Washington, DC, London, Paris, Tokyo, Beijing, Hong Kong

John F. Breglio . . . . .Chairman/Partner, Entertainment
Peter L. Felcher . . . . .Partner, Entertainment
Charles H. Googe Jr. . . . . .Partner, Entertainment
Deborah Hartnett . . . . .Counsel, Entertainment
Helene Gaulrapp . . . . .Assistant to John F. Breglio

PERLBERGER LAW OFFICES

515 N. Arden Dr.
Beverly Hills, CA 90210
PHONE 310-859-1511
FAX 310-859-1512
EMAIL . . . . .mpesq@perlberger.com
WEB SITE . . . . .www.perlberger.com

ENTERTAINMENT LAW SERVICES	Full Service Representation - Acquisitions & Mergers - Arbitration & Mediation - Contract Negotiation & Drafting - Financing - Licensing - Motion Picture & TV Law - Music Law - Partnerships/Joint Ventures - Talent Representation - Transactional Law

Martin Perlberger . . . . .Attorney

PHILLIPS, ERLEWINE & GIVEN LLP

One Embarcadero Center, Ste. 2350
San Francisco, CA 94111
PHONE 415-398-0900
FAX 415-398-0911
WEB SITE . . . . .www.phillaw.com

ENTERTAINMENT LAW SERVICES	Contract Negotiation & Drafting - Copyright & Trademark Matters - Intellectual Property Law - Licensing - Litigation - Royalty Law

David C. Phillips . . . . .Partner (dcp@phillaw.com)
R. Scott Erlewine . . . . .Partner (rse@phillaw.com)
David M. Givens . . . . .Partner (dmg@phillaw.com)
Spencer C. Martinez . . . . .Attorney
John C. Espedal . . . . .Of Counsel

LAW OFFICE OF ROBERT PRESKILL

400 S. Beverly Dr., Ste. 214
Beverly Hills, CA 90212
PHONE .415-377-3919/310-949-9234
FAX 413-638-6878
EMAIL . . . . .preskilllaw@hotmail.com
WEB SITE . . . . .www.preskilllaw.com

ENTERTAINMENT LAW SERVICES	Full Service Representation - Contract Negotiation & Drafting - Copyright & Trademark Matters - Corporate Matters - Employment/Labor Law - Financing - Intellectual Property Law - Licensing - Motion Picture & TV Law - Music Law - Partnerships/Joint Ventures - Talent Representation - Transactional Law
REPRESENTS	Authors - Animators - Start-up Music Labels - Music Artists - Merchandisers - Licensers - Publishers - Filmmakers - Dance Troupes - Theatres - Studio Musicians
COMMENTS	Book publishing/literary rights; Founding member of literary agency Lit West Group, LLC

Robert Preskill . . . . .Attorney at Law

RODRIGUEZ & RICCI, LLC

82 E. Allendale Rd., Ste. 2B
Saddle River, NJ 07458
PHONE 201-327-1820
FAX 201-327-1824
WEB SITE . . . . .www.rrlaw.biz

ENTERTAINMENT LAW SERVICES	Full Service Representation - Contract Negotiation & Drafting - Copyright & Trademark Matters - Licensing - Music Law - Partnerships/Joint Ventures - Talent Representation

Judith A. Ricci Esq. . . . . .Attorney
Michael A. Rodriguez Esq. . . . . .Attorney
Amanda J. Martinez . . . . .Assistant
Jaclyn D. Munier . . . . .Assistant

ATTORNEYS

ATTORNEYS

LAW OFFICE OF HENRY W. ROOT, PC
1541 Ocean Ave., Ste. 200, Paseo del Mar
Santa Monica, CA 90401-2104
PHONE 310-395-6800
FAX 310-393-7777
EMAIL . . . . .henry@grrlaw.com
WEB SITE . . . . .www.grrlaw.com
ENTERTAINMENT LAW SERVICES   Contract Negotiation & Drafting
- Motion Picture & TV Law -
Music Law - Partnerships/Joint
Ventures - Transactional Law

Henry W. Root . . . . .Attorney
Lynn Quarterman . . . . .Attorney
Derrick K. Lee . . . . .Attorney

ROSEN, FEIG, GOLLAND & LUNN, LLP
9454 Wilshire Blvd., Ste. 850
Beverly Hills, CA 90212
PHONE 310-275-0562
FAX 310-275-0563
EMAIL . . . . .flunn@rfgllaw.com
WEB SITE . . . . .www.rfgllaw.com
ENTERTAINMENT LAW SERVICES   Copyright & Trademark Matters -
Intellectual Property Law - Music
Law - Talent Representation -
Transactional Law
REPRESENTS   Writers - Producers - Composers
- Actors
COMMENTS   Development, distribution, guilds
and unions, merchandising,
internet, publishing, theatre;
Previous experience includes in-
house business and legal affairs
at both Disney and 20th Century
Fox

Adam Rosen .Partner (arosen@rfgllaw.com)
Eric Feig . . . . .Partner (efeig@rfgllaw.com)
Michael H. Golland . . . . .Parnter (mgolland@rfgllaw.com)
Frank M. Lunn . . . . .Partner (flunn@rfgllaw.com)
Sarah Conley . . . . .Of Counsel (sconley@rfgllaw.com)

ROSENFELD, MEYER & SUSMAN, LLP
9601 Wilshire Blvd.
Beverly Hills, CA 90210-5211
PHONE 310-858-7700
FAX 310-860-2430
EMAIL . . . . .rms@rmslaw.com
WEB SITE . . . . .www.rmslaw.com
ENTERTAINMENT LAW SERVICES   Intellectual Property Law -
Licensing - Litigation
REPRESENTS   Individual Talent - Independent
Production/Distribution
Companies - Music
COMMENTS   Literary material clearance;
Completion guarantees

Marvin B. Meyer . . . . . .Founding Partner, Entertainment & Trusts/Estates
Renee A. Farrell . . . . .Partner, Entertainment
Lawrence Kartiganer . . . . .Partner, Entertainment & Music
Jeffrey L. Nagin . .Partner, Entertainment, Business/Corporate, Real Estate
Ron Dolecki . . . . .Sr. Counsel, Entertainment

SAYEGH & PHAM, PLC
5895 Washington Blvd.
Culver City, CA 90232
PHONE 310-895-1188
FAX 310-895-1180
EMAIL .srabin@spattorney.com
WEB SITE . . . . .www.spattorney.com
ENTERTAINMENT LAW SERVICES   Contract Negotiation & Drafting
- Copyright & Trademark Matters
- Corporate Matters - Intellectual
Property Law - Licensing -
Litigation - Misappropriation of
Name, Voice, Likeness - Motion
Picture & TV Law - Music Law -
Partnerships/Joint Ventures -
Right of Publicity - Royalty Law -
Talent Representation -
Transactional Law
REPRESENTS   Film and music production com-
panies, music publishers, com-
posers, recording artists, screen-
writers, broadcasters, including
digital streaming and subscrip-
tion services, literary authors,
visual artists

F. Freddy Sayegh . . . . .Partner
Christopher Q. Pham . . . . .Partner
Susan Rabin . . . . .Of Counsel
Miguel del Rosario . . . . .Associate
Hani Naser . . . . .Certified Mediator

SCHLEIMER & FREUNDLICH, LLP
9100 Wilshire Blvd., Ste. 615E
Beverly Hills, CA 90212
PHONE 310-273-9807
FAX 310-273-9809
WEB SITE . . . . .www.schleimerlaw.com
ENTERTAINMENT LAW SERVICES   Contract Negotiation & Drafting
- Copyright & Trademark Matters
- Intellectual Property Law -
Litigation - Right of Publicity -
Royalty Law
COMMENTS   Profit participation; Artist/manag-
er disputes; Guild and talent
agency arbitrations

Joseph D. Schleimer . . . . .Partner
Kenneth D. Freundlich . . . . .Partner

SEDGWICK, DETERT, MORAN & ARNOLD LLP
801 S. Figueroa St., 18th Fl.
Los Angeles, CA 90017
PHONE 213-426-6900/212-422-0202
FAX 213-426-6921/212-422-0925
EMAIL . . . . .firstname.lastname@sdma.com
WEB SITE .www.sdma.com
ENTERTAINMENT LAW SERVICES — Full Service Representation - Arbitration & Mediation - Contract Negotiation & Drafting - Copyright & Trademark Matters - Corporate Matters - Employment/Labor Law - Financing - First Amendment Issues - Intellectual Property Law - Libel & Privacy Matters - Licensing - Litigation - Misappropriation of Name, Voice, Likeness - Motion Picture & TV Law - Music Law - Right of Publicity - Royalty Law - Talent Representation - Transactional Law
COMMENTS — East Coast office: 125 Broad St., 39th Fl., New York, NY 10004-2400

Craig S. Barnes . . . . .Partner, Entertainment
Robert F. Helfing . . . . .Partner, Entertainment
James J.S. Homes . . . . .Partner, Media/Entertainment
John F. Stephens . . . . .Partner, Media/Entertainment
Alan C. Chen . . . . .Associate, Media/Entertainment
Stacy Goldscher . . . . .Associate, Media
Philip M.W. Pailey Jr. . . . . .Associate, Media/Entertainment
Aaron Rudin . . . . .Associate, Media/Entertainment

SEDLMAYR & ASSOCIATES, PC
200 Park Avenue South, Ste. 1408
New York, NY 10003
PHONE 212-925-3456
FAX 212-925-0554
WEB SITE . . . . .www.csentlaw.com
ENTERTAINMENT LAW SERVICES — Music Law

Theo Sedlmayr .Partner

SELVERNE, MANDELBAUM & MINTZ, LLP
1775 Broadway, Ste. 2300
New York, NY 10019
PHONE 212-259-3900
FAX 212-259-3910
ENTERTAINMENT LAW SERVICES — Copyright & Trademark Matters - Intellectual Property Law - Music Law

Michael Selverne . . . . .Partner
Thomas I. Mandelbaum . . . . .Partner
Alan M. Mintz . . . . .Partner (Retired)
Whitney C. Broussard . . . . .Attorney
David D. Gold . . . . .Attorney
Kristin L. Daily . . . . .Associate
Stephanie R. Morris . . . . .Associate
Monika A. Tashman . . . . .Associate
Roger L. Cramer . . . . .Of Counsel

SENDROFF & ASSOCIATES, P.C.
1500 Broadway, Ste. 2001
New York, NY 10036
PHONE 212-840-6400
FAX 212-840-6401
EMAIL . . . . .welcome@sendroff.com
WEB SITE . . . . .www.sendroff.com
ENTERTAINMENT LAW SERVICES — Contract Negotiation & Drafting - Copyright & Trademark Matters - Intellectual Property Law - Motion Picture & TV Law - Music Law - Talent Representation

Mark D. Sendroff . . . . .Owner
Eric Goldman . . . . .Associate

SERLING ROOKS & FERRARA, LLP
254 W. 54th St., 14th Fl.
New York, NY 10019
PHONE 212-245-7300
FAX 212-586-5175
ENTERTAINMENT LAW SERVICES — Full Service Representation - Copyright & Trademark Matters - Intellectual Property Law - Music Law

Joseph Lloyd Serling . . . . .Sr. Partner
Wayne D. Rooks . . . . .Partner
Nicholas C. Ferrara . . . . .Partner
Michael L. McKoy . . . . .Partner
J. Reid Hunter . . . . .Partner
Jeffrey A. Worob . . . . .Partner
Greg W. Brooks P.C. . . . . .Associate
Nicole L. Giacco . . . . .Associate
Stacey Lager .Associate
Theodore D. Weis . . . . .Associate
Wallace Collins . . . . .Of Counsel
Harold Rosenblum . . . . .Of Counsel

LISA A. SHAPIRO, ESQ.
16662 Oldham Pl.
Encino, CA 91436
PHONE 818-817-0066
FAX 818-995-6200
EMAIL . . . . .lisashapiroesq@earthlink.net
ENTERTAINMENT LAW SERVICES — Full Service Representation - Contract Negotiation & Drafting - Motion Picture & TV Law - Music Law - Talent Representation - Transactional Law
REPRESENTS — Writers - Directors - Producers; Client list: Broken Sky Films - Apex Entertainment - Gold Circle Films - Evolution Entertainment - XTeam Productions - Niki Marvin Productions
COMMENTS — Full-service business affairs for small entertainment companies without in-house legal staff

Lisa Shapiro .Attorney

ATTORNEYS

SHEPPARD MULLIN RICHTER & HAMPTON LLP
1901 Avenue of the Stars, Ste. 1600
Los Angeles, CA 90067
PHONE 310-228-3700
FAX 310-228-3701
WEB SITE . . . . .www.sheppardmullin.com
ENTERTAINMENT LAW SERVICES   Full Service Representation -
Acquisitions & Mergers -
Arbitration & Mediation -
Contract Negotiation & Drafting
- Copyright & Trademark Matters
- Corporate Matters -
Employment/Labor Law -
Financing - First Amendment
Issues - Intellectual Property Law
- Libel & Privacy Matters -
Licensing - Litigation -
Misappropriation of Name,
Voice, Likeness - Motion Picture
& TV Law - Music Law -
Partnerships/Joint Ventures -
Right of Publicity - Royalty Law -
Tax Law - Transactional Law
COMMENTS   Main office: 333 S. Hope St.,
48th Fl., Los Angeles, CA 90071

Robert A. Darwell . . . . .Attorney
Martin D. Katz . . . . .Attorney

SHERMAN & NATHANSON
9454 Wilshire Blvd., Ste. 820
Beverly Hills, CA 90212
PHONE 310-246-0321
FAX 310-246-0305
EMAIL . . . . .rsherman@snmlaw.com
WEB SITE . . . . .www.lawyers.com/sn&mlaw
ENTERTAINMENT LAW SERVICES   Full Service Representation -
Arbitration & Mediation -
Contract Negotiation & Drafting
- Copyright & Trademark Matters
- Corporate Matters -
Employment/Labor Law -
Intellectual Property Law - Libel &
Privacy Matters - Litigation -
Misappropriation of Name,
Voice, Likeness - Motion Picture
& TV Law - Music Law -
Partnerships/Joint Ventures -
Right of Publicity - Royalty Law -
Talent Representation -
Transactional Law

Richard Sherman . . . . .Partner
Ken Nathanson . . . . .Partner
Craig Englander . . . . .Associate
Cameron Totten . . . . .Associate
Elda Fernandez . . . . .Paralegal

SKRZYNIARZ & MALLEAN
9601 Wilshire Blvd., Ste. 650
Beverly Hills, CA 90210
PHONE 310-786-8876
FAX 310-786-8878
ENTERTAINMENT LAW SERVICES   Contract Negotiation & Drafting
- Copyright & Trademark Matters
- Financing - First Amendment
Issues - Intellectual Property Law
- Libel & Privacy Matters -
Licensing - Misappropriation of
Name, Voice, Likeness - Motion
Picture & TV Law - Music Law -
Partnerships/Joint Ventures -
Talent Representation
COMMENTS   Entertainment business matters

William J. Skrzyniarz .Owner, Entertainment
Tanya M. Mallean .Attorney, Entertainment

LAW OFFICE OF MIRIAM STERN
303 E. 83rd St.
New York, NY 10028
PHONE 212-794-1289
ENTERTAINMENT LAW SERVICES   Arbitration & Mediation -
Contract Negotiation & Drafting
- Copyright & Trademark Matters
- Intellectual Property Law -
Licensing - Motion Picture & TV
Law - Music Law -
Partnerships/Joint Ventures -
Talent Representation -
Transactional Law

Miriam Stern . . . . .Attorney

JOEL R. STROTE LAW OFFICES
4333 Park Terrace Dr., Ste. 200
Westlake Village, CA 91361
PHONE .818-707-1923/818-259-2939
FAX 805-707-8884/805-494-4809
EMAIL . . . . .jstrote@liberace.org
ENTERTAINMENT LAW SERVICES   Arbitration & Mediation -
Contract Negotiation & Drafting
- Licensing - Music Law
COMMENTS   Music industry contract negotiation

Joel R. Strote . . . . .Principal

LAW OFFICES OF NEIL SUSSMAN
10727 Interlake Ave. North
Seattle, WA 98133
PHONE 206-363-8070
FAX 206-363-7519
EMAIL . . . . .neilsussman@mindspring.com
ENTERTAINMENT LAW SERVICES   Contract Negotiation & Drafting
- Copyright & Trademark Matters
- Licensing - Music Law - Royalty
Law - Tax Law
REPRESENTS   Honey Tongue - Nevermore -
Queensrÿche - The Souvenirs -
The Toucans - Too Slim & the
Taildraggers
COMMENTS   Business management; Income
taxes and return preparation;
Business Law

Neil Sussman . . . . .Entertainment Law

PETER M. THALL
1740 Broadway, 22nd Fl.
New York, NY 10019
PHONE 212-245-6221
FAX 212-245-6406
WEB SITE . . . . .www.thallentlaw.com
ENTERTAINMENT LAW SERVICES   Contract Negotiation & Drafting
                              - Intellectual Property Law -
                              Music Law

Peter M. Thall . . . . .Attorney
Terri F. Baker . . . . .Of Counsel
Alexander Murphy Jr. .Of Counsel
Jackie J. Kim . . . . .Associate

JOHN J. TORMEY III, PLLC
217 E. 86th St., PMB 221
New York, NY 10028
PHONE 212-410-4142/845-735-9691
FAX 212-410-2380/845-735-0476
EMAIL . . . . .brightline@att.net
SECOND EMAIL . . . . .jtormey@optonline.net
WEB SITE . . . . .www.tormey.org
SECOND WEB SITE . . . . .www.tormey.net
ENTERTAINMENT LAW SERVICES   Full Service Representation -
                              Acquisitions & Mergers -
                              Contract Negotiation & Drafting
                              - Copyright & Trademark Matters
                              - Corporate Matters -
                              Employment/Labor Law -
                              Financing - Intellectual Property
                              Law - Libel & Privacy Matters -
                              Licensing - Misappropriation of
                              Name, Voice, Likeness - Motion
                              Picture & TV Law - Music Law -
                              Partnerships/Joint Ventures -
                              Right of Publicity - Royalty Law -
                              Talent Representation -
                              Transactional Law
COMMENTS   Merchandising

John J. Tormey III, Esq. . . . . .Attorney

HARRIS TULCHIN & ASSOCIATES, LTD.
11377 W. Olympic Blvd., 2nd Fl.
Los Angeles, CA 90064
PHONE 310-914-7900
FAX 310-914-7927
EMAIL . . . . .entesquire@aol.com
SECOND EMAIL . . . . .info4tulchinent@aol.com
WEB SITE . . . . .www.medialawyer.com
ENTERTAINMENT LAW SERVICES   Full Service Representation -
                              Acquisitions & Mergers -
                              Arbitration & Mediation -
                              Contract Negotiation & Drafting
                              - Copyright & Trademark Matters
                              - Financing - Intellectual Property
                              Law - Licensing -
                              Misappropriation of Name,
                              Voice, Likeness - Motion Picture
                              & TV Law - Music Law -
                              Partnerships/Joint Ventures -
                              Talent Representation
COMMENTS   Producer representation services

Harris Tulchin . . . . .Owner/Attorney
Robert Yu . . . . .VP, Acquisitions & Sales
Kathy Morozova . . . . .Director, Acquisitions & Sales

VALENSI, ROSE, MAGARAM, MORRIS & MURPHY
2029 Century Park East, Ste. 2050
Los Angeles, CA 90067-3031
PHONE 310-277-8011
FAX 310-277-1706
EMAIL . . . . .mrm@vrmlaw.com
WEB SITE . . . . .www.vrmlaw.com
ENTERTAINMENT LAW SERVICES   Full Service Representation -
                              Acquisitions & Mergers -
                              Arbitration & Mediation -
                              Contract Negotiation & Drafting
                              - Copyright & Trademark Matters
                              - Corporate Matters -
                              Employment/Labor Law -
                              Intellectual Property Law -
                              Licensing - Litigation - Music Law
                              - Partnerships/Joint Ventures -
                              Royalty Law - Talent
                              Representation - Tax Law

Michael R. Morris . . . . .Attorney, Music/Certified Tax Specialist
Michael A. Tonya . . . . .Attorney, Employment/Labor Law
Stephen F. Moeller . . . .Attorney, Entertainment Litigation & Transactions/
                                                          Labor Issues
Bruce D. Sires . . . . .Attorney, Employment of Minors in the
                              Entertainment Industry/Estate Planning

WEISSMANN, WOLFF, BERGMAN, COLEMAN, GRODIN & EVALL, LLP
9665 Wilshire Blvd., Ste. 900
Beverly Hills, CA 90212
PHONE 310-858-7888
FAX 310-550-7191
WEB SITE . . . . .www.weissmannwolff.com
ENTERTAINMENT LAW SERVICES   Full Service Representation -
                              Acquisitions & Mergers -
                              Arbitration & Mediation -
                              Contract Negotiation & Drafting
                              - Copyright & Trademark Matters
                              - Corporate Matters -
                              Employment/Labor Law -
                              Financing - First Amendment
                              Issues - Intellectual Property Law
                              - Libel & Privacy Matters -
                              Licensing - Litigation -
                              Misappropriation of Name,
                              Voice, Likeness - Motion Picture
                              & TV Law - Partnerships/Joint
                              Ventures - Right of Publicity -
                              Talent Representation - Tax Law -
                              Transactional Law

Eric Weissmann . . . . .Partner
Michael D. Bergman . . . . .Partner
Stanley M. Coleman . . . . .Partner
Alan L. Grodin . . . . .Partner
Mitchell Evall . . . . .Partner
David Burg . . . . .Partner
Howard Hart . . . . .Partner
Anjani Mandavia . . . . .Partner
Abraham Rudy . . . . .Partner
Andrew Schmerzler . . . . .Partner
Todd Stern . . . . .Partner
Julie Waldman . . . . .Partner
Matthew Sugarman . . . . .Associate
Peter Dekom . . . . .Of Counsel

ATTORNEYS

ATTORNEYS

WENZLAU LAW GROUP, PLLC
10575 N. 114th St., Ste. 103
Scottsdale, AZ 85259
PHONE 480-344-7788
FAX 602-870-2090
EMAIL . . . . .info@arizonamusiclaw.com
WEB SITE .www.arizonamusiclaw.com
ENTERTAINMENT LAW SERVICES   Full Service Representation -
Contract Negotiation & Drafting
- Copyright & Trademark Matters
- Corporate Matters -
Employment/Labor Law -
Financing - Intellectual Property
Law - Motion Picture & TV Law -
Music Law

Matthew B. Wenzlau . . . . .Sr. Attorney

LAW OFFICES OF DAVID WERCHEN
845 Third Ave., Ste. 1400
New York, NY 10022
PHONE 212-308-1999
FAX 212-593-1318
EMAIL . . . . .dw@davidwerchen.com
WEB SITE .www.davidwerchen.com
ENTERTAINMENT LAW SERVICES   Full Service Representation -
Contract Negotiation & Drafting
- Music Law - Royalty Law -
Talent Representation -
Transactional Law

David Werchen . . . . .Owner

THE WINOGRADSKY COMPANY
11240 Magnolia Blvd., Ste. 104
North Hollywood, CA 91601
PHONE 818-761-6906
FAX 818-761-5719
EMAIL . . . . .steve@winogradsky.com
WEB SITE .www.winogradsky.com
ENTERTAINMENT LAW SERVICES   Contract Negotiation & Drafting
- Licensing - Motion Picture & TV
Law - Music Law
REPRESENTS   Composers
COMMENTS   Also handles music clearance
and publishing administration

Steven Winogradsky Esq. . . . . .President
Kathryn Morrow . . . . .Director, Administration
Amy MacDonald .Manager, Licensing

WOLF, RIFKIN, SHAPIRO & SCHULMAN, LLP
11400 W. Olympic Blvd., Ste. 900
Los Angeles, CA 90064
PHONE 310-478-4100
FAX 310-479-1422
EMAIL . . . . .mwolf@wrslawyers.com
WEB SITE .www.wrslawyers.com
ENTERTAINMENT LAW SERVICES   Acquisitions & Mergers -
Arbitration & Mediation -
Contract Negotiation & Drafting
- Copyright & Trademark Matters
- Corporate Matters -
Employment/Labor Law -
Financing - Intellectual Property
Law - Licensing - Litigation -
Motion Picture & TV Law -
Partnerships/Joint Ventures -
Talent Representation - Tax Law -
Transactional Law
COMMENTS   Merchandising; Advertising and
related corporate and business
matters

Roy Rifkin . . . . .Partner, Entertainment Litigation
Neal Tabachnick . . . . .Partner, Talent, Licensing & Merchandising
Michael Wolf . . . . .Partner, Transactional Matters
David Hochman . . . . .Associate, Entertainment
Joseph Petro . . . . .Associate, Licensing & Trademark

WYMAN & ISAACS LLP
8840 Wilshire Blvd., 2nd Fl.
Beverly Hills, CA 90211
PHONE 310-358-3221
FAX 310-358-3224
ENTERTAINMENT LAW SERVICES   Full Service Representation

Robert A. Wyman . . . . .Attorney, Entertainment Transactional
Bruce Isaacs . . . . .Attorney, Litigation
Cheryl Nelson . . . . .Attorney, Entertainment Transactional
Janna O. Smith . . . . .Attorney, Litigation
David H. Boren . . . . .Attorney, Litigation
Lee N. Rosenbaum . . . . .Of Counsel
Richard N. Blumenthal . . . . .Of Counsel
Diana Alikas . . . . .Assistant to Ms. Nelson
Marla Foreman . . . . .Assistant to Mr. Wyman
Lina Pearmain . . . . .Assistant to Mr. Isaacs

ZIFFREN, BRITTENHAM, BRANCA, FISCHER, GILBERT-LURIE, STIFFELMAN & COOK, LLP
1801 Century Park West
Los Angeles, CA 90067
PHONE 310-552-3388
FAX 310-553-7068
ENTERTAINMENT LAW SERVICES   Full Service Representation

Ken Ziffren . . . . .Partner
Skip Brittenham . . . . .Partner
John Branca . . . . .Partner
Sam Fischer . . . . .Partner
Cliff Gilbert-Lurie . . . . .Partner
Gary Stiffelman . . . . .Partner
Steve Burkow . . . . .Partner
Jamey Cohen . . . . .Partner
Melanie Cook . . . . .Partner
Kathy Hallberg . . . . .Partner
Matt Johnson . . . . .Partner
David Lande . . . . .Partner
Dennis Luderer . . . . .Partner
David Nochimson . . . . .Partner
Mitch Tenzer . . . . .Partner
Bryan Wolf . . . . .Partner
Jamie Young . . . . .Partner

ZUBER & TAILLIEU LLP
9595 Wilshire Blvd., 9th Fl.
Beverly Hills, CA 90212
PHONE 310-300-8480
FAX 310-300-8481
EMAIL . . . . .contact@zuberlaw.com
WEB SITE . . . . .www.zuberlaw.com
ENTERTAINMENT LAW SERVICES   Full Service Representation -
Acquisitions & Mergers -
Arbitration & Mediation -
Contract Negotiation & Drafting
- Copyright & Trademark Matters
- Corporate Matters - Financing
- Intellectual Property Law - Libel
& Privacy Matters - Licensing -
Litigation - Misappropriation of
Name, Voice, Likeness - Motion
Picture & TV Law - Music Law -
Partnerships/Joint Ventures -
Right of Publicity - Talent
Representation - Transactional
Law
REPRESENTS   Distribution Companies -
Production Companies -
Producers - Directors - Writers -
Actors - Crew - Musicians -
Financiers

Josh Lawler Esq. . . . . .Partner
Olivier A. Taillieu Esq. . . . . .Partner
Jeffrey J. Zuber Esq. . . . . .Partner
Thomas F. Zuber Esq. . . . . .Partner

ZUMWALT, ALMON & HAYES, PLLC
1014 16th Ave. South
Nashville, TN 37212
PHONE 615-256-7200
FAX 615-256-7106
WEB SITE . . . . .www.zahlaw.com
ENTERTAINMENT LAW SERVICES   Full Service Representation -
Music Law

James G. Zumwalt . . . . .Sr. Partner
Orville Almon Jr. . . . . .Partner
Craig Hayes . . . . .Partner
Kent Marcus . . . . .Attorney

ATTORNEYS

WORKSHEET

DATE	PROJECT	CONTACT	NOTES

Available online at www.hcdonline.com

SECTION C

FILM & TV MUSIC

— **Studios/Networks**

— Music Supervisors

— Clearance & Licensing

— Composers

Asterisks (*) next to companies denote new listings.

ABC TELEVISION NETWORK
500 S. Buena Vista St.
Burbank, CA 91521-4653
PHONE 818-460-6446/212-456-4355
FAX 818-460-5375/212-456-3084
SUBMISSION POLICY   No unsolicited submissions
COMMENTS   Music Publisher; East Coast office: 30
W. 67th St., 9th Fl., New York, NY
10023

Peter DiCecco . . . . .VP, Music/Business Affairs
Sylvia Webster . . . . .Executive Director, Production Music
Alessandra Springer . . . . .Executive Director, Music Rights/Licensing
Fae Kopacka . . . . .Director, ABC Music Publishing

CBS TELEVISION NETWORK (LOS ANGELES)
7800 Beverly Blvd., Rm. M3
Los Angeles, CA 90036
PHONE 323-575-2345
FAX 323-575-2525
WEB SITE . . . . .www.cbs.com
SUBMISSION POLICY   No unsolicited submissions accepted

Roni Mueller . . . . .Sr. VP, Business Affairs
Cindy Badell-Slaughter . . . . . . .Director, Music Operations, West Coast
Karen Takata . . . . .Director, Production Music, West Coast
Joan Mateo . . . . .Music Administrator
Aldrex G.M. Caparros . . . . .Music Administrator
Bob Tsai . . . . .Music Administrator

CBS TELEVISION NETWORK (NEW YORK)
1515 Broadway, 49th Fl.
New York, NY 10036
PHONE 212-846-3376
FAX 212-846-1903
EMAIL . . . . .firstinitiallastname@cbs.com

Don Steever . . . . .Music Manager, East Coast
Lydia Segundo . . . . .On-Air Promotions Coordinator, Music Operations,
East Coast
Jim Black . . . . .Licensing Manager
Sol Leistner . . . . .Music Coordinator

WALT DISNEY MUSIC & DISNEYTOON STUDIOS
500 S. Buena Vista St.
Animation Bldg., 2E16
Burbank, CA 91521-1759
PHONE 818-560-7495
FAX 818-560-2500

Chris Montan . . . . .President, Walt Disney Music
Matt Walker . . . . .Sr. VP Music, DisneyToon Studios
Tom MacDougall . . . . .VP, Walt Disney Music (818-460-9552)
Jay Stutler .VP, Music, TV Animation
Brett Swain . . . . .VP, Music Supervisor, DisneyToon Studios
Steven Gizicki . . . . .Music Supervisor, DisneyToon Studios
Kim Oliver . . . . .Music Supervisor, DisneyToon Studios

WALT DISNEY PICTURES & TELEVISION/BUENA VISTA MOTION PICTURES GROUP
500 S. Buena Vista St., Ink and Paint Bldg.
Burbank, CA 91521-3400
PHONE 818-560-1000
FAX 818-560-5737
WEB SITE . . . . .www.disney.com

Mitchell Leib . . . . . .President, Music/Soundtracks, Walt Disney Pictures &
Television/Buena Vista Music Group
Scott Holtzman . . . . . .Executive VP Music Affairs, Walt Disney Pictures &
Television
Glen Lajeski . . . . . .Executive VP Music Creative/Marketing, Walt Disney
Pictures & Television
Lesley Allery . . . . . .VP, Music Licensing, Walt Disney Pictures & Television
Cheryl Foliart . . . . .VP, TV Music, Walt Disney Pictures & Television
Kaylin Frank . . . .VP, Creative, Music/Soundtracks, Walt Disney Pictures &
Television
Reggie Wilson . . . . . .VP, Music Production/Administration, Walt Disney
Pictures & Television
Monica Zierhut . .VP Music Production, Walt Disney Pictures & Television
Desiree Craig-Ramos . . . . .Director, Soundtracks, Walt Disney Pictures &
Television

*WALT DISNEY TELEVISION ANIMATION MUSIC DEPARTMENT
500 S. Buena Vista St.
Burbank, CA 91521-3400
PHONE 818-560-0600
FAX 818-846-8066

Matt Walker . . . . .Sr. VP Music, DisneyToon Studios
Jay Stutler .VP, Music, TV Animation
Brett Swain . . . . .VP, Music Supervisor, DisneyToon Studios
Steven Gizicki . . . . .Music Supervisor, DisneyToon Studios
Kim Oliver . . . . .Music Supervisor, DisneyToon Studios

STUDIOS/NETWORKS

DREAMWORKS
1000 Flower St.
Glendale, CA 91201-3007
PHONE 818-695-5000
FAX 818-695-6570
WEB SITE . . . . .www.dreamworks.com

Lenny Wohl . . . . .Executive in Charge of Music for DreamWorks Studios
Sunny Park . . . .Executive in Charge of Music for DreamWorks Animation
Julie Butchko . . . . .Music Clearance
Cindi Smith . . . . .Scoring Supervisor
Ken Smith . . . . .Production Coordinator
Julie Keel . . . . .Production Coordinator for DreamWorks Animation
Marisa Barela . . . . .Licensing
Silvia Torres-Baker . . . . .Assistant to Julie Butchko
Vince Villanueva . . . . .Assistant to Lenny Wohl

FOX MUSIC
10201 W. Pico Blvd.
Los Angeles, CA 90035
PHONE 310-369-1000
FAX 310-369-1137
WEB SITE . . . . .www.foxmusic.com
SUBMISSION POLICY   No unsolicited materials; Submissions
                        must have representation

Robert Kraft . . . . .President
Geoff Bywater . . . . .Executive VP
Lance Grode . . . . .Executive VP, Legal & Business Affairs
Carol Farhat . . . . .VP, TV Music
Mike Knobloch . . . . .VP, Film Music
Jacquie Perryman . . . . .VP, TV Creative

LIFETIME TELEVISION
2049 Century Park East, Ste. 840
Los Angeles, CA 90067
PHONE 310-556-7500
FAX 310-557-8317
WEB SITE . . . . .www.lifetimetv.com
SUBMISSION POLICY   No unsolicited materials

Marianne Goode . . . . .VP, Music

LIONS GATE ENTERTAINMENT CORP.
4553 Glencoe Ave., Ste. 155B
Marina del Rey, CA 90292
PHONE 310-581-7339
FAX 310-581-7326
EMAIL . . . . .jhigh@lgf.com
WEB SITE . . . . .www.lionsgatefilms.com

Joel C. High . . . . .Sr. VP, Music/Soundtracks
Rebecca Rienks . . . . .Music Coordinator (310-581-7341)

MILLENNIUM FILMS
6423 Wilshire Blvd.
Los Angeles, CA 90048
PHONE 310-388-6900
FAX 310-388-6901
EMAIL . . . . .ashm@earthlink.net
SUBMISSION POLICY   No phone calls; Send CDs in labeled
                        jewel case, with contact info and one-
                        page presskit; No materials will be
                        returned

Ashley Miller .Executive in Charge of Music

MIRAMAX FILMS
8439 Sunset Blvd., 2nd Fl.
West Hollywood, CA 90069
PHONE 323-822-4150/917-606-5500
FAX 323-822-4151
WEB SITE . . . . .www.miramax.com
COMMENTS   East Coast office: 161 Avenue of the
                        Americas, 15th Fl., New York, NY
                        10013-2338

Randy Spendlove . . . . .President, Motion Picture Music
Theodore Rand . . . . .Coordinator, Motion Picture Music

MTV NETWORKS MUSIC GROUP
1515 Broadway
New York, NY 10036
PHONE 212-258-8000/310-752-8000
WEB SITE . . . . .www.mtv.com
COMMENTS   West Coast office: 2600 Colorado Ave.,
                        Santa Monica, CA 90404

Tom Freston . . . . .Co-President/Co-COO, Viacom Entertainment Group
Judith McGrath . . . . .Chairman/CEO, MTV Networks
Bill Roedy . . . . .Co-Chairman, MTV Networks Group/President,
                        MTV Networks International, MTV Music Group & LOGO
Van Toffler   President, MTV Networks Music Group, LOGO & MTV Films
Brian Graden . . . .President, Entertainment, MTV Music Group & LOGO
Christina Norman . . . . .President, MTV
Michael J. Wolf . . . . .President/COO, MTV Networks
Jason Hirschhorn . . . . .Chief Digital Officer, MTV Networks
David Cohn . . . . .General Manager, MTV2

(Continued)

MTV NETWORKS MUSIC GROUP (Continued)

Stephen Friedman . . . . .General Manager, mtvU
Richard Eigendorff . . . .Executive VP/COO, MTV Music Group & LOGO
Brian Phillips . . . . .Executive VP/General Manager, CMT
Nancy Newman . . . . . .Executive VP, Strategy & Organizational Planning,
MTV Music Group & LOGO
John Shea . . . . .Executive VP, Sponsorship Development &
Integrated Marketing, MTVN Music Group
Sabrina Silverberg . . . . .Executive VP, Music Strategy & Relations
Michele Dix . . . . .Sr. VP, Music & Talent Programming
Jeannie Kedas . . . . .Sr. VP, MTV Networks Music Group
Nicholas Lehman . .Sr. VP, Strategy & Operations, Digital Music & Media
Jose Tillan . . . . .Sr. VP, Music & Talent, MTV Networks Latin America
Peter Baron . . . . .VP, Label Relations
Michael Bloom . . . . .VP, Digital Music
Amy Doyle . . . . .VP, Music Programming Initiative/360
Fernando Hernandez . . . . .VP, Music Series Development
Jesse Ignjatovic . . . . .VP, Music & Talent Development, MTV
Jesus Lara . . . . .VP, Music Marketing/Talent/Artist Relations
Michele Roberts . . . . .VP, MTV/VH1/CMT Radio
Julio Muniz . . .Sr. Director, Music & Talent, MTV Networks Latin America
Marc Zimet . . . . .Sr. Director, International Music Talent & Content

NBC UNIVERSAL STUDIOS

100 Universal City Plaza, Bldg. 1320 West, 3rd Fl.
Universal City, CA 91608
PHONE 818-777-1000
FAX 818-733-3810
WEB SITE . . . . .www.nbcuni.com
SECOND WEB SITE . . . . .www.universalrecords.com

Kathy Nelson . . . . .President, Film Music
Steve Scott . . . . .Executive VP, Music Publishing/Music Operations,
Universal Pictures
Harry Garfield . . . . .Sr. VP, Music
Philip M. Cohen . . . . .Sr. VP, Music Business Affairs
David Buntz . . . . .VP, Film Music
Robert Gasper . . . . .Director, Music Business Affairs
Chris Saranec . . . . .Director, Music Licensing
Tiffany Jones . . . . .Music Scoring Manager

NBC UNIVERSAL TELEVISION (LOS ANGELES)

3000 W. Olive Ave., Ste. 600
Burbank, CA 91505
PHONE 818-840-3532
FAX 818-840-4293
WEB SITE . . . . .www.nbc.com
SUBMISSION POLICY   No unsolicted materials accepted

Martha Hanrahan . . . . .Sr. VP, Music Services
Alicen Catron Schneider . . . . .Director, Music Supervision
Nicole de la Torriente . . . . .Director, Music Services
Janine Kerr . . . . .Director, Music Services
Dennis McCafferty . . . . .Director, Music Services
Mary Oatman . . . . .Director, Music Services
Kerri Kirchheimer . . . . .Manager, Music Services
Dan Rimas . . . . .Manager, Music Services
Dave Madden . . . . .Administrator, Music Services
Tumara Stockey .Administrator, Music Services
Emily Winnie . . . . .Coordinator, Music Services

NBC UNIVERSAL TELEVISION (NEW YORK)

30 Rockefeller Plaza
New York, NY 10112
PHONE 212-664-2445
FAX 212-664-6644
WEB SITE . . . . .www.nbc.com
SUBMISSION POLICY   No unsolicited materials accepted

Ciru Limoli . . . . .Director, Music Services
Amie Bond . . . . .Music Licensing/Administrator, Music Services

NEW LINE CINEMA (LOS ANGELES)

116 N. Robertson Blvd.
Los Angeles, CA 90048
PHONE 310-854-5811
FAX 310-854-0422
WEB SITE . . . . .www.newline.com

Paul Broucek . . . . .President, Music
Jason Linn . . . . .Executive VP, New Line Records
Robert Bowen . . . . .Sr. VP, Music
Erin Scully . . . . .Sr. VP, Music
Jason Cienkus . . . . .VP, Soundtracks
Kevin Kertes . . . . .VP, Promotions, New Line Records
Genevieve Morris . . . . .VP, Sales, New Line Records

NEW LINE CINEMA (NEW YORK)

888 Seventh Ave.
New York, NY 10106
PHONE 212-649-4900
FAX 212-956-1931

Lori Silfen . . . . .Executive VP, Music/Sr. VP, Business & Legal Affairs
Mark Kaufman . . . . .Executive VP, Production & Theatre
John Walsh . . . . .Sr. VP, Music Business Affairs
Jessica Dolinger . . . . .VP, Music Licensing

PARAMOUNT PICTURES MUSIC DEPARTMENT

The Crosby Building
5555 Melrose Ave.
Los Angeles, CA 90038
PHONE 323-956-5000
FAX 323-862-2014
WEB SITE . . . . .www.paramount.com

Burt Berman . . . . .President, Music Department
David Helfant . . . . .Sr. VP, Music, Business Affairs & Legal
John Kirkpatrick . . . . .Sr. VP, Music Creative Affairs
Linda Springer . . . . .Sr. VP, Music Production
Linda Wohl . . . . .Sr. VP, Music/Legal
Denise Carver . . . . .VP, Music Clearance
Elizabeth McNicoll . . . . .VP, Business Affairs/Legal
Marty Olinick . . . . .VP, Licensing & Special Projects
Matt Lilley .Director, Music Clearance
Bernardo Silva . . . . .Atttorney, Music Department

STUDIOS/NETWORKS

*REVOLUTION STUDIOS
2900 W. Olympic Blvd.
Santa Monica, CA 90404
PHONE 310-255-7136
FAX 310-255-7139
EMAIL ....breeab@revolutionstudios.com

Denise Luiso ....Head, Music
Justin Reeve ....Music Coordinator
Breea Burtch ....Executive Assistant

SONY PICTURES ENTERTAINMENT - FEATURES
10202 W. Washington Blvd.
Culver City, CA 90232
PHONE 310-244-4000
FAX 310-244-7129

Lia Vollack ....President, Worldwide Music
Raul Perez ....Sr. VP, Music Administration
Don Kennedy ....VP, Music Licensing
Pilar McCurry ....Sr. VP, Music Creative Affairs
Monica Brautovich ....Director, Music Licensing
Rachel Thompson ....Manager, Music Creative Affairs

SONY PICTURES ENTERTAINMENT - MUSIC GROUP
10202 W. Washington Blvd.
Culver City, CA 90232
PHONE 310-244-8389
FAX 310-244-2258
WEB SITE ....www.sonypictures.com

Shelly Bunge ....Executive VP
Larry Stephens ....Sr. VP
Larry Kohorn ....VP
Paul Friedman ....VP
Jennifer Rick ....VP
Michael Frisby ....VP
Rita Zak ....VP
Susan Slamer ....VP

SONY PICTURES TELEVISION MUSIC
10202 W. Washington Blvd., WWD 2319
Culver City, CA 90232
PHONE 310-244-4000
FAX 310-244-0082
WEB SITE ....www.sonypicturestelevision.com

Margie C. Paris ....VP, TV Music
Tony Scudellari ....Director, TV Music Licensing
David Castle ....Manager, TV Music Licensing
Vikki Jacobs ....Manager, TV Music Licensing
Diana Randell ....Director, TV Ancillary Music Licensing
Felicity Bath ....Assistant
Kari Ferris ....Assistant

WARNER BROS. MUSIC
4000 Warner Blvd.
Burbank, CA 91522
PHONE 818-954-5523
FAX 818-954-5525
WEB SITE ....www.warnerbros.com

Doug Frank ....President, Music Operations (818-954-5523)
Gary LeMel ....President, Worldwide Music (818-954-3456)
Keith Zajic ....Executive VP, Business Affairs/Legal (818-954-3701)

WARNER BROS. TELEVISION MUSIC
300 Television Plaza, Bldg. 137, Rms. 2061/2053
Burbank, CA 91505
PHONE 818-954-7338
FAX 818-954-3469

Bronwyn Savasta ....VP, TV Music
Gay DiFusco ....Director, Music Clearance & Licensing
Tamar Chammou ....Manager, TV Music
Joe Fischer ....Manager, TV Music
Cindy Rodriguez ....Manager, Clearance & Licensing

THE WB TELEVISION NETWORK
4000 Warner Blvd., Bldg. 4R
Burbank, CA 91522
PHONE 818-977-5000
FAX 818-977-0210

Leonard Richardson ....VP, Music
Bekki Newton ....Sr. Coordinator, Music

SECTION C

FILM & TV MUSIC

- Studios/Networks
- **Music Supervisors**
- Clearance & Licensing
- Composers

Asterisks (*) next to companies denote new listings.

GEORGE ACOGNY INC.
c/o First Artists Management
16000 Ventura Blvd.
Encino, CA 91436
PHONE 818-377-7750
RECENT CREDITS   Step Into Liquid - The Wild Thornberrys
                        Movie - Rabbit-Proof Fence - Rugrats in
                        Paris: The Movie

George Acogny . . . . .Music Supervisor

*AGORAPHONE MUSIC DIRECTION
401 Broadway, Ste. 1606
New York, NY 10013
PHONE 212-966-2790
FAX 212-966-2791
WEB SITE . . . . .www.agoraphone.com

Dawn Sutter Madell . . . . .No Title
Beth A. Urdang . . . . .No Title

*JASON ALEXANDER
c/o First Artists Management
16000 Ventura Blvd.
Encino, CA 91436
PHONE 818-377-7750
RECENT CREDITS   Film: Flicka - Goal! - 11:14 - City by the
                        Sea - Mean Mach - Festival in Cannes -
                        Universal Soldier: The Return; TV: North
                        Shore - Cold Case - Jake 2.0 - Out of
                        Order - Platinum - Without a Trace -
                        CSI: Miami - CSI: Crime Scene
                        Investigation

Jason Alexander . . . . .Music Supervisor

ALPHABAE MUSIC
c/o Creative Artists Agency
9830 Wilshire Blvd.
Beverly Hills, CA 90212
PHONE 310-288-4545
RECENT CREDITS   WWE videogame series - Tony Hawk 4 -
                        Mat Hoffman's Pro BMX 1&2 - The
                        Hitchhiker Chronicles (FX)

Nelson Bae . . . . .Music Supervisor

DEVA ANDERSON
c/o Creative Artists Agency
9830 Wilshire Blvd.
Beverly Hills, CA 90212
PHONE 310-288-4545
RECENT CREDITS   Last Holiday - Because of Winn-Dixie -
                        The Truth About Charlie - My Big Fat
                        Greek Wedding - Murder by Numbers -
                        Center of the World - Anywhere But
                        Here - My Dog Skip - Beloved - From
                        the Earth to the Moon

Deva Anderson . . . . .Music Supervisor

APERTURE MUSIC
c/o First Artists Management
16000 Ventura Blvd.
Encino, CA 91436
PHONE 818-377-7750
WEB SITE . . . . .www.aperture-music.com
RECENT CREDITS   Stuck on You - Stealing Harvard -
                        Orange County - The Majestic - Shallow
                        Hal - Me, Myself & Irene

Manish Raval . . . . .Music Supervisor
Tom Wolfe . . . . .Music Supervisor

*DONDI BASTONE
c/o Soundtrack Music Associates
15760 Ventura Blvd., Ste. 2021
Encino, CA 91436
PHONE 818-382-3300
RECENT CREDITS   Sideways - The Breed - The Human Stain
                        - City of Ghosts - Pollack

Dondi Bastone . . . . .Music Supervisor

BEYOND
1545 N. Wilcox Ave., 2nd Fl.
Hollywood, CA 90028
PHONE 323-856-7073
FAX 323-856-5917
EMAIL . . . . .office@musicbeyond.com
WEB SITE . . . . .www.musicbeyond.com
RECENT CREDITS   Thunderbirds Trailer - Progressive Auto
                        Insurance - Apple - Tylenol
COMMENTS   Independent music library specializing in
                        high-end production music

Jonathan Parks .Head, Music Development

JOHN BISSELL
c/o Creative Artists Agency
9830 Wilshire Blvd.
Beverly Hills, CA 90212
PHONE 310-288-4545
RECENT CREDITS   10th & Wolf - Lord of War - American
                        Wedding - Ladder 49 - The Banger
                        Sisters - The Rookie - Hearts in Atlantis -
                        The Dangerous Lives of Altar Boys - The
                        Legend of Bagger Vance - The Horse
                        Whisperer

John Bissell . . . . .Music Supervisor

*BLACK MILK
1/57 Doughty St.
London WC1 N2LS United Kingdom
PHONE 44-207-2424233/44-7905254-787
EMAIL . . . . .jason@blackmilkonline.com
SECOND EMAIL . . . . .ant@blackmilkonline.com
WEB SITE .www.blackmilkonline.com
RECENT CREDITS   Aquamarine - One Perfect Day - Moulin
                        Rouge

Anton Monsted . . . . .Music Supervisor
Jason Lamont . . . . .Music Supervisor

GARY CALAMAR
c/o First Artists Management
16000 Ventura Blvd.
Encino, CA 91436
PHONE 818-377-7750
RECENT CREDITS   Six Feet Under - After the Sunset

Gary Calamar . . . . .Music Supervisor

THE CHOP SHOP
812 Fremont, #203
South Pasadena, CA 91030
PHONE 626-441-0600
EMAIL .chopshop66@hotmail.com
RECENT CREDITS   The O.C.

Alexandra Patsavas . . . . .Music Supervisor

MUSIC SUPERVISORS

MUSIC SUPERVISORS

*BARRY COLE
c/o First Artists Management
16000 Ventura Blvd.
Encino, CA 91436
PHONE 818-377-7750
RECENT CREDITS   Roll Bounce - Beauty Shop - Club Dread
                        - You Got Served - Brown Sugar -
                        Drumline - Session 9 - Daddy and Them
                        - O - Julie Johnson - Super Troopers -
                        All the Pretty Horses - American Psycho -
                        You Can Count on Me - The Minus Man
                        - Strangeland - Next Stop Wonderland -
                        Two Girls and a Guy - Niagara, Niagara
                        - Sling Blade

Barry Cole ....Music Supervisor

COMMOTION RECORDS
126 Fifth Ave., 7th Fl.
New York, NY 10011
PHONE 212-243-2100
FAX 212-243-2329
EMAIL ....info@arecordcommotion.com
WEB SITE ....www.arecordcommotion.com
RECENT CREDITS   A Dirty Shame - End of the Century: The
                        Story of the Ramones - The Ice Harvest -
                        My Architect

Tracy McKnight ....Partner
Walter Yetnikoff ....Partner
Aram Goldberg ....No Title
Matt Havron ....No Title

CHRISTOPHER COVERT
c/o Evolution Music Partners
9100 Wilshire Blvd., Ste. 201, East Tower
Beverly Hills, CA 90212
PHONE 310-623-3388
RECENT CREDITS   Broken Lizard's Club Dread - Drumline -
                        Brown Sugar - Songcatcher - You Can
                        Count on Me

Christopher Covert ....Music Supervisor

CREATIVE LICENSE
71 Eighth Ave., Ste. 2R
New York, NY 10014
PHONE 212-741-6703
FAX 212-741-6704
EMAIL ....info@creativelicense.com
SECOND EMAIL ....jennifer@creativelicense.com
WEB SITE ....www.creativelicense.com
RECENT CREDITS   Chevrolet - Gatorade - MCI - Intel -
                        Hewlett-Packard

MAUREEN CROWE
c/o Gorfaine/Schwartz Agency
4111 W. Alameda Ave., Ste. 509
Burbank, CA 91505
PHONE 818-260-8500
RECENT CREDITS   Poseiden Adventure - Heart of Summer -
                        Molly Gunn - A Guy Thing - Chicago -
                        Juwanna Man - The Banger Sisters - The
                        Breakers - The Perfect Storm - The
                        Replacements - True Romance - The
                        Bodyguard - Wayne's World - Newsies

Maureen Crowe ....Music Supervisor

DANCING MICE PRODUCTIONS
1234 Delaware Ave.
Buffalo, NY 14209
PHONE 716-885-3030/716-885-5050
FAX 716-885-4040
EMAIL ....info@dancingmice.net
SECOND EMAIL ....canadafilm@dancingmice.net
WEB SITE ....www.dancingmice.net
RECENT CREDITS   Head in the Clouds
SUBMISSION POLICY   Open

Scottpatrick J. Sellitto ....President (scott@dancingmice.net)

DEEPMIX
6255 Sunset Blvd., Ste. 1024
Hollywood, CA 90028
PHONE 323-769-3500
FAX 323-417-5134
EMAIL ....info@deepmix.com
WEB SITE ....www.deepmix.com
SUBMISSION POLICY   Email or mail submissions directly
COMMENTS   Licensing

Brad Colerick ....Managing Partner
David Curtin ....Creative Director/Partner
Caitlin Andrea ....Executive Producer
David Garcia ....Music Supervisor
Marc Morris ....Producer (NY)
Laurel Bogner ....Assistant Producer

DILBECK ENTERTAINMENT
5855 Green Valley Circle, Ste. 310
Culver City, CA 90230-6969
PHONE 310-670-0704
FAX 310-670-0164
EMAIL ....md90230@aol.com
RECENT CREDITS   Click - Benchwarmers - Grandma Boy -
                        Deuce Bigalow 1&2 - The Longest Yard -
                        50 First Dates - Dickie Roberts: Former
                        Child Star - Anger Management -
                        Master of Disguise - Mr. Deeds - Joe Dirt
                        - Scary Movie - The Animal - Little Nicky
                        - Big Daddy - Lost & Found - The
                        Wedding Singer - The Waterboy - Bad
                        Boys - Bulletproof - My Fellow Americans
                        - Money Train

Michael Dilbeck ....President
Bryan Bonwell ....Associate Music Supervisor
Tom Iannessa ....Associate Music Supervisor

CHRIS DOURIDAS
c/o Gorfaine/Schwartz Agency
4111 W. Alameda Ave., Ste. 509
Burbank, CA 91505
PHONE 818-260-8500
WEB SITE ....www.chrisdouridas.com
RECENT CREDITS   Shrek 2 - American Beauty - Down with
                        Love - Girl Next Door - One Hour Photo
SUBMISSION POLICY   No unsolicited material

Chris Douridas ....Music Supervisor

KEVIN EDELMAN
c/o First Artists Management
PHONE 818-377-7750
RECENT CREDITS   Film: The Butterfly Effect; TV: My Name
                        Is Earl - Reunion - Kevin Hill - North
                        Shore - Tru Calling - Carnivàle - She
                        Spies - Popular - Roswell - Boston Public
                        - Providence - V.I.P. - Baywatch

Kevin Edelman ....Music Supervisor

EMOTO
c/o Hampton/Adair
1615 16th St.
Santa Monica, CA 90404
PHONE 310-399-6900
EMAIL .lindsay@emotomusic.com
SECOND EMAIL . . . . .hpaar@emotomusic.com
RECENT CREDITS   Daltry Calhoun - Monster - DEBS - Herbie - Sueño - Party Monster - Garage Days - Ken Park - Miss Match

Howard Paar . . . . .Music Supervisor
Lindsay Froemke . . . . .Assistant (lindsay@admusic.biz)

*NORA FELDER
c/o Gorfaine/Schwartz Agency
4111 W. Alameda Ave., Ste. 509
Burbank, CA 91505
PHONE 818-260-8500
RECENT CREDITS   The Fog - The King - Hotel Rwanda - The Last Shot

Nora Felder . . . . .Music Supervisor

ARLENE FISHBACH ENTERPRISES
1223 Wilshire Blvd., Ste. 304
Santa Monica, CA 90403-5400
PHONE 310-451-5916
FAX 310-393-5313
EMAIL . . . . .afent@att.net
RECENT CREDITS   Riding the Bullet - Swimming Upstream

Arlene Fishbach . . . . .President

FRANK FITZPATRICK
c/o Envisage Entertainment, Inc.
2118 Wilshire Blvd., Ste. 198
Santa Monica, CA 90403
PHONE . . . . .310-623-3388 (Evolution Music, Seth Kaplan)
EMAIL . . . . .info@frankfitzpatrick.com
WEB SITE . . . . .www.frankfitzpatrick.com
RECENT CREDITS   Proud Family Movie - Scary Movie 3 - Lil' Pimp - Queen of the Damned - In Too Deep - The Larry Sanders Show - The Players Club - Friday

Frank Fitzpatrick .Music Supervisor
Daniel Birczynski . . . . .No Title

DAVID FRANCO INTERNATIONAL MUSIC PRODUCTIONS
4342 Redwood Ave., Ste. 310
Marina del Rey, CA 90292-7650
PHONE 310-823-5547
FAX 310-821-0707
EMAIL . . . . .dfintlprod@aol.com
RECENT CREDITS   Gods and Generals (WB) - When Billie Beat Bobby (ABC TV) - The Art of War (WB) - Together (UA) - American Family (PBS)
SUBMISSION POLICY   No unsolicited material; Call first
COMMENTS   Clearance & Licensing

David Franco . . . . .Music Supervisor/Producer
Creyna Katzef .Production Assistant

G CLEF MUSIC SUPERVISION & EDITING, INC.
5030 Riverton Ave., Ste. 4
North Hollywood, CA 91601
PHONE 818-752-7489
FAX 818-752-3527
EMAIL . . . . .mxmxmx@earthlink.net

Celia Weiner . . . . .President

LIZ GALLACHER
c/o Greenspan Artist Management
8748 Holloway Dr., 2nd Fl.
West Hollywood, CA 90069
PHONE 310-289-3990
EMAIL . . . . .mail@greenartman.com
WEB SITE .www.greenartman.com
RECENT CREDITS   Resident Evil: Apocalypse - Happily Never After - Where the Truth Lies

Liz Gallacher . . . . .Music Supervisor

*GENERATION MUSIC/GIMBEL MUSIC GROUP
661 N. Harper Ave., Ste. 205
Los Angeles, CA 90048
PHONE 323-966-4433
FAX 323-653-5111
EMAIL . . . . .info@gimbelmusic.com

Tony Gimbel . . . . .President
Joel Alvarez . . . . .Creative

*RANDY GERSTON
c/o First Artists Management
16000 Ventura Blvd.
Encino, CA 91436
PHONE 818-377-7750
RECENT CREDITS   The Wedding Date - Jiminy Glick in Lalawood - The Man from Elysian Fields - The Weight of Water - The Opposite of Sex - Titanic - Strange Days - Sleep with Me - Renaissance Man - Tombstone; TV: Jake 2.0 - Robbery Homicide Division - Dark Angel

Randy Gerston . . . . .Music Supervisor

*JANICE GINSBERG
c/o The Agency Group Ltd.
9348 Civic Center Dr., 2nd Fl.
Beverly Hills, CA 90210
PHONE 310-385-2800
RECENT CREDITS   Carlito's Way: Rise to Power - Back to Gaya - The Dreamers - Young Adam - All the Real Girls

Janice Ginsberg .Music Supervisor

THOMAS GOLUBIC
c/o Creative Artists Agency
9830 Wilshire Blvd.
Beverly Hills, CA 90212
PHONE 310-288-4545
EMAIL . . . . .thomas@supermusicvision.com
WEB SITE . . . . .www.supermusicvision.com
RECENT CREDITS   Six Feet Under - After the Sunset

Thomas Golubic .Music Supervisor

MARK GOODMAN
c/o Evolution Music Partners
9100 Wilshire Blvd., Ste. 201, East Tower
Beverly Hills, CA 90212
PHONE 310-623-3388
RECENT CREDITS   Desperate Housewives - Something's Gotta Give - What Women Want

Mark Goodman . . . . .Music Supervisor

MUSIC SUPERVISORS

GOODNIGHT KISS MUSIC
10153-1/2 Riverside Dr., Ste. 239
Toluca Lake, CA 91602
PHONE 831-479-9993
EMAIL . . . . .hlywdgrl@aol.com
WEB SITE .www.goodnightkiss.com
RECENT CREDITS   Yard Sale - Good Luck - Road Ends
COMMENTS   Film & TV soundtracks; Music coordina-
                        tor; Genre-specific CDs, needle drops,
                        quality access

Janet Fisher . . . . .Owner
Kelie McIver . . . . .Administrative Assistant

BILLY GOTTLIEB
c/o Playback Music
109 S. Kilkea Dr.
Los Angeles, CA 90048
PHONE 323-852-1838
FAX 323-852-1094
EMAIL .billyg@playbackmusic.net
RECENT CREDITS   Film: The Cooler - Bring It On - Like
                        Mike - The Tuxedo - The Perfect Man;
                        TV: Head Cases - Bones - Alias - Huff
SUBMISSION POLICY   No unsolicited material; Email first

Billy Gottlieb .Music Supervisor
Jenee DeAngellis . . . . .Assistant

DON GRIERSON
7651 Woodrow Wilson Dr.
Los Angeles, CA 90046-1251
PHONE 323-874-6992
FAX 323-874-7655
EMAIL . . . . .donunda@earthlink.net
RECENT CREDITS   Slap Her, She's French
COMMENTS   A&R and Creative Consultant/Executive
                        Producer

Don Grierson .Music Supervisor

HAIKU ENTERTAINMENT
PO Box 16215
Beverly Hills, CA 90209-2215
PHONE 310-837-1451
FAX 310-402-0880
EMAIL . . . . .jonjaz@aol.com
RECENT CREDITS   Interscope Presents The Next Episode
                        (Showtime)

Jonathan Weiss . . . . .Music Supervisor
David Was . . . . .Composer/Music Supervisor

DARREN HIGMAN
c/o Gorfaine/Schwartz Agency
4111 W. Alameda Ave., Ste. 509
Burbank, CA 91505
PHONE 818-260-8500
RECENT CREDITS   Win a Date with Tad Hamilton - Shark
                        Tale - Madagascar

Darren Higman .Music Supervisor

ANDY HILL FILM + MUSIC
c/o Modern Music
7080 Hollywood Blvd., Ste. 600
Hollywood, CA 90028
PHONE 323-666-5108
EMAIL . . . . .ahillmusic@earthlink.net
RECENT CREDITS   The Complete Guide to Guys - Princess
                        Stories - My First Mister - Annie -
                        Adventures of Elmo in Grouchland -
                        Message in a Bottle - Happy Feet

Andy Hill . . . . .Music Supervisor

HOLLOWAY HOUSE
PO Box 48645
Los Angeles, CA 90048-0645
PHONE 213-384-0269
EMAIL . . . . .hollowayhouse@aol.com

Danny Holloway . . . . .Music Supervisor

HOOKED RECORDINGS/35 SOUND
PO Box 217
Pacific Palisades, CA 90272
PHONE 310-454-1280
FAX 310-230-0132
EMAIL . . . . .adam@35sound.com
RECENT CREDITS   Auto Focus - Spy Game - Sweet
                        November - Pay It Forward - Bring It On

G. Marq Roswell . . . . .President
Adam Swart . . . . .Coordinator

HOT HOUSE MUSIC LTD.
Greenland Pl.
115-123 Bayham St.
London NW1 0AG United Kingdom
PHONE 44-20-7446-7446
FAX 44-20-7446-7448
EMAIL . . . . .info@hot-house-music.com
WEB SITE . . . . .www.hot-house-music.com
RECENT CREDITS   The Children of Men - The Constant
                        Gardener - Stoned - Proof - Hotel
                        Rwanda

Becky Bentham . . . . .Managing Director
Karen Elliott .Managing Director
Nyree Pinder . . . . .Composer Enquiries
Becca Catrell . . . . .Music Supervison/Score Coordination Enquiries
Abbie Lister . . . . .General Enquiries

HOULIHAN FILM MUSIC 1
3250 Dona Maria Dr.
Studio City, CA 91604
PHONE 323-848-8205
FAX 323-848-8203
EMAIL .houliwood@aol.com
RECENT CREDITS   2gether - Roswell - Delivered - I'll Be
                        Home for Christmas - Malcolm in the
                        Middle - Bernie Mac - Wonderfalls
SUBMISSION POLICY   Does not always respond to unsolicited
                        submissions; Prefers acts with label and
                        management

Julie Glaze Houlihan . . . . .Music Supervisor

HOULIHAN FILM MUSIC 2
12031 Ventura Blvd., Ste. 1
Studio City, CA 91604
PHONE 818-509-2494
FAX 818-509-2493
RECENT CREDITS   Get Rich of Die Tryin' - Two for the
                        Money - The Thing About My Folks -
                        Miss Congeniality 2 - Assault on Precinct
                        13
SUBMISSION POLICY   Accepts unsolicited material, but will only
                        respond if interested

John Houlihan .Music Supervisor
Lizzy Gerber .Music Coordinator

*JOHN HOULIHAN
c/o First Artists Management
16000 Ventura Blvd.
Encino, CA CA
PHONE 818-377-7750
RECENT CREDITS　　　　　　　Get Rich or Die Tryin' - Two for the
　　　　　　　　　　　　　　　　Money - The Thing About My Folks - 13
　　　　　　　　　　　　　　　　Going On 30 - The Sweetest Thing -
　　　　　　　　　　　　　　　　Training Day - Charlie's Angels 1&2 - I
　　　　　　　　　　　　　　　　Still Know What You Did Last Summer -
　　　　　　　　　　　　　　　　Austin Powers 1-3

John Houlihan . . . . .Music Supervisor

*HUM MUSIC + SOUND DESIGN
1547 Ninth St.
Santa Monica, CA 90401
PHONE 310-260-4949
FAX 310-260-4944
WEB SITE . . . . .www.humit.com
COMMENTS　　　　　　　　　　Music supervision for commercials, video
　　　　　　　　　　　　　　　　games

Tricia Halloran . . . . .Music Supervisor/Director, A&R
Jennifer Mandel . . . . .Music Supervisor

IMMORTAL ENTERTAINMENT
12200 Olympic Blvd., Ste. 400
West Los Angeles, CA 90064
PHONE 310-481-1871
FAX 310-481-1444
RECENT CREDITS　　　　　　　White Chicks
SUBMISSION POLICY　　　　　Call before submitting

Lisa Brown . . . . .Music Supervisor
Jennifer Ross . . . . .Music Coordinator
Amanda Sobeck . . . . .Assistant

INAUDIBLE
14724 Ventura Blvd., Ste. 440
Sherman Oaks, CA 91403
PHONE 818-385-3400
FAX 818-385-3456
RECENT CREDITS　　　　　　　Runaway Jury - The Girl Next Door - The
　　　　　　　　　　　　　　　　Passion of the Christ - Hellboy - The Hot
　　　　　　　　　　　　　　　　Chick - Eight Legged Freaks - Lara Croft:
　　　　　　　　　　　　　　　　Tomb Raider - Road Trip - Private Parts

Peter Afterman . . . . .Music Supervisor
Margaret Yen . . . . .Music Supervisor
Alison Litton . . . . .Music Supervisor

*INDEPENDENT MUSIC DEPARTMENT
2455 Marie St.
Simi Valley, CA 93065
PHONE 818-470-1018
FAX 818-337-7435
EMAIL . . . . .mason@imusicdepartment.com
RECENT CREDITS　　　　　　　Annie: Life After Tomorrow - All In - CMT
　　　　　　　　　　　　　　　　20 Sexiest Videos of 2005

Mason Cooper . . . . .Music Supervisor

INTERMUSIC
8562 Wonderland Ave.
Los Angeles, CA 99946
PHONE 323-654-9972
FAX 323-654-9972
EMAIL . . . . .rich@intermusic.us
RECENT CREDITS　　　　　　　What's New Scooby Doo? - Paid in Full
　　　　　　　　　　　　　　　　- Fogbound - Queen of the Damned -
　　　　　　　　　　　　　　　　Stanley's Gig

Rich Dickerson . . . . .Composer/Producer/Music Supervisor

SUE JACOBS
c/o Creative Artists Agency
9830 Wilshire Blvd.
Beverly Hills, CA 90212
PHONE 310-288-4545
RECENT CREDITS　　　　　　　It Runs in the Family - Monsoon
　　　　　　　　　　　　　　　　Wedding - Unbreakable - Before Night
　　　　　　　　　　　　　　　　Falls Happiness 51 Basquiat
　　　　　　　　　　　　　　　　Kansas City - Short Cuts - The Village

Sue Jacobs . . . . .Music Supervisor

JELLYBEAN
235 Park Avenue South, 10th Fl.
New York, NY 10003-1405
PHONE 212-777-5678
FAX 212-777-7788
EMAIL . . . . .info@jellybeanrecordings.com
SECOND EMAIL . . . . .promo@jellybeanrecordings.com
WEB SITE . . . . .www.jellybean-recordings.com
RECENT CREDITS　　　　　　　Dummy - Angel Eyes - Get Carter - One
　　　　　　　　　　　　　　　　Tough Cop - 2 Days in the Valley

Jellybean Benitez . . .President (x117, jbenitez@jellybeanrecordings.com)

DAVID JORDAN
c/o Kraft-Engel Management
15233 Ventura Blvd., Ste. 200
Sherman Oaks, CA 91403
PHONE 818-380-1918
RECENT CREDITS　　　　　　　Fantastic Four - Elektra - Fat Albert - The
　　　　　　　　　　　　　　　　Punisher - Cheaper by the Dozen -
　　　　　　　　　　　　　　　　Harold and Kumar Go to White Castle -
　　　　　　　　　　　　　　　　Johnson Family Vacation - Daredevil -
　　　　　　　　　　　　　　　　American Pie 2 - The Fast and the
　　　　　　　　　　　　　　　　Furious

David Jordan . . . . .Music Supervisor

JULIANNE JORDAN
c/o Soundtrack Music Associates
15760 Ventura Blvd., Ste. 2021
Encino, CA 91436
PHONE 818-382-3300
RECENT CREDITS　　　　　　　Mr. & Mrs. Smith - Without a Paddle -
　　　　　　　　　　　　　　　　The Italian Job - The Bourne Identity
SUBMISSION POLICY　　　　　No unsolicited material

Julianne Jordan . . . . .Music Supervisor

MATT KIERSCHT
c/o Soundtrack Music Associates
15760 Ventura Blvd., Ste. 2021
Encino, CA 91436
PHONE 818-382-3300
RECENT CREDITS　　　　　　　Committed - America's Next Top Model
　　　　　　　　　　　　　　　　- America Or Busted - Reunited

Matt Kierscht . . . . .Music Supervisor

*EVYEN KLEAN
c/o First Artists Management
16000 Ventura Blvd.
Encino, CA 91436
PHONE 818-377-7750
RECENT CREDITS　　　　　　　Warm Springs - Lackawanna Blues -
　　　　　　　　　　　　　　　　Angels in America - Starring Pancho Villa
　　　　　　　　　　　　　　　　as Himself - S.W.A.T. - Normal - Live
　　　　　　　　　　　　　　　　From Baghdad - Real Women Have
　　　　　　　　　　　　　　　　Curves - Crazy/Beautiful - 61*; TV: Las
　　　　　　　　　　　　　　　　Vegas - The Shield

Evyen Klean . . . . .Music Supervisor

MUSIC SUPERVISORS

MUSIC SUPERVISORS

KUSHNICK ENTERTAINMENT
1779 Wells Branch Pkwy., #110B-316
Austin, TX 78728
PHONE 512-255-7700
EMAIL .kushnickent@sbcglobal.net
RECENT CREDITS   40 - Down to Earth - Muppets From
                      Space - Twilight - Breakdown

Ken Kushnick . . . . .President

MICHELLE KUZNETSKY-SILVERMAN
c/o Soundtrack Music Associates
15760 Ventura Blvd., Ste. 2021
Encino, CA 91436
PHONE 818-382-3300
RECENT CREDITS   Surviving Christmas - Kill Bill - The
                      Station Agent - National Security

Michelle Kuznetsky-Silverman . . . . .Music Supervisor

JON LESHAY
c/o The Firm
9465 Wilshire Blvd.
Beverly Hills, CA 90212
PHONE 310-860-8000
RECENT CREDITS   Saved - How to Deal - A Walk to
                      Remember
COMMENTS   Manager

Jon Leshay . . . . .Music Supervisior

*TAMI LESTER
c/o Gorfaine/Schwartz Agency
4111 W. Alameda Ave., Ste. 509
Burbank, CA 91505
PHONE 818-260-8500
RECENT CREDITS   Barbershop 2 - Drive - The First to Go

Tami Lester . . . . .Music Supervisor

LUCKY DUCK MUSIC
9977 Robbins Dr.
Beverly Hills, CA 90212
PHONE 310-788-3454
FAX 310-788-9554
EMAIL . . . . .jpdaisy@earthlink.net
RECENT CREDITS   Las Vegas - My Boss's Daughter - The
                      Perfect Score - Tarzan - One Tree Hill -
                      Alias - Smallville - Repli-Kate - Soul
                      Survivors - Lush - The Sterling Chase -
                      Stag - Summerland

Jennifer Pyken . . . . .Music Supervisor (jpdaisy@earthlink.net)

LUKE HITS
137 N. Larchmont Blvd., #555
Los Angeles, CA 90004
PHONE 310-236-5853
EMAIL . . . . .info@lukehits.com
WEB SITE . . . . .www.lukehits.com

Luke Eddins . . . . .Music Supervisor

ELLIOT LURIE
4041 Ventura Canyon Ave.
Sherman Oaks, CA 91423-4714
PHONE 310-274-4825
FAX 818-981-9545
RECENT CREDITS   The Lizzie McGuire Movie - I Spy -
                      Riding in Cars with Boys - Get Over It -
                      Loser

Elliot Lurie . . . . .Music Supervisor

MACHINE | HEAD
1410 Abbot Kinney Blvd.
Venice, CA 90291
PHONE 310-392-8393
FAX 310-392-9676
EMAIL . . . . .info@machinehead.com
SECOND EMAIL . . . . .production@machinehead.com
WEB SITE .www.machinehead.com
RECENT CREDITS   Raise Your Voice - The Chronicles of
                      Riddick - Dark Fury - The Yank - Full
                      Spectrum Warrior - On the Road -
                      Boarding House: North Shore - The
                      Matrix 1-3 - Blind Horizon - Freddy vs.
                      Jason - Timeline - The Animatrix - Narc -
                      Black Hawk Down - Traffic - Jacob's
                      Ladder - Sneakers - Black Rain -
                      Mothman Prophecies - Twister - Jackie
                      Brown - Exit Wounds - The Laramie
                      Project - Crazy/Beautiful - Cheaters -
                      Point of Origin - City of Industry

Stephen Dewey . . . . .Owner/Sound Designer/Composer
Jason Bentley . . . . .Music Supervisor/Soundtrack Producer
Marcus Brown . . . . .Composer
Adam Schiff . . . . .Composer
Vicki Ordeshook .Executive Producer
Maggie Tran . . . . .Associate Producer
Millie Christie . . . . .Business Affairs

MICHAEL MCQUARN
c/o Soundtrack Music Associates
15760 Ventura Blvd., Ste. 2021
Encino, CA 91436
PHONE 818-382-3300
RECENT CREDITS   Elvis Has Left the Building - Havoc - Love
                      Don't Cost a Thing - Bringing Down the
                      House - Bad Company
SUBMISSION POLICY   No unsolicited material

Michael McQuarn . . . . .Music Supervisor

*JULIA MICHELS
c/o Kraft-Engel Management
15233 Ventura Blvd., Ste. 200
Sherman Oaks, CA 91403
PHONE 818-380-1918
RECENT CREDITS   Jellybeans - The Devil Wears Prada -
                      Daredevil - Be Cool - Beauty Shop

Julia Michels . . . . .Music Supervisor

THE MUSIC BRIDGE LLC
PO Box 661918
Los Angeles, CA 90066
PHONE 310-398-9650
FAX 310-398-4850
EMAIL . . . . .thabridge@aol.com
WEB SITE .www.themusicbridge.com
COMMENTS   Clearance & Licensing

David G. Powell . . . . .President

MUSIC MAKES PICTURES
12128 Hartsook St.
Valley Village, CA 91607-3057
PHONE 818-753-9872
FAX 818-753-9872
EMAIL . . . . .gregatz@aol.com
RECENT CREDITS   Door to Door - Boomtown - Elvis
                      (Miniseries) - Sleeper Cell - Friends - ER
                      - American Dreams - Reefer Madness

Greg Sill . . . . .Music Supervisor

MUSIC RESOURCES, INC.
6671 Sunset Blvd., Ste. 1574-A
Los Angeles, CA 90028-7123
PHONE 323-993-9915
FAX 323-993-9921
EMAIL . . . . .mr@musicresources.com
WEB SITE . . . . .www.musicresources.com
RECENT CREDITS   The Benefactor - Supernanny - Virgin -
                     Gram Parsons Return to Sin City - A Little
                     Trip to Heaven
SUBMISSION POLICY   No unsolicited submissions

Nancie Stern . . . . .President
Tony Abner . . . . .Executive VP
Brandon Schott . . . . .Assistant

MUSIC SUPERVISION SERVICES
A Division of S.L. Feldman & Associates
Ste. 200, 1505 W. Second Ave.
Vancouver, BC V6H 3Y4 Canada
PHONE 604-734-5945
FAX 604-732-0922
WEB SITE . . . . .www.slfa.com

Janet York . . . . .VP, Film Music (jyork@direct.ca)
Amy Fritz Music Supervisor/Composer Manager (Toronto) (fritz@slfa.com)
Sarah Webster . . . . .Music Supervisor (webster@slfa.com)
Jane Muckle . . . . .Contracts, Film Music (muckle@slfa.com)
Stacey Horricks . . . . .Music Supervisor (horricks@slfa.com)

MUSICOM MEDIA
131 N. Croft Ave., Ste. 302
Beverly Hills, CA 90048
PHONE 310-204-4881
FAX 310-204-4884
EMAIL . . . . .musicommedia@yahoo.com
COMMENTS   Specializes in music composition, scor-
                     ing & production for TV, film, video
                     games & commercials; All genres of
                     music available

Earl Cole . . . . .CEO/Music Supervisor
Greg Anderson . . . . .Creative Director
Chris Manley . . . . .A&R Manager
Shinobu Bridges . . . . .Financial & Licensing Manager

NEOPHONIC, INC.
9320 Wilshire Blvd., Ste. 200
Beverly Hills, CA 90212
PHONE 310-550-0124
FAX 310-550-8376
WEB SITE . . . . .www.neophonic.com
RECENT CREDITS   Nip/Tuck - Angels in America - The Life
                     and Death of Peter Sellers - The Ballad
                     of Bettie Page - The Shield
SUBMISSION POLICY   No unsolicited material

Evyen Klean . . . . .Executive Music Producer/Music Supervisor
P.J. Bloom . . . . .Soundtrack Producer/Music Supervisor
Ray Espinola Jr. . . . . .Music Supervisor
Jennifer Reeve . . . . .Music Coordinator

THE OVERSEER
17600 Burbank Blvd., Ste. 300
Burbank, CA 91316
PHONE 310-903-0213
FAX 818-990-8648
EMAIL . . . . .g@theoverseer.com
WEB SITE . . . . .www.theoverseer.com
RECENT CREDITS   Man on Fire - King's Ransom - Phone
                     Booth - Kate & Leopold
SUBMISSION POLICY   No unsolicited submissions
COMMENTS   Music production supervisor for com-
                     posers & production studios

Gretchen O'Neal . . . . .President

JEFFREY POLLACK
c/o Gorfaine/Schwartz Agency
4111 W. Alameda Ave., Ste. 509
Burbank, CA 91505
PHONE 818-260-8500
RECENT CREDITS   Music Consultant: Constantine - Lara
                     Croft Tomb Raider: Cradle of Life - Love
                     Actually - As Good As It Gets - You've
                     Got Mail

Jeffrey Pollack . . . . .Music Consultant

REEL MUSIC
23297 Park Ensenada
Calabasas, CA 91302
PHONE 818-225-8166
FAX 818-225-1175
EMAIL . . . . .rurdang@reelmusic.us
RECENT CREDITS   Beer League - Wristcutters - Great New
                     Wonderful - Mean Creek - Intorducing
                     Dorothy Dandridge - A Midsummer
                     Night's Dream - Soldier's Girl - The
                     Prince and Me - People I Know - Glitter -
                     The Anniversary Party - 3000 Miles to
                     Graceland
SUBMISSION POLICY   No unsolicited material

Robin Urdang . . . . .Music Supervisor

BRIAN REITZELL
c/o Evolution Music Partners
9100 Wilshire Blvd., Ste. 201, East Tower
Beverly Hills, CA 91212
PHONE 310-623-3388
RECENT CREDITS   Thumbsucker - The Virgin Suicides - CQ

Brian Reitzell . . . . .Composer

LIZA RICHARDSON
c/o Greenspan Artist Management
8748 Holloway Dr., 2nd Fl.
PHONE 310-289-3990
EMAIL . . . . .mail@greenartman.com
WEB SITE .www.greenartman.com
RECENT CREDITS   Lords of Dogtown - Wicker Park - Levity -
                     Y Tu Mama Tambien - The Mothman
                     Prophecies - The Assassination of
                     Richard Nixon - Curious George

Liza Richardson . . . . .Music Supervisor/Consultant

ROCK-IT SCIENCE MUSIC SUPERVISION
PO Box 39500
Los Angeles, CA 90039
PHONE 323-468-8888
FAX 323-468-8889
EMAIL .info@mediacreature.com
RECENT CREDITS   Black Cloud - Word Wars - Dahmer -
                     Devil's Playground: Amish Teenagers -
                     Last Days of The San Jose
COMMENTS   Music consulting, clearance & licensing

Sharal Churchill . . . . .Founder/CEO
Renee Travis . . . . .VP

MUSIC SUPERVISORS

ROSS ENTERTAINMENT
937 N. Cole Ave., Ste. 3
Los Angeles, CA 90038
PHONE 323-871-4800
FAX 323-464-8699
EMAIL . . . . .brian@ross-entertainment.com
RECENT CREDITS   Clubhouse - Suspect Zero - The Last
                        Ride - Miracle - The Slaughter Rule

Brian Ross . . . . .Music Supervisor

RUBY BEAT, INC.
1950 Weepah Way
Los Angeles, CA 90046-1437
PHONE 323-650-2116
FAX 323-650-2120
RECENT CREDITS   Arrested Development - Welcome to
                        Collinwood - Wicked - The Grass Harp -
                        Andy Richter Controls the Universe -
                        Twins - Wild at Heart
SUBMISSION POLICY   No unsolicited material

Diane Wessel . . . . .Music Supervisor

RUDOLPH PRODUCTIONS
1321 Seventh St., Ste. 300
Santa Monica, CA 90401-1682
PHONE 310-458-9861
FAX 310-458-9862
EMAIL . . . . .west@musicsales.com
RECENT CREDITS   Imaginary Heroes - The Gary and Mike
                        Show
SUBMISSION POLICY   No unsolicited submissions

Ricardo Rudolph .Music Supervisor
Karen Kloack . . . . .Music Supervisor
Wendy Crompton . . . . .Assistant

SATURDAY, INC.
7080 Hollywood Blvd., Ste. 600
Los Angeles, CA 90028
PHONE 323-603-5166
FAX 323-603-5192
EMAIL . . . . .tritone00@aol.com
RECENT CREDITS   Prison Break - Never Been Kissed - Clay
                        Pigeons - Digging to China - Cop Land -
                        Kill Bill Vols. 1&2 - National Security -
                        Surviving Christmas
SUBMISSION POLICY   Email introduction first

Mary Ramos . . . . .Music Supervisor
Wendi Morris . . . . .Music Coordinator
Kasey Truman . . . . .Assistant

STEVE SCHNUR
c/o Gorfaine/Schwartz Agency
4111 W. Alameda Ave., Ste. 509
Burbank, CA 91505
PHONE 818-260-8500
RECENT CREDITS   Film: Miss Congeniality - Cruel
                        Intentions - Excess Baggage - Teaching
                        Mrs. Tingle; Videogames: Madden 2004
                        - Nascar Thunder 2003 - NHL 2003 -
                        NBA Live 2003

Steve Schnur . . . . .Music Supervisor

*ROCHELLE SHARPE
c/o First Artists Management
16000 Ventura Blvd., Ste. 605
Encino, CA 91436
PHONE 818-377-7750
RECENT CREDITS   Santa's Slay - Americano - 50 Says to
                        Leave Your Lover - Queer Eye for the
                        Straight Girl

Rochelle Sharpe .Music Supervisor

DAVID SIBLEY
c/o The Agency Group Ltd.
9348 Civic Center Dr., 2nd Fl.
Beverly Hills, CA 90210
PHONE 310-385-2800
RECENT CREDITS   Desperate Housewives - Once Upon a
                        Wedding - American Family - Luis
                        Guzman Show - The Little Richard Story
                        - Vibe
SUBMISSION POLICY   No unsolicited submissions

David Sibley . . . . .Music Supervisor

JOEL SILL
c/o Gorfaine/Schwartz Agency
4111 W. Alameda Ave., Ste. 509
Burbank, CA 91505
PHONE 818-260-8500
RECENT CREDITS   Terminator 3 - Basic - Dark Blue - Cast
                        Away - What Lies Beneath - Return to
                        Me - Wag the Dog

Joel Sill . . . . .Music Supervisor

DAWN SOLÉR
c/o Gorfaine/Schwartz Agency
4111 W. Alameda Ave., Ste. 509
Burbank, CA 91505
PHONE 818-260-8500
RECENT CREDITS   Dramarama - Sisterhood of the
                        Travelling Pants - Princess Diaries 1&2 -
                        Confessions of a Teenage Drama Queen
                        - Raising Helen - Hollywood Homicide -
                        Big Trouble - Being John Malkovich -
                        Notting Hill - Sweet Home Alabama

Dawn Solér . . . . .Music Supervisor

SOUNDSTRIPE INC.
PO Box 34172
Los Angeles, CA 90034
PHONE 323-953-4984
FAX 323-953-4984
EMAIL . . . . .info@soundstripe.com
SECOND EMAIL .soundstripe@yahoo.com
WEB SITE . . . . .www.soundstripe.com
SUBMISSION POLICY   Send all CDs by US Mail
COMMENTS   Composition, production and supervi-
                        sion
facility

M. Paul Larson . . . . .Chief Composer/Producer (paul@soundstripe.com)
Ian MacKinnon . . . . .Music Supervisor (ian@soundstripe.com)

*PAUL STEWART
c/o The Agency Group Ltd.
9348 Civic Center Dr., 2nd Fl.
Beverly Hills, CA 90210
PHONE 310-385-2800
RECENT CREDITS Four Brothers - Hustle and Flow -
 Barbershop 1&2 - 2 Fast 2 Furious -
 Men of Honor - Poetic Justice

Paul Stewart . . . . .Music Supervisor

SUPERSONIC MUSIC, INC.
PO Box 6355
Malibu, CA 90264
PHONE 310-457-2777
FAX 310-457-8823
EMAIL . . . . .michelle@supersonicmusic.net
WEB SITE . . . . .www.supersonicmusic.net

Michelle Norrell .Music Supervisor
Clif Norrell . . . . .Music Producer, Engineer & Mixer

MELODEE SUTTON
c/o Soundtrack Music Associates
15760 Ventura Blvd., Ste. 2021
Encino, CA 91436
PHONE 818-382-3300
RECENT CREDITS Soul Plane - Black Knight - Baby Boy -
 Love and Basketball

Melodee Sutton .Music Supervisor

JEREMY SWEET MUSIC SERVICES
4826 Beeman Ave.
Valley Village, CA 91607
PHONE 818-705-3279
EMAIL . . . . .jeremy@smashtrax.com
WEB SITE . . . . .www.smashtrax.com

Jeremy Sweet . . . . .Music Supervisor

SWELL
PO Box 249, Station C
Toronto, ON M6J 3P4 Canada
PHONE 416-533-3864
EMAIL . . . . .jeff@handsomeboy.com
WEB SITE . . . . .www.handsomeboy.com
SECOND WEB SITE . . . . .www.thedrakehotel.ca
COMMENTS Movie soundtracks; Live entertainment;
 Events; The Drake Hotel (Showcase
 room in Toronto)

Jeff Rogers . . . . .President

TEQUILA MOCKINGBIRD MUSIC & SOUND DESIGN
306 W. 16th St.
Austin, TX 78701
PHONE 512-499-8655
FAX 512-499-8057
EMAIL . . . . .info@tequilamockingbird.com
WEB SITE . . . . .www.tequilamockingbird.com
COMMENTS Music production house; ADR recording

Angela Johnson .Executive Producer
Danny Levin . . . . .Head Composer
Wally Williams . . . . .Creative Director

TILTED WORLD MUSIC
742 Milwood Ave.
Venice, CA 90291-3829
PHONE 310-745-2343
FAX 310-745-2470
RECENT CREDITS Nine Lives - Bigger Than the Sky -
 Cracking Up - The Lone Gunmen -
 Guinevere - Mr. Holland's Opus

Barklie K. Griggs .Music Supervisor

TRAILER PARK
1741 N. Ivar Ave.
Los Angeles, CA 90028
PHONE 323-461-4232
FAX 323-461-2632
WEB SITE . . . . .www.trailerpark.com

Pete Hasty . . . . .Music Supervisor

TYRELL MUSIC GROUP
10866 Wilshire Blvd., 10th Fl.
Los Angeles, CA 90024
PHONE 323-656-7244
FAX 310-474-0478
EMAIL .tyrellmusic@aol.com
WEB SITE . . . . .www.stevetyrell.com
RECENT CREDITS Dudley Do-Right - And the Beat Goes
 On: The Sonny and Cher Story - 20
 Dates - Once Upon a Time...When We
 Were Colored - The Heights

Steve Tyrell . . . . .Music Supervisor
Jon Allen . . . . .Project Coordinator

CHRIS VIOLETTE
c/o Soundtrack Music Associates
15760 Ventura Blvd., Ste. 2021
Encino, CA 91436
PHONE 818-382-3300
RECENT CREDITS Eulogy - The Deal - Imagining Argentina
 - Jeepers Creepers 2 - The Good Girl -
 National Lampoon's Van Wilder
SUBMISSION POLICY No unsolicited material

Chris Violette . . . . .Music Supervisor

LAURA Z. WASSERMAN
12100 Olympic Blvd., 4th Fl.
Los Angeles, CA 90064
PHONE 310-407-0293
FAX 310-407-0295
RECENT CREDITS xXx: State of the Union - A Lot Like Love
 - Shark Tale - Alex & Emma - Sweet
 Home Alabama
SUBMISSION POLICY No unsolicited material

Laura Z. Wasserman . . . . .Music Supervisor (lzw@wh-ent.com)
Diane Stata . . . . .Music Supervisor (ds@wh-ent.com)
Laura Webb . . . . .Music Coordinator (lwebb@wh-ent.com)

WHIRLY GIRL MUSIC
c/o Soundtrack Music Associates
15760 Ventura Blvd., Ste. 2021
Encino, CA 91436
PHONE 818-382-3300
RECENT CREDITS The Santa Clause 2&3 - Matador -
 Believe in Me - Mrs. Harris - Aurora
 Borealis

Frankie Pine . . . . .Music Supervisor
Wendy Crowley .Music Supervisor

WORKSHIRT MUSIC
1680 N. Vine St., Ste. 1014
Hollywood, CA 90028
PHONE 323-466-6046
FAX 323-466-6086
EMAIL . . . . .workshirt2@earthlink.net
WEB SITE .www.workshirtmusic.com

Chris Anderson . . . . .Music Supervisor, Composer

ZOO STREET MUSIC
2701 W. Willow St.
Burbank, CA 91505
PHONE 818-955-5268
FAX 818-295-5001
EMAIL . . . . .music@zoostreet.com
WEB SITE . . . . .www.zoostreet.com
COMMENTS   Music library and custom original music
                  scoring

Marc Jackson . . . . .Director, Music/Music Supervisor
Mike Contreras . . . . .Music Supervisor
Omar Herrera . . . . .Music Supervisor
Yosuke Kitazawa . . . . .Music Supervisor
Jeffrey Hepker . . . . .Composer

SECTION C

FILM & TV MUSIC

- Studios/Networks
- Music Supervisors
- **Clearance & Licensing**
- Composers

Asterisks (*) next to companies denote new listings.

615 MUSIC LIBRARY
1030 16th Ave. South
Nashville, TN 37212
PHONE .888-615-TRAX/818-846-1615 (LA)
FAX 615-242-2455
EMAIL . . . . .info@615music.com
SECOND EMAIL . . . . .fern@615music.com
WEB SITE www.615music.com
GENRES   All Genres
RECENT PROJECTS   "Live for Today" (Today Show theme
                           song)
COMMENTS   Full-service music scoring and sound
                           design company with over 90 national
                           awards

Randy Wachtler . . . . .President/CEO
Laura Palmer . . . . .VP, Operations
Fern Helms . . . . .Sales Representative (LA)

*7-OUT-MUSIC
8350 Santa Monica Blvd., #108
Hollywood, CA 90069
PHONE 323-650-0767
FAX 323-650-2906
EMAIL . . . . .info@7outmusic.com
SECOND EMAIL . . . . .mark@7outmusic.com
WEB SITE www.7outmusic.com
GENRES   All Genres
RECENT PROJECTS   TV: ER - Friends - CSI - Law & Order -
                           The Shield - Malcolm in the Middle -
                           Scrubs; Trailers: Just Like Heaven -
                           Chicken Little

Mark Pariser . . . . .President

AIRCRAFT PRODUCTION MUSIC LIBRARY
162 Columbus Ave.
Boston, MA 02116
PHONE 617-303-7600/800-343-2514
FAX 617-303-7666
EMAIL . . . . .info@aircraftmusiclibrary.com
WEB SITE . . . . .www.aircraftmusiclibrary.com
COMMENTS   Music Library; Per project plans for TV
                           and film

Paul Greenberg . . . . .Managing Director

*ALLCLEAR
2022 Cliff Dr., Box 196
Santa Barbara, CA 93105
PHONE 805-569-2538
FAX 805-569-7128
EMAIL . . . . .cjallclear@earthlink.net

Chad Jensen . . . . .President

*ALLMEDIA LICENSING WORLDWIDE LLC
4635 SW Hillside Dr., 21st Fl.
Portland, OR 97221
PHONE 503-291-0165
FAX 1-503-292-8462
EMAIL . . . . .allmedia@hevanet.com

Bart Day . . . . .President

AMERICAN MUSIC COMPANY INC.
2901 Long Beach Rd., Ste. 6
Oceanside, NY 11572
PHONE 516-764-1466
FAX 516-764-2648
EMAIL . . . . .info@americanmusicco.com
WEB SITE .www.americanmusicco.com
COMMENTS   Music Library; Full service music produc-
                           tion, copyright research, arranging for
                           permission to clear popular music

Mitchel J. Greenspan . . . . .President

AMERITONE ENTERTAINMENT
6958 Halbrent Ave.
Van Nuys, CA 91405-3560
PHONE 818-335-4410
FAX 818-908-9421
EMAIL . . . . .freddie.vasquez@ameritone.com
WEB SITE . . . . .www.ameritone.com
GENRES   All Genres
RECENT PROJECTS   One Tree Hill - Summerland
SUBMISSION POLICY   No unsolicited materials; Email first
COMMENTS   Independent licensing for Film, TV and
                           Commercials; Publisher; Management

Freddie Vasquez .Founder/President
J.J. Garcia . . . . .Creative Director
Lacy Ostendorf . . . . .Assistant to Freddie Vasquez

AMUSICOM
22817 Ventura Blvd., Ste. 319
Woodland Hills, CA 91364-1202
PHONE 818-883-8376
FAX 818-883-4535
EMAIL . . . . .info@amusicom.com
WEB SITE . . . . .www.amusicom.com
GENRES   Alternative - Blues - Christian - Classical
                           - Country - Electronica - Folk - Gospel -
                           Jazz - Latin - New Age - Pop - R&B -
                           Rap/Hip-Hop - Reggae - Rock - Roots -
                           Urban - World

Linda Lawley . . . . .President (linda@amusicom.com)

ASHLEY & FRISBY
841 Victoria Ave.
Venice, CA 90291
PHONE 310-306-6217
FAX 310-827-6007

Steven Ashley . . . . .No Title

CLEARANCE & LICENSING

ASSOCIATED PRODUCTION MUSIC
6255 Sunset Blvd., Ste. 820
Hollywood, CA 90028
PHONE 323-461-3211/800-543-4276
FAX 323-461-9102
EMAIL . . . . .accountservices@apmmusic.com
SECOND EMAIL . . . . .firstinitiallastname@apmmusic.com
WEB SITE . . . . .www.apmmusic.com
COMMENTS   East Coast office: 240 Madison Ave.,
                           11th Fl., New York, NY 10016, phone:
                           800-276-6874, fax: 212-856-9807

Adam Taylor . . . . .President
George Macias . . . . .VP, Sales
Richard Judice . . . . .Music Director
Robert Navarro . . . . .Music Director
Georgia Robertson . . . . .Music Director
Edwina Travis-Chin . . . . .Music Director
Lauren Bell . . . . .Account Executive
Rob Cairns . . . . .Account Executive
Deborah Fisher . . . . .Account Executive
Bob Frymire . . . . .Account Executive
Craig Giummarra . . . . .Account Executive
Connie Red . . . . .Account Executive
Tia Sommer . . . . .Account Executive
Dale Suss . . . . .Account Executive
Erin Collins . . . . .Director, Marketing

THE AUDIO DEPARTMENT
119 W. 57th St., 4th Fl.
New York, NY 10019
PHONE 212-586-3503
FAX 212-245-1675
EMAIL . . . . .scheduling@theaudiodepartment.com
WEB SITE . . . . .www.theaudiodepartment.com
COMMENTS   Music Library; Original scoring

BIG SOUNDS INTERNATIONAL
5225 Wilshire Blvd., Ste. 407
Los Angeles, CA 90036
PHONE 323-954-0274
FAX 323-954-0277
EMAIL . . . . .info@bigsoundsintl.com
SECOND EMAIL . . . . .licensing@bigsoundsintl.com
WEB SITE . . . . .www.bigsoundsintl.com
RECENT PROJECTS   Sunday Driver (Documentary) - Must
                      Love Dogs (Feature)
SUBMISSION POLICY   No unsolicited material

Jonathan Hafter . . . . .President

HELENE BLUE MUSIQUE LTD.
421 Seventh Ave., Ste. 901
New York, NY 10001
PHONE 212-724-5900
FAX 212-501-0360
EMAIL . . . . .helene@helenebluemusic.com

Helene Blue . . . . .Owner (helene@helenebluemusic.com)
Susan Berlowitz . . . . . .Creative Director (susan@helenebluemusic.com)

BLUE WAVE RECORDS
3221 Perryville Rd.
Baldwinsville, NY 13027
PHONE 315-638-4286
FAX 315-635-4757
EMAIL . . . . .bluewave@localnet.com
WEB SITE . . . . .www.bluewaverecords.com
GENRES   Blues
SUBMISSION POLICY   Accepts unsolicited material
COMMENTS   Record Company; Publishing

Greg Spencer . . . . .President

BZ/RIGHTS & PERMISSIONS, INC.
121 W. 27th St., Ste. 901
New York, NY 10001
PHONE 212-924-3000
FAX 212-924-2525
EMAIL . . . . .info@bzrights.com
WEB SITE . . . . .www.bzrights.com

Barbara Zimmorman . . . . .No Title

*CELLULOID JUKEBOX
2653 S. Halm Ave.
Los Angeles, CA 90034
PHONE 310-838-3495
FAX 310-836-3653
EMAIL . . . . .tristana@celljuke.com

Tristana Ward . . . . .Owner/President

*CHRISTMAS AND HOLIDAY MUSIC
24351 Grass St.
Lake Forest, CA 92630
PHONE 949-859-1615
FAX 949-859-1615
EMAIL . . . . .justinwilde@christmassongs.com
WEB SITE . . . . .www.christmassongs.com

Justin Wilde . . . . .President

MONICA CIAFARDINI MUSIC CLEARANCE
3727 W. Magnolia Blvd., PMB 829
Burbank, CA 91510-7711
PHONE 818-563-9843
FAX 818-563-9832
EMAIL . . . . .ciafardini@covad.net

Monica Ciafardini . . . . .No Title

CINECALL SOUNDTRACKS, INC.
3 White St., Ste. 100
Red Bank, NJ 07701
PHONE 732-450-8882
FAX 732-450-8884
EMAIL . . . . .mail@cinecall.com
WEB SITE . . . . .www.cinecall.com
GENRES   All Genres

George McMorrow . . . . .President
Daniel Fulton . . . . .Creative Support
Michael Sternbach . . . . .Creative Support

CINETRAX
8033 Sunset Blvd., Ste. 400
Los Angeles, CA 90046
PHONE 323-874-9590
EMAIL . . . . .info@cinetrax.com
WEB SITE . . . . .www.cinetrax.com
COMMENTS   Production Music Library; Original scor-
                      ing

Daniel Cossu .Creative Director/Composer

DICK CLARK MEDIA ARCHIVES
3003 W. Olive Ave.
Burbank, CA 91505
PHONE 818-841-3003
FAX 818-566-7313
GENRES   Country - Pop - R&B - Rock

Jeff James . . . . .No Title

CLEAR CUT INC.
9490 Crockett Rd.
Brentwood, TN 37027
PHONE 615-370-3760
FAX 615-507-2003
EMAIL . . . . .barbara@thentertainment.com
SECOND EMAIL . . . . .kristen@thentertainment.com

Barbara Hall . . . . .President
Kristen Topping . . . . .No Title

CLEARANCE CONSULTANTS
10565 Esther Ave.
Los Angeles, CA 90064
PHONE 310-253-5085
FAX 310-253-5086
EMAIL . . . . .jeanne.fay@comcast.net

Jeanne Fay . . . . .Principal

CLEARANCE QUEST
2112 Sunset Pl.
Nashville, TN 37212
PHONE 615-298-2463
FAX 615-298-2327
EMAIL . . . . .clearancequest@comcast.net

Cheryl Melton-Smith . . . . .President

*CLEARING SKY
254 Reservoir Ave.
Providence, RI 02907
PHONE 800-759-0841
EMAIL .music@clearingsky.com
WEB SITE .www.clearingsky.com
GENRES   All Genres

Benjamin Aleman . . . . .Director, Licensing
Kathleen Faron . . . . .Music Supervisor

CLEARVISION UNLIMITED
8300 Beverly Blvd.
Los Angeles, CA 90048
PHONE 323-651-4478
FAX 323-651-3614
EMAIL . . . . .clearrights@aol.com
COMMENTS   Music Supervision; Media Copyright
                                Clearance

Lana Hale . . . . .President

COMBUSTION MUSIC
1609 17th Ave. South
Nashville, TN 37212-2812
PHONE 615-515-5490
FAX 615-269-6883
EMAIL . . . . .firstname@combustionent.com
WEB SITE . . . . .www.windsweptpacific.com
GENRES   Alternative - Country - Gospel - Jazz -
                                Pop - R&B - Rock - Urban

Chris Farren . . . . .Co-President
Ken Levitan . . . . .Co-President (ken@vectormgmt.com)
Chris Van Belkom . . . . .Office/Catalogue Manager
                                (chrisvb@combustionent.com)
John Anderson . . . . . VP, Film/TV (LA) (janderson@windsweptpacific.com)
LeAnn Phelan . . . . .VP, Creative (leann@combustionent.com)
Jameson Clark . . . . . .Creative Director (jameson@combustionent.com)

COPYRIGHT CLEARINGHOUSE, INC.
405 Riverside Dr.
Burbank, CA 91506
PHONE 818-558-3480, x126
FAX 818-558-3474
EMAIL .anita@musicreports.com
WEB SITE .www.musicreports.com

Anita Hunsaker . . . . .VP
Ronald H. Gertz Esq. . . . . .President/CEO
Douglas J. Brainin MBA . . . . .Executive VP/COO

COPYRIGHT MUSIC & VISUALS
61 Hoyle Ave.
Toronto, ON M4S 2X5 Canada
PHONE 416-979-3333
FAX 416-979-2559
EMAIL .info@copyrightmv.com
SECOND EMAIL . . . . .john@copyrightmv.com
WEB SITE .www.copyrightmv.com
GENRES   All Genres
COMMENTS   Combines music supervision/consulting
                                with leading expertise in copyright clear-
                                ance, music, film clips, art, etc.

John Ciccone . . . . .President

CREATIVE CLEARANCE
4570 Van Nuys Blvd., Ste. 594
Sherman Oaks, CA 91403
PHONE 818-728-4622
FAX 818-479-9696
EMAIL . . . . .contact@creativeclearance.com
WEB SITE . . . . .www.creativeclearance.com

Llyswen Vaughan . . . . .No Title

CREATIVE MUSICAL SERVICES
13547 Ventura Blvd., Ste. 358
Sherman Oaks, CA 91423-3825
PHONE 818-762-4222
EMAIL . . . . .info@creativemusicalsvcs.com
WEB SITE . . . . .www.creativemusicalsvcs.com

Dana Ferandelli . . . . .Music Clearance

CSS MUSIC/D.A.W.N. MUSIC
1948 Riverside Dr.
Los Angeles, CA 90039
PHONE 323-660-2070/800-468-6874
FAX 323-660-2070
EMAIL . . . . .info@cssmusic.com
SECOND EMAIL . . . . .sales@dawnmusic.com
WEB SITE . . . . .www.cssmusic.com
COMMENTS   Music Library

Mike Fuller . . . . .Creative Director
David Wurst . . . . .Head, Administration
Brian Fuller . . . . .IT Specialist

DELTA ENTERTAINMENT CORPORATION
1663 Sawtelle Blvd.
Los Angeles, CA 90025
PHONE 310-268-1205
FAX 310-268-1279
EMAIL . . . . .info@deltamusic.com
WEB SITE . . . . .www.deltaentertainment.com
GENRES   Adult Contemporary - Blues - Classical -
                                Country - Jazz - Pop - Rock - World

Michelle Justice . . . . .Executive VP
Anne Wettig . . . . .Production Administrator

CLEARANCE & LICENSING

*DEMON MUSIC GROUP
33 Foley St.
London W1W 7TL United Kingdom
PHONE 44-207-612-3303
FAX 44-207-612-3366
EMAIL . . . . .glen.d'souza@demonmusicgroup.co.uk
SECOND EMAIL . . . . .david.bass@demonmusicgroup.co.uk
WEB SITE . . . . .www.tracklicensing.com

Glen D'Souza . . . . .Licensing Manager
Elliott Tucker . . . . .Licensing Manager

DEWOLFE MUSIC
25 W. 45th St., Ste. 801
New York, NY 10036
PHONE 800-221-6713/212-382-0220
FAX 212-382-0278
EMAIL . . . . .info@dewolfemusic.com
WEB SITE . . . . .www.dewolfemusic.com
GENRES   All Genres

Andy Jacobs . . . . .President
Marcie Jacobs . . . . .Sr. VP
Jon Lettis . . . . .VP
Mike Michaels . . . . .No Title
Joel Feinberg . . . . .Sales
Richard Jankovich . . . . .Sales
Jaime Gillespie . . . . .Manager, Music Sales
Jerry La Rosa .Engineer, Sales

DIAMOND TIME
73 Spring St., Ste. 504
New York, NY 10012
PHONE 212-274-1006/310-828-9201
FAX 212-274-1938/310-828-9203
EMAIL . . . . .info@diamondtime.net
WEB SITE . . . . .www.diamondtime.net
COMMENTS   Music Supervisor; West Coast office:
                            1610 Colorado Ave., Ste. 200, Santa
                            Monica, CA 90404

Cathy Carapella . . . . .Licensing
Chris Robertson . . . . .Licensing
Jennifer Reves . . . . .Licensing
Norman Cohen . . . . .Licensing
Rick Eisenstein . . . . .Licensing (LA)
Chris Potter . . . . .Assistant

*DL MUSIC
3575 Cahuenga Blvd.
Los Angeles, CA 90068
PHONE 323-878-0400
FAX 323-878-0444
EMAIL . . . . .customerservice@dl-music.com
WEB SITE . . . . .www.dl-music.com
GENRES   All Genres
COMMENTS   Music Publishing and Creative Services;
                            Music Library; Original Composition

Derek Luff . . . . .CEO
Richard Gelles . . . . .President
David Zumsteg . . . . . . .Music Coordinator/Sales Representative
Mick Mahan .Sales Representative
Anfinn Skulevold . . . . .Mastering & Distribution
Steve Kim . . . . .Assistant Music Coordinator

DMG CLEARANCES INC.
13 Robin Dr.
Hockessin, DE 19707
PHONE 302-239-6337
FAX 302-239-6875
EMAIL . . . . .info@dmgclearances.com
WEB SITE . . . . .www.dmgclearances.com
RECENT PROJECTS   School of Rock - The Aviator - Christmas
                           with the Kranks - White Chicks - In Her
                           Shoes

Deborah Mannis-Gardner . . . . .President

EASTWEST
9000 Sunset Blvd., Ste. 1550
West Hollywood, CA 90069
PHONE 800-833-8339
FAX 310-271-6968
EMAIL . . . . .sales@eastwestsounds.com
WEB SITE . . . . .www.soundsonline.com

Doug Rogers . . . . .President/CEO
Stefan Leiste . . . . .VP, Sales

EXTREME PRODUCTION MUSIC
1547 14th St.
Santa Monica, CA 90404
PHONE 310-395-0408/800-542-9494
FAX 310-395-0409
EMAIL . . . . .la@extrememusic.com
WEB SITE . . . . .www.extrememusic.com

Luke Rowland . . . . .Contact

*FINTAGE PUBLISHING & COLLECTION
Stationsweg 32
Leiden 2312 AV The Netherlands
PHONE 31-71-565-9999
FAX 31-71-565-9990
EMAIL . . . . .niels.teves@fintagehouse.com
SECOND EMAIL . . . . .ernstjacob.bakker@fintagehouse.com
WEB SITE . . . . .www.fintagehouse.com
SECOND WEB SITE . . . . .www.fintagemusic.com

Robbert Aarts . . . . .Co-CEO
Niels Teves . . . . .Co-CEO
Ernst Jacob Bakker . . . . .Head, Music/Secondary Rights
Paul Rogers . . . . .Representative

FIRSTCOM MUSIC, INC.
8750 Wilshire Blvd., 2nd Fl.
Beverly Hills, CA 90211
PHONE 310-358-4915/310-358-4916
FAX 310-358-4314
EMAIL . . . . .info@firstcom.com
WEB SITE . . . . .www.firstcom.com
COMMENTS   Music Production Library

Carol Riffert . . . . .VP/General Manager
Sam Kling . . . . .VP, Film & TV Music (samk@firstcom.com)
John Lentz .Music Director (800-858-8880)
Jerome Spence . . . . .Director, Film & TV Music (310-358-4918)

DAVID FRANCO INTERNATIONAL MUSIC PRODUCTIONS
4342 Redwood Ave., Ste. 310
Marina del Rey, CA 90292-7650
PHONE 310-823-5547
FAX 310-821-0707
EMAIL . . . . .dfintlprod@aol.com

David Franco . . . . .Music Supervisor/Producer

FREEPLAY MUSIC
5532 Freeman Ave.
La Crescenta, CA 91214
PHONE 818-248-7018/212-974-0548
FAX 818-248-1596
EMAIL . . . . .deborah@freeplaymusic.com
WEB SITE . . . . .www.freeplaymusic.com
COMMENTS   East Coast office: 630 Ninth Ave., Ste.
                        1408, New York, NY 10036

Deborah Cally . . . . .Director, West Coast Music Operations

FRICON ENTERTAINMENT COMPANY
11 Music Square East, Ste. 301
Nashville, TN 37203
PHONE 615-826-2288/323-931-7323
FAX 615-826-0500/323-938-2030
EMAIL . . . . .fricon@comcast.net
GENRES   All Genres
RECENT PROJECTS   Ambulance Girl - The Hunt for BTK - For
                        One Night - Vampire Bats
SUBMISSION POLICY   Call for permission
COMMENTS   West Coast office: 1048 S. Ogden Dr.,
                        Los Angeles, CA 90019-6501

Terri Fricon . . . . .President
Jan Morales . . . . .Creative Director

G&E MUSIC
36 E. 23rd St., Ste. 7R
New York, NY 10010
PHONE 212-673-9274
FAX 212-673-9140
EMAIL . . . . .info@gemusic.com
WEB SITE . . . . .www.producerstoolbox.com

Erik Blicker . . . . .Creative Partner (erik@gemusic.com)
Glenn Schloss . . . . .Creative Partner (glenn@gemusic.com)
Ben Stivers . . . . .Composer (ben@gemusic.com)
Eric de Picciotto . . . . .Client Relations (edp@gemusic.com)

*GREEN & GREEN
1000 Fourth St., Ste. 595
San Rafael, CA 94901
PHONE 415-457-8300
FAX 415-457-8757
EMAIL . . . . .bev@musiclawyer.com
WEB SITE . . . . .www.musiclawyer.com

Beverly Robin Green . . . . .Director, Business/Legal Affairs

EVAN M. GREENSPAN, INC. (EMG)
4181 Sunswept Dr.
Studio City, CA 91604
PHONE 818-762-9656
FAX 818-762-2624
EMAIL . . . . .emginc@clearance.com
WEB SITE . . . . .www.clearance.com

Evan M. Greenspan . . . . .President
E. Shain . . . . .Director, Music Clearance
Suzi Barry . . . . .Manager, Clearance Operations

GROOVE ADDICTS
12211 W. Washington Blvd.
Los Angeles, CA 90066
PHONE 800-400-6767/310-572-4646
FAX 310-572-4647
EMAIL . . . . .info@grooveaddicts.com
WEB SITE . . . . .www.grooveaddicts.com
COMMENTS   Music Library

Cindy Rosmann . . . . .Head, Marketing

*GROUP MUSICWORKS
8539 Sunset Blvd., Ste. 141
West Hollywood, CA 90069
PHONE 310-652-0650
FAX 310-652-0651
COMMENTS   No unsolicited material accepted

Suzan Mann . . . . .President

THE HARRY FOX AGENCY INC.
711 Third Ave.
New York, NY 10017
PHONE 212-370-5330/212-834-0100
FAX 212-953-2384
EMAIL . . . . .client_relations@harryfox.com
WEB SITE . . . . .www.harryfox.com
GENRES   All Genres
COMMENTS   U.S. mechanical rights agent; Provides
                        licensing for the use of its represented
                        publishers' compositions for recordings,
                        downloads and certain other digital uses

Gary L. Churgin . . . . .President/CEO
Alfred Pedecine . . . . .Sr. VP, Finance/CFO
Michael Simon . . . . . . .Sr. VP, Licensing/Chief, Strategic Development &
                                                          Marketing
Frank Wander . . . . .Sr. VP, IT/CIO
Edward Hunt . . . . .Sr. VP, Index & Client Relations
Michele Olton . . . . .Sr. VP, Human Resources & Administration
Jacqueline Charlesworth . . . . .Sr. VP/General Counsel
Nat Annamalai . . . . .VP, Royalty Compliance
Lauren Apolito . . . . .VP, Business Development
Christos Badavas .VP/Senior Counsel
Paul Gilbert . . . . .VP, Index & Client Relations
Maurice Russell . . . . .VP, Licensing
Laurie Jakobsen . . . . .Sr. Director, Communications
Sean Parlakian . . . . .Sr. Director, Collections
Matt Wuolle .Director, Distribution

HEADROOM DIGITAL AUDIO
11 E. 26th St.
New York, NY 10010
PHONE 212-246-8400
FAX 212-245-0370
EMAIL . . . . .info@headroomdigi.com
WEB SITE . . . . .www.headroomdigi.com

Lynn Antizzo . . . . .Studio Manager/Producer (lynn@headroomdigi.com)
Jessica Poland . . . . .Scheduling (jessica@headroomdigi.com)
Gigi Lacks . . . . .Accounting (gigi@headroomdigi.com)
Jerry Plotkin Composer/Sound Designer/Mixer (jerry@headroomdigi.com)
Alan Varner . . . . . . .Mixer/Sound Designer (alan@headroomdigi.com)
Jesse Hammer . . . . . .Mixer/Sound Designer (jesse@headroomdigi.com)
Evan Spear . . . . .Assistant Engineer (evan@headroomdigi.com)
Sam Bair . . . . .Assistant Engineer/Technician (sam@headroomdigi.com)

*HOGAN MEDIA & MUSIC, INC.
712 Bancroft Rd., PMB 517
Walnut Creek, CA 94598
PHONE 925-685-9535
FAX 925-676-8195
EMAIL . . . . .hmmshelly@astound.net
WEB SITE . . . . .www.hoganmediaandmusic.com

Shelly Hogan . . . . .No Title
Mary Rogers . . . . .No Title

CLEARANCE & LICENSING

*HOT HOUSE MUSIC LTD.
Greenland Place, 115-123 Bayham St.
London NW1 0AG United Kingdom
PHONE 44-207-446-7446
FAX 44-207-446-7448
EMAIL . . . . .info@hot-house-music.com
WEB SITE . . . . .www.hot-house-music.com

Becky Bentham . . . . .Executive
Karen Elliott . . . . .Executive

*IDM MUSIC/BIXIO MUSIC GROUP & ASSOCIATES
111 E. 14th St., Ste. 140
New York, NY 10003
PHONE 212-695-3911
FAX 212-967-6284
EMAIL .sales@idmmusic.com
SECOND EMAIL . . . . .sales@bixio.com
WEB SITE . . . . .www.idmmusic.com
SECOND WEB SITE . . . . .www.bixio.com

Johannes In der Muhlen . . . . .General Manager
Miriam Westercappel . . . . .Managing Director
Ana Starcevic . . . . .Clearance Department
Dus . . . . .Creative/IT
Dijana Dobras . . . . .Copyright/Administration

IMAGINARY FRIENDS MUSIC PARTNERS
1158 26th St., Ste. 242
Santa Monica, CA 90403
PHONE 310-281-7812
FAX 310-315-1984
EMAIL . . . . .beth@imaginaryfriends.com
WEB SITE . . . . .www.imaginaryfriends.com
GENRES   All Genres
SUBMISSION POLICY   No unsolicited submissions
COMMENTS   Independent artists only

Beth Wernick . . . . .No Title

INSTANT ACCESS MUSIC
44 Music Square East, Ste. 503
Nashville, TN 37203
PHONE 615-974-3158/877-342-6721
FAX 215-895-9672
EMAIL . . . . .info@iamusic.com
WEB SITE . . . . .www.iamusic.com

JECO MUSIC
62 W. 45th St.
New York, NY 10036
PHONE 212-768-8501/310-315-3626
FAX 212-768-8505
EMAIL . . . . .gus@jecomusic.com
SECOND EMAIL . . . . .jeco@jecomusic.com
WEB SITE . . . . .www.jecomusic.com
GENRES   All Genres
RECENT PROJECTS   Allegra - Pillsbury - Nike - Listerine -
                             Bose - Caress - Reeses - Accuvue
COMMENTS   Commercial Music Library; West Coast
                             office: 2936 Nebraska Ave., Santa
                             Monica, CA 90404

Gus Reyes . . . . .Contact

*JEFF WAYNE MUSIC GROUP
Oliver House, 8-9 Ivor Place
London NW1 6BY United Kingdom
PHONE 44-207-724-2471
FAX 44-207-724-6245
EMAIL . . . . .info@jeffwaynemusic.com
WEB SITE . . . . .www.jeffwaynemusic.com

Mandy Hughes . . . . .Head, Production

JRT MUSIC
648 Broadway, Ste. 504
New York, NY 10012
PHONE 212-253-8908
FAX 212-353-9317
EMAIL . . . . .info@jrtmusic.com
WEB SITE . . . . .www.jrtmusic.com
GENRES   Classical - Country - Electronica - Folk -
                             Jazz - Latin - New Age - Pop - R&B -
                             Rap/Hip-Hop - Reggae - Roots - Urban -
                             World
SUBMISSION POLICY   Submissions accepted only upon direct
                             request; Unsolicited submissions will not
                             be opened
COMMENTS   Music Library, music publishing, custom
                             music composition

Jerome Tokarz . . . . .Partner
Roger Tokarz . . . . .Partner
Catherine Bogin . . . . .GM
Marc Goldberg .Client Manager

JUNE STREET ENTERTAINMENT
4111 W. Alameda Ave., Ste. 501
Burbank, CA 91505
PHONE 818-972-1112
FAX 818-972-9011
EMAIL . . . . .reception@junestentertainment.com
WEB SITE . . . . .www.junestentertainment.com
GENRES   All Genres
RECENT PROJECTS   My Baby's Daddy - Confessions of a
                             Teenage Drama Queen - New York
                             Minute
SUBMISSION POLICY   No unsolicited material accepted
COMMENTS   Independent marketing and licensing for
                             Film, TV and Commercials; Publishing:
                             June Street Publishing (ASCAP), June
                             Street Global Songs (BMI)

Art Ford . . . . .President
Brooke Lizotte . . . . .VP
Amanda Johnson . . . . .Project Coordinator
Lachlan McClain . . . . .Online Catalog Manager/Office Manager

*JUST SONGS
The Studio, Coombe House, Cudworth, Nr. Illminster
Somerset TA 19 OPR United Kingdom
PHONE 44-1460-259-312
FAX 44-01460-259-312
EMAIL . . . . .info@justsongs.co.uk
SECOND EMAIL . . . . .bj@justsongs.co.uk

Brian Justice . . . . .President
Kieron Forgerty . . . . .Executive Logistics

KID GLOVES MUSIC
20106 Via Cellini
Porter Ranch, CA 91326
PHONE 818-700-0292
FAX 818-700-0294
EMAIL . . . . .submissions@kidglovesmusic.com
GENRES   Alternative - Blues - Christian/Gospel -
                             Classical - Country - Electronica - Folk -
                             Jazz - Latin - New Age - Pop - R&B -
                             Rap/Hip-Hop - Reggae - Rock - Roots -
                             Urban - World

Nathalie Stebleton . . . . .President

KILLER TRACKS
6534 Sunset Blvd.
Hollywood, CA 90028
PHONE 323-957-4455
FAX 323-957-4470
EMAIL . . . . .production@killertracks.com
SECOND EMAIL . . . . .sales@killertracks.com
WEB SITE . . . . .www.killertracks.com
GENRES   All Genres

Gary Gross . . . . .President
Dennis Dunn .Sr. Director, Sales
Dennis Pontillano . . . . .Sr. Director, Marketing

K-TEL INTERNATIONAL, INC.
2655 Cheshire Lane North, Ste. 100
Plymouth, MN 55447
PHONE 763-268-0226
FAX 763-559-5505
EMAIL . . . . .mkuehn@k-tel.com
WEB SITE . . . . .www.k-tel.com
GENRES   Adult Contemporary - Children's -
                               Classical - Country - Electronica -
                               Gospel - Jazz - R&B - Rock

Mary Kuehn . . . . .VP/General Manager

LATIN MUSIC SPECIALISTS
5943 Melvin Ave.
Tarzana, CA 91356
PHONE 818-774-1441
FAX 818-774-9172
EMAIL . . . . .sara@indartmusic.com
WEB SITE . . . . .www.indartmusic.com
GENRES   Latin
RECENT PROJECTS   The Sopranos - The Shield - Carnivale -
                               The Handler - S.W.A.T. - Spy Hard - The
                               Bachelor
COMMENTS   Licensing division of LMS Records

Daniel Indart . . . . .President
Sara Traina . . . . .VP

LICENSE IT ...
9899 Santa Monica Blvd., Ste. 1103
Beverly Hills, CA 90212
PHONE 310-289-7232
FAX 310-772-0985
EMAIL . . . . .licenseit@aol.com
RECENT PROJECTS   Charmed - Ballistic: Ecks vs. Sever -
                               Global Lounge - Global Destination
COMMENTS   Record label; Music publisher; Music
                               supervisor

Lauren Brown . . . . .No Title

*THE LICENSING TEAM, INC.
7958 Beverly Blvd.
Los Angeles, CA 90048
PHONE 323-658-6580/44-1923-234-021
FAX 323-653-0482/44-1923-249-251
EMAIL .info@thelicensingteam.com
WEB SITE .www.thelicensingteam.com
SECOND WEB SITE . . . . .www.musicmoves.net
COMMENTS   UK office: 23 Capel Rd., Watford,
                               WD19 4FE UK

Celine Palavioux . . . . .President
Lucy Winch . . . . .President (UK) (lucy@thelicensingteam.com)
Miguel Govea Jr. . . . . .VP, Music Supervisor

*LONGO MUSIC SERVICES LLC
10718 White Oak Ave., Ste. 4
Granada Hills, CA 91344
PHONE 818-368-4018
FAX 818-366-2968
EMAIL . . . . .alongo@socal.rr.com

Angela Longo . . . . .President
Gloria Longo . . . . .VP
Michael Mercy . . . . .No Title

LOS ANGELES POST MUSIC INC.
15030 Ventura Blvd., Ste. 22-473
Sherman Oaks, CA 91403
PHONE 818-501-8329/800-527-6781
FAX 818-990-7661
EMAIL . . . . .info@lapostmusic.com
WEB SITE . . . . .www.lapostmusic.com
GENRES   Blues - Pop - Punk - R&B - Rap/Hip-Hop
                               - Reggae - Rock

MANHATTAN PRODUCTION MUSIC
355 W. 52nd St., 6th Fl.
New York, NY 10019
PHONE 800-227-1954/212-333-5766
FAX 212-262-0814
EMAIL . . . . .info@mpmmusic.com
WEB SITE . . . . .www.mpmmusic.com

Ron Goldberg . . . . .VP, Sales & Marketing

MEGATRAX PRODUCTION MUSIC
7629 Fulton Ave.
North Hollywood, CA 91605
PHONE 818-255-7100/888-MEGA-555
FAX 818-255-7199
EMAIL . . . . .info@megatrax.com
WEB SITE . . . . .www.megatrax.com
RECENT PROJECTS   Features: Crash - Mr. & Mrs. Smith -
                               House of Wax; TV: Las Vegas - The
                               Shield - Arrested Development - Without
                               a Trace - American Idol - 2004 Kids
                               Choice Awards - American Family -
                               9/11: Life on the Line (TLC) - The
                               Sopranos - The Other Half - Arliss -
                               Primetime Glick; Trailers: Dark Water -
                               Valiant - Fun with Dick & Jane - I, Robot
                               - The Notebook - Home On The Range
                               - Little Black Book - Princess Diaries 2 -
                               Vanity Fair - Sky Captain and the World
                               of Tomorrow
SUBMISSION POLICY   No unsolicited submissions
COMMENTS   Production music for film, TV advertising
                               and multimedia with more than 500
                               CDs across 6 libraries

J.C. Dwyer . . . . .Composer/Executive Producer
Ron Mendelsohn . . . . .Composer/Executive Producer
Andrew Robbins . . . . .Licensing Director, Film & TV
Aaron Davis . . . . .Licensing Director, TV Broadcast & Network Promotion
Cassidy Richey . . . . .Licensing Manager, Broadcast AV
Leisa Korn . . . . .Director, Publishing & Administration
Jennifer Vallens . . . . .Director, Human Resources

CLEARANCE & LICENSING

METRO MUSIC PRODUCTION, INC.
37 W. 20th St.
New York, NY 10011
PHONE 212-229-1700/800-697-7392
FAX 212-229-9063
EMAIL .info@metromusicinc.com
WEB SITE .www.metromusicinc.com
GENRES   Alternative - Jazz - Pop - R&B - Rock
COMMENTS   Production Library

Mitch Coodley . . . . .President & Composer
Michael Swanson . . . . .Licensing Manager

JILL MEYERS MUSIC CONSULTANTS
1551 Ocean Ave., Ste. 260
Santa Monica, CA 90401
PHONE 310-576-1387
FAX 310-576-6989
EMAIL . . . . .jill@jillmeyersmusic.com

Jill Meyers . . . . .No Title
Lisa Feldman . . . . .No Title
Mike Mallen . . . . .No Title
Lisa Wasiak . . . . .No Title

*MARC MILLER
4454 Strohm Ave.
Toluca Lake, CA 91602
PHONE 818-395-9160
EMAIL . . . . .mmiller@earthlink.net

Marc Miller . . . . .Owner

MUSIC 2 HUES
PO Box 1068
Agawam, MA 01001
PHONE 888-821-7515
FAX 413-821-8717
EMAIL . . . . .info@music2hues.com
WEB SITE www.music2hues.com
GENRES   All Genres
COMMENTS   Music Library; Sound Effects Library;
                          Production Music, sold as buy-out or
                          custom scored; Royalty-free music

Andy Wells . . . . .Sales Manager

THE MUSIC BAKERY
7522 Campbell Rd., Ste. 113
Dallas, TX 75248
PHONE 972-578-7863/800-229-0313
FAX 972-424-3680
EMAIL . . . . .jackw@musicbakery.com
WEB SITE . . . . .www.musicbakery.com
COMMENTS   Royalty-free production music and sound
                          effects

Jack Waldenmaier . . . . .President & Executive Producer
                          (jackw@musicbakery.com)
Kelly Atkinson . . . . .Sales & Licensing (kelly@musicbakery.com)

*THE MUSIC BRIDGE LLC
PO Box 661918
Los Angeles, CA 90066
PHONE 310-398-9650
FAX 310-398-4850
EMAIL . . . . .thabridge@aol.com
WEB SITE .www.themusicbridge.com

David G. Powell . . . . .President

MUSIC RESOURCES, INC.
6671 Sunset Blvd., Ste. 1574-A
Los Angeles, CA 90028
PHONE 323-993-9915
FAX 323-993-9921
EMAIL . . . . .mr@musicresources.com
WEB SITE . . . . .www.musicresources.com
GENRES   All Genres
RECENT PROJECTS   Virgin - A Little Trip to Heaven - The
                          Benefactor - Supernanny - Gram
                          Parsons: Return to Sin City
SUBMISSION POLICY   No unsolicited submissions

Nancie Stern . . . . .President
Tony Abner . . . . .Executive VP
Brandon Schott . . . . .Assistant

MUSIC RIGHTZ
556 S. Fair Oaks Ave., Ste. 342
Pasadena, CA 91105
PHONE 626-345-0046/818-769-4829
FAX 626-604-0420/818-337-0482
EMAIL . . . . .suzannecoffman@sbcglobal.net
WEB SITE . . . . .www.musicrightz.com
COMMENTS   Second office: 4804 Laurel Canyon
                          Blvd., Ste. 578, Valley Village, CA
                          91607

Suzanne Coffman . . . . .Co-Owner
Micki Stern . . . . .Co-Owner
Yolanda Ferraloro . . . . .Director, Licensing

MUST HAVE MUSIC
PO Box 801181
Santa Clarita, CA 91380
PHONE 661-645-7618
FAX 661-799-3732
EMAIL . . . . .info@musthavemusic.com
WEB SITE . . . . .www.musthavemusic.com
GENRES   Country - Pop - R&B - Rock
COMMENTS   Music Library specializing in pop/R&B,
                          pop country, rock and AAA songs for use
                          in film and TV

Ken Klar . . . . .Managing Director

NATURAL ENERGY LAB
7424-1/2 Sunset Blvd., #5
Los Angeles, CA 90046
PHONE 323-876-2408/323-876-2070
FAX 323-874-0442
WEB SITE .www.naturalenergylab.com
SUBMISSION POLICY   Contact by telephone or email prior to
                          submitting

Danny Benair . . . . . . .Sr. Lab Technician (danny@naturalenergylab.com)
Heather Kreamer . . .Jr. Lab Technician (heather@naturalenergylab.com)

NETWORK MUSIC
8750 Wilshire Blvd.
Beverly Hills, CA 90211
PHONE 310-358-4982/800-854-2075
FAX 310-358-4311
EMAIL . . . . .sales@networkmusic.com
WEB SITE . . . . .www.networkmusic.com
SUBMISSION POLICY   Send composer demos to Carl Peel,
                          Network Music, 6534 Sunset Blvd.,
                          Hollywood, CA 90028

Gary Gross . . . . .President
Dennis Dunn . . . . .VP, Sales
Todd Kern . . . . .Director, Marketing
Carl Peel . . . . .Director, Music Production

NIGHTINGALE MUSIC PRODUCTIONS INC.
5460 Yonge St., Ste. 1004
Toronto, ON M2N 6K7 Canada
PHONE 416-221-2393
FAX 416-221-2676
EMAIL . . . . .info@nightingalemusic.com
WEB SITE . . . . .www.nightingalemusic.com
COMMENTS   Award-winning music, songs and sound
                         effects for film, television and multi-
                         media; Over 1500 CDs; Original music
                         and production music

Caron Nightingale . . . . .Founder & President

NOMA MUSIC
23705 Vanowen St., Ste. 239
West Hills, CA 91307
PHONE 818-883-1878
FAX 818-883-1878
EMAIL . . . . .musicplacement@nomamusic.com
SECOND EMAIL . . . . .licensing@nomamusic.com
WEB SITE . . . . .www.nomamusic.com
GENRES   All Genres
SUBMISSION POLICY   See Web site
COMMENTS   Publishing, Composer Representation,
                         Music Supervision, Soundtracks

NON-STOP MUSIC LIBRARY
4605 Lankershim Blvd., Ste. 305
North Hollywood, CA 91602
PHONE 818-752-1898/801-531-0060
FAX 818-752-1899/801-531-0346
EMAIL . . . . .info@nonstopmusic.com
SECOND EMAIL . . . . .firstname@nonstopmusic.com
WEB SITE . . . . .www.nonstopmusic.com
GENRES   All Genres
COMMENTS   Salt Lake City office: 915 W. 100 South,
                         Salt Lake City, UT 84104; East Coast
                         office: 134 W. Ninth St., Ste. 906, New
                         York, NY 10001, phone: 212-242-
                         1155, fax: 212-290-7612

Tim Arnold .West Coast Regional Manager
Mike Hicks   Agencies, Post, Corporate (SLC) (mikeh@nonstopmusic.com)
Micki Stefanik . . . . .East Coast
Dana Buhr . . . . .TV Program/Feature Film, Advertising (LA)

NORTH STAR MEDIA
12650 Riverside Dr., Ste. 200
Studio City, CA 91607
PHONE 818-766-2100
FAX 818-766-2105
FMAIL .info@northstarmedia.com
WEB SITE . . . . .www.northstarmedia.com
RECENT PROJECTS   Desperate Housewives - The O.C. - Sex
                         and the City - The Shield - North Shore

Ron Sobel . . . . .President
Dan Kirkpatrick .VP, Administration
Joyce Lapinsky . . . . .VP, Creative
Marty Silverstone .Film & TV Music
Adam Wolf . . . . .Film & TV Licensing

NOW HEAR THIS
250 W. 49th St., Ste. 704
New York, NY 10019
PHONE 212-265-1188
FAX 212-265-6363
EMAIL . . . . .larry@nhtsound.com
WEB SITE . . . . .www.nhtsound.com
COMMENTS   Original music, sound design, mix; Full
                         service audio production

Larry Buksbaum . . . . .President
Katie Cassidy . . . . .Studio Manager

OCEAN PARK MUSIC GROUP
1119 Colorado Ave., Ste. 21
Santa Monica, CA 90401
PHONE 310-576-7424
FAX 310-576-7434
EMAIL . . . . .info@oceanparkmusic.com
WEB SITE .www.oceanparkmusic.com
GENRES   All Genres
RECENT PROJECTS   Closer - Volvo Europe - The Aviator trail-
                         er - Mr. 3000 - Vodaphone - Huff - The
                         Wire - Six Feet Under - The O.C.
SUBMISSION POLICY   No unsolicited material accepted

Carol Sue Baker . . . . .No Title
Rhonda Jones . . . . .No Title
Chris Jerde . . . . .No Title
Gary Mecija . . . . .No Title

OGM PRODUCTION MUSIC
6464 Sunset Blvd., Ste. 790
Hollywood, CA 90028
PHONE 323-461-2701/800-421-4163
FAX 323-461-1543
EMAIL . . . . .info@ogmmusic.com
SECOND EMAIL . . . . .ogmmusic@ogmmusic.com
WEB SITE . . . . .www.ogmmusic.com
RECENT PROJECTS   TV: Desperate Housewives - Arrested
                         Development - The West Wing - CSI -
                         Six Feet Under - Scrubs - Passions;
                         Features: Old School - The Banger
                         Sisters
COMMENTS   Library includes all musical genres
                         designed for Internet, film, broadcast,
                         video and multimedia

Ole Georg . . . . .President

OMNIMUSIC
52 Main St.
Port Washington, NY 11050
PHONE 800-828-6664
FAX 516-883-0271
EMAIL . . . . .omni@omnimusic.com
WEB SITE . . . . .www.omnimusic.com
GENRES   All Genres
COMMENTS   Music Library

Doug Wood . . . . .President & Sr. Music Producer
Patti Wood . . . . .VP/Executive Director
Shawn Green . . . . .VP, Operations/Tech Support
Barbara Ring .Director, Marketing
Sally Hogenauer .Customer Service
Kathe O'Connor .Customer Service
Gesine Stross . . . . .Customer Service
Deborah Anderson . . . . .Executive Assistant
Jon Anderson . . . . .Web Administrator

OPUS 1 MUSIC LIBRARY
12711 Ventura Blvd., Ste. 170
Studio City, CA 91604
PHONE 818-508-2040/888-757-6787
FAX 818-508-2044
EMAIL ....office@opus1musiclibrary.com
WEB SITE www.opus1musiclibrary.com

Alan Ett . . . . .President/CEO (alan@opus1musiclibrary.com)
Mitch Rabin . . . . .VP, Sales & Marketing (mitch@opus1musiclibrary.com)
Marrsha Sill . . . . . .VP, Film/TV Music (marrsha@opus1musiclibrary.com)
Ryan Neill . . . . .VP, Production (ryan@opus1musiclibrary.com)
Levon Broussalian . . . . .Director, Music Supervision
(levon@opus1musiclibrary.com)
Evan Cooney . . . . . . .Digital Integration (evan@opus1musiclibrary.com)
Sheila Hall . . . . .Royalties Administrator (sheila@opus1musiclibrary.com)
Daniel Kristofferson . . . . .New Business Development
(daniel@opus1musiclibrary.com)
Alan Cooper . . . . .Music Licensing Associate
(cooper@opus1musiclibrary.com)
Rodney Gordy . . . . .Manager, Licensing & Royalty Administration
(rodney@opus1musiclibrary.com)
Lourdes (Lou) Vitor . . . .Sales & Marketing (lou@opus1musiclibrary.com)
Katie Johnson . . . . .Operations (katie@opus1musiclibrary.com)

PARADISE ARTISTS
PO Box 1821
Ojai, CA 93024-1821
PHONE 805-646-8433
FAX 805-646-3367
EMAIL ....john@paradiseartists.com
WEB SITE ....www.paradiseartists.com
GENRES　　　　　　　Pop - Rock
COMMENTS　　　　　Specializes in classic rock and pop from
　　　　　　　　　　the '60s, '70s and '80s

John Lappen . . . . .Executive VP, Music Licensing

PARKER MUSIC GROUP
2934-1/2 Beverly Glen Circle, Ste. 220
Bel Air, CA 90077
PHONE 818-905-9552
FAX 818-905-7807
EMAIL ....randy@musicclearance.com
WEB SITE ....www.musicclearance.com
COMMENTS　　　　　Provides music supervision, clearance,
　　　　　　　　　　licensing, composing and production for
　　　　　　　　　　all media; Independent music depart-
　　　　　　　　　　ment with a mix of creative and business
　　　　　　　　　　affairs

Randy Parker . . . . .President
Kathleen Merrill . . . . .Executive VP

PATCO RESOURCES, INC.
9 Washington Circle
Suffern, NY 10901
PHONE 845-357-5300
FAX 845-357-6427
EMAIL ....musicinfo@patcoresources.com
WEB SITE ....www.patcoresources.com
GENRES　　　　　　　All Genres
COMMENTS　　　　　Music research; Advertising agencies
　　　　　　　　　　and production houses all over the US

Peter Tracton . . . . .President

THE PERMISSIONS PLACE
2315 Fox Meadow Dr.
Allentown, PA 18104
PHONE 610-439-3410/323-960-4397
FAX 610-439-3412
EMAIL ....lisa@thepermissionsplace.com
WEB SITE ....www.thepermissionsplace.com
GENRES　　　　　　　Adult Contemporary - Gospel - Jazz -
　　　　　　　　　　Pop - R&B - Rock
RECENT PROJECTS　　I Love the '80s (VH1) - I Love the '90s
　　　　　　　　　　Part Deux (VH1)

Lisa A. Merlo . . . . .Owner
Carol Chesko . . . . .Manager, West Coast
Jeannie Fitzpatrick . . . . .Research Manager

DIANE PRENTICE MUSIC CLEARANCE, INC.
9010 Corbin Ave., Ste. 14A
Northridge, CA 91324
PHONE 818-678-0471
FAX 818-678-0475
EMAIL ....diane.p@dpmci.com

Diane Prentice . . . . .Owner

PROMUSIC, INC.
941-A Clint Moore Rd.
Boca Raton, FL 33487
PHONE 800-322-7879/561-995-0331
FAX 561-995-8434
EMAIL ....mail@promusiclibrary.com
WEB SITE ....www.promusiclibrary.com

Alain Leroux . . . . .President
Mike Spitz . . . . .Director, Sales

RAFELSON MEDIA CONSULTING
10713 Burbank Blvd.
North Hollywood, CA 91601
PHONE 818-753-9300
FAX 818-753-9966
EMAIL ....info@rafelson.com
WEB SITE ....www.rafelson.com
SUBMISSION POLICY　　No unsolicited material
COMMENTS　　　　　Film, TV and music production company
　　　　　　　　　　with large music catalog, full post pro-
　　　　　　　　　　duction facilities and recording
　　　　　　　　　　studio/soundstage; In-house record
　　　　　　　　　　label: RM Records; Music distributor,
　　　　　　　　　　publisher, producer, licensing, clearance

Peter Rafelson . . . . .President
Yongbae Cho . . . . .VP, International A&R
Michael Brooks . . . . .Head, Production
Wyatt Peabody . . . . .Director, Operations
Brad Houshour . . . . .Label Manager

REEL MUSIC
23297 Park Ensenada
Calabasas, CA 91302
PHONE 818-225-8166
FAX 818-225-1175
EMAIL ....rurdang@reelmusic.us

Robin Urdang . . . . .President/Music Supervisor

RIPPLE FX
6330 Ferguson St.
Indianapolis, IN 46220
PHONE 317-255-7618
FAX 317-255-7663
EMAIL . . . . .billmallers@ripplefx.com
WEB SITE . . . . .www.ripplefx.com
COMMENTS   Custom Tracks

Bill Mallers . . . . .No Title

RIVER CITY SOUND PRODUCTIONS
PO Box 750786
Memphis, TN 38175
PHONE 901-274-7277/800-755-8729
FAX 901-274-8494
EMAIL . . . . .info@rivercitysound.com
WEB SITE . . . . .www.rivercitysound.com
COMMENTS   Music Library

Bob Pierce . . . . .Creative Director

ROCK-IT SCIENCE MUSIC SUPERVISION
PO Box 39500
Los Angeles, CA 90039
PHONE 323-468-8888
FAX 323-468-8889
EMAIL .info@mediacreature.com

Sharal Churchill . . . . .Founder/CEO
Renee Travis . . . . .VP

RON ROSE PRODUCTIONS, INC.
1101 N. Himes Ave.
Tampa, FL 33607
PHONE 813-873-7700
FAX 813-875-6633
EMAIL . . . . .info@ronroseproductions.com
WEB SITE . . . . .www.ronroseproductions.com
COMMENTS   Custom production music

Travis Hearne . . . . .No Title
Dan Mockensturm . . . . .No Title
Don Poole . . . . .No Title
Chris Swere . . . . .No Title
Kristen Walters . . . . .No Title

SAMPLE CLEARANCE LTD.
162 W. 56th St., Ste. 306
New York, NY 10019
PHONE 212-707-8804
FAX 212-707-8952
EMAIL . . . . .drubin@sampleclearanceltd.com
COMMENTS   Clearance for music, film, DVD, video
                      games

Daniel Rubin .Associate Licensing

SCHERZO MUSIC
710 N. Hillcrest Rd.
Beverly Hills, CA 90210
PHONE 310-278-0733
FAX 310-278-6542
EMAIL . . . . .gotheresa@aol.com
WEB SITE . . . . .www.schifrin.com
GENRES   Classical - Jazz
COMMENTS   Soundtracks; Film and TV Music; Owns
                      mastering and publishing rights to over
                      100 songs

Theresa Eastman . . . . .Licensing

SCREENMUSIC INTERNATIONAL
18034 Ventura Blvd., Ste. 450
Encino, CA 91316
PHONE 818-789-2954
FAX 818-789-5801
EMAIL . . . . .screenmusic@aol.com
WEB SITE . . . . .www.screenmusic.com
GENRES   All Genres
COMMENTS   Over 5,000 CDs of film & TV music
                      available for licensing

Melissa Bree .Production Coordinator

*SEARCH
A Division of Jeff Wayne Music Group
Oliver House, 8-9 Ivor Place
London NW1 6BY United Kingdom
PHONE 44-207-724-2471
FAX 44-207-724-6245
EMAIL . . . . .info@jeffwaynemusic.com
WEB SITE . . . . .www.jeffwaynemusic.com

Jane Jones . . . . .Group Director

SELECTRACKS
10327 Santa Monica Blvd.
Los Angeles, CA 90025
PHONE 310-201-0015/410-685-0470
FAX 310-201-0126/410-685-0472
EMAIL . . . . .info@selectracks.com
WEB SITE . . . . .www.selectracks.com
RECENT PROJECTS   Ladder 49 - Bruce Almighty - The Girl
                      Next Door - Miracle - The Punisher -
                      Alien vs. Predator - Lost in Translation
COMMENTS   Music Library

Terri Lynn Rosa . . . . .Contact

*SESSING MUSIC SERVICES
639 N. Larchmont Blvd., Ste. 204
Los Angeles, CA 90004
PHONE 323-461-5508
FAX 818-688-8119
EMAIL . . . . .julie@sessingmusicservices.com
WEB SITE . . . . .www.sessingmusicservices.com

Julie Sessing-Turner . . . . .No Title

SIGNATURE SOUND, INC.
71 W. 23rd St., Ste. 902
New York, NY 10010
PHONE 212-989-0011
FAX 212-989-3576
EMAIL . . . . .info@signature-sound.com
WEB SITE . . . . .www.signature-sound.com

Elliot Schrager . . . . .President
Alex Battles . . . . .Director, Music Clearance Services

SMASHTRAX MUSIC LLC
4826 Beeman Ave.
Valley Village, CA 91607
PHONE 818-705-3279
EMAIL . . . . .info@smashtrax.com
SECOND EMAIL . . . . .jeremy@smashtrax.com
WEB SITE . . . . .www.smashtrax.com
GENRES   All Genres

Jeremy Sweet . . . . .No Title

CLEARANCE & LICENSING

*SONGFINDER
446 Peachtree Battle Ave.
Atlanta, GA 30305
PHONE 404-876-2967/404-841-0303
FAX 404-876-5644/404-841-0404
EMAIL . . . . .chrisbailey@musicsongfinder.com
SECOND EMAIL . . . . . .lukecrampton@musicsongfinder.com
WEB SITE . . . . .www.musicsongfinder.com
SECOND WEB SITE . . . . .www.original-media.net
GENRES   All Genres

Luke Crampton . . . . .President
Chris Bailey . . . . .VP

*SONICFREQ
PO Box 1003
South Pasadena, CA 91031
PHONE 626-403-3911
FAX 626-403-3911
EMAIL . . . . .director@sonicfreq.com
WEB SITE . . . . .www.sonicfreq.com
SECOND WEB SITE . . . . .www.projecthollywood.com
GENRES   All Genres
COMMENTS   Music Library

Rob Bryton . . . . .Partner
Neil Cross . . . . .Partner
Brad Goodman . . . . .Partner

SONY BMG MUSIC LICENSING
2100 Colorado Ave.
Santa Monica, CA 90404
PHONE 310-449-2555/212-833-7100
FAX 310-449-2570
EMAIL . . . . .firstname_lastname@sonymusic.com
WEB SITE . . . . .www.sonymusic.com
SECOND WEB SITE . . . . .www.sonymusicfinder.com
GENRES   All Genres
COMMENTS   East Coast office: 550 Madison Ave.,
                              New York, NY 10022

Keith D'Arcy . . . . .VP
Paula Erickson . . . . .Sr. VP
Joanna Zachary . . . . .Sr. Director, Contact Administration
Abby Lia . . . . .Director
Wendy Turnbull . . . . .Director
Elena Byington . . . . .Associate Director
Millie Hsyu . . . . .Manager
Kate Naylor . . . . .Manager
Margo Plotkin . . . . .Manager
Jonathan Hecht . . . . .Assistant
David Heredia . . . . .Assistant
Matt Mufalli . . . . .Assistant
Tiffany Nesson . . . . .Assistant

SONY BMG STRATEGIC MARKETING
1540 Broadway, 35th Fl.
New York, NY 10036
PHONE 212-833-8000/310-449-2100
WEB SITE . . . . .www.sonybmg.com
COMMENTS   West Coast office: 2100 Colorado Ave.,
                              Santa Monica, CA 90404; Additional
                              East Coast office: 550 Madison Ave.,
                              New York, NY 10022

Joe DiMuro . . . . .Executive VP/GM
Paula Erickson . . . . .Sr. VP, Master Licensing, Film & TV (LA)
Tim Pearson . . . . .Sr. VP, Sony BMG Direct (212-833-4151)
Matt Stringer . . . . .Sr. VP, Marketing & New Product Development
Kimberly Allison-Hopkins . . . . .VP, Strategic Business Development
Kendra Commander . . . . .Sr. Director, Strategic Business Development

SOPERSOUND MUSIC LIBRARY
PO Box 869
Ashland, OR 97520
PHONE 541-552-0830/800-227-9980
FAX 541-552-0832
EMAIL . . . . .info@sopersound.com
WEB SITE . . . . .www.sopersound.com
GENRES   All Genres
RECENT PROJECTS   Six Feet Under - Marvel Comics Web site
                              - Inside Edition - Jack Hanna's Animal
                              Adventures - Buckmasters
SUBMISSION POLICY   No unsolicited submissions

John Robertson . . . . .Sales Manager

*SOUND THINKING MUSIC RESEARCH
1534 N. Moorpark Rd., PMB 333
Thousand Oaks, CA 91360
PHONE 805-495-3306
FAX 805-495-3306
EMAIL . . . . .soundthink@earthlink.net
WEB SITE . . . . .home.earthlink.net/~soundthink

Cary Ginell . . . . .Director

SOURCE/Q
11288 Ventura Blvd.
Studio City, CA 91604
PHONE 818-763-9095
FAX 818-763-4737
EMAIL . . . . .marty@sourceq.com
WEB SITE . . . . .www.sourceq.com
GENRES   Classical - Country - Gospel - Pop - R&B
                              - World
COMMENTS   Classical, opera, world, movie scores,
                              '50s/'60s pop original hits, Christmas

Marty Wekser . . . . .President

STARBORN RECORDS INTERNATIONAL
3884 Franklin Ave.
Los Angeles, CA 90027-4661
PHONE 323-662-3121
COMMENTS   Licenses to 1800 music and record com-
                              panies in 55 countries

Brian Ross . . . . .CEO/Chairman

*SUGAROO!
3650 Helms Ave.
Culver City, CA 90232
PHONE 310-842-9151
FAX 310-842-7393
EMAIL . . . . .info@sugaroo.com
WEB SITE . . . . .www.sugaroo.com
COMMENTS   Represents independent labels, artists,
                              and publishers for visual media music
                              licensing; Places music in films, TV,
                              advertising, interactive/Internet media
                              and other visual mediums

Michael Nieves . . . . .Managing Director
Michelle Bayer . . . . .Head, East Coast Office

*SYNCRONICITY
10739 Acama St.
Toluca Lake, CA 91602
PHONE 818-985-2555
EMAIL . . . . .rhodia@hotmail.com

Robin Kaye . . . . .No Title

*TAKE NOTE
725 Washington St., Ste. 211
Oakland, CA 94607
PHONE 510-836-4554
FAX 510-836-4580

Patricia Phillips . . . . .President

TIMES SQUARE PRODUCTIONS
520 Washington Blvd., #199
Marina Del Rey, CA 90292
PHONE 323-876-7487
EMAIL . . . . .timesx@aol.com
SECOND EMAIL . . . . .music@rocketcityrecords.com
WEB SITE . . . . .www.rocketcityrecords.com
GENRES   Rock
RECENT PROJECTS   Dawson's Creek Season 4 DVD - Cabin
                             Fever - Butterfly - Buffy the Vampire
                             Slayer
SUBMISSION POLICY   See Web site

Mara Fox . . . . .President

TKO GROUP
4501 Connecticut Ave., NW, Ste. 711
Washington, DC 20008
PHONE 202-966-3280/44-0-1273-550088
FAX 202-364-1367/44-0-1273-540969
EMAIL . . . . .mac@tkogroup.com
WEB SITE . . . . .www.thekrugerorganisation.com
GENRES   All Genres
COMMENTS   UK office: PO Box 130, Hove, East
                             Sussex, BN3 6QU United Kingdom

Howard Kruger . . . . .CEO (hkruger@tkogroup.com)
Jeffrey Kruger . . . . .CEO (jkruger02@aol.com)
Michael Cohn . . . . .CFO (mac@tkogroup.com)
Warren Heal . . . . .Licensing (warren@tkogroup.com)
Roland Rogers . . . . .Publishing (jestersong@msn.com)

TM CENTURY, INC.
2002 Academy Lane
Dallas, TX 75234
PHONE 972-406-6800
FAX 972-406-6890
EMAIL . . . . .tmci@tmcentury.com
WEB SITE . . . . .www.tmcentury.com
COMMENTS   Music Libraries, Jingles, Production
                             Music

David Graupner . . . . .President/CEO
Teri James . . . . .President/CFO
Marcus Hill . . . . .VP, Operations
John Kuykendoll . . . . .VP, Facilities
Eve Mayer Orsburn . . . . .VP, Sales & Marketing
John Noble . . . . .Director, Domestic Sales & Marketing
Karyn Fairris . . . . .Assistant to President/HR
Alison Dempsey . . . . .Sales Assistant

TRAX CONNECTION
PO Box 618
Stratford, NJ 08084-0618
PHONE 856-783-2245
FAX 856-783-2247
EMAIL . . . . .info@traxconnection.com
SECOND EMAIL . . . . .tomadams@traxconnection.com
WEB SITE . . . . .www.traxconnection.com
GENRES   All Genres
COMMENTS   Music library; Composer services

Tom Adams . . . . .Composer
Sandy Adams . . . . .Licensing

TRF PRODUCTION MUSIC LIBRARIES
747 Chestnut Ridge Rd.
Chestnut Ridge, NY 10977
PHONE 845-356-0800/800-899-MUSIC
FAX 845-356-0895
EMAIL . . . . .info@trfmusic.com
WEB SITE .www.trfmusic.com
GENRES   All Genres

Eric Nurko . . . . .Creative Director

TUNEDGE MUSIC SERVICES
15303 Ventura Blvd., Bldg. C, Ste. 1070
Sherman Oaks, CA 91403
PHONE 800-279-0014
FAX 877-886-3343
EMAIL . . . . .info@tunedge.com
WEB SITE .www.tunedge.com
GENRES   All Genres
COMMENTS   Music Library

Brandon D'Amore . . . . .CEO
Rod West . . . . .COO
Joel Thatcher . . . . .President

TWISTED MEDIA, INC.
5556 N. Wayne Ave., 1st Fl.
Chicago, IL 60640
PHONE 773-944-9510
EMAIL . . . . .music@twistedtracks.com
WEB SITE . . . . .www.twistedtracks.com
COMMENTS   Royalty-free Music Library

Derek Frederickson . . . . .Founder

*UNDERTOW MUSIC - LICENSING & PRODUCTION
5 Old Conant Rd.
Lincoln, MA 01773
PHONE 617-395-7746
FAX 617-249-0830
EMAIL . . . . .jeff@undertowmusic.com
WEB SITE . . . . .www.undertowmusic.com
GENRES   Alternative - Blues - Rock - Roots
SUBMISSION POLICY   Submissions welcome

Jeff Macklin . . . . .Partner

*UNIVERSAL MUSIC PRODUCTION LIBRARY
2440 Sepulveda Blvd., Ste. 100
Los Angeles, CA 90064
PHONE 310-235-4860
EMAIL . . . . .umpl.licensing@umusic.com
WEB SITE .www.umplmusic.com

Jonathan Firstenberg . . . . .Creative Director

SUZY VAUGHAN ASSOCIATES, INC.
6848 Firmament Ave.
Van Nuys, CA 91406
PHONE 818-988-5599
FAX 818-988-5577/818-475-1903
EMAIL . . . . .srvaughan@suzyvaughan.com
SECOND EMAIL . . . . .suzy@clearances.net
WEB SITE .www.clearances.net
SECOND WEB SITE . . . . .www.suzyvaughan.com
GENRES   All Genres
RECENT PROJECTS   Sonny & Cher Ultimate Collection - Tom
                             Jones DVDs - Color Honeymooners -
                             Ellen
COMMENTS   Clears talent clips, still photos and
                             scripts; Copyright and title searches

Suzy Vaughan Esq. . . . . .Principal
Lacey Beers . . . . .Manager, Clearance Department

CLEARANCE & LICENSING

VIDEOHELPER

18 W. 21st St., 7th Fl.
New York, NY 10010
PHONE 212-633-7009
FAX 212-633-9014
EMAIL . . . . .info@videohelper.com
WEB SITE . . . . .www.videohelper.com
COMMENTS   Production music library

Betsy Todd . . . . .No Title

WILD WHIRLED

10017 N. 16th Ave.
Phoenix, AZ 85021
PHONE 602-595-3582
FAX 602-595-3590
EMAIL . . . . .jeff@wildwhirled.com
WEB SITE . . . . .www.wildwhirled.com
RECENT PROJECTS   Harold and Kumar Go to White Castle -
                         CSI: Miami - Navy N.C.I.S. - Law &
                         Order - Scrubs - King of the Hill - The
                         Simple Life - Smallville
COMMENTS   Music library/song catalog

Jeff Freundlich . . . . .Licensing

THE WINOGRADSKY COMPANY

11240 Magnolia Blvd., Ste. 104
North Hollywood, CA 91601
PHONE 818-761-6906
FAX 818-761-5719
EMAIL . . . . .steve@winogradsky.com
WEB SITE . . . . .www.winogradsky.com

Steven Winogradsky Esq. . . . . .President
Kathryn Morrow . . . . .Director, Administration
Amy MacDonald .Manager, Licensing
Tamara Hutcherson . . . . .Assistant

YESSIAN MUSIC SEARCH

33117 Hamilton Court, Ste. 175
Farmington Hills, MI 48334
PHONE 248-553-4044/888-YESSIAN/212-633-4881
FAX 248-893-4044/212-533-3443
EMAIL . . . . .info@yessianmusic.com
WEB SITE . . . . .www.yessianmusic.com
COMMENTS   Music Library; East Coast office: 57 E.
                  11th St., 3rd Fl., New York, NY 10003;
                  West Coast office: 333 Costa Del Sol
                  Way, Malibu, CA 90265

Dan Yessian . . . . .Creative Director/Composer/Arranger
Brian Yessian . . . . .Executive Producer
Michael Yessian . . . . .Creative Director
Randy Monday . . . . .Engineer/Sound Designer
Gerard Smerek .Producer/Engineer
Marlene Bartos . . . . .Producer

ZOOPHORIA MUSIC

7559 Willoughby Ave., Ste. 10
West Hollywood, CA 90046
PHONE 323-851-0786
FAX 323-851-0786
EMAIL .brian@zoophoriamusic.com
WEB SITE . . . . .www.zoophoriamusic.com

Brian Black . . . . .Founder/President

SECTION C

FILM & TV MUSIC

- Studios/Networks
- Music Supervisors
- Clearance & Licensing
- **Composers**

Asterisks (*) next to companies denote new listings.

*TREE ADAMS
c/o First Artists Management
PHONE 818-377-7750
RECENT CREDITS   Film: Walking Tall - Killer Diller - Dawn of the Dead - Baadasssss! - Auto Focus - Poor White Trash - Drowning Mona - The Breaks; TV: The Hunt for the BTK Killer - Reba - Felicity

BRIAN ADLER
c/o Evolution Music Partners
PHONE 310-623-3388
RECENT CREDITS   Ordinary Sinner - Slam - Married to the Kellys

*MARK ADLER
c/o Soundtrack Music Associates
PHONE 818-382-3300
RECENT CREDITS   Marilyn Hotchkiss Ballroom Dancing & Charm School - When Do We Eat? - Life of the Party - Follow the Stars Home

AEONE
c/o The Agency Group Ltd.
PHONE 310-385-2800
RECENT CREDITS   The Mists of Avalon - Witchblade - Spy Girls

ERIC ALLAMAN
c/o The Agency Group Ltd.
PHONE 310-385-2800
RECENT CREDITS   Latter Days - One Kill - True Heart - Mike Hammer Private Eye - High Tide

*JOHN ALTMAN
c/o First Artists Management
PHONE 818-377-7750
RECENT CREDITS   Film: Shall We Dance - Town & Country - Beautiful Joe - RKO 281 - The MatchMaker - Beautiful Thing - Funny Bones; TV: The Reagans

TORI AMOS
c/o Creative Artists Agency
PHONE 310-288-4545
RECENT CREDITS   Great Expectations (2 songs)

CHRIS ANDERSON
c/o Evolution Music Partners
PHONE 310-623-3388
RECENT CREDITS   Keep Your Distance - The Scheme - Wake - The Box

*LARS ANDERSON
c/o Gorfaine/Schwartz Agency
PHONE 818-260-8500
RECENT CREDITS   Hellraiser: Hellworld - Rancid

MICHAEL ANDREWS
c/o First Artists Management
PHONE 818-377-7750
RECENT CREDITS   Max and Grace - Me and You and Everyone We Know - Wonderfalls (TV) - Freaks & Geeks (TV)

ANDY BUSH & DAVID GALE
c/o The Kaufman Agency
PHONE 818-506-6013
RECENT CREDITS   Days That Shook the World - Castle - Boston Law - Hiroshima - C'est pas moi...C'est l'autre!

THE ANGEL
c/o Soundtrack Music Associates
PHONE 818-382-3300
RECENT CREDITS   The Heart of the Game - Kidulthood - Boiler Room - Gridlock'd - 'Til There Was You

MARC ARAMIAN
3000 W. Olympic Blvd.
Santa Monica, CA 90404
PHONE 310-449-4037
EMAIL . . . . .marc@aramian.com
WEB SITE . . . . .www.aramian.com
RECENT CREDITS   Framed - Small Change - Blacklist: Hollywood on Trial

*STEVEN ARGILA
c/o Soundtrack Music Associates
PHONE 818-382-3300
RECENT CREDITS   The Thing About My Folks - Memron - Teenage Mutant Nina Turtles (live action)

CRAIG ARMSTRONG
c/o First Artists Management
PHONE 818-377-7750
RECENT CREDITS   Must Love Dogs - Fever Pitch - Ray - Love Actually - Moulin Rouge

DAVID ARNOLD
c/o First Artists Management
PHONE 818-377-7750
RECENT CREDITS   Ghost Rider - Stoned - Four Brothers - The Stepford Wives - Man on Fire

ERIC AVERY
c/o Creative Artists Agency
PHONE 310-288-4545
RECENT CREDITS   Sex with Strangers (TV)

LUIS BACALOV
c/o Kraft-Engel Management
PHONE 818-380-1918
RECENT CREDITS   Bride of the Sea - Dust Factory - Kill Bill Vols. 1&2 (Additional Music) - The Love Letter - Il Postino

ANGELO BADALAMENTI
c/o Kraft-Engel Management
PHONE 818-380-1918
RECENT CREDITS   A Very Long Engagement - Dark Water - Secretary - Mullholland Drive - Lost Highway - The Straight Story

DAVID BAERWALD
c/o Evolution Music Partners
PHONE 310-623-3388
RECENT CREDITS   Around the Bend - The Weather Man - Wannabe - The King

COMPOSERS

RICK BAITZ
c/o The Kaufman Agency
PHONE 818-506-6013
RECENT CREDITS   The Vagina Monologues - Life After Life -
Hope and a Little Sugar - Heart of Africa
- Guns & Mothers

KLAUS BALDET
c/o Gorfaine/Schwartz Agency
PHONE 818-260-8500
RECENT CREDITS   The Promise - Constantine - Pirates of
the Caribbean - Ned Kelly

LESLEY BARBER
c/o Creative Artists Agency
PHONE 310-288-4545
RECENT CREDITS   Being Julia - We Don't Live Here
Anymore - Hysterical Blindness - You
Can Count on Me - Mansfield Park

NATHAN BARR
c/o First Artists Management
PHONE 818-377-7750
RECENT CREDITS   Hostel - The Dukes of Hazzard - 2001
Maniacs - Club Dread - Cabin Fever

JOHN BARRY
c/o Kraft-Engel Management
PHONE 818-380-1918
RECENT CREDITS   Indecent Proposal - Out of Africa -
Dances with Wolves - Goldfinger -
Midnight Cowboy

STEVE BARTEK
c/o Kraft-Engel Management
PHONE 818-380-1918
RECENT CREDITS   Carolina - Novocaine - Snow Day - An
Extremely Goofy Movie

LIAM BATES
c/o The Agency Group Ltd.
PHONE 310-385-2800
RECENT CREDITS   The Puppet - La Jalouise - Echo -
Promethus - Miss-Adventures of
Margaret

TYLER BATES
c/o Soundtrack Music Associates
PHONE 818-382-3300
RECENT CREDITS   The Devil's Rejects - Dawn of the Dead -
Baadasssss! - Half Past Dead - Get
Carter

JEFF BEAL
c/o First Artists Management
PHONE 818-377-7750
RECENT CREDITS   Emmanuel's Gift - Stone Cold - The
Wool Cap - Rome - Monk

JOHN BEAL
c/o The Winogradsky Company
11240 Magnolia Blvd., Suite 104
North Hollywood, CA 91601
PHONE 818-761-6906
RECENT CREDITS   Salmon Run - Weird TV (Series) -
Countdown to Invasion - A Journey In
Faith - Terror in the Aisles - The
Funhouse

CHRISTOPHE BECK
c/o Kraft-Engel Management
PHONE 818-380-1918
RECENT CREDITS   Two for the Money - The Pink Panther -
Elektra - Cheaper by the Dozen - Under
the Tuscan Sun

DAVID BELL
c/o Gorfaine/Schwartz Agency
PHONE 818-260-8500
RECENT CREDITS   Cops and Roberts - There Goes the
Neighborhood - Dead Man's Walk (TV) -
Enterprise (TV) - Star Trek: Voyager (TV)

ROGER BELLON
c/o The Agency Group Ltd
PHONE 310-385-2800
RECENT CREDITS   The Highlander (Series) - The Carl
Foreman Letter - The Last Don - Final
Jeopardy - Without Limits

*MARCO BELTRAMI
c/o Greenspan Artist Management
PHONE 310-289-3990
RECENT CREDITS   XXX: State of the Union - Red Eye - Flight
of the Phoenix - I, Robot - Hellboy

*CHARLES BERNSTEIN
c/o Soundtrack Music Associates
PHONE 818-382-3300
RECENT CREDITS   A Matter of Family - Profoundly Normal -
A Christmas Visitor - Out of the Ashes

PETER BERNSTEIN
c/o Soundtrack Music Associates
PHONE 818-382-3300
RECENT CREDITS   Happy Face Murders - Wild Wild West -
Susan's Plan

*RYAN BEVERIDGE
c/o First Artists Management
PHONE 818-377-7750
RECENT CREDITS   Film: Dirty - Boy Culture - L.A. Dicks -
Rampage - Race You to the Bottom -
Zyzzyx Rd. - Frankenfish - Valentine Man
- Nightstalker - Taboo; TV: Breaking
News - Brutally Normal

*AMIN BHATIA
c/o Soundtrack Music Associates
PHONE 818-382-3300
RECENT CREDITS   Rescue Heroes - Detention - Taking It
Global - Queer as Folk

*WENDY BLACKSTONE
c/o Soundtrack Music Associates
PHONE 818-382-3300
RECENT CREDITS   Backroads - Love Walked In - Sixteen -
Into the Volcano

COMPOSERS

TERENCE BLANCHARD
c/o First Artists Management
PHONE 818-377-7750
RECENT CREDITS   Film: Inside Man - Drum - She Hate Me - 25th Hour - Dark Blue - People I Know - Barbershop - Jim Brown All American - Glitter - Original Sin - The Caveman's Valentine - Bamboozled - Love & Basketball - Next Friday - Summer of Sam - Eve's Bayou - 4 Little Girls - 'Til There Was You - Get on the Bus - Clockers - Crooklyn - The Inkwell - Sugar Hill - Malcolm X - Jungle Fever - Mo' Better Blues; TV: Their Eyes Were Watching God - Gia

CHRIS BOARDMAN
c/o Soundtrack Music Associates
PHONE 818-382-3300
RECENT CREDITS   Spy Kids (Themes) - Bruno - Payback - Tales from the Crypt: Bordello of Blood

WES BORLAND
c/o Creative Artists Agency
PHONE 310-288-4545
RECENT CREDITS   Constantine - Underworld (2 Songs) - Mission Impossible 2 (Song)

*SCOTT BORMAR
c/o First Artists Management
PHONE 818-377-7750
RECENT CREDITS   Black Snake Moan - Hustle & Flow

JON BRION
c/o Kraft-Engel Management
PHONE 818-380-1918
RECENT CREDITS   Head Games - I Heart Huckabees - Eternal Sunshine of the Spotless Mind - Punch Drunk Love - Magnolia

MICHAEL BROOK
c/o First Artists Management
PHONE 818-377-7750
RECENT CREDITS   Charlotte Sometimes - Crime and Punishment in Suburbia - Affliction - Albino Aligator - Deadwood

*BIL BROWN
c/o First Artists Management
PHONE 818-377-7750
RECENT CREDITS   Film: Ali - Any Given Sunday; TV: CSI: NY

*SAMM BROWN
c/o Carefree Management & Associates
PHONE 818-769-4498
RECENT CREDITS   Michael Jackson: A Remarkable Life - Nat Love: Seminole Indian Scout - Tranche de Vie - Discovery - Makin' It

JERRY BRUNSKILL
c/o Evolution Music Partners
PHONE 310-623-3388
RECENT CREDITS   Supercross - Jingle All the Way - The Next Great Champ - Crossing Jordan

BT
c/o Kraft-Engel Management
PHONE 818-380-1918
RECENT CREDITS   Stealth - Underclassman - Monster - The Fast and the Furious

DAVID BUCHBINDER
c/o The Kaufman Agency
PHONE 818-506-6013
RECENT CREDITS   The Stone of Folly - Bleacher Bums - Club Land - The Fishing Trip - Jerry and Tom

PAUL BUCKLEY
c/o Evolution Music Partners
PHONE 310-623-3388
RECENT CREDITS   Will & Grace - Reba - Oliver Beene

PAUL BUCKMASTER
c/o Whatever...Talent Agency
PHONE 818-360-4843
RECENT CREDITS   12 Monkeys - Mean Streak - Most Wanted - Cinderella 2

VELTON RAY BUNCH
c/o Gorfaine/Schwartz Agency
PHONE 818-260-8500
RECENT CREDITS   Dance With Me - Lost in Space - Nash Bridges - The Pretender - Country Music Awards

*JUSTIN BURNETT
c/o The Agency Group Ltd.
PHONE 310-385-2800
RECENT CREDITS   Man on Fire - Phone Booth - Spy Game - Dungeons and Dragons - Fight Club

CARTER BURWELL
c/o Creative Artists Agency
PHONE 310-288-4545
RECENT CREDITS   Kinsey - The Alamo - Adaptation - The Rookie - Being John Malkovich - Fargo

ROB CAIRNS
c/o First Artists Management
PHONE 818-377-7750
RECENT CREDITS   Film: Bigger Than the Sky - Billy's Dad Is a Fudge-Packer - Rockfish; TV: Bands Reunited - Cracking Up - I Love the '70s - The Bachelorette - I Love the '80s - Tough Crowd with Colin Quinn - Girls Club - The Bachelor -Thieves

SEAN CALLERY
c/o Gorfaine/Schwartz Agency
PHONE 818-260-8500
RECENT CREDITS   24 - Blow Back - Freedom - Sheena: Queen of the Jungle - La Femme Nikita

COMPOSERS

DAVID CARBONARA
c/o Gorfaine/Schwartz Agency
PHONE 818-260-8500
RECENT CREDITS   The Village - An Unfinished Life -
Queenie in Love - Fast Food, Fast
Women - The Guru

JEFF CARDONI
c/o First Artist Management
PHONE 818-377-7750
RECENT CREDITS   Just Friends - Siete Dias - Love For Rent -
Behind the Camera: The Charlie's
Angels Story

TEDDY CASTELLUCCI
c/o Greenspan Artist Management
PHONE 310-289-3990
RECENT CREDITS   The Longest Yard - Rebound - White
Chicks - 50 First Dates - Anger
Management

*GARY CHANG
c/o Soundtrack Music Associates
PHONE 818-382-3300
RECENT CREDITS   Word of Honor - Path to War - Stephen
King's Kingdom Hospital - Rose Red

STEVEN CHESNE
c/o The Kaufman Agency
PHONE 818-506-6013
RECENT CREDITS   Close Call - No Turning Back - The Trip
- Zen Noir - Monsoon Wife

PAUL CHIHARA
c/o The Agency Group Ltd.
PHONE 310-385-2800
RECENT CREDITS   Romance & Cigarettes - Strip Search -
100 Centre Street - American Family -
China Beach

*EDMUND CHOI
c/o Greenspan Artist Management
PHONE 310-289-3990
RECENT CREDITS   Nola - The Dish - Down to You - The
Castle

*CLAK
c/o Soundtrack Music Associates
PHONE 818-382-3300
RECENT CREDITS   Stay Alive - Rise - Knights of the Bronx

Leo Ross . . . . .Composer
Atticus Ross . . . . .Composer
Claudia Sarne . . . . .Composer

*ALF CLAUSEN
c/o Soundtrack Music Associates
PHONE 818-382-3300
RECENT CREDITS   The Simpsons - Half-Baked - She Knows
Too Much

*SCOTT CLAUSEN
c/o Soundtrack Music Associates
PHONE 818-382-3300
RECENT CREDITS   Mindstorm - Antibody - Less Than Perfect
- According To Jim - What I Like About
You

GEORGE S. CLINTON
c/o First Artists Management
PHONE 818-377-7750
RECENT CREDITS   The Cleaner - Life of the Party - A Dirty
Shame - The Santa Clause 2&3 - Austin
Powers 1&2

CHARLIE CLOUSER
c/o Evolution Music Partners
PHONE 310-623-3388
RECENT CREDITS   Saw - Deepwater - Las Vegas - Fastlane

ELIA CMIRAL
c/o First Artists Management
PHONE 818-377-7750
RECENT CREDITS   The Cutter - The Mechanik - Iowa -
Species 3 - Wrong Turn - Ronin

TODD COCHRAN
c/o Evolution Music Partners
PHONE 310-623-3388
RECENT CREDITS   Woman Thou Art Loosed - The Best Man
- Five Heartbeats - Cat Chasers - Keep
the Faith, Baby

ADAM J. COHEN
c/o Gorfaine/Schwartz Agency
PHONE 818-260-8500
RECENT CREDITS   Grilled - Martha Stewart Inc. - Behind
the Camera: The Story of Three's
Company - Captain Sturdy - Long
Night's Journey into Day

ERIC COLVIN
c/o First Artists Management
PHONE 818-377-7750
RECENT CREDITS   Knit Wits - NASCAR (IMAX) - Monte
Walsh

*JOSEPH CONLAN
c/o Soundtrack Music Associates
PHONE 818-382-3300
RECENT CREDITS   Mortuary - Deadly Visions - 14 Hours -
The Book Of Ruth - The Rosa Parks Story

MICHAEL CONVERTINO
c/o Soundtrack Music Associates
PHONE 818-382-3300
RECENT CREDITS   We Don't Live Here Anymore - Straight
Into Darkness - Dance with Me - Bed of
Roses - Things to Do in Denver When
You're Dead

STEWART COPELAND
c/o First Artists Management
PHONE 818-377-7750
RECENT CREDITS   I Am David - On the Line - Pecker - Very
Bad Things - Gridlock'd - Fresh - Wide
Sargasso Sea - Afterburn - She's Having
a Baby - Wall Street - Rumble Fish; TV:
Dead Like Me - Babylon 5: The
Gathering - The Equalizer

COMPOSERS

NORMAND CORBEIL
c/o Kraft-Engel Management
PHONE 818-380-1918
RECENT CREDITS   The Statement - A Different Loyalty -
Double Jeopardy - Hitler: The Rise of
Evil

JOHN CORIGLIANO
c/o Gorfaine/Schwartz Agency
PHONE 818-260-8500
RECENT CREDITS   The Red Violin - Revolution - Altered
States

*JANE ANTONIA CORNISH
c/o Soundtrack Music Associates
PHONE 818-382-3300
RECENT CREDITS   Sports Century - Five Children and It

JEFF DANNA
c/o First Artists Management
PHONE 818-377-7750
RECENT CREDITS   Tideland - Ripley Underground -
Resident Evil: Apocalypse - O - The Kid
Stays in the Picture - The Boondock
Saints - Spinning Boris

MYCHAEL DANNA
c/o First Artists Management
PHONE 818-377-7750
RECENT CREDITS   Capote - Where the Truth Lies - Being
Julia - Shattered Glass - Monsoon
Wedding

MASON DARING
c/o First Artists Management
PHONE 818-377-7750
RECENT CREDITS   Silver City - Casa De Los Babys - Music
of the Heart - The Opposite of Sex -
Sunshine State - A Walk on the Moon

MARTY DAVICH
c/o Gorfaine/Schwartz Agency
PHONE 818-260-8500
RECENT CREDITS   Instant Karma - Crossing the Line - The
Killing Jar - Jackie, Ethel, Joan: The
Women of Camelot (TV)

CARL DAVIS
c/o The Kaufman Agency
PHONE 818-506-6013
RECENT CREDITS   The French Lieutenant's Woman - Pride
and Prejudice - The Great Gatsby -
Widow's Peak - Topsy-Turvy

DON DAVIS
c/o First Artists Management
PHONE 818-377-7750
RECENT CREDITS   The Matrix Reloaded - The Matrix
Revolutions - Behind Enemy Lines -
Jurassic Park 3 - Anti-Trust

MARIUS DE VRIES
c/o Gorfaine/Schwartz Agency
PHONE 818-260-8500
RECENT CREDITS   Romeo + Juliet - The Eye of the
Beholder

DICK DEBENEDICTIS
c/o Soundtrack Music Associates
PHONE 818-382-3300
RECENT CREDITS   Diagnosis Murder - Matlock - Father
Dowling - Jake and the Fatman

JOHN DEBNEY
c/o Kraft-Engel Management
PHONE 818-380-1918
RECENT CREDITS   Dreamer - Chicken Little - Zathura - The
Passion of the Christ - Elf - Bruce
Almighty - The Princess Diaries 1&2 -
Spy Kids 1&2

BEN DECTER
c/o Gorfaine/Schwartz Agency
PHONE 818-260-8500
RECENT CREDITS   Heartland - Hollywood Palms - The
Quarry

CHRISTOPHER DEDRICK
c/o Marks Management
PHONE 805-882-1116
RECENT CREDITS   The Saddest Music in the World -
Childstar - Shattered City - Walter and
Henry

*TOM DELAUGHTER
c/o Gorfaine/Schwartz Agency
PHONE 818-260-8500
RECENT CREDITS   Thumbsucker

JOE DELIA
c/o Soundtrack Music Associates
PHONE 818-382-3300
RECENT CREDITS   A Jersey Tale - The Tao of Steve - The
Addiction - The Funeral - Bad Lieutenant

ALEXANDRE DESPLAT
c/o Kraft-Engel Management
PHONE 818-380-1918
RECENT CREDITS   Syriana - Birth - Hostage - The Upside of
Anger - Girl With a Pearl Earring

JAMES DI PASQUALE
c/o Gorfaine/Schwartz Agency
PHONE 818-260-8500
RECENT CREDITS   Armed and Dangerous - One Crazy
Summer - Rad - See Jane Run (TV) -
Untamed Love (TV)

RAMIN DJAWADI
c/o Gorfaine/Schwartz Agency
PHONE 818-260-8500
RECENT CREDITS   Ask the Dust - Blade: Trinity - The Devil
and Daniel Webster - Beat the Drum

JAMES MICHAEL DOOLEY
c/o Gorfaine/Schwartz Agency
PHONE 818-260-8500
RECENT CREDITS   Ordinary Miracles - The Mars
Underground - Aqua Dulce

STEVE DORFF
c/o Gorfaine/Schwartz Agency
PHONE 818-260-8500
RECENT CREDITS   Cactus Kid - Dudley Do-Right - Tin Cup
- Reba (TV) - Maverick

COMPOSERS

*HOWARD DROSSIN
c/o The Agency Group Ltd.
PHONE 310-385-2800
RECENT CREDITS   Blade Trinity - She Hate Me - Raising Helen - Barbershop - Sidewalk

*GEORGE DUKE
c/o The Agency Group Ltd.
PHONE 310-385-2800
RECENT CREDITS   Never Die Alone - Good Fences - Count on Me - Generations

TAN DUN
c/o Gorfaine/Schwartz Agency
PHONE 818-260-8500
RECENT CREDITS   Hero - Crouching Tiger, Hidden Dragon - Fallen

ROBERT DUNCAN
c/o Gorfaine/Schwartz Agency
PHONE 818-260-8500
RECENT CREDITS   Return of the Living Dead - Destroy the Light - Vampire Effect - Tru Calling - Buffy the Vampire Slayer (TV)

*JOHN DUPREZ
c/o Gorfaine/Schwartz Agency
PHONE 818-260-8500
RECENT CREDITS   Surf's Up - The Wind in the Willows - A Good Man in Africa

IAN DYE
c/o Gorfaine/Schwartz Agency
PHONE 818-260-8500
RECENT CREDITS   20 - Lilo & Stitch (TV) - Teamo Supremo - The Tick - Dilbert - NYPD Blue

E (THE EELS)
c/o Creative Artists Agency
PHONE 310-288-4545
RECENT CREDITS   Levity - The Grinch (Additional Music)

RANDY EDELMAN
c/o Gorfaine/Schwartz Agency
PHONE 818-260-8500
RECENT CREDITS   Son of the Mask - Miss Congeniality 2 - Surviving Christmas - Gods & Generals - Shanghai Knights - XXX

GREG EDMONSON
c/o The Agency Group Ltd.
PHONE 310-385-2800
RECENT CREDITS   Firefly - King of the Hill - Lucky Town Blues - Blue Ridge Falls - Undercover Angel

STEVE EDWARDS
c/o Gorfaine/Schwartz Agency
PHONE 818-260-8500
RECENT CREDITS   Today You Die - Raging Sharks - Shadow of Fear - Target of Opportunity - Straight Jacket

JON EHRLICH
c/o First Artists Management
PHONE 818-377-7750
RECENT CREDITS   Invasion - House, M.D. - The Mountain - Hawaii - Party of Five

CLIFF EIDELMAN
c/o First Artists Management
PHONE 818-377-7750
RECENT CREDITS   The Sisterhood of the Traveling Pants - Sexual Life - The Lizzie McGuire Movie - One True Thing - Crazy People - Star Trek VI

DANNY ELFMAN
c/o Kraft-Engel Management
PHONE 818-380-1918
RECENT CREDITS   Corpse Bride - Charlotte's Web - Desperate Housewives - Charlie and the Chocolate Factory - Spiderman 1&2 - Chicago

STEPHEN ENDELMAN
c/o First Artists Management
PHONE 818-377-7750
RECENT CREDITS   De-Lovely - The Blue Butterfly - I'm with Lucy

THE ENGINE ROOM
c/o Creative Artists Agency
PHONE 310-288-4545
RECENT CREDITS   Nip/Tuck Theme

EVAN EVANS
c/o The Kaufman Agency
PHONE 818-506-6013
RECENT CREDITS   Fear of Clowns - Table for One - Killers - Miss Wonton - Revelation

KURT FARQUHAR
c/o First Artists Management
PHONE 818-377-7750
RECENT CREDITS   Keke & Jamal - Gas - All of Us - The Proud Family - Soul Food

LOUIS FEBRE
c/o Soundtrack Music Associates
PHONE 818-382-3300
RECENT CREDITS   Control - Nine Lives - 3: The Dale Earnhardt Story - Desperate Housewives

GEORGE FENTON
c/o Gorfaine/Schwartz Agency
PHONE 818-260-8500
RECENT CREDITS   Last Holiday - Valiant - Bewitched - Hitch - Stage Beauty

JAY FERGUSON
c/o First Artists Management
PHONE 818-377-7750
RECENT CREDITS   Film: Paradise, Texas - Tremors 4 - N.T.S.B.; TV: The Office - Too Legit: MC Hammer

BRAD FIEDEL
c/o Gorfaine/Schwartz Agency
PHONE 818-260-8500
RECENT CREDITS   Eden - Johnny Mnemonic - True Lies - The Real McCoy - Gladiator

CHRISTOPHER FIELD
c/o Gorfaine/Schwartz Agency
PHONE 818-260-8500
RECENT CREDITS   Vlad - Madigan Men

COMPOSERS

*CHAD FISHER
c/o Greenspan Artist Management
PHONE 310-289-3990
RECENT CREDITS   Little Manhattan - Kicking and
                        Screaming - Garden State

CLAUDE FOISY
c/o Soundtrack Music Associates
PHONE 818-382-3300
RECENT CREDITS   The Outer Limits - We'll Meet Again -
                        The 4400 - White Noise - First Wave

*RUY FOLGUERA
c/o Gorfaine/Schwartz Agency
PHONE 818-260-8500
RECENT CREDITS   Zapata - The Kiss - Picking Up the Pieces

*DAN FOLIART
c/o Soundtrack Music Associates
PHONE 818-382-3300
RECENT CREDITS   8 Simple Rules - Seventh Heaven -
                        Home Improvement - Roseanne

ROBERT FOLK
c/o Soundtrack Music Associates
PHONE 818-382-3300
RECENT CREDITS   Kung Pow: Enter the Fist - Boat Trip -
                        Major League 3 - Nothing to Lose -
                        Maximum Risk

CHARLES FOX
c/o Marks Management
PHONE 805-882-1116
RECENT CREDITS   Zorro - 9 to 5 - Barbarella - Foul Play

DAVID MICHAEL FRANK
c/o Soundtrack Music Associates
PHONE 818-382-3300
RECENT CREDITS   Slap Her, She's French - You Lucky Dog -
                        The Last Patrol - Celebrity Mole - Hard
                        To Kill

CHRISTOPHER FRANKE
c/o First Artists Management
PHONE 818-377-7750
RECENT CREDITS   Firefighter - Hooligans - Berkeley - The
                        Amazing Race (TV)

JASON FREDERICK
c/o Soundtrack Music Associates
PHONE 818-382-3300
RECENT CREDITS   Jackhammer - 2 B Perfectly Honest -
                        Terror Toons 2 - News from the Church -
                        Good Girls Don't

JOHN FRIZZELL
c/o First Artists Management
PHONE 818-377-7750
RECENT CREDITS   Black Irish - Four Minutes - The Woods -
                        Wal-Mart: The High Cost of Low Price -
                        The Prizewinner of Defiance, Ohio

*NATHAN FURST
c/o First Artists Management
PHONE 818-377-7750
RECENT CREDITS   Christmas Vacation 2: Cousin Eddie's
                        Island Adventure - Birds of Prey - The
                        Real World

GRANT GEISSMAN
c/o Marks Management
PHONE 805-882-1116
RECENT CREDITS   Two and a Half Men - The Ponder Heart
                        - Call Me Claus - Monday Night
                        Mayhem

LISA GERRARD
c/o First Artists Management
PHONE 818-377-7750
RECENT CREDITS   A Thousand Roads - Layer Cake -
                        Collateral - Tears of the Sun - Whale
                        Rider

MICHAEL GIACCHINO
c/o Gorfaine/Schwartz Agency
PHONE 818-260-8500
RECENT CREDITS   Mission: Impossible 3 - Sky High - The
                        Incredibles - Sin - Lost - Alias

*RICHARD GIBBS
c/o Soundtrack Music Associates
PHONE 818-382-3300
RECENT CREDITS   The Honeymooners - Fat Albert -
                        Johnson Family Vacation - Barbershop 2

*PHILIP GIFFIN
c/o Soundtrack Music Associates
PHONE 818-382-3300
RECENT CREDITS   Topa Topa Bluffs - The Spring -
                        Summerland - Boomtown

STEFAN GIRADET
c/o Evolution Music Partners
PHONE 310-623-3388
RECENT CREDITS   An American Reunion - Spanish Fly - The
                        Confessional - The Animal Room -
                        Keeping Mum (TV)

PHILIP GLASS
c/o Kraft-Engel Management
PHONE 818-380-1918
RECENT CREDITS   Neverwas - Taking Lives - Secret Window
                        - The Hours - The Truman Show -
                        Kundun

NICK GLENNIE-SMITH
c/o First Artists Management
PHONE 818-377-7750
RECENT CREDITS   A Sound of Thunder - Laura Stern - Ella
                        Enchanted - We Were Soldiers - The
                        Man in the Iron Mask

BARRY GOLDBERG
c/o The Kaufman Agency
PHONE 818-506-6013
RECENT CREDITS   Street Time - L.A. Johns - Smart House -
                        Pow Wow Highway - Flashback

*JONATHAN GOLDBERGER
c/o First Artists Management
PHONE 818-377-7750
RECENT CREDITS   The Hawk Is Dying - Fossil - The Eulipion
                        Chronicles - Trans

COMPOSERS

ELLIOT GOLDENTHAL
c/o Gorfaine/Schwartz Agency
PHONE 818-260-8500
RECENT CREDITS S.W.A.T. - The Good Thief - Frida - Titus - The Butcher Boy

JOEL GOLDSMITH
c/o First Artists Management
PHONE 818-377-7750
RECENT CREDITS Haunting Sarah - Helen of Troy - Kull the Conqueror - Stargate: Atlantis - Stargate SG-1

JONATHAN GOLDSMITH
c/o The Agency Group Ltd.
PHONE 310-385-2800
RECENT CREDITS Sex Traffic - Play On - Rare Birds - The Mary Kay Story - The Man Who Saved Christmas

JOSEPH JULIAN GONZALEZ
c/o Soundtrack Music Associates
PHONE 818-382-3300
RECENT CREDITS Cowboy del Amore - Price of Glory - Curdled - Fish Outta Water - Resurrection Blvd.

JOEL GOODMAN
c/o Evolution Music Partners
PHONE 310-623-3388
RECENT CREDITS Disorder - Evenhand - Undermind - Born Rich

MICHAEL GORE
c/o Evolution Music Partners
PHONE 310-623-3388
RECENT CREDITS Camp - Superstar - Mr. Wonderful - Defending Your Life - The Butcher's Wife

ADAM GORGONI
c/o Evolution Music Partners
PHONE 310-623-3388
RECENT CREDITS 95 Miles to Go - Blue Car - Easy Six - Judge Koan - Happy Family

MARK GOVERNOR
c/o The Agency Group Ltd.
PHONE 310-385-2800
RECENT CREDITS ShAme - Possessed - Casino Royale - The Brave - Notes From the Underground

*RON GRANT
c/o Gorfaine/Schwartz Agency
PHONE 818-260-8500
RECENT CREDITS Air Time - In Dark Places - The Accident

HARRY GREGSON-WILLIAMS
c/o Gorfaine/Schwartz Agency
PHONE 818-260-8500
RECENT CREDITS Deja Vu - Kingdom of Heaven - Team America: World Police - The Lion, the Witch and the Wardrobe

ANDREW GROSS
c/o First Artists Management
PHONE 818-377-7750
RECENT CREDITS Venus & Vegas - The Act - Off the Lip - Shut Up and Kiss Me! - DisFunktional Family

JONATHAN GROSSMAN
c/o First Artists Management
PHONE 818-377-7750
RECENT CREDITS Joan of Arcadia - Judging Amy

LAWRENCE GROUPE
c/o First Artists Management
PHONE 818-377-7750
RECENT CREDITS Line of Fire - The Search for John Gissing - The Contender - I Woke Up Early the Day I Died

DAVE GRUSIN
c/o Gorfaine/Schwartz Agency
PHONE 818-260-8500
RECENT CREDITS Jump Shot - Dinner with Friends - Random Hearts - Hope Floats - Selena

JAY GRUSKA
c/o First Artists Management
PHONE 818-377-7750
RECENT CREDITS Supernatural - Wildfire - Hack - Charmed - The Division

*ANDREA GUERRA
c/o First Artists Management
PHONE 818-377-7750
RECENT CREDITS Pursuit of Happyness - Hotel Rwanda

GARY G-WIZ & AMANI K. SMITH
c/o First Artists Management
PHONE 818-377-7750
RECENT CREDITS Method & Red - Save Virgil - Volcano High - Luis - Dark Angel

CHRIS HAJIAN
c/o First Artists Management
PHONE 818-377-7750
RECENT CREDITS Inspector Gadget 2 - Queens Supreme - Chairman of the Board - Mr. Vincent

*PAGE HAMILTON
c/o Creative Artists Agency
PHONE 310-288-4545
RECENT CREDITS Hellcab

HAMPTON/ADAIR
1615 16th St.
Santa Monica, CA 90404
PHONE 310-399-6900
FAX 310-399-5333
EMAIL . . . . .brad@hamptonadair.com
RECENT CREDITS Barbershop: The Series - Stacked - Last Comic Standing - Just Shoot Me - Greg the Bunny; Song Placement: Sex in the City - Dawson's Creek - Alias - Joan of Arcadia - Queer Eye
COMMENTS Representation: Soundtrack Music Associates, phone: 818-382-3300

John Adair . . . . .Partner/Composer
Steve Hampton . . . . .Partner/Composer
Howard Paar . . . . .Music Supervisor
Brad Hamilton . . . . .Executive Producer/Music Editor

COMPOSERS

*RICHARD HARTLEY
c/o Soundtrack Music Associates
PHONE 818-382-3300
RECENT CREDITS   Puckoon - The Martins - The Lion in
                        Winter - Alice in Wonderland

PAUL HASLINGER
c/o First Artists Management
PHONE 818-377-7750
RECENT CREDITS   Into the Blue - Underworld - Blue Crush
                        - Crazy/Beautiful

TODD HAYEN
c/o The Kaufman Agency
PHONE 818-506-6013
RECENT CREDITS   Pittsburgh's Big Picture - Finding Kelly -
                        Fly Boy - Treasure of Pirate's Point -
                        Waking Up Horton

HEAVY MELODY MUSIC & SOUND DESIGN
307 Seventh Ave., Ste. 1203
New York, NY 10001
PHONE 212-675-9585
FAX 212-675-9565
EMAIL . . . . .cpeterson@heavymelodymusic.com
WEB SITE .www.heavymelodymusic.com
RECENT CREDITS   A Tale in the Desert 2 (Online Game)
COMMENTS   Original music and sound design prima-
                        rily for television commercials and long
                        form programming, film and video
                        games

Chris Peterson . . . . .Producer
David Fraser .Composer/Sound Designer
Neil Goldberg . . . . .Composer/Sound Designer

ALEX HEFFES
c/o Evolution Music Partners
PHONE 310-623-3388
RECENT CREDITS   The Last King of Scotland - Click - Dear
                        Frankie - Touching the Void - Trauma

REINHOLD HEIL & JOHNNY KLIMEK
c/o Creative Artists Agency
PHONE 310-288-4545
RECENT CREDITS   Iron-Jawed Angels - Swimming
                        Upstream - One-Hour Photo - The
                        Princess & the Warrior - Run Lola Run

*ERIC HESTER
c/o The Kaufman Agency
PHONE 818-506-6013
RECENT CREDITS   The Swap - Jack - Marcus Apple

PETER HIMMELMAN
c/o Evolution Music Partners
PHONE 310-623-3388
RECENT CREDITS   Ash Tuesday - Porn N' Chicken - Judging
                        Amy - A Slipping Down Life

*DICKON HINCHLIFFE
c/o First Artists Management
PHONE 818-377-7750
RECENT CREDITS   Keeping Mum - Forty Shades of Blue -
                        Intimacy

DAVID HIRSCHFELDER
c/o Gorfaine/Schwartz Agency
PHONE 818-260-8500
RECENT CREDITS   Aquamarine - The Weight of Water -
                        Hanging Up - Elizabeth - Sliding Doors

MICHAEL HOENING
c/o Gorfaine/Schwartz Agency
PHONE 818-260-8500
RECENT CREDITS   Dracula 3000: Infinite Darkness - The
                        Crossing Guard - The District (TV) -
                        Ultraviolet (TV) - Rag & Bone (TV)

*LEE HOLDRIDGE
c/o Soundtrack Music Associates
PHONE 818-382-3300
RECENT CREDITS   The Long Way Home - The Mists Of
                        Avalon - Into Thin Air - 10.5

DAVID HOLMES
c/o First Artists Management
PHONE 818-377-7750
RECENT CREDITS   Ocean's 12 - Code 46 - Buffalo Soldiers
                        - Analyze That - Ocean's 11 - Out of
                        Sight

JAMES HORNER
c/o Gorfaine/Schwartz Agency
PHONE 818-260-8500
RECENT CREDITS   All the King's Men - Flight Plan - The
                        New World - Troy - House of Sand and
                        Fog

JAMES NEWTON HOWARD
c/o Gorfaine/Schwartz Agency
PHONE 818-260-8500
RECENT CREDITS   Lady in the Water - Freedomland -
                        Batman Begins - Interpreter - The Village

JEEHUN HWANG
c/o First Artists Management
PHONE 818-377-7750
RECENT CREDITS   James Cameron's Aliens of the Deep -
                        Quest for Columbus - James Cameron's
                        Expedition: Bismarck - Tart

DICK HYMAN
c/o The Kaufman Agency
PHONE 818-506-6013
RECENT CREDITS   Moonstruck - The Purple Rose of Cairo -
                        Sweet and Lowdown - Hannah and Her
                        Sisters - Mighty Aphrodite

*ALBERTO IGLESIAS
c/o Gorfaine/Schwartz Agency
PHONE 818-260-8500
RECENT CREDITS   Constant Gardener - Bad Education -
                        Comandante - Talk to Her

*DAMON INTRABARTOLO
c/o Creative Artists Agency
PHONE 310-288-4545
RECENT CREDITS   Bare

COMPOSERS

*PAT IRWIN
c/o First Artists Management
PHONE 818-377-7750
RECENT CREDITS   Trekkies 2 - Drop Back Ten - But I'm a Cheerleader; TV: The Groovenians

MARK ISHAM
c/o First Artists Management
PHONE 818-377-7750
RECENT CREDITS   In Her Shoes - Running Scared - Crash - Racing Stripes - Miracle

IVY
c/o Evolution Music Partners
PHONE 310-623-3388
RECENT CREDITS   Shallow Hal

STEVE JABLONSKY
c/o Gorfaine/Schwartz Agency
PHONE 818-260-8500
RECENT CREDITS   The Island - The Amityville Horror - Steamboy - Live From Baghdad - Desperate Housewives

JOE JACKSON
c/o The Agency Group Ltd.
PHONE 310-385-2800
RECENT CREDITS   The Greatest Game Ever Played - Tucker - Three of Hearts - I'm Your Man - Queens Logic - Mike's Murder

MAURICE JARRE
c/o Kraft-Engel Management
PHONE 818-380-1918
RECENT CREDITS   Sunshine - Ghost - Witness - Dead Poets Society - Fatal Attraction

CARL JOHNSON
c/o Soundtrack Music Associates
PHONE 818-382-3300
RECENT CREDITS   Piglet's Big Movie - June - The Hunchback of Notre Dame 2 - Toonsylvania - Winnie The Pooh: Pooh's Grand Adventure

ADRIAN JOHNSTON
c/o Soundtrack Music Associates
PHONE 818-382-3300
RECENT CREDITS   If Only - This Is Not a Love Song - The Lawless Heart - Me Without You - The House Of Mirth

RON JONES
c/o The Kaufman Agency
PHONE 818-506-6013
RECENT CREDITS   Fairly Odd Parents - Family Guy - Star Trek: Starfleet Academy - Star Trek: The Next Generation - American Dad

*DAVID JULYAN
c/o Soundtrack Music Associates
PHONE 818-382-3300
RECENT CREDITS   Inside I'm Dancing - Insomnia - Memento

BENOIT JUTRAS
c/o Gorfaine/Schwartz Agency
PHONE 818-260-8500
RECENT CREDITS   Alegria, The Movie - Ultimate G's - The Hunger (TV)

JAN A.P. KACZMAREK
c/o Greenspan Artist Management
PHONE 310-289-3990
RECENT CREDITS   Finding Neverland - Unfaithful - Quo Vadis

*TUOMAS KANTELINEN
c/o Gorfaine/Schwartz Agency
PHONE 818-260-8500
RECENT CREDITS   Midhunters - The Threat - Certainly Not a Fairytale - The Pelican Man

JOHN KEANE
c/o Gorfaine/Schwartz Agency
PHONE 818-260-8500
RECENT CREDITS   CSI - The Amazing Race - A Better Way to Die - A Vow to Kill - One Woman's Courage

ROLFE KENT
c/o First Artists Management
PHONE 818-377-7750
RECENT CREDITS   Wedding Crashers - Mean Girls - Sideways - About Schmidt - Nurse Betty

RANDY KERBER
c/o Gorfaine/Schwartz Agency
PHONE 818-260-8500
RECENT CREDITS   Wild Thornberrys

KEVIN KLIESCH
c/o The Kaufman Agency
PHONE 818-506-6013
RECENT CREDITS   Popeye's Voyage: The Quest for Pappy - Dracula 3: Legacy - Wes Craven Presents Dracula 2: The Ascension

WILLIAM KIDD
c/o Soundtrack Music Associates
PHONE 818-382-3300
RECENT CREDITS   Mohammed (Animated) - The King And I (Animated) - Tough & Deadly

WOJCIECH KILLAR
c/o Kraft-Engel Management
PHONE 818-380-1918
RECENT CREDITS   The Pianist - Bram Stoker's Dracula - Ninth Gate - Portrait of a Lady

KEVIN KINER
c/o First Artists Management
PHONE 818-377-7750
RECENT CREDITS   CSI: Miami - Star Trek: Enterprise - Madison - Wing Commander

*JOHN KING
c/o Gorfaine/Schwartz Agency
PHONE 818-260-8500
RECENT CREDITS   Tenacious D Movie- - Li'l Pimp - Orgazmo - Push, Nevada

COMPOSERS

*KITARO
c/o The Agency Group Ltd.
PHONE 310-385-2800
RECENT CREDITS   Song jia huang sho - Heven & Earth -
                        Shang Hai yijiu er ling - Samuel Lount -
                        Sishui liunian

DAVID KITAY
c/o Kraft-Engel Management
PHONE 818-380-1918
RECENT CREDITS   Art School Confidential - Relative
                        Strangers - The Ice Harvest - Harold and
                        Kumar Go to White Castle - Bad Santa

HARALD KLOSER
c/o Gorfaine/Schwartz Agency
PHONE 818-260-8500
RECENT CREDITS   Alien Vs. Predator - Tomorrow - 13th
                        Floor - Rudy's War (TV) - Little Brother
                        (TV)

JOE KRAEMER
c/o First Artists Management
PHONE 818-377-7750
RECENT CREDITS   Open House - The Hitcher 2 - The Way
                        of the Gun

*NICK LAIRD-CLOWES
c/o First Artist Management
PHONE 818-377-7750
RECENT CREDITS   Fierce People - The Invisible Circus

RUSS LANDAU
c/o Evolution Music Partners
PHONE 310-623-3388
RECENT CREDITS   Lost - Survivor - The Assistant - Fear
                        Factor - The Restaurant 1&2

ROB LANE
c/o The Kaufman Agency
PHONE 818-506-6013
RECENT CREDITS   The Lost World - Charles II : The Last
                        King - Henry VIII - Red Dust - Aileen:
                        The Life and Death of a Serial Killer

BRIAN LANGSBARD
c/o Creative Artists Agency
PHONE 310-288-4545
RECENT CREDITS   The Specials - Frozen - First of May -
                        Johnny Skidmarks

DANIEL LANOIS
c/o First Artists Management
PHONE 818-377-7750
RECENT CREDITS   The Million Dollar Hotel - Sling Blade

NATHAN LARSON
c/o First Artists Management
PHONE 818-377-7750
RECENT CREDITS   A Love Song for Bobby Long - The
                        Woodsman - Dirty Pretty Things - Boys
                        Don't Cry - Prozac Nation

JIM LATHAM
c/o Whatever...Talent Agency
PHONE 818-360-4843
RECENT CREDITS   Columbo Likes the Night Life - The
                        Almost Guys - South of Heaven West of
                        Hell - Maniac McGee

DAVID LAWRENCE
c/o First Artists Management
PHONE 818-377-7750
RECENT CREDITS   La La Wood - National Lampoon's Van
                        Wilder - American Pie 1&2 - Miss Match

MICHEL LEGRAND
c/o Kraft-Engel Management
PHONE 818-380-1918
RECENT CREDITS   Madeline - Yentl - The Thomas Crown
                        Affair - Summer of '42

CHRISTOPHER LENNERTZ
c/o First Artists Management
PHONE 818-377-7750
RECENT CREDITS   Sledge - The Pearl - The Deal - Soul
                        Plane - Tortilla Heaven

CORY LERIOS
c/o First Artists Management
PHONE 818-377-7750
RECENT CREDITS   ToddWorld - What's New Scooby Doo -
                        Child's Play 3 - Kim Possible (TV) - The
                        Mummy (TV) - Baywatch (TV)

STEWART LEVIN
c/o Marks Management
PHONE 805-882-1116
RECENT CREDITS   The Practice - Picket Fences - 30
                        Something - Wonder Years

MICHAEL K. LEVINE
c/o First Artists Management
PHONE 818-377-7750
RECENT CREDITS   Close to Home - Cold Case - Drew
                        Carey's Green Screen Show

DANIEL LICHT
c/o Evolution Music Partners
PHONE 310-623-3388
RECENT CREDITS   Soul Survivors - Amityville: A New
                        Generation - Cowboy Up - Splendor -
                        Permanent Midnight - The Winner

HAL LINDES
c/o Soundtrack Music Associates
PHONE 818-382-3300
WEB SITE . . . . .www.hallindes.com
RECENT CREDITS   Girl 27 - Local Boys - Quicksand - Lucky
                        13 - The Infiltrator

JEFF LIPPENCOTT & MARK T. WILLIAMS
c/o Gorfaine/Schwartz Agency
PHONE 818-260-8500
RECENT CREDITS   The Apprentice - The Apprentice Martha
                        Stewart - Rock Star: INXS

COMPOSERS

ANDREW LOCKINGTON
c/o First Artists Management
PHONE 818-377-7750
RECENT CREDITS   Cake - St. Ralph - Touch of Pink - Long
Life, Happiness and Prosperity

JOSEPH LODUCA
c/o Kraft-Engel Management
PHONE 818-380-1918
RECENT CREDITS   Devour - Boogeyman - Brotherhood of
the Wolf - Army of Darkness - Evil Dead
1&2

HENNING LOHNER
c/o First Artists Management
PHONE 818-377-7750
RECENT CREDITS   Blood Rayne - Santa's Slay - Incident at
Loch Ness - Hellraiser: Deader - Ned
Kelly - The Ring

DEBORAH LURIE
c/o Kraft-Engel Management
PHONE 818-380-1918
RECENT CREDITS   An Unfinished Life - Mozart & The Whale
- Sleepover - Imaginary Heroes -
Whirlygirl

EVAN LURIE
c/o Soundtrack Music Associates
PHONE 818-382-3300
RECENT CREDITS   Famous - Happy Accidents - The Whole
She-Bang - Joe Gould's Secret - Tree's
Lounge

MARK MANCINA
c/o Gorfaine/Schwartz Agency
PHONE 818-260-8500
RECENT CREDITS   Asylum - Brother Bear - Haunted
Mansion - Reckoning - Training Day

HUMMIE MANN
c/o The Kaufman Agency
PHONE 818-506-6013
RECENT CREDITS   Robin Hood: Men In Tights - Thomas
and the Magic Railroad - The Wooly
Boys - In Cold Blood - Cyber World In
3-D

CLINT MANSELL
c/o First Artists Management
PHONE 818-377-7750
RECENT CREDITS   The Fountain - Sahara - Sonny -
Abandon - Requiem for a Dream

DAVID MANSFEILD
c/o First Artists Management
PHONE 818-377-7750
RECENT CREDITS   The Divine Secrets of the Ya-Ya
Sisterhood - Songcatcher - Tumbleweeds
- The Apostle

MARILYN MANSON
c/o Creative Artists Agency
PHONE 310-288-4545
RECENT CREDITS   Resident Evil

SUSAN MARDER
c/o The Agency Group Ltd.
PHONE 310-385-2800
RECENT CREDITS   Any Day Now - The Division - Leaving
L.A. - Equal Justice - Murder 101

ANTHONY MARINELLI
c/o First Artists Management
PHONE 818-377-7750
RECENT CREDITS   The Mayor of the Sunset Strip - The Man
from Elysian Fields - Hotel - 15 Minutes
- Time Code - Two Days in the Valley

*DONNY MARKOWITZ
c/o Soundtrack Music Associates
PHONE 818-382-3300
RECENT CREDITS   Jesus, Mary And Joey - Dragon Storm -
Jake 2.0 - The Chronicle

RICK MAROTTA
c/o Evolution Music Partners
PHONE 310-623-3388
RECENT CREDITS   Everybody Loves Raymond - Yes, Dear -
Abby - The Jennifer Estes Story

*PHILIP MARSHALL
c/o Soundtrack Music Associates
PHONE 818-382-3300
RECENT CREDITS   Wired To Win - Blind Guy - Twin Towers
- Kicking And Screaming

*CLIFF MARTINEZ
c/o Soundtrack Music Associates
PHONE 818-382-3300
RECENT CREDITS   First Snow - Havoc - Wicker Park -
Wonderland - Traffic

RICHARD MARVIN
c/o First Artists Management
PHONE 818-377-7750
RECENT CREDITS   The Battle for Shaker Heights -
Clubhouse - Empire - Six Feet Under -
U-571

MARK MCKENZIE
c/o The Kaufman Agency
PHONE 818-506-6013
RECENT CREDITS   Blizzard - The Last Castle - Mi Familia
(aka My Family) - Frank and Jesse -
Dragonheart: A New Beginning

JOEL MCNEELY
c/o First Artists Management
PHONE 818-377-7750
RECENT CREDITS   Ghosts of the Abyss - Holes - Return to
Neverland - Soldier - Dark Angel

JAMES MCVAY
c/o The Kaufman Agency
PHONE 818-506-6013
RECENT CREDITS   Snap Decision - Living Dolls: The
Making of a Child Beauty - Queen
One-Eyed King - Freaky Friday -
Breaking Through

COMPOSERS

BRAD MEHLDAU
c/o First Artists Management
PHONE 818-377-7750
RECENT CREDITS   Ma Femme est une Actrice

PETER MELNICK
c/o The Kaufman Agency
PHONE 818-506-6013
RECENT CREDITS   L.A. Story - Call Waiting - West of Here - Indictment: The McMartin Trial - Grand Avenue

ALAN MENKEN
c/o Kraft-Engel Management
PHONE 818-380-1918
RECENT CREDITS   Shaggy Dog - Noel - Home on the Range - The Little Mermaid - Beauty and the Beast

MESSY
c/o Creative Artists Agency
PHONE 310-288-4545
RECENT CREDITS   Robbery Homicide - Our Town - Extreme Team - LAX

MICHAEL SUBY
c/o First Artists Management
PHONE 818-377-7750
RECENT CREDITS   A Cool Breeze on the Underground - Tamara - The Zodiac - Able Edwards - The Butterfly Effect

MARCUS MILLER
c/o First Artists Management
PHONE 818-377-7750
RECENT CREDITS   King's Ransom - Head of State - Ladies Man - Deliver Us from Eva - Boomerang - The Brothaz

SHELDON MIROWITZ
c/o The Kaufman Agency
PHONE 818-506-6013
RECENT CREDITS   The Nazi Officer's Wife - Woodcutter - Johnson County War - Evolution - Outside Providence

AHRIN MISHAN
c/o Gorfaine/Schwartz Agency
PHONE 818-260-8500
RECENT CREDITS   Claire Dolan - Maryam - Whoopi - Ed - Fling

JUN MIYAKE
c/o Creative Artists Agency
PHONE 310-288-4545
RECENT CREDITS   The Story of Pu Pu - Itashi No Half Moon - Memories/Stink Bomb

*CHARLIE MOLE
c/o Greenspan Artist Management
PHONE 3610-289-3990
RECENT CREDITS   Goose! - Only Human - The Importance of Being Earnest

FRED MOLLIN
c/o Soundtrack Music Associates
PHONE 818-382-3300
RECENT CREDITS   Daydream Believers (The Monkey's Story) - Liar, Liar - Tucker & the Horse Thief

DEBORAH MOLLISON
c/o Creative Artists Agency
PHONE 310-288-4545
RECENT CREDITS   East Is East - Simon Magus - Boys of Sunset Ridge - Earth Story - Witch's Daughter

*GUY MOON
c/o Soundtrack Music Associates
PHONE 818-382-3300
RECENT CREDITS   A Very Brady Sequel - The Brady Movie - The Fairly Odd Parents - Danny Phantom - Jimmy Neutron

MARK MORGAN
c/o Gorfaine/Schwartz Agency
PHONE 818-260-8500
RECENT CREDITS   Hawaii - The District - Hoop Life - Ellen - Ink

ANDREA MORRICONE
c/o Gorfaine/Schwartz Agency
PHONE 818-260-8500
RECENT CREDITS   Funny Money - Capturing the Friedmans

ENNIO MORRICONE
c/o Gorfaine/Schwartz Agency
PHONE 818-260-8500
RECENT CREDITS   Ripley's Game - Malena - Vatel - Lolita - Bulworth

*TREVOR MORRIS
c/o Gorfaine/Schwartz Agency
PHONE 818-260-8500
RECENT CREDITS   Rancid - 3 Neddles - The Lost Angel - The Artificial Feast

MARK MOTHERSBAUGH
c/o Greenspan Artist Management
PHONE 310-289-3990
RECENT CREDITS   Herbie Fully Loaded - The Big White - Lords of Dogtown - The Life Aquatic with Steve Zissou

*JOHN MURPHY
c/o First Artists Management
PHONE 818-377-7750
RECENT CREDITS   The Man - A Lot Like Love - Millions - The Perfect Score - Intermission

SUJIN NAM
c/o Evolution Music Partners
PHONE 310-623-3388
RECENT CREDITS   The Visit - Shanghai Ghetto - Menace - One Last Run

*GREGOR NARHOLZ
c/o First Artist Management
PHONE 818-377-7750
RECENT CREDITS   The SpongeBob SquarePants Movie

COMPOSERS

*ME'SHELL NDEGÉOCELLO
c/o Evolution Music Partners
PHONE .310-623-3388
RECENT CREDITS Lackawanna Blues - Disappearing Acts

BLAKE NEELY
c/o Gorfaine/Schwartz Agency
PHONE .818-260-8500
RECENT CREDITS Wedding Date - Jack & Bobby - Everwood

ROGER NEILL
c/o Gorfaine/Schwartz Agency
PHONE .818-260-8500
RECENT CREDITS King of the Hill - Simple Life - A.U.S.A - Lone Ranger - Chicago Hope

DAVID NEWMAN
c/o First Artists Management
PHONE .818-377-7750
RECENT CREDITS The Pink Panther - The Cat in the Hat - How to Lose a Guy in 10 Days - Daddy Day Care - Scooby Doo - Ice Age

JOEY NEWMAN
c/o Gorfaine/Schwartz
PHONE .818-260-8500
RECENT CREDITS Pursued - Stealing Time - Once and Again - Providence - Anna's Dream

RANDY NEWMAN
c/o Gorfaine/Schwartz Agency
PHONE .818-260-8500
RECENT CREDITS Cars - Meet the Fockers - Seabiscuit - Monsters, Inc. - Meet the Parents

THOMAS NEWMAN
c/o Gorfaine/Schwartz Agency
PHONE .818-260-8500
RECENT CREDITS Jarhead - Cinderella Man - Lemony Snicket's A Series of Unfortunate Events - Angels in America - Finding Nemo

*LENNIE NIEHAUS
c/o Soundtrack Music Associates
PHONE .818-382-3300
RECENT CREDITS Bloodwork - Space Cowboys - Midnight in the Garden of Good and Evil

JOHN NORDSTROM
c/o Gorfaine/Schwartz Agency
PHONE .818-260-8500
RECENT CREDITS Nearing Grace - Black Cloud - Spy Game - Five Days to Midnight - Prince William

MICHAEL NYMAN
c/o First Artists Management
PHONE .818-377-7750
RECENT CREDITS The Libertine - The Piano - Gattaca - The End of the Affair

*PAUL OAKENFOLD
c/o Soundtrack Music Associates
PHONE .818-382-3300
RECENT CREDITS Victims - Elvis Has Left the Building - Collateral - Shrek 2 - The Matrix Reloaded

GREG O'CONNOR
c/o First Artists Management
PHONE .818-377-7750
RECENT CREDITS Blue Collar TV - 10-8 - Mad TV - The Jamie Kennedy Experiment

ATLI ÖRVARSSON
c/o Gorfaine/Schwartz Agency
PHONE .818-260-8500
RECENT CREDITS Stuart Little 3 - Strike the Tent - Jacob's Sound - Just Legal - Dragnet

JOHN OTTMAN
c/o Kraft-Engel Management
PHONE .818-380-1918
RECENT CREDITS Superman Returns - Fantastic Four - X-Men 2 - Gothika - The Usual Suspects - Apt Pupil

VAN DYKE PARKS
c/o First Artists Management
PHONE .818-377-7750
RECENT CREDITS Color Me Kubrick - The Company - Bastard Out of Carolina - Harold and the Purple Crayon

DANNY PELFREY
c/o First Artists Management
PHONE .818-377-7750
RECENT CREDITS American Dreams - Strong Medicine - That's Life - Spin City - Joseph: King of Dreams

DAVE PELMAN MUSIC PRODUCTION
11830 Dorothy St., #7
Los Angeles, CA 90049
PHONE 310-826-3999/310-508-1313
FAX 310-826-7091
EMAIL . . . . .d.pel@verizon.net
SECOND EMAIL . . . . .davepelman@hotmail.com
WEB SITE . . . . .www.davepelman@hotmail.com

Dave Pelman . . . . .Owner/Producer/Composer

MICHAEL PENN
c/o The Agency Group Ltd.
PHONE .310-385-2800
RECENT CREDITS Boogie Nights - Hard Eight - The Anniversary Party - Melvin Goes to Dinner - Sydney

HEITOR PEREIRA
c/o Gorfaine/Schwartz Agency
PHONE .818-260-8500
RECENT CREDITS Curious George - Havana Nights - Haven - Real Women Have Curves - Spy Kids

*GRANT LEE PHILLIPS
c/o First Artists Management
PHONE .818-377-7750
RECENT CREDITS Easy - ZigZag

*STEPHEN PHILLIPS
c/o First Artists Management
PHONE .818-377-7750
RECENT CREDITS B.M.O.C.: Big Man on Campus - The Wool Cap - Short on Sugar

COMPOSERS

*MICHAEL PICTON
c/o The Kaufman Agency
PHONE 818-506-6013

SCOOTER PIETSCH
c/o First Artists Management
PHONE 818-377-7750
RECENT CREDITS   The CMT Music Awards - Extreme
Makeover - Who Wants to Marry My
Dad? - Manhunt

*NICHOLAS PIKE
c/o Soundtrack Music Associates
PHONE 818-382-3300
RECENT CREDITS   Masters of Horror - Love Object -
Desperation - Life With Bonnie

*EGO PLUM
c/o Whatever...Talent Agency
PHONE 818-360-4843
RECENT CREDITS   The Ghastly Love of Johnny X - Black
Dahlia - noTORIous - Haunted Boat -
Wit's End

BASIL POLEDOURIS
c/o Creative Artists Agency
PHONE 310-288-4545
RECENT CREDITS   For Love of the Game - Cecil B.
Demented - Les Misérables - Mickey
Blue Eyes - The Hunt for Red October

CONRAD POPE
c/o Whatever...Talent Agency
PHONE 818-360-4843
RECENT CREDITS   Seabiscuit - Lloyd - The Rising Place -
Pavilion of Women - Amati Girls

STEVE PORCARO
c/o Gorfaine/Schwartz Agency
PHONE 818-260-8500
RECENT CREDITS   Emmett's Mark - Almost Dead - My First
Mister - Metro - North Shore

*RACHEL PORTMAN
c/o Kraft-Engel Management
PHONE 818-380-1918
RECENT CREDITS   The Little Prince - The Manchurian
Candidate - Mona Lisa - Human Stain -
Chocolat - Cider House Rules   Emma

MIKE POST
c/o Gorfaine/Schwartz Agency
PHONE 818-260-8500
RECENT CREDITS   Blind Justice - Law & Order: Trial by Jury
- Law & Order: SVU

JOHN POWELL
c/o Kraft-Engel Management
PHONE 818-380-1918
RECENT CREDITS   Mr. and Mrs. Smith - Robots - Alfie - The
Bourne Supremacy - The Italian Job -
The Bourne Identity

REG POWELL
c/o The Kaufman Agency
PHONE 818-506-6013
RECENT CREDITS   Cahoots - Alaska - Caitlin's Way -
Beyond Chance - The Romeo Show -
The Pathfinder

PRAY FOR RAIN
c/o Soundtrack Music Associates
PHONE 818-382-3300
RECENT CREDITS   Never Trust a Serial Killer - Three
Businessmen - Roadside Prophets -
Straight to Hell - Sid and Nancy

SIGUR RóS
c/o First Artists Management
PHONE 818-377-7750
RECENT CREDITS   Hlemmur - Vanilla Sky - Angels in the
Universe

TREVOR RABIN
c/o Kraft-Engel Management
PHONE 818-380-1918
RECENT CREDITS   The Great Raid - Glory Road - Coach
Carter - National Treasure - Remember
the Titans - Armageddon

J.A.C. REDFORD
c/o Gorfaine/Schwartz Agency
PHONE 818-260-8500
RECENT CREDITS   George of the Jungle 2 - The Joyriders -
The Mighty Ducks 3 - A Kid in King
Arthur's Court - Bye Bye, Love

ALAN REEVES
c/o The Kaufman Agency
PHONE 818-506-6013
RECENT CREDITS   Ocean Oasis - To Walk with Lions -
Rainbow - Bethune: Hero to a Nation -
For Hire

VERNON REID
c/o The Agency Group Ltd.
PHONE 310-385-2800
RECENT CREDITS   Mr. 3000 - Paid in Full - Fresh Kill

GRAEME REVELL
c/o Kraft-Engel Management
PHONE 818-380-1918
RECENT CREDITS   The Fog - Harsh Times - Pitch Black -
Daredevil - Blow

*DAVID REYNOLDS
c/o First Artists Management
PHONE 818-377-7750
RECENT CREDITS   Heavens Fall - Tides of War - Beauty
Shop - The Novice

*CRAIG RICHEY
c/o First Artists Management
PHONE 818-377-7750
RECENT CREDITS   Friends with Money - Journey Into Night
- Dream a Little Dream for Me

COMPOSERS

COMPOSERS

DAVID ROBBINS
c/o Evolution Music Partners
PHONE 310-623-3388
RECENT CREDITS   The Prime Gig - Cradle Will Rock -
Dead Man Walking - How to Kill Your
Neighbor's Dog

*J. PETER ROBINSON
c/o Soundtrack Music Associates
PHONE 818-382-3300
RECENT CREDITS   The World's Fastest Indian - Beeper -
Identity Theft - Twelve Days Of Terror -
Charmed

PETER MANNING ROBINSON
c/o Evolution Music Partners
PHONE 310-623-3388
RECENT CREDITS   Flypaper - Hit Me - Without a Trace -
Robbery Homicide Division

EDWARD ROGERS
c/o Soundtrack Music Associates
PHONE 818-382-3300
RECENT CREDITS   Kiss Me Goodnight - Guy In Row Five -
Elvis Took a Bullet - NYPD Blue - Law &
Order

JEFF RONA
c/o Soundtrack Music Associates
PHONE 818-382-3300
RECENT CREDITS   The Quiet - Urban Legend 3: Bloody
Mary - Stephen King's The Dead Zone -
Profiler

*BRETT ROSENBERG
c/o First Artists Management
PHONE 818-377-7750
RECENT CREDITS   Half Light - Josh Jarman - Liquid Bridge

LAURENCE ROSENTHAL
c/o The Agency Group Ltd.
PHONE 310-385-2800
RECENT CREDITS   Master Spy: The Robert Hanssen Story -
Wild Iris - Inherit the Wind - The Man
Who Captured Eichmann - The Miracle
Worker

WILLIAM ROSS
c/o Gorfaine/Schwartz Agency
PHONE 818-260-8500
RECENT CREDITS   Kicking and Screaming - Ladder 49 -
Tuck Everlasting - My Dog Skip - Tin
Cup

BRUCE ROWLAND
c/o Soundtrack Music Associates
PHONE 818-382-3300
WEB SITE . . . . .www.bruce.rowland.net
RECENT CREDITS   The Man From Snowy River 1&2 - Andre
- Zeus & Roxanne - Phar Lap - Lightning
Jack

DAVID RUSSO
c/o Evolution Music Partners
PHONE 310-623-3388
RECENT CREDITS   Sin City - Assault on Precint 13 - The
Chronicles of Riddick - CSI: Miami

DANNY SABER
c/o Soundtrack Music Associates
PHONE 818-382-3300
RECENT CREDITS   Cruel World - The Hillside Strangler -
Blade 2

*CRAIG SAFAN
c/o Soundtrack Music Associates
PHONE 818-382-3300
RECENT CREDITS   A Time of Fear - Delivering Milo -
Operation Splitsville - Mr. Wrong -
Major Payne

RYUICHI SAKAMOTO
c/o Creative Artists Agency
PHONE 310-288-4545
RECENT CREDITS   Snake Eyes - Little Buddha - High Heels
- The Sheltering Sky - The Last Emperor

H. SCOTT SALINAS
c/o The Kaufman Agency
PHONE 818-506-6013
RECENT CREDITS   Latin Dragon - Laugh, Clown, Laugh -
Forgetting Aphrodite - The Squaw Man

BENNETT SALVAY
c/o Gorfaine/Schwartz Agency
PHONE 818-260-8500
RECENT CREDITS   Mr. 3000 - Jeepers Creepers 1&2 - Love
Stinks - Boomtown - Providence

ANTON SANKO
c/o Evolution Music Partners
PHONE 310-623-3388
RECENT CREDITS   One Last Thing... - Voices in Wartime -
Saving Face - Scotland, PA - Bad Apple
- Wonderland

GUSTAVO SANTAOLALLA
c/o First Artists Management
PHONE 818-377-7750
RECENT CREDITS   North Country - Brokeback Mountain -
21 Grams - The Motorcycle Diaries -
Amores Perros - The Insider

*ANDREA SAPAROFF
c/o Soundtrack Music Associates
PHONE 818-382-3300
RECENT CREDITS   Borrowing Time - The Art of a Bullet -
Appointment with Fear - Perfect Match

KEVIN SARGENT
c/o Evolution Music Partners
PHONE 310-623-3388
RECENT CREDITS   Crush - Fakers - The Canterbury Tales

LALO SCHIFRIN
c/o First Artists Management
PHONE 818-377-7750
RECENT CREDITS   X-Men 3 - Mission: Impossible 3 - After
the Sunset - Shrek 2 - Rush Hour 1&2

DAVID SCHWARTZ
c/o First Artists Management
PHONE 818-377-7750
RECENT CREDITS   Deadwood - Arrested Development -
Hidden Hills - Leap of Faith - The Ellen
Show - Wolf Lake - Northern Exposure

*NAN SCHWARTZ
c/o Soundtrack Music Associates
PHONE 818-382-3300
RECENT CREDITS   Something Borrowed, Something Blue -
Prison of Secrets - Color Me Perfect

TOM SCOTT
c/o Soundtrack Music Associates
PHONE 818-382-3300
RECENT CREDITS   Shakes the Clown - Soul Man - The Sure
Thing - Just One of the Guys - Fast
Forward

SCULPTURED MUSIC
2445 N. Vermont Ave.
Los Angeles, CA 90027
PHONE 323-666-1183
FAX 323-913-0345
EMAIL . . . . .contact@sculpturedmusic.com
WEB SITE . . . . .www.sculpturedmusic.com
RECENT CREDITS   Seven and a Matche - Ole - Now
Chinatown - Epoch of Lotus

ERIC SERRA
c/o Kraft-Engel Management
PHONE 818-380-1918
RECENT CREDITS   Bulletproof Monk - The Fifth Element -
GoldenEye - The Professional

MARC SHAIMAN
c/o Kraft-Engel Management
PHONE 818-380-1918
RECENT CREDITS   Rumor Has It - Hairspray (Broadway) -
South Park: Bigger, Longer and Uncut -
Sleepless in Seattle - A Few Good Men

THEODORE SHAPIRO
c/o Gorfaine/Schwartz Agency
PHONE 818-260-8500
RECENT CREDITS   Fun with Dick and Jane - Idiocracy -
Dodgeball - 13 Going on 30 - Old
School

EDWARD SHEARMUR
c/o Gorfaine/Schwartz Agency
PHONE 818-260-8500
RECENT CREDITS   Derailed - Four Brothers - Bad News
Bears - The Skeleton Key - Sky Captain
and the World of Tomorrow

DAVID SHIRE
c/o Evolution Music Partners
PHONE 310-623-3388
RECENT CREDITS   The Tollbooth - Ash Wednesday - Two
Against Time - These Old Broads - Thin
Air

*HANK SHOCKLEE
c/o The Agency Group Ltd.
PHONE 310-385-2800
RECENT CREDITS   Juice - Friday Night Lights - He Got
Game - CB4 - Mo' Money - House Party
- Do the Right Thing

HOWARD SHORE
c/o Gorfaine/Schwartz Agency
PHONE 818-260-8500
RECENT CREDITS   History of Violence - King Kong - The
Aviator - The Lord of the Rings - Gangs
of New York

RYAN SHORE
c/o First Artists Management
PHONE 818-377-7750
RECENT CREDITS   Headspace - Confession - Prime - Call
Me: The Rise and Fall of Heidi Fleiss -
Harvard Man

LAWRENCE SHRAGGE
PHONE 818-382-3300
RECENT CREDITS   Frontline - The Wrong Guy - The
Assistant - The Christmas Blessing -
Merlin's Apprentice

CARLO SILIOTTO
c/o Soundtrack Music Associates
PHONE 818-382-3300
RECENT CREDITS   Nomad - The Punisher - Fluke

ALAN SILVESTRI
c/o Gorfaine/Schwartz Agency
PHONE 818-260-8500
RECENT CREDITS   The Wild - The Polar Express - Van
Helsing - Something's Gotta Give -
Tomb Raider 2

MIKE SIMPSON
c/o Kraft-Engel Management
PHONE 818-380-1918
RECENT CREDITS   Fight Club - Saving Silverman - Road
Trip

MICHAEL SKLOFF
c/o Gorfaine/Schwartz Agency
PHONE 818-260-8500
RECENT CREDITS   Just Looking - Bob Patterson - Jesse -
Holding the Baby - Friends

*CEZARY SKUBISZEWSKI
c/o Evolution Music Partners
PHONE 310-623-3388
RECENT CREDITS   Hating Alison Ashley - The Rage in
Placid Lake - Black and White

BC SMITH
c/o Soundtrack Music Associates
PHONE 818-382-3300
RECENT CREDITS   Kids in America - Standing Still - United
States of Leland - Edge of America

STANLEY A. SMITH
c/o Gorfaine/Schwartz Agency
PHONE 818-260-8500
RECENT CREDITS   The Gospel - Constellation - Hustle and
Heat - Love and a Bullet - The Bernie
Mac Show

COMPOSERS

NEIL SMOLAR
c/o The Kaufman Agency
PHONE 818-506-6013
RECENT CREDITS   Varian's War - The Boys of St. Vincent - Dieppe - Captive Heart: The James Mink Story - A Question of Privilege

MARK SNOW
c/o Gorfaine/Schwartz Agency
PHONE 818-260-8500
RECENT CREDITS   The X-Files (Feature) - Disturbing Behavior - Stranger in My House - One Tree Hill - Smallville

*SOLARFUNK STUDIOS
1402 Veteran Ave., Ste. B
Los Angeles, CA 90024
PHONE 661-645-8072
FAX 310-478-1528
EMAIL .mikeraznick@gmail.com
WEB SITE . . . . .www.solarfunk.com
RECENT CREDITS   TV: First 48 (A&E) - Dead Tenants (TLC); Film: Cacerina (Yukio Ogata) - Red Letters (Erik Ryerson) - Crosswalk (Inkee Shinn) - Josephine's Medicine (Samuel M. Littenberg-Weisberg) - Silence (Dan Bogosian) - Stop at the Greenlight (Dennis Chang) - I Want You Lucy (Elliott Breedon)
COMMENTS   Specializing in electronic, orchestral and ambient music composition; Custom sound creation for film and TV
Mike Raznick . . . . .Principal

ERIC SPEIER
c/o First Artists Management
PHONE 818-377-7750
RECENT CREDITS   Goldfish - The Mullets - The Pitts - Complete Savages

*FRANKIE BLUE SPOSATO
c/o Soundtrack Music Associates
PHONE 818-382-3300
RECENT CREDITS   How the Garcia Girls Spent Their Summer - Jackson - Crazy/Beautiful - Venus Rising

DOUGLAS ROMAYNE STEVENS
c/o The Agency Group Ltd.
PHONE 310-385-2800
RECENT CREDITS   Buffy the Vampire Slayer - Angel - Miracles - The Skulls 2&3

JAN STEVENS
c/o Gorfaine/Schwartz Agency
PHONE 818-260-8500
RECENT CREDITS   A State of Mind - Scrubs

DAVE STEWART
c/o Gorfaine/Schwartz Agency
PHONE 818-260-8500
RECENT CREDITS   Alfie - Cookie's Fortune - Grace of My Heart - Beautiful Girls - The Ref

FRANK STRANGIO
c/o The Kaufman Agency
PHONE 818-506-6013
RECENT CREDITS   Paradise Found - Power Rangers Ninja Storm - Dalkeith - Young Blades - Snowy River: The McGregor Saga

*STUART KOLLMORGEN
c/o The Kaufman Agency
PHONE 818-506-6013

*JEFF SUDAKIN
c/o Greenspan Artist Management
PHONE 310-289-3990
RECENT CREDITS   The Grubbs - Off Centre - Grounded for Life - Normal, Ohio

MARK SUOZZO
c/o The Kaufman Agency
PHONE 818-506-6013
RECENT CREDITS   Shelter Dogs - American Splendor - Metropolitan - The Last Days of Disco - Barcelona

*STANISLAS SYREWICZ
c/o The Agency Group Ltd.
PHONE 310-385-2800
RECENT CREDITS   Walk Through the Woods - Strictly Sinatra - The Clandestine Marriage - True Blue

*MICHAEL TAVERA
c/o First Artists Management
PHONE 818-377-7750
RECENT CREDITS   On Native Soil - The Fix - Lilo & Stitch

*STEPHEN JAMES TAYLOR
c/o Soundtrack Music Associates
PHONE 818-382-3300
RECENT CREDITS   The Adventures of Br'er Rabbit - Mickey's Twice Upon A Christmas - 10,0000 Black Men Named George - Teacher's Pet - Mouseworks

NIC. TENBROEK
c/o Marks Management
PHONE 805-882-1116
RECENT CREDITS   The Moguls - Who's the Man - American Ninja IV - Spinning Out of Control

JEANINE TESORI
c/o Creative Artists Agency
PHONE 310-288-4545
RECENT CREDITS   Thoroughly Modern Millie - Caroline or Change - Twelfth Night - Mulan II - Lilo & Stitch 2

KEVIN THORNE
c/o The Kaufman Agency
PHONE 818-506-6013
RECENT CREDITS   Love Comes Softly - Superman 2 - HELP - Mary, Mother of Jesus - Return to Lonesome Dove

*MARTIN TILLMAN
c/o First Artists Management
PHONE 818-377-7750
RECENT CREDITS   The Ring 1&2 - Admissions

COMPOSERS

*PINAR TOPRAK
c/o First Artists Management
PHONE 818-377-7750
RECENT CREDITS   Ninety-Nine Nights (Vldeo Game) -
When All Else Fails - Headbreaker -
Hold the Rice

DAVID TORN
c/o Evolution Music Partners
PHONE 310-623-3388
RECENT CREDITS   Friday Night Lights - The Order

COLIN TOWNS
c/o The Kaufman Agency
PHONE 818-506-6013
RECENT CREDITS   D.H. Lawrence's Sons and Lovers -
Vampire's Kiss - The Puppet Masters -
Angelina Ballerina - The Beatrix Potter
Stories

ERNEST TROOST
c/o First Artists Management
PHONE 818-377-7750
RECENT CREDITS   The Creature of Sunny Side Up Trailer
Park - Fallen Angel - Wilder Days -
Martin and Lewis - A Lesson Before
Dying - Amy and Isabelle

TIM TRUMAN
c/o Soundtrack Music Associates
PHONE 818-382-3300
RECENT CREDITS   Inferno - Angel's Dance - Boogie Boy -
Charmed - Stargate SG-1

JONATHAN TUNICK
c/o The Kaufman Agency
PHONE 818-506-6013
RECENT CREDITS   The Last Good Time - The Birdcage -
Reds - Endless Love - The Fantasticks

BRIAN TYLER
c/o Gorfaine/Schwartz Agency
PHONE 818-260-8500
RECENT CREDITS   The Greatest Game Ever Played -
Constantine - Paparazzi - Final Cut -
Godsend

*CHRISTOPHER TYNG
c/o Soundtrack Music Associates
PHONE 818-382-3300
RECENT CREDITS   Bookies - The Bumblebee Flies Anyway -
Attack of the 5'2" Women - The O.C. -
Futurama

NERIDA TYSON-CHEW
c/o Soundtrack Music Associates
PHONE 818-382-3300
RECENT CREDITS   Anacondas: Search for the Wild Orchid
- Visitors - Crocodile Hunter: Collision
Course

JOHN VAN TONGREN
c/o First Artists Management
PHONE 818-377-7750
RECENT CREDITS   Wanted - Twitches - Empire - Miss
Congeniality 2 - Jesus the Driver

DAVID VANACORE
c/o First Artists Management
PHONE 818-377-7750
RECENT CREDITS   The Apprentice: Martha Stewart - The
Contender - The Apprentice - Survivor -
Temptation Island

BEN VAUGHN
c/o Creative Artists Agency
PHONE 310-288-4545
RECENT CREDITS   Psycho Beach Party - The Independent -
Off Center - Inside Schwartz - That 70's
Show

JAMES L. VENABLE
c/o Kraft-Engel Management
PHONE 818-380-1918
RECENT CREDITS   Venom - Deuce Bigalow: European
Gigolo - Scary Movie 3 - Jersey Girl -
Eurotrip - Jay and Silent Bob Strike Back

VISIONSOUND
13547 Ventura Blvd., Ste. 110
Sherman Oaks, CA 91423
PHONE 818-786-4800
EMAIL . . . . .info@visionsound.com
WEB SITE . . . . .www.visionsound.com
RECENT CREDITS   Powershift (PBS)
COMMENTS   Specializes in 5.1 composition and syn-
thesis for TV, Film and DVD

Benjamin Dowling . . . . .Composer/Producer
Kit Thomas . . . . .Producer

JOSEPH VITARELLI
c/o Creative Artists Agency
PHONE 310-288-4545
RECENT CREDITS   My Architect - And Starring Pancho Villa
as Himself - Nobody's Baby - She's So
Lovely - The Substance of Fire

W.G. SNUFFY WALDEN
c/o Gorfaine/Schwartz Agency
PHONE 818-260-8500
RECENT CREDITS   Homage - Leaving Normal - Huff - The
West Wing - The George Lopez Show

SHIRLEY WALKER
c/o First Artists Management
PHONE 818-377-7750
RECENT CREDITS   Final Destination 1-3 - Willard -
Turbulence - Mad About You

BENNIE WALLACE
c/o The Agency Group Ltd.
PHONE 310-385-2800
RECENT CREDITS   The Hoop Life - White Men Can't Jump -
Blaze - Bull Durham - Little Surprises

MICHAEL WANDMACHER
c/o Evolution Music Partners
PHONE 310-623-3388
RECENT CREDITS   Over the Hedge - Night Stalker -
Madagascar (Video Game) - Cry Wolf -
From Justin to Kelly

COMPOSERS

NATHAN WANG
c/o Soundtrack Music Associates
PHONE 818-382-3300
RECENT CREDITS   Tom & Jerry: The Fast and The Furry - Reefer Madness - Charlie's War - The Last Days - An American Family

*STEPHEN WARBECK
c/o Soundtrack Music Associates
PHONE 818-382-3300
RECENT CREDITS   MickyBo & Me - Proof - Quills - Billy Elliot - Shakespeare In Love

CHRISTOPHER WARD
c/o Soundtrack Music Associates
PHONE 818-382-3300
RECENT CREDITS   Walk the Line - From the Earth to the Moon: Apollo 1 - Flight of the Phoenix

*MERVYN WARREN
c/o Soundtrack Music Associates
PHONE 818-382-3300
RECENT CREDITS   Honey - The Wedding Planner - A Walk to Remember - Marci X

MARK WATTERS
c/o Gorfaine/Schwartz Agency
PHONE 818-260-8500
RECENT CREDITS   Dinotopia: Quest for the Ruby Sunstone - Doug's First Movie - The Pebble and the Penguin - All Dogs Go to Heaven 2

*CRAIG WEDREN
c/o Soundtrack Music Associates
PHONE 818-382-3300
RECENT CREDITS   P.S. - School of Rock - Laurel Canyon - Roger Dodger - Wet Hot American Summer

WENDY AND LISA
c/o First Artists Management
PHONE 818-377-7750
RECENT CREDITS   Cavedweller - Juwanna Mann - Soul Food - Hav Plenty - Dangerous Minds

MICHAEL WHALEN
c/o The Kaufman Agency
PHONE 818-506-6013
RECENT CREDITS   The Shape of Life - Slavery and the Making of America - The Lost Liners - Inside the Space Station - Chasing Destiny

BILLY WHITE ACRE
c/o The Agency Group Ltd.
PHONE 310-385-2800
RECENT CREDITS   Love & Sex - Cookers - Noon Blue Apples - Beyond the City Limits - Denial

ALAN WILLIAMS
c/o The Kaufman Agency
PHONE 818-506-6013
RECENT CREDITS   The Princess and the Pea - Kilimanjaro: To the Roof of Africa - Amazon - Crab Orchard - Island of the Sharks

DAVID WILLIAMS
c/o Soundtrack Music Associates
PHONE 818-382-3300
WEB SITE . . . . .www.davidwilliamsmusic.com
RECENT CREDITS   Planet Ibsen - Manticore - The Benedict Arnold Story - LA Law: Stay of Execution - Glimpse of Hell

JOHN WILLIAMS
c/o Gorfaine/Schwartz Agency
PHONE 818-260-8500
RECENT CREDITS   Memoirs of a Geisha - War of the Worlds - Star Wars Episode 3: Revenge of the Sith - Terminal - Harry Potter and the Prisoner of Azkaban

JOSEPH STANLEY WILLIAMS
c/o Gorfaine/Schwartz Agency
PHONE 818-260-8500
RECENT CREDITS   Miracles - Roswell - Felicity

PATRICK WILLIAMS
c/o Gorfaine/Schwartz Agency
PHONE 818-260-8500
RECENT CREDITS   Julian Po - That Old Feeling - The Grass Harp - Cry Baby - Monk

NANCY WILSON
c/o Creative Artists Agency
PHONE 310-288-4545
RECENT CREDITS   Vanilla Sky - Almost Famous - Jerry Maguire - Say Anything

DEBBIE WISEMAN
c/o Kraft-Engel Management
PHONE 818-380-1918
RECENT CREDITS   Arsene Lupin - Wilde - Tom and Viv - Tom's Midnight Garden

PETER WOLF
c/o Evolution Music Partners
PHONE 310-623-3388
RECENT CREDITS   Nutcracker & Mouse King - Weekend at Bernie's 2 - Neverending Story 3 - To Err Is a Male Thing

RICHARD WOLF
c/o Gorfaine/Schwartz Agency
PHONE 818-260-8500
RECENT CREDITS   Three Kings - Presumed Innocent - King of the Hill - The Sharon Osbourne Show - One Life to Live

MICHAEL WOLFF
c/o Evolution Music Partners
PHONE 310-623-3388
RECENT CREDITS   The Bitiminous Coal Queen Pageant - Made Up - The Tic Code - Who's the Man? - Dark Angel

*LYLE WORKMAN
c/o First Artists Management
PHONE 818-377-7750
RECENT CREDITS   The 40 Year Old Virgin - Woman at the Beach - Made

COMPOSERS

ALEX WURMAN
c/o Evolution Music Partners
PHONE 310-623-3388
RECENT CREDITS　　　　　March of the Penguins - A Lot Like Love -
Anchorman: The Legend of Ron
Burgandy - Criminal

*WYCLEF
c/o The Agency Group Ltd.
PHONE 310-385-2800
RECENT CREDITS　　　　　7eventy 5ive - Rock the Paint - The
Agronomist - Shottas - Love Jones

DAVE WYNDORFF
c/o Creative Artists Agency
PHONE 310-288-4545
RECENT CREDITS　　　　　Torque

GABRIEL YARED
c/o Evolution Music Partners
PHONE 310-623-3388
RECENT CREDITS　　　　　Breaking and Entering - Decameron -
Shall We Dance? - Cold Mountain

CHRISTOPHER YOUNG
c/o First Artists Management
PHONE 818-377-7750
RECENT CREDITS　　　　　Lucky You - The Exorcism of Emily Rose -
Beauty Shop - Unfinished Life - The
Hurricane - Exorcist: The Beginning

MARCELO ZARVOS
c/o Gorfaine/Schwartz Agency
PHONE 818-260-8500
RECENT CREDITS　　　　　Four Lane Highway - The Race - The
Door in the Floor - The Mudge Boy -
Kissing Jessica Stein

AARON ZIGMAN
c/o Kraft-Engel Management
PHONE 818-380-1918
RECENT CREDITS　　　　　Dying for Dolly - My Friend Flicka -
Alpha Dog - The Notebook - John Q. -
Raise Your Voice

HANS ZIMMER
c/o Gorfaine/Schwartz Agency
PHONE 818-260-8500
RECENT CREDITS　　　　　The Da Vinci Code - Pirates of the
Caribbean 2 - Madagascar - The Ring 2
- Batman Begins

DAVID ZIPPEL
c/o Kraft-Engel Management
PHONE 818-380-1918
RECENT CREDITS　　　　　Hercules - Mulan - City of Angels

COMPOSERS

WORKSHEET

DATE	PROJECT	CONTACT	NOTES

SECTION D

MUSIC PUBLISHERS

Asterisks (*) next to companies denote new listings.

5TH AVE. MEDIA
60 Madison Ave., Ste. 1026
New York, NY 10010
PHONE 212-691-5630
FAX 212-645-5038
EMAIL . . . . .bruce@thefirm.com
SECOND EMAIL . . . . .jeff@thefirm.com
WEB SITE . . . . .www.thefirm.com
ARTIST ROSTER   Sly & Robbie - Freddie McGregor -
                       Bernard Purdie - Mick Taylor - Isreal
                       Vibration - Marty Balin
GENRES   All Genres
SUBMISSION POLICY   Send SASE for return of materials
COMMENTS   Producer

Bruce Colfin . . . . .President
Jeffrey Jacobson . . . . .VP

*"A" SIDE MUSIC LLC
133 W. 25th St., 5th Fl.
New York, NY 10001-7287
PHONE 212-459-2996/212-683-8775
FAX 212-656-1767/212-414-0525
EMAIL . . . . .info@asidemusic.com
WEB SITE . . . . .www.asidemusic.com
GENRES   All Genres

Dan Coleman . . . . .Partner
Bob Donnelly . . . . .Partner

AFFILIATED PUBLISHING, INC. (API)
1508 South St.
Nashville, TN 37212
PHONE 615-291-5007
FAX 615-291-5008
EMAIL . . . . .apiimage@mindspring.com
GENRES   Country - Pop - Roots
SUBMISSION POLICY   No unsolicited submissions
COMMENTS   API is a group of publishing companies

Johnny Slate . . . . .President
Janet Slate . . . . .VP
Wyatt Easterling . . . . .Creative Director

AIR DELUXE MUSIC GROUP
23 Music Square East, Ste. 301
Nashville, TN 37203-4346
PHONE 615-726-1204
EMAIL . . . . .bob@airdeluxemusic.com
WEB SITE .www.airdeluxemusic.com
GENRES   Blues - Country - Pop - R&B

Bob Berg . . . . .President
Gail Lund . . . . .Assistant

ARC MUSIC GROUP
254 W. 54th St., 13th Fl.
New York, NY 10019-5516
PHONE 212-246-3333
FAX 212-262-6299
EMAIL . . . . .info@arcmusic.com
WEB SITE . . . . .www.arcmusic.com
GENRES   All Genres
COMMENTS   Administers and represents the Jewel
                       Music, Conrad, Sunflower and Regent
                       catalogues worldwide; Arc Music West:
                       150 Camino Seco, Ste. 103A, Tucson,
                       AZ 85710

Kenneth Higney . . . . .VP, Copyright Licensing
Jim Leavitt . . . . .Director, Catalog Exploitation & Licensing

ARHOOLIE PRODUCTIONS, INC.
10341 San Pablo Ave.
El Cerrito, CA 94530
PHONE 510-525-7471
FAX 510-525-1204
EMAIL . . . . .info@arhoolie.com
WEB SITE . . . . .www.arhoolie.com
GENRES   Blues - Christian - Country - Folk -
                       Gospel - Latin - Roots - World
COMMENTS   Record Company; Affiliated with
                       Tradition Music Co.

Chris Strachwitz . . . . .President
Tom Diamant . . . . .Label Manager/Publicity
Annie Johnston . . . . .Office Manager

ASH STREET MUSIC
1508 16th Ave. South
Nashville, TN 37212
PHONE 615-383-8775/818-720-5692
FAX 615-269-4138
EMAIL . . . . .june@ashstreetmusic.com
ARTIST ROSTER   Irene Kelly - Bob Rea
GENRES   Bluegrass - Blues - Country - Pop - Roots
SUBMISSION POLICY   No unsolicited submissions
COMMENTS   West Coast office: 5719 Beck Ave.,
                       North Hollywood, CA 91601

June McHugh CIC
Tom Gould . . . . .President
Greg Gallo . . . . .Creative
Antionette Olesen . . . . .Creative
Jimmy Yessian . . . . .Creative (West Coast)
Bruce Burch . . . . .Creative Consultant
Robyn Lail . . . . .Office Administrator
Alex Heddle . . . . .Intern

GENE AUTRY MUSIC GROUP
4383 Colfax Ave.
Studio City, CA 91604
PHONE 818-752-7770
FAX 818-752-7779
EMAIL . . . . .kbuhlman@autry.com
WEB SITE . . . . .www.autry.com
GENRES   Country
SUBMISSION POLICY   Vintage country catalog; Does not
                       accept new songs
COMMENTS   Gene Autry's Western Music Publishing
                       Company; Golden West Melodies, Inc.;
                       Melody Ranch Music Company, Inc.;
                       Ridgeway Music Company; Gene Autry
                       Music Company

Karla Buhlman . . . . .Director

BACHARACH MUSIC
10585 Santa Monica Blvd., 3rd Fl.
Los Angeles, CA 90025-4950
PHONE 310-441-8699
FAX 310-470-3232
EMAIL . . . . .bob_fead@warnerchappell.com
COMMENTS   Administers Burt Bacharach's catalog

Bob Fead . . . . .President
Janis Schifter . . . . .Assistant

*BASS KING MUSIC

13012 Haas Ave.
Gardena, CA 90249
PHONE 323-360-5335
FAX 310-327-7587
EMAIL . . . . .dfw329@aol.com
GENRES   Gospel - Jazz - Latin - R&B - Rap/Hip-
                          Hop - Reggae
SUBMISSION POLICY   Accepts unsolicited materials; Submit CD
                          with photo and bio

Charles Weathersby . . . . .A&R Director

BEVERLYFAX MUSIC

c/o CBS
7800 Beverly Blvd., Mezzanine Level
Los Angeles, CA 90036-2165
PHONE 323-575-2345/212-846-3376
FAX 323-575-2525/212-846-1903
WEB SITE . . . . .www.cbs.com
GENRES   Alternative - Blues - Christian - Classical
                          - Country - Electronica - Folk - Gospel -
                          Jazz - Latin - New Age - Pop - R&B -
                          Rap/Hip-Hop - Reggae - Rock - Roots -
                          Urban - World
SUBMISSION POLICY   Does not accept unsolicited submissions
COMMENTS   East Coast office: 1515 Broadway, New
                          York, NY 10036

Roni Mueller . . . . .Sr. VP, Business Affairs
Cindy Badell-Slaughter . . . . .Director, Music Operations
Karen Takata . . . . .Director, Production Music
Aldrex G.M. Caparros . . . . .Music Administrator
Joan Mateo . . . . .Music Administrator
Bob Tsai . . . . .Music Administrator

BICYCLE MUSIC COMPANY

449 S. Beverly Dr., Ste. 300
Beverly Hills, CA 90212
PHONE 310-286-6600
FAX 310-286-6622
EMAIL .info@bicyclemusic.com
WEB SITE . . . . .www.bicyclemusic.com
GENRES   Alternative - Blues - Christian - Classical
                          - Country - Electronica - Folk - Gospel -
                          Jazz - Latin - New Age - Pop - R&B -
                          Rap/Hip-Hop - Reggae - Rock - Roots -
                          Urban - World

Jon Rosner . . . . .Co-President
Jake Wisely . . . . .Co-President

BIG FISH MUSIC PUBLISHING GROUP

11927 Magnolia Blvd., Ste. 3
North Hollywood, CA 91607
PHONE 818-984-0377
FAX 818-984-0377
GENRES   Adult Contemporary - Alternative - Blues
                          - Christian - Classical - Country -
                          Electronica - Folk - Gospel - Jazz - Latin
                          - New Age - Pop - R&B - Reggae - Rock
                          - Roots - Urban - World
SUBMISSION POLICY   Write first for permission to submit new
                          material; No calls
COMMENTS   Two different publishing companies: Big
                          Fish Music (BMI) and California Sun
                          Music (ASCAP)

Chuck Tennin . . . . .President/CEO
Laura Sprague .Music Manager
Gary Black . . . . .Producer
Darryl Harrelson . . . . .Producer

BLACK ROSE PRODUCTIONS, INC.

409 Rte. 112
Port Jefferson Station, NY 11776
PHONE 631-928-0660
EMAIL . . . . .titobatista@blackroseproductions.com
WEB SITE . . . . .www.blackroseproductions.com
SECOND WEB SITE . . . . .www.titobatista.com
ARTIST ROSTER   Sabrina Asher - Slava - Raymond Parker
                          - Split Leaf - U-Turn - Roger Evans -
                          Doug Gordon Band
GENRES   Country - Electronica - Jazz - Pop - R&B
                          - Reggae - Rock
COMMENTS   Second office: 15 Gloria Lane, Fairfield,
                          NJ 97994

Tito Batista . . . . .President
Thomas Anderer . . . . .Director, A&R
Josh Freeman . . . . .A&R
Daniel Oliverio . . . . .A&R
Brett Aaron .Business Affairs
Chris Hand . . . . .Web Designer
Barbera Bauer . . . . .Office Manager

BLUE JACKEL ENTERTAINMENT

PO Box 87
Huntington, NY 11743
PHONE 516-624-6095
FAX 516-624-6096
EMAIL . . . . .bluejackel@earthlink.net
SECOND EMAIL . . . . .info@bluejackel.com
WEB SITE . . . . .www.bluejackel.com
GENRES   Folk - Jazz - Latin - Roots - World
SUBMISSION POLICY   Send to Jack O'Neil
COMMENTS   Record Company; Producer

Jack O'Neil . . . . .Owner

HELENE BLUE MUSIQUE LTD.

421 Seventh Ave., Ste. 901
New York, NY 10001
PHONE 212-724-5900
FAX 212-564-3113
EMAIL . . . . .helene@helenebluemusic.com
GENRES   Alternative - Blues - Christian - Classical
                          - Country - Electronica - Folk - Gospel -
                          Jazz - Latin - New Age - Pop - R&B -
                          Rap/Hip-Hop - Reggae - Rock - Roots -
                          Urban - World

Helene Blue . . . . .Owner (helene@helenebluemusic.com)
Susan Berlowitz . . . . . .Creative Director (susan@helenebluemusic.com)

BLUE WAVE RECORDS

3221 Perryville Rd.
Baldwinsville, NY 13027
PHONE 315-638-4286
FAX 315-635-4757
EMAIL .bluewave@localnet.com
WEB SITE . . . . .www.bluewaverecords.com
ARTIST ROSTER   Downchild Blues Band - Kim Simmons
                          - Jony James Blues Band - Kim Lembo -
                          The Kingsnakes - Jimmy Cavallo
GENRES   Blues
SUBMISSION POLICY   Accepts unsolicited material
COMMENTS   Record Company; Licensing

Greg Spencer . . . . .President

BMG FILM & TELEVISION MUSIC (LOS ANGELES)
8750 Wilshire Blvd., 2nd Fl.
Beverly Hills, CA 90211-2313
PHONE 310-358-4731
FAX 310-358-4733
EMAIL . . . . .firstname.lastname@bmg.com
WEB SITE . . . . .www.bmgmusicsearch.com
GENRES   Alternative - Blues - Christian - Classical
     - Country - Electronica - Folk - Gospel -
     Jazz - Latin - New Age - Pop - R&B -
     Rap/Hip-Hop - Reggae - Rock - Roots -
     Urban - World

Ron Broitman . . . . .VP, Film & TV (310-358-4747)
Michelle Belcher . . . . .Sr. Director, Film (310-358-4726)
Wendy Christiansen . . . . .Sr. Director, Film (310-358-4710)
Stacy Wallen-McCarthy . . . . .Director, Film (310-358-4760)
Renee Dabbah . . . . .Director, TV (310-358-4748)
Christian Wiseman . . . . . .Manager, TV & Videogames (310-358-4770)
Lauren Haber . . . . .Administrative Assistant (310-358-4731)

BMG MUSIC PUBLISHING (LOS ANGELES)
8750 Wilshire Blvd.
Beverly Hills, CA 90211
PHONE 310-358-4700
FAX 310-358-4742
EMAIL . . . . .firstname.lastname@bmg.com
WEB SITE . . . . .www.bmgmusicsearch.com
GENRES   Alternative - Blues - Christian - Classical
     - Country - Electronica - Folk - Gospel -
     Jazz - Latin - New Age - Pop - R&B -
     Rap/Hip-Hop - Reggae - Rock - Roots -
     Urban - World

Scott Francis . . . . .President
Ron Broitman . . . . .VP, Film & TV Music
Monti Olson . . . . .VP, A&R
Derrick Thompson . . . . .VP, A&R (Urban)

BMG MUSIC PUBLISHING (NASHVILLE)
1600 Division St., Ste. 225
Nashville, TN 37203
PHONE 615-687-5800
FAX 615-687-5839
EMAIL . . . . .firstname.lastname@bmge.com
WEB SITE . . . . .www.bmgmusicsearch.com
GENRES   Country - Pop

Ron Stuve . . . . .VP
Michelle Berlin . . . . .A&R Representative
Martha Irwin . . . . .A&R Representative
Aaron Rathbone . . . . .A&R Representative
Karen Conrad . . . . .Consultant

BMG MUSIC PUBLISHING (NEW YORK)
245 Fifth Ave., 8th Fl.
New York, NY 10016
PHONE 212-930-4000
FAX 212-930-4263
EMAIL . . . . .firstname.lastname@bmg.com
WEB SITE . . . . .www.bmgmusicsearch.com
GENRES   All Genres
SUBMISSION POLICY   No unsolicited material

Nicholas Firth . . . . .Chairman/CEO
Andrew Jenkins   President, BMG Music Publishing International (London)
Laurent Hubert .Executive VP/COO
Carol Lipkin . . . . .CFO
Jennifer L. Press . . . . .Director, Communications

BOK MUSIC
PO Box 8339
Calabasas, CA 91372-8339
PHONE 818-222-9969
FAX 818-222-0853
EMAIL .monica@bokmusic.com
WEB SITE . . . . .www.bokmusic.com
GENRES   All Genres
SUBMISSION POLICY   Submissions on CD only with lyric sheets
     included

Monica Benson . . . . .President
Dany O'Bryan . . . . .Assistant

BOOSEY & HAWKES
35 E. 21st St., 9th Fl.
New York, NY 10010-6212
PHONE 212-358-5300
FAX 212-358-5301
EMAIL .info.ny@boosey.com
WEB SITE . . . . .www.boosey.com
GENRES   Classical
COMMENTS   Orchestral, opera, chorus, wind ensem-
     bles and chamber ensembles

Jenny Bilfield . . . . .President
Mark Ostrow . . . . .VP, Business Affairs
Helane Anderson . . . . .Promotion Manager
Steven Swartz .Publicity Manager
Kenneth Krasner . . . . .Synchronization Manager

BRASSHEART MUSIC
256 S. Robertson Blvd., Ste. 2288
Beverly Hills, CA 90211-2898
PHONE 323-932-0534
FAX 323-937-6884
EMAIL . . . . .brassheartmusic@aol.com
WEB SITE . . . . .www.brassheartmusic.com
SECOND WEB SITE . . . . .www.dreamaworld.com
GENRES   Alternative - Children's - Christian -
     Country - Gospel - Jazz - Latin - New
     Age - Pop - R&B - Reggae - Rock -
     Urban - World
SUBMISSION POLICY   No unsolicited submissons
COMMENTS   Record Label: Dream A World;
     Licensing; Partial client list: CBS, NBC,
     ABC, Universal, Paramount, Tristar,
     Spelling, 20th Century Fox, HBO,
     Showtime, Lifetime

Bunny Hull . . . . .Owner

BRENTWOOD-BENSON MUSIC PUBLISHING
741 Coolsprings Blvd.
Franklin, TN 37067-2697
PHONE 615-261-3300
FAX 615-261-3384
WEB SITE . . . . .www.brentwood-bensonmusic.com
GENRES   Christian - Country - Gospel
SUBMISSION POLICY   No unsolicited materials; Industry referral
     only

Dale Mathews . . . . .President (dmathews@brentwoodbenson.com)
Marty Wheeler . . . . . . .VP, Creative (mwheeler@brentwoodbenson.com)
Ross Asher . . . . .Director, A&R (rasher@brentwoodbenson.com)
Holly Zabka . . . . . . .Creative Director (hzabka@brentwoodbenson.com)

BUG MUSIC (LOS ANGELES)
7750 Sunset Blvd.
Los Angeles, CA 90046
PHONE 323-969-0988
FAX 323-969-0968
EMAIL .buginfo@bugmusic.com
SECOND EMAIL . . . . .See staff list
WEB SITE . . . . .www.bugmusic.com
GENRES   Alternative - Blues - Christian - Classical
                                 - Country - Electronica - Folk - Gospel -
                                 Jazz - Latin - New Age - Pop - R&B -
                                 Rap/Hip-Hop - Reggae - Rock - Roots -
                                 Urban - World

Dan Bourgoise . . . . .Chairman/CEO (danb@bugmusic.com)
Fred Bourgoise . . . . .President (fredbo@bugmusic.com)
David Hirshland . . . . .Executive VP (dhirsh@bugmusic.com)
Steve Toland . . . . .VP/General Manager (stevet@bugmusic.com)
Beth Allison . . . . .VP, Finance (beth@bugmusic.com)
Eddie Gomez . . . . .VP, Creative (x223, eddieg@bugmusic.com)
Jamie Purpora . . . . .VP, Administration (jamie@bugmusic.com)
Elizabeth Herndon . . . . .Director, Film & TV Licensing
                                       (elizabeth@bugmusic.com)
Pamela Lillig . . . . .Sr. Director, Business Affairs/Film & TV
                                       (x208, pamela@bugmusic.com)
Mara Schwartz . .Director, Film, TV & New Media (mara@bugmusic.com)
Kyle Staggs . . . .Director, Business & Legal Affairs (kyle@bugmusic.com)
Sasha Ross . . . . .Creative Manager, Film & TV (sasha@bugmusic.com)
Diane Kornarens . . . . .Manager, Business & Legal Affairs
                                       (diane@bugmusic.com)
Crystal Fallon . . . . .Assistant Manager, Finance (crystal@bugmusic.com)
Nissa Pedraza . . . . .Creative Assistant (nissa@bugmusic.com)

BUG MUSIC (NASHVILLE)
1910 Acklen Ave.
Nashville, TN 37212
PHONE 615-279-0180
FAX 615-279-0184
EMAIL .buginfo@bugmusic.com
SECOND EMAIL . . . . .firstnamelastinitial@bugmusic.com
WEB SITE . . . . .www.bugmusic.com
GENRES   Alternative - Blues - Christian - Classical
                                 - Country - Electronica - Folk - Gospel -
                                 Jazz - Latin - New Age - Pop - R&B -
                                 Rap/Hip-Hop - Reggae - Rock - Roots -
                                 Urban - World

Kim Hylick . . . . .General Manager
Dave Durocher . . . . .VP
John Allen . . . . .Creative Director
Drew Hale . . . . .Creative Manager

BUG MUSIC (NEW YORK)
347 W. 36th St., Ste. 1203
New York, NY 10018
PHONE 212-643-0925
FAX 212-643-0897
EMAIL .buginfo@bugmusic.com
SECOND EMAIL . . . . .firstnamelastinitial@bugmusic.com
WEB SITE . . . . .www.bugmusic.com
GENRES   Alternative - Blues - Christian - Classical
                                 - Country - Electronica - Folk - Gospel -
                                 Jazz - Latin - New Age - Pop - R&B -
                                 Rap/Hip-Hop - Reggae - Rock - Roots -
                                 Urban - World

Gary Velletri . . . . .Sr. VP
William Daniels . . . . .Liaison Manager/Creative Assistant

BUGLE MUSIC
14724 Ventura Blvd., PH
Sherman Oaks, CA 91403
PHONE 323-512-4080
FAX 323-512-4089
EMAIL . . . . .stevo@ark21.com
GENRES   Country - Pop - Rock - World

Stevo Glendinning . . . . .Sr. VP

CARLIN AMERICA
126 E. 38th St.
New York, NY 10016
PHONE 212-779-7977
FAX 212-779-7920
EMAIL . . . . .sscharf@carlinamerica.com
WEB SITE . . . . .www.carlinamerica.com
GENRES   Alternative - Blues - Christian - Classical
                                 - Country - Electronica - Folk - Gospel -
                                 Jazz - Latin - New Age - Pop - R&B -
                                 Rap/Hip-Hop - Reggae - Rock - Roots -
                                 Urban - World
COMMENTS   Showtunes

Steven Scharf . . . . .Sr. VP, Creative
Sophia Kim . . . . .Assistant

CHERRY LANE MUSIC PUBLISHING (NEW YORK)
6 E. 32nd St., 11th Fl.
New York, NY 10016-5415
PHONE 212-561-3000
FAX 212-683-2040
EMAIL . . . . .firstinitiallastname@cherrylane.com
WEB SITE . . . . .www.cherrylane.com
GENRES   All Genres

Aida Gurwicz . . . . .President
Michael Connelly . . . . .Sr. VP, Business Development
Phil Cialdella . . . . .VP, Administration & Licensing
Richard Stumpf . . . . .VP, Creative Services & Marketing
Keith Hauprich . . . . .Sr. Director, Business & Legal Affairs
Brooke Primont . . . . .Director, Film & TV Music
Christa Shaub . . . . .A&R
Jennifer Balfus . . . . .Creative Services

CHRISTMAS AND HOLIDAY MUSIC
24351 Grass St.
Lake Forest, CA 92630
PHONE 949-859-1615
FAX 949-859-1615
EMAIL . . . . .justinwilde@christmassongs.com
WEB SITE . . . . .www.christmassongs.com
SUBMISSION POLICY   Accepts all unsolicited material

Justin Wilde . . . . .President

CHRYSALIS MUSIC GROUP
8500 Melrose Ave., Ste. 207
Los Angeles, CA 90069-5145
PHONE 310-652-0066
FAX 310-652-5428
WEB SITE . . . . .www.chrysalismusic.co.uk
ARTIST ROSTER   OutKast - Black Rebel Motorcycle Club - Longwave - Black Keys - Velvet Revolver - Ray LaMontagne - Helmet - Daniel Lanois - Joe Henry - Rahsaan Patterson - Jahnta Austin - Roy Ayers
GENRES   All Genres

Kenny MacPherson . . . . .President
Valerie Patton . . . . .Sr. VP, A&R, Urban Music
David Ellman . . . . .VP/General Manager
Dave Ayers . . . . .VP, A&R (NY)
Jeffrey Brabec . . . . .VP, Business Affairs
Scott Cresto . . . . .VP, Film & TV/A&R
Mark Friedman . . . . .VP, Creative Services
James Cerreta . . . . .Sr. Director, A&R
Jessica Hobbs . . . . .Sr. Director, Licensing
Carol King . . . . .Sr. Director, Copyright
David Kawanishi . . . . .Director, Royalties
Jane Ventom . . . . .Director, Licensing
Sara Kapuchinski . . . . .Director, A&R
Kira Williams .A&R Assistant
Patricia Wittmer . . . . .Assistant to Mr. MacPherson

CRC JIANIAN PUBLISHING
1680 Vine St., Ste. 1200
Hollywood, CA 90028
PHONE 323-960-0830
FAX 323-960-0840
EMAIL .info@crcjianian.com
WEB SITE . . . . .www.chinarecords.com
GENRES   World
SUBMISSION POLICY   Email for permission
COMMENTS   Representing the largest catalog of Chinese music from China Record Corporation

Frank Mayor . . . . .CEO
Peter Jansson . . . . .COO

CRITERION
6124 Selma Ave.
Hollywood, CA 90028-6497
PHONE 323-469-2296
FAX 323-962-5751
EMAIL . . . . .criterion_la@earthlink.net
GENRES   All Genres

Michael Goldson . . . . .CEO
Bo Goldson . . . . .President
Stacey Neisig . . . . .Assistant
Delda Sciurba . . . . .Assistant

CRUTCHFIELD MUSIC
1106 17th Ave. South
Nashville, TN 37212-2288
PHONE 615-321-5558
FAX 615-321-5598
GENRES   Adult Contemporary - Alternative - Bluegrass - Blues - Christian - Country - Gospel - Pop - Roots

Jerry Crutchfield . . . . .President
Martin Crutchfield . . . . .VP, A&R
Christy C. Fields . . . . .VP, Administration
Jennifer Yates . . . . .Executive Assistant

CURB MAGNATONE
2630 Elm Hill Pike, Ste. 115
Nashville, TN 37214
PHONE 615-884-8673
FAX 615-884-8676
WEB SITE . . . . .www.curb.com
GENRES   Country

Jeffrey J. Nelson . . . . .Creative Director

CURB PUBLISHING
48 Music Square East
Nashville, TN 37203
PHONE 615-321-5080
FAX 615-742-3152
WEB SITE . . . . .www.curb.com
GENRES   Christian - Country - Pop

Drew Alexander . . . . .Director, Publishing
Portis Tanner . . . . .Publishing Administration

DE WALDEN MUSIC INTERNATIONAL, INC.
11324 Ventura Blvd.
Studio City, CA 91604-3137
PHONE 818-763-6995
FAX 818-763-6997
EMAIL .zigwal@pacbell.net
GENRES   Alternative - Blues - Christian - Classical - Country - Electronica - Folk - Gospel - Jazz - Latin - New Age - Pop - R&B - Rap/Hip-Hop - Reggae - Rock - Roots - Urban - World

Christian de Walden . . . . .President
Lindsay J. Little . . . . .Assistant

DIMENSIONAL MUSIC PUBLISHING
321 S. Beverly Dr., Ste. T
Beverly Hills, CA 90212
PHONE 310-277-7722
FAX 310-277-0828
EMAIL . . . . .bridget@dmusicpublishing.com
WEB SITE . . . . .www.dmusicpublishing.com
ARTIST ROSTER   Jimmy Eat World - Lifehouse - The Sounds
GENRES   All Genres
SUBMISSION POLICY   Does not accept unsolicited material

Bridget O'Gara . . . . .Director, Film & TV
Debra Delshad . . . .Manager, Film & TV (debra@dmusicpublishing.com)

WALT DISNEY MUSIC
500 S. Buena Vista St.
Burbank, CA 91521-6182
PHONE 818-569-3228
FAX 818-569-3358
EMAIL . . . . .firstname.lastname@disney.com
WEB SITE . . . . .www.disney.com
GENRES   Alternative - Blues - Christian - Classical - Country - Electronica - Folk - Gospel - Jazz - Latin - New Age - Pop - R&B - Rap/Hip-Hop - Reggae - Rock - Roots - Urban - World
SUBMISSION POLICY   Request permission to submit; No unsolicited submissions

Julie Enzer . . . . .Sr. VP, Music Publishing
Brian Rawlings . . . . .Sr. VP, Creative
Sandy Hoag . . . . .Assistant to Julie Enzer
Ashley Saunig . . . . .Assistant to Brian Rawlings

EMI MUSIC PUBLISHING (LOS ANGELES)
2700 Colorado Blvd., Ste. 100
Santa Monica, CA 90404-3521
PHONE 310-586-2700/310-586-2740
FAX 310-586-2795/310-586-2758
EMAIL . . . . .losangeles@emimusicpub.com
SECOND EMAIL . . . . . . .firstinitiallastname@emimusicpub.com
WEB SITE .www.emimusicpub.com
GENRES   All Genres

Jody Gerson . . . . .Executive VP/General Manager, Creative
Big Jon Platt . . . . .Sr. VP, Creative
Alan Warner . . . . .Sr. VP, Music Resources & Catalogue Exploitation
Matt Messer . . . . .VP, Creative
Dan McCarroll . . . . .Sr. Director, Creative
Benjamin Groff . . . . . . .Sr. Director, Creative/Writer Development
Summer Zimberg .Creative Manager
Jennifer Wolf . . . . .Manager, Creative Administration
Eliza Smith . . . . .Executive Assistant
Pat Lucas . . . . .Executive VP/General Manager, Film/TV
Alison Whitlin O'Donnell . . . . .VP, Film Soundtracks
Doug James . . . . .VP, EMI Film Soundtracks
Oscar Mazzola . . . . .Manager, Film/TV Music
Tami Lester . . . . .Manager
Jeff Moreno . . . . .Assistant
Ayiko Carmichael . . . . .Assistant
Greg James . . . . .Assistant
Aaron Monty . . . . .Assistant
Brian Sapp . . . . .Assistant

EMI MUSIC PUBLISHING (NEW YORK)
1290 Avenue of the Americas, 42nd Fl.
New York, NY 10104
PHONE 212-492-1288
FAX 212-492-1240
EMAIL . . . . .firstinitiallastname@emimusicpub.com
WEB SITE . . . . .www.emimusicpub.com
GENRES   All Genres
SUBMISSION POLICY   Does not accept unsolicited submissions

Martin Bandier . . . . .Chairman & CEO
Evan Lamberg . . . . .Executive VP, Creative, North America
Brooke Morrow .Sr. VP, International
Kevin Hershey . . . . .VP, Talent Acquisitions & Marketing
Neil Lasher . . . . .VP, Promotion, Marketing & Artist Relations
Debi Wylde . . . . .Sr. Director, Creative/Administration
Jake Ottmann . . . . .Creative Director
Jessica Rivera . . . . .Director, Creative & Acquisitions

ESTEFAN MUSIC PUBLISHER, INC.
420 Jefferson Ave.
Miami Beach, FL 33139
PHONE 305-695-7000
FAX 305-534-5220
WEB SITE . . . . .www.estefan.com
GENRES   Latin - R&B - Rock - Urban

Patricia Wemyss . . . . .Sr. Director, Publishing
Valerie Pozo .Publishing Manager

FAMOUS MUSIC PUBLISHING (LOS ANGELES)
10635 Santa Monica Blvd., Ste. 300
Los Angeles, CA 90025-4900
PHONE 310-441-1300/212-654-7418
FAX 310-441-4729/310-441-4722
EMAIL . . . . .firstname_lastname@paramount.com
WEB SITE . . . . .www.syncsite.com
SECOND WEB SITE . . . . .www.paramount.com
GENRES   Alternative - Blues - Christian - Classical
                           - Country - Electronica - Folk - Gospel -
                           Jazz - Latin - New Age - Pop - R&B -
                           Rap/Hip-Hop - Reggae - Rock - Roots -
                           Urban - World
COMMENTS   East Coast office: 1633 Broadway, 11th
                           Fl., New York, NY 10019, fax: 212-
                           654-4748; Nashville office: 65 Music
                           Square East, Nashville, TN 37203,
                           phone: 615-329-0500, fax: 615-321-
                           4121

Irwin Z. Robinson . . . . .Chairman/CEO (NY)
Ira Jaffe . . . . .President/COO
Kent Klavens . . . . .Sr. VP, Legal & Business Affairs
Stacey Palm .Sr. VP, Film/TV Music
Billy Calloway . . . . .Sr. Creative Director, Urban
Claribell Cuevas-Brasileiro . . .Sr. Creative Director, Latin Music (Miami)
Chad Greer . . . . .Sr. Director, Film/TV Music
Carol Spencer .Sr. Creative Director
Eleanor Antes . . . . .Assistant to Stacey Palm

FANTASY INC.
2600 10th St.
Berkeley, CA 94710
PHONE 510-549-2500
FAX 510-486-2015
EMAIL . . . . .info@fantasyjazz.com
WEB SITE . . . . .www.fantasyjazz.com
GENRES   Blues - Jazz - R&B

Bill Belmont . . . . .No Title

THE FITZGERALD HARTLEY COMPANY
34 N. Palm St., Ste. 100
Ventura, CA 93001
PHONE 805-641-6441
FAX 805-641-6444
WEB SITE . . . . .www.fitzhart.com

Chad Jensen . . . . .Manager

FOREIGN IMPORTED PRODUCTIONS & PUBLISHING
420 Jefferson Ave.
Miami Beach, FL 33139-6503
PHONE 305-695-7000
FAX 305-534-5220
WEB SITE . . . . .www.estefan.com
GENRES   Jazz - Pop - R&B - Rock - Urban

Patricia Wemyss . . . . .Sr. Director, Publishing
Valerie Pozo .Publishing Manager

FOUR JAYS
443 S. San Pedro St., Ste. 304
Los Angeles, CA 90013
PHONE 213-236-9222
FAX 213-614-6801
EMAIL .fourjayscom@earthlink.net
WEB SITE .www.harrywarrenmusic.com
GENRES   Jazz - Pop
COMMENTS   Standards 1926-1960

Julia J. Riva . . . . .President
Jophe Jones-Gaddis . . . . .VP
Robert Walls . . . . .VP

MUSIC PUBLISHERS

FOX MUSIC PUBLISHING
10201 W. Pico Blvd., Bldg. 18
Los Angeles, CA 90035-2625
PHONE 310-369-2541
WEB SITE . . . . www.foxmusic.com
GENRES   Alternative - Blues - Classical - Country -
                    Electronica - Folk - Jazz - Latin - New
                    Age - Pop - R&B - Rap/Hip-Hop -
                    Reggae - Rock - Roots - Urban - World
COMMENTS   Licensing and Clearance

Cathy Merenda . . . . .Executive Director, Administration
Greg Curtis . . . . .Executive Director, Creative
Ted Spellman . . . . .Director, Licensing
Dale Melidosian . . . . .Sr. Counsel
Fran Block . . . . .Manager

LEN FREEDMAN MUSIC, INC.
1482 E. Valley Rd., Ste. 400
Santa Barbara, CA 93108-1200
PHONE 805-966-6999
FAX 805-966-0768
EMAIL . . . . .salterst@aol.com
GENRES   All Genres
SUBMISSION POLICY   No unsolicited material

Len Freedman . . . . .President

GOODNIGHT KISS MUSIC
10153-1/2 Riverside Dr., Ste. 239
Toluca Lake, CA 91602
PHONE 831-479-9993
EMAIL . . . . .hlywdgrl@aol.com
WEB SITE . . . . www.goodnightkiss.com
RECENT SOUNDTRACKS   Good Luck - Road Ends
COMMENTS   Film and TV Soundtracks; Music
                    Coordinator; Music Supervisor; Genre-
                    specific CDs, needle drops, quality
                    access

Janet Fisher . . . . .Owner
Kelie McIver . . . . .Administrative Assistant

GROUND BREAKING MUSIC, INC.
2135 Defoor Hills Rd. NW, Ste. I
Atlanta, GA 30318-2218
PHONE 404-350-1669
FAX 404-350-9044
EMAIL . . . . .gbmpublishing@aol.com
SECOND EMAIL . . . . .information@gbmpublishing.com
WEB SITE . . . . .www.gbmpublishing.com
ARTIST ROSTER   Shamora Crawford - French - Tezz - Li Li
                    - Jason Bowen - Angie Irons - Chrissy
                    Conway - Duve Hummel - Kenny Wray
GENRES   Pop - R&B
SUBMISSION POLICY   No direct submissions; Must be submit-
                    ted by attorney or label

Albert McKissack . . . . .President

*HERE! TUNES
10990 Wilshire Blvd., PH
Los Angeles, CA 90024
PHONE 310-806-4283
FAX 310-806-4268
EMAIL . . . . .info@heretv.com
WEB SITE . . . . .www.heretv.com
GENRES   All Genres

Brian Goldman . . . . .President, A&R & Artist Relations

HARLAN HOWARD SONGS
1902 Wedgewood Ave.
Nashville, TN 37212-3733
PHONE 615-321-9098
FAX 615-327-1748
WEB SITE . . . . .www.harlanhoward.com
ARTIST ROSTER   Lori McKenna - Mary Gauthier
GENRES   Country - Folk

Melanie Howard . . . . .Owner (melanie@harlanhoward.com)
Sara Johnson . . . . . .Administrative Assistant (sara@harlanhoward.com)

IDOL RECORDS
PO Box 720043
Dallas, TX 75372
PHONE 214-321-8890
FAX 214-321-8889
EMAIL . . . . .info@idolrecords.com
WEB SITE .www.idolrecords.com
GENRES   Alternative - Pop - Rock
COMMENTS   Record Company

Erv Karwelis . . . . .President

INSPIRED DISTRIBUTION, LLC
A Division of the Inspired Corporation
103 Eisenhower Pkwy., 2nd Fl.
Roseland, NJ 07068
PHONE 800-738-3747/973-226-1234
FAX 973-226-6696
EMAIL . . . . .inspiredsales@inspiredcorp.com
WEB SITE .www.inspiredcorp.com
GENRES   Children's - Jazz - Latin - New Age -
                    Reggae - Urban
SUBMISSION POLICY   On a per project basis; Submission poli-
                    cy available on Web site
COMMENTS   Distributor, Music Library; Affiliate labels:
                    Compose, Tiffton, Tinkerbell, Peter Pan
                    and Compose Tropico

Steven King . . . . .VP, Music Publishing (sking@inspiredcorp.com)
George Bauman VP, Sales Administration (gbauman@inspiredcorp.com)
Mike Cuthill . . . . .VP, Manufacturing & Fulfillment
                    (mcuthill@inspiredcorp.com)

QUINCY JONES MUSIC
6671 Sunset Blvd., Ste. 1574A
Los Angeles, CA 90028
PHONE 323-957-6601
FAX 323-962-5231
EMAIL . . . . .info@quincyjonesmusic.com
WEB SITE . . . . .www.quincyjonesmusic.com
GENRES   Alternative - Blues - Christian - Classical
                    - Country - Electronica - Folk - Gospel -
                    Jazz - Latin - New Age - Pop - R&B -
                    Rap/Hip-Hop - Reggae - Rock - Roots -
                    Urban - World

Nancy Stern . . . . .VP
Marc Cazorla . . . . .Creative

JUNE STREET ENTERTAINMENT
4111 W. Alameda Ave., Ste. 501
Burbank, CA 91505
PHONE 818-972-1112
FAX 818-972-9011
EMAIL . . . . .reception@junestentertainment.com
WEB SITE . . . . .www.junestentertainment.com
ARTIST ROSTER   Quincy Jones - Mystikal - Jim Croce -
                       Roy Orbison - Paul Oakenfold - Sophie
                       B. Hawkins
GENRES   All Genres
SUBMISSION POLICY   No unsolicited material accepted
COMMENTS   Film, TV and Commercial independent
                       licensing

Art Ford . . . . .President
Brooke Lizotte . . . . .Creative
Lachlan McLean . . . . .Online Catalog Manager

KID GLOVES MUSIC
20106 Via Cellini
Porter Ranch, CA 91326
PHONE 818-700-0292
FAX 818-700-0294
EMAIL . . . . .submissions@kidglovesmusic.com
GENRES   Alternative - Blues - Christian - Classical
                       - Country - Electronica - Folk - Gospel -
                       Jazz - Latin - New Age - Pop - R&B -
                       Rap/Hip-Hop - Reggae - Rock - Roots -
                       Urban - World

Doug Stebleton . . . . .President

KOCH ENTERTAINMENT
740 Broadway, 7th Fl.
New York, NY 10003
PHONE 917-757-9937
FAX 201-221-7917
EMAIL . . . . .michelle.bayer@kochent.com
SECOND EMAIL . . . . .mbayer@sugaroo.com
WEB SITE . . . . .www.kochentertainment.com
SECOND WEB SITE . . . . .www.sugaroo.com
GENRES   Country - R&B - Rap/Hip-Hop - Rock -
                       Urban
SUBMISSION POLICY   No unsolicited material
COMMENTS   Record Company; Distributor

Michael Koch . . . . .CEO
Bob Frank . . . . .President (x216)
Larry Offsey . . . . .COO/CFO
Alan Grunblatt . . . . .Executive VP (x211)
Cliff Cultreri .Sr. VP, A&R (x229)
Ed Franke . . . . .Sr. VP, Sales
Rick Meuser .VP, Business Affairs
Chuck Oliner . . . . .VP, Promotion
Susan Del Giorno . . . . .Director, Classics
John Franck .Director, Marketing
Gio Melchiore . . . . .Director, Media Relations (x257)
Catania Whalen . . . . .Director, International
Scott Kuchler . . . . .Label Manager
Michelle Bayer . . . . .TV/Film Licensing
Michael Healy . . . . .Controller
Naomi Yoshii . . . . .Product Manager
Marleny Dominguez . . . . .Assistant

LEIBER & STOLLER MUSIC PUBLISHING
9000 Sunset Blvd., Ste. 1107
Los Angeles, CA 90069-5811
PHONE 310-273-6401
FAX 310-273-1591
EMAIL . . . . .firstname.lastname@leiberstoller.com
WEB SITE . . . . .www.smokeyjoescafe.com
GENRES   Blues - Country - Folk - Jazz - Pop - R&B
                       - Rap/Hip-Hop - Reggae - Rock - Roots
                       - Urban
SUBMISSION POLICY   No unsolicited submissions

Randy Poe . . . . .President
Helen Mallory . . . . .VP, Licensing

WENDY LEVY
C/O First Artist Mangement
16000 Ventura Blvd., Ste. 605
Encino, CA 91436
PHONE 818-377-7750
RECENT CREDITS   South Beach - Sex, Love & Secrets

Wendy Levy . . . . .Music Supervisor

MAJOR BOB MUSIC COMPANY, INC.
1111 17th Ave. South
Nashville, TN 37212
PHONE 615-329-4150
FAX 615-329-1021
GENRES   Country

Bob Doyle . . . . .Owner

MEDIA CREATURE MUSIC
PO Box 39500
Los Angeles, CA 90039
PHONE 323-468-8888
FAX 323-468-8889
EMAIL . . . . .info@mediacreature.com
WEB SITE . . . . .www.mediacreature.com
GENRES   All Genres
SUBMISSION POLICY   By mail

Sharal Churchill . . . . .President/CEO
Renee Travis . . . . .VP
Sean Mulligan . . . . .Manager, Copyrights
Leo Medrano . . . . .Creative Associate
Melanie Sanchez . . . . .Creative Associate
J.P. Lacasse . . . . .Executive Assistant

*MEMORY LANE MUSIC GROUP
928 Broadway
New York, NY 10010
PHONE 212-460-8677
FAX 212-614-0166
EMAIL . . . . .info@memorylanemusicgroup.com
WEB SITE . . . . .www.memorylanemusicgroup.com
GENRES   Adult Contemporary - Alternative - Blues
                       - Jazz - Latin - Pop - R&B - Rock - Urban

Mark Spier . . . . .President
Heather Trussell . . . . .Licensing Manager
Eric Konzelman . . . . .Associate

MPL MUSIC PUBLISHING, INC.
41 W. 54th St.
New York, NY 10019
PHONE 212-246-5881
FAX 212-246-7852
EMAIL . . . . .info@mplcommunications.com
WEB SITE . . . . .www.mplcommunications.com
ARTIST ROSTER   Active Writer/Client list: Martin Briley -
                       Russ DeSalvo

GENRES   Blues - Jazz - Pop - R&B - Rock
SUBMISSION POLICY   No unsolicited material
COMMENTS   Collection includes works by Buddy
                       Holly, Carl Perkins, Jerry Herman, Frank
                       Loesser, Harold Arlen, Meredith Willson,
                       Bessie Smith & Paul McCartney

William Porricelli . . . . .Sr. VP, Promotions/New Product Development
Peter Silvestri . . . . .VP, Licensing & Royalties
Jessica Bumsted .Creative Services

MUSIC & MEDIA INTERNATIONAL, INC.
8756 Holloway Dr.
Los Angeles, CA 90069
PHONE 310-360-7777
FAX 310-360-7778
WEB SITE . . . . .www.musicmediaintl.com

Billy Meshel . . . . .Owner/CEO
John Massa . . . . .President
Roberta Meshel . . . . .Office Manager
David Meshell . . . . .Creative Manager
Madelaine Kelley . . . . .Copyright Department

MUSIC SALES EAST
257 Park Ave. South, 20th Fl.
New York, NY 10010-7304
PHONE 212-254-2100
FAX 212-254-2013
WEB SITE . . . . .www.musicsales.com
GENRES   Alternative - Blues - Christian - Classical
                       - Country - Electronica - Folk - Gospel -
                       Jazz - Latin - New Age - Pop - R&B -
                       Rap/Hip-Hop - Reggae - Rock - Roots -
                       Urban - World

Denise Maurin . . . . .VP, Administration/Operations
Philip Black . . . . .Manager, Creative
Iris Torres . . . . .Manager, Synchronization Licensing

MUSIC SALES WEST
1321 Seventh St., Ste. 300
Santa Monica, CA 90401-1682
PHONE 310-458-9861
FAX 310-458-9862
EMAIL . . . . .west@musicsales.com
WEB SITE . . . . .www.musicsales.com
SUBMISSION POLICY   No unsolicited submissions
COMMENTS   Full service office with a catalogue span-
                       ning nine decades and over 250,000
                       songs

Robert Knight .VP, Film, TV & Advertising
Karen Kloack . . . . .Director, Film, TV & Advertising
Wendy Crompton . . . . .Creative Assistant

MUSICSOOPZ MUSIC SUPERVISION
2540 Shore Blvd.
Astoria, NY 11102
PHONE 917-952-3063
FAX 718-721-663
E-MAIL . . . . .arahmaan@musicsoopz.com
WEBSITE . . . . .www.musicsoopz.com
SUBMISSION POLICY   Accepted via US mail
COMMENTS   Music Licensing

Akinah Rahmaan . . . . .Co-Founder/Music Supervisor
Ali Muhammad . . . . .Co-Founder/Music Supervisor

NETTWERK SONGS PUBLISHING LTD.
1650 W. Second Ave.
Vancouver, BC V6J 4R3 Canada
PHONE 604-654-2929/44-207-424-7500
FAX 604-654-1993/44-207-424-7501
EMAIL . . . . .publishing@nettwerk.com
WEB SITE . . . . .www.nettwerksongspublishing.com
GENRES   Pop - Rock
SUBMISSION POLICY   See Web site
COMMENTS   London Office: Clearwater Yard, 35
                       Inverness St., London NW1 7HB UK

Craig Horton . . . . .No Title (Vancouver)
Mark Jowett . . . . .No Title (Vancouver)
Blair McDonald . . . . .No Title (London)

NICK-O-VAL MUSIC COMPANY
254 W. 72nd St., Ste. 1A
New York, NY 10023
PHONE 212-873-2179
FAX 212-799-6926
GENRES   Alternative - Blues - Christian - Classical
                       - Country - Electronica - Folk - Gospel -
                       Jazz - Latin - New Age - Pop - R&B -
                       Rap/Hip-Hop - Reggae - Rock - Roots -
                       Urban - World

Nickolas Ashford . . . . .Owner
Valerie Simpson . . . . .Owner

OLD PANTS PUBLISHING, INC. (BMI)/NEW PANTS PUBLISHING, INC. (ASCAP)
102 E. Pikes Peak Ave., Ste. 200
Colorado Springs, CO 80903
PHONE 719-632-0227
FAX 719-634-2274
EMAIL . . . . .rac@hpi.net
WEB SITE . . . . .www.oldpants.com
SECOND WEB SITE . . . . .www.newpants.com
ARTIST ROSTER   Chris Clarke - Tech T - Stephanie
                       Aramburo - Chad Steele - Sherwen
                       Greenwood - Brian Stewart - Silence -
                       Kathy Watson - James Becker
GENRES   All Genres
SUBMISSION POLICY   Through manager or lawyer

Rob Case . . . . .President

BARBARA ORBISON PRODUCTIONS
1625 Broadway, Ste. 200
Nashville, TN 37203-3137
PHONE 615-242-4201
FAX 615-242-0942
EMAIL . . . . .info@orbison.com
WEB SITE . . . . .www.orbison.com
GENRES   Blues - Country - Pop - R&B - Rock -
                       Roots
COMMENTS   Record Company/Label

Barbara Orbison . . . . .President

THE CLYDE OTIS MUSIC GROUP INC.
PO Box 325
Englewood, NJ 07631-0325
PHONE 201-567-7538
FAX 201-567-5948
EMAIL . . . . .clo3@tcomg.com
SECOND EMAIL . . . . .dro@tcomg.com
WEB SITE . . . . .www.tcomg.com
GENRES   Blues - R&B - Rap/Hip-Hop

Isidro Otis . . . . .President
Clyde Otis III . . . . .Legal

MUSIC PUBLISHERS

PEERMUSIC (LOS ANGELES)
5358 Melrose Ave., Ste. 400
Los Angeles, CA 90038-3147
PHONE 323-960-3400
FAX 323-960-3410
EMAIL . . . . .losangeles@peermusic.com
WEB SITE . . . . .www.peermusic.com
GENRES   Alternative - Blues - Christian - Classical
                        - Country - Electronica - Folk - Gospel -
                        Jazz - Latin - New Age - Pop - R&B -
                        Rap/Hip-Hop - Reggae - Rock - Roots -
                        Urban - World

Kathy Spanberger . . . . .President/COO
Brady L. Benton . . . . .VP, Film, TV & Special Markets
Frank Petrone . . . . .Creative Director/National Director
Nicole Bayless . . . . .Creative Director, Film & TV
Karima Torres . . . . .Creative Manager, Film/TV & Advertising
Kim Draper . . . . .Manager, Film & TV Licensing
Yvonne Gomez . . . . .Manager, Latin Creative, West Coast

PEERMUSIC (NASHVILLE)
1207 16th Ave. South
Nashville, TN 37212
PHONE 615-329-0603
FAX 615-320-0490
EMAIL .nashville@peermusic.com
SECOND EMAIL . . . . .firstinitiallastname@peermusic.com
WEB SITE . . . . .www.peermusic.com
GENRES   Alternative - Blues - Christian - Classical
                        - Country - Electronica - Folk - Gospel -
                        Jazz - Latin - New Age - Pop - R&B -
                        Rap/Hip-Hop - Reggae - Rock - Roots -
                        Urban - World

Kevin Lamb . . . . .VP

PEERMUSIC (NEW YORK)
810 Seventh Ave., 10th Fl.
New York, NY 10019
PHONE 212-265-3910
FAX 212-489-2465
EMAIL . . . . .newyork@peermusic.com
SECOND EMAIL . . . . .firstinitiallastname@peermusic.com
WEB SITE . . . . .www.peermusic.com
GENRES   Alternative - Blues - Christian - Classical
                        - Country - Electronica - Folk - Gospel -
                        Jazz - Latin - New Age - Pop - R&B -
                        Rap/Hip-Hop - Reggae - Rock - Roots -
                        Urban - World

Jenny Ortiz . . . . .Creative

PEN MUSIC GROUP, INC.
589 N. Larchmont Blvd., 2nd Fl.
Los Angeles, CA 90004
PHONE 323-871-9200
FAX 323-460-2333
EMAIL . . . . .info@penmusic.com
WEB SITE . . . . .www.penmusic.COO
GENRES   All Genres
SUBMISSION POLICY   No unsolicited submissions

Michael Eames . . . . .President (michael@penmusic.com)
Connie Ambrosch-Ashton . . . . .VP
Richard Hellstern . . . . .Office & Royalties Manager
Cassie Wickham . . . . .Licensing & Creative Manager

PUTUMAYO
411 Lafayette St., 4th Fl.
New York, NY 10003
PHONE 212-625-1400
FAX 212-460-0095
EMAIL . . . . .info@putumayo.com
WEB SITE . . . . .www.putumayo.com
GENRES   World

John McQueeney . . . . .Licensing Director (x208, john@putumayo.com)

RAFELSON MEDIA CONSULTING
10713 Burbank Blvd.
North Hollywood, CA 91601
PHONE 818-753-9300
FAX 818-753-9966
EMAIL . . . . .info@rafelson.com
WEB SITE . . . . .www.rafelson.com
GENRES   All Genres
COMMENTS   Full post production facilities and record-
                        ing studio/soundstage; Music distributor,
                        supervisor, producer, licensing, clearance

Peter Rafelson . . . . .President
Yongbae Cho . . . . .VP, International A&R
Michael Brooks .Head, Production
Wyatt Peabody . . . . .Director, Operations
Brad Houshour . . . . .Label Manager

REALSONGS
6363 Sunset Blvd., 8th Fl.
Los Angeles, CA 90028-7318
PHONE 323-462-1709
FAX 323-462-1713
WEB SITE . . . . .www.realsongs.com
GENRES   Alternative - Blues - Christian - Classical
                        - Country - Electronica - Folk - Gospel -
                        Jazz - Latin - New Age - Pop - R&B -
                        Rap/Hip-Hop - Reggae - Rock - Roots -
                        Urban - World

Diane Warren . . . . .Owner
Julie Horton . . . . .Executive VP
Michael Anthony . . . . .Sr. VP, Creative Affairs

RED QUEEN MUSIC
443 S. San Pedro St., Ste. 406
Los Angeles, CA 90013
PHONE 213-236-9222
FAX 213-614-6801
EMAIL . . . . .webmasterbob@earthlink.net
GENRES   R&B - Rap/Hip-Hop - Urban
COMMENTS   Easy license; All master and publishing
                        rights

Julia J. Riva . . . . .President
Robert Walls . . . . .VP

RIGHTEOUS BABE RECORDS
PO Box 95, Ellicott Station
Buffalo, NY 14205-0095
PHONE 716-852-8020
FAX 716-852-2741
EMAIL . . . . .info@righteousbabe.com
WEB SITE . . . . .www.righteousbabe.com
GENRES   Alternative - Folk - Jazz - Latin - Pop -
                        Rock
SUBMISSION POLICY   No unsolicited submissions

Ani DiFranco . . . . .Founder
Scot Fisher . . . . .President
Mary Begley . . . . .Label Manager

ROADRUNNER PUBLISHING
902 Broadway, 8th Fl.
New York, NY 10010
PHONE 212-274-7500
FAX 212-505-7469
EMAIL . . . . .roadrunner@roadrunnerrecords.com
SECOND EMAIL . . . . .lastname@roadrunnerrecords.com
WEB SITE .www.roadrunnerrecords.com
GENRES   Alternative - Rock

David Bason . . . . .Director

ROGERS & HAMMERSTEIN/WILLIAMSON MUSIC
1065 Avenue of the Americas, Ste. 2400
New York, NY 10018-2506
PHONE 212-541-6600
FAX 212-489-6637
EMAIL . . . . .concert@rnh.com
WEB SITE . . . . .www.rnh.com
GENRES   Alternative - Blues - Christian - Classical
                                - Country - Electronica - Folk - Gospel -
                                Jazz - Latin - New Age - Pop - R&B -
                                Rap/Hip-Hop - Reggae - Rock - Roots -
                                Urban - World
COMMENTS   Annex: 229 W. 28th, St., 11th Fl., New
                                York, NY 10001

Maxyne Berman Lang . . . . .President (mlang@rnh.com)
Nancy Di Turo . . . . .Director, World Wide Sync (ndituro@rnh.com)

RONDOR MUSIC INTERNATIONAL/ALMO IRVING MUSIC
A Universal Music Group Company
2440 Sepulveda Blvd., Ste. 119
Los Angeles, CA 90064
PHONE 310-235-4800
FAX 310-235-4801
WEB SITE . . . . .www.umusicpub.com
GENRES   Alternative - Blues - Christian - Classical
                                - Country - Electronica - Folk - Gospel -
                                Jazz - Latin - New Age - Pop - R&B -
                                Rap/Hip-Hop - Reggae - Rock - Roots -
                                Urban - World

Lance Freed . . . . .President
Linda Chelgren . . . . .VP, Creative Licensing
Ron Moss . . . . .VP, A&R
Randall Rumage . . . . .VP, Business Affairs
Kevin Hall . . . . .A&R, Urban

THE ROYALTY NETWORK
224 W. 30th St., Ste. 1007
New York, NY 10001
PHONE 212-967-4300/323-938-4349
FAX 212-967-3477/323-938-7556
EMAIL . . . . .mail@roynet.com
WEB SITE . . . . .www.roynet.com
GENRES   Alternative - Blues - Christian - Classical
                                - Country - Electronica - Folk - Gospel -
                                Jazz - Latin - New Age - Pop - R&B -
                                Rap/Hip-Hop - Reggae - Rock - Roots -
                                Urban - World
COMMENTS   West Coast office: 7223 Beverly Blvd.,
                                Ste. 205, Los Angeles, CA 90036-2500

Frank Liwall . . . . .President (NY)
Steven Weber . . . . .President/West Coast Representative (LA)
Marshall Murphy . . . . .Director, Media Relations (NY)
Renato Olivari . . . . .Director, Operations (NY)

RYKOMUSIC (LOS ANGELES)
8335 Sunset Blvd., Ste. 302
Los Angeles, CA 90069
PHONE 323-337-9012
FAX 323-337-9013
EMAIL .donna.young@rykodisc.com
WEB SITE . . . . .www.rykomusic.com
GENRES   All Genres

Donna Young . . . . .Head, Creative
Nili Freeman . . . . .Creative Manager
Natalie Cervelli . . . . .Creative Coordinator

RYKOMUSIC (NEW YORK)
30 Irving Pl., 3rd Fl.
New York, NY 10003
PHONE 212-287-6143
FAX 212-287-6199
EMAIL . . . . .jeff.pachman@rykogroup.com
WEB SITE . . . . .www.rykomusic.com
GENRES   All Genres

Jeff Pachman . . . . .Director, Creative

SABAN MUSIC GROUP
10100 Santa Monica Blvd., 26th Fl.
Los Angeles, CA 90067
PHONE 310-557-5177
FAX 310-557-5172
EMAIL . . . . .teri@saban.com
WEB SITE . . . . .www.saban.com
COMMENTS   Film/TV Music Catalog

Ron Kenan . . . . .President
Teri Nelson Carpenter . . . . .Sr. VP, Music Publishing
Debbie Eisenberg . . . . .Director, Music Royalties
Chris Hicks . . . . .Executive Assistant
Chuck Keenum .Executive Assistant

SANCTUARY MUSIC PUBLISHING
45-53 Sinclair Rd.
London W14 ONS UK
PHONE 44-207-300-1866
FAX 44-207-300-1881
EMAIL . . . . .musicpub@sanctuarygroup.com
SECOND EMAIL . . . . .firstname.lastname@sanctuarygroup.com
WEB SITE . . . . .www.sanctuarygroup.com
GENRES   Alternative - Blues - Christian - Classical
                                - Country - Folk - Gospel - Jazz - Latin -
                                New Age - Pop - R&B - Rap/Hip-Hop -
                                Reggae - Rock - Roots - Urban - World
COMMENTS   Additional genres: Dance/DJ

Deke Arlon . . . . .CEO/President
Aky Najeeb . . . . .Joint CEO
Maria Forte . . . . .Director, Commercial Business
Jamie Arlon . . . . .Director, A&R
Matt Bolton . . . . .Royalty & Copyright Administrator
Jess Hamilton .Publishing Assistant

SILVER BLUE MUSIC
3940 Laurel Canyon Blvd., Ste. 441
Studio City, CA 91604-3709
PHONE 818-980-9588
FAX 818-980-9422
EMAIL . . . . .jdiamond20@aol.com
WEB SITE . . . . .www.joeldiamond.com
ARTIST ROSTER   Engelbert Humperdink - Gloria Gaynor -
                                David Hasselhoff - Howard Hewett - The
                                5 Browns
SUBMISSION POLICY   No return
COMMENTS   Publisher; Producer; Music Supervisor;
                                Manager

Joel Diamond . . . . .President

*SMOKING CATERPILLAR MUSIC/HAVE ANOTHER HIT MUSIC
222 E. 44th St., 9th Fl.
New York, NY 10017
PHONE 212-573-6000
FAX 212-370-7174
EMAIL . . . . .smokingcaterpillar@earthlink.net
WEB SITE . . . . .www.smokingcaterpillarmusic.com

David Reich . . . . .Founding Partner
Steven I. Rosenfeld . . . . .Founding Partner
Marcy Drexler . . . . .Executive VP, Creative
Robert Stewart .Creative Director

SONY/ATV MUSIC (LOS ANGELES)
2120 Colorado Ave., Ste. 100
Santa Monica, CA 90404-3504
PHONE 310-449-2120
FAX 310-449-2541
EMAIL . . . . .firstname_lastname@sonymusic.com
WEB SITE . . . . .www.sonyatv.com
SECOND WEB SITE . . . . .www.sonymusic.com
GENRES   Alternative - Blues - Christian - Classical
                             - Country - Electronica - Folk - Gospel -
                             Jazz - Latin - New Age - Pop - R&B -
                             Rap/Hip-Hop - Reggae - Rock - Roots -
                             Urban - World

Kathleen Carey . . . . .Sr. VP, A&R
Becky Mancuso-Winding . . . . .Sr. VP, Film, TV & Advertising
Esther Friedman . . . . .VP, Film, TV & Advertising
Mack Hill . . . . .VP, Film, TV & Advertising
Marni Coudro . . . . .Director, Film & TV
Jonathan Palmer . . . . .Director, Film & TV
Hillary Bernstein . . . . .Film & TV
Dorothy Joo . . . . .Assistant to Becky Mancuso-Winding

SONY/ATV MUSIC (NEW YORK)
550 Madison Ave., 18th Fl.
New York, NY 10022
PHONE 212-833-8000/212-833-4729
FAX 212-833-5552
EMAIL . . . . .info@sonyatv.com
SECOND EMAIL . . . . .firstname_lastname@sonymusic.com
WEB SITE . . . . .www.sonyatv.com
SECOND WEB SITE . . . . .www.sonymusic.com
GENRES   Pop - Rock - Urban

David Hockman . . . . .Chairman
Danny Strick . . . . .President
Kathleen Carey . . . . .Sr. VP, Creative
Becky Mancuso-Winding . . . . .Sr. VP, Film, TV & Advertising
Lauren Berkowitz . . . . .VP, Global Digital Business

SONY/ATV TREE MUSIC (NASHVILLE)
8 Music Square West
Nashville, TN 37203-3204
PHONE 615-726-8300
FAX 615-242-3441
EMAIL . . . . .firstname_lastname@sonymusic.com
WEB SITE . . . . .www.sonyatv.com
SECOND WEB SITE . . . . .www.sonymusic.com
GENRES   Christian - Country - Folk - Gospel -
                             Rock
COMMENTS   Tree & Cross Keys Publishing, Acuff Rose
                             & Milene Music

Donna Hilley . . . . .President/CEO
Woody Bomar . . . . .Sr. VP/General Manager, Creative
Troy Tomlinson . . . . .VP
Mike Whelan . . . . .Sr. Director, Creative Services
Alisa Graner . . . . .Associate Director, Film & TV Licensing

SPIRIT MUSIC GROUP
137 Fifth Ave., 8th Fl.
New York, NY 10010-7103
PHONE 212-533-7672
FAX 212-979-8566
EMAIL . . . . .info@spiritmusicgroup.com
WEB SITE . . . . .www.spiritmusicgroup.com
GENRES   All Genres

Mark Fried . . . . .President
Buckley Hugo . . . . .General Manager/Administration
Justin Kalifowitz . . . . .Sr. Director, A&R
Peter Shane . . . . .Sr. Director, Film & TV Music
Jedd Katrancha . . . . .Creative Manager
Anita Nimoh . . . . .Manager, Mechanical Licensing

STAGE THREE MUSIC (U.S.) INC.
1616 Vista del Mar St.
Los Angeles, CA 90028
PHONE 323-467-9794
FAX 323-467-9793
ARTIST ROSTER   Aerosmith - ZZ Top
GENRES   Alternative - Country - Electronica - Pop
                             - R&B - Rock

Lionel Conway . . . . .President
Michael Pizzuto . . . . .Creative Director

STOKESONGS
9454 Wilshire Blvd., Ste. 624
Los Angeles, CA 90212
PHONE 310-278-3092
FAX 310-388-4689
EMAIL .stokesongs@gmail.com
SECOND EMAIL . . . . .publishing@billbottrell.com
WEB SITE . . . . .www.billbottrell.com
SUBMISSION POLICY   Industry referral
COMMENTS   Stokesongs - Ignorant Music

Bill Bottrell . . . . .Owner
Gary Wishik . . . . .No Title

SUNSET BLVD. ENTERTAINMENT
740 N. La Brea Ave., 1st Fl.
Los Angeles, CA 90038-3339
PHONE 818-992-7910
EMAIL . . . . .alanmelina@newheightsent.com
GENRES   Electronica - Latin - Pop - R&B -
                             Rap/Hip-Hop - Reggae - Rock - Urban

Alan Melina . . . . .Partner
Laurent Besencon . . . . .Director, A&R

DALE TEDESCO MUSIC
16020 Lahey St.
Granada Hills, CA 91344
PHONE 818-360-7329
FAX 818-832-4292
GENRES   Alternative - Blues - Christian - Classical
                             - Country - Electronica - Folk - Gospel -
                             Jazz - Latin - New Age - Pop - R&B -
                             Rap/Hip-Hop - Reggae - Rock - Roots -
                             Urban - World
SUBMISSION POLICY   Please send material with SASE

Dale Tedesco . . . . .President

TEN TEN MUSIC GROUP
33 Music Square West, Ste. 110
Nashville, TN 37203-3226
PHONE 615-255-9955
FAX 615-255-1209
EMAIL . . . . .music@tentenmusic.com
WEB SITE . . . . .www.tentenmusic.com
ARTIST ROSTER   Keith Urban - Cory Mayo - Bobby Huff -
                       Angela Kaset - Angaleena Presley -
                       Harley Allen
GENRES   Country - Electronica - Rock - Urban

Barry Coburn . . . . .Co-President
Jewel Coburn . . . . .Co-President
Jill Napier . . . . .VP, Business Affairs
Joe Saul . . . . .Publishing Assistant
Amanda Cirotto . . . . .Administrative Assistant

THIRD STORY MUSIC
740 N. La Brea Ave.
Los Angeles, CA 90038
PHONE 323-938-5000
FAX 323-936-6354
GENRES   Rock

Herb Cohen . . . . .Principal

TKO GROUP
4501 Connecticut Ave., NW, Ste. 711
Washington, DC 20008
PHONE 202-966-3280/44-0-1273-550088
FAX 202-364-1367/44-0-1273-540969
EMAIL . . . . .mac@tkogroup.com
WEB SITE . . . . .www.thekrugerorganisation.com
GENRES   All Genres
COMMENTS   UK office: PO Box 130, Hove, East
                      Sussex, BN3 6QU UK

Howard Kruger . . . . .CEO (hkruger@tkogroup.com)
Jeffrey Kruger . . . . .CEO (jkruger02@aol.com)
Michael Cohn . . . . .CFO (mac@tkogroup.com)
Warren Heal . . . . .Licensing (warren@tkogroup.com)
Roland Rogers . . . . .Publishing (jestersong@msn.com)

TMC MUSIC PRODUCTIONS
5230 San Pedro Ave.
San Antonio, TX 78212
PHONE 210-829-1909
EMAIL . . . . .axbar@stic.net
WEB SITE . . . . .www.axbarmusic.com
GENRES   Bluegrass - Country - Gospel
COMMENTS   Axbar Productions (BMI) - Axhandle
                      Music (ASCAP) - Scate & Blanton (BMI)

Joe Axbar . . . . .Owner

TRACE ELEMENTS/SHRUB MUSIC
3953 Sendero Dr.
Austin, TX 78735-6390
PHONE 512-891-0789
FAX 512-891-9396
EMAIL . . . . .ahalbreich@aol.com
WEB SITE . . . . .www.shrubmusic.com
GENRES   Alternative - Blues - Christian - Classical
                       - Country - Electronica - Folk - Gospel -
                       Jazz - Latin - New Age - Pop - R&B -
                       Rap/Hip-Hop - Reggae - Rock - Roots -
                       Urban - World

Andrew Halbreich . . . . .Director

TRANSITION MUSIC CORPORATION
11288 Ventura Blvd., Ste. 709
Studio City, CA 91604
PHONE 323-860-7074
FAX 323-860-7986
EMAIL . . . . .onestopmus@aol.com
WEB SITE . . . . .www.transitionmusic.com
GENRES   All Genres
SUBMISSION POLICY   Five master quality tracks only per sub-
                       mission; No demos
COMMENTS   Creative Entertainment Music & Pushy
                       Publishing

Donna Ross-Jones . . . . .President
David Alan Jones . . . . .VP
Jennifer Brown . . . . .Director, FIlm & TV Music
Michael Dobson . . . . .Music Publishing/A&R
Todd Johnsen . . . . .FIlm & TV Music

TVT MUSIC/TVT SOUNDTRACKS
23 E. 4th St., 3rd Fl.
New York, NY 10003-7028
PHONE 212-979-6410
FAX 212-979-6489
EMAIL . . . . .info@tvtrecords.com
WEB SITE . . . . .www.tvtrecords.com
ARTIST ROSTER   213 - Lil Jon & the Eastside Boyz - Ying
                       Tang Twins - Pitbull - Jacki-O - The
                       Eastsidaz - Ambulance - The Baldwin
                       Brothers - Blue Epic - Default -
                       Sevendust - The Blue Van - The Kicks
GENRES   Alternative - Blues - Christian - Classical
                       - Country - Electronica - Folk - Gospel -
                       Jazz - Latin - New Age - Pop - R&B -
                       Rap/Hip-Hop - Reggae - Rock - Roots -
                       Urban - World

Patricia Joseph . . . . .VP, Soundtracks/A&R (pjoseph@tvtrecords.com)
Jackie Sussman . . . . .VP, Business & Legal Affairs (jackie@tvtrecords.com)

UNIVERSAL MUSIC PUBLISHING GROUP
2440 S. Sepulveda Blvd., Ste. 100
Los Angeles, CA 90064-1712
PHONE 310-235-4700/212-841-8000
FAX 310-235-4905/212-841-8072
EMAIL .umpg.newmedia@umusic.com
SECOND EMAIL . . . . .firstname.lastname@umusic.com
WEB SITE . . . . .www.umusicpub.com
GENRES   Alternative - Blues - Christian - Country -
                       Electronica - Folk - Gospel - Jazz - Latin
                       - Pop - R&B - Rap/Hip-Hop - Reggae -
                       Rock - Roots - Urban - World
SUBMISSION POLICY   No unsolicited material
COMMENTS   East Coast office: 1755 Broadway, 8th
                       Fl., New York, NY 10019-3743

David Renzer . . . . .Chairman/CEO
Mike Sammis . . . . .Executive VP/CFO
Linda Newmark . . . . .Executive VP, Acquisitions & Strategic Projects
Tom Sturges . . . . .Executive VP, Creative Affairs
Scott James . . . . .Sr. VP, Film, TV & New Technologies
Donna Caseine . . . . .VP, Creative Services
Andrew Fuhrmann . . . . .VP, Creative Affairs/General Manager,
                                                         East Coast (NY)
Irwin Griggs . . . . .VP, Special Projects
Brian Lambert . . . . .VP, FIlm & TV Music
Gary Miller . . . . .VP, Film & TV Clearance & Licensing
Tom Eaton . . . . .Sr. Director, Advertising, Film & TV Music (NY)
Maani Edwards . . . . .Sr. Director, Urban Music, West Coast
Kevin McManus . . . . .Sr. Director, Creative Affairs (NY)
Carianne Brown . . . . .Director, Film & TV Music
Heather Brown . . . . .Director, Marketing & Communications
Jackie Curry . . . . .Director, Music Licensing
Ethiopia Habtemariam . . . . .Director, Urban Music, East Coast (NY)
Gary Helsinger . . . . .Director, A&R, West Coast
Suzanne Moss . . . . .Director, Music Licensing
(Continued)

UNIVERSAL MUSIC PUBLISHING GROUP (Continued)

Nanci Walker . . . . .Director, Creative Affairs, West Coast
Rita Brock . . . . .Sr. Manager, Film & TV Licensing
Paul Brooks . . . . .Sr. Manager, Music Clearance
Chris Lakey . . . . .Manager, Music Licensing
Brent Locke . . . . .Manager, Special Markets
Neil Morris . . . . .Manager, Catalog Services
Lori Rosolino . . . . .Manager, Music Clearance
Jenna Voorhees . . . . .Manager, Music Clearance
Joanna Puglisi . . . . . . .Associate Manager, Advertising, Film & TV Music
James Cheney . . . . .Creative Coordinator
Melinda Mondrala . . . . .Coordinator, Music Publishing & TV Clearance/
Assistant to Scott James
Marilyn Alkire . . . . .Assistant to Paul Brooks, Film & TV Clearance
Louella De Los Angeles . . . .Assstant to Jackie Curry, Film & TV Licensing
Ross Donadio . . . . .Assistant to Andrew Fuhrmann (NY)
Nancy Dovan . . . . .Assistant to Linda Newmark & Irwin Griggs
Judie Grucella . . . . .Assistant to David Renzer
Elizabeth Henderson . . . . .Assistant to Jenna Vorhees & Lori Rosolino,
Film & TV Clearance
Joseph Krauss . . . . . . .Assistant to Suzanne Moss, Film & TV Clearance
Lindsey Lanier . . . . . . .Assistant to Maani Edwards & Gary Helsinger
Mark Lennon   Assistant to Heather Brown, Marketing & Communications
Dani Lopez . . . . .Assistant to Donna Caseine & Nanci Walker
Mandy Sewell . . . . .Assistant to Tom Eaton (NY)
Michael Swartz . . . . .Assistant to Brian Lambert & Carianne Brown
Nicole Taher . . . . .Assistant to Gary Miller, Film & TV Clearance
Jill Tschogl . . . . . .Administrative Assistant to Ethiopia Habtemariam (NY)

UNIVERSAL MUSIC PUBLISHING GROUP (NASHVILLE)

1904 Adelicia St.
Nashville, TN 37212
PHONE 615-340-5400
FAX 615-340-5491
EMAIL . . . . .pat.higdon@umusic.com
WEB SITE . . . . .www.umpgnashville.com
SECOND WEB SITE . . . . .www.umusicpub.com
GENRES   Country

Pat Higdon .Sr. VP/General Manager

V2 PUBLISHING

14 E. 4th St., 3rd Fl.
New York, NY 10012-1155
PHONE 212-320-8500/44-207-471-3000
FAX 212-320-8600/44-207-603-4796
EMAIL .information@v2music.com
WEB SITE www.v2music.com
GENRES   Alternative - Blues - Christian - Classical
- Country - Electronica - Folk - Gospel -
Jazz - Latin - New Age - Pop - R&B -
Rap/Hip-Hop - Reggae - Rock - Roots -
Urban - World
COMMENTS   UK office: 131-133 Holland Park Ave.,
London W11 4UT UK

Rob Stangroom . . . . . . .Licensing (UK) (rob.stangroom@v2music.com)
David Steel . . . . .VP, Publishing (NY) (david.steel@v2music.com)

WARNER/CHAPPELL (LOS ANGELES)

10585 Santa Monica Blvd., 3rd Fl.
Los Angeles, CA 90025-4950
PHONE 310-441-8600
FAX 310-470-3232
EMAIL . . . . .firstname.lastname@warnerchappell.com
WEB SITE . . . . .www.warnerchappell.com
GENRES   Alternative - Blues - Christian - Classical
- Country - Electronica - Folk - Gospel -
Jazz - Latin - New Age - Pop - R&B -
Rap/Hip-Hop - Reggae - Rock - Roots -
Urban - World
COMMENTS   No unsolicited material

Richard Blackstone . . . . .Chairman/CEO
Rick Shoemaker . . . . .President
Jay Morgenstern . . . . .Executive VP/General Manager
Ed Pierson . . . . .Executive VP, Legal & Business Affairs
Guy Blake . . . . .Sr. VP, Legal & Business Affairs
Brad Rosenberger . . . . .Sr. VP, Film & TV
Jack Rosner . . . . .Sr. VP, Special Projects
Nick Thomas . . . . .Sr. VP/CFO
Scott Allender . . . . .VP, Human Resources
Jeremy Blietz . . . . .VP, Administration
Tony DeNeri . . . . .VP, Tracking
Steven Holmberg . . . . .VP, Finance
Scott McDowell . . . . .VP, Legal & Business Affairs
Chia Park . . . . .VP, Information Technology Worldwide
Greg Sowders . . . . .VP, A&R Services
Judy Stakee . . . . .VP, A&R Services
Denise Weathersby . . . . .VP, A&R Services
Paulette Hawkins . . . . .Sr. Director, Licensing
Pat Woods . . . . .Sr. Director, Licensing
Jeff Conroy . . . . .Director, Production
Dhira Dharman . . . . .Director, Information Technology
Stephanie Salcedo . . . . .Manager, Legal & Business Affairs
Ralph Smith . . . . .Production Manager
Scott Blietz . . . . .Foreign Licensing, Karaoke & Video
Margaret Rosato . . . . .Financial Controller, US & Canada

WARNER/CHAPPELL (NASHVILLE)

20 Music Square East
Nashville, TN 37203
PHONE 615-733-1880
FAX . . . . .615-733-1885/615-733-1875 (A&R)
EMAIL . . . . .firstname.lastname@warnerchappell.com
WEB SITE . . . . .www.warnerchappell.com
GENRES   Country - Folk
SUBMISSION POLICY   No unsolicited material

Dale Bobo . . . . .Sr. VP, A&R
Kos Weaver . . . . .VP, A&R
Cris Lacy . . . . .Sr. Director, A&R
BJ Hill . . . . .Director, A&R
Lu Ann Inman . . . . .Director, Copyright & Licensing
Matt Michiels .Productions Director
Karen Harrison-Hite . . . . .A&R/Contracts Coordinator
Neena Wright . . . . .Office Manager/Accounting Manager
Patricia Ragan Mainello . . . . .Administrative Services/Copyright Assistant

WARNER/CHAPPELL (NEW YORK)
1290 Avenue of The Americas
New York, NY 10104
PHONE 212-707-2600
FAX .212-405-5428/212-405-5429
EMAIL . . . . .firstname.lastname@warnerchappell.com
WEB SITE . . . . .www.warnerchappell.com
GENRES   Alternative - Blues - Christian - Classical
                            - Country - Electronica - Folk - Gospel -
                            Jazz - Latin - New Age - Pop - R&B -
                            Rap/Hip-Hop - Reggae - Rock - Roots -
                            Urban - World
SUBMISSION POLICY   No unsolicited material

John Titta . . . . .Sr. VP/General Manager, A&R, East
Neil Gillis . . . . .Sr. VP, Creative Music Solutions
Michael Lau . . . . .Manager, Creative Music Solutions
Frank Military . . . . .Consultant

WELK MUSIC PUBLISHING
120 31st Ave. North
Nashville, TN 37203
PHONE 615-297-4322/615-297-2588
FAX 615-297-8575
EMAIL . . . . .info@welkmg.com
ARTIST ROSTER   Scott Miller - Joy Lynn White - Greg
                            Trooper - Steve Forbert - Sean Locke -
                            Amy Rigby - Pamela Brown Hayes -
                            Brian Maher - Stacy Dean Campbell

Bob Kirsch . . . . .Head, Publishing
Tuttie Jackson .Executive Assistant
Jessi Heisler .Publishing Assistant

WESTWOOD MUSIC GROUP
521 Fifth Ave., 17th Fl.
New York, NY 10175-0038
PHONE 212-619-3500/800-340-7611
FAX .212-619-3588/562-684-4615
EMAIL . . . . .filmmusic@westwoodmusicgroup.com
SECOND EMAIL . . . . .filmmusicla@westwoodmusicgroup.com
WEB SITE . . . . .www.westwoodmusicgroup.com
ARTIST ROSTER   Soul Engines - One Found Day - Brad
                            Hodge - Kidd Skruff - Evan Keith -
                            Stikmen - Brian Clayton
GENRES   Alternative - Blues - Christian - Classical
                            - Country - Electronica - Folk - Jazz -
                            Latin - New Age - Pop - R&B - Rap/Hip-
                            Hop - Reggae - Rock - Roots - Urban -
                            World
SUBMISSION POLICY   Request permission; Three song limit
COMMENTS   West Coast office: 1223 Wilshire Blvd.,
                            Ste. 830, Santa Monica, CA 90403-
                            5400

Victor Kaply . . . . .Manager, Film & TV Music (x14)
Kevin McCabe . . . . .Music Coordinator (x25)
Jim Carolan . . . . .International Licensing Coordinator (x45)
Toke Kates Jr. . . . . .A&R Manager, R&B (x35)

WINDSWEPT PACIFIC MUSIC
9320 Wilshire Blvd., Ste. 200
Beverly Hills, CA 90212-3216
PHONE .310-550-1500/615-313-7676
FAX .310-247-0195/615-313-7670
EMAIL . . . . .info@windsweptpacific.com
SECOND EMAIL . . . . .firstinitiallastname@windsweptpacific.com
WEB SITE . . . . .www.windsweptpacific.com
GENRES   Alternative - Blues - Christian - Classical
                            - Country - Electronica - Folk - Jazz -
                            Latin - New Age - Pop - R&B - Rap/Hip-
                            Hop - Reggae - Rock - Roots - Urban -
                            World
COMMENTS   Nashville office: 33 Music Square West,
                            Ste. 104-B, Nashville, TN 37215

Evan Meadow . . . . .CEO
John Anderson . . . . .Sr. VP, Film & TV
Debby Dill .Sr. VP, Creative Affairs
Steve Markland . . . . .VP, Creative Affairs
Carol Dunn . . . . .Director, Film & TV Music
Lola Jordan . . . . .Director, Synch. Licenses
Marina Mena . . . . .Creative Coordinator, Film & TV
Priya Perera . . . . .Synch. Licensing Manager
Brad Rains . . . . .Manager, Film & TV Music
Julie Foist . . . . .Licensing Assistant

WORD MUSIC PUBLISHING
25 Music Square West
Nashville, TN 37203
PHONE 615-687-6831
FAX 615-726-7888
WEB SITE . . . . .www.wordmusicpublishing.com
GENRES   Christian

Shari Saba .VP/General Manager
Cindy Wilt . . . . .VP
Joel West . . . . .Creative Manager
Amy Pelphrey . . . . .Executive Assistant to VP/General Manager

ZOMBA MUSIC PUBLISHING
245 Fifth Ave., 8th Fl.
New York, NY 10016
PHONE 212-287-1300
FAX 646-486-1480
EMAIL . . . . .firstname.lastname@zomba.com
WEB SITE . . . . .www.bmgmusicsearch.com
GENRES   Alternative - Blues - Christian - Classical
                            - Country - Electronica - Folk - Jazz -
                            Latin - New Age - Pop - R&B - Rap/Hip-
                            Hop - Reggae - Rock - Urban - World
COMMENTS   West Coast office: 8750 Wilshire Blvd.,
                            Beverly Hills, CA 90211, phone: 310-
                            358-4700, fax: 310-358-4742

David Mantel . . . . .President
Bob Bortnick . . . . .Sr. VP, Creative
Jennifer Blakeman . . . . .VP, Creative
Andrea Torchia . . . . .VP, A&R (LA)
Lisa Piacenti . . . . .Director, Creative (Urban)

WORKSHEET

DATE	PROJECT	CONTACT	NOTES

SECTION **E**

RECORDING STUDIOS

Asterisks (*) next to companies denote new listings.

4TH STREET RECORDING
1211 Fourth St.
Santa Monica, CA 90401
PHONE 310-395-9114
FAX 310-394-7772
EMAIL . . . . .kathleen@4thstreetrecording.com
WEB SITE www.4thstreetrecording.com
CLIENTS   Incubus - Fiona Apple - Hoobastank -
                           Nelly Furtado - Live - No Doubt -
                           George Clinton - Brian Setzer - Alice
                           Cooper - Shelby Lynne - Chris Robinson
GENRES   All Genres

Kathleen Robinson Wirt . . . . .Owner

AB AUDIO VISUAL ENTERTAINMENT
3765 Marwick Ave.
Long Beach, CA 90808
PHONE 562-429-1042/877-222-8346
FAX 562-429-2401
EMAIL . . . . .media@abaudio.com
WEB SITE . . . . .www.abaudio.com

Arlan Boll . . . . .President
Linda Rippee . . . . .Studio Manager

ABERDEEN RECORDING STUDIOS
116 S. Main St, #309
Aberdeen, SD 57401
PHONE 605-622-4890
FAX 605-622-4891
EMAIL . . . . .info@aberdeenrecording.com
WEB SITE . . . . .www.aberdeenrecording.com
GENRES   All Genres

Tim Andersen . . . . .Owner/CEO/Chief Engineer
Janet Preus . . . . .COO
Angela Spear . . . . .Office Manager
Gordy Zens . . . . .CFO/Assistant Engineer

AMERAYCAN STUDIOS
5719 Lankershim Blvd.
North Hollywood, CA 91601
PHONE 818-760-8733/323-465-4000
FAX .818-760-2524/323-469-1905
WEB SITE . . . . .www.paramountrecording.com
CLIENTS   Sarah McLachlan - Sum 41 - Jet -
                           Brandy - Nas - Macy Gray - Dave
                           Matthews - Tears for Fears - Nickel
                           Creek
GENRES   All Genres
COMMENTS   Music mixing; Music tracking; Large-
                           scale tracking room; Orchestra work

Adam Beilenson . . . . .Owner
Mike Kerns . . . . .Owner

ARDENT STUDIOS
2000 Madison Ave.
Memphis, TN 38104-2794
PHONE 901-725-0855
FAX 901-725-7011
EMAIL . . . . .jstephens@ardentstudios.com
WEB SITE . . . . .www.ardentstudios.com
SECOND WEB SITE . . . . .www.ardentrecords.com
GENRES   Alternative - Bluegrass - Blues - Christian
                           - Country - Pop - R&B - Rock - Roots

Jody Stephens . . . . .Studio Manager

ARTISAN SOUND RECORDERS
19941 Hiawatha St.
Chatsworth, CA 91311
PHONE 818-832-1951
EMAIL . . . . .bluesman@socal.rr.com
WEB SITE . . . . .www.artisansoundrecorders.com

John Lowry . . . . .Owner/Manager

ATLANTIS GROUP RECORDING
429 Santa Monica Blvd., Ste. 250
Santa Monica, CA 90401
PHONE 310-458-9098
FAX 310-458-9048
WEB SITE . . . . .www.atlantisgrouprecording.com
CLIENTS   THQ - Leap Frog - Blue Frog Mobile -
                           Dailey & Associates

John Chominsky . . . . .President
Sean Graham . . . . .Studio Manager

AUDIO VISION STUDIOS
13385 W. Dixie Hwy.
North Miami, FL 33161
PHONE 305-893-9191
FAX 305-895-2647
EMAIL .sales@audiovisionstudios.com
WEB SITE .www.audiovisionstudios.com
CLIENTS   Beyoncé - Lil Jon - Tweet - P. Diddy -
                           Ghostface - 19 Entertainment -
                           Alejandro Fernandez - Warner Bros. -
                           Elektra - Sony Music

Steve Alaimo . . . . .Partner
Ron Albert . . . . .Partner
Howard Albert . . . . .Partner
Mack Emerman . . . . .Partner
Karl Richardson . . . . .Partner
Ricky Taylor . . . . .Partner

BAY RECORDS RECORDING STUDIOS
1741 Alcatraz Ave.
Berkeley, CA 94703
PHONE 510-428-2002
FAX 510-428-1196
EMAIL . . . . .mcogan@bayrec.com
WEB SITE . . . . .www.bayrec.com

Michael Cogan . . . . .Owner
Jeremy Goody . . . . .Engineer
Bob Shumaker . . . . .Engineer

BEAR CREEK STUDIO AND MUSIC PRODUCTION, INC.
6313 Maltby Rd.
Woodinville, WA 98072-8345
PHONE 425-481-4100
FAX 425-486-2718
EMAIL . . . . .bearcreek@seanet.com
WEB SITE . . . . .www.bearcreekstudio.com
CLIENTS   Josh Ritter - The Dead Silence - Jack
                           Endino - Holy Ghost Revival - Andy
                           Chatterley - Pretty Girls Make Graves
COMMENTS   Film work, licensing, commercials, rock
                           bands; Producer and management of
                           The Strokes, Regina Spektor and
                           Pussycat Dolls

Ryan Hadlock . . . . .Producer/Engineer/Composer
                           (ryanhadlock@hotmail.com)
Joe Hadlock . . . . .Producer/Engineer/Composer
                           (joehadlock@hotmail.com)
Gordon Raphael . . . . .Producer/Engineer
                           (gordonraphael@rockfeedback.com)
Brandon Eggleston . . . . .Engineer
Manny Hadlock . . . . .Director, Sales/Commercial Production
                           (mannyhadlock@hotmail.com)

BELL SOUND STUDIO
916 N. Citrus Ave.
Los Angeles, CA 90038
PHONE 323-461-3036
FAX 323-461-8764
EMAIL ....bellsound@bellsound.com
WEB SITE ....www.bellsound.com

John Osiecki ....Chief Engineer
Beth Quimby ....Office Manager

BLUE MOON STUDIO
28205 Agoura Rd.
Agoura Hills, CA 91301
PHONE 818-889-8920
FAX 818-889-1208
GENRES   All Genres

Diane Ricci ....Studio Manager

CAN-AM RECORDERS, INC.
18730 Oxnard St., Ste. 211
Tarzana, CA 91356
PHONE 818-342-2626
FAX 818-342-7474

Larry Cummins ....No Title

CAPITOL STUDIOS
1750 N. Vine St.
Hollywood, CA 90028
PHONE 323-871-5001
FAX 323-871-5058
EMAIL ....paula.salvatore@capitolrecords.com
WEB SITE ....www.capitolstudios.com
CLIENTS   Al Schmitt - Geoff Emerick - Ed Cherney
                          - Burt Bacharach - Faith Hill - Coldplay -
                          Ozzy Osbourne - Diana Krall - Harry
                          Connick, Jr. - The Vines - Green Day -
                          Oasis

Paula Salvatore ....Sr. Director/Manager
Louise Glover ....Manager, Administration
David Stern ....Assistant

CHALICE RECORDING STUDIO
845 N. Highland Ave.
Los Angeles, CA 90038
PHONE 323-957-7100
FAX 323-957-7110
EMAIL ....info@chalicerecording.com
WEB SITE ....www.chalicerecording.com

Irit Zarutsky ....Booking Manager
Stacey Dodds ....Manager, Technical Operations

CHEROKEE STUDIOS
751 N. Fairfax Ave.
Los Angeles, CA 90046
PHONE 323-653-3412
FAX 323-653-3546
EMAIL ....info@cherokeestudios.com
WEB SITE ....www.cherokeestudios.com

Joe Robb ....Owner
Dee Robb ....Owner
Bruce Robb ....Owner

CLEAR LAKE AUDIO
10520 Burbank Blvd.
North Hollywood, CA 91601
PHONE 818-762-0707
FAX 818-762-0256
EMAIL ....cla@clearlakeaudio.com
WEB SITE ....www.clearlakeaudio.com
CLIENTS   Asia - Dishwalla - Terry Gibbs
GENRES   All Genres

Brian Levi ....Owner
Preston Boebel ....Chief Engineer

BILLY COBB RECORDING & MASTERING
2899 Agoura Rd., Ste. 299
Westlake Village, CA 91361
PHONE 818-410-2458
FAX 805-482-7784
EMAIL ....billyc777@aol.com
WEB SITE ....www.billycobbrecording.com

Billy Cobb ....Owner/Engineer

THE COMPLEX STUDIOS
2323 Corinth Ave.
West Los Angeles, CA 90064
PHONE 310-477-1938
FAX 310-473-2485
WEB SITE ....www.thecomplexstudios.com

Mike Seros ....Director, Operations
Dawn Abraham ....Manager, Marketing
Tim Treadway ....Business Manager

CONWAY RECORDING
5100 Melrose Ave.
Hollywood, CA 90038
PHONE 323-463-2175
FAX 323-463-2479
EMAIL ....info@conwayrecording.com
WEB SITE ....www.conwayrecording.com
CLIENTS   Blink-182 - Morrissey - Black Eyed Peas
                    - Meat Loaf - Denver Harbor - Mana
GENRES   Alternative - Latin - Metal - Punk -
                    Rap/Hip-Hop - Rock

John Musgrave ....Technical Director/General Manager
Lisa Stuck ....Studio Bookings/Traffic Manager
                        (lisa@conwayrecording.com)

CORNERSTONE RECORDERS
9626 Lurline Ave., Ste. K
Chatsworth, CA 91311
PHONE 818-341-1358
FAX 818-341-1358
COMMENTS   SSL 72 input console with ProTools and
                    48-track analog facility

Ken Koroshetz ....Studio Manager

DIFFERENT FUR RECORDING STUDIO
3470 19th St.
San Francisco, CA 94110
PHONE 415-864-1967
FAX 415-864-1966
EMAIL . . . . .recording@kleptorecords.com
WEB SITE . . . . .www.differentfur.com
CLIENTS   Bill Frisell - Primus - Kronos Quartet -
                         Joan Jeanrenaud - Tuck & Patty -
                         George Winston
GENRES   Alternative - Blues - Christian -
                         Electronica - Folk - Gospel - Jazz - New
                         Age - Pop - R&B - Rap/Hip-Hop - Rock -
                         Roots - Urban - World

Jeromy Smith . . . . .Owner/Engineer
Enrique Perez . . . . .Engineer
Duane Ramos . . . . .Engineer

DOPPLER STUDIOS
1922 Piedmont Circle
Atlanta, GA 30324
PHONE 404-873-6941
FAX 404-249-7148
EMAIL . . . . .info@dopplerstudios.com
WEB SITE . . . . .www.dopplerstudios.com
CLIENTS   Mary J. Blige - Toni Braxton - Usher - U2
                         - Mos Def - Brandi - Third Day - Incubus
                         - Ciara - T.D. Jakes - Monica
GENRES   All Genres

Bill Quinn . . . . .Studio Manager
Joe Neil . . . . .Chief Engineer
Beverly Kennerly . . . . .Scheduling

EASTWOOD SCORING STAGE
c/o Warner Bros. Postproduction Services
4000 Warner Blvd., Bldg. 6
Burbank, CA 91522
PHONE 818-954-6800
FAX 818-954-1652
EMAIL . . . . .wbscoring@warnerbros.com
SECOND EMAIL . . . . .wbpostproduction@warnerbros.com
WEB SITE .www.wbpostproduction.com

Greg Dennen . .Post-Production Services (greg.dennen@warnerbros.com)

ENTOURAGE MUSIC GROUP
11115 Magnolia Blvd.
North Hollywood, CA 91601
PHONE 818-505-0001
FAX 818-761-7956
EMAIL . . . . .info@e51.biz
WEB SITE . . . . .www.entouragestudios.com

Guy Paonessa . . . . .Owner
Andy Waterman . . . . .Producer/Engineer
David Brown . . . . .Chief Technician
Josh Lynch . . . . .Systems Director

FANTASY STUDIOS
2600 10th St.
Berkeley, CA 94710
PHONE 510-486-2038
FAX 510-486-2248
EMAIL . . . . .nbombardier@fantasyjazz.com
WEB SITE . . . . .www.fantasystudios.com

Nina Bombardier . . . . .Studio Manager
Stephen Hart . . . . .Chief Engineer
Guy Lento . . . . .Chief Technician

FIREHOUSE RECORDING STUDIOS INC.
30 W. Green St.
Pasadena, CA 91105
PHONE 626-405-0411
FAX 626-405-0413
EMAIL . . . . .lindsay@firehouserecordingstudios.com
WEB SITE . . . . .www.firehouserecordingstudios.com

Tena Clark . . . . .Owner
Lindsay Tomasic . . . . .Studio Manager

FOX STUDIOS POSTPRODUCTION SERVICES
The Newman Scoring Stage
10201 W. Pico Blvd.
Los Angeles, CA 90035
PHONE 310-369-5665/310-369-7678
FAX 310-369-4407
EMAIL . . . . .foxinfo@fox.com
WEB SITE . . . . .www.foxpost.com

Andy Nelson . . . . .Sr. VP, Sound Operations
Stacey Robinson . . . . .Executive Director, Sound Operations

FOXFIRE RECORDING
16760 Stagg St.
Van Nuys, CA 91406-1642
PHONE 818-787-4843
WEB SITE . . . . .www.foxfirerecording.com
GENRES   All Genres

Rudi Ekstein . . . . .Owner

GLENWOOD PLACE STUDIOS
619 S. Glenwood Pl.
Burbank, CA 91506
PHONE 818-260-9555
FAX 818-260-9507
EMAIL . . . . .kit@glenwoodstudios.com
WEB SITE . . . . .www.glenwoodstudios.com
GENRES   Alternative - Blues - Classical - Country -
                         Folk - Jazz - Latin - Pop - Rock - World

Kit Rebhun . . . . .Studio Manager

GOLD STREET
649 Bethany Rd.
Burbank, CA 91504
PHONE 818-567-1911
EMAIL . . . . .music@goldstreet.net
WEB SITE . . . . .www.goldstreetentertainment.com
CLIENTS   TeleStoryTOONS/EMI Christian Music -
                         Laurice Monica - Life After Death
                         Records - Nathan Sassover - Passport
                         Productions - Goodnight Kiss - Bruce
                         Michael Hall & Donn Swaby - Rosy
                         Morales - Devotion - Strunz & Farah -
                         Amanda McBroom - Tai Lewis
GENRES   Christian - Electronica - Gospel - Latin -
                         Pop - R&B - Rap/Hip-Hop
COMMENTS   Music production, recording, mixing,
                         mastering, video/DVD

Eric Michael Cap . . . . .Manager/Producer

GRANDMASTER RECORDERS
1520 N. Cahuenga Blvd.
Hollywood, CA 90028
PHONE 323-462-6136
FAX 323-462-6137

Alan Dickson . . . . .Owner

HEADROOM AUDIO
7513-1/2 Santa Monica Blvd.
West Hollywood, CA 90046
PHONE 323-874-2447
FAX 323-874-0715
EMAIL . . . . .headroomaudio@aol.com
WEB SITE . . . . .www.headroomaudio.com

Eric Arm . . . . .No Title

HILLTOP RECORDING STUDIOS
902 Due West Ave.
Nashville, TN 37115
PHONE 615-865-5272
FAX 615-865-5553
EMAIL . . . . .studio@hilltopstudio.com
WEB SITE . . . . .www.hilltopstudio.com
CLIENTS . . . . A&E - Columbia Records - Rounder
Records - Vivaton Records
GENRES . . . . Bluegrass - Children's - Christian -
Country - Folk - Gospel - Jazz - Pop -
R&B - Rock
COMMENTS . . . . Album production, jingles, voice-overs,
analog to digital transfers, ADR

John Nicholson . . . . .Owner/Chief Engineer
Steve Chandler . . . . .Engineer
Jim Stewart . . . . .Assistant/ProTools Engineer

HOLLYWOOD SOUND RECORDERS
6367 Selma Ave.
Los Angeles, CA 90028
PHONE 323-467-1411
FAX 323-462-8562
EMAIL . . . . .info@hollywoodsound.net
WEB SITE . . . . .www.hollywoodsound.net
CLIENTS . . . . Flogging Molly - Gavin Rossdale - Rock
Kills Kid - Kelly Clarkson - (hed) pe -
Chris Isaak

Jonathan Hodges . . . . .Studio Manager

HOUSE OF BLUES STUDIOS
4431 Petit Ave.
Encino, CA 91436
PHONE 818-990-1296
FAX 818-990-3309
EMAIL . . . . .hobstudios@aol.com
WEB SITE . . . . .www.houseofbluesstudios.com
CLIENTS . . . . Jessica Simpson - Macy Gray - Justin
Timberlake - Sergio Mendes - Pink
GENRES . . . . All Genres
COMMENTS . . . . Vintage and modern equipment

Gary Belz . . . . .Owner

HYDE STREET STUDIOS
245 Hyde St.
San Francisco, CA 94102
PHONE 415-441-8934
FAX 415-441-8943
EMAIL . . . . .hydestreet@hotmail.com
WEB SITE . . . . .www.hydestreet.com
CLIENTS . . . . Green Day - Cake - George Clinton -
Chris Isaak
GENRES . . . . All Genres

Jeff Cleland . . . . .Studio Manager

IRONWOOD STUDIOS
601 NW 80th St.
Seattle, WA 98117
PHONE 206-789-7569
FAX 206-784-2880
EMAIL . . . . .avast@comcast.net
WEB SITE . . . . .www.ironwoodstudios.com
CLIENTS . . . . Blues Traveler - Evanescence -
Supersuckers - Maktub - Craving Theo -
The Divorce - Chris Cornell
COMMENTS . . . . Studio A: 22'x32'x15'h live room with 2
isolation booths, 20'x26' control room,
Procontrol and Manley mixer/Preamp;
Studio B: 36'x34'x17'h live room with 2
isolation booths, 20'x24' control room,
fully-restored 48 channel Neve console,
ProTools HD and Studer A827

Donn DeVore .Chief Engineer
Kelly Campbell . . . . .Engineer
Owen Strain . . . . .Engineer

JEL RECORDING STUDIOS
6100 West Coast Hwy.
Newport Beach, CA 92663
PHONE 949-631-4880
FAX 949-548-1622
EMAIL . . . . .firstname@jelrecording.com
WEB SITE . . . . .www.jelrecording.com
GENRES . . . . All Genres

Edo Guidotti . . . . .Owner
Shelly Guidotti . . . . .Booking/Billing

KAS MUSIC & SOUND
34-12 36th St.
Astoria, NY 11106
PHONE 718-786-3400
FAX 718-729-3007
EMAIL . . . . .info@kasmusic.com
WEB SITE . . . . .www.kasmusic.com

Joe Castellon . . . . .Executive Creative Director

L.A. FX RECORDING STUDIO
5634 Cleon St.
North Hollywood, CA 91601
PHONE 818-769-5239
FAX 818-769-7288
EMAIL . . . . .info@lafx.com
WEB SITE . . . . .www.lafx.com

Dan Vicari . . . . .Owner/Engineer

LARRABEE NORTH
4162 Lankershim Blvd.
North Hollywood, CA 91602
PHONE 818-753-0717
FAX 818-753-8046
EMAIL . . . . .larrabeemanager@yahoo.com
WEB SITE . . . . .www.larrabeestudios.com

Madeline Marotto . . . . .Studio Manager

THE LODGE
740 Broadway, Ste. 605
New York, NY 10003
PHONE 212-353-3895
FAX 212-353-2575
EMAIL . . . . .info@thelodge.com
WEB SITE . . . . .www.thelodge.com

Emily Lazar . . . . .Chief Mastering Engineer
Scotty Lee . . . . .Sales & Marketing Manager

MAD DOG STUDIOS
291 S. Lake St.
Burbank, CA 91502-2111
PHONE 818-557-0100
FAX 818-557-6383
EMAIL . . . . .info@maddogstudio.com
WEB SITE . . . . .www.maddogstudio.com

Dusty Wakeman . . . . .Owner
Brian Kohl . . . . .Manager

MARCUSSEN MASTERING
1545 N. Wilcox Ave.
Hollywood, CA 90028
PHONE 323-463-5300
FAX 323-463-5600
EMAIL . . . . .ew@marcussenmastering.com
WEB SITE . . . . .www.marcussenmastering.com

Stephen Marcussen . . . . .Owner
Eddie Wisztreich . . . . .General Manager

MASTER GROOVE STUDIOS
1419 California St., Ste. 2
Huntington Beach, CA 92648
PHONE 818-830-3822
FAX 714-536-8515
EMAIL . . . . .leafcake@att.net
SECOND EMAIL . . . . .davejavu@att.net
WEB SITE . . . . .www.mastergroovestudios.com
CLIENTS   Incubus- Warrant - Van Halen - David
                         Bowie - Red Hot Chili Peppers - Ice
                         Cube - Sony - Warner Bros. - Geffen -
                         Priority
COMMENTS   Mastering, mixing, tracking, production

Dave Morse . . . . .Studio Manager

METROPOLIS DIGITAL STUDIOS
1120 Westchester Pl.
Los Angeles, CA 90019
PHONE 323-373-1537
FAX 323-373-1583
EMAIL . . . . .onfilm1@pacbell.net
WEB SITE www.onfilm1.com

John Gocha . . . . .CEO/Owner

THE MIX ROOM
2940 W. Burbank Blvd.
Burbank, CA 91505
PHONE 818-846-8900
FAX 818-846-0015
EMAIL . . . . .info@themixroom.com
WEB SITE . . . . .www.themixroom.com
GENRES   All Genres
COMMENTS   Full-service studios with Solid State Logic
                         J&K consoles

Laura Dore . . . . .Studio Manager

NRG RECORDING SERVICES
11128 Weddington St.
North Hollywood, CA 91601
PHONE 818-760-7841
FAX 818-760-7930
EMAIL . . . . .annette@nrgrecording.com
WEB SITE . . . . .www.nrgrecording.com

Annette Scott . . . . .Studio Manager

OCEAN STUDIOS BURBANK
435 S. San Fernando Blvd.
Burbank, CA 91502
PHONE 818-955-9010
FAX 818-955-8301
EMAIL . . . . .info@oceanstudiosburbank.com
WEB SITE . . . . .www.oceanstudiosburbank.com
CLIENTS   Mark Trombino - Jimmy Eat World - Lou
                         Giodano - The Ataris - Oliver Lieber -
                         Dave Fortman - Evanescence
GENRES   Alternative - New Age - Pop - Rock

Smith Craig . . . . .Studio Manager

OCEAN WAY NASHVILLE
1200 17th Ave. South
Nashville, TN 37212
PHONE 615-320-3900
FAX 615-320-3910
EMAIL . . . . .information@oceanwaystudios.com
WEB SITE . . . . .www.oceanwaystudios.com
CLIENTS   George Strait - Matchbox Twenty - Harry
                         Connick, Jr. - Faith Hill - The Mavericks
                         - Willie Nelson - Train - Yo-Yo Ma -
                         Montgomery Gentry - Toby Keith -
                         Juvenile - Sheryl Crow - Kings of Leon

Gelnda Cones . . . . .Studio Manager (cones@mail.belmont.edu)
Sal Greco . . . . .Technical Coordinator (x22, grecos@mail.belmont.edu)

OCEAN WAY RECORDING
6050 W. Sunset Blvd.
Hollywood, CA 90028
PHONE 323-467-9375/818-788-7751
FAX 323-467-3962/818-788-3528
EMAIL . . . . .kelly@oceanwayrecording.com
WEB SITE . . . . .www.oceanwayrecording.com
COMMENTS   2 studio complexes: Ocean Way
                         (Hollywood) & Record One (Sherman
                         Oaks)

Kelly Erwin . . . . .Studio Manager (kelly@oceanwayrecording.com)
Ernie Woody . . . .General Manager (infoowr@oceanwayrecording.com)
Alan Yoshida . .Mastering Engineer (mastering@oceanwayrecording.com)

O'HENRY SOUND STUDIOS
4200 W. Magnolia Blvd.
Burbank, CA 91505
PHONE 818-563-4200
FAX 818-842-5763
EMAIL . . . . .ohenrysound@earthlink.net
WEB SITE . . . . .www.ohenrystudios.com

Melissa Firestone . . . . .Studio Manager

PARAMOUNT PICTURES SCORING STAGE M
5555 Melrose Ave., The Crosby Bldg.
Los Angeles, CA 90038
PHONE 323-956-7267
FAX 323-862-1000
EMAIL . . . . .stephanie_murray@paramount.com
CLIENTS   Paramount Pictures & Television -
                         Universal Studios - Disney Films &
                         Television - Miramax - DreamWorks -
                         MGM - New Line - Sony

Stephanie Murray . . . . .Executive Director
Norm Dlugatch . . . . .Technical Engineer
Paul Wertheimer . . . . .Recordist
Dominic Gonzales .Floor Person

PARAMOUNT RECORDING STUDIOS
6245 Santa Monica Blvd.
Hollywood, CA 90038
PHONE 323-465-4000
FAX 323-469-1905
EMAIL . . . . .info@paramountrecording.com
WEB SITE . . . . .www.paramountrecording.com

Mike Kerns . . . . .No Title
Adam Beilenson . . . . .No Title

THE PASS STUDIOS
3249 Cahuenga Blvd. West
Hollywood, CA 90068
PHONE 323-851-1244
FAX 323-851-8604
EMAIL .thepassstudios@aol.com
WEB SITE . . . . .www.thepassstudios.com
CLIENTS   Roseanne Cash - The Rolling Stones -
                     India.Arie - Wolfmother - Chris Isaak -
                     Thrice

Anne Kadrovich-Johnson . . . . .Studio Manager

THE PLANT RECORDING STUDIOS
2200 Bridgeway
Sausalito, CA 94965
PHONE 415-332-6100
FAX 415-332-5738
EMAIL . . . . .alexa@plantstudios.com
WEB SITE . . . . .www.plantstudios.com
CLIENTS   Mudvayne - P.O.D. - Journey - The
                     Noisettes

Alexa Schlittgen . . . . .Studio Manager
Perry Lancaster .Technical Engineer
John Cuniberti .Mastering Engineer

PRECISION MASTERING, LLC
1008 N. Cole Ave.
Los Angeles, CA 90038
PHONE 323-464-1008
FAX 323-464-4579
EMAIL . . . . .info@precisionmastering.com
SECOND EMAIL . . . . .firstname@precisionmastering.com
WEB SITE . . . . .www.precisionmastering.com
GENRES   All Genres
COMMENTS   Mastering studio

Larry Emerine . . . . .No Title
Tom Baker . . . . .Engineer
Ron Boustead . . . . .Engineer
Don C. Tyler . . . . .Engineer
Claudia Lagan . . . . .Project Manager

PRIVATE ISLAND TRAX/ROBYNOPOLY
6671 Sunset Blvd., Ste. 1550
Los Angeles, CA 90028
PHONE 323-856-8729
FAX 323-856-0309
EMAIL . . . . .info@privateislandtrax.com
WEB SITE .www.privateislandtrax.com
CLIENTS   Solomon Burke - Bone Thugs-N-
                     Harmony - Steve Torme - Jim Belushi -
                     Michael Wolff - Patti LaBelle - Arsenio
                     Hall - Francisco Aguabella
GENRES   All Genres
COMMENTS   Four studios; Tracking in orchestra sized
                     room; Mastering, restoration, mixing,
                     voice-overs, Audiopost; 25 editors and
                     engineers on staff

Michael McDonald .Chief Engineer

Q DIVISION STUDIOS
363 Highland Ave.
Somerville, MA 02144-2574
PHONE 800-284-2964/617-625-9900
FAX 617-625-2224
EMAIL . . . . .info@qdivision.com
WEB SITE . . . . .www.qdivision.com
CLIENTS   Fountains of Wayne - James Taylor -
                     Mission of Burma - The Click Five -
                     Howie Day - Pixies - Aimee Mann -
                     Guster
GENRES   Alternative - Pop - Rock
COMMENTS   Record Company; Producer

Michael Denneen . . . . .Owner
Jon Lupfer . . . . .Owner
Dave Sakowki . . . . .Studio Manager

RECORD PLANT
1032 N. Sycamore Ave.
Hollywood, CA 90038
PHONE 323-993-9300
FAX 323-466-8835
EMAIL . . . . .kimkennedy@recordplant.com
WEB SITE . . . . .www.recordplant.com

Rose Mann . . . . .President
Kim Kennedy . . . . .Booking Manager

RFI/CD MASTERING
3136 E. Madison St., Ste. 300N
Seattle, WA 98112
PHONE 206-325-5212
FAX 206-325-3334
EMAIL . . . . .info@rficd.com
WEB SITE . . . . .www.rficd.com
COMMENTS   Mastering lab

Ed Brooks . . . . .Engineer (ed@rficd.com)
Rick Fisher . . . . .Engineer (rick@rficd.com)

RIGHT TRACK RECORDING
168 W. 48th St.
New York, NY 10036
PHONE 212-944-5770
FAX 212-944-7258
EMAIL . . . . .info@righttrackrecording.com
WEB SITE . . . . .www.righttrackrecording.com

Simon Andrews . . . . .Owner
Barry Bongiovi . . . . .General Manager
Donna Kloepfer . . . . .Studio Manager

SCORPIO SOUND LLC
8286 Mannix Dr.
Los Angeles, CA 90046
PHONE 323-650-6028 x11
FAX 323-650-6457
EMAIL . . . . .info@scorpiosound.com
WEB SITE . . . . .www.scorpiosound.com
GENRES   Classical - Electronica - Rock - World

Gregory Hainer . . . .CEO/Creative Director/Composer/Sound Designer

SIGNATURE STUDIO/SIGNATURE SOUNDS RECORDINGS
227 Peterson Rd.
Pomfret, CT 06259
PHONE 860-974-2016/413-283-2587
EMAIL . . . . .mthayer814@aol.com
WEB SITE . . . . .www.signaturesounds.com

Mark Thayer . . . . .Studio Manager (mthayer814@aol.com)

SIGNET SOUND
7317 Romaine St.
Los Angeles, CA 90046
PHONE 323-850-1515
FAX 323-874-1420
EMAIL . . . . .ddubow@signetsound.com
WEB SITE .www.ascentmedia.com
GENRES   All Genres
COMMENTS   Neve/Flying Faders automated consoles;
                          Stereo to 5.1 mixing

David Dubow .Managing Director

SKYWALKER SOUND
PO Box 3000
San Rafael, CA 94912
PHONE 415-662-1353
FAX 415-662-2429
EMAIL . . . . .info@skysound.com
SECOND EMAIL . . . . .lajones@skysound.com
WEB SITE . . . . .www.skysound.com
CLIENTS   Kronos Quartet - Herbie Hancock
GENRES   All Genres
COMMENTS   Full-service recording studio and scoring
                          stage; 5.1 mixing

Glenn Kiser . . . . .VP/General Manager
Leslie Ann Jones . . . . . . .Director, Recording & Scoring/Engineer/Mixer
Judy Kirschner .Recording Engineer
Dann Thompson . . . . .Recording Engineer
Andre Zweers . . . . .Recording Engineer/ProTools Editor

A SMOOTH SOUND RECORDING STUDIO
13649 Vanowen St.
Van Nuys, CA 91405
PHONE 818-779-1259
FAX 818-779-1207
EMAIL . . . . .jerryjackson@earthlink.net
WEB SITE . . . . .www.smoothsoundstudio.com
COMMENTS   Analog and digital recording

Jerry Jackson . . . . .Owner

SONY MUSIC STUDIOS
460 W. 54th St.
New York, NY 10019
PHONE 212-833-7373
FAX 212-833-8412
EMAIL . . . . .brian_mckenna@sonymusic.com
WEB SITE . . . . .www.sonymusicstudios.com
CLIENTS   Roc-A-Fella - Billy Joel - Destiny's Child -
                          Kanye West - John Legend - Alicia Keys -
                          Norah Jones - Aerosmith - Lauryn Hill -
                          Harry Connick, Jr. - The Ravonettes -
                          Swizz Beatz - Rodney Jerkins - Nas

Andy Kadison . . . . .Sr. VP, Sony Music Studios
Brian McKenna . . . . .Sr. Director, Audio Operations/Marketing

SONY PICTURES SCORING STAGE - BARBRA STREISAND SCORING STAGE
10202 W. Washington Blvd.
Culver City, CA 90232
PHONE 310-244-5714
FAX 310-244-0770
EMAIL . . . . .julianne_mccormack@spe.sony.com
WEB SITE . . . . .www.sonypictures.com/studio/postprod

Julianne McCormack . . . . .VP, Operations

SOUND CITY RECORDING STUDIOS
15456 Cabrito Rd.
Van Nuys, CA 91406
PHONE 818-787-3722
FAX 818-787-3981
EMAIL .soundcty@aol.com
SECOND EMAIL . . . . .shivaun@soundcitystudios.com
WEB SITE . . . . .www.soundcitystudios.com

Shivaun O'Brien .Studio Manager

SOUND FACTORY
6357 Selma Ave.
Hollywood, CA 90028
PHONE 323-467-2500
FAX 323-467-3103
EMAIL .phil@sunsetsound.com
SECOND EMAIL . . . . .mail@sunsetsound.com
WEB SITE . . . . .www.sunsetsound.com

Phil MacConnell . . . . .General Manager
Craig Hubler . . . . .General Manager, Sunset Sound

SOUNDCASTLE RECORDING STUDIOS
2840 Rowena Ave.
Los Angeles, CA 90039
PHONE 323-665-5201
FAX 323-662-4273
EMAIL . . . . .scmanager@earthlink.net
WEB SITE . . . . .www.soundcastle.com

Pat Kane . . . . .No Title
Thom Roy . . . . .No Title

SOUNDELUX DMG
7080 Hollywood Blvd., Ste. 100
Hollywood, CA 90028
PHONE 323-603-5100
FAX 323-603-5101
EMAIL . . . . .sgershin@soundeluxdmg.com
WEB SITE .www.soundeluxdmg.com
CLIENTS   Sony Computer Entertainment America -
                          Capcom - Ichiat Day
COMMENTS   Music and sound design house;
                          Commercials, games and film sound-
                          tracks

Scott Gershin . . . . .Creative Director/Founder
Darlene Gorzela . . . . .Executive Producer
Mikael Sandgren . . . . .Composer/Creative Director

STRATOSPHERE SOUND
239 11th Ave.
New York, NY 10001-1206
PHONE 212-924-2193
FAX 646-486-7695
EMAIL . . . . .debb@stratospheresound.com
WEB SITE . . . . .www.stratospheresound.com
CLIENTS   Depeche Mode - The Damnwells -
                          Michael Stipe - Nada Surf - James Iha -
                          Ben Hillier

Debb Hanks . . . . .Studio Manager

STUDIO ATLANTIS
1140 N. Western Ave.
Hollywood, CA 90029
PHONE 323-462-7761
FAX 323-462-3393
EMAIL .jon@studio-atlantis.com
WEB SITE .www.studio-atlantis.com
CLIENTS   Usher - Jermaine Dupri - Faith Evans - J
                           Records - Interscope - Def Jam - Sony -
                           Capitol Records
GENRES   All Genres
COMMENTS   SSL J9000 Architecture by Studio
                           Bauton; Pro-Tools HD; 2 machines;
                           Vintage & modern equipment

Jon Newkirk . . . . .Manager/Partner
Demetrius Spencer . . . . .Partner
Colin Miller . . . . .Staff Engineer/Assistant Engineer

STUDIO CITY SOUND
4412 Whitsett Ave.
Studio City, CA 91604
PHONE 818-505-9368
FAX 818-761-4744
EMAIL . . . . .eharrison@studiocitysound.com
WEB SITE .www.studiocitysound.com
CLIENTS   Tom Morello - David Zucker - Toots &
                           the Maytals - Willie Nelson - Bonnie
                           Raitt - Pete Yorn - Gwen Stephani -
                           Phantom Planet - Eric Clapton - Chuck
                           Negron
GENRES   All Genres
COMMENTS   Mastering

Tom Weir . . . . .Chief Engineer/Owner
Estelle Harrison . . . . .Studio Manager

STUDIO D RECORDING, INC.
425 Coloma St.
Sausalito, CA 94964
PHONE 415-332-6289
FAX 415-332-0249
WEB SITE .www.studiodrecording.com
CLIENTS   Huey Lewis - Chris Isaak - Ringo Starr -
                           DJ QBert - The Four Tops - Smashmouth
                           - Third Eye Blind
GENRES   Alternative - Blues - Jazz - Pop - R&B -
                           Urban
COMMENTS   Mastering and restoration; Mixing;
                           Producer

Joel Jaffe . . . . .President
Dan Godfrey . . . . .VP

STUDIO LITHO
348 NW 54th St.
Seattle, WA 98117
PHONE 206-632-8157
FAX 206-632-3491
EMAIL . . . . .info@studiolitho.com
WEB SITE . . . . .www.studiolitho.com

Jim Haviland . . . . .Founder
Ed Brooks . . . . .Manager
Floyd Reitsma . . . . .Producer
Dave Fisher . . . . .Producer/Engineer

STUDIOMEDIA RECORDING CO.
1030 Davis St.
Evanston, IL 60201
PHONE 847-864-4460/847-864-4461
FAX 847-864-4836
EMAIL . . . . .studiomedia@studiomediarecording.com
SECOND EMAIL . . . . .s2domedia@aol.com
WEB SITE . . . . .www.studiomediarecording.com
GENRES   All Genres
COMMENTS   Audio & video services; ISDN digital
                           phone patch; Fairlight Dream Station &
                           Satellite workstations; Recording & mix-
                           ing for audio & video; ADR

Scott Steinman . . . . .President/Engineer
Mike Stuckmyer . . . . .Manager
Andrew Arbetter . . . . .Engineer
John Buehler . . . . .Engineer
Choate Hoyle . . . . .Assistant Engineer
Aaron Seckman . . . . .Assistant Engineer

SUNBURST RECORDING
10313 W. Jefferson Blvd.
Culver City, CA 90232
PHONE 310-204-2222
EMAIL . . . . .sunburstrecording@sbcglobal.net
SECOND EMAIL . . . . .bob@sunburstrecording.com
WEB SITE . . . . .www.sunburstrecording.com

Bob Wayne . . . . .Director
Geoff Schroer . . . . .Staff Engineer

SUNSET SOUND
6650 Sunset Blvd.
Hollywood, CA 90028
PHONE 323-469-1186
FAX 323-465-5579
EMAIL .mail@sunsetsound.com
WEB SITE . . . . .www.sunsetsound.com

Craig Hubler . . . . .General Manager, Sunset Sound
Phil MacConnell . . . . .General Manager, Sound Factory

TERRA NOVA DIGITAL AUDIO
5446 Hwy. 290 West, Ste. 270
Austin, TX 78735
PHONE 512-891-8010
FAX 512-891-8014
EMAIL .terranova@austin.rr.com
WEB SITE .www.terranovamastering.com
CLIENTS   Susan Tedeschi - Lucinda Williams -
                           Robert Earl Keen - Steve Earle -
                           Flatlanders - Susan Gibson - Weary Boys
                           - Willie Nelson - Ray Price - New West
                           Records - Palo Duro Records
GENRES   All Genres
COMMENTS   Mastering studio; Digital and analog;
                           DVD surround, CD mastering,
                           archival/restoration editing, transfers

Jerry Tubb . . . . .CEO/Chief Mastering Engineer
Diane Tubb . . . . .VP, Studio Operations/Business Manager
Nick Landis . . . . .Mastering Engineer/DVD Authoring Specialist
Sari Hayes . . . . .Administrative Assistant

THRESHOLD SOUND & VISION
2260 Centinela Ave.
West Los Angeles, CA 90064
PHONE 310-571-0500
FAX 310-571-0505
EMAIL . . . . .threshold@thresholdsound.com
WEB SITE .www.thresholdsound.com
CLIENTS   MGM - Paramount - Universal - HBO
                         MTV - VH1 - Sony - Interscope - Warner
                         - Maverick - Geffen - Casablanca

David Moss . . . . .President

TODD-AO HOLLYWOOD
900 N. Seward St.
Hollywood, CA 90038
PHONE 323-962-4000
FAX 323-466-4062
EMAIL . . . . .rward@toddao.com
WEB SITE . . . . .www.toddao.com

Ron Ward . . . . .Managing Director (323-962-4129)

TODD-AO RADFORD
4024 Radford Ave.
Studio City, CA 90046
PHONE 818-487-6069
FAX 818-487-6088
EMAIL . . . . .kirsten.smith@toddao.com
WEB SITE . . . . .www.toddao.com
SECOND WEB SITE . . . . .www.ascentmedia.com

Kirsten Smith . . . . .Managing Director

A TOUCH OF JAZZ
444 N. Third St., Ste. C9
Philadelphia, PA 19123-4107
PHONE 215-928-9192
FAX 215-928-9487
EMAIL . . . . .irize@atojazz.com
WEB SITE . . . . .www.atojazz.com
SECOND WEB SITE . . . . .www.djjazzyjeff.com
GENRES   Urban
COMMENTS   4 Studios

Jeff Townes . . . . .CEO

TRACK RECORD STUDIOS
5102 Vineland Ave.
North Hollywood, CA 91601
PHONE 818-761-0511
FAX 818-761-0539
EMAIL . . . . .alan@trackrecordstudios.com
SECOND EMAIL . . . . .inquiry@trackrecordstudios.com
WEB SITE . . . . .www.trackrecordstudios.com
CLIENTS   Petey Pablo - Maroon 5 - Matchbox
                         Twenty - Taproot - Evanescence - Rush -
                         Brandy - Goo Goo Dolls - The Offspring
                         - Jane's Addiction - Tori Amos - Blink-
                         182 - Tupac - Snoop Dogg - Wu-Tang
                         Clan - Aerosmith - Kiss - Foreigner -
                         Dwight Yoakam
GENRES   All Genres

Alan Morphew . . . . .Studio Manager

TREE SOUND
4610 Peachtree Industrial Blvd.
Norcross, GA 30071
PHONE 770-242-8944
FAX 770-242-0155
EMAIL . . . . .nina@treesoundstudios.com
WEB SITE . . . . .www.treesoundstudios.com
COMMENTS   live sound stage; 4 studios with lounges,
                         2 kitchens, billiards, pinball, foosball,
                         basketball, climbing atrium

Paul Diaz . . . . .Owner
Nina Baldridge .Studio Manager
Zack Odom . . . . .Lead Engineer
John Holmes . . . . .Lead Engineer
Travis Daniels .Assistant Engineer
Ryan McDavid . . . . .Live Engineer/Remote Engineer

THE VILLAGE RECORDER
1616 Butler Ave.
West Los Angeles, CA 90025
PHONE 310-478-8227
FAX 310-479-1142
EMAIL . . . . .villagerec@aol.com
WEB SITE . . . . .www.villagerecorder.com
CLIENTS   Nine Inch Nails - Oasis - Liz Phair -
                         Lenny Kravitz - Ringo Starr - Hot Hot
                         Heat
GENRES   All Genres

Jeff Greenberg . . . . .CEO
Darren Frank . . . . .Manager

WESTLAKE RECORDING STUDIOS AND TECHNICAL SERVICES
7265 Santa Monica Blvd.
Los Angeles, CA 90046
PHONE 323-851-9800
FAX 323-851-9386
EMAIL . . . . .bookings@thelakestudios.com
WEB SITE . . . . .www.thelakestudios.com
GENRES   All Genres
COMMENTS   Replication

Steve Burdick . . . . .President

WORKSHEET

DATE	PROJECT	CONTACT	NOTES

SECTION **F**

INDEX BY NAME

WORKSHEET

NAME	COMPANY	PHONE #	FAX #